HQ   Rohrbaugh, Joanna
1206   Bunker, 1943-
.R63
       Women, psychology's
       puzzle

DATE		
MAR 4 '82		
MAY 27 '82		
APR 18 '8		
FEB 22 2015		
MAR 23 2015		
APR 13 2015		

Women: Psychology's Puzzle

WOMEN: PSYCHOLOGY'S PUZZLE

Joanna Bunker Rohrbaugh

Basic Books, Inc., Publishers   New York

Library of Congress Cataloging in Publication Data

Rohrbaugh, Joanna Bunker, 1943–
Women, psychology's puzzle.

Bibliography: p. 469
Includes index.
1. Women—Psychology   2. Women—United States—
Social conditions.   I.   Title.
HQ1206.R63   301.41'2   79–7345
ISBN: 0–465–09206–3

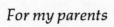

For my parents

Contents

Figures and Tables

Preface

"Women are a fad." These words seem preposterous today. But the psychologist who barked them at me in 1971 was not kidding. He had just read my first paper on the psychology of women and was appalled. How could I waste my time on such a frivolous project, examining the view of women in various personality theories? Why was I not content to stick to my other research interests? If I persisted in such a foolhardy endeavor, I would be a laughingstock. And he, for one, wanted nothing to do with me. At the time he was speaking for most of academic psychology. Women's issues were not serious. If those "radicals" insisted on protesting about women's issues, let them. But no social scientist worth his salt was going to pay much attention.

Times have changed. The Women's Movement has raised many controversial issues over the past ten years, and social scientists have begun to pay attention. Courses on women's studies have flourished. Exciting new research is being done on many aspects of women's lives. More women are entering the field, and those who are interested in studying women and gender roles are not being intimidated into concentrating on research that men define as more "serious."

Not that women's issues are not controversial; they are. In fact, they often seem to be emotionally explosive—for both sexes. Because whatever we learn about sex differences, gender roles, and traditional femininity is bound to affect real human lives. The questions reflect concerns and anxieties we all live with. Are women as aggressive as men? Or as independent, competitive, and achievement-oriented? If they are, why has no one acknowledged it? And what happens when these characteristics and needs are thwarted and ignored? Should a woman marry, have children, hold a paying job outside the home? How will each of these choices affect her life—and the lives of those close to her?

The questions go on and on—about sexuality, life styles, physical assault and rape, pregnancy and childbirth, mental health and psychotherapy. But we are no longer in the quandary of wondering what is myth and what reality; for a sizable body of research addresses these questions. The purpose of this book is to examine this research critically so that we can begin to answer some of the questions that are crucial to the lives of women today.

xi

I have summarized the major themes and studies that relate to five key areas of female psychology and gender differences: biology, personality, social roles, bodily functions, and mental health. After examining the formal theories and studies, I have compared them with women's own opinions and experiences. Sometimes the contrast is startling, at other times infuriating, for only recently have social scientists begun to ask women themselves about the female experience.

This female experience is extremely diverse, as we will see. And yet there are common themes—themes that suggest that our female gender has a profound impact on our everyday thoughts, feelings, and actions.

Joanna Bunker Rohrbaugh
Boston

Acknowledgments

I should like to thank my students and my friends in the Women's Movement for inspiring me to write this book. I should also like to thank Matina Horner for her confidence, encouragement, and warm support during my graduate work at Harvard. Many people have stimulated, challenged, and influenced my thinking throughout this project, including Elliot Mishler, Brendan Maher, Sunny Yando, Clara Mayo, Roger Brown, Ronnie Littenberg, and my patients, friends, and colleagues at the Massachusetts General Hospital and the Freedom Trail Clinic. I am especially grateful to Anne Verdon for her helpful criticisms and suggestions at each stage of the manuscript, and to Judy Arnold for her patience and enthusiasm. Margaret Erickson typed the manuscript with amazing efficiency and cheerfulness. Herb Reich of Basic Books was a consistent source of friendly encouragement and sound advice, and Phoebe Hoss was extremely helpful in the final stages of the manuscript.

I gratefully acknowledge permission to reprint excerpts from the following:

Alexis M. Herman, "Money: Still . . . Small Change for Black Women," *Ms.* (February 1979) 7(8): 96,98. Copyright © 1979 by Alexis M. Herman. Reprinted by permission of *Ms.* Magazine Corporation.

Gloria Steinem, "If Men Could Menstruate—A Political Fantasy," *Ms.* (October 1978) 7(4): 110. Copyright © 1978 by *Ms.* Magazine Corporation. Excerpts reprinted with permission.

Patricia A. Schmuck, "Deterrents to Women's Careers in School Management," *Sex Roles* (1975) 1(4): 339–53. By permission of the author and Plenum Publishing Corporation.

Alice Walker, Sandra Flowers, Christine Bond, and Audre Lorde, "Other Voices, Other Moods," *Ms.* (February 1979). Reprinted by permission of Alice Walker and *Ms.* Magazine Corporation.

Michele Wallace, "Black Macho and the Myth of the Superwoman," *Ms.* (January 1979). Reprinted by permission of the author and *Ms.* Magazine Corporation.

Debra Renee Kaufman, "Associational Ties in Academe: Some Male and Female Differences," *Sex Roles* (1978) 4(1): 9–21. By permission of the author and Plenum Publishing Corporation.

A. N. Groth, A. W. Burgess, and L. L. Holmstrom, "Rape: Power, Anger, and Sexuality, _American Journal of Psychiatry_ (1977) 134: 1240–43. Copyright © 1977 by the American Psychiatric Association. Reprinted by permission.

Pat Mainardi, "The Politics of Housework," in _Notes from the Second Year: Women's Liberation_ (New York: Notes from the Second Year, Radical Feminism, 1970), edited by S. Firestone and A. Koedt.

Judy Syfers, "Why I Want a Wife." In _Notes from the Third Year: Women's Liberation_ (New York: Notes from the Second Year, Inc., 1971).

Ellen Goodman, "Estrogen on Patrol." Copyright © 1976 by The Boston Globe Newspaper Company. Reprinted by permission of the Washington Post Writers Group.

Ruth Moulton, "A Survey and Reevaluation of the Concept of Penis Envy," _Contemporary Psychoanalysis_ (1970) 7 (1): 84–104. By permission of the author and Academic Press, Inc.

Helene Deutsch, _The Psychology of Women,_ vol. I (New York: Grune & Stratton, 1944). By permission of the author.

Edna I. Rawlings and Dianne K. Carter, "Feminist and Nonsexist Psychotherapy," in _Psychotherapy for Women: Treatment toward Equality_ (1977), edited by Edna I. Rawlings and Dianne K. Carter. Courtesy of Charles C Thomas, Publisher, Springfield, Illinois.

Wilma Scott Heide, "Feminism for a Sporting Future," in _Women and Sport: From Myth to Reality,_ edited by Carole A. Oglesby (Philadelphia: Lea & Febiger, 1978).

Our Bodies, Ourselves by The Boston Women's Health Book Collective. Copyright © 1971, 1973, 1976 by The Boston Women's Health Book Collective, Inc. Reprinted by permission of Simon and Schuster, a Division of Gulf & Western Corporation.

Wife Beating: The Silent Crisis by Roger Langley and Richard C. Levy. Copyright © 1977 by Roger Langley and Richard C. Levy. By permission of E. P. Dutton.

Anita Diamant, "The Women's Sports Revolution: Change for the Better? Or Only for the Best?" This article first appeared in _The Real Paper_ (24 March 1979), Boston, Mass.

John Money, "Statement on Antidiscrimination regarding Sexual Orientation," _Journal of Homosexuality_ (Winter 1976–77) 2(2): 159–61.

Lucia H. Bequaert, _Single Women: Alone & Together._ Copyright © 1976 by Lucia H. Bequaert. Reprinted by permission of Beacon Press.

Anne Steinmann, "Cultural Values, Female Role Expectancies and Therapeutic Goals: Research and Interpretation"; Aaron T. Beck and Ruth L. Greenberg, "Cognitive Therapy with Depressed Women"; Arnold A. Lazarus, "Women in Behavior Therapy"; and Barbara Kirsh, "Consciousness-raising Groups as Therapy for Women"—from _Women in Therapy: New Psychotherapies for a Changing Society,_ edited by Violet Franks and Vasanti Burtle (New York: Brunner/Mazel, 1974).

Del Martin, _Battered Wives._ Copyright © 1976 by Del Martin. All rights reserved. Published by Glide Publications, 330 Ellis Street, San Francisco, Calif. 94102. ($7.95) Used with permission.

Cynthia Fuchs Epstein, "Positive Effects of the Multiple Negative: Explaining the Success of Black Professional Women." Reprinted from *Changing Women in a Changing Society*, edited by Joan Huber, by permission of The University of Chicago Press. Copyright © 1973 by the University of Chicago.

Walter R. Gove and Jeanette F. Tudor, "Adult Sex Roles and Mental Illness." Reprinted from *Changing Women in a Changing Society*, edited by Joan Huber, by permission of The University of Chicago Press. Copyright © 1973 by The University of Chicago.

Diane K. Lewis, "A Response to Inequality: Black Women, Racism, and Sexism," *Signs* (1977) 3(2), by permission of The University of Chicago Press. Copyright © 1977 by The University of Chicago.

Matina S. Horner, "The Motive to Avoid Success and Changing Aspirations of College Women," in *Women on Campus: 1970*, a symposium (Ann Arbor, Michigan, Center for the Continuing Education of Women, 1970).

Susan Griffin, "Rape: The All-American Crime," *Ramparts* (September 1971) 10 (3): 26–35.

Shere Hite, *The Hite Report*. Reprinted with permission of Macmillan Publishing Co., Inc. Copyright © 1976 by Shere Hite.

Phyllis Chesler, *Women and Madness*. Copyright © 1972 by Phyllis Chesler. Reprinted by permission of Doubleday & Company, Inc.

Our Right to Love: A Lesbian Resource Book by Virginia Vida and National Gay Task Force. Copyright © 1978 by Virginia Vida. Published by Prentice-Hall, Inc., Englewood Cliffs, New Jersey 07632.

Walter Mischel, "A Social-Learning View of Sex Differences in Behavior"; and Lawrence Kohlberg, "A Cognitive-Developmental Analysis of Children's Sex-Role Concepts and Attitudes"—from *The Development of Sex Differences*, edited by Eleanor E. Maccoby, with the permission of the publishers, Stanford University Press. Copyright © 1966 by the Board of Trustees of the Leland Stanford Junior University.

E. E. Maccoby and C. N. Jacklin, *The Psychology of Sex Differences*, Stanford University Press, 1974.

Robert S. Weiss, *Marital Separation*. Copyright © 1975 by Basic Books, Inc., Publishers, New York.

Paper 17, "Some Psychological Consequences of the Anatomical Distinction Between the Sexes," in *Collected Papers of Sigmund Freud*, Volume 5, edited by Ernest Jones, authorized translation by Alix and James Strachey, published by Basic Books, Inc., by arrangement with The Hogarth Press and The Institute for Psycho-Analysis, London.

Paper 24, "Female Sexuality," in *Collected Papers of Sigmund Freud*, Volume 5, edited by Ernest Jones, authorized translation by Alix and James Strachey, published by Basic Books and The Institute of Psycho-Analysis, London.

Chapter 9, "Ambivalence: The Socialization of Women," by Judith M. Bardwick and Elizabeth Douvan, in *Woman in Sexist Society: Studies in Power and Powerlessness*, ed. by Vivian Gornick and Barbara K. Moran. Copyright © 1971 by Basic Books, Inc., Publishers, New York.

Chapter 17, "Patient and Patriarch: Women in the Psychotherapeutic Relationship" by Phyllis Chesler, in *Woman in Sexist Society: Studies in Power and Powerlessness*, edited by Vivian Gornick and Barbara K. Moran. Copyright © 1971 by Basic Books, Inc., Publishers, New York.

The Female Orgasm: Psychology, Physiology, Fantasy by Seymour Fisher. Copyright © 1973 by Basic Books, Inc., Publishers, New York.

New Introductory Lectures on Psychoanalysis by Sigmund Freud. Translated and edited by James Strachey. Used with the permission of W. W. Norton & Company, Inc. Copyright © 1965, 1964 by James Strachey. Copyright 1933 by Sigmund Freud. Copyright renewed 1961 by W. J. H. Sprott.

Norman Cameron, *Personality Development and Psychopathology: A Dynamic Approach.* Copyright © 1963 by Norman Cameron. Reprinted by permission of Houghton Mifflin Company.

Linda La Rue, "The Black Movement and Women's Liberation," *The Black Scholar* (May 1970). Reprinted by permission of The Black World Foundation.

Mae C. King, "The Politics of Sexual Stereotypes," *The Black Scholar* (March–April 1973). Reprinted by permission of The Black World Foundation.

Karen Horney, "The Flight from Womanhood: The Masculinity Complex in Women as Viewed by Men and by Women." Originally published in the *International Journal of Psycho-Analysis* (1926). Reprinted by permission of W. W. Norton.

Women: Psychology's Puzzle

INTRODUCTION

Sex and Identity

NO TWO AMERICAN women are quite alike. Each lives her life in a different way. Some women are married, some are not; some have children, some do not; some are straight, others are gay. Although the majority work at paid jobs outside the home, their training and their job situations vary tremendously. And millions belong to economic and racial groups whose problems often go unnoticed. These missing millions live with pressures and life demands that are very different from those experienced by the white, affluent groups that make up the theories about women, write most of the books, and participate in most of the social science studies.

In spite of this diversity, each woman has something in common with her sisters: each exists in a male-dominated culture. Gender has a profound impact on how others perceive a woman and on how she views herself, on what she can expect from life, and on whether, indeed, she can even expect to survive from day to day. Although the importance of gender varies from one area of life to another, from one setting to another, and from one group of women to another, gender is inescapable. It is probably the most important determinant of any individual's life experience. For the two sexes exist in different social worlds with widely

3

divergent pressures, rewards, and expectations. In many areas of life there is no truly human experience. There is only female experience and male experience.

Are Women and Men
Really Different?

If women exist in a different social world from that of men, does this mean that they are different as individuals? Are female characteristics, personalities, and behaviors different from male ones? If we did put a man and a woman in an identical setting, would they feel, think, and act the same way? Or are women basically different from men, regardless of the environment?

MYTHIC WOMAN

Many people certainly think women are different. In fact, throughout history women have been described as being worlds apart from men—mysterious creatures who are somehow both weak and strong, sexy and virginal, subservient and threatening. Juanita Williams (1977) summarizes a number of myths that have been used to categorize these inexplicable creatures. There is woman as earth mother, a fertile creature who is somehow more in tune with nature than is her male counterpart. Then there is woman as seductress, another magical creature whose charms lure the man away from the narrow path of rectitude and responsibility.

The stereotype of the virtuous woman is diametrically opposed to that of the seductress. The virtuous woman is perceived as "a faithful, loyal and submissive wife; a dedicated, loving mother; a competent, diligent housewife; and an unquestioning supporter of the moral and religious values of society" (Williams 1977, p. 8). Williams points out that this stereotype emphasizes womanly characteristics that distinguish the female from the male and underscore her subordinate status—piety, purity, submissiveness, and domesticity. As long as such a woman stays in her "proper" place, all is well. In fact, in some historical periods the virtuous woman has been placed on a pedestal, where men could romanticize about the feminine qualities that were so different from their own.

Most pervasive of all, however, is the popular myth of woman as mystery. This myth supplements the others, for when rational explanations fail to account for the female, she can be set apart as a creature not governed by the normal patterns of thought and behavior. Given her mysterious powers, capricious moods, and feminine wiles, what baffled man can understand woman? Clearly she is from a separate world.

Simone de Beauvoir (1953) maintains that the myth of feminine "mystery" has several advantages—for the male. He can dismiss inexplicable moods, behaviors, and feelings by saying, "Oh, women! Who can understand them anyway?" He does not have to admit ignorance; he can simply point to the perennial mystery of femininity. In this way he also protects himself from disturbing insights: after all, if he did understand a woman's feelings and actions, he might become disillusioned about her nature and feelings toward him. All this leaves man as the sole judge of reality. "In the company of a living enigma man remains alone—alone with his dreams, his hopes, his fears, his love, his vanity" and his view of life (de Beauvoir 1953, p. 240). Since woman cannot be understood, man cannot be expected to build an authentic relationship with her. He is free to relate to her in terms of his *own* perceptions, fantasies, and desires.

Where does the myth of woman as mystery come from? And why has it persisted throughout much of history? Williams attributes it to women's economic and social dependence on men.

> When a woman is kept by a man, she is a passive recipient of the advantages he bestows upon her as long as he cares about her. But this role is not a vocation and does not bestow identity upon the woman. Her dependency causes her to dissemble, as all subordinates learn to dissemble with their masters, concealing their real thoughts and feelings under an enigmatic exterior. . . .
>
> By defining her as mysterious Other, man spares himself the necessity of analyzing her behavior and understanding it as a consequence of her position vis-à-vis him. To do that would require acknowledgement of her oppression, and a possible shift in their power relationship. The price would be very high. (1977, p. 7)

MODERN WOMAN

Myths about women are part of our history. But do they apply to women today? Surely no one believes in these myths any more, for women are no longer relegated to the realm of mystery and enigma. They participate in the mainstream of American life—in the workplace, in cultural activities, in public life. Women's thoughts, feelings, and personalities *are* being analyzed. A quick trip to any bookstore will prove it, as will even a cursory inspection of many newspapers, magazines, and television schedules.

The changes in the activities of women do not eliminate the basic issues, however; for "femininity" and "masculinity" are still central to everyone's self-definition. As a little girl begins to realize that the world is divided into two groups of people, female and male, she starts to wonder where she fits in. Does she have the characteristics that are expected for her gender group? This question is unavoidable, because gender is the main focus for the organization of social perceptions and activities.

But what characteristics should she have? Defining them has become problematic, for the role of women has changed dramatically in the past few decades. As anthropologist Margaret Mead put it, America "is a society in which hardly anyone doubts the existence of a different 'natural' behavior for the sexes, but no one is very sure what that 'natural' behavior is" (Mead 1935, p. 283).

People are no longer willing to accept at their face value the myths about women and have begun to turn to psychologists for a delineation of the "natural" behavior of females.

WOMEN IN PSYCHOLOGY

There have been thousands of studies comparing women and men, and the results have begun to fit a clear pattern. When women and men are put in the same situation, with clearly defined expectations and demands, they respond in remarkably similar ways. Women are no more mysterious, unpredictable, capricious, or baffling than men. Mythic woman is a thing of the past.

Or is she? Have the notions of woman as earth mother, seductress, and paragon of virtue really disappeared? Not entirely. For these images persist—and seem to be shared by both men *and* women. They are reflected in the lingering double standard about sexuality, in the popular view of rape, and in the tendency to condone wife beating. They are expressed—albeit in modified form—in the current stereotypes of femininity and masculinity. In fact modern versions of these myths are reflected in almost every area of our lives.

The tendency to exaggerate the differences between the sexes also lingers on. Anyone who doubts this has only to listen to the debate about the biological basis for sex differences in personality. In spite of many technical studies and review articles that indicate that males and females have essentially the same abilities—except of course for their genitalia and reproductive capacities—both scientists and the general public continue to argue that anatomy is destiny. They seem to feel that since women and men act, feel, and think so differently, that since indeed they lead such different lives, there must be some inherent, biological reason. Surely the reason cannot be social and environmental.

But it seems to be. Certainly there are many biological differences between females and males. But none of these differences is important enough to explain the dramatic disparity between the personalities, behavior, attitudes, and life styles of women and men. Something else must be causing the female/male divergence. And that something seems to be cultural customs, child-rearing practices, and social expectations.

Many social scientists are thus coming around to the view long espoused by feminists: social factors account for the huge gap between the sexes. The essential ingredient in those social factors is power: power as access to money, prestige, and advancement; power as the ability and the right to control the behavior of others; power as the expression of dominance and ownership. And in all these areas the male comes out on top. He has the power, and the woman has none.

Does this mean that women and men are not so different after all? Only in the sense of potential abilities. For women live in a separate world from men. Their experiences are different, their feelings and thoughts are different, their life choices and options are different. The fact that the female world is created primarily by social factors does not make it any less real for women. Nor does it lessen the psychological implications of life in that world. Female oppression does indeed exist, and it influences every aspect of our existence.

But one may ask, "Isn't oppression a rather strong word? Doesn't it exaggerate just a bit?" Perhaps, although I think not. Certainly things have changed a lot over the past fifty years. Women in the United States today have more options and freedom than they have ever had before; and increasingly, they are choosing to exercise that new freedom. On the other hand, their personal lives are in many ways still frustrating and limiting.

A New Psychology

of Women

Until quite recently most psychologists shared the popular myths about women. Freud, for instance, tended to view women as mysterious and more enigmatic than men, as we can see from his widely quoted comment: "The great question that has never been answered and which I have not yet been able to answer, despite my thirty years of research into the feminine soul, is 'What does a woman want?' " (Jones 1955, p. 421).

Freud's writings about women generated a great deal of discussion and research. The controversy surrounding the Women's Movement has intensified this interest over the past ten years, leading to new questions and research strategies. Many studies have examined the biological differences between the sexes. Others have considered social differences— how girls and boys grow up and how their growing up shapes their personalities and experiences as adults. And more recently interest has turned to areas of women's lives that were previously neglected: the way women themselves experience sexuality, pregnancy, and childbirth; the emotional experience of being wife, mother, and worker; and the psychological effects of rape and physical abuse.

The results of this new research are startling. For the researchers have examined not only women but also the ways in which women have been viewed, and have found that psychologists are people just like everyone else: they share the attitudes, the prejudices, and the assumptions of their culture, all of which biases creep into their work. Since most psychologists are male and live in a male-dominated culture, these biases have been male-oriented. The older studies tended to take the male as the norm with which the female was compared; any difference in the female was defined as a deficiency. This pattern is found throughout psychology—in studies of biological sex differences, in theories of personality development, and in studies of numerous areas of everyday life. The underlying assumption is clear: since whatever is male is best, whatever is female must therefore be second-rate. Even the conception of mental health has been affected by this bias: traditional masculinity is viewed as healthier than traditional femininity.

Many researchers have responded to this pervasive male bias by calling for the development of a new psychology of women. We need to focus on the unique aspects of female experience and on how these are perceived by women themselves. We need to continue examining how myths and stereotypes influence not only social science but our daily lives as well. And we need to consider how the changes in woman's role over the past fifty years have affected women—and what further changes the future can and should bring.

A related question then arises. If there is to be a separate psychology of women, why not a psychology of men, too? The answer is that we already have a psychology of men, but it is simply called "psychology." The major theories have been developed by men, the subjects in most experiments have been men, and the model of human development has, in reality, been male development.

Not that men are unaffected by cultural myths and stereotypes. They, too, have been viewed in terms of the cultural norms of what a man should be. This stereotype of masculinity is often personally limiting and can certainly cause a man to feel threatened by the changes that women are now going through. Research is being done on the male response to gender role changes, and rightly so.

But for women there is an even more pressing need. The view of woman has been so distorted in traditional male psychology that it bears only a slight resemblance to real life. Only when women have been studied separately and have begun to define themselves apart from men, can we come to any realistic understanding of how and why the two sexes really differ. When we know more about women as separate beings, we can begin to answer the question, What does woman want? And with this answer we can begin to speculate about how women and men might relate to each other in more positive, caring, and humane ways in the future.

PART I

BIOLOGY AND
FEMALE BEHAVIOR

IN EVERY ARGUMENT about women entering new activities outside the home, someone is always sure to say, "But it's just a matter of biology. You *know* women are different from men—they're more intuitive, nurturant, emotional, but also weaker and subject to fits of weeping once a month. What it really comes down to is women are naturally made to be mothers. Men are stronger, both physically and psychologically, and therefore more fit for work and leadership roles. Look at the baboons. The males are socially dominant and physically aggressive; they run things and protect their females whose function is to have the babies."

After sputtering through a defense of women as human beings with other attributes besides their reproductive organs, we are often left wondering just what are the basic biological differences between the sexes. In recent years more people have been turning to psychologists for an answer. But here, too, controversy abounds. Some psychologists say no sex differences are biologically determined, while others stoutly maintain that all the key ones are. The only difference everyone agrees on is reproduction: only men can impregnate women, and only women can give birth and lactate.

The debate about the biological basis for sex differences has been raging for a long time. Scientists have searched everywhere for definitive evidence of biological determinism and have contrasted biology with learning in many ways. First there is the attempt to eliminate social influences—by studying animal groups, for instance, or human newborns who are not yet socialized. Then there is the attempt to equalize the social influences by looking at human behavior in a variety of cultures: if *all* females tend to behave differently from *all* males, the assumption is that these sex differences must be due to biology rather than to social factors.

Some researchers have responded by raising the question of gender identity itself. Is everyone born female or male, or does everyone actually have to learn to think of him- or herself in terms of only one gender? For if one has to learn what gender one is, one has also to learn the behaviors that go with that gender.

Other researchers have examined biological factors directly rather than contrasting them with learning. How do hormones influence the behavior of adults, for instance? Do male hormones cause "male" behavior, while female hormones cause "female" behavior? Does the menstrual cycle have a dramatic effect on female personality? And finally there is the whole issue of intellectual abilities. Do females have different intellectual abilities from males, differences that are caused by genes, hormones, and physical development?

In spite of all this research, controversy continues. No one has been able to demonstrate a clear biological basis for sex differences. One researcher finds this; another challenges it with that. But in spite of the confusion, there is a certain pattern to the information available. This pattern is seldom, however, the one intended by the researchers. Instead of biological determinism we find social determinism, and instead of scientific objectivity we find male bias.

The story of this research effort is thus one of failure—failure to isolate a biological basis for women's personality, behavior, and position in society. This failure does not mean, however, that we should ignore the research; for it illustrates the way social attitudes can creep into research, coloring both the research design and the interpretation of results. No study is immune to cultural bias, even a study concerned with concrete physical differences. Researchers are people, too, and they share the attitudes of those around them. These attitudes often determine what they study and how they study it, as we will see.

Chapter 1

Is a Woman Born

to Be Dominated?

WHEN A MAN argues that a woman's personality and social role are "just a matter of biology," he often bolsters his statement with examples of unlearned and hence biologically based male dominance. "Males are dominant in natural animal groups," he states, "and in most human societies as well. Even male babies are bigger, stronger, and more aggressive than female babies. Face it—male dominance is inborn, biological, natural, and inevitable."

Let us turn to the research on animal groups, human societies, and human newborns to see if it bears out this assumption.

Animal Behavior—

The Baboon Argument

Studies of the social organization and behavior of wild animals continue to be a favorite source of ammunition for those who think that giving birth and raising children is the proper and the only role for

13

women. "Look at the baboons," they will say, and a heated argument begins. Actually these data have been so thoroughly discredited as indicating determinants of gender roles in humans (Weisstein 1971; M. Rosenberg 1973) that they are no longer a source of real controversy among researchers who specialize in the psychology of women. Since the popular press continues to make much of these studies, however, it is important to understand the issues involved.

The basic rationale for studying sex differences in animals is that these differences reflect pure biology without the interference of socialization. This assumption is questionable at best, because coherent systems of social organization have been found in many animal groups studied, and these systems vary from one species to another and even from one group to another within a species. Thus animals are not necessarily unsocialized; they are merely socialized differently from humans.

Furthermore, in trying to avoid the effects of socialization by turning to animals, these researchers assume that anything that animals do is necessary, natural, and desirable in humans. Weisstein (1971) has pointed out that this reasoning would lead to the conclusion that since monkeys cannot read, we should not teach children to read because it is unnatural. To put it another way, the idea that animal life reflects a less complex combination of the primarily biological determinants of human behavior "implies that the 'lower animals' are 'on the way' to becoming human, when they are actually on the way to becoming something else, different in each case" (B. G. Rosenberg and B. Sutton-Smith 1972, p. 9).

But, if we accept the assumption that we can extrapolate from animals to humans, what do these studies show? The essential result is disappointing for the biological reductionists. Every conceivable type of social organization and sex difference has been found, from the male marmoset who does most of the child care and the female lion who does most of the hunting and killing to the female baboon who does the child care while the male does the fighting and food gathering (M. Rosenberg 1973; Weisstein 1971). Thus even in nonhumans the fact that a female gives birth does not necessarily mean that she cares for the infant, much less spends all her time on this nurturant function.

The broad differences among species are themselves a source of difficulty in trying to draw conclusions from animal studies; for each researcher tends to concentrate on a species whose behaviors support that researcher's underlying assumptions and attitudes about sex differences. The most popular object of studies is the rhesus monkey species, whose males are extremely aggressive and dominant, and whose females are passive, submissive, and primarily involved in child care. Yet the rhesus monkey is more distant from humans in the evolutionary scheme than is the gibbon, whose males and females are scarcely distinguishable from each other in behavior or physical appearance (M. Rosenberg 1973).

Observer bias is also a problem in animal studies. Miriam Rosenberg (1973) points out that researchers (mostly male), raised in a culture that places a premium on male aggressiveness, are likely to choose male-oriented behaviors that exaggerate any existing sex differences, and then to expect the male animals to display these behaviors more than the female animals do. Of course no research area is free of this problem, as Rosenthal (1966) has dramatized by showing how the outcome of behavioral studies can be changed by altering the observer's expectations of the results. But the cause of sex differences is often emotionally charged for psychologists as well as for the public and hence is probably even more subject to experimenter bias than are other areas. Our confidence in the scientific objectivity of these studies is further weakened when we read such comments as:

> "However, let us not belittle the female, for they also serve who only stand and wait."
> "Females show no respect for a male they can dominate."
> "We had assigned the evening care to Kathy, a maternal bit of fluff who had worked for several years as a monkey tester while studying to become an elementary school teacher."
> "Combining our human and male-monkey talents, we are winning the good fight and imparting to naive and even resistant female monkeys the priceless gift of motherhood."

These remarks were not made in a heated cocktail party debate or even in a media misquote but were printed as part of "scientific" reports of serious research by the famous psychologist Harry Harlow (1962, pp. 5–9). After raising newborn rhesus monkeys in isolation for two months and then observing their play, Harlow claimed that males were naturally more aggressive and rough than females. He also compared the effects on the isolated neonates of wire mothers with an attached bottle, who thus provided nourishment but no cuddling, and of terrycloth mothers with no attached bottle, who thus provided cuddling but no nourishment. All the monkeys deprived of real mothers had difficulty engaging in mating behaviors later on (Harlow 1962; Harlow and Suomi 1970; Harlow and Zimmerman 1959). These studies are standard reading for psychology courses and are usually interpreted as proof that human infants need an ever-present mother, in spite of other studies that show that although *nurturance* is essential, the *gender* of the parenting figure is not a crucial factor.

There are other problems with animal research, too. Animals observed by a human with a camera and other paraphernalia are probably not acting naturally, as anyone can tell after making obvious and surreptitious observations of a household pet. Furthermore, in laboratory experiments the animals are in a totally artificial environment and have often been bred specially for experimental use. Finally, one could maintain that genetic mutations affecting social behaviors are different in various species, so that the eminently social *Homo sapiens* may have genetic underpinnings for social behaviors different from those of other species (M. Rosenberg 1973).

But the essential problem is the diversity of animals and behaviors studied, which provide a myriad of contradictory results. For a particular question, one has only carefully to choose a species and a target behavior in order to obtain the desired answer. It is tempting to conclude that certain species are studied more for their "fantasy value" than for any objective, scientific reasons (Weisstein 1971, p. 142).

Human Societies—

The Ever-Dominant Male?

If we survive the "battle of the baboons" in our initial argument, we are likely to be faced next with, "Okay, so maybe animals do vary a lot. But you've got to admit that men have always had the powerful positions in *human* societies. That's because they're bigger and naturally stronger." The issue here is not whether men are bigger (since they obviously are),* but whether this biological sex difference is the inevitable basis for sex-role stereotyping. If it is, then the same sex roles should be found in all societies. The rationale is that if we examine a variety of societies in which the cultural influences vary widely, the social factors should cancel each other out, leaving a clear biological basis for the sex-role differentiation.

CROSSCULTURAL PATTERNS

Margaret Mead's research has become the classic evidence in this dispute. In 1931, while she was on her way to study the kinship system of a tribe beyond the Torricelli Mountains in New Guinea, Mead's native carriers left her stranded among the mountain Arapesh. Here she found both men *and* women to be gentle, trained to be cooperative, nonaggressive, and responsive to the needs of others—nurturant people in

* Some people may think that it is not at all "obvious" that men are bigger and stronger because of their *biology*, since most cultures encourage men to develop their musculature through sports and other activities while discouraging women from developing theirs (or even dramatically weakening women through practices such as foot binding among the ancient Chinese). They may be right, but we cannot know what men and women would look like without this cultural intervention, since we cannot study them in a cultural vacuum. For now, we will have to consider biological sex differences as they are currently manifested within various human societies. And it is true that among existent cultures men are generally larger and more physically powerful than women.

whom sexual desire was not seen as a powerful driving force. In the river-dwelling Mundugumor tribe nearby, however, Mead found that both men and women had personalities similar to the American masculine stereotype: all were ruthless, aggressive, viewed as sexually driven, and only minimally nurturant. In a third tribe, the lake-dwelling Tchambuli, she did find sex differences in personality types—but in the reverse direction from those of our culture. Here the women were dominant, impersonal, and economically powerful, while the men were emotionally, economically, and sexually dependent, preoccupied with decorating themselves for ritualistic dramas and engaging in much of the backbiting pettiness and emotionality that many Americans associate with helpless female "bitchiness." As Mead put it:

> If those temperamental attitudes which we have traditionally regarded as feminine—such as passivity, responsiveness, and a willingness to cherish children—can so easily be set up as the masculine pattern in one tribe, and in another be outlawed for the majority of women as well as for the majority of men, we no longer have any basis for regarding such aspects of behavior as sex-linked. . . .
>
> The material suggests that we may say that many, if not all, of the personality traits which we have called masculine or feminine are as lightly linked to sex as are the clothing, the manners, and the form of head-dress that a society at a given period assigns to either sex. . . . We are forced to conclude that human nature is almost unbelievably malleable, responding accurately and contrastingly to contrasting cultural conditions. . . . Standardized personality differences between the sexes are of this order, cultural creations to which each generation, male and female, is trained to conform. (Mead 1935, pp. 259–60)

Of course the evidence from these small tribes cannot be interpreted as showing that a broad pattern of sex differences in personality and social roles does not exist across cultures. Such a pattern does indeed exist and indicates that, by and large, males tend to be more sexually active, more dominant, more deferred to, more aggressive, less responsible, less nurturant, and less emotionally expressive than females. Males are also more likely to perform the basic subsistence tasks, to control the property involved in these economic activities, and to live together in a descent group. The extent of these sex differences varies by culture, however, and in some cultures the differences do not exist or are reversed (D'Andrade 1966). These reversals are the point at issue. If the pattern can be reversed for entire cultures, then it cannot be based purely or even primarily on biological sex differences.

GROWING UP FEMALE

Having established that cultural or environmental factors are crucial to sex differences, researchers began to ask what these social factors are and how they affect behavior and personality. They began to concentrate on identifying the *cultural norms and learning experiences* that help to differentiate the two sexes, magnifying whatever biological sex differences may be present at birth. For instance, Barry, Bacon, and Child (1957) examined crosscultural sex differences in socialization, using published ethnographic reports of 110 societies distributed around the world. They found that although the two sexes were usually treated similarly in infancy, from four or five years of age until puberty there was a widespread pattern of greater pressure toward nurturance, obedience, and responsibility in girls and toward self-reliance and achievement striving in boys. The researchers attributed these differences in the upbringing of boys and girls to training in the personality characteristics and skills required for the economic tasks the boys and girls would perform as adults.

> The observed differences in the socialization of boys and girls are consistent with certain universal tendencies in the differentiation of adult sex role. In the economic sphere, men are more frequently allotted tasks that involve leaving home and engaging in activities where a high level of skill yields important returns; hunting is a prime example. Emphasis on training in self-reliance and achievement for boys would function as preparation for such an economic role. Women, on the other hand, are more frequently allotted tasks at or near home that minister most immediately to the needs of others (such as cooking and water carrying); these activities have a nurturant character, and in their pursuit a responsible carrying out of established routines is likely to be more important than the development of an especially high order of skill. Thus training in nurturance, responsibility, and, less clearly, obedience, may contribute to preparation for this economic role. (1957, pp. 328–29)

Of course, trained chefs (who are usually male) might quarrel with the assertion that cooking requires obedience rather than skill. One might even maintain that the researchers' characterization of male versus female tasks reflects male-oriented values. But here our concern is with the existence of general cultural practices that encourage the development of different personality characteristics and abilities in male and female children. The existence of these cultural patterns, which channel males and females into personality patterns matching common sexual stereotypes, challenges the idea that these sexual stereotypes are based entirely or even primarily on biological sex differences. As these researchers themselves conclude, "There are a few reversals of sex differences, and many instances of no detectable sex differences; these facts tend to confirm the cultural rather than directly biological nature of the differences" (1957, p. 332).

By comparing the crosscultural sex differences in behavior that are present at different ages, other researchers have tried to tease out the biological, as opposed to the social, factors causing sex differences. The reasoning goes like this: if the differences exist from birth, they are probably due to innate biological factors; if they appear only later in childhood, they are probably due to differences in the upbringing of boys and girls. For instance, Beatrice Whiting and Carolyn Pope Edwards (1973) examined the behavior of children between three and six and between seven and eleven years old in natural settings in seven different parts of the world. In the younger age group these researchers found sex differences in the manner of initiating physical contact: girls tended to initiate contact by seeking help or by physical touching, whereas boys tended to do it through rough-and-tumble play. At this age boys were also more verbally aggressive than girls and were likely to assert their dominance over peers directly, while girls were likely to assert their dominance indirectly by citing social rules. There were no differences in sociability, passivity, withdrawal from aggression, or nurturance (offering help and support) in this younger group.

The only consistent sex differences that still held true in the seven-to-eleven age group were the boys' greater tendencies to engage in rough-and-tumble play and to use verbal aggression. By then boys were seeking help and physical touching as much as girls were and seeking attention even more. New sex differences appeared in this age group, in that the older girls had become more nurturant (offered help and support more often) and were more compliant toward their mothers than were boys, while the older boys had become more ready than girls to respond to peer aggression with counteraggression. There continued to be no sex difference in sociability, while the sex difference in mode of asserting dominance had disappeared.

Thus boys began by being more physically aggressive than girls and seeking physical touching and help less than girls did. By the ages of seven to eleven both sexes were seeking an equal amount of physical touching and help from adults, while boys continued to be more physically aggressive to peers and began to seek attention more than girls did. Meanwhile, the older girls had begun to be more nurturant to their peers than were the older boys. Whiting and Edwards point out that "the difference in many of the types of behavior seems to be one of style rather than intent: i.e., seeking help ('feminine') rather than attention ('masculine'), and justifying dominance by appealing to the rules ('feminine') rather than straight egoistic dominance ('masculine')" (1973, p. 171).

Whiting and Edwards suggest that the two sexes may start out with a biological difference in energy level which causes girls to seek skin contact with others through a quieter mode than boys—that is, through touching or cuddling rather than through rough-and-tumble play. This initial sex difference then appears to be magnified by an encouragement of altruistic, nurturant behavior in girls as opposed to an encouragement of self-serving, physical assertiveness in boys. The authors focus on the differential pressure to be nurturant as a key theme of socialization that results from the different social interactions accompanying the childhood tasks assigned to the two sexes. Girls are usually expected to take care of infants and children and perform domestic chores that keep them in the vicinity of the house and yard and thus bring them into contact with infants and female adults. Boys, on the other hand, are expected to do farming and animal husbandry chores that bring them into contact primarily with male peers rather than with infants or adults of either sex. The authors hypothesize that the acts directed toward adults and infants are typically feminine in character—seeking and offering help, support, and attention; while the acts directed toward male peers are typically masculine in character—rough-and-tumble play and self-assertive aggressiveness. They support this hypothesis by noting that in both their own and others' studies fewer sex differences are found in societies where boys take care of infants, cook, and perform other domestic chores. This decrease in behavioral sex differences is due primarily to a decrease of masculine behavior in the boys. Furthermore, in the one social group in which Whiting and Edwards found that young girls did not care for infants or children, the behavioral sex differences were minimal due to a lower incidence of feminine behaviors and a higher incidence of masculine behaviors in these girls than they found in the other societies in their sample.

CULTURE AND BIOLOGY

How, then, do we determine which sex differences are biological in origin? Certainly we can reject the assertion that "men have always had the powerful positions in human societies because they are bigger and more aggressive." Margaret Mead's study demonstrates dramatically that men do not *always* hold the positions of power, nor do they *always* display personalities and behaviors that would be called masculine in our culture. The variability of sex differences from culture to culture clearly shows that size and strength—or any other sex-linked physical characteristics for that matter—are not the inevitable basis for sex-role stereotyping.

Furthermore, the later crosscultural studies suggest that there are broad patterns of child rearing that encourage females to be nurturant and altruistic but males to be aggressive and self-reliant. These socialization pressures appear to be strong enough to account for the entire range and degree of sex differences in society today.

On the other hand, Whiting and Edwards suggest that the cultural patterns of socialization magnify and elaborate an innate biological sex difference in levels of physical energy or activity. Is energy or activity level the essential element in biological sex differences? Perhaps. But their argument rests on their finding these energy differences in children between three and six years old—an age by which the socialization process may already be well under way. Then how about sex differences noted earlier in life, before the expectations and treatment begin to differ for males and females? For an answer to this question we must turn to psychologists' observations of human newborns.

At this point someone may argue that I still have not explained either the source of the crosscultural patterns of socialization or the fact that male-female differences are central to social organization in all cultures, regardless of the fact that the exact nature of those differences may vary from culture to culture. Are there indeed no basic biological differences that cause the universal male-female division?

These are important points. I certainly would not argue that there are no basic biological differences between the sexes. The question, however, is whether there are biological differences that affect other areas of life besides reproduction. Are there biological differences between the sexes that serve as a basis for sex roles, or do the expectations surrounding traditionally masculine and feminine personality and behavior represent a generalization from reproductive differences? The latter seems to be the case. While the smaller female is occupied having babies and bringing them up, the larger male is occupied with physically strenuous, dangerous activities that take him away from home and provide the food and money (or bartering objects) for the family. Since he usually performs the subsistence activities, the male also tends to control the property. This control, or dominance, is perpetuated by the cultural encouragement of aggression, sexual activity, and authority in males, combined with the encouragement of nurturance, responsibility, and emotional expressiveness in females (D'Andrade 1966).

These crosscultural patterns refer to the social roles and personalities of women and men in existing cultures. Does it follow that males have been socially dominant throughout history? Many anthropologists think so, for the sex differences in reproductive function and size and strength were probably crucial in primitive cultures. As societies have become more technically sophisticated, the early sexual divisions have been perpetuated in spite of their decreasing relevance to everyday life. Gender is less relevant to factory work than to hunting, for instance.

Some feminists have, however, begun to challenge the primacy of male dominance. They maintain that the earliest societies were matriarchal, with women controlling reproduction and the subsistence tasks and hence forming a descent group and controlling the property (Newton and Webster 1973).

A discussion of the historical development of sex-role differentiation will not help with the question of biological differences. For even if we knew exactly what happened in earlier cultures, we still would not be able to separate biological from cultural factors in the personality and behavior patterns of those cultures. For any examination of the biological factors in current female personality, then, we are still left with (1) great variation in sex differences across cultures; (2) common themes of greater male dominance, aggression, and sexual activity and greater female nurturance, responsibility, and emotional expressiveness; and (3) the suggestion that innate sex differences in levels of energy and activity are magnified by socialization patterns.

Human Newborns—Are Males Born to Be Macho?

Then there is the argument that male babies are bigger, stronger, and more aggressive than female babies. Is this true, and does it prove that male dominance is inborn, biological, natural, and inevitable?

This argument is not limited to casual conversation. Many social scientists who believe in biological determinism also use it. Their reasoning goes like this: since a number of sex differences have been found in the unsocialized, newborn infant, obviously they point to the biological basis for all the major sex differences in adult behavior and social roles.

A number of investigators have indeed reported sex differences in newborns. If one considers only such isolated studies while ignoring other studies that found no differences or differences in the opposite direction, one can assemble a wide array of supposedly innate sex-linked characteristics. This approach has been deplorably common among psychologists. As recently as 1972, Rosenberg and Sutton-Smith stated that earlier research suggested that male newborns are larger, have more muscular development, are more active, and have a higher pain threshold than females, and also referred to studies that have found males to be less sensitive to touch and less susceptible to comforting and to have higher basal metabolism rates that may indicate higher energy levels.

But in order to state that a sex difference has been clearly established, one must survey *all* the available data, not just those that support one viewpoint or another. After the most exhaustive and authoritative review of the literature to date, Eleanor Maccoby and Carol Jacklin (1974) conclude that the results are so contradictory that none of these sex differences can be viewed as clearly established in infancy. The results vary not only for males and females from study to study but also for the same infant over time. For instance, those infants who appear to be the most active as newborns are often the ones who are least active as preschoolers. If we cannot even predict the same infant's behavior in a few months or years, how can we predict differences between groups of male and female infants?

For the moment, however, let us assume that the preceding sex differences do really exist in newborns. How, then, do these differences relate to sex-role stereotypes in adults? Are females uniquely suited for child rearing, and only for child rearing, because they are smaller, less muscular, and more sensitive to touch? Lifting heavy weights is an inherently male capacity according to this argument, but in terms of sheer physical strength, how does lifting a forty-pound load of bricks differ from lifting a forty-pound child?

Even if we grant that the sex differences sometimes found in newborns are crucial to adult sex-role behaviors, we run into the same difficulty as in the study of animals: these differences do not reflect pure biology, uncontaminated by cultural factors. Sex-role stereotyping begins the moment a baby is labeled male or female; it does not even wait for the pink and blue clothes or décor that go with the label. Three researchers from Tufts University demonstrated this by interviewing thirty pairs of first-time parents, fifteen with newborn sons and fifteen with daughters, within twenty-four hours of delivery (Rubin, Provenzano, and Luria 1974). Daughters were described as softer, finer-featured, littler, and more inattentive than sons, even though there was no difference in size or weight between male and female infants.

Whether male and female babies actually do vary predictably according to gender, they are perceived by adults as doing so and are, in turn, brought up accordingly. Some researchers have suggested that differences in perception and response to male and female newborns magnify whatever sex differences may be present at birth. This more moderate position maintains that the initial, innate biological sex differences may be too small to be assessed through current measurement techniques, yet are translated into major sex differences in personality and behavior through a complex interaction of biological and social factors.

This position is compatible with recent research on child-rearing practices that stresses the *interaction* between the behavior of the baby and its caretaker. In a typical study Howard Moss (1967) observed thirty first-born infants and their mothers over the first three months of life. He found that the male infants slept less and cried more than the females and had more stimulating interaction with their mothers. When the infant's own behavior was controlled (that is, was held statistically constant), the mothers showed a tendency to treat the males and the females differently: they were more likely to stimulate and arouse the males to be more active but to repeat the vocalizations of the females. Since physical activity in infancy has been interpreted as a forerunner of aggressiveness, and vocal imitation has been interpreted as encouraging verbal fluency, these sex differences can be viewed as significant precursors of later sex differences; that is, male infants may have a biological predisposition to greater activity which is encouraged by mothers and hence leads to more aggressiveness in later life. Female infants, on the other hand, may have a biological predisposition to less activity and not be encouraged to be more active, while they are encouraged to be more verbal, hence leading to less aggressiveness and greater verbal fluency in later life.

Moss also found that mothers were more likely to respond to crying and fussing in females than in males—perhaps because females are more easily comforted, or because mothers think only females should be coddled. In either case this maternal response may foster a female tendency to turn to others for help and hence be interpreted as a precursor to the (supposedly) greater sociability of women.

Moss's study helps us visualize how child-rearing practices magnify any innate biological differences between the sexes. This does not necessarily mean that there *are* important biological sex differences at birth; the same social shaping could take place even if the two sexes were initially indistinguishable in their behavior. In fact, Maccoby and Jacklin (1974) point out that later studies have failed to substantiate the two innate sex differences suggested by Moss—greater activity in males and greater susceptibility to comforting in females. There is no evidence of sex differences in degree of activity during the first year of life. From this age on, studies vary widely regarding sex differences in this area; but when differences are reported, boys are more active. However, under certain conditions boys are more active, and under others the two sexes are much alike; activity has not been studied in situations that might prove especially stimulating to girls.

The idea that girls are more easily comforted is usually based on their greater sensitivity to touch. Maccoby and Jacklin point out that not only is the sex difference in response to touch questionable, but "being highly sensitive to touch could mean that touch is either more irritating or more soothing than for insensitive persons. It is not intuitively obvious which way the effect should go" (1974, p. 22).

As for the differences in the way mothers treat male and female infants, Moss reports that mothers were more likely to stimulate boys to higher activity levels, to encourage vocalization in girls, and to respond to crying and fussing in girls. Among infants only the first difference is supported by a consistent trend for parents to elicit "gross motor behavior" more from sons than from daughters; or as Maccoby and Jacklin put it, "the continuing theme appears to be that girls are treated as though they were more fragile than boys" (1974, pp. 307, 309). The findings on vocalization and comforting are mixed and confusing, varying from study to study and according to factors such as the parent's sex, socioeconomic level, and subcultural group.

What do these observations of newborns add to the argument about innate biological sex differences? When *all* the available data are considered, we find that there are no clearly established differences in the behavior of male and female newborns. There *is* a difference in the way parents treat these newborns, however, and it revolves around the perception and treatment of females as more fragile. These "fragile" babies are handled in a more gingerly fashion—a fact that is probably related to preschool girls being less involved in rough-and-tumble play and in other behavior indicative of high levels of activity and physical aggression.

Thus our biological determinist's appeal to sex differences in the newborn has backfired. Not only does the latest research suggest that no discernible sex differences exist at birth, but in addition it points toward a pervasive tendency for parents to perceive infants in terms of gender. If any real biological sex differences do serve as the starting point for the socialization process, we cannot know what they are as long as sex-role stereotyping is so deeply ingrained that babies are perceived in terms of gender.

Gender Identity—Learning That

One Is Female

In most arguments about biological sex differences, neither side knows what to make of the occasional adult who undergoes a sex-change operation. Millions of Americans have seen people on television who look and act like demure, attractive women—but these "women" grew up as boys, participated in sports and other "male" activities, had successful careers as men, even married and fathered children. Is such a person *really* a woman? If genital surgery, dress, and makeup can turn a man into a woman, what exactly *is* a woman as opposed to a man?

During the past twenty years this question has been addressed through the study of hermaphrodites, people who are born with poorly developed, ambiguous genitalia. These rare individuals are labeled boys or girls according to the predominant appearance of their external genitals and are reared accordingly, so that their sex of rearing may not match their internal sexual anatomy and chromosomes. The studies focus on cases of such a mismatch. When these mismatched individuals reach puberty, the development of secondary sex characteristics such as breasts or a beard contradicts the gender label they have learned to apply to themselves. In spite of this contradiction, however, almost all these people continue to think of themselves as being of the sex within which they were raised, and they go on to work, play, and marry as a person of that sex.

The interpretation of this amazing phenomenon is based on the "critical period" hypothesis, which asserts that humans, like other animals, go through specific and limited periods of early learning that have a permanent effect on later social behavior. These periods are believed to be set by a biological clock that opens the door to special types of learning during a given period. When this critical period ends, the door shuts and whatever was learned is set for life. When a duckling is biologically ready to learn to follow its mother, for instance, it latches onto whatever moving object first appears. From then on it continues to respond to that object as to a mother, even if the object is a human being or a wooden duck on a string. This formulation implies that one's gender identity is as irreversible as the identity of a duckling's mother. Once a person learns that she or he is female or male, it is extremely difficult, if not impossible, to change this basic perception.

Of course, most people believe that gender is a simple matter—that one is born either female or male, and that's that. Well, certainly most of us are unequivocally of one gender or the other, but there are actually six determinants of gender. These determinants are: (1) chromosomes, XX for females and YY for males; (2) gonads, testes in males and ovaries in females; (3) hormone level, more androgens in males and more estrogens and progesterone in females; (4) internal accessory organs, which are the uterus as the organ of menstruation in females and the prostate gland and seminal vesicles involved in the secretion of seminal fluid in males; (5) external genital appearance; and (6) assigned sex and rearing, usually based solely on external genital appearance (Hampson and Hampson 1961).

During the first six weeks of intrauterine life, the tissues that later develop into internal and external genitalia follow the female pattern in all fetuses. After the sixth week the developing testes in males secrete one substance that inhibits further female differentiation and another substance (testosterone) that initiates male differentiation. Thus to masculinize a fetus something must be added; without this (and with no addition of female hormones) female differentiation will occur. In a genetically male fetus, inadequate secretion of the female-inhibiting substance can result in a boy's being born with incompletely formed genitals that resemble the female's, and even with female as well as male internal anatomy. In a genetically female fetus, rare conditions involving increased secretion of testosterone can interfere with normal development, causing the absence of internal female anatomy and/or enlargement of the clitoris and fusion of the labial lips so that the external genitalia resemble the male's.

When a baby is born with inadequately differentiated sexual anatomy, the condition is called "hermaphroditism," regardless of whether the internal and/or external genitalia are involved.* The classic studies

---

* Some writers distinguish between "hermaphrodites," who possess internal genitalia of both sexes, and "pseudohermaphrodites," who have internal sexual anatomy of only one sex but whose external genitalia resemble the opposite sex at birth (M. Rosenberg 1973). John Money points out that this distinction is due to

in this area have focused on babies whose external genitalia are affected and hence look ambiguous or resemble the opposite sex. John Money and his colleagues (Hampson and Hampson 1961) studied over one hundred such hermaphrodites whose external genital appearance and sex of rearing contradicted the other biological determinants of their gender. All but seven developed the gender identity that their parents had brought them up to have. Furthermore, they showed the interests, the fantasies, and the behavior typical of their socially assigned, rather than of their biological, sex. From this the researchers concluded that perception of one's own gender is based on learning rather than on biology. This learning is so thorough, moreover, that attempts to re-assign such individuals to their biological sex after about eighteen months of age often result in extreme confusion, emotional distress, and even psychosis.

But if one's gender itself is learned, how can the behavior and characteristics associated with that gender be biologically determined? Obviously they cannot. As two of these researchers put it,

> In the human psychologic sexuality is not differentiated when the child is born. Rather, psychologic sex becomes differentiated during the course of the many experiences of growing up, including those experiences dictated by his or her own bodily equipment. Thus, in the place of the theory of an innate, constitutional psychologic bisexuality such as that proposed by Freud . . . we must substitute a concept of psychologic sexual neutrality in humans at birth. Such psychosexual neutrality permits the development and perpetuation of divers patterns of psychosexual orientation and functioning in accordance with the life experiences each individual may encounter and transact. (Hampson and Hampson 1961, p. 1406)

But what of the adults who have successfully functioned within one sex and then undergone genital surgery? They seem to be abandoning their sex of rearing, unlike most of the hermaphrodites studied by Money and his colleagues. Some of these transsexuals may be physical hermaphrodites who were assigned to the wrong sex and are now fol-lowing the promptings of their basic biology. But their behavior can also be explained in terms of learning one's gender identity and sex-role characteristics. For instance, some may have been born with ambiguous external genitalia that caused some confusion within their family in spite of the assignment of a correct gender label. For them, the sex-change operation would be an attempt to deal with socially induced confusion and conflict and would have the effect of contradicting their basic biology. Others with normal sexual anatomy may have learned

---

the mistaken belief that only the gonads determine gender (Money and Ehrhardt 1972). To dismiss studies of pseudohermaphrodites as not showing true biological contradiction is beside the point in any case, for the important dimension is the contradiction between *biological* and *social* determination of gender.

such strict criteria for sex roles that they feel that, to acknowledge and display any characteristics that they associate with the opposite sex, they must physically become part of that sex. (This feeling seems to have contributed to the dilemma of Jan Morris, whose autobiography *Conundrum* was published in 1974 and received extensive publicity.) In such cases the sex-change operation would be a result not of social confusion but of social rigidity, while its results would also contradict the person's biology.*

Furthermore, after surgery a dramatic change is often observed in the appearance, the behavior, and even the personalities of such transsexuals. If the characteristics associated with sex roles can be altered merely by removing or rearranging a small amount of genital tissue (and by making the changes in dress and social interaction that accompany this operation), how can these characteristics be entirely or even primarily determined by biological factors present from birth? One could maintain, of course, that the hormone changes involved in sex-change operations cause these alterations in behavior and personality. Certainly the hormone balance is drastically altered both by removal of the testicles or ovaries and by the supplementary hormone therapy that is usual both before and after surgery. But hormone levels are only one factor in the biological determination of gender. Furthermore, the biological view of sex differences implies a certain immutability of personality, contrary to the marked flexibility observed over the life span of many transsexuals, not to mention to the flexibility and variation observed within and between ordinary people of each sex.

So is the male-to-female transsexual really a woman? In terms of self-perception, the answer is clearly yes. For the studies of hermaphrodites show that while each of us is born with a body of one gender or the other, each of us has to learn which gender that is. If for some reason learning clashes with biology, learning wins hands down. Biology is no match for feelings and self-perceptions in this area.

---

* Ross, Rogers, and McCulloch recently suggested that a few homosexuals may seek sex-change operations because of such a reaction to social rigidity or stigma. "Where normative social pressure is internalized, the homosexual may, in an extreme case, believe that sexual relations can only be male-female, and rationalize in line with this pressure that if he desires a male, he must become a female. Thus, he may opt for changing to a female rather than adopting alternative male behaviors" (1978, p. 324). Kando (1974) came to a similar conclusion after finding that transsexuals showed significantly more conservative attitudes toward gender-linked norms than did matched females or males.

Chapter 2

Hormones

No ARGUMENT about biological sex differences is complete without someone's saying, "In my opinion it's all a matter of hormones. Everyone knows that men are more aggressive and highly sexed because of their male hormones, while women are naturally fitted for child rearing because of their female hormones. Not only that, women are notoriously unpredictable, moody, and even hysterical once a month, while men are reliable and steady." This comment is likely to spark the sort of heated debate that has been going on for over a decade in both the popular press and scientific journals.

There are two basic questions here. First, how are differences in hormone levels reflected in the personalities and the behavior of different individuals? This question involves male-female differences as well as comparisons of individuals within each sex, and studies addressing it have examined behavior related to nurturance, power and aggression, and strength of the sex drive. The second question is, how do variations in hormone levels over time—hormone cycles—within one individual affect that person's behavior and mood? Efforts to answer this question have focused on the effects of the female menstrual cycle.

The Role of Hormones in Physical Growth,

Behavior, and Emotions

Before turning to the debate itself, I shall consider the role of hormones in normal human development. I have already discussed the sexual differentiation of the fetus, which operates on an additive principle: all fetuses develop as female unless male testicular substances are added after the sixth week of development. Hamburg and Lunde (1966) have summarized evidence that indicates that after birth secretion of sex hormones is regulated by the brain. The hypothalamus controls the action of the anterior lobe of the pituitary gland, which produces hormones (gonadotrophins) that in turn prompt development and secretion of sex hormones in the ovaries and testes and regulate the female menstrual cycle. Puberty seems to be initiated by an interaction between the sex hormones and certain cells of the brain.

In normal childhood, both male (androgenic) and female (estrogenic) sex hormones are almost undetectable in the urine until the child is eight to ten years of age. At this point the male hormones sharply increase in both sexes, while the female hormones increase only in females. In girls the production of sex hormones becomes cyclic at about the eleventh year and is accompanied by the beginning of menstruation, the appearance of secondary sexual characteristics, and a growth spurt. Thus in terms of hormones measurable through urinalysis, there are no appreciable differences between males and females until puberty. After puberty both androgenic and estrogenic hormones are present in both sexes, but in different proportions. Males have high levels of androgens and low levels of estrogens, while females have high levels of estrogens and moderate levels of androgens.

Even this brief outline of hormonal development shows that, in order to explain prepubertal sex differences in terms of hormones circulating in the bloodstream, one would have to assume that the hormone levels of boys and girls vary significantly. Nevertheless, since these absolute differences in hormone secretion are too small to be measured through analysis of urine content, this assumption, however reasonable on the surface, cannot be the basis for scientific statements about sex differences. For if assumed differences have authoritative explanatory value, any argument can be proven scientifically.

Abandoning this assumption, we could examine hormonally linked behaviors in adults only. But here we run into a second assumption: that bodily chemistry, or physiological state, is directly translated into personality and behavior. In other words, the hormonal argument again ignores social factors. Now the biological determinist says, "Hormones are a pretty simple matter. They give us energy and direct that energy into natural channels such as sex and fighting. Socialization doesn't enter into the relationship between our behavior and moods and our own bodily state." We cannot be so sure, however, that socialization is irrelevant. Extensive research has shown that even our private emotions and their interpretation are shaped by the reactions of those around us. While visceral sensations such as heart palpitations, flushing, and tremor tell us that we are emotionally aroused, we have to learn whether that arousal means that we are excited, angry, or happy. And we learn to apply these verbal labels by observing others while we are experiencing the physical sensations.

The classic experiment in this area was done by Schachter and Singer (1962) using injections of adrenalin, a stimulating drug that mimics the visceral sensations underlying emotion—heart palpitations, flushing, and tremor. The basic idea was to see whether people who did not know the source of these sensations would use the social context to interpret them as emotional arousal. The experimenters wanted to induce visceral arousal that could be emotional, while letting some people know this arousal was drug-induced but concealing the fact from others. To do this, they gave adrenalin injections to three kinds of subject: (1) informed subjects who were told about the actual side effects; (2) misinformed subjects who were led to expect side effects but were told that there would be itching, numbness in the feet, and a slight headache; and (3) uninformed subjects who were not told to expect side effects. The subjects were told that the experiment was concerned with the effects of the drug Suproxin on their vision, and were asked to wait twenty minutes between the injection and the vision test. For these twenty minutes each subject was joined by another person who was supposedly also a subject waiting for the Suproxin to take effect. This second person was actually a stooge prepared to show either rage by railing at the experimenter and behaving in a disagreeable, aggressive way, or extreme high spirits by laughing and engaging in such shenanigans as shooting baskets with crumpled paper balls and flying folded paper airplanes. The subjects' actions were observed through a one-way mirror, while their descriptions of their moods were obtained by questionnaires.

The experimenters' expectations were supported: the uninformed and the misinformed subjects, who did not anticipate their symptoms, behaved like the stooge and reported that they had experienced a mood similar to the one expressed by the latter's behavior. These results suggest that when we experience a physical sensation for which we have no explanation, we are likely to label this sensation in terms of our social surroundings.

Some internal cues are necessary, however, for emotion to be experienced. A fourth group of subjects who were injected with a placebo (a saline solution producing no physical effects) tended to copy the stooge less than did either misinformed or uninformed subjects injected with adrenalin.

The implications of this research have been called the "juke box theory of emotion" (Mandler 1962). To play a juke box one must first insert a coin and then select a tune. Visceral arousal is analagous to the insertion of the coin that energizes the machine; this physical condition is necessary for emotional arousal but not specifically patterned for any one emotion. Interpretation of the social situation is analagous to the selection of a tune; if others are laughing, the tune will be happiness; if others are frowning, the tune will be anger.

Thus, a simple, one-to-one relationship does not always exist between body chemicals and their physical effects, on the one hand, and between behavior and mood, on the other. Like all body chemicals, hormones produce a physiological state that must be translated into personality and behavior through a specific social context. Given the pervasiveness of gender as a filter of perceptions and expectations from birth on, we can reasonably assume that sex roles determine many of these social contexts. Thus, sex roles probably enter into the very way we perceive and interpret our own bodily sensations, including those sensations due to hormones.

Take the case of the hormone androgen, found in greater quantities in males than in females. Because males are typically more physically aggressive than females, androgen is thought to be associated with greater physical activity and aggressiveness. But Moss (1967) found that mothers tend to comfort crying or fussing female babies more than they do crying or fussing males. It may be that the male infant experiences visceral sensations, such as the stomach contractions of hunger pangs, within the social context of lack of maternal response. He then learns that crying is not enough; he has to assert himself physically to attract the mother's attention. Over a period of months or years the male child may then come to associate these visceral sensations with greater activity or aggressiveness; this aggressiveness in turn may lead the male to interpret the underlying visceral sensation as the emotion of anger.

The female infant, on the other hand, may begin by experiencing the same visceral sensations due to stomach contractions; but when she cries, her mother comforts her. The female infant then learns that crying will attract attention in this situation. Over a period of time the female may come to associate these visceral sensations with comforting and its resulting quiescence; this comforting, in turn, may lead her to interpret the underlying visceral sensations as the emotion of happiness. Thus, from the same visceral sensation, the male infant could derive a tendency to respond to visceral discomfort with physical activity, aggressiveness, and anger, and the female infant a tendency to respond to visceral discomfort with appeals for help, physical passivity, and happiness.

This example is hypothetical and somewhat farfetched. But it does outline one of the ways in which the social context may cause a particular internal cue to lead to different personal interpretations and behavior in the two sexes. This is not to say that hormone levels are irrelevant to personality and behavior. It merely suggests that, even in dealing with such presumably purely biological differences as hormones, we need to keep a sharp eye out for ways in which social factors help translate these biological factors into everyday behavior.

Hormonal Research Strategies

Keeping in mind the intervention of social factors, we now turn to sex differences in behavior caused by differences in hormone levels. But here we run into yet another problem in this area: there is no simple, reliable method for determining the amount of hormones present in the human body. In the past ten years biochemical methods have been developed that can measure hormone levels in the blood or the urine. But these are in the early stages of development, so that much of the data already reported in scientific journals are based on bioassay. This method involves injecting human urine or blood into a laboratory animal and measuring subsequent changes in some tissue known to respond to a given hormone. (For example, the internal sexual anatomy of the female mouse changes in response to female hormones, while that of the male mouse changes in response to male hormones.) Even when such bioassay studies are completed, however, they measure the *activity* of the injected hormones rather than the total amount or level of the hormones present in the human body. Furthermore, such bioassay studies are notoriously difficult to standardize, because the animal's response must be taken into account: responses to the same hormone injection vary among individual animals, among genetic strains of a given species, and among species.

Faced with these difficulties, most researchers have not attempted to measure hormone levels directly. Instead, they have turned to four major alternatives. The first involves experimental studies of animal behavior following massive injections of hormones. This strategy differs from the naturalistic studies of animal groups in that the animal is studied in the laboratory rather than in its natural habitat, and also that the measures focus on *changes* in behavior caused by the injections rather than on the natural behavior and social organization observed without artificial intervention.

Laboratory studies of animals suffer from many of the same difficulties that hamper naturalistic studies. Species vary not only in the natural behavior to be altered but also in their responses to the hormone injections. Researchers often follow their own biases both in choosing a species to study and in selecting a "masculine" or a "feminine" behavior pattern to alter by male or female hormones. We seldom know how the laboratory environment affects the animal's behavior to confound the impact of the hormone injections. And there is still the basic difficulty of extrapolating from animals to humans.

On the other hand, hormone injection studies do not necessarily assume that animals are unsocialized, and thus do not assume that the behavior observed before administering hormones is totally determined by biological as opposed to social factors. The crucial point is the change in gender-linked behavior after hormone injection. If behavior does change significantly, it must be strongly influenced by hormones. Of course, the existence of hormonal linkage does not eliminate other simultaneous causes for behavior: hormonally linked behavior can be shaped by social factors as much as nonhormonally linked behavior. The concept of hormonal linkage is important, however, and therefore the results of these animal studies deserve careful consideration.

The second hormonal research strategy also examines the effects of massive doses of hormones, but in humans rather than in animals. Since it is not feasible to inject hormones into human subjects, the researchers take advantage of accidents of nature that involve similar "overdoses." They compare normal girls with female hermaphrodites, whose ambiguous genitalia suggest the presence of excess male hormones (at least during the hermaphrodites' fetal development).

The third hormonal research strategy attempts to relate changes in behavior to natural changes in hormone levels due to menstruation, pregnancy, or childbirth in humans. Here the hormone "injection" also occurs without experimental manipulation but involves same-sex hormones (female hormones in females) rather than opposite-sex hormones. And rather than "injected" subjects being compared with "noninjected" subjects, the same individual is studied at different times: when her level of female hormones is high and when her level of female hormones is moderate or low.

The fourth research method examines the effects of hormone deficiencies rather than overdoses. Using human subjects, these studies examine the effects of surgical removal of the testicles or the ovaries. This research strategy has focused on sexual behavior and desires, omitting extensive discussion of other supposedly hormonally linked behavior.

Using these four major types of data, let us see whether the research supports the idea that sex differences are all a matter of hormones. I shall first examine sex differences in nurturance, aggression, and the sex drive and then turn to studies of the effects of the menstrual cycle itself.

Nurturance

The idea that a woman is naturally fitted for child rearing because of her female hormones rests on two assertions. First, the hormones associated with pregnancy and childbirth are seen as preparing the woman to take care of the newborn child. Second, the female hormones present in a woman even when not pregnant are seen as making her uniquely equipped for childcare.

Experimental research with rats suggests that the hormones involved in pregnancy and giving birth do indeed "prime" the female in some way for taking care of the young. Maccoby and Jacklin (1974) have summarized evidence that pregnant rats show a gradually increasing responsiveness to foster pups (newborn rats) during the course of their pregnancy, and that injecting a virgin female with blood plasma from a female who has just given birth decreases the time required for the virgin rat to respond to foster pups by such maternal behavior as retrieving, nest building, and licking pups. However, these authors go on to point out that

> the hormonal impetus to maternal behavior in rats is superimposed upon a base level of responsiveness that is greater than zero and is *not* hormonally controlled. Both virgin females and males will show maternal behavior towards pups after about five days if a fresh litter of newborns is given to them each day. And this is true even if they have been deprived of the glands that produce sex hormones. A female that has just given birth to pups, of course, is responsive immediately. (Maccoby and Jacklin 1974, p. 216)

Thus, in rodents, pregnancy hormones appear to lower the threshold of maternal response, shortening the time period between presentation of newborns and the beginning of nurturant behaviors. But pregnancy hormones are not necessary to nurturance, since both males and untreated virgin females respond positively to newborns. I should note, however, that male rats tend to be more aggressive toward pups and are likely to kill the first litters given to them. Only after this aggressive response has been extinguished do the males begin to take care of the foster pups.

Although findings with rodents are suggestive, there is little data available on other animal species to corroborate these initial impressions. If it is risky to generalize from a number of species to humans, it is even more risky to generalize from only one species, and one that is rather low on the phylogenetic scale. This note of caution seems particularly appropriate when we turn to the sparse data available on pregnancy hormones in humans. These data rely on comparisons of parental responses to newborns: if pregnancy hormones prime women for child rearing, then mothers who have just given birth should show more nurturant behaviors than do the babies' fathers. In the only relevant study reported by Maccoby and Jacklin (1974), a hospital nurse brought a baby in and asked which parent wanted to hold it. The researchers noted which parent initially took the child and how much that parent engaged in nurturant interaction (looking, touching, rocking, holding, and smiling). With the exception of smiling, fathers engaged in *as much or more* nurturant interaction than mothers did, both when the parents were together and when each parent was observed alone with the baby. The results were the same for one group of well-educated fathers who had taken a course in natural childbirth and observed the delivery and for a second group of working-class fathers who did not take the course and were not present at the delivery (Parke and O'Leary 1974).

What of the effects of the comparative levels of male and female hormones outside the period of pregnancy and childbirth? There are few observational studies comparing males and females in this area, because nurturance is viewed as feminine and hence is usually studied only within all-female groups. Sandra Bem (1974) has begun such a research program, however, and found no sex differences in college students' responses to an eight-week-old kitten.

Some researchers have suggested that male hormones may actually suppress nurturant behavior. As I said, male rats tend to kill the first few litters of pups placed in their cages and only begin to groom and care for the pups after this aggressive response has been extinguished by exposure to several litters. The suppression hypothesis can be examined indirectly by studying females with unusually high levels of male hormones; if male hormones suppress nurturance, these females should show less nurturant behaviors than normal females show.

The standard evidence offered for the suppression hypothesis is Money and Ehrhardt's (1972) study of twenty-five genetic females inadvertently masculinized *in utero* by excessive androgen production or by the administration of hormones to prevent miscarriage. At birth most of these hermaphrodites had enlarged clitorises and a certain amount of labial fusion, although in some the masculinization extended to a fully formed penis and empty scrotum. All the infants were raised as girls and had entirely female internal sexual anatomy. Surgery and hormone therapy were used to correct the genital ambiguity. As compared to a control group of nonmasculinized girls, the hermaphrodites showed more evidence of "tomboyism," defined as (1) high energy expenditure and involvement in sports, (2) self-assertiveness and rivalry with boys in the dominance hierarchy of childhood, (3) preference for functional rather than self-adorning clothing, (4) little interest in or involvement with dolls, and (5) focus on achievement and career rather than on romance and marriage as adolescents. Money and Ehrhardt attribute this tomboyism to a masculinizing effect on the fetal brain. Thus, this study does not compare the effects of current hormone levels in the bloodstream but rather examines the effects of a prenatal hormone difference on behavior in childhood, assuming that the behavioral differences are mediated by structural changes caused by the hormones at an earlier, crucial stage of development.

For the purposes of considering the relationship between hormones and nurturance, the relevant finding is the hermaphrodites' relative lack of interest in dolls. But can we assume that doll play is actually nurturant behavior? Dolls are used to act out a variety of fantasized behavior, including wrestling, fighting, and killing (remember the toy G.I. Joe). Maccoby and Jacklin put it this way:

> It is true that dolls are hugged and tucked into bed, which are nurturant actions by any definition: however, they are also scolded, spanked, subjected to surgical operations, and (in the personal experience of one of the authors) even scalped. If girls choose dolls as a vehicle for acting out a variety of fantasies, this is not in itself evidence that the fantasies are more nurturant than those of boys, although they may be. (1974, p. 220)

But if we ignore the doll playing, what other behaviors remain to differentiate the hermaphrodites from normal girls their age? Differentiating behavior revolves around two themes: various manifestations of high levels of physical energy and assertiveness, summarized by the term "tomboyism," and a heightened interest in careers rather than in romance and marriage. The researchers may be assuming that high levels of physical energy and assertiveness are antithetical to nurturance, while an interest in romance and marriage are precursors of the nurturant behavior of child rearing. The argument that androgens suppress nurturant behavior appears to rest on this assumption, in that the low interest in dolls, high degree of tomboyism, and high interest in careers are all attributed to androgen levels.

But what of social factors affecting interests and activities in childhood? The social pressures on hermaphrodites were probably as unusual as their initial genitalia. The parents of the hermaphrodites certainly knew about their children's medical histories. Although the hermaphrodites were labeled and reared as girls, their parents may well have permitted and even encouraged them to participate in "boyish" activities more than their nonmasculinized sisters and friends, of which less doll play could merely be a consequence. Tomboys express their feelings and energies through direct, assertive manipulation of the physical environment. With greater physical expression tomboys may not need to rely as much on the fantasized expressions of doll play.

Furthermore, the corrective surgery and hormone therapy required in all cases may well have affected the hermaphrodites' self-perceptions. Concern about their own sexual anatomy might make these children anxious about romantic involvements, so that a career would seem a safer outlet for their energies and aspirations. The parents might also have been worried about the hermaphrodites' future sexual performance and might well have encouraged career interests more in these than in their other female children.

Social factors could certainly account for an increase in tomboyish behavior and career plans that are viewed as acceptable, if not necessarily highly desirable, in female children. Even a marked difference from normal controls could thus be due to social influences rather than to differences in androgen levels in the hermaphrodites.*

Does all this add up to a firm hormonal basis for nurturance? Hardly. Although the studies of rats are suggestive, the studies of humans either are inconclusive or contradict the hormonal hypothesis. The study of hermaphrodites is flawed by the use of doll play as the central measure of nurturance as well as by the parents' knowledge of the children's medical histories, while the observation of new parents suggests that new fathers without pregnancy hormones actually act *more* nurturant than new mothers act.

My skepticism increases when I consider the studies that show that in most cultures females are encouraged to be nurturant and altruistic, while males are encouraged to be aggressive and self-reliant (Barry, Bacon, and Child 1957; Whiting and Edwards 1973). With only weak and contradictory data to support a hormonal basis for nurturant behavior, it is sensible to rely on the extensive data that point to learning and socialization as the basis for such behavior.

Aggression

The controversy surrounding aggression is not about whether males act more aggressive than females but about the causes for these sex differences, for regardless of how aggression is defined and measured, males of all ages show a consistent tendency to be more aggressive than their female peers (Maccoby and Jacklin 1974; Mischel 1970; Oetzel 1966; Terman and Tyler 1954). Males are more apt to express their hostile feelings in daydreams and fantasies, in socially disguised forms of dominance and competition, and in direct physical attacks. This greater male aggression is expressed not only in a variety of behavioral modes but also in a variety of situations and cultures.

Furthermore, not only is aggression the most striking sex difference, it is also the one with the strongest evidence of biological causation. This evidence involves the observation of aggressive behavior in animals and humans with varying levels of male hormones. The basic rationale is that since males are the more aggressive sex, the male hormones must be linked to this behavior.

Three main research strategies have been used. The first examines females who have received an abnormally high (for females) *prenatal*

---

* I should also note that these female hermaphrodites all developed a gender identity consistent with their sex of rearing. This result matches earlier studies of hermaphrodites which suggest that social factors involved in child rearing are the crucial variables in developing self-perception of gender.

dose of male hormones. After birth these females generally show elevated levels of threat behavior and rough-and-tumble play. This effect has been demonstrated in rhesus monkeys, rodents, and chickens, and even in human hermaphrodites. Maccoby and Jacklin (1974) conclude that these studies suggest that male sex hormones present before birth program the individual so as to affect behavior in childhood and adulthood, producing a "male brain" that predisposes the individual to learn and more readily to exhibit aggressive threat behavior.

Although the research on animals is fairly persuasive, the research on human hermaphrodites is less convincing. As I have already noted in discussing Money and Ehrhardt's (1972) classic study of twenty-five girls who received excess male hormones *in utero*, the observation of higher levels of physical aggression in these girls was based on their involvement in rough-and-tumble play, an activity often observed in young female tomboys. With their knowledge of the girls' medical histories, which included hormone treatments and sometimes surgery to correct the masculinized appearance of the female genitals at birth, the mothers of these hermaphrodites may well have permitted and even expected greater tomboyism in their daughters. The strongest point of the argument that androgens cause a "male brain" is thus the animal data, with which the somewhat equivocal human data appear to agree.

The second area of research on hormones and aggression focuses on increased aggressive behavior in females who are administered male hormones *postnatally*, without prenatal sensitization. In a typical study Joslyn (1973) took three female and three male rhesus monkeys who were separated from their mothers at three to four months of age. The three females were given regular injections of testosterone from six and one half months until fourteen and one half months of age, while the three males were untreated. Aggressive responses were studied as part of the establishment of social dominance patterns at ages five to nine and one half months, thirteen and one half to sixteen months, and twenty-five to twenty-seven and one half months. Before the administration of testosterone began, the males were dominant and showed more aggression than the females. During the hormone treatment the frequency of the females' aggressive behavior gradually increased until it equaled that of the males at nine months of age. Shortly after this, two of the treated females attacked and subdued the two most dominant males. These two females then assumed the positions of dominance and were still maintaining them a year after treatment ended.

The change in the aggressive behavior and dominance patterns of Joslyn's monkeys was, moreover, not due merely to weight changes. Although the treated females gained weight until they outweighed the untreated males, the two aggressive females continued to dominate the males after the weight difference had disappeared. Furthermore, the third treated female who did not attack and dominate the males during treatment was the one who gained the most weight of all, and she began to dominate the two initially dominant males only *after* the treatment period, when she had already lost some weight.

This study of dominance and testosterone levels in rhesus monkeys raises questions about studies that use increased rough-and-tumble play as a measure of aggression. While the androgen-treated females became more physically aggressive toward males, they did not engage in more masculine sexual behavior or in more rough-and-tumble play among themselves than they did before treatment. And after they had been attacked and subdued by the newly aggressive females, the males engaged in less rough-and-tumble play among themselves and also in less sexual behavior than did normal males their age. Thus, administering male hormones to these female monkeys did not *increase* the frequency of their rough-and-tumble play or their masculine sexual behavior; it only *decreased* the frequency of such behavior in the untreated males. This suggests that social factors, such as the response to physical attack, may play an important part in behavior like rough-and-tumble play which is often used as a measure of aggression.

The third research strategy used to examine the role of hormones in aggression involves the measurement of current levels of androgens in adult males who engage in differing amounts of aggressive behavior. Most of this work again uses animals. For instance, Rose et al. (1971) found that the dominant members of a monkey troupe had higher levels of testosterone in their blood than had less dominant members. However, this correlation means only that position in a dominance hierarchy varies with androgen levels; it does not show what causes this covariance. In fact, the relationship between male hormones and dominance appears to be rather circular, for these same researchers found that when they put low-dominance male monkeys in cages with female monkeys whom the males could dominate and mate with, the males' androgen levels rose markedly and remained high. If the males were defeated in a fight, however, their androgen levels fell and remained low. Thus, while aggressive dominance behavior appears to be linked to male hormone levels in animals, we do not know whether the high hormone levels *cause* the aggressive behavior or whether they result from successful aggressive behavior.

But how do female hormones affect aggression? Unfortunately we know little about the answer to this question. Having begun with the observation that males tend to act more aggressive than females, most researchers have assumed that male and female hormones have opposite effects: that male hormones increase aggression, while female hormones decrease it. These researchers then set out to study only male hormones in relation to aggression, either injecting females with this (supposedly) foreign substance or measuring levels of androgens in males with differing levels of aggression.

We do know enough, however, to contradict the assumption that the action of female hormones is simply opposite to that of male hormones. For example, Bronson and Desjardins (1968) found that administering female hormones to newborn mice *decreased* the aggressiveness of males but *increased* the aggressiveness of females. Thus, in females the estrogens may mimic the effect of androgens in males; when given to males, however, estrogens may interfere with the action of the androgens.

However, injections of male hormones may have different effects upon the two sexes, just as injections of female hormones do. In this regard, Maccoby and Jacklin (1974) report Ehrhardt's finding that fetally androgenized boys were no more aggressive than their nonandrogenized brothers. There could be a ceiling effect here, with a certain minimal level of prenatal male hormone needed to masculinize an individual's behavior, and with male hormones beyond this level having little effect.

Furthermore, male androgens administered shortly before or after birth seem to increase aggressive behavior in females but not in males, while female hormones administered at that time also seem to increase aggressive behavior in females while decreasing it in males. Thus excess hormones, whether androgens or estrogens, seem to increase aggressive behavior in females more than in males. Rather than conclude that only *male* hormones underlie aggression, one could just as easily conclude that *both* male and female hormones underlie aggression (at least in women). This second conclusion would then suggest that it is the absolute level of *all* hormones, androgens and estrogens together, that underlies aggression in women, rather than the level of androgens relative to that of estrogens.

Where does this all lead the argument that hormones cause greater male aggression? Not to a definitive answer certainly. The study of hermaphrodites is no more conclusive in establishing a hormonal basis for aggression than it is in establishing a hormonal basis for nurturance. The animal studies do suggest a strong link between hormones and aggression, but the exact nature of this link is still shrouded in mystery. We will not solve this mystery until new studies examine the role of estrogens and androgens in both sexes. And even then we will be left with the problem of extrapolating from animals to humans.

Faced with so much confusing evidence, many researchers have turned to learning and socialization to account for the pervasive male tendency to be more physically aggressive than females. The basic argument is that the two sexes are actually equally aggressive in their underlying motivation but carry out the desire to hurt others in different ways. This argument takes two basic forms. The first maintains that the two sexes are reinforced for different forms of aggression: girls are allowed to show hostility only in subtle ways, while boys are encouraged to show it more directly by physical attack. The second form of the argument maintains that aggression in general is less acceptable and hence more discouraged for girls, leading to greater female anxiety and conflict over aggression. The research bearing on this issue will be outlined in the later chapter on social learning theory and female personality. Here I will simply note that although the hormonal explanation of aggression is suggestive, there are persuasive alternate explanations.

It is often assumed that female hormones cause problems while male hormones do not. The male androgens—and the aggression with which they are popularly associated—are taken as the desirable norm, so that few people have seriously investigated the possible harmful effects of androgen levels. Ellen Goodman makes a humorous comment on this state of affairs in her "At Large" column in the *Boston Globe*.

Estrogen on Patrol

They're going to study hormones in Philadelphia. To be more precise about it, they're going to study Hormones on Patrol—and if you think that sounds like science fiction, you're right.

Earlier this month, in response to a sex-discrimination suit, the City of Brotherly (sic) Love finally agreed to hire 100 women as police officers for patrol duty. In order, of course, to study them.

Since 1968 when Indianapolis became the first American city to put them in patrol cars police women have been researched more closely than Jane Goodall's chimpanzees. They have been studied in San Francisco. They have been studied in Cleveland. They have been studied in St. Louis. They have been studied in Washington, New York and New Jersey. At last count there were no more than half a dozen female patrol officers without a social researcher to call their own.

The results that have been published in Washington and New York prove the same thing—men and women have roughly the same effectiveness.

Nevertheless, under the leadership of that eminent biologist Frank Rizzo, Philadelphia is determined to confront once again the issues of anatomy, destiny and The Estrogen Factor.

The city fathers, including their lawyer, one Stephen Arinson believe that women aren't biologically strong enough for the job. It's not their fault, you understand, it's just the way God made them. As Arinson bellowed long distance into his speaker phone, "It's a question of biology. There is estrogen in women that is accountable for their lack of muscle tone."

Now, we are all in favor of researching estrogen. Some of us have been trying to get the Federal Drug Administration to do it properly for years. But this research is more discriminatory than the original situation. Once again women are going to have to prove that they can do the job despite their hormonal "flaw."

Men on the other hand are being allowed to labor on as if they were normal. In fact, they have "a problem"—testosterone poisoning.

As Alan Alda once so accurately and sympathetically described it, "Everyone knows that testosterone, the so-called male hormone, is found in both men and women. What is not so well known is that men have an overdose."

Alda—and that man's a M*A*S*H doctor!—went on to describe the distressing symptoms—a tendency to violence, competitiveness, and chicken legs (on their feet, not their plates). He said, "Until now it has been thought that the level of testosterone in men is normal simply because they have it. But, if you consider how abnormal their behavior is, then you are led to the hypothesis that almost all men are suffering from testosterone poisoning."

So, the fact of the matter is that we have been worrying about the wrong Hormones on Patrol. Much of the prejudice against women has hung on the idea that police officers must be able to win in hand-to-hand combat on the streets of San Francisco. Not to mention Clevelend, Washington, St. Louis and Philadelphia.

This notion was propagated by fellow sufferers like Arinson, Kojak and the entire cast of S.W.A.T. But, as Alda put it, "Testosterone poisoning is particularly cruel because its sufferers usually don't know they have it. . . . They even give each other medals for exhibiting the most advanced symptoms of the illness." Therefore, we must discount their definition of the problem.

The truth is that the vast majority of police situations call for tact, flexibility and the ability to read a touchy situation. In the case of unavoidable violence, well, they didn't call the Colt 45 "The Great Equalizer" for nothing.

Testosterone sufferers are more likely to produce or to escalate violence. They tend—through no fault of their own, you understand—to respond chiefly in terms of more violence.

Women, however, blessed with estrogen, may, as the New York and Washington studies suggest, have greater success in cooling down violent situations.

Thus the real question is whether the citizens of our great land should allow those who are under the sway of this raging hormonal imbalance to have command of a patrol car, a gun or even a billy club.

Should we allow cities to hire victims of this genetic disorder, without at least some special training to compensate for what they lack? Or, in the most extreme cases, some hormone therapy?

Certainly they shouldn't let them stalk the streets alone, or in pairs. They must each be assigned a partner who isn't born with the disease and can't catch it. Perhaps someone with just the right level of estrogen.

Source: Published in the *Boston Evening Globe* on 30 March 1976. © 1976, The Boston Globe Newspaper Company.

Sex Drive

Americans today seem to be obsessed with physical attractiveness and sexual prowess. It is difficult to get through a day without seeing an advertisement, an article, or a book on how to look, act, and feel sexier.

In spite of the current flurry of articles stressing women's sexuality, however, many people still agree when someone says, "Everyone knows that men are more highly sexed than women because of their male hormones." When we turn to the research, however, we find complex results.

THE AROUSAL OF LUST

Human sexual arousal and behavior are not automatically triggered by external sights, sounds, and smells or by internal hormones, as they are in lower animals. Money (1961) has explained that there are three major components of human sexual functioning: local genital sensations, brain cognitions, and hormones. Although the failure of any one of these components limits the sexual response, it does not destroy it entirely. Human sexuality is extremely complex and variable, adapting to wide variations in physical state and external circumstances.

Money (1961) reports on a number of studies demonstrating that although genital sensations are important, sexual response can continue without them. The major source of evidence involves the experiences of paraplegics, who have lost sensation and movement in their lower bodies through severe spinal cord injuries. The physical state of these patients varies, as does their gonadal secretion of hormones. Nevertheless, researchers have found that among 500 male paraplegics and quadraplegics (whose loss of function involves all four limbs), two-thirds were capable of achieving erection and, of these 330, about 100 actually had successful vaginal penetration in intercourse (Talbot 1955; Zeitlin, Cottrell, and Lloyd 1957). These sexual experiences did not, however, provide the gratification obtained before the injury.

Many paraplegic patients continue to have erotic thoughts, images, fantasies, and dreams in spite of the fact that their genitals—indeed a large portion of their bodies—are paralyzed and without feeling. Money himself interviewed a nineteen-year-old paraplegic man who, ten months earlier, had lost all feeling and movement from the nipples down. This patient reported that he experienced the same erotic arousal as before his injury—when his girlfriend kissed him he felt as though his penis were becoming erect and throbbing. "But when I would look down, nothing was there—it was all in my mind, or something" (1961, p. 1394). The discontinuity between cognitive and genitopelvic eroticism was further illustrated by the man's description of sexual daydreams, when he would also experience physical sensations, whereas in reality no erection occurred. In nocturnal dreams of intercourse and orgasm, the feelings accompanying the dream orgasm were also the same as in an ordinary nocturnal emission. But here again there was neither erection nor ejaculation.

Sexual response not only continues without genital sensations; it also occurs when there is a deficiency of sex hormones. This is shown by the effects of castration, which involves the surgical removal of the testicles in males and of the ovaries in females. Male testicular castration has been practiced throughout history—on enemies captured in war, on youths assigned as harem attendants, and as a badge of membership and commitment in obscure religious sects. In eighteenth-century Europe boys were still being castrated to provide virtuoso sopranos for adult female opera roles, and castration was part of the "pseudomedical fake experimentation" performed in Hitler's concentration camps (Money and Ehrhardt 1972, p. 217). Today male castration is performed primarily to treat cancer of the testes or as adjunct therapy for cancer of the prostate; although some castrations result from physical injuries, and others have been performed on prison inmates or mentally retarded males.

There is no historical tradition of female castration, which is a more complex medical procedure than male castration. Today it is usually performed on diseased ovaries, although "adult ovariectomy has been, and sometimes still is, recklessly included in surgery for hysterectomy" (Money and Ehrhardt 1972, p. 219).

The effects of castration vary dramatically depending on when it is done. If a male is castrated before puberty, his internal and external sexual organs fail to mature and he does not develop the usual secondary sexual characteristics. Such a man (a eunuch) retains his high voice and grows no beard, and his arms and legs often grow disproportionately long in relation to his trunk. He will not experience masculine balding later in life and develops a femalelike distribution of subcutaneous fat deposits. Although he may develop pubic and armpit hair, the pattern will be similar to the female's. As an adult a eunuch is usually sexually apathetic, although exceptional cases do occur. In spite of the lack of data on female prepubertal castration, the effects would probably be similar: failure to develop both primary and secondary sexual character-istics, such as menstruation and breasts, and lessened sexual impulse (Money 1961; Money and Ehrhardt 1972).

The physical effects of postpubertal castration are also quite pre-dictable. Males usually lose their ability to ejaculate first, since this is more hormone-dependent than erection. Ejaculation may, however, be replaced by a "dry-run orgasm" accompanied by the same subjective feelings (Money and Ehrhardt 1972, p. 219). Erectile potency is lost only gradually, over a period of weeks, months, or years. Females stop men-struating and experience less vaginal lubrication during sexual arousal. All these physical effects can be reversed by hormone therapy in both sexes (Money 1961; Money and Ehrhardt 1972).

In spite of the physical effects of castration, however, some men and women who undergo postpubertal castration retain their usual sexual capacities and responsiveness without hormone therapy, and a few actually show increased sexual expression. Others show a decrease in or total loss of sex drive (Money 1961; Money and Ehrhardt 1972; Rosenberg and Sutton-Smith 1972; West 1967). How can the same operation have such varying results? The answer seems to lie in the mind. Sexually mature adults have already accumulated memories of sexual sensation and the feelings accompanying arousal, orgasm, and ejaculation, as well as a network of habitual sexual responses. The drastic reduction of sex hormones does not eradicate these memories and habits, nor does it eliminate localized genital sensations. Social factors also complicate the response to castration—factors such as previous sexual experience, the nature of the castrate's ongoing sexual relationship, the cultural background of expectations regarding castration, and the relief of being freed of pregnancy fears (Money 1961).

The effects of hormone deficiency can also be examined by studying the sexual behavior of people whose ovaries or testes fail to secrete sex hormones. Money (1961) studied eleven males and ten females suffering from such gonadal failure. They were all totally hormone-deficient at age sixteen, when normal pubertal development was initiated by administering androgen substitutes to males and estrogen substitutes to females. Five of the hypogonadal men later discontinued hormone treatment for three months or longer. The absence of androgen made a decided difference to them: their ejaculatory emissions gradually diminished in volume; they had fewer erections and felt less impetus to masturbate or initiate intercourse. But their eroticism did continue—in imagery, sensations, and behavior. It simply became less frequent, in terms of both erections and more voluntary erotic actions.

Four of the hypogonadal women also discontinued hormone therapy for three months or longer. All of them eventually stopped menstruating and experienced less vaginal lubrication. They did not report the malaise or hot flashes typical of menopause, however. And their erotic sensations, imagery, and actions, including reaching orgasm, continued just as before.

The studies of paraplegia, castration, and gonadal failure demonstrate that sexual response can continue in the human adult without either hormones or local genital sensations. Psychological, social, and cognitive factors seem to be crucial to human sexuality (Ross, Rogers, and McCulloch 1978; Swyer 1968). Is sex, then, all in our heads? Are hormones not important? Money points out that such an extreme view is unwarranted:

> Some writers have suggested that psychologic stimuli are sufficient, that in man there has been an emancipation from hormonal control. If it is true, however, as a number of the same writers have postulated, that the sex hormones have a direct effect on the genitalia, maintaining them erotically functional, and on the generation of genitopelvic tactile and somesthetic signals that are relayed to the brain, the role of sex hormones

in erotic arousal cannot properly be claimed to have been completely replaced by psychologic stimuli, for indeed the two are not mutually separable. (1961, p. 1397)

WHICH HORMONES INCREASE LUST?

Hormones do seem to be related to the level of the sex drive. In males, androgen deficiency, however created, predictably leads to a decrease in sex drive, ejaculation, and erectile potency. In females, however, the picture is more complicated. Females have both high levels of estrogens and moderate levels of androgens in their bodies. Surprisingly enough, it seems to be the androgens that underlie female sexual arousal; for when androgens are administered to women for various medical reasons, one predictable side effect is an increase of sex drive (Money 1961; Money and Ehrhardt 1972; West 1967). When females suffer estrogen deficiencies, on the other hand, the only area of sexual functioning that suffers is vaginal lubrication; sexual imagery, arousal, and behavior are unchanged. In reviewing these data, Money says, "The relationship of estrogen to eroticism in the adult female seems, after the pubertal estrogenic function of maturing the reproductive tract and feminizing the body morphology in general, to be restricted to maintaining the lubricant secretions of the vagina preparatory to copulation" (1961, p. 1390).

Money concludes that androgens must therefore be responsible for sexual arousal in the female, and suggests that they originate in the female adrenal gland. To support this suggestion, he cites a study of twenty-nine women who had both adrenals and both ovaries removed in the treatment of breast cancer (Waxenberg, Drellich, and Sutherland 1959). Loss of the ovaries and their hormone secretions had no adverse effect on sexual drive, arousal, or activity. But when the adrenals were also removed, all three areas of sexual functioning were diminished or even abolished.

THE DIRECTION OF LUST

Although androgens appear to activate the sex drive, they do not seem to determine the form or the direction in which it is expressed (Hampson and Hampson 1961; Money 1961). In other words, higher levels of androgen are linked to more sexual behavior but not to the gender of the desired partner or to the specific sexual behavior. Thus, homosexual males do not have lower levels of androgen predisposing them to more "female" sexual behavior, nor do homosexual women have higher levels of androgen predisposing them to more "male" sexual behavior. After many years of research, scientists have concluded that there is no consistent relationship between circulating hormone levels and sexual orientation (Hampson and Hampson 1961; Money and Ehrhardt 1972; Ross et al. 1978; West 1967, 1977).

Studies that involve the administration of extra sex hormones show the same results. When male homosexuals are given androgen, for instance, their homosexual desires increase, but there is no shift toward heterosexuality and no change in attitudes, interests, or behavior (Hampson and Hampson 1961; West 1967). Administering opposite-sex hormones also shows that hormones do not affect sexual orientation. When estrogen is administered to heterosexual males, sex drive decreases but there is no shift toward homosexuality (Money 1961; Money and Ehrhardt 1972; West 1967). A similar effect is observed when androgens are given to heterosexual women: sex drive increases, but there is no shift toward lesbianism (Money 1961; Money and Ehrhardt 1972).

These studies substantiate the idea that level of androgen is related to level of lust. What a man or a woman does with that lust is another matter.

IS THE MALE SEX DRIVE STRONGER?

The role of androgen in sexual activation offers a plausible basis for the argument that men are more "highly sexed" than women. The androgens are called male hormones precisely because after puberty they are found at higher levels in males than in females. Thus, if androgens are the essential sex-stimulating substance, their higher levels in males would suggest a stronger sex drive in males.

On the other hand, it is possible that androgens are more crucial to sexual arousal in males than in females. It may be that estrogens also influence female sexual arousal, combining with androgens to produce a female sex drive equal to that of the male. The data on hormonal deficiency do not support this hypothesis, however. As I have already noted, when adult women are deprived of estrogens through gonadal failure or menopause, their sexual functioning seems to continue much as before. Postcastration responses also seem to be more variable in females than in males, with a tendency toward greater maintenance of female sexual functioning. This suggests that loss of estrogen through ovariectomy does not destroy or even seriously impair female sexuality.

Perhaps female sexual arousal is more dependent on learning and social factors than is male sexual arousal. It seems more likely, however, that Money (1961) is right: estrogen simply initiates vaginal lubrication, while androgen (which may continue to be produced by the adrenal glands after ovariectomy) initiates sexual arousal. This suggests that female sexual arousal is maintained by an adrenal source of androgens after ovariectomy, while male sexual arousal has no source of androgens to sustain it after testicular castration. If Money is correct in his idea that estrogen plays this limited a role in female sexuality, it is doubtful that estrogen compensates for lower levels of androgen in the female.

The implication thus remains that higher levels of androgen in males underlie a stronger sex drive (or at least a greater potential for arousal) in males.

Another possibility is that estrogen not only plays a limited role in sexual arousal but is actually antagonistic to sexual activation. This does seem to be the case in the human male; for when he is given estrogen, his sex drive decreases (Money 1961; Money and Ehrhardt 1972; West 1967). It is not true for the female, however, for estrogen therapy restores the normal sex drive in postmenopausal women and certainly does not interfere with sexual arousal in hypogonadal women (Money 1961). After noting these results, however, Money goes on to suggest that the restorative nature of estrogen therapy is due to a localized effect on the genital tract. In other words, we have come back to the hypothesis stated earlier: that estrogens only initiate vaginal lubrication, while androgens are primarily responsible for general sexual arousal.

A third possibility is that androgens underlie the *aggressive* expression of sexuality. Money and Ehrhardt (1972) summarize a number of studies in which androgens were administered to a variety of female animals prenatally, postnatally, or both. In infancy and later development these androgenized females (hermaphrodites) sometimes showed increased levels of physical activity and roughness when compared with normal females. In one study, for instance, juvenile hermaphroditic macaque monkeys showed increased levels of play initiative, rough-and-tumble play, chasing play, and playful threats (Goy 1970; Phoenix, Goy, and Young 1967). They also engaged in more sexual mounting play than normal females and were likely to lift their feet off the ground while mounting, whereas normal females stayed on all fours.

The increase and modification of mounting behavior in these macaque hermaphrodites is especially interesting. Monkeys of both sexes engage in mounting behavior as well as in receptive rump-presenting postures; the sex difference involves the greater frequency of mounting in males and the greater frequency of presenting in females. Thus, the female hermaphrodites were not engaging in male behavior rarely seen in females but rather were increasing the frequency of behavior all females exhibit to some degree. They also seemed to be carrying out this mounting behavior in a more aggressive way by clasping the presenting monkey's shanks with their feet rather than leaving all four feet on the ground. Since mounting in general is a more aggressive and forceful act than presenting, this shift involves a more aggressive expression of sexuality. It seems fair to conclude, then, that the macaque hermaphrodites showed a general increase in physical initiative and aggression which was reflected in both sexual and nonsexual behaviors.

This study of monkey hermaphrodites suggests that there is a link between aggression and male sexual behaviors. As we saw in the section on hormones and aggression, male androgens also seem to be related to nonsexual aggression in animals. Thus, the animal data raise the possibility that androgens underlie aggression in both sexual and nonsexual behavior.

What about humans? If the androgens are responsible for both aggression and sexual arousal, are they also responsible for the aggressive as opposed to the passive and receptive expression of sexuality? The available data cannot really tell us. But the studies of androgen deficiency in human males are suggestive. For as Money (1961) pointed out, the primary difficulty of adult males with untreated hypogonadalism is a decrease in sexual initiative; their ability to attain erections and ejaculations is less impaired. Perhaps androgen is responsible for the more forceful aggressive expression of sexuality. This could mean that men are more *aggressively* sexed because of their male hormones rather than that men are more *highly* sexed because of their male hormones.

The link between aggression and male sexual behavior is more than a matter of hormones. It is also a matter of social attitudes. In American society sexuality tends to be viewed in aggressive terms. The fusion of aggression and sexuality is evident in our cultural view of sexual fulfillment and rape, as I shall discuss in chapters 12 and 15. This view is not, however, shared by all cultures. I have mentioned the Arapesh whom Margaret Mead studied and who viewed sex as a more gentle physical need shared equally by men and women. Our cultural view of sexuality may bias the research in this area by predisposing observers to perceive and label only aggressively loaded acts as sexual in nature while overlooking nonaggressive sexual acts. By focusing on sexuality expressed in the male as opposed to the female mode, these studies may be overestimating the sexual drive evident in males as opposed to females.

Cultural factors not only influence the form in which the sex drive is expressed; they also shape the level or degree of that expression. This shaping often takes opposite forms for males and females: males are taught to express their sexuality freely, while females are taught to hide and even deny their sexuality. As Maccoby and Jacklin put it:

> In most cultures there is a double standard of adult sexual morality. Women are expected to be modest and, to some degree, chaste. Men are allowed (or even expected) to have a more active sex life and engage in more sexual exploration. In encounters between the sexes, men are expected to take the initiative. . . .
>
> We do not know precisely how early in a child's life the socialization for his adult role in courtship and sex might be expected to begin, but it would not be surprising if, even in early childhood, parents emphasized the importance of modesty more with daughters, and were less permissive toward them in dealing with overt displays of sexual activity and interest. (1974, p. 329)

These authors point out that, unfortunately, direct observation of parent-child interaction in this area is almost impossible; since the child's sexual behavior usually occurs when adults are not present, and is revealed only when the parents "catch" the child at it. Maccoby and Jacklin note that the three interview studies that have obtained detailed information about parents' reactions to their children's sexuality found no sex differences in parental response. Regardless of the sex of the child, parents were equally severe in their reactions to masturbation, were equally likely to give the child information about sex, were equally unlikely to allow other family members to see the child in the nude, and reacted similarly to instances of sex play with neighborhood children.

Studies of sexual responsiveness in adults suggest that females may repress their sexuality more than males do. Thus, in discussing female orgasmic dysfunction, Masters and Johnson point out:

> During her formative years the female dissembles much of her developing functional sexuality in response to societal requirements for a "good girl" facade. Instead of being taught or allowed to value her sexual feelings in anticipation of appropriate and meaningful opportunity for expression, thereby developing a realistic sexual value system, she must attempt to repress or remove them from their natural context of environmental stimulation under the implication that they are bad, dirty, etc. She is allowed to retain the symbolic romanticism which usually accompanies these sexual feelings, but the concomitant sensory development with the symbolism that endows the sexual value system with meaning is arrested or labeled—for the wrong reasons—objectionable. . . .
>
> Since, as far as is known, elevated levels of female sexual tension are not technically necessary to conception, the natural function of woman's sexuality has been repressed in the service of false propriety and restricted by other unnecessary psychosocial controls for equally unsupportable reasons. (1970, pp. 215–16)

How, then, can we respond to the assertion that men are more highly sexed because of their male hormones? The available data suggest a connection between male hormones and the aggressive expression of sexuality. Therefore, *if* sexuality is defined in terms of American culture—as an aggressive sexuality—we would have to agree that men appear to be more highly sexed than women. But the idea of sexual repression suggests that this may be appearance only, for not only may there be a natural female mode of sexual expression that is less aggressive—and less recognized—than the male mode, but culturally induced repression of sexual impulses may also interfere with the recognition, the expression, and hence the measurement of sexuality in females.

The Menstrual Cycle

When I hear people say that women are notoriously unpredictable, moody, and even hysterical once a month while men are reliable and steady, I want to shout, "Ridiculous! Women are no more at the mercy of raging hormones than men are. Look at female work records—women are actually out sick *less* than men. They're tougher than men because they're used to being in pain and discomfort once a month, while most men think they're going to die if they get so much as a head cold. And . . . and . . ."

But where is this argument leading? Does anyone seriously believe that there are an "estrogen personality" found in all women—a personality characterized by fits of weeping and irrational behavior which follow the phases of the moon—and an "androgen personality" found in all men—a personality characterized by emotional stability, reliability, and even tempers? Even if there were such personalities, would they spring from the hormonal differences between the sexes?

Unfortunately any thoughtful attempt to find a hormonal basis for sex differences by looking at the research on hormone cycles is doomed to failure, for this research begins with the assumption that only women have cycles—an incorrect assumption, as it turns out. Biologist Estelle Ramey (1972) has pointed out that men have hormone cycles, too. These seem to be about thirty days long, corresponding to four- to six-week cycles in mood. In addition, Ramey mentioned that over forty years ago Rex Hersey studied mood changes in male factory workers and found a predictable twenty-four-hour cycle within a larger monthly rhythm. Finally, we should note that not only do men have cycles, but also there is increasing evidence of general human *biorhythms*—natural cycles of activity and mood that seem to be biologically based and also to fluctuate on a daily, weekly, and monthly schedule. Although the mechanisms underlying biorhythms are still being investigated, their effects are familiar to all of us—male and female—who have predictable ups and downs in our schedules.

Why, then, has so much recent research and publicity been focused on hormonal cycles in women only? The major reason is that the "raging hormone theory of female personality" reflects and strengthens cultural attitudes toward women as mysterious, unpredictable creatures who are somehow closer to nature than are their male counterparts. The major symbol of this female earthiness is menstruation, that mysterious monthly bleeding that serves as a visible reminder of the power of growth and reproduction. But popular imagination does not attribute purely positive powers to menstrual blood. On the contrary, female sexual processes, genitals, and menstrual blood are perceived as not only powerful but dangerous as well. In ancient times the danger was attributed to supernatural powers and was considered especially threatening for males.

> The menstrous woman is possessed by an evil spirit; the spirit resides in her blood, and by the medium of her menstrual blood may exert its influence, for good or for harm, on her environment. The evil spirit may

effect its entry into the woman in the form of a bird, or a lizard, or a serpent; hence the folk association of these animals with menstruation. It was the serpent that marred the primordial bliss of Eden. (Crawfurd 1915, p. 1331)

This perception of menstrual blood led to the menstrual taboo, which required that menstruating women be physically segregated, and that utensils women had touched be purified before they could be safely reused. The Old Testament states the taboo clearly, as in the following passage:

> When a woman has a discharge of blood which is her regular discharge from her body, she shall be in her impurity for seven days, and whoever touches her shall be unclean until the evening.
> And everything upon which she lies during her impurity shall be unclean; everything also upon which she sits shall be unclean. . . .
> And if any man lies with her, and her impurity is on him, he shall be unclean seven days; and every bed on which he lies shall be unclean. (Leviticus 15: 19–20, 24)*

In the United States today the menstrual taboo is reflected in the lingering belief that menstruation is unclean, causing women to go to great lengths to hide their menstruation and making most couples reluctant to have intercourse during this period (Paige 1973; Weideger 1975). Although both men and women usually attribute their reluctance to the "mess" of menstruation, the roots of this attitude can be seen in ancient religious beliefs and prohibitions. As one writer put it:

> The belief, of very ancient lineage, that coitus during menstruation led to the birth of monsters was formerly very widespread. . . . Ancient mythology attributed the deformity of Vulcan to the union of Jupiter with Juno during her menstrual period. The Talmud went further and assigned disorders of the mind, such as epilepsy, cretinism, and insanity to the same cause. The belief is not wholly dead nowadays. . . . (Crawfurd 1915, p. 1335)

Our culture's current view of menstruation as something unclean or indecent to be mentioned only indirectly is also reflected in the common

---

* In the Old Testament the menstrual taboo is presented as part of more general laws aimed at prevention of infection and disease. All bodily discharge is considered unclean, including discharge of semen. Thus, men are not exempted from the connections among sex, disease, and uncleanliness. However, only women have a discharge on a monthly basis regardless of their sexual activity, while men most often become unclean through sex with a woman. The strictures surrounding sex and genitalia are therefore more closely associated with the basic bodily functions and personal characteristics of women than with those of men. Furthermore, blood has many complex connotations of power and danger. The fear, the loathing, and the strictures surrounding menstruation are thus more powerful than those for other discharges.

euphemisms for a menstruating woman who has a "period" or a "visit from a friend," or more negatively "falls off the roof," "rides the rag," or "is unwell." The most damning saying of all is that she has "the curse" (Weideger 1975, p. 4). Just in case we do not grasp this portrayal of God-given suffering for female evil, Archie Bunker explains it in the television show "All in the Family":

> Read your Bible. Read about Adam and Eve. . . . Going against direct orders, she makes poor Adam take a bite out of that apple. So God got sore and told them to get their clothes on and get outta there. So it was Eve's fault God cursed women with this trouble. That's why they call it, what do you call it, the curse. (Quoted in Weideger 1975, p. 91)

Of course, modern behavioral science does not study menstruation in moral or religious terms. The search is for hormonal underpinnings of female behavior and personality, not for evidence of supernatural powers. Yet the influence of these old superstitions is still perceptible. For if menstruation is seen as a curse, it follows that changes in mood and behavior associated with this curse will be negative. And this is what researchers have been asking—what *negative* changes in mood and behavior occur during the days just prior to and during menstruation? Practically no one has asked what *positive* changes in mood and behavior occur at different points in the menstrual cycle. Thus, there are many studies of negative emotional states, physical discomfort of all types, and increases in antisocial acts just before menstruation. There are practically no studies of positive emotional changes, feelings of physical well-being, or increases in constructive activities or creativity.

The general approach involves measuring a woman's emotional state and behavior when she is either at midcycle (during ovulation) or just beginning to menstruate. Figure 2.1 shows that the levels of estrogen and progesterone rise gradually during the twenty-eight-day cycle, with a sharp drop just before menstrual bleeding starts. Thus, the level of female hormones is generally high at midcycle and low premenstrually. The general idea is that a woman's emotional state and behavior are expected to vary with these hormone levels: pleasant moods and socially acceptable behavior at midcycle, unpleasant moods and antisocial behavior at menstruation.

One of the most frequently quoted studies used this approach to examine mood changes during the menstrual cycle. Ivey and Bardwick (1968) asked twenty-six female college students to tell about *any* personal experience that came to mind, at midcycle and just before menstruation over two complete cycles for each student. These researchers taped responses and then scored them for themes related to death, mutilation, separation, guilt, shame, and diffuse anxiety. The following typical responses were reported by four women at (*a*) midcycle and (*b*) just before menstruation:

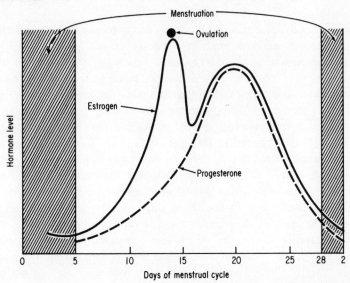

Figure 2.1   Level of Female Hormones during the Menstrual Cycle

1*a*.   We took our skis and packed them on top of the car and then we took off for up North. We used to go for long walks in the snow and it was really great, really quiet and peaceful.

1*b*.   . . . came around a curve and did a double flip and landed upside down. I remember the car coming down on my hand and slicing it right open and all this blood was all over the place.

2*a*   . . . talk about my trip to Europe. It was just the greatest summer of my life. We met all kinds of terrific people everywhere we went and just the most terrific things happened.

2*b*.   . . . talk about my brother and his wife. I hated her. I just couldn't stand her. I couldn't stand her mother. I used to do terrible things to separate them.

3*a*.   . . . so I was elected chairman. I had to establish with them the fact that I knew what I was doing. I remember one particularly problematic meeting, and afterwards, L. came up to me and said "you really handled the meeting well." In the end it came out the sort of thing that really bolstered my confidence in myself.

3*b*.   They had to teach me how to water ski. I was so clumsy it was really embarrassing 'cause it was kind of like saying to yourself you can't do it and the people were about to lose patience with me.

4*a*.   Well, we just went to Jamaica and it was fantastic the island is so lush and green. . . . and the natives are just so friendly.

4*b*.   I'll tell you about the death of my poor dog M. . . . oh, another memorable event, my grandparents died in a plane crash. That was my first contact with death and it was very traumatic for me. (Ivey and Bardwick 1968, pp. 341, 343)

The pattern of sample responses is clear: optimistic, self-affirming, confident thoughts are expressed near ovulation, while morbid, pessimistic, hostile, and self-doubting thoughts are expressed near menstruation. When the researchers combined the scores for all subjects, they found that the premenstrual anxiety scores were significantly higher than the anxiety scores at ovulation, the difference being so large that it would occur fewer than five times out of ten thousand by chance alone. Ivey and Bardwick also identified a number of recurring themes illustrated in the preceding responses: feelings of self-satisfaction or ability to cope at ovulation (3a) as opposed to feelings of hostility (2b), death anxiety (4b), and mutilation anxiety (1b) before menstruation.

In discussing this study in her textbook *Psychology of Women* (1971), Bardwick suggests that depression, anxiety, and irritability increase premenstrually due to the sharp drop in estrogen production at this point in the cycle. This interpretation is supported by one of Karen Paige's early studies (1969), in which she compared mood changes of menstruating women with mood changes of women using oral contraceptives. Paige collected verbal samples by interviewing 102 married women at four different times in the cycle: the fourth day of menstruation, the tenth day of the cycle, the sixteenth day (midcycle), and two days before the next menstrual period. Three groups of subjects were formed: one group of thirty-eight who had never used oral contraceptives, a second group of fifty-two who were using the combination pill, and a third group of twelve who were using sequential pills. Combination-pill therapy involves twenty consecutive days of pills containing both synthetic estrogen and synthetic progesterone followed by approximately seven days off the pill; combination pills thus level off the usual rise and fall of estrogen and progesterone during the menstrual cycle. Sequential-pill therapy involves fifteen days of pills containing only estrogen, followed by five days of pills containing both estrogen and progesterone, and then approximately seven days off; sequential pills thus mimic the usual rise and fall of estrogen and progesterone during the menstrual cycle.

Paige scored the verbal samples according to the Gottschalk scales for anxiety and hostility used by Ivey and Bardwick. Her hypothesis was that the levels of hostility and anxiety would vary inversely with the levels of estrogen and progesterone. The combination-pill group was expected to show no fluctuation since levels of estrogen and progesterone were relatively constant, while the no-pill and sequential-pill groups were expected to show low levels of hostility and anxiety at midcycle and high levels of hostility and anxiety premenstrually. A statistical analysis of the results supported this hypothesis.

In discussing the study she did with Ivey, Bardwick (1971) commented on the striking absence of individual differences in reactions to the menstrual cycle. In most psychological studies the differences due to core personality characteristics are marked; so that only when the scores or responses of all subjects are combined, does a trend emerge that can be attributed to the effects of whatever social or physiological factors are being studied. Bardwick concluded that the individual personality differences in her college sample were overshadowed by the hormonal changes during the menstrual cycle. The overshadowing factor may well have been social rather than hormonal, however, for the women participating in both the Ivey and Bardwick study and Paige's study were asked to come in on certain days of their cycle. They were thus encouraged to focus on the day of their cycle while being interviewed. Their heightened awareness of their cycle could be expected to make them especially sensitive to social attitudes toward menstruation and lead them to "spontaneously" produce verbal materials that express those attitudes and their resulting self-perceptions.

Paige herself began to speculate that social attitudes toward menstruation shape the personal menstrual experience. Several years later she investigated this social-influence interpretation by comparing questionnaire responses about menstruation obtained from 298 unmarried college students who were Jewish (54), Protestant (181), or Catholic (63). The questions elicited information about physical and emotional health, feelings about family and motherhood, sexual experience, and acceptance of the menstrual taboo.

Paige (1973) found that the Jewish women most likely to have difficulties with menstruation were those who accepted the ban on sexual intercourse during menstruation. Among Catholic women, the more fully they lived out the feminine role ideal with which they were brought up—to marry, to have children, and to have no substantial goal outside the home—the more frequent were their premenstrual difficulties. Paige found no clear pattern of premenstrual difficulties among the Protestant women in her study and attributed this to a failure to subdivide them according to the various Protestant sects. In all three groups of women, however, menstrual distress was associated with frequency of church attendance and various factors related to traditional femininity, such as adherence to norms regarding virginity, menstrual sex taboos, and "feminine hygiene." In other words, "the traditionally feminine woman is the one who tends to get the cramps and the blues" (1973, p. 46).

Paige's later study suggests that attitudes toward menstruation and the menstrual taboo are closely tied to concepts of appropriate femininity, and that femininity so defined is crucial to one's self-perception and response to menstruation. Paige concludes:

> I have come to believe that the "raging hormones" theory of menstrual distress simply isn't adequate. . . . Nor do I agree with the "raging neurosis" theory, which argues that women who have menstrual symptoms are merely whining neurotics, who need only a kind pat on the head to cure their problems.
>
> We must instead consider the problem from the perspective of women's subordinate social position, and of the cultural ideology that so

narrowly defines the behaviors and emotions that are appropriately "feminine." Women have perfectly good reasons to react emotionally to reproductive events. Menstruation, pregnancy and childbirth—so sacred, yet so unclean—are the woman's primary avenues of achievement and self-expression. Her reproductive abilities define her femininity; other routes to success are only second best in this society. (1973, p. 46)

Paula Weideger (1975) has speculated on the interplay between a woman's self-perception and her response to menstruation by discussing the "premenstrual uglies"—those subtle changes in appearance that often occur a few days before menstruation. She points out that since looks are a woman's most widely acknowledged asset, women often become anxious at the slightest loss of attractiveness. When a woman looks in the mirror just before menstruation and sees slightly limp hair, sallow skin, and a flare-up adolescent acne, she tends to exaggerate these changes and experience a real sense of anxiety and loss. Thus, "the premenstrual uglies provide a particularly clear example of the way in which a minor aspect of the premenstrual phase becomes more substantial because of the social evaluation of the female role" (p. 186).

The profound influence of attitudes toward menstruation, reproduction, female sexuality, and the female role in general suggests that the hormone changes during menstruation are not the only or even the major cause for the predictable cyclicity in female behavior and moods. There are numerous other problems in the research studies done in this area. Perhaps most important is the failure to consider the social context in which women live. This context itself involves many pressures that vary in a rhythmic way. In one study, for instance, Rossi (1974) reported the usual ups and downs in mood that correlated with the menstrual cycle, but went on to comment that the *day of the week* was even more important than the day of the menstrual cycle in determining these changes: the young women studied reported a lift in mood over weekends, with Wednesday (the day furthest from the weekend) showing the lowest mood ratings. In fact, only when menstruation fell on a Wednesday was there a marked mood effect for the menstrual cycle.

Another major problem is the lack of agreement as to just what the "premenstrual syndrome" is. Over 150 variables have been used to assess the presence of this syndrome in study participants, including a variety of (negative) moods, behaviors, and physical symptoms. The time period used to delineate this phase of the menstrual cycle also varies, from two days to seven days before flow starts. The measuring instruments introduce many difficulties. Most studies have been done with questionnaires that ask women to rate their behaviors and moods just before and during menstrual flow. The physical symptoms and moods listed are usually negative, so that women are asked how "depressed" they feel rather than how "happy" they feel at that time. Thus, their attention is directed to the negative effects of this particular stage of their cycle.

When women have been asked to fill out a preliminary questionnaire about their usual premenstrual symptoms and then daily questionnaires throughout the cycle, major discrepancies in reported symptoms have been found (McCance, Luff, and Widdowson 1937). Since most of the studies on the premenstrual syndrome use anticipatory or retrospective questionnaires only, they may well be telling us more about how women *expect* menstruation to affect them than about how it actually *does* affect them.

Other studies fail to distinguish between women taking combination or sequential types of birth control pill, or even between women taking pills and those not taking pills. Without specific information about pill usage, no inferences can be made about the relationship between hormone levels and other variables.

The lack of pill/no-pill comparisons brings us to the general issue of comparison or control groups. Without comparing mood shifts for menstruating women with mood shifts for nonmenstruating women and for men, we cannot know whether these shifts are greater or lesser during menstruation. Furthermore, what period of the menstrual cycle should be viewed as a baseline for behavior and mood? Suppose a group of women were found to be more irritable and to score lower on a timed arithmetic task during menstruation than at midcycle. Should this difference in mood and performance be viewed as a decrease in functioning at menstruation or as an increase in functioning at midcycle? And how would the menstruating women's performance compare with that of nonmenstruating individuals? Perhaps the menstruating women's average arithmetic score might be higher than the average score of men—would this still constitute a menstrual deficit?

One could go on and on outlining the many aspects of the menstrual experience that are overlooked in most research studies. Almost all the researchers start out by assuming that hormonal factors and negative moods at menstruation are the (only) relevant factors. They not only ignore social factors but also conclude that because hormones and moods fluctuate on a monthly schedule, the hormones must cause the mood fluctuations. This conclusion cannot be drawn, because most studies of the menstrual cycle are correlational: that is, they report the extent to which variable *a* (stage of the menstrual cycle) is related to variable *b* (level of anxiety, depression, irritability), so that when variable *a* changes, so does variable *b*. This type of study cannot establish causation—we cannot tell whether *a* causes *b* to change, *b* causes *a* to change, or a third unstudied variable *c* causes both *a* and *b* to change simultaneously. In this regard, we cannot automatically assume that hormone levels change moods rather than that moods themselves change hormone levels. It is commonly accepted that menstruation may stop entirely or be delayed under stress (Sherman 1971). This is not surprising when we recall that plasma testosterone levels of monkeys introduced into an established social group have been shown to drop as the newcomer becomes submissive (Rose et al. 1971). There is undoubtedly a complex relationship among hormone levels, moods, and social behavior—and it is too soon (and too simplistic) to conclude that hormones alone have the force to change the other factors.

Even if we knew for sure that some biological aspect of the menstrual cycle caused the observed fluctuations in behavior and mood, we would still be left with the question of *how* menstruation causes these changes. Are they due to the total level of female hormones in the body at any given time? Or are they caused by the interaction between the levels of estrogen and progesterone? Perhaps the cause lies not in the hormones themselves but in the physical symptoms that often accompany menstruation: abdominal cramping, water retention, nausea, and constipation (Dalton 1969). At the present time, researchers have only opinions and hypotheses about the causal mechanism, with no definitive data.

Assuming that some aspect of hormonal changes had been isolated as the major cause of mood changes, would this eliminate social influences? Unfortunately it would not. Earlier I described Schachter and Singer's (1962) study of the importance of cognitive factors in determining emotions. The juke box theory of emotion would suggest that a woman interprets the physiological state caused by hormone changes in terms of the behavior of those around her. When menstruation is called "the curse" and women report feeling depressed and irritable at menstruation, it is hardly surprising that a developing female learns to interpret her own physiological state in similar negative terms. The same female growing up in a culture where menstruation and reproduction are more positively viewed might well learn to interpret the same internal physiological state in more positive emotional terms.

When menstruation is viewed negatively, it can also become a convenient scapegoat for other sources of malaise. Thus Paige (1973) found that women who experience physical and emotional distress during menstruation tend to report these symptoms in other situations as well. Similarly, Brown (1976) found that women who reported menstrual depression had lower mood scores throughout the month and showed a lift in mood on the first day of menstruation rather than on the day before, as most other subjects did. This suggests that women who report menstrual depression may be more depressed generally and merely attribute this low mood to menstruation.

Once a woman has learned to associate certain emotions and behavior with menstruation, it may be difficult to unlearn them. Parlee (1973) reports that many drug treatments have been used, with little success, to treat severe menstrual distress; even hysterectomy has failed to be effective and can make the menstrual symptoms worse. If the causal factor were purely or even primarily hormonal, such treatments should be effective. The conclusion that learned, social factors are crucial to menstrual mood and behavior seems unavoidable.

The "raging hormone theory of female personality" sounds logical at first. What could be more obvious than the idea that the fluctuating levels of female hormones over the menstrual cycle cause a predictable cyclicity in female moods and behavior? But this logic is culture-bound; the whole idea of studying the menstrual cycle is based on the menstrual taboo and the negative view of female reproduction it reflects. Unless male cycles and general human biorhythms are examined, no conclusions can be drawn about sex differences in cyclicity.

We can use these studies to ask whether female hormones cause cyclic changes in emotions and behavior, without claiming that this cyclicity is true for women only. Here we find, however, that menstruation is a social phenomenon as well as a biological event. Both women and men have strong feelings and ingrained attitudes toward menstruation that color their perception of menstrual "symptoms." The onset of menstruation still serves as the symbol for the onset of female adulthood, and throughout life menstruation is used as a convenient cultural explanation for innumerable "female" characteristics and discriminatory social practices. Until we sort out the social factors that influence responses to menstruation, we cannot differentiate between biological and social causation. Yes, women do seem to experience a monthly ebb and flow in their behavior and moods, but it is not clear that this ebb and flow is due to the ebb and flow of hormones.

This is not to say that studies of the menstrual cycle are not important. On the contrary, they demonstrate the immense impact that perceptions of reproduction and the female role have on both physical and psychological functioning. The importance of these studies thus lies not so much in uncovering sex differences as in exemplifying the subtle interrelationship between a woman's body and her social environment.

Chapter 3

Intellectual Abilities

ALTHOUGH OCCASIONALLY someone will claim that men are smarter than women, it is widely known that there are no sex differences in overall scores on intelligence tests. Some psychologists have suggested, however, that the sex hormones influence general intellectual capacity. The most popular view has been that male hormones enhance intellectual functioning and development in both sexes and perhaps is based on the assumption that, since levels of male hormones are related to aggressive physical and social behavior, they must also be related to aggressive or energetic intellect. The hypothesis of a link between male hormones and increased intelligence is based on a study in which Ehrhardt and Money (1967) found that fetally androgenized girls had intelligence quotas (IQs) averaging 125, which the authors believed was higher than would be expected of the girls' socioeconomic backgrounds. No control group of nonfetally androgenized girls from similar backgrounds was included in this early study, however.

Other psychologists argue that female hormones may underlie intellectual abilities. They refer to a study in which Dalton (1968) worked with a group of children whose mothers had received large amounts of progesterone during pregnancy. These fetally progesteronized children of both sexes scored significantly higher than matched controls on general aptitude tests.

A later study contradicts both the male and the female hormone advocates. Ehrhardt and Baker (1973) found that although fetally androgenized girls had higher-than-average IQs, so did their normal sisters used as a control group. Thus, although children exposed to excess male *or* female hormones may tend to have higher IQs than other children of their socioeconomic background, they do not necessarily tend to have higher IQs than their own siblings have. This suggests that something unusual about the families of children who receive excess hormones *in utero* causes *all* the children in the family to have high IQs.

Specific Intellectual Abilities

The fact that males and females obtain similar overall scores on intelligence tests does not mean that there are no sex differences in intellectual abilities, for the *pattern* of intellectual abilities that makes up the overall IQ score differs for the two sexes. In fact, IQ tests have been carefully constructed to weight the various portions on which men and women typically score higher in such a way that their average overall scores will be equivalent.

A pattern of sex differences emerges from the subtests of general intelligence tests and from studies using tests of specific intellectual abilities. Females generally excel in verbal ability, while males excel in visual-spatial and mathematical abilities. These sex differences do not usually appear during the grade school years but begin in junior high school and show increasing sexual divergence through high school and perhaps beyond (Maccoby and Jacklin 1974).

The female superiority in verbal ability is found in both "lower-level" measures (fluency) and "higher-level" tasks (analogies, comprehension of difficult written material, and creative writing). The male visual-spatial advantage is about equal in nonanalytical tasks (matching similar shapes and completing routine numerical operations) and analytical measures (perceiving and manipulating parts and completing complex numerical operations). Since the two sexes are similar in their acquisition of quantitative concepts and mastery of arithmetic in grade school, the greater rate of male improvement in math beginning in junior high involves more sophisticated tasks that build upon these basic abilities. Although the magnitude of the sex difference in math scores varies greatly from one social group to another, initial studies suggest that it is not entirely a function of the number of math courses taken. The variability in the size of the male advantage may be partly due to the fact that both visual-spatial and verbal processes are often involved in the solution of math problems; that is, a math problem may be expressed in words as well as numbers and may also require reading a graph or a chart (Maccoby and Jacklin 1974).

Maccoby and Jacklin (1974) point out that the mixture of basic cognitive abilities involved in many math problems raises a general difficulty in this area. How can we distinguish between verbal and quantitative skills or between spatial and nonspatial abilities? The manipulation of symbols (verbal or numerical), the consideration of "if-then" possibilities, and the restructuring of problem elements are often required for high-level tasks in all these areas. The differences among the specific intellectual abilities appear to be based on test labeling as much as on basic strategies or types of thinking.

In spite of some confusion about the distinctions among verbal, quantitative, and spatial abilities, however, the pattern of sex differences is fairly consistent when the standard tests are used. Even with somewhat mixed abilities involved in each test, the focus of each is usually on one specific ability. The question thus remains: What causes this pattern of sex differences in test scores?

Hormones and Spatial Ability

The onset of puberty in early adolescence coincides with the emergence of sex differences in intellectual ability scores. This coincidence has led to speculation that the increased production and circulation of sex hormones may cause sex differences. The major proponents of this viewpoint are Broverman and his colleagues, who attribute lower spatial-ability scores in females to interference from female hormones. Their argument centers on the relationship between the activating and the inhibiting functions of the sympathetic and the parasympathetic nervous systems. They claim that the sex hormones are activators and hence *facilitate* performance of type A tasks, "simple, overlearned, repetitive behaviors." Sex hormones *interfere* with the performance of type B tasks, which require inhibition of initial responses to allow for the reorganization of stimulus materials that is required in more complex information processing. The researchers label type B behaviors as visual-spatial and assert that males excel in these because female hormones are more powerful than male hormones and hence are more likely to interfere with complex information processing by enhancing intellectual impulsiveness (Broverman et al. 1968).

When Broverman's theory is translated into plain English, we find that familiar stereotype: women are naturally equipped to do well at dull, routine (and low-status) tasks like typing and filing; "raging hormones" prevent women from thinking analytically and performing well on complex intellectual (and high-status) tasks that require calm, objective reasoning. The common view of women as being more impulsive and labile because of female hormones has merely been applied to internal mental processes.

But even though Broverman's theory is reminiscent of social attitudes and stereotypes about women, it could still be correct; these stereotypes could reflect some underlying biological sex differences. This does not seem to be the case, however, as Maccoby and Jacklin (1974) point out. First of all, Broverman's classification of tasks into types A (repetitive, nonanalytical) and B (complex, analytical) does not make sense in view of the overlapping basic skills and levels of complexity involved in verbal, math, and visual-spatial abilities. Nor do the findings on sex differences in performance after grade school fit into Broverman's classification. The verbal abilities on which women do better *and* the visual-spatial and math abilities on which men do better involve both lower-level (simple or repetitive type A) and higher-level (complex or analytical type B) skills.

If sex hormones do interfere with complex mental processes, there should also be within-sex differences: low-estrogen females should do better than high-estrogen females, and low-androgen males should do better than high-androgen males. There is some indication that this may be true for males, in that highly "masculine" physiques and personalities tend to be associated with low spatial scores (Maccoby and Jacklin 1974). But what little is known about females is confusing. One study (Peterson 1973) did find that less "feminine" physiques in late adolescence were associated with higher spatial scores, but these physiques could be caused by low estrogen or high androgen levels compared with those of female age mates.

Maccoby and Jacklin (1974) point out that the timing of the sexual divergence in visual-spatial and math scores is also puzzling.

> Boys experience their greatest rise in spatial ability—and their greatest rate of divergence from girls' scores—from the beginning of adolescence until late adolescence, precisely when their androgen levels are rising most steeply. If androgens exercise a negative influence upon spatial ability, then there must be other powerful forces operating in an opposite direction to stimulate spatial development in adolescence and to more than neutralize the effects of the increasing androgens. (1974, p. 125)

What could these "other powerful forces" be? Sex-role pressures seem a likely possibility, since they increase dramatically during this age period. Adolescent boys having muscular, tall, and athletic ("masculine," high-androgen) physiques may try to assert their manhood through sports and hence divert their attention and energies from intellectual pursuits including spatial and math tasks. This movement away from academics might be especially marked in boys from racial minorities and economically deprived backgrounds, since sports are one of the few avenues to success available to them. Adolescent boys with nonathletic (less "masculine," low-androgen) physiques may try to assert their manhood through aggressive pursuit of academics, especially in the math and spatial tasks viewed as masculine. This movement toward aggressive academic achievement might be especially marked in boys from white and more affluent backgrounds who have greater access to college and white-collar jobs as avenues of advancement.

And what of sex-role pressures for adolescent girls? Those who experience early puberty (high estrogen levels and "feminine" physiques) may become more successfully involved in dating as a way to assert their femininity, thus diverting their energies from intellectual pursuits. Less sexually developed (low-estrogen) girls may continue to focus on academic achievement as a key area of competence and self-esteem, being less motivated or less successful at the dating game. In general, however, school becomes less important for girls as dating and marriage pressures increase. Their grade advantage over boys begins to decline as successful academic achievement tends to be viewed as the result of competitively aggressive and hence unfeminine behavior. Math and visual-spatial tasks are likely to be particularly eschewed as highly masculine. The increasing avoidance of academic competition and "male" fields might be especially marked in girls from more conservative, poorer, and minority backgrounds who are not expected (and who do not have the opportunity) to go to college. They receive the message most strongly: Stop competing with boys; you marry success, you don't make it for yourself.

But these sex-role pressures are not the "other powerful forces" needed to buttress Broverman's argument, for they do not counteract the effects of rising androgen levels; they simply compound them. The sex-role pressures themselves could be expected to produce the observed pattern of increasing sexual divergence in intellectual abilities. Thus, Maccoby and Jacklin seem to be on the right track when they comment that the rising levels of male androgens and the increasing sexual divergence in spatial ability "may actually be physiologically unrelated, even though both are sex-linked and occur at the same time" (1974, p. 125).

In summary, then, Broverman's hormone theory involves an inaccurate classification of basic intellectual abilities, does not fit the established pattern of sex differences in intellectual abilities, and ignores the powerful social forces that could account for the increasing sexual divergence in adolescence. Even if his predictions fitted the evidence, however, Broverman's theory would still not be substantiated. The crux of his argument is that although all sex hormones interfere with complex mental processes, estrogens do so *more* than androgens. If the sex hormones all interfered equally, there would be no reason to expect higher male scores on spatial tasks (or other measures of complex processing). Unfortunately there has been no research on this crucial point.

Genetic Factors

High and low IQ scores tend to run in families; that is, parents with high IQs tend to have children with high IQs, while parents with low IQs tend to have children with low IQs. These family similarities used to be attributed to genetic inheritance. In the last ten or fifteen years, however, psychologists have become increasingly aware that scores on intelligence tests reflect one's general socioeconomic level and cultural background. This awareness has led to attempts to develop "culture-free" IQ tests that are not biased against the poor, the less educated, and those from ethnic and racial minorities. These culture-free tests have not, however, been successful in eliminating bias, and IQ scores continue to measure intellectual ability as developed and filtered through a cultural milieu. This means that the similarity in IQ scores within families and also within racial and ethnic groups is due to both *social inheritance* and *genetic inheritance*.

A GENE FOR VERBAL ABILITY?

To get around the problem of social inheritance, researchers have compared the scores of different members of a given family who presumably all share the same social milieu but have differing percentages of shared genes. This approach has demonstrated high levels of "heritability" in verbal ability scores (Vandenberg 1968); that is, the higher the percentage of genes shared by two people, the greater the similarity between their verbal ability scores. This result has been shown in studies of monozygotic (single-egg) twins who share 100 percent of their gene pool as compared with 50 percent shared by parent-child pairs and 25 percent shared by dyzygotic (two-egg) twins and nontwin sibling pairs.

This measure of heritability does not totally eliminate social factors, however, for as genetic similarity increases so does social similarity. Monozygotic ("identical") twins are always of the same sex and frequently so similar in appearance that they are confused with one another, while dyzygotic twins can be of opposite sexes and do not necessarily resemble one another more than they resemble other family members. The identical twins are more apt to be dressed alike and treated the same; their social environments are much more similar than those of dyzygotic twins.

Sex roles also influence the social environment of family members. Parents have markedly different perceptions of girls and boys and expect them to do different things. Brothers and sisters thus live in quite different social worlds in spite of the genes and the family experiences they share.

This is not to say that heritability does not demonstrate genetic linkage, but merely to point out that such genetic linkage does not eliminate the possibility of simultaneous social inheritance or linkage.

SPATIAL ABILITY: A SEX-LINKED GENE?

Spatial ability also appears to be inherited. In addition, Stafford (1961) has suggested that it is tied to a sex-linked recessive gene carried on the female X chromosome. The genetic mechanisms of this sex linkage would be similar to those of color blindness: girls receive one female X chromosome from each parent, while boys receive one female X chromosome from the mother and one male Y chromosome from the father. The spatial trait carried on the recessive female chromosome would only be displayed in behavior if no dominant X without the recessive trait were inherited. Thus, boys would show the recessive high spatial ability trait if their mother carried it in her genes (whether or not she displayed it), while girls would show the recessive high ability trait only if both parents carried it (and if he carried it, the father would always show it).

Using this model of a sex-linked recessive gene, researchers have worked out and substantiated fairly precise predictions about the correlations of spatial ability scores between children and their opposite-sex or same-sex parents (Bock and Kolakowski 1973; Corah 1965; Hartlage 1970; Stafford 1961).

If spatial ability is inherited in a way similar to (predominantly male) color blindness, is it a male trait? Maccoby and Jacklin warn us not to jump to this conclusion.

> To say that there is a genetic component in spatial ability does *not* imply that it is something, like male genitals, that men have and women do not. With respect to a spatial gene that is sex-linked and recessive, some women will of course have two space-recessives, and their genetic potential for spatial ability will be the same as that of men who have a single recessive space gene on the X chromosome. The *proportion* of persons so endowed will be different for the two sexes—Bock and Kolakowski estimate that the ratio may be approximately 2 to 1, with 50 percent of men and 25 percent of women showing the trait phenotypically [in behavior]. But it should be noted that spatial ability, like all other human abilities, is genetically multidetermined. As noted above, Bock and Kolakowski hypothesize two specific determiners (only one of which is sex-linked), and there may very well be more. (1974, p. 121)

Maccoby and Jacklin go on to point out that spatial ability is usually positively correlated with other kinds of cognitive performance in which females do as well as or better than males. These other components of spatial ability show no genetic sex linkage. They also remind us that many intellectual tasks can be approached in several ways, so that people with high spatial ability might use a different (but equally successful) strategy from that used by those with low spatial ability. And, finally, Maccoby and Jacklin refer to the importance of training and experience, which we will return to after considering sex differences in the brain structures underlying intellectual performance.

The Male-Female Brain

Other researchers have considered genetic factors indirectly by studying sex differences in brain structure which are assumed to be caused by sex-linked genetic factors or by the long-lasting effects that past levels of circulating hormones have had upon the development of various parts of the brain.

This research elaborates on the existence of "cerebral dominance," a concept that refers to the specialization of functions within the human brain: perception and production of speech in the left hemisphere and perception of spatial elements and nonverbal sounds in the right hemisphere. Such specialization, or "lateralization," increases with age and has been found in children as young as four years old. The verbal (left-hemisphere) and nonverbal/spatial (right-hemisphere) functions may become specialized at different rates in the same person. The most common line of reasoning is that females should show greater lateralization for verbal materials and males should show greater lateralization for nonverbal materials, since greater lateralization is assumed to underlie higher task performance.

Levy-Agresti and Sperry (1968) maintain that strong cerebral dominance facilitates performance of spatial tasks. They report finding weaker lateralization in females, who thus have lower spatial scores than males have.

Buffery and Gray (1972), on the other hand, maintain that verbal skills are maximized by strong lateralization, while spatial skills call for a more bilateral representation in the brain. They report finding earlier and stronger lateralization in females and argue that this facilitates female verbal development, while the more bilateral brain functions that they report in males supposedly facilitate male spatial skills.

These two theories are contradictory. In attempting to account for male superiority on spatial tasks, Levy-Agresti and Sperry point to *weaker* lateralization in females, whereas Buffery and Gray point to *stronger* lateralization in females. The difference in their findings could be due to the populations studied: Levy-Agresti and Sperry studied epileptic patients, while Buffery and Gray studied nonpatients.

Sherman (1967) has made a third suggestion that involves the timing as well as the strength of lateralization. Agreeing with Buffery and Gray that females show earlier and stronger left-hemisphere dominance than males, Sherman suggests that this dominance orients girls toward verbal modes of problem solving. She thinks that early verbal development inhibits the girl's development of nonverbal (and especially spatial) abilities. Her argument assumes a critical period in intellectual development during which a verbal or nonverbal orientation to problem solving is established—an orientation that is later maintained when its biological basis has disappeared. Thus, even though boys do catch up in lateralization in adolescence, they have already been "imprinted" with nonverbal modes of problem solving, and hence their subsequent left-hemisphere dominance does not inhibit their established spatial orientation.

The major problem with Sherman's hypothesis is that sex differences in verbal and nonverbal ability scores do not appear until adolescence, after the period when she is suggesting that greater left-hemisphere dominance in girls causes their verbal orientation. These sex differences thus appear at the most unlikely period, when cerebral dominance is supposedly the same for both sexes.

Yet a fourth approach focuses on right-hemisphere specialization. Sandra Witelson (1976) reports that among one hundred males and one hundred females aged six to thirteen years, boys showed right-hemisphere dominance for processing nonlinguistic spatial information by age six, while girls did not show this dominance even by age thirteen. Witelson asserts that the earlier and stronger right-hemisphere dominance in males underlies superior male performance on spatial tasks. The argument here is thus that *stronger* lateralization—but on the *right*—causes male spatial superiority.

Careful examination of Witelson's results brings us back to the problems that plague this area of research. Boys performed a tactile shape-recognition task better with their left than with their right hands, while girls performed equally well with both hands. This suggests stronger right-hemisphere dominance in boys, since each hemisphere of the brain controls the hand on the opposite side of the body. The problem is that *in spite of stronger right-hemisphere lateralization, the boys did not receive higher spatial scores than the girls* when the scores of both hands were combined. Here, then, we have a study that seems to establish stronger right-hemisphere dominance in males, but this hemispheric dominance does not affect spatial performance.

Waber (1977) has extended the investigation of lateralization by examining the relationship among rate of physical maturation, brain lateralization, and verbal and spatial abilities. She expected to find that faster physical maturation would be associated with less brain lateralization and hence would favor verbal abilities, while slower maturation would be associated with greater brain lateralization and hence would favor spatial abilities. Since girls typically mature faster than boys, this difference in growth rates might cause the sex differences in intellectual abilities.

Waber studied forty boys and forty girls ten to sixteen years of age who were classified as either early or late maturers: that is, they showed significantly more or less development of secondary sexual characteristics than other children of their age and sex. She assessed their mental abilities with three verbal and three spatial tasks and assessed brain lateralization with a dichotic listening task. The dichotic listening involved simultaneous presentation of different nonsense syllables to both ears; lateralization was defined as a clear ear advantage, or a greater number of correct identifications of syllables for one ear. Waber found that late maturers of both sexes exceeded early maturers in brain lateralization (single-ear advantage in dichotic listening) and also in spatial scores, but the two groups did not differ in verbal abilities. When she compared the verbal and the spatial scores for each student, Waber found that late maturers did better in spatial than in verbal tasks, while early maturers did better in verbal than in spatial tasks. There were no significant sex differences when the rate of maturation was ignored.

Waber's study suggests that the rate of maturation is more important than sex in determining an individual's performance on spatial as compared with verbal tasks. Slower maturation may underlie greater lateralization, which is in turn associated with better spatial performance. It is well known that boys mature more slowly than girls from birth on. The slower physical maturation in boys may underlie greater male brain lateralization, which is in turn associated with the male superiority in spatial tasks.

The theories about brain lateralization and intellectual abilities are confusing. Is stronger or weaker lateralization the cause of greater spatial abilities? The question needs to be refined—do we mean lateralization of the right hemisphere or the left? If we mean the right, we should assess lateralization through nonlinguistic materials (as Witelson did); if the left, we should assess it through linguistic materials (as Waber did). Even this clarification would not be enough, however, for current research suggests that the left hemisphere is not only more verbal but also more analytical. On the other hand, the literature on sex differences in intellectual abilities has associated analytical thinking with the right hemisphere and spatial processing. Extensive research on brain functioning per se must be done in order to clarify the relationship between hemispheric dominance and the standard tests of specialized intellectual abilities. Only then can these brain functions be correlated with sex differences in intellectual performance.

For now, we are left with no clear evidence of sex differences in the degree or the timing of lateralization. Even if these sex differences in lateralization were definitively demonstrated, we would not know how they affect performance on standard measures of intellectual ability that seem to tap a mixture of functions carried out in both hemispheres. The suggestion of intervening variables like rate of physical maturation is promising but far from conclusive.

The idea of differences in male and female brains continues to have popular appeal and has been hotly debated and researched for over a decade in spite of numerous contradictions in both theory and data. As usual, the sex difference research started with a relatively simple idea—that male and female brains are different—only to find that the issue is extremely complicated and does not offer any conclusive evidence that biological sex differences cause differences in intellectual performance.

Training the Intellect

Can the sex differences in intellectual abilities be erased through altered social experience or specific training? If they can, these differences might be attributed to differences in the training that males and females receive in the usual course of growing up in our culture.

Our entire educational system is based on the premise that training is crucial, that without it children would not be able to reason clearly or to complete complex verbal *and* nonverbal tasks. Yet every teacher knows that there is a limit to what the best instruction can accomplish with each child. There seems to be a basic intellectual capacity that sets the limits for the rate and perhaps for the total amount of learning. With no instruction few children will develop complex skills, yet with the best instruction not all children will become highly skilled. No one would argue that instruction is useless. The issue is whether instruction helps a child use basic cognitive abilities he or she already possesses, or whether instruction can affect the development of these basic intellectual abilities themselves.

Research on training effects has focused on the Embedded Figures Test (EFT) and the Rod and Frame Test (RFT) developed by Witkin (1950). These tests assess spatial decontextualization, or the ability to extract key elements of a stimulus from a confusing background. In the EFT one is asked to identify a familiar object or shape buried within a larger patterned picture, while in the RFT one is asked to adjust a rod to a true horizontal position when it is contained within a somewhat skewed rectangular frame. Other tests expand the measurement to one's own body, requiring adjustment to an upright position while seated in a slanted chair or within a small asymmetrical room. All these tests are measuring "field dependence" versus "field independence"—one's ability to assess external or internal stimulation independently of the environment.

Measures of field independence are a basic component of tests of visual-spatial ability. They are interpreted as tapping the capacity for restructuring spatial elements that is thought to underlie abstract reasoning. Most summaries of this literature over the past two decades have reported that women are more field-dependent than men (in other words, women have lower spatial ability scores than men have), and that field independence does not increase with training. These findings and interpretations have recently been challenged by a growing number of psychologists. For instance, Mary Brown Parlee (1973–74) conducted a thorough review of all published studies and concluded that the sex differences were not nearly so conclusive as usually reported, partly because writers keep citing Witkin's work as if it encompassed numerous studies when in reality his writings appear to be based upon only one study. Furthermore, Parlee maintains that field independence scores tend to improve with practice or training.

Another way to approach social influences on spatial ability is to look at the scores obtained by people from differing cultural backgrounds. Kagan and Kogan (1970) have summarized this work, which indicates that, within a given population from the same genetic pool, those groups that are in the process of adopting a modern life style receive higher spatial scores than groups continuing in a traditional life style. This suggests that formal education, which accompanies the shift to modern life styles, may enhance spatial ability scores.

Personality and the Intellect

Crosscultural research also sheds some light on the personality characteristics associated with spatial ability (or lack of it). The greater field dependence in women has been interpreted as an indication both of basic female dependence on others for emotional support and social stimulation and of a general lack of "psychological differentiation" or development of a clearly defined and separate self-identify. The crosscultural argument is that people living in cultures that encourage dependence in children should have more field-dependent scores than have those living in cultures that encourage greater autonomy. Kagan and Kogan (1970) conclude that not only are child-rearing practices associated with spatial ability scores in the predicted fashion, but sex roles are also implicated: that is, men tend to score higher in spatial ability in those cultures with marked differences between the social roles assigned to the two sexes. The assumption is that greater sex-role differentiation is associated with greater encouragement of dependence in females, and this dependence in turn interferes with spatial ability as measured by field independence and other measures.

The crosscultural argument is organized around the theme of dependence and assumes that the trait of dependence interferes with the restructuring of external physical and social stimulation and hence inhibits abstract reasoning. When cultures begin to adopt a modern life style, allow children more autonomy, or define the proper role of the sexes less strictly, they are increasing the independence of their population. This more independent population then scores higher on field independence and other spatial-ability measures. But increased childhood autonomy, decreased sex-role differentiation, and increased technological innovation are all associated with higher levels of formal education for the population in general and for women in particular. Thus, increases in visual-spatial ability scores may be reflecting increased formal education rather than a personality trait of independence.

If independence were the key to high spatial ability, we would expect the most assertive and independent men *and* women to have the highest spatial-ability scores. This is not the case, however, for after ten years of research high scores on *all* intellectual ability measures continue to be associated with cross-sex typing (Maccoby and Jacklin 1974): that is, within-sex comparisons show that women who are *more* traditionally masculine and men who are *less* so receive higher scores. Independence, assertiveness, competitiveness, and dominance are key dimensions of "masculinity" measures. Thus, if dependence is the key dimension, it appears to operate differently in men and women.

At this point a critical observer often objects. Why is attentiveness to one's social or physical context described as "dependence"? And why is this a negative quality? If the most accomplished people paid no attention to their surroundings, where would society be? The answer to the "why" appears to be male cultural bias: that is, the traditional feminine orientation toward other people is devalued, compared with the traditional masculine focus on people and things in isolation. This "feminine" orientation is defined as "dependence" and proposed as a basic flaw or deficit that interferes with thinking in the logical and abstract ways associated with masculinity and strength.

For that matter, why has so much research been devoted to explaining the supposed male advantage in spatial ability? Why not focus on the female advantage in verbal ability, and then search for deficits in male personality that interfere with that ability?

Are the Sexes So Different?

Those who argued for biological underpinnings of intellectual sex differences are in somewhat of a quandary. Starting with the dictum that men and women think differently, they looked for biological mechanisms to explain these differences. Focusing on the male advantage in spatial ability scores beginning in adolescence, they looked at hormone levels, genetic linkage, and brain lateralization. All these investigators began with the "established" pattern of sex differences in spatial scores and tried to match it with a pattern that would be expected if the proposed hormonal, genetic, and brain lateralization differences did exist. The whole line of reasoning is refuted by the facts that the existing tests of intellectual abilities do not clearly differentiate among verbal, spatial, and mathematical abilities, and that recent reviews of the spatial ability literature suggest that the sex differences themselves do not exist, since spatial ability scores are often based on field-independence scores for which the sex differences are extremely doubtful.

The investigation of personality and intellect presents a similar situation. If there were clear personality differences between the sexes that were correlated with differences in intellectual abilities, we could at least begin to ask whether these personality correlates were due to biological sex differences. But here again the sex differences in intellectual abilities that served as the starting point for this line of reasoning do not appear to exist. And the personality differences traditionally used to explain these apparently nonexistent sex differences in intellectual ability have now been challenged as well.

Over a single decade of research there has been a major reversal of thinking. Few psychologists have confronted this change as openly and honestly as has Eleanor Maccoby of Stanford University. Speaking of her own review of sex differences in intellectual abilities written in 1966—and still cited by others as the authoritative summary in this area—she writes:

> The earlier argument began by assuming the existence of certain sex differences in intellectual performance that have not turned out to be consistently present; it then attempted to explain these on the basis of personality differences that have also proved to be more myth than reality. In view of this, the senior author can do little more than beg the reader's indulgence for previous sins. (Maccoby and Jacklin 1974, p. 133)

The lack of sex differences in intellectual functioning and personality does not mean, on the other hand, that the personal characteristics fostered in men and women do not affect their intellectual development differently; cross-sex typing still continues to be associated with higher scores on all measures of intellectual performance in both men and women. Maccoby goes on to address this issue:

> However, the studies on personality correlates of intellectual performance have continued to suggest that intellectual development in girls is fostered by their being assertive and having a sense that they can control, by their own actions, the events that affect their lives. These factors appear

to be less important in the intellectual development of boys—perhaps because they are already sufficiently assertive and have a sufficient sense of personal control over events, so that other issues (e.g., how well they can control aggressive impulses) become more important in how successfully they can exploit their intellectual potential. (P. 133)

Can we say, then, that men think differently than women? Or better than women? Not with any assurance. Do biological sex differences underlie any possible differences? It seems unlikely. The only clear theme is the familiar one of social factors. When owing to traditional sex roles females are discouraged from being assertive and independent, their intellectual development and performance seems to be inhibited.

Does Biology Make the Difference?

The entire area of biology and female behavior shares the problems that Maccoby outlines for intellectual abilities. Beginning with assumed sex differences in behavior, investigators have looked for biological differences that might cause these differences. Most of the behavioral differences used as a starting point have proved to be illusory, while the biological differences thought to underlie them have not been substantiated either.

The one exception is aggression. Here the initial idea that males act more aggressively than females continues to be supported by a variety of measures in many different situations, although the biological basis for this greater male aggressiveness is still a puzzle. The hormonal explanation is promising, especially in view of the link between male hormones and aggressive sexual behavior. But the hormonal research is plagued by the same difficulties that hamper other investigations of biology and sex-linked behavior. Researchers have looked only at sex-appropriate behavior—the effects of male hormones on traditionally masculine behavior and the effects of female hormones on traditionally feminine behavior. This difficulty is compounded by the coexistence of both male and female hormones in people of each gender. We do not know how progesterone might affect aggression or how androgen might affect nurturance; nor do we know whether the two types of hormones might affect the two sexes differently. Furthermore, it is difficult to draw definitive conclusions from separate studies of male and female hormones which ignore their relative levels and possible interactions. Perhaps the absolute level of both types of hormone combined may be more important than the separate levels of each.

For aggression, as for the more illusory sex differences, the biological explanation has to compete with a plausible social explanation. We know that parents treat male and female newborns differently, encouraging gross motor behavior in males while viewing females as littler, cuter, cuddlier, and generally more fragile. The crosscultural research echoes this social theme by demonstrating that most cultures encourage males to be independent and assertive while encouraging females to be dependent, nurturant, and responsible.

The social influences are not all in the environment. All types of research, even in such a purely physical area as biology, reflect the socially determined assumptions and viewpoints of the researchers themselves. As awareness of this cultural distortion has grown, psychologists have begun to make it an object of research in itself. The question is no longer the simple one of whether males and females are different, but has split into two: How do the social roles and stereotypes assigned to each sex shape the behavior, personalities, and lives of individuals? and, How do these same sex roles determine the way scientists study these sex differences?

I will take the second question first and consider the current theories that psychologists use to explain how personality and behavior develop differently in males and females. Once I have clarified some of the cultural themes embedded in these theories, I will be better able to evaluate the impact that cultural forces and life situations have on women today.

PART II

THEORIES OF

FEMALE PERSONALITY

WHAT HAPPENS as women grow up to make them different from men? Are women born with a female personality that is inherently different from the male personality? Should we encourage girls to climb trees and play Little League baseball, or is this going against nature? We often hear these issues discussed with a psychologist on radio and television talk shows. When people listen to this so-called expert, they seldom realize that he or she is expressing only one of several psychological truths. There are actually three major camps in psychology today, each with its own theory about how and why sex differences develop.

Thus, we have "female personality" as defined by psychoanalytic, cognitive-developmental, and social learning theories. Each theory reflects different assumptions about human nature—how it is determined by anatomy, sexual desires, emotions, thoughts, or behavior. These assumptions determine which areas of experience the theories focus on and how they study this experience.

In spite of their differences, these theories of female personality all have something in common: they highlight the sexual bias that determines how psychologists regard the female. Both the psychoanalytic and the cognitive-developmental theories treat the male body and personality as the norm. Freud begins with the premise that not having a male genital is a catastrophe almost beyond imagining. And Kohlberg's cognitive-developmental view is just as male-oriented, only now it is the entire male body, not just the penis, that contains or connotes much of what it means to be human.

Social learning theory highlights the sexual bias of our culture in an entirely different way—by studying it directly. Rather than attributing sex differences to some inherent body image (genital or nongenital), this theory attributes them to the social environment in which we live. Thus, girls and boys learn the same things, envy the same things, want the same things. But they *do* different things because other people expect them to. The psychological processes are the same for both sexes, then, but result in different behavior patterns.

I shall take each theory separately, examining the basic ideas used to explain the development of sex differences. Then I shall evaluate the theory in terms of the research literature and consider how persuasive it is in explaining female personality.

Chapter 4

Women in

Psychoanalytic Theory

MANY WOMEN are appalled when they first encounter Sigmund Freud's writings about women, which appear to be the sexist ramblings of a late Victorian patriarch, a way of dressing up cultural bias in fancy theoretical clothes, rather than the meditations of a great thinker on the female personality. Some feminists will not discuss Freud at all, preferring to spend their time and energy on developing new theories about female personality.

The psychoanalytic view of women can certainly be infuriating. But to ignore it is to ignore a major part of our cultural heritage, for not only have Freud's ideas dominated American psychiatry for the past fifty years, they have permeated our entire society as well. Our conversations and literature are sprinkled with references to "Freudian slips," the "oedipal complex," and the "unconscious" aspects of our thoughts and actions. Every time we search for our *real*, or unconscious, as opposed to our *obvious*, or stated, reasons for doing something, we are using the Freudian approach.

If Freud's ideas have had such an extensive influence on the society at large, we would expect them to have profoundly influenced psychologists as well—and they have. Much research on sex roles and sex differences is based on Freudian assumptions—assumptions about what is important to study, how to study it, and how to explain what is found. Thus, psychoanalytic theory has served as one of the most important filters through which psychologists look at the world of female experience. To get a clearer view of that world, we need to understand the nature of that filter.

Before turning to Freud's specific ideas about women, however, let us consider some central elements of his theory, which form a backdrop for those ideas. Sigmund Freud (1856–1939) was a Viennese physician who proposed that dreams could be used systematically to study the inner workings of the mind, and that these workings were the same for both normal and pathological behavior. His two greatest contributions were his ideas about the unconscious and the psychosexual stages. Early in his career Freud suggested that there are differing degrees of awareness of thoughts, feelings, or external events: "conscious" phenomena we are aware of at any given moment, "preconscious" phenomena we can become aware of if we attend to them, and "unconscious" phenomena that we are not aware of and that are expressed only indirectly through dreams. Freud went on to outline the properties of the unconscious and how it influences everyday behavior. The unconscious is illogical, so that opposites can represent the same thing; it disregards time, so that events from different time periods occur together; and it ignores space and distance, so that large objects seem to fit into small spaces, and distant places appear together. In general, then, the unconscious operates according to the symbolic expression of wishes without regard to external limitations and realities (Freud 1933b).

In 1923, Freud went beyond this concept of levels of awareness to propose separate mental functions or structures: the *id*, the *ego*, and the *superego* (Freud 1923, 1933b). The id represents the biological instincts or drives, primarily sexual and aggressive, and seeks to discharge excitation through the "pleasure principle" (the uninhibited pursuit of pleasure and the avoidance of pain). The superego is the conscience that seeks to control behavior in accordance with society's standards. The ego is reality-oriented, trying to satisfy the demands of the id within the limits imposed by the superego and external circumstances. The ego develops many strategies for moderating the demands of the id, such as delaying gratification until an appropriate time, displacing energy into socially acceptable outlets, and allowing release of energy only gradually. These strategies require perceptual and cognitive skills: the ability to distinguish wish from fantasy and to tolerate tension, conflict, and compromise. Later psychoanalysts such as Anna Freud (1946) and other "ego psychologists" have elaborated on Freud's early conception of the ego, emphasizing its importance in conflict resolution and viewing it as having some energy of its own not derived from the id.

According to Freud, a human being is not born with an ego or a superego but has to develop both over time, during the progress through the "psychosexual stages." These stages reflect Freud's biological bias, for he saw people as having a variety of instinctual drives whose sources were different bodily regions or "erotogenic zones" (1933a). An erotogenic or erogenous zone is a very sensitive area of skin or mucous membrane that accumulates irritation or arousal which must be discharged through physical manipulation. There are three such zones: the lips and oral cavity, the anal region, and the sex organs.

Freud suggested that there is a natural developmental sequence or series of psychosexual stages through which everyone passes during the first few years of life. In each stage the *libido* or sexualized life force focuses on a particular erogenous zone for which the stage is named—that is, the oral, the anal, the phallic-urethral, and the genital stages. During the first year of life, for instance, most of one's experiences and pleasures are focused on the mouth region. In the second year this oral stage gives way to the anal stage when bowel movements are a central source of pleasure and when the handling of these experiences (as in toilet training) shapes the personality and attachment to others. The phallic stage begins around three or four and focuses on self-stimulation of the genitals. Although these stages occur in a fixed sequence, the shift from one to another occurs gradually and at somewhat different ages in different individuals. If the needs of the libido are not met at one stage (for example, by sucking in the oral stage), some energy will remain "fixated" at that stage, causing later conflicts and a lessened amount of libidinal energy to be directed toward gratification at a later stage.

Freud viewed male and female development as similar during the oral, the anal, and the phallic stages. After the phallic stage, however, the sexes begin to diverge as they enter the oedipal stage in their fourth or fifth year. This stage involves attachment to the opposite-sex parent and is named after the mythic Greek, Oedipus, a son who kills his father and later marries his mother without being aware they are related to him. According to Freud, the sexual divergence in the oedipal stage forms the basis for dramatic differences in male and female personality development, as we will see (Freud 1925, 1931, 1933c).

Freud on Women

"Freud was the first to recognize what he didn't know about women" (Strouse 1974, p. 3). Freudian apologists often begin with this statement and go on to argue that although Freud obviously took the male as the norm in all things, the very fact that he viewed women as different is one of his major contributions, since male and female development are bound to differ in a sexist society (Mitchell 1974). Certainly Freud did hedge his bets by pleading some ignorance. Thus, he concluded one of his major articles focusing on female development with the words:

> That is all I had to say to you about femininity. It is certainly incomplete and fragmentary and does not always sound friendly. But do not forget that I have only been describing women in so far as their nature is determined by their sexual function. It is true that that influence extends very far; but we do not overlook the fact that an individual woman may be a human being in other respects as well. If you want to know more about femininity, enquire from your own experiences of life, or turn to the poets, or wait until science can give you deeper and more coherent information. (1965 [1933c], p. 135)

This disclaimer seems somewhat insincere, however, in the light of the authoritative tone of Freud's statements about women. It is true that of his voluminous writings Freud devoted only three articles to women, while other psychoanalysts have written many books and articles expanding and modifying his original concepts. But all discussion inevitably refers back to what Freud himself did and said. Here I will summarize his own statements and then go on to discuss their empirical support (or nonsupport) and consider whether recent modifications in psychoanalytic theory warrant a reconsideration of their empirical validity.

OUTLINE OF MALE AND FEMALE DEVELOPMENT

Let us consider the male first, since Freud takes his development as the norm. During the first few years of life the child's experience is focused on sucking and eliminating. He becomes emotionally attached to the mother as she nurses, bathes, and changes him. Her ministrations arouse his genital sensations; and as he enters the phallic stage at three or four he begins to masturbate. At four or five the boy connects his genital pleasure with the mother and becomes sexually attached to her, wanting to have her for himself. This desire is not specifically for intercourse, since young children have no understanding of the mechanics of the act, but rather for a generalized sexual possession. The arrival of a younger brother or sister usually initiates the boy's desire to have a child by the mother. At this age the boy perceives his father as a rival for the mother's attentions and hears many threats of punishment for his own masturbatory activities. The masturbating boy thus passes from the phallic stage to the oedipal stage when he begins to desire his mother and compete with his father.

The crucial event occurs when the boy in the oedipal stage sees the genitals of a sister or female playmate. At first he ignores the genital sex differences or discounts them as unimportant. Eventually, however, he connects them with the parental threats about his own masturbation:

the boy perceives the girl as having lost the organ that he himself values so highly—that is, as having already been castrated for masturbating with her penis. The perception of his sister as castrated arouses fear of castration or *castration anxiety* in the boy. Since the father is the primary disciplinarian and is seen as a rival, this threat of castration seems to come from him. Faced with a choice between having his mother and losing his own penis, the boy gives up his mother and identifies with his father. This identification with the aggressor causes the boy to incorporate the father's attributes, including his morals and sex-role characteristics. The boy thus forms a strong superego and sexual identity and goes on to want a wife of his own.

What of the girl? She, too, becomes emotionally and sexually attached to the mother through nursing, bathing, and changing in the first three years of life. As her libido begins to focus on the genitals in the phallic stage, she, too, masturbates, but with her clitoris, since "in the phallic phase of girls the clitoris is the leading erotogenic zone" (1965 [1933c], p. 118). Thus in the phallic stage both boys and girls masturbate, or as Freud puts it, "the little girl is a little man" (1965 [1933c], p. 118). The girl in the phallic stage also connects her sexual pleasure with the mother, wants the mother for herself, wants to have a baby by the mother, and sees the father as a rival.

For the girl the crucial event is also seeing the genitals of an opposite-sex sibling. But when she sees her brother's penis, the girl does not fear castration; instead, she perceives herself as already castrated. Freud describes her reaction this way:

> [Girls] notice the penis of a brother or playmate, strikingly visible and of large proportions, at once recognize it as the superior counterpart of their own small and inconspicuous organ, and from that time forward fall a victim to envy for the penis. . . . She makes her judgement and her decision in a flash. She has seen it and knows that she is without it and wants to have it. (1959 [1925], pp. 190–91)

Having seen "the boy's far superior equipment" (1965 [1933c], p. 126), the girl develops *penis envy* and stops masturbating because her female masturbation, like her female organ, is obviously second-rate. Since Freud views masturbation as an active, masculine form of sexuality, this means a turn from masculinity to femininity for the girl. As Freud puts it,

> I cannot explain the opposition which is raised in this way by little girls to phallic masturbation except by supposing that there is some concurrent factor which turns her violently against that pleasurable activity. Such a factor lies close at hand in the narcissistic sense of humiliation which is bound up with penis-envy, the girl's reflection that after all this is a point on which she cannot compete with boys and that it would there-

fore be best for her to give up the idea of doing so. Thus the little girl's recognition of the anatomical distinction between the sexes forces her away from masculinity and masculine masturbation on to new lines which lead to the development of femininity. (1959 [1925], p. 194)

These "new lines" lead to a focus on the vagina as the primary female sexual organ. Freud maintains that while females have two sexual organs—the clitoris and the vagina—the clitoris is merely a "penis-equivalent," while the vagina is the "truly feminine" organ (1965 [1933b], p. 118). The idea that vaginal sexuality is somehow more naturally feminine than clitoral sexuality is still prevalent today and underlies the continuing controversy about vaginal versus clitoral orgasms, as we will see in Chapter 12.

Penis envy not only causes the girl to stop masturbating; it also causes her to turn from her mother out of shame, anger, and disappointment that the mother brought her into the world without a penis. She turns to the father hoping to get a penis from him; failing in this, she eventually comes to want a baby from her father as a symbolic equivalent of a penis. Thus:

> But now the girl's libido slips into a new position by means—there is no other way of putting it—of the equation "penis = child." She gives up her wish for a penis and puts in place of it a wish for a child: and *with this purpose in view* she takes her father as a love-object. Her mother becomes the object of her jealousy. (1959 [1925], p. 195)

> Her happiness is great if later on this wish for a baby finds fulfillment in reality, and quite especially so if the baby is a little boy who brings the longed-for penis with him. (1965 [1933c], p. 128)

Thus, penis envy pushes the girl into the oedipal stage of sexual desire for the opposite-sex parent and of jealousy and rivalry for the same-sex parent.

CENTRAL POINT OF SEX DIFFERENCES

The diagram in Figure 4.1 shows that while the discovery of opposite-sex genitalia is crucial for both boys and girls, the "castration complex" or response to this traumatic event has a dramatically different effect on the two sexes. The masturbating boy is already in the oedipal stage when he sees his sister; fear of castration forces him to give up his mother to save his penis and hence abruptly *ends* his oedipal complex. The masturbating girl is still in the phallic stage when she sees her brother; penis envy pushes her *into* the oedipal stage, and there is no fear of castration to make her give up her father abruptly (since she is already castrated and has nothing to fear). Consequently, the girl's oedipal complex lingers on, and she has no strong impetus to identify with her mother; she does not incorporate her mother's attributes as

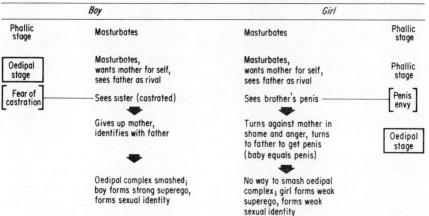

Figure 4.1 Freud's View of Male and Female Development

thoroughly as the boy does the father's, and she fails to develop a strong superego or sexual identity. Freud states this difference strongly:

> In girls the Oedipus complex is a secondary formation. The operations of the castration complex precede it and prepare for it. As regards the relation between the Oedipus and castration complexes there is a fundamental contrast between the two sexes. *Whereas in boys the Oedipus complex succumbs to the castration complex, in girls it is made possible and led up to by the castration complex.* . . .
>
> In boys . . . the complex is not simply repressed, it is literally smashed to pieces by the shock of threatened castration. Its libidinal cathexes [sexualized attachments] are abandoned, desexualized and in part sublimated; its objects are incorporated into the ego, where they form the nucleus of the super-ego and give that new structure its characteristic qualities. In normal, or rather in ideal cases, the Oedipus complex exists no longer, even in the unconscious; the super-ego has become its heir. . . .
>
> In girls the motive for the destruction of the Oedipus complex is lacking. Castration has already had its effect, which was to force the child into the situation of the Oedipus complex. Thus the Oedipus complex escapes the fate which it meets with in boys: it may either be slowly abandoned or got rid of by repression, or its effects may persist far into women's normal mental life. I cannot escape the notion (though I hesitate to give it expression) that for women the level of what is ethically normal is different from what it is in men. Their super-ego is never so inexorable, so impersonal, so independent of its emotional origins as we require it to be in men. (1959 [1925], pp. 195, 196)

CHANGES REQUIRED OF GIRLS ONLY

To negotiate Freud's stages of sexual development successfully, a girl must go through three major changes not required of the boy. First,

she must stop masturbating with her "masculine" clitoris and change
her sexual zone to the "truly feminine" vagina.

> The [male] has only one principal sexual zone—only one sexual organ
> —whereas the [female] has two: the vagina, the true female organ, and the
> clitoris, which is analogous to the male organ. We believe that we may
> justly assume that for many years the vagina is virtually non-existent and
> possibly does not produce sensations until puberty. . . . Thus in female
> development there is a process of transition from the one phase to the
> other, to which there is nothing analogous in males. (1959 [1931], p. 255)

> . . . With the change to femininity the clitoris should wholly or in part
> hand over its sensitivity, and at the same time its importance, to the vagina.
> This would be one of the two tasks which a woman has to perform in the
> course of her development, whereas the more fortunate man has only to
> continue at the time of his sexual maturity the activity that he has previ-
> ously carried out at the period of the early efflorescence of his sexuality.
> (1965 [1933c], p. 118)

The change of sexual zone is accompanied by a change from an active
to a passive sexuality.

> The turning-away from the mother is a most important step in the
> little girl's development: it is more than a mere change of object. . . . we
> observe, hand in hand with it, a marked diminution in the active and an
> augmentation of the passive sexual impulses. . . . Frequently, with the
> turning-away from the mother there is cessation of clitoridal masturbation,
> and very often when the little girl represses her previous masculinity a
> considerable part of her general sexual life is permanently injured. The
> transition to the father-object is accomplished with the assistance of the
> passive tendencies so far as these have escaped overthrow. (1959 [1931],
> pp. 267, 268)

This change from active to passive sexuality does not imply a change
in the substance of libido, or sexual energy, since "psycho-analysis
teaches us to manage with a single libido, though its aims, *i.e.* its modes
of gratification, are both active and passive" (1959 [1931], pp. 268–69).
However, it does seem to imply a general decrease in sexual activity due
to severe repression (and, I might add, to the supposed insensitivity of
the vagina until puberty).

Not only must the girl change her sexual zone and become sexually
passive, she must also change the gender of her "object choice," or
sexual attachment. While the boy must renounce his mother, he does not
need to renounce females in general. The girl, however, has to renounce
her mother *and all females*, turning to her father and then to other males.
Freud puts it this way:

> Parallel with this first great difference there is another, which con-
> cerns the love-object. The first love-object of the male is the mother, be-

cause it is she who feeds and tends him, and she remains his principal love-object until she is replaced by another which resembles her or is derived from her. With the female too the mother must be the first object, for the primary conditions of object-choice are the same for all children. But at the end of the girl's development it is the man—the father—who must come to be the new love-object; *i.e.* as she changes in sex, so must the sex of her love-object change. (1959 [1931], p. 256)

In the course of time, therefore, a girl has to change her erotogenic zone and her object—both of which a boy retains. (1959 [1933c], p. 119)

RESOLUTIONS OF THE FEMALE OEDIPAL COMPLEX

What becomes of girls after they go through these rather tortuous changes? The outcome for boys is simple: most of them identify with their aggressive, powerful fathers and eventually assume the sexually active, dominant male role in their own marriages. Freud suggests three different paths for girls—all rather pessimistic and demeaning. The first ends in sexual frigidity and a general inhibition of activity.

The first leads to her turning her back on sexuality altogether. The budding woman, frightened by the comparison of herself with boys, becomes dissatisfied with her clitoris and gives up her phallic activity and therewith her sexuality in general and a considerable part of her masculine proclivities in other fields. (1959 [1931], p. 257)

The second path leads to the "masculinity complex." The girl refuses to stop masturbating, deluding herself into thinking that she has the proper equipment for this male activity. She continues to be assertive in other areas as well, revealing her hopeless desire to get a penis and be a man. This female difficulty is quite common, as evidenced by the number of women who insist on entering the male domain of careers. Freud suggests that in its most extreme form the masculinity complex may lead to female homosexuality, where the woman tries to take on the role of a man in relating to other women. As Freud describes it:

If she pursues the second line, she clings in obstinate self-assertion to her threatened masculinity; the hope of getting a penis sometime is cherished to an incredibly late age and becomes the aim of her life, whilst the phantasy of really being a man, in spite of everything, often dominates long periods of her life. This "masculinity complex" may also result in a manifestly homosexual object-choice. (1959 [1931], p. 257)

From this point [of seeing and wanting the boy's penis] branches off what has been named the masculinity complex of women, which may put great difficulties in the way of their regular development towards femininity, if it cannot be got over soon enough. The hope of some day obtaining a penis in spite of everything and so of becoming like a man may persist to an incredibly late age and may become a motive for the strangest and otherwise unaccountable actions. Or again, a process may set in which might be described as a "denial," a process which in the mental life of children seems neither uncommon nor very dangerous but which in an adult would mean the beginning of a psychosis. Thus a girl may refuse to accept the fact of being castrated, may harden herself in the conviction that she *does* possess a penis, and may subsequently be compelled to behave as though she were a man. (1959 [1925], pp. 191–92)

Only the third "very circuitous path" leads to the "normal feminine attitude" (1959 [1931], p. 257). Here the girl neither refuses to stop masturbating nor renounces sexuality altogether. Instead she acknowledges her "organic inferiority" (1959 [1931], p. 259), switches from active (clitoral) to passive (vaginal) sexuality, rejects her mother, and turns to her father to get a penis/baby. The girl pays a high price for this normal development, however; for the penis envy that motivates it also leads naturally to permanent feelings of shame, inferiority, and jealousy.

The psychical consequences of penis-envy, in so far as it does not become absorbed in the reaction-formation of the masculinity complex, are various and far-reaching. After a woman has become aware of the wound to her narcissism, she develops, like a scar, a sense of inferiority. When she has passed beyond her first attempt at explaining her lack of a penis as being a punishment personal to herself and has realized that that sexual character is a universal one, she begins to share the contempt felt by men for a sex which is the lesser in so important a respect, and, at least in the holding of that opinion, insists upon being like a man.

Even after penis envy has abandoned its true [physical] object, it continues to exist: by an easy displacement it persists in the character-trait of *jealousy*. Of course, jealousy is not limited to one sex and has a wider foundation than this, but I am of opinion that it plays a far larger part in the mental life of women than of men and that that is because it is enormously reinforced from the direction of displaced penis-envy. (1959 [1925], p. 192)

Freud goes on to say that lingering penis envy causes the female to be physically vain and morally deficient.

The effect of penis-envy has a share, further, in the physical vanity of women, since they are bound to value their charms more highly as a late compensation for their original sexual inferiority. Shame, which is considered to be a feminine characteristic *par excellence* but is far more a matter of convention than might be supposed, has as its purpose, we believe, concealment of genital deficiency. We are not forgetting that at a later time shame takes on other functions. It seems that women have made few contributions to the discoveries and inventions in the history of civilization; there is, however, one technique which they may have invented—that of plaiting and weaving. If that is so, we should be tempted to guess the unconscious motive for the achievement. Nature herself would seem to have given the model which this achievement imitates by causing the growth at maturity of the pubic hair that conceals the genitals. The step that remained to be taken lay in making the threads adhere to one another, while on the body they stick into the skin and are only matted together.

The fact that women must be regarded as having little sense of justice is no doubt related to the predominance of envy in their mental life; for the demand for justice is a modification of envy and lays down the condition subject to which one can put envy aside. (1965 [1933c], pp. 132, 134)

The effects of envy are added to a more basic problem: women do not have adequate consciences anyway. Freud says that the boy forms a strong superego, or conscience, when his oedipal complex is smashed, while the girl's superego is always weak because her oedipal complex lingers on indefinitely. He expands on this point by saying:

Character-traits which critics of every epoch have brought up against women—that they show less sense of justice than men, that they are less ready to submit to the great necessities of life, that they are more often influenced in their judgements by feelings of affection or hostility—all these would be amply accounted for by the modification in the formation of their super-ego which we have inferred. (1959 [1925], p. 197)

To defend himself against accusations of male bias, Freud hastens to add that even the majority of men fail to live up to the "masculine ideal" of justice and that this "masculine" quality can exist in both sexes.

We must not allow ourselves to be deflected from such conclusions by the denials of the feminists, who are anxious to force us to regard the two sexes as completely equal in position and worth; but we shall, of course, willingly agree that the majority of men are also far behind the masculine ideal and that all human individuals, as a result of their bisexual disposition and of cross-inheritance, combine in themselves both masculine and feminine characteristics, so that pure masculinity and femininity remain theoretical constructions of uncertain content. (1959 [1925], p. 197)

The "normal" woman is not only plagued by envy, jealousy, shame, feelings of inferiority, and a defective sense of justice. She is also passive and masochistic, deriving pleasure from being offended, mistreated, dominated, and embarrassed. When the girl abandons her active (clitoral) sexuality, she gives up her active strivings in all other areas as well. The passive mode of (vaginal) sexual expression generalizes, so that the girl generally eschews active, aggressive, and hence traditional masculine behavior and thus turns her repressed aggression inward in the self-destructive attitudes and behaviors of masochism. Freud puts it this way:

The suppression of women's aggressiveness which is prescribed for them constitutionally and imposed on them socially favours the development of powerful masochistic impulses, which succeed, as we know, in binding erotically the destructive trends which have been diverted inwards. Thus masochism, as people say, is truly feminine. (1965 [1933c], p. 116)

But even this does not complete Freud's derogatory view of women, for he maintains that the normal woman is also passive and less urgently sexed than the normal man. This is partly due to the side effects of renouncing clitoral masturbation: in repressing her active sexuality, the girl often represses much of her passive sexuality as well. In addition, Freud suggests that the libido, or sex drive, may be anatomically weaker in females than in males. He supports this view with the observation that men are primarily responsible for reproduction, since their aggressive nature enables them to force women to have sexual intercourse whether they want to or not. This remarkable argument is contained in the following passage:

> There is only one libido, which serves both the masculine and the feminine sexual functions. To it itself we cannot assign any sex; if, following the conventional equation of activity and masculinity, we are inclined to describe it as masculine, we must not forget that it also covers trends with a passive aim. Nevertheless the juxtaposition "feminine libido" is without any justification. Furthermore, it is our impression that more constraint has been applied to the libido when it is pressed into the service of the feminine function, and that—to speak teleologically—Nature takes less careful account of its [that function's] demands than in the case of masculinity. And the reason for this may lie—thinking once again teleologically—in the fact that the accomplishment of the aim of biology has been entrusted to the aggressiveness of men and has been to some extent independent of women's consent.
>
> The sexual frigidity of women, the frequency of which appears to confirm this disregard, is a phenomenon that is still insufficiently understood. Sometimes it is psychogenic and in that case accessible to influence; but in other cases it suggests the hypothesis of its being constitutionally determined and even of there being a contributory anatomical factor. (1965 [1933c], pp. 131–32)

MOTHERS AND DAUGHTERS

Just like the boy, the girl starts out with a strong attachment to her mother. What could make the girl turn against this powerful person who has provided physical comfort and emotional support? Freud points to three sources of resentment in the child. First, there is the insatiable nature of the child's desires: she always feels that "the mother gave the child too little milk and did not suckle her long enough" (1959 [1931], p. 262). Then, there is jealousy: the girl resents that the mother pays attention to her brothers, sisters, and father because "childish love knows no bounds; it demands exclusive possession, is satisfied with nothing less than all" (1959 [1931], p. 259). And, finally, there is the rebellion fostered by the mother herself—first she introduced the girl to sexual pleasure through bathing and other caretaking activities; then she prohibited the child's pursuit of sexual pleasure through masturbation.

The girl shares these reproaches with the boy. But the boy can project his hostility onto the father, from whom he fears castration. The girl, however, looks to the father for a penis and is not so free to direct hostility toward the person from whom she hopes to get this magical organ. Nevertheless, these negative feelings serve only to make the girl feel somewhat ambivalent toward the mother; they are not strong enough to make her reject the mother.

The boy gives up his mother to save his penis. What strong motivation does the girl develop that matches the overwhelming fear of castration? Freud proposes two uniquely female motivations that serve this purpose. First, the girl blames the mother for bringing her into the world without a penis. This blaming soon turns into animosity, so that "the turning away from the mother is accompanied by hostility; the attachment to the mother ends in hate" (1965 [1933c], p. 121). Second, the girl comes to devalue the mother, because the mother herself does not have a penis. This second motivation takes longer, because at first the girl thinks that she alone has been castrated for her sins. Only gradually does she understand that all females share her fate. As Freud puts it:

> Invariably the child regards castration in the first instance as a misfortune peculiar to herself; only later does she realize that it extends to certain other children and at length to certain adults. When the universality of this negative character of her sex dawns upon her, womanhood, and with it also her mother, suffers a heavy loss of credit in her eyes. (1959 [1931], p. 261)

> This means, therefore, that as a result of the discovery of women's lack of a penis they are debased in value for girls just as they are for boys and later perhaps for men. (1965 [1933c], p. 127)

Having a penis is thus the key for both the boy and the girl. The boy turns away from the mother *to retain* his penis. The girl turns away from the mother *to get* a penis from the father and, in addition, comes to hate the mother for not providing her with one and to devalue the mother for not having one herself.

Freud suggests that the preoedipal attachment to the mother is more important in females than it is in males because of the "circuitous" nature of female development. Many girls fail to complete the difficult transition to the father and therefore remain fixated in a more primitive attachment to the mother. This close mother-daughter relationship is extremely ambivalent, however, due to the girl's hostility toward and devaluing of the mother. Thus, Freud portrays girls and their mothers as locked into a continuing, immature love-hate relationship.

RELATIONSHIPS BETWEEN MEN AND WOMEN

Freud's picture of male-female relationships is no more encouraging. After the boy sees his castrated sister, he reacts with "horror of the mutilated creature or triumphant contempt for her"; and these attitudes "permanently determine the boy's relations to women" (1959 [1925], p. 191). The girl comes to share this view; she develops a "sense of inferiority" and begins to "share the contempt felt by men for a sex which is the lesser in so important a respect" (1959 [1925], p. 192).

Freud's picture of marriage is also rather bleak. Both sexes choose a spouse on the basis of the oedipal complex: the man chooses a wife who reminds him of his mother, while the woman chooses a husband who reminds her of her father. The husband provides the wife with her longed-for penis, and all is well. But gradually the wife begins to relate to her husband not as to her father, but as to her mother; the wife regresses to the preoedipal phase and becomes hostile. The wife's hostility may flare into rebellion.

> The woman's husband, who to begin with inherited from her father, becomes after a time her mother's heir as well. So it may easily happen that the second half of a woman's life may be filled by the struggle against her husband, just as the shorter first half was filled by her rebellion against her mother. (1965 [1933c], p. 133)

This rebellion, of course, is an immature continuation of the girl's rebellion against her "organic inferiority."

If the couple has a baby—especially a male baby—things are better, for a woman's relationship with a son is portrayed as warm and unambivalent because of the symbolic equivalence, penis = baby. But otherwise a woman may begin to treat her husband like a baby in an attempt to feel that his penis belongs to her and makes up for her "genital deficiency."

The following psychoanalytic case history reported by Moulton (1970) illustrates how the difficulties of a young professional woman would be analyzed in terms of penis envy and its derivatives—continuing feelings of jealousy and inferiority; inhibited sexuality; a long-lasting, sexualized attachment to the father; an ambivalent relationship with the mother characterized by strong preoedipal attachment, hostility, and contempt; and a desperate attempt to make up for organic inferiority by having a baby.

An unsuccessful actress who had always resented being a woman came to treatment very depressed and anxious at having allowed herself to become pregnant. Her husband had recently become extremely successful, and her envy and competition with him were enormous, especially since she was blocked in her own professional development. She felt that the best way to "show up" her husband was to do the one thing he could not do—bear a child.

She expressed only hatred and contempt for her mother, who had been a dependent, ineffectual housebound woman. This resentment seemed to have started at the birth of her sister, three years younger, at which time the patient hid herself and refused to talk for days. The mother, a masochistic woman dependent on her own mother, was hospitalized for depression when the patient was fifteen. The father was an unsuccessful actor, an exciting, talented person whom the patient adored. She turned away from her mother and spent the next ten years of her life trying to be her father's son. He encouraged her acting and took her to performances, partly to get away from the mother. However, he was very inconsistent and bitter, given to terrifying rages; he would alternate between leading her on and slapping her down. Her fantasy of being like a boy was brutally crushed at a time when she was preparing for a bas mitzvah; she thought she would be allowed to have one "as good as a boy's" but was suddenly humiliated publicly at puberty and sent home from the synagogue on the Sabbath because it was decided that she was now a woman and could no longer stay and compete with the men and boys. Menarche intensified her resentment of female functions but she compensated with fantasies of having a son and traveling around the world with him—self-sufficient, no longer needing her family or her father. While in Europe on a scholarship, she fell in love and, while petting with the boy, had the only orgasm she has ever experienced. She feared his increasing power over her, experienced a resurgence of dependency needs and fled home, presumably because her father was ill. She felt she had spent her life trying to win her father's approval. But when she finally "made" Broadway, he taunted her, "Why not give it up, go home, and make babies?"

After his death and her professional failure, she became increasingly depressed. At the age of thirty, she decided to get pregnant—after having been married four years. (She had previously been phobic about pregnancy and remained a virgin until her marriage.) She felt that her baby was conceived out of emptiness, not fullness, and then feared that the child would take her life from her, would deplete rather than fulfill her. Having a baby trapped her, she felt; she could no longer try to be like a man. It was as though she had had a fantasy penis which she finally had to relinquish. . . . She also feared that motherhood would transform her into a person like her own mother—a fate desperately to be avoided. She found herself unconsciously imitating many of her mother's patterns, which aggravated her self-contempt and depression.

There was plenty of evidence of typical penis envy in this case. As a girl, the patient even tried to compete with boys in urinary contests, and was furious because she always lost. She first associated her bed-wetting with rage at not having a penis, but finally viewed it as a way to punish mother for turning to [her] sister, and as an effort to recover the maternal solicitude she had lost. She envied, and was attracted to, men who had powerful drives for achievement and were free to pursue them. The penis was for her as a symbol of such drives; to possess it would also save her from being like her mother. In one sense, she wanted a baby as a substitute for not having a penis; but she also had a burning wish to be a good mother—to prove her own validity as well as to "undo" her past. Her difficulty in achieving this wish forced her to work through her relationship with her mother, which she had contemptuously shelved, finding competition with men more exciting and less anxiety-provoking. (Moulton 1970, pp. 97–99)

Research Challenges Freud

What research evidence is needed to substantiate Freud's theory? The crux of the matter is the castration complex—penis envy in girls and castration anxiety in boys; so it is necessary to establish that children notice the genital differences between the sexes at about four or five years of age and react to those differences with intense fear or envy. Since Freud maintains that these emotional reactions shape the adult personality and persist throughout life, at least on an unconscious level, it is also necessary to examine the emotional life of adults for signs of these reactions.

Innumerable psychoanalytic case histories address these issues. These reports are similar to Moulton's (1970) and involve an analyst's reporting on his or her memory of a series of sessions and interpreting the material in psychoanalytic terms. There are many problems with this approach. One cannot generalize from a single case nor can one assume that someone in therapy is the same as the general population (the person in therapy must have enough money for private therapy, perceive his or her behavior as "symptoms" of illness, and be motivated to seek help from an analyst). The analyst also chooses what aspects of the patient's life and personality are important and then guides the exploration of them in therapy, describing them, along with dreams and free associations, in Freudian terms. Such case histories take on the character of self-fulfilling prophesies; they make fascinating reading but abominable science.

Here I shall consider only empirical studies that follow the standard methods of research: objective measures that can be understood and repeated by other researchers, groups of comparison subjects matched for relevant characteristics, and accepted methods of data analysis. Some Freudians have used this more systematic approach to explore the way the castration complex is expressed in everyday behavior, dreams, and responses to material designed to evoke sexual conflicts. I shall discuss some typical studies that illustrate common research strategies; and I shall focus on the critical dimensions of the various research designs, since other writers have already provided comprehensive reviews of this literature (Fisher and Greenberg 1977; Kline 1972). Then I shall go on to consider research that examines the assumptions underlying Freud's concept of penis envy—assumptions about children's knowledge of anatomical sex differences and about the nature of female sexuality.

THE CASTRATION COMPLEX: PROBING THE UNCONSCIOUS

There are many studies of the ways penis envy and castration anxiety are expressed in everyday behavior. Eugene Landy (1967) observed the way men and women opened a pack of cigarettes and removed the first cigarette. He described his study this way:

> It was predicted that for women, having penis envy and the desire to possess a penis would constitute reaction formation; they would reject phallic images in everyday life and recreate by repetition compulsion the cavity (vaginal fenestra) to have within them a child. Freud explains this as the sublimation of penis envy. Thus, female smokers should tend to open an unopened pack of cigarettes and obtain a cigarette by lifting open the folded part of the cigarette pack, lifting the flaps up to make a form similar to a cavity, and pushing the bottom of the pack up to expel the cigarette from the top. In this manner the female creates a cavity in the bottom of the pack and expels the cigarette (the penis object). . . . (1967, p. 576)

Landy found what he expected: women did tend to open a pack this way more than men did. But he also found that this method of opening was more common among nonsmokers than among smokers, and women were more apt to be nonsmokers. He blithely ignored the smoker-nonsmoker difference, however, and concluded that "the observed behaviors are consistent with the Freudian hypothesis that castration complex in males and penis envy in females is expressed in everyday living" (Landy 1967, p. 579).

Landy's study illustrates a serious problem in studies of Freudian theory: How can one know whether the behavior being measured reflects the Freudian concept? The usual approach is through symbols: anything longer than it is wide is considered a penis symbol, while anything elliptical or round is considered a womb symbol. If one objects to the symbolic equivalence, one is accused of denying the unconscious reality. Since the unconscious does not follow the rules of logic, anything goes. Noticing a "penis symbol" expresses "penis envy"; ignoring it still expresses "penis envy" through the mechanisms of displacement, denial, or projection. Thus, Freudian theory can predict the result of A or the opposite of A in the same experiment. This "damned if you do, damned if you don't" quality of Freudian predictions makes the theory difficult to test empirically and leads some psychologists to call it a "rubber-band theory."

A second approach is to use projective measures. The basic idea is to assess the response to penis or castration symbols, on the assumption that the individual automatically "projects" his or her own personal feelings onto the situation in which the symbols are depicted. Gerald Blum (1949) developed the Blacky Test which uses cartoon drawings of a supposedly neutral-sex black dog (Blacky), a blonde neutral-sex sibling dog (Tippy), and two parent dogs. Blum showed drawings of various situations to about two hundred male and female students at Stanford University and asked them to choose one of two or three sentences that described the situation. Each cartoon supposedly represented an important dimension of the castration complex and its derivatives. For instance, of a drawing of Blacky watching the parent dogs holding hands, the students were asked, "Which one of the following makes Blacky most unhappy?" The choices were: (a) "Papa keeping Mama all to himself," or (b) "The idea that Mama and Papa seem to be ignoring him." More males than females chose the "oedipal" alternative (a), while more females than males chose the "preoedipal" alternative (b). Similarly, a cartoon of Blacky licking his genitals was described as, "Here Blacky is discovering sex." When asked "How does Blacky feel here?" more males than females chose the guiltless alternative (a) among three choices: (a) "Happy, without a care in the world," (b) "Enjoying himself, but a little worried," and (c) "Mixed up and guilty." This was interpreted as evidence that females have greater masturbation guilt due to penis envy and to the resulting renunciation of "male" sexuality.

Blum's study shares the problem of symbolic meaning raised by Landy's study of smoking behavior. How do we know that the Blacky cartoons symbolize what Blum says they do? In addition, Blum found the sex differences and *then* consulted Freudian theory for a prediction. This is putting the cart before the horse. Careful research requires one to make theoretical predictions and then devise a study to test them; it is not legitimate to find results and then see how a theory can justify them.

Friedman (1952) tried to tap unconscious material with a variation of the projective technique used by Blum. Friedman asked 305 school children five to sixteen years old to tell a story about a picture of a monkey who was "very fond of his tail" and then "something different happened." Since 75 percent of the children ended their stories with loss or damage of the tail, he concluded that castration anxiety was indeed prevalent (although less so in girls than in boys). There are two problems with this study. First, the instructions are biased, in that they predispose the subjects to envision something bad happening to the tail. These instructions violate the assumptions of projective techniques:

the examiner and the material must be neutral, so that the subjects can project their own feelings and reactions onto the situation. Second, how do we know that the tail represented a phallic symbol to the children as well as to the researcher? The children may have reacted much as they would to the loss of any bodily extremity such as an arm or a leg. With this research method it is impossible to differentiate between a threat to general bodily integrity and a threat to the penis per se. This second difficulty, of course, is the same one of symbolic meaning found in both Landy's and Blum's studies.

Sarnoff and Corwin (1959) used Blum's Blacky Test in a more sophisticated study designed to test Freud's proposal that fear of having a fatal illness is a characteristic derivative of repressed castration anxiety. They first assessed the degree of castration anxiety in fifty college men by having them tell how much anxiety Blacky felt when he was watching a large knife hovering over the tail of a neutral-sex, blindfolded dog. At this point they also administered a questionnaire to assess fear of death. A few weeks later they showed photos of nude females to one group of men and showed photos of clothed females to a second group. Both groups then filled out the fear-of-death questionnaire again. Freud's proposal would suggest that sexual arousal should be associated with fear of death, so that the men with initially high castration anxiety should show a greater increase in fear-of-death scores after sexual arousal. The researchers found this was true: men with high castration anxiety did show a greater increase in fear-of-death scores in the sexually aroused group shown nude photos but not in the unaroused group shown clothed photos.

When I discuss this study in class, some students always point out that we should not assume that nudes are more arousing than clothed women. After all, the coyly exposed ankle can be very alluring. But there is a far more serious difficulty with the study—the problem of symbolic meaning. How do we know that the Blacky cartoon arouses a specific fear of castration rather than a general fear of bodily mutilation? What makes cutting a tail represent cutting the genitals? If we do not assume the tail is a phallic symbol, the study results still make sense. Those men who show the most concern about being mutilated increase that concern under sexual arousal; the sexual arousal may serve to increase their attention to the test materials, or it may arouse general concern about bodily appearance and functioning. Any bodily mutilation is threatening to one's feeling of sexual attractiveness and prowess. Those men who are already worried about being mutilated might well become even more anxious about it under sexual arousal. The threatened mutilation does not need to be genital for this to happen.

A third approach uses dream analysis rather than everyday behavior or projective measures to assess castration anxiety and penis envy. The symbolic problem is the same here: How do we determine what the different elements of the dream stand for? The usual method is totally arbitrary; the researcher simply decides that *x, y,* and *z* are symbolic representations of penis envy and so on. Thus, when Hall and Van deCastle (1966) tell us that they found more evidence of castration wish and penis envy in the dreams of sixty college women than in the dreams of sixty college men, we do not know exactly what has been measured. Our skepticism is increased when we consider that their conclusion is based on evidence of penis envy's occurring thirty-two times in 956 female dreams and sixteen times in 953 male dreams, and this in college students who were enrolled in psychology classes that may have discussed Freudian theory.

Some studies report on more specific dream content. Thus, in another study Hall and Domhoff (1963) counted the male and female characters in dreams collected from males and females two to eighty years old. They found that men dream more about their own sex, while women dream equally about both sexes. What does this prove? Are women more likely to dream about opposite-sex people because of their desire to have a penis? Or are they more likely to dream about men because men are more likely to be socially powerful? The latter seems more probable, since Maccoby and Wilson (1957) found that teenagers watch movie characters of their own sex but tend to identify with characters of a slightly higher socioeconomic status to which they aspire. Women attend to socially important people they want to be like; these people tend to be men, but it is not necessarily their penises that women want.

These studies of the castration complex in adults are unconvincing, to say the least. Let us turn to studies of children four to five years old who are presumably in the oedipal period. Do they know that girls do not have penises, and do they react to this knowledge with "shame" or with "horror of the mutilated creature"?

DO CHILDREN KNOW GIRLS LACK PENISES?

Early attempts to answer the question whether children know girls lack penises used doll play interviews with children four to twelve years old. The basic idea is that when children are asked to act out situations, they will express their own feelings and reactions through the words and actions of the dolls. Conn (1940) interviewed 128 boys and 72 girls in this way and found that three-fourths of them had seen the genitalia of the opposite sex. One-third of those who had observed genital sex differences were willing to discuss them, and the majority of these showed no particular emotional reaction to their observation. Conn and Kanner (1947) followed this up with a similar study dividing children into separate age groups. This time they were able to elicit knowledge of genital sex differences from 50 percent of the children four to six years old, 72 percent of the children six to eight years old, and 86 percent of the children eleven to twelve years old. These studies suggest that many children four to six years old do not even know that girls do not have penises, and that those who do know are not traumatized by this information.

Katcher (1955) devised a clever and more direct way to assess knowledge of genital differences. First he painted pictures of one nude and one clothed adult and child of each sex. The body outlines of the figures were similar: the nude was emerging from the shower, while the clothed figure was descending steps outdoors. Then he cut the pictures into sections: two for the clothed adults and both clothed and nude children (cut below the neck) and three for the nude adults (cut below the neck and above the waist). The sex of each picture segment could thus be determined by only one factor: hair, clothes, naked chest, or naked genitals. He presented pairs of these segments to 149 boys and 117 girls three to nine years old and asked them to "show me the boy (girl, man, woman)."

Katcher found that an amazing percentage of the children made errors in identifying the genital segments: 88 percent at age three, 69 percent at age four, 49 percent at age five, and 29 percent at age six. Not only did they have difficulty identifying the gender of the genital segment, but they also had difficulty matching it with the gender of the hair and trunk sections of the unclothed figure. Thus Katcher found the same thing Conn and Kanner did: one-half of the children in the oedipal age period (four to five years) are not fully aware of the genital sex differences that are supposed to be so traumatic and crucial to their emotional development.

Other aspects of Katcher's study also undercut Freud's argument. Freud maintains that seeing the genitals of a sibling or a parent is the crucial event that leads to penis envy or castration anxiety. If this is so, children with opposite-sex siblings and those with both parents in the home should have shown more accurate knowledge of genital differences, since they were more probably exposed to those differences. But Katcher found that the number of parents and opposite-sex siblings in the home made no difference in children's ability to identify the genital segments. In fact, after age three, children with one parent at home were *more* accurate in matching the segments than were children with two parents at home.

Katcher also found a regular pattern of increasing knowledge of body parts with age. The order of ease of identification was clothing, hair, genitals, and chest. At age three few children made errors in assigning gender by clothing or hair, while many were still making errors using genitals and chests when they were six years old. Freudian theory would predict that the traumatic nature of genital differences would make them more difficult to distinguish than chests; here again the data do not support Freud.

DO WE HAVE TO LEARN WHAT GENDER WE ARE?

Freud's theory not only assumes that children four to five years old know that girls do not have penises. It also assumes that children have an innate, instinctual knowledge of their own genders at even younger ages. The emotions and behavior of the child are supposedly based upon biological urges that express the profound sex differences embedded in anatomy.

But does a child automatically know its gender? In the studies of hermaphrodites I discussed in Chapter 1 (Hampson and Hampson 1961; Money and Ehrhardt 1972), it was found that these children who are born with undeveloped or sexually ambiguous genitalia grow up to show the interests, behaviors, and personality characteristics of the sex in which they are raised, regardless of their biological gender. This research indicates that children have to *learn* what their gender is; after they have done this in the first few years of life, they have to learn about the genital sex differences that usually determine gender labels. Since many four- and five-year-olds do not know that girls do not have penises, they are obviously still in the process of acquiring this information about genitals. When I discuss Kohlberg's cognitive-developmental theory, I shall examine the reasons that this learning is still incomplete at that age.

But if gender itself has to be learned, how can the characteristics and behavior associated with that gender be biologically determined? Obviously they cannot. Female anatomy alone cannot determine the girl's behavior; female socialization is crucial.

FEAR OF CASTRATION OR GENERAL MUTILATION?

Castration is crucial to Freud's theory: fear of it in the boy, recognition of it in the girl. Studies of penis envy and castration anxiety assume that all bodily mutilation represents specifically genital mutilation—recall the dog and the monkey tails. Certainly we are all afraid of being maimed, but is the imagined damage necessarily genital?

The fact that children must learn their own gender and then learn the genital differences used to assign gender labels suggests that the threat is to our entire anatomy, not just to our genitals; for the child naturally fears any damage to the body. Kohlberg calls this a threat to "anatomical constancy" or bodily integrity and views it as a natural outgrowth of other learning about the body, as I shall discuss.

But scientific studies are not really necessary for the raising of this issue. Logic is enough. Psychoanalytic case histories also challenge the assumption that all bodily mutilation represents genital mutilation, as later Freudians have pointed out. Ruth Moulton, for instance, says that "fears of mutilation precede knowledge of the penis, and may refer to a diffuse dread of bodily injury rather than just sexual injury" (1970, p. 92). She goes on to argue that after a girl discovers the penis, fears of mutilation do center on the genitals for a time, but this penis envy is transitory unless other reinforcing factors lead to conflicts about femininity—factors like sibling rivalry, unusually strong dependency needs for the mother, a rejecting or remote father, and anything else that increases the "dread of becoming a woman" (1970, p. 91).

CAN ENVY BE PHYSIOLOGICAL?

Freud maintains that the girl stops masturbating with her clitoris because she realizes that her female masturbation, like her female organ, is second-rate. She envies the physical sensations that the boy experiences when he masturbates with his penis, and she knows that they are superior to the pleasure she gets from her clitoris.

But how can one envy a physical sensation one has not experienced? How can the girl "know" the boy's pleasure is superior when she has not felt it? This idea seems patently absurd.

But perhaps it is merely the erections and the other observable physical characteristics of the penis that the girl wants. She sees the penis and wants it as a physical appendage she does not have. This desire would not assume physiological envy, since it would be based on envy not of physical sensations but rather of physical appearance and observable movement. Once this envy developed, the girl might feel the "shame" Freud suggests and then denigrate anything connected with her own organ, including the pleasure it provided her through masturbation.

Even this reinterpretation is questionable, however, for what makes the girl "know" that penile erections are desirable? Why should she want the penis more than other physical appendages she lacks—breasts, for instance? The obvious answer is that the penis is valued by others around her as a sign of maleness. Since males have more social status and power, the penis becomes a symbol for these advantages. She does not envy the male anatomy; she envies the male sociocultural advantages.

Rachel Levin (1966) did a study that provides a comparison of the anatomical and social sources of penis envy. She took two groups of women of equal intelligence and psychological adjustment who had all graduated from college. Twenty-six were unmarried women with careers in traditionally masculine occupations who could be expected to show penis envy or "masculine protest"; twenty-five were married, full-time homemakers with two or more children. Levin devised a female-castration complex measure based on the Rorschach Test, a projective measure that taps unconscious motivation through perception of ink blots. There were differences in only one of four indices meant to assess reaction to anatomical sex differences: the career women were "more disturbed in their reactions to male sexuality" (p. 186). There were differences in two out of four nonanatomical personality factors: the career women were "more active and assertive" and "more oriented towards status and achievement" (p. 186). Of all eight indices, the one most clearly differentiating the two groups was that of the need for achievement.

Levin's study suggests that social factors may be more crucial to penis envy than anatomical factors are; but it does not provide a clear test of the social versus the physical source of penis envy, as Levin herself points out. For Levin's data cannot tell us whether the differences between the two groups of women led them to adopt their feminine and masculine roles, or whether these differences were a consequence of the roles themselves. In other words, were the single career women uncomfortable with male genitals because of their unmarried status, and did they become more assertive and achievement-oriented because their jobs required them to do so? Or did their inherent feelings of penis envy lead to these attitudes and life choices?

I should also note that Levin's study shares the usual problem of defining the symbolic measures of unconscious factors. Thus while the study is far from definitive, it does demonstrate that even projective measures fail to provide clear support for Freud's conception of penis envy if they do not start from the assumption that all signs of activity, competition, and assertiveness in women reflect the desire to have a male genital.

IS PENIS ENVY TYPICAL OF WOMEN?

If Freud is right about penis envy, the phenonemon should be found more typical of women than of men. After all, even a man can envy the size of another man's penis; but a woman's envy should be more intense, since she lacks this crucial organ entirely. And this intense envy should affect other areas of a woman's life.

As Fisher and Greenberg (1977) point out, no major studies have compared the degree of penis envy imagery in the two sexes. Nor have studies asked whether women who display "blatantly compensatory phallic behavior"—such as female professional athletes, police, or army recruits—also show the expected "high degree of penis-envy preoccupation" (p. 202). And researchers need to test the Freudian proposition that women who have hostile, derogatory, and envious attitudes toward men also show "unusually intense penis-envy imagery" (p. 202).

On the other hand, there *has* been extensive research on the way the two sexes feel about their bodies; and it does not support Freud. "It can be immediately declared that Freud was wrong in his assumption that the average woman perceives her body in more negative and depreciated terms than the average man . . . if anything, women are more comfortable with their body experiences than are men" (Fisher and Greenberg 1977, p. 199).

IS FEMALE SEXUALITY PASSIVE?

According to Freud, the shift from the "masculine" clitoris to the "truly feminine" vagina is essential to normal female development, because it initiates a general shift to appropriately passive femininity. The passive/receptive vagina, which supposedly has no sensations until puberty, is the prototype for the female personality—passive, dependent, masochistic, and sexually inactive.

Psychoanalyst Helene Deutsch elaborated on Freud's original statements by describing at length how female reproductive anatomy inevitably makes women passive, masochistic, and weak, leaving the aggressive male properly in control of all sexual activity. Her comments are rather startling:

> The theory that I have long supported—according to which femininity is largely associated with passivity and masochism—has been confirmed in the course of years by clinical observations.
>
> The woman's sexual activity no longer follows the stirrings of her own rhythm or the summons of the reproductive function. She has obviously subordinated herself to the sexual will and domination of the male.
>
> This [passive female] behavior is repeated in the functions of the sexual cells: the ovum is relatively motionless, passively expectant, while the spermatozoid is active and mobile. The behavior of the sexual partners during intercourse continues this differentiation between the masculine-active and the feminine-passive. The anatomy of the sex organs leaves no doubt as to the character of their aims: the masculine organ is made for active penetration, the feminine [vagina] for passive reception. The objection that many and even most normal women develop a high degree of activity during sexual intercourse does not refute the view presented here.
>
> It might be assumed that either the little girl's sexual excitability is from the outset less active and intensive than the boy's, or that she has an inferior [clitoral] organ with which to attain the same instinctual goals. Actually it seems that both these assumptions are correct.
>
> The vagina—a completely passive, receptive organ—awaits an active agent to become a functioning excitable organ.
>
> The awakening of the vagina to full sexual functioning is entirely dependent upon the man's activity; and this absence of spontaneous vaginal activity constitutes the physiologic background of feminine passivity. The competition of the clitoris, which intercepts the excitations unable to reach the vagina, and the genital trauma [penis envy] then create the dispositional basis of a permanent sexual inhibition, i.e. frigidity. (1944, pp. 220, 221, 223–24, 228, 230, 233)

The essential distinction in Deutsch's argument is still between clitoral and vaginal sexuality. Sensations and orgasms experienced through the clitoris are immature and imitate the male, a vestige of preoedipal phallic sexuality; all those experienced through the vagina are mature and appropriately feminine.

But where does this distinction come from? Apparently from Freud's rather active and traditionally masculine imagination, for modern science has established what many women knew all along: there is no physical difference between clitoral and vaginal orgasms. Regardless of where a woman's body is stimulated, the resulting excitation occurs *throughout* the genital tissue. A stroke on the clitoris, in the vagina, on a breast, a thigh, or even a foot all lead to the same result—vasocongestion through-out the genital area caused by a rush of body fluids, followed by the physical release of rhythmic contractions in the uterus and the lower third of the vagina. Although the subjective experience of orgasm varies somewhat due to psychological factors, clitoral and vaginal orgasms cannot be distinguished from one another on a physiological basis (Kaplan 1974; Masters and Johnson 1966; Sherfey 1972).*

What about structural differences between clitoris and vagina? Here, too, the organs are remarkably similar, composed of highly sensitive mucous membranes developed from the same tissues in the fetus. The concentration of nerve endings is even greater in the tip of the clitoris (glans) than in the vagina, whose lower third has so few that "it is doubtful that stimulation of the lower third of the vagina alone could produce anything but infrequent and weak orgasmic reactions at best" (Sherfey 1972, p. 126).

And what of the argument that the male sperm is active in swimming up the vagina, while the female egg is "relatively motionless" and "pas-sively expectant"? One could just as easily argue that the egg is active in traveling down the fallopian tubes. Furthermore, the vagina itself is not biologically passive. As a later female analyst has pointed out:

> More important is Deutsch's acceptance of Freud's view that activity (libido) is masculine, and his confusion of passivity with receptivity. As always, Freud wanted to base his thinking on biology. Yet there is even no biological reason for thinking that the vagina is passive. It is a re-ceptive organ; but unless it is unaroused, it is certainly active, and in fact its contractions are apparently at least as responsible as the motility of the sperm for the latter's reaching the ovum. There are as many ways of being active as there are of being human. To pierce and to enter are one kind of activity. To grasp and to hold are another. (Cavell 1974, p. 164)

And then there is Freud's assertion that the vagina is insensitive until puberty, to which Deutsch adds that only a male penis can awaken it. Research on the sexual response in humans and primates does sug-gest that "it is extremely doubtful that vaginal sensations would occur in prepubertal girls" (Sherfey 1972, p. 126). The development of vaginal

---

* The physiology of the female sexual response will be discussed more fully in chapter 12.

sensuality is dependent on biology rather than on male initiative, however, for the dramatic rise in female hormones which occurs during puberty causes the maturation of female sexual/reproductive structures. To attribute this maturation to the male penis is absurd. It is a physical expression of the underlying assumption found in fairy tales: that the female is totally passive and that, to experience life fully, she requires a male; even female nerve endings are asleep, waiting for Prince Charming to awaken them.

If the clitoral glans has more nerve endings than the vagina, and if the physical response to stimulation is so generalized, why define vaginal stimulation and orgasm as the only natural feminine sexuality? The answer seems to lie in the Victorian idea that sex is acceptable only when its purpose is reproduction. Thus, Deutsch (1925) suggests that while men derive maximum pleasure from intercourse, when they both experience orgasm and complete their role in reproduction, women derive maximum pleasure only when reproduction is finalized in childbirth. Giving birth is thus presented as the ultimate sexual pleasure for women.

Feminists point out that not only has our culture viewed sex as acceptable only for reproductive purposes, it has also used the male definition of female sexuality to keep women sexually repressed and subservient. Susan Lydon comments on this state of affairs:

> Dr. William Masters had searched for a woman co-worker for his research because, as he said, "No male really understands female sexuality." Before Masters and Johnson [1966], female sexuality had been objectively defined and described by men; the subjective experience of women had had no part in defining their own sexuality. And men defined feminine sexuality in a way as favorable to themselves as possible. If woman's pleasure was obtained through the vagina, then she was totally dependent on the man's erect penis to achieve orgasm; she would receive her satisfaction only as a concomitant of man's seeking his. With the clitoral orgasm, woman's sexual pleasure was independent of the male's, and she could seek her satisfaction as aggressively as the man sought his, a prospect which didn't appeal to too many men. The definition of normal feminine sexuality as vaginal, in other words, was a part of keeping women down, of making them sexually, as well as economically, socially, and politically subservient. (1970, pp. 200–201)

Neo-Freudians Make Amends

Freud's ideas about women have never gone unchallenged. Freud himself tacitly acknowledged their controversial, male-oriented nature when he said that he refused to be dissuaded by "the denials of the feminists" (1959 [1925], p. 197). Many of these feminist "denials" have been voiced by the neo-Freudians, who have proposed revisions in various aspects of Freud's theory. Their central objection to his theory of female personality is the same as the objection of political feminists outside the mental health profession: that Freud takes the male as the basic pattern for health and normality. Kate Millett states this objection succinctly; she says that Freud fails "to acknowledge that woman is born female in a masculine-dominated culture which is bent upon extending its values even to anatomy and is therefore capable of investing biological phenomena with symbolic force" (1970, p. 180).

Some feminists have responded to Freud's focus on male genital anatomy by insisting that *female* anatomy is actually the basic human form: all fetuses are biologically female until the sixth week of life; after that, the developing testes in males secrete hormones that initiate male differentiation. Thus, Moulton points out that "embryologically speaking . . . it would be correct to say that the penis is an exaggerated clitoris rather than the reverse" (1970, p. 88). Most writers go on to warn, however, that to argue that the female is therefore the norm for all human development merely perpetuates Freud's fallacy of anatomical determinism and one-upmanship (Moulton 1970; Sherfey 1972).

Rather than try to turn the tables by asserting female anatomical superiority, most neo-Freudians have focused instead on how male cultural bias is reflected in Freud's theory. Karen Horney raised this issue right after Freud wrote his first major article on women: she said that "like all sciences and all valuations, the psychology of women has hitherto been considered only from the point of view of men" (1926, p. 326). She went on to illustrate how the analytical picture of feminine development corresponds to the typical ideas that little boys have about little girls. This boy's-eye view of women (Table 4.1) is hardly a sound basis for a sophisticated theory about female personality development.

Many neo-Freudians have followed Horney's lead in discussing how social factors influence both the theory and the reality of female development. Since penis envy is the central concept in Freud's view of women, these writers have focused on alternate interpretations of this phenomenon. Then they have gone on to discuss other sexual and reproductive differences between the sexes and how these shape the female personality.

THE PENIS AS A SYMBOL OF POWER

The major theme of neo-Freudian writings is that penis envy is social rather than anatomical. The girl envies male social status and power and hence desires a penis that represents maleness. As I suggested before, she does not envy the male anatomy; she envies the male sociocultural advantages. According to Clara Thompson, Freud maintains that it is the actual physical male organ which women are demanding . . . whereas it seems to me that when such a wish is expressed the woman is but demanding in this symbolic way some form of equality with men. . . .

In this specific, limited sense Freud's idea that women have envy because they have no penis is symbolically true in this culture. The woman envies the greater freedom of the man, his greater opportunities and his relative lack of conflict about his fundamental drives. The penis as a symbol of aggression stands for the freedom to be, to force one's way, to get what one wants. These are the characteristics which a woman envies in a man. (1942, pp. 332, 337)

So, the attitude called penis envy is similar to the attitude of any underprivileged group towards those in power. (1943, p. 124)

TABLE 4.1
Psychoanalysis: A Boy's-Eye View of Women

The Boy's Ideas	Our [Psychoanalytic] Ideas of Feminine Development
Naïve assumption that girls as well as boys possess a penis	*For both sexes it is only the male genital which plays any part*
Realization of the absence of the penis	*Sad discovery of the absence of the penis*
Idea that the girl is a castrated, mutilated boy	*Belief of the girl that she once possessed a penis and lost it by castration*
Belief that the girl has suffered punishment that also threatens him	*Castration is conceived of as the infliction of punishment*
The girl is regarded as inferior	*The girl regards herself as inferior. Penis envy*
The boy is unable to imagine how the girl can ever get over this loss or envy	*The girl never gets over the sense of deficiency and inferiority and has constantly to master afresh her desire to be a man*
The boy dreads her envy	*The girl desires throughout life to avenge herself on the man for possessing something which she lacks*

Source: Karen Horney, "The flight from womanhood: The masculinity-complex in women as viewed by men and by women," in Karen Horney, *Feminine psychology* (New York: W. W. Norton, 1967), pp. 57–58. Originally published in the *International Journal of Psycho-Analysis* (1926) 7 (3/4): 326.

Ruth Moulton (1970) has pointed out that in a less patriarchal culture where women had more prestige and power, the penis would not be a power symbol and might therefore elicit female contempt rather than envy and shame. This possibility has not escaped feminists, who have humorously proposed such concepts as "penis pity" (Walsh 1977).

Elizabeth Janeway has extended the argument that penis envy is social by suggesting that Freud himself may have meant to imply that women are "social castrates":

By insisting, falsely, on female deprivation of the male organ, Freud is pointing to an actual deprivation, and one of which he was clearly aware. In Freud's time the advantages enjoyed by the male sex over the inferior female were, of course, even greater than at present and they were also accepted, to a much larger extent, as being inevitable, inescapable. Women were evident *social* castrates, and the mutilation of their potentiality as achieving human creatures was quite analogous to the physical wound, reference to which recurs both in Freud's 1925 and 1931 papers. . . .

. . . We must allow that women's inferiority, in Freud's mind, was somewhere understood to be the result of her lack of power; and that her lack of a penis did not simply *denote* this, but *stood* for it. (1974, pp. 58, 65)

Janeway goes on to wonder whether Freud might have felt compelled to refer to female oppression in this indirect way because he himself was oppressed and powerless as a Jew in Hapsburg Vienna. This seems a bit farfetched, since Freud's writings certainly sound as though he believed in female "organic inferiority" as the *cause* of female social inferiority. But a reinterpretation of Freud's idea of physical castration in terms of social castration seems logical, if a bit overly dramatic.

"SECONDARY" PENIS ENVY: REJECTING FEMININITY?

While neo-Freudians view penis envy as social envy, they do not entirely discount the idea that little girls desire a penis per se. But they maintain that this anatomical envy is transitory, since it is based on a natural childish curiosity and desire to possess everything one sees. This transitory anatomical penis envy is usually called "primary penis envy" to distinguish it from the continuing, unconscious desire to be a man that is found in neurotic adult women. Thus, primary, anatomical penis envy is found in young girls, while secondary, social penis envy is found in adult women. Karen Horney (1926) outlined this distinction, and it was repeated by later writers like Clara Thompson (1943) and Ruth Moulton (1970).

According to Horney's definition, "secondary" penis envy is basically a new version of Freud's "masculinity complex," for neo-Freudians talk about how social disadvantages reinforce a girl's primary (anatomical) penis envy, interfering with her normal female development. The adult woman's resulting secondary penis envy, or desire to be a man, is interpreted as a reflection of her deep-seated doubts about her own femininity (Moulton 1970; Thompson 1943) or as an unconscious attempt to repress her continuing sexual desire for her father (Horney 1926). The adult woman is no longer seen as neurotic because she wants a male genital; she is now seen as neurotic because she rejects her passive, powerless feminine role.

The redefinition of penis envy as social rather than anatomical does not necessarily eliminate the assumption that women are naturally (biologically and anatomically) passive and dependent. The writings of neo-Freudians are still full of references to natural "feminine" passivity. Beulah Bosselman, for instance, agrees that penis envy is social but views it as an expression of female resentment at not being allowed to exercise one's "feminine prerogatives" (1960, p. 259). These prerogatives, it turns out, are to be in a "protected-dependent role" in which one "dares to be passive-receptive" (p. 256). The woman displaying penis envy does not really want to be a man; she wants the man in her life to be more dominant and competitive so that she can be "allowed to be a woman" (p. 257).

REPRODUCTIVE VERSUS GENITAL SEX DIFFERENCES

The second major theme of neo-Freudian writings is that Freud emphasized the genitals and intercourse while ignoring reproduction. After all, only women can give birth—surely the human achievement most obvious to young children. One would think that boys would develop envy of the female womb, uterus, and breasts that represent this reproductive capacity. Horney maintains that males actually do develop an "intense envy of motherhood" that is much stronger than the female penis envy. The strength of this male envy leads to a "greater necessity to depreciate women than conversely" and to strenuous attempts to compensate for males' inability to give birth by engaging in worldly achievements (1926, pp. 330, 331).

Margaret Mead elaborates on this idea by pointing out that in cultures where women's reproductive role is recognized and respected, one finds "womb envy," rituals like the *couvade* in which men imitate pregnancy and childbirth, and myths about man-making powers that were invented by a woman and stolen from her by men (1974, pp. 96–97).

Of course Freud does discuss reproduction, but not as a distinct female capability. Instead, he views childbirth as yet another expression of penis envy, through the symbolic equivalence penis = baby. As Kate Millett puts it, "Freudian logic has succeeded in converting childbirth, an impressive female accomplishment, and the only function its rationale permits her, into nothing more than a hunt for a male organ. It somehow becomes the male prerogative even to give birth, as babies are but surrogate penises" (1970, p. 185). Is motherhood really just another way of becoming a man by obtaining a penis? Many of us share Horney's dismay at this idea.

> At this point I, as a woman, ask in amazement, and what about motherhood? And the blissful consciousness of bearing a new life within oneself? And the ineffable happiness of the increasing expectation of the

appearance of this new being? And the joy when it finally makes its appearance and one holds it for the first time in one's arms? And the deep pleasurable feeling of satisfaction in suckling it and the happiness of the whole period when the infant needs her care? (1926, p. 329)

What could make anyone suggest, or accept, the ludicrous idea that a woman has a baby in order to get a penis? Here we return again to the issue of male power and prestige. As Mead has pointed out, whatever males do is seen as achievement; whatever females do is discounted.

> However, in all cultures, without any known exception, male activity is seen as achievement; whatever women do—gathering seeds, planting, weeding, basket-making, pot-making—is valued less than when the same activity, in some other culture, is performed by men. When men cook, cooking is viewed as an important activity; when women cook it is just a household chore. And correspondingly, if an activity once performed by women becomes more important in a society, it may be taken over by men. For example, midwifery, once a profession in which the female practitioners were both constricted and feared, has been taken over by male obstetricians. (Mead 1974, pp. 99–100)

This valuing of maleness does not apply only to activities; it extends even to anatomy: whatever men have women must want, and whatever women do must be motivated by envy of maleness. If men could menstruate, someone would propose "menstruation envy," as Gloria Steinem illustrates in her humorous article entitled "If Men Could Menstruate: A Political Fantasy":

> A white minority of the world has spent centuries conning us into thinking that a white skin makes people superior—even though the only thing it really does is make them more subject to ultraviolet rays and to wrinkles. Male human beings have built whole cultures around the idea that penis-envy is "natural" to women—though having such an unprotected organ might be said to make men vulnerable, and the power to give birth makes womb-envy at least as logical.
>
> In short, the characteristics of the powerful, whatever they may be, are thought to be better than the characteristics of the powerless—and logic has nothing to do with it.
>
> What would happen, for instance, if suddenly, magically, men could menstruate and women could not?
>
> The answer is clear—menstruation would become an enviable, boast-worthy, masculine event:
>
> Men would brag about how long and how much.
>
> Boys would mark the onset of menses, that longed-for proof of manhood, with religious ritual and stag parties.
>
> Congress would fund a National Institute of Dysmenorrhea to help stamp out monthly discomforts. . . .
>
> Military men, right-wing politicians, and religious fundamentalists

would cite menstruation ("*men*-struation") as proof that only men could serve in the Army ("you have to give blood to take blood"), occupy political office ("can women be aggressive without that steadfast cycle governed by the planet Mars?"), be priests and ministers ("how could a woman give her blood for our sins?"), or rabbis ("without the monthly loss of impurities, women remain unclean")....

And how would women be trained to react? One can imagine traditional women agreeing to all these arguments with a staunch and smiling masochism. ("The ERA would force housewives to wound themselves every month": Phyllis Schlafly. "Your husband's blood is as sacred as that of Jesus—and so sexy, too!": Marabel Morgan.) ...

In fact, if men could menstruate, the power justifications could probably go on forever.

If we let them. (Steinem 1978a, p. 110)

THE ACTIVE VAGINA

Along with their emphasis on the uniquely female capacity to give birth, neo-Freudians stress also that the vagina is an active organ that plays a major part in the sexuality of the preoedipal girl (Cavell 1974; Horney 1926; Moulton 1970). At the same time, however, they point out difficulties that supposedly stem from the fact that the vagina is an internal organ. Vaginal sensations are often described as "vague, amorphous, and anxiety-provoking"; and since the girl cannot observe the vagina as the boy can his penis, it is difficult for her to establish "organ constancy," to learn that she will always have a vagina rather than a penis (Moulton 1970, pp. 86, 87). The internal nature of the vagina also makes the girl uncertain about the "dreaded consequences" of masturbation, which "contributes to the peculiar inner uncertainty so often met with in women" (Horney 1926, p. 335).

Recent neo-Freudians acknowledge that there is no physiological difference between vaginal and clitoral orgasms, and some even stress that while the penis functions as a separate organ, the clitoris functions inseparably from the vagina (Moulton 1970). After saying this, however, some quickly add that the vagina is still the truly feminine organ. Cavell, for instance, maintains:

Surely Deutsch is right in saying that the woman who consciously or unconsciously regards her clitoris as her primary sexual organ has something to hide, some reason to deny the existence or the importance of her invisible vagina and uterus, and that she may indeed think of herself as a defective male. Phantasied castration amounts to real psychological castration and is a cry for help. Deutsch's answer to such women—though it's an answer which may take years of therapy for them to hear—is that "the final phase of attaining to a definitively feminine attitude is not gratification through the sexual act of the infantile desire for a penis, but full realization of the vagina as an organ of pleasure—an exchange of the desire for a penis for the real and equally valuable possession of a vagina." (1974, p. 165)

WOMAN'S INNER SPACE

The new emphasis on social factors and reproductive differences does not really eliminate the male bias in Freudian theory. The writings of psychoanalyst Erik Erikson are a case in point. Erikson is known for his discussion of social influences in psychological development and has called for a "shift of theoretical emphasis from the loss of an external organ to a sense of vital inner potential" (1968, p. 275). Erikson believes that the anatomy of reproduction inevitably makes men and women dramatically different. The male's penis orients him aggressively toward conquering the external world of objects; the female's "inner space" orients her passively toward nurturing the internal world of children, family, and interpersonal relationships. Erikson describes it this way:

> But how does the identity formation of women differ by dint of the fact that their somatic design harbors an "inner space" destined to bear the offspring of chosen men and, with it, a biological, psychological, and ethical commitment to take care of human infancy? Is not the disposition for this commitment (whether it be combined with a career, and even whether or not it be realized in actual motherhood) the core problem of female fidelity?
>
> Young women often ask whether they can "have an identity" before they know whom they will marry and for whom they will make a home. Granted that something in the young woman's identity must keep itself open for the peculiarities of the man to be joined and of the children to be brought up, I think that much of a young woman's identity is already defined in her kind of attractiveness and in the selective nature of her search for the man (or men) by whom she wishes to be sought. This, of course, is only the psychosexual aspect of her identity, and she may go far in postponing its closure while training herself as a worker and a citizen and while developing as a person within the role possibilities of her time. . . . A true moratorium must have a term and a conclusion: womanhood arrives when attractiveness and experience have succeeded in selecting what is to be admitted to the welcome of the inner space "for keeps."
>
> Am I saying, then, that "anatomy is destiny"? Yes, it is destiny, insofar as it determines not only the range and configuration of physiological functioning and its limitation but also, to an extent, personality configurations. The basic modalities of woman's commitment and involvement naturally also reflect the ground plan of her body. (1968, pp. 266, 283, 285)

Woman's nature, then, is still wholly determined by her anatomy— only now it is the uterus and womb rather than the clitoris. Woman is still naturally suited only for marriage and motherhood, although she can make temporary forays into the external world of men while waiting for the right man to come along and complete her true feminine identity. Again the fairy tale motif holds true only instead of the vagina waiting to be awakened to sensation by Prince Charming, the womb and uterus await his coming to give the sleeping woman her feminine identity. Erikson still views woman solely in terms of her relationships with men.

THE NEO-FREUDIAN PREDICAMENT

Neo-Freudians have, however, a more serious problem than male bias. Without anatomical penis envy, what makes a girl turn to her father? What initiates the female oedipal complex which is central to the Freudian view of female development? Perhaps the transitory anatomical penis envy of the girl is the answer. She is happily masturbating, sees her brother's penis, develops a temporary envy of his organ, and turns to her father to get one like it. Social penis envy then might keep her oriented to her father once the anatomical penis envy fades; she would still want her father because he is powerful. But the problems here are the same as in Freud's formulation. At the crucial age many children do not know that a girl lacks a penis.

Could envy of male power accomplish the girl's turn to the father? (We cannot view envy of the penis as a *symbol* of that power at ages four to six, since children are not sure about genital sex differences at that age.) Here we have the happily masturbating girl who perceives that her father is powerful, and turns her erotic attentions to him. But this turn would not be caused by basic instincts and drives with a clear biological source. Such a social motivation lacks the force of biological drives and hence is incompatible with the rest of the biologically based Freudian theory. To suggest that social forces are more powerful than innate sexual drives is to undercut the biological underpinnings of Freudian theory.

Which brings us to the reproductive sex differences and the active vagina. Now we have both clitoral and vaginal sexuality recognized as natural, active, and physiologically inseparable. But again, what makes the girl change her sexual desires to focus on her father instead of on her mother? Perhaps the female organs naturally yearn for the male—but no, that would mean the girl would be oriented to her father from the beginning. We are once more left with male power—a social perception rather than a biological urge.

Chapter 5

Cognitive-Developmental Theory and Female Personality

AFTER FREUD'S EMPHASIS on anatomy and sexual drives, cognitive-developmental theory often seems like a breath of fresh air. Now it seems that we can discuss female development logically by examining how women learn to think rather than by appealing to vague, overwhelming urges somehow based on "natural" feminine biology; for this theory focuses on how the growing child perceives the world and slowly comes to understand that it is composed of males and females who are very different creatures. Surely, one may suppose, basic thought processes are sexless, so here the female will not be at a disadvantage.

Or does this theory, too, assume that males are somehow more "normal"? Unfortunately the answer is yes. In spite of its emphasis on thought processes, cognitive-developmental theory makes some basic male-oriented assumptions that define the male as somehow more human than the female.

In order to see how this theory is applied to female personality development, we must first examine its basic tenets.

The Development of Thought
and Self-Concept

Cognitive-developmental theory is the brainchild of a Swiss philosopher, logician, and psychologist named Jean Piaget (born 1896). The basic thrust of this theory is that children do not think like adults. Although a baby is born with the ability to perceive the world, its initial impressions are a confusion of sights, smells, noises, and activity. Only gradually does it develop the intellectual or cognitive structures needed to organize these impressions in a coherent and logical way (Piaget 1929, 1952, 1954).

Intellectual development requires both biological maturation and the child's own efforts: as the child interacts with people and objects in the environment, an orderly pattern of relationships emerges. For instance, the infant first accidentally hits a rattle suspended over the cradle. The resulting noise is interesting, so the infant deliberately repeats the action. Gradually the child learns that the sequence reach-hit-noise is predictable and develops a mental schema or structure for this cause-effect sequence. Once this schema is well established for the rattle, it can be used on other objects. New objects are then assimilated into the schema; they are treated as things to be reached for and hit to make noise. Some objects do not quite fit; they make no noise when hit, for instance, but may do so when shaken. So the infant then accommodates the schema to the new object: instead of reach-hit-noise, there is reach-shake-noise. The growth of intelligence proceeds according to this pattern of "equilibration," or progress toward ever more complex and stable levels of mental functioning. The child develops more and more schemas and begins to connect them into a network; as these networks become well established, the world seems more orderly as things are perceived and acted on in terms of the schemas.

Piaget's theory divides intellectual development into four major stages. In the "sensorimotor period" (birth to two years) the infant begins with reflex reactions (hits the rattle accidentally), comes to create events deliberately (hits the rattle purposefully to make noise), and begins to use one schema to attain another goal (uses the reach-hit-noise sequence to get mother's attention and initiate a reach-suck-satisfaction schema for breastfeeding). At this point, then, the child can act on objects in the environment in an orderly way and can use one physical object to deal with another.

In the "preoperational period" (two to seven years) the child develops mental images for objects. He or she no longer has to have the rattle right there but can imagine it and act *as if* it were there. At first a child moves parts of his or her own body to imitate the rattle or other object, which is "out of sight, out of mind": if it falls underneath the cradle, the child immediately loses interest as if it has ceased to exist. Then a child comes to be able to think of the rattle without having to mimic it, and thus to understand that it still exists even if it cannot be seen or touched. Now the child continues to search for the object.

The "period of concrete operations" (seven to eleven years) involves an increasing ability to relate one mental schema to another without depending on physical objects to initiate thought and action. Now the child can group both schemas and objects into classes and can "think" about them without any overt action. There are groups of people or things that have certain characteristics, and those characteristics are related to one another in an orderly way.

"Formal operations" develop after eleven years. Now the child can solve complex problems with symbols. He or she can systematically analyze the movement of a pendulum, for instance, and can mentally alter various factors (length of string, size of suspended weight, height of arc) to predict changes in its movement.*

Harvard psychologist Lawrence Kohlberg (1966a) has applied cognitive-developmental theory to the development of sexual identity and personality characteristics. He maintains that just as a child must learn about the inanimate objects in the world, so must a child also learn about human bodies. At the same age (two to seven years) when a child learns that physical objects always exist independently of their physical presence, he or she learns that people also exist when they are not present. And when a child is learning about the unchangeable nature of physical objects, he or she is also learning about the unchangeable characteristics of human bodies. For instance, a young child watching water being poured from a short, fat glass into a tall, thin one initially thinks that there is more water in the taller glass, even though it is the same water. A child must learn the same thing about people: when they stand up, they are not bigger than they are when sitting; height, weight, and volume are constants in the physical world. And, similarly, a child has to learn that once a male, always a male. Changing haircuts or clothing does not make a boy a girl, or vice versa.

Once the physical constancies of human bodies are understood, a child can begin to connect behavior and emotions with those physical characteristics. Thus by age four a child learns that the world is made up of people who are physically male or physically female. Applying this category to himself or herself, a child develops "gender identity," or

* This brief sketch gives only the general flavor of an extremely complicated and rather mathematical theory. Although Piaget has written numerous books, the best introductions to this complex subject are found in H. Ginsburg and S. Opper, *Piaget's theory of intellectual development: An introduction* (Englewood Cliffs, N.J.: Prentice-Hall, 1969) and J. H. Flavell, *The developmental psychology of Jean Piaget* (New York: Van Nostrand Reinhold, 1963).

a stable self-categorization as male or female. A child, once having understood that he or she will always be of one gender, begins to value objects and characteristics that go with that gender.

The boy thus notices that his father is also male and values male things, and begins to identify with his father. The order of events could be summarized this way: "I am a male (gender identity), I like male things (sex-typed interests); my father is a male, he does male things; therefore I want to do things that my father does (imitation) and be like him (identification)." Thus, sexual identification is the product of cognitive growth, not of sexual attachments, and takes place in three clear stages: gender identity, sex typing, and parental identification.

Before examining each stage, I should explain why I am going to use male pronouns in discussing the development of sexual identification. The reason is the inevitable one: the model is inherently male. Although Kohlberg's male bias is not as blatant as Freud's, it is there nevertheless. I tried to couch the discussion in female terms, only to find it became a jumble as female pronouns were paired with examples of male development, quotes from male children, and discussions of only male body types. Better to be realistic, I decided, and present the theory first and then try to fit the female in afterward, just as Kohlberg does. Although I agree that using male terms in everyday language perpetuates male-oriented thinking, changing the gender of words will not change the basic thrust of a theory. Women *are* an afterthought in Kohlberg's model, just as they are in most of psychology.

Stages of Sexual Identification

GENDER IDENTITY: "I'M MALE"

During the first two years of life a child begins to notice that people are either big or little: there are babies, boys and girls, and adults. Since he thinks of everything in terms of concrete objects, he perceives social and behavioral attributes in terms of these bodily differences: big people are powerful, strong, and aggressive. But age, sex, and physical size remain confused in his mind, as four-year-old Philip shows when he says to his mother:

> "When you grow up to be a Daddy, you can have a bicycle, too (like Daddy)." On another occasion, Philip climbed on a chair so as to be higher than his seated parents and said, "Look, I'm higher than a grown-up, I'm older than a grown-up now." These comments taken together are quite typical illustrations of the young child's fusion of the age, sex, and size dimension of status. (Kohlberg 1966a, p. 102)

Toward the end of the second year the child also learns his "gender label." He has been called "boy" repeatedly and associates the word with himself just as he does his name. Gesell (1940) demonstrated this learning when he found that while the majority of two-and-one-half-year-olds did not answer correctly when asked "Are you a little girl or a little boy?" two-thirds to three-quarters of three-year-olds did answer correctly. The three-year-old does not yet understand, however, that everyone is a boy *or* a girl. As Kohlberg explains:

> At this early age, however, correct self-labeling does not imply correct self-classification in a general physical category. The label "boy" may be a name just like the name "Johnny." The child may recognize that there are other boys in the world, just as there may be other Johnnies, but this recognition need not imply a basic criterion for determining who is a boy any more than it does for determining who is a Johnny; nor does it necessarily imply that everyone in the world is either a boy or a girl, or a Johnny or a non-Johnny.
>
> [For example] a 2½-year-old boy, Tommy, observed by the writer, would go around the family circle saying "I'm boy," "Daddy boy," "Mommy boy," "Joey (brother) boy." After correction he eliminated his mother from the list, but did not label people outside the family correctly. (1966a, pp. 93–94)

During the third year a child begins to generalize the gender labels to others, using a loose criterion of superficial characteristics like clothing and hair style. He now knows that everyone is either male *or* female. But he does not realize that gender cannot be changed. Kohlberg illustrates this with an anecdotal observation.

> The following comments were made by Jimmy, just turning four, to his 4½-year-old friend Johnny:
> JOHNNY: I'm going to be an airplane builder when I grow up.
> JIMMY: When I grow up, I'll be a Mommy.
> JOHNNY: No, you can't be a Mommy. You have to be a Daddy.
> JIMMY: No, I'm going to be a Mommy.
> JOHNNY: No, you're not a girl, you can't be a Mommy.
> JIMMY: Yes, I can.
>
> (1966a, p. 95)

In a more formal study Kohlberg asked children four to eight years old whether a pictured girl could be a boy if she wanted to, if she played boys' games, or if she wore a boy's haircut or clothes. Most of the four-year-olds thought she could be a boy, but the six- to seven-year-olds were certain a girl could not be a boy regardless of changes in appearance or behavior (Kohlberg 1966b).

Children of four to five not only think gender can be changed; they think other aspects of the anatomy can be changed as well. This result is similar to Piaget's finding that children of this age think physical objects change their height or other dimensions just by being moved from one place to another. Again, Kohlberg provides us with an anecdotal example of Jimmy, just turned five, who spontaneously said, "I can be a girl, you know. I can. I can wear a wig and have my throat so I can talk like a girl." On another occasion Jimmy showed the same illogical and perhaps wishful thinking about body size as opposed to gender:

EXPERIMENTER: Do airplanes get small when they fly away in the sky?
JIMMY: Yes, they get real tiny.
EXPERIMENTER: Do they really get small, or do they just look small?
JIMMY: They really get small.
EXPERIMENTER: What happens to the people inside?
JIMMY: They shrink.
EXPERIMENTER: How can they shrink and get small?
JIMMY: They cut their heads off.

(Kohlberg 1966a, p. 97)

At this age (four to five) children also think species is changeable. Thus when DeVries (1969) took a live cat and covered it with a dog mask, the children thought it had become a dog. Kohlberg (1967) got similar results by asking four-year-olds whether a pictured cat could be a dog if it wanted to or if its whiskers were cut off. Only at ages six to seven do children realize that once a cat, always a cat. Six to seven is also the age at which they realize that once a boy, always a boy. Thus the child learns about "gender constancy" at the same time and in the same ways that he learns about other unchanging aspects of physical objects. This learning process cannot be hurried up, either, for children who have been exposed to information about anatomical sex differences still think gender is changeable. When Kohlberg asked children of four to seven "how you could tell boys from girls when they had clothes on" and "when they had clothes off," those who answered correctly were no more aware that gender could not be changed than were those who answered incorrectly (Kohlberg 1967). Simply showing the child anatomical sex differences is not sufficient; the child must be mentally developed enough to see those differences as unchanging physical attributes that serve as the basis for grouping people into male and female categories.

Once he has learned his own gender label, generalized it to others by categorizing them as male or female, and realized that gender is unchangeable, a child has developed "gender identity"—the knowledge that he is and always will be physically male as opposed to female. Forming this gender identity is irreversible because it involves such a central cognitive judgment about himself. The boy has gradually learned that he is male, and has come to view himself and the world in male terms; to change this perception is almost impossible. We have encountered this irreversibility already in studies of the critical period in hermaphrodites (Hampson and Hampson 1961; Money and Ehrhardt 1972). When there is a mismatch between biology and socially assigned sex, attempts to change the socially assigned sex creates severe psychological problems after about eighteen months of age (when the child develops language).

Gender identity is not initially based on genital sex differences, however, but on general anatomical sex differences. Since a child does not know about (or pay much attention to) genital sex differences while his gender identity is developing, his image of why one is male or female is based first on superficial appearance and later on general, nongenital anatomical sex differences. Only at the end of this process does a child realize that genitals are the central basis of gender categorization. Once he realizes this, of course, genitals take on an added importance for him.

> The fact that children are still confused about genital differences at an age (four-five) when they clearly stereotype sex-roles in terms of size, strength, aggression, and power strongly suggests that genital concepts do not form the direct basis for these other connotations of gender differences. The research does suggest a confused early awareness of genital differences that fuses with other sex-typed physical attributes in early stereotyping, but which is neither causally nor developmentally essential to the formation of these stereotypes. The traditional psychoanalytic approach to the problem assumes that the genital and sexual imagery of adults and adolescents develops in early childhood. It is more plausible, however, to assume that the genitals acquire added significance and centrality, first when the child realizes that they are the central basis of gender categorization (at around age six-seven), then when the child develops a definite conception of sexual intercourse (at a slightly older age), and finally when the child experiences actual sexual drives in adolescence.
>
> (Kohlberg 1966a, p. 104)

SEX-TYPING: "I'M MASCULINE"

Once a boy understands that he is male, he automatically wants to do things that are consistent with his gender. He thinks, "I'm male. I want to do male things." This preference for masculine activities does not wait until the boy develops an understanding of gender as an unchanging category based on anatomy; for as a child becomes vaguely aware that he is male, he starts doing male things, and these early preferences are then reinforced by the natural tendency to repeat one's actions (or in Piaget's terms, the tendency to fit new objects and experiences into an existing schema).

But what are male things? Kohlberg maintains that these are determined by sexual stereotypes based on the universal connotations of nongenital body images. He argues that people have a natural tendency to create abstract concepts and to use concrete objects to symbolize those concepts. For example, "wisdom universally connotes light (and light, wisdom) because abstract concepts of knowing are related to concrete concepts of seeing" (Kohlberg 1966a, p. 99). Similarly, the male body image universally connotes activity, aggression, power, and prestige. These symbolic qualities of the male body are derived from the child's early perception of social power as based on physical differences in age/size. As Kohlberg puts it:

> The stereotype of masculine aggressiveness has a body-image basis because it is linked to the child's belief that males are physically more powerful and more invulnerable than females. By age five-six, all children seem to express this belief. Almost every one of twenty-four first-grade children said that boys fight more than girls. When asked "Why don't girls fight like boys?" the most frequent response was "because girls get hurt easier than boys." (1966a, p. 101)

These universal body images are also expressed in crosscultural patterns of social roles: males engage in aggressive and dangerous activities outside the home, while females engage in nurturant activities inside the home. The child views these male-female role differences as being based on body image differences. The child abstracts the sexual stereotypes from the body images and social role patterns; he does not learn what is male or female from simply observing his own parents.

> Stereotypes of masculine aggression derive not only from body concepts, but also from highly visible differences in extra-familial roles. By age four-five, almost all of a group of sixteen American children showed awareness of the fact that only males play the extra-familial roles (policeman, soldier, fireman, robber, etc.) involving violence and danger (Kohlberg, unpublished data). This cross-culturally universal male specialization in roles of violence far outweighs subtle family differences in minor expressions of verbal and physical hostility in determining the child's basic sex-role stereotypes. (Kohlberg 1966a, p. 101)

But once he has perceived the universal sexual stereotypes, what motivates a child to conform to them? This again is a matter of natural thought processes: one naturally values things that are consistent with or like the self. As a child's gender identity develops, he increasingly expresses his self-perceptions and valuations in relation to his gender. Thus, in the first two years of life the child has a "tendency to respond to new activities and interests that are consistent with old ones" (Kohlberg 1966a, p. 112). Since he is just learning to associate the word "boy" with himself, the child does not think of these activities in terms of maleness. But by age three or four he knows that he is male and applies gender categories to others on the basis of superficial appearance. So now he begins to view people and activities as male or female and to value them accordingly. As Kohlberg describes it:

> As we have seen, the child by the age of three has a concept of self and a concept of gender that he relates to himself. By age three-four, the child also tends to make judgments of good and bad about things, and to maintain that whatever he makes, does, or owns is as good or better than those things other children do, make, or own. . . . At this age, then, the child has a naive or egocentric tendency to value anything associated with or like himself. Accordingly, the child tends to value positively objects and activities that represent his gender identity because his gender identity is part of himself. (1966a, p. 113)

Children themselves recognize this valuing of the like-self. When a four-year-old boy expressed a preference for a male babysitter, for instance, his seven-year-old brother explained to the parents that it was "because he's a boy himself, of course" (Kohlberg 1966a, p. 113).

The four- to five-year-old realizes that gender is based on anatomy but still thinks both are changeable. At this point he values things and people because they are male, not merely because he participates in or is like them. But he still "values the masculine as it is identified with himself; he does not value the masculine as an absolute stereotype, standard, or category" (Kohlberg 1966a, p. 115).

By six to seven the child realizes that both gender and anatomy are unchangeable. At this age he begins to separate the masculine stereotype from himself and to value it per se: he now thinks not only that it is best to be male because he is male, but that it is best to be male because male is inherently better. By now he perceives and values the sexual stereotype based on the male body image, associating "masculinity with values of strength and power" (Kohlberg 1966a, p. 111).

Once the boy perceives himself in terms of the abstract masculine stereotype of power and prestige, he begins to imitate adults who also fit that stereotype. This imitation simply enhances the boy's existent masculinity but does not cause it, for his masculinity grows naturally out of his desire to behave in a way that is consistent with his male body image.

PARENTAL IDENTIFICATION: "I'M LIKE DAD"

The same sense of "we males" that makes the boy value and imitate masculine things also makes him want to be like his father. Thus, attachment to the father develops out of the boy's autonomous cognitive development and comes *after* gender identity and sex-typed interests. The boy does not learn to be masculine by watching his father, nor does he want to be masculine because this loved or feared person is masculine (as Freud suggests). The boy wants to be like the father simply because they are both males; rewards, sexual drives, and a previous emotional relationship are not important.

The boy's sense of "we males" develops gradually during years four to eight. As he begins to separate the abstract masculine stereotype from himself and to perceive it as being based on the male body image, the boy comes to see maleness as extending across age lines: both boys and men are male and hence powerful, aggressive, and prestigious. During these same years power and prestige become increasingly important to the child. Children notice the greater power of the male about age four to five; as their awareness of this power increases so does their valuing and imitation of males. In the boy's growing awareness, abstract sexual stereotypes and power and prestige combine to make the father more important. Here is a person who is perceived as powerful and also like the self.

Kohlberg does not ignore the impact of the emotional relationship between parent and child; he merely views it as secondary. Thus he reminds us of the research that shows that imitation of adult models is enhanced by emotional warmth (Bandura and Walters 1963). Paternal warmth is viewed as increasing but not causing the boy's identification with his father; the basic cause is the boy's own thought processes.

What About the Female?

Kohlberg's entire theory is couched in male terms. The pronouns are male, the body type discussed is male, even the anecdotal examples are all about male children. Is the theory equally applicable to both sexes? Kohlberg maintains that it is—with certain modifications for the irregular nature of female development, of course. Let us follow the female through the three stages of sexual identification to see what these modifications are.

GENDER IDENTITY: "I'M FEMALE"

The girl progresses through this stage in the same way as the boy. At two she begins to associate the label "girl" with herself and at three she realizes that everyone is either male or female and starts to use superficial appearance to categorize people by gender. At four to five she realizes that gender is based on physical anatomy but still thinks both are changeable. At six to seven she learns that gender and anatomy are unchangeable, that once a girl always a girl. And in the years six to nine she becomes aware that genitals are the basic criterion for determining gender.

Gender identity is based on the same thought processes as awareness of other physical constancies, and these have been carefully researched in both sexes. Kohlberg himself has studied both boys and girls with the same results, even though he devotes most of his discussion to boys (Kohlberg 1966a, 1966b, 1967, 1969; Kohlberg and Zigler 1967). Clearly the girl learns that "I'm female and will always be female" in the same way and at the same age that the boy learns that "I'm male and will always be male."

SEX TYPING: "I'M FEMININE"

Once the girl understands that she is female, she too wants to do things that are consistent with her gender. She thinks, "I'm female. I want to do female things." The problem is, what are "female things"? Kohlberg maintains that these are determined by the universal connotations of nongenital body images. But the only examples he gives are for the male body, which connotes activity, aggression, power, and prestige. Does the female body image then connote the opposite?

Kohlberg seems to imply that it does, for he goes right from a discussion of body image connotations to a description of the expression of those connotations in crosscultural social roles. Here he says:

> In general, males are connotatively perceived to be more active, powerful, and aggressive than women in all countries so far studied. . . .
> Not only are there a number of apparent universals in the connotations of gender role, but these universals are found very early (by age five-six) among American children. Fathers are perceived as more powerful, punitive, aggressive, fearless, instrumentally competent, and less nurturant than females. . . . Thus power and prestige appear as one major attribute of children's sex-role stereotypes, aggression and exposure to danger as another major attribute, and nurturance and child care as a third. Associated with recognition of child care as a feminine function is the general differentiation of maternal, inside-the-home functions from paternal, outside-the-home functions. (1966a, p. 99)

The female body image, then, connotes nurturance and child care—as well as a relative lack of activity, competence, power, and aggression.

Having perceived the universal sexual stereotypes based on nongenital body images, the girl is motivated to conform to them in the same way as the boy is. She, too, naturally values things that are consistent with or like the self; and as her gender identity develops, she expresses this principle of consistency increasingly in terms of gender. By three she values things that are female simply because she does them, and at four to five she values female things because she is female. By the time she realizes that gender and anatomy are unchangeable, at ages six to seven, the girl values femaleness in and of itself. By this time she, too, has separated the sexual stereotype from herself and thinks not only that it is best to be female because she herself is female, but that it is best to be female because female is better.

But does the girl perceive female as better? Not necessarily, for at the same time that the awareness of "we females" is developing in the years four to eight, the awareness of power and prestige is developing also. And power and prestige are part of the masculine stereotype. Thus, while self-consistency and power and prestige work together to draw boys toward masculinity, they work against each other in girls. Kohlberg suggests that this contradiction causes the preferences of girls to become less sex-typed in the years five to eight, when all children are becoming increasingly aware of the power and prestige dimensions of the male role. The boy's preferences, on the other hand, become steadily more sex-typed during this period.

PARENTAL IDENTIFICATION: "I'M LIKE MOM"

The sense of "we females" makes the girl want to be like her mother, just as the sense of "we males" makes the boy want to be like his father. But "we females" means we who are inherently nurturant and lack power, prestige, or competence. All children tend "to imitate or model persons who are valued because of prestige and competence, and who are perceived as like the self" (Kohlberg 1966a, p. 111). For the girl like-self and prestige and competence are contradictory. Should she imitate her mother who is female like herself, or should she imitate her father who is powerful?

During the years five to eight the answer seems to be "imitate your father." Kohlberg maintains that the increase in father-orientation and corresponding decrease in sex-typed female preferences during this period actually consolidate rather than weaken the girl's feminine values and self-definition. This is because of what could be called "complementary modeling": the girl contrasts herself to the masculine stereotype and learns to interact with males in an appropriately feminine way. As Kohlberg puts it:

> . . . the girl's sex-role identification is based more on identification with the complementary (father) role than is the boy's. While the boy defines his masculinity in terms of competitive achievement and acceptance in male groups (i.e., being "one of the boys"), the girl defines her femininity in terms of male acceptance and approval. (1966a, p. 163)

In proposing the idea of complementary modeling, Kohlberg reverses the basic principle that he uses to explain male development. The boy values and imitates people who are *similar* to himself, while the girl values and accommodates her behavior to people who are *opposite* to herself.

This inconsistency in his own thinking apparently makes Kohlberg uncomfortable, for he goes on to search for some valued female similarity that will make the girl imitate the mother. His major argument is that the mother is perceived as having *some* power and prestige, so that the like-self and the power and prestige principles do come together for the girl. First he points out that although the mother has less power and prestige than the father, she has decidedly more than a child.

> More basically, however, adult female stereotypes are positive enough to make femininity attractive to young girls, even though adult females are perceived as less powerful and competent than males. While the stereotype of adult femininity is inferior in power and competence to the male, it is still superior to that of a child of either sex. (1966a, p. 121)

Kohlberg maintains that this adult-child status difference is especially important in the first four years, when the child's life is bounded by the home where the mother is the caretaker and controller. We should note, however, that the child does not have a clear concept of gender categories before age four. As these develop at age four to five the child also begins to interact with the outside world of school and playground and becomes aware of the power and prestige of the male role. Thus the perception of maternal power occurs when the child has no gender concept to attach to it; by the time the child does have this gender concept, female power is perceived to be trifling compared to male power.

Kohlberg's second suggestion is that the female stereotype includes its own subtle form of prestige, which he calls "niceness." He describes it this way:

> It should also be noted that stereotypes of femininity rate higher than stereotypes of masculinity in a number of important areas of value or prestige. The fact that the male role is associated with aggression and the female role with nurturance and dependence relations suggests that females are stereotyped as "nicer" than males. Since aggression is a major component of "badness," it is not surprising that almost all girls and most boys of six-seven say boys do more bad things than girls (Kohlberg, unpublished data). Mothers are said to be "nicer" than fathers by a majority of both boys and girls of four-seven (Kagan and Lemkin 1960). "Niceness" is a very important value to school-age American girls, connoting nonaggression, interpersonal conformity, restraint, and nurturance or helpfulness. (1966a, p. 121)

Kohlberg's formulation involves two assertions: that "niceness" involves a subtle form of prestige and therefore will induce children to imitate adults who display it, and that girls value "niceness" more than boys and therefore will imitate "nice" adults more than boys will. And what is "feminine moral-niceness" (p. 122)? It consists of being nurturant and dependent.

What makes girls value "niceness" more than boys? Kohlberg does not address this question directly. Presumably, however, this valuing is based on the nongenital female body image. This body image connotes nurturance and child care and hence would lead to an inherent female valuing of nurturance and the dependence that Kohlberg associates with nurturance.

POWER VERSUS SUBSERVIENCE

What is the essential difference between Kohlberg's male and female models of development? The difference can be stated in one word: *power*. Whereas boys and girls develop gender identity in the same way, the body images and sexual stereotypes that derive from their gender identities differ dramatically. The boy sees himself as male and hence as inherently powerful, aggressive, and competent. The girl sees herself as female and hence as inherently powerless, nurturant, and dependent. They both imitate adults who are perceived as like themselves and also enviable. The boy envies power and aggression, however, while the girl envies nurturance and dependence. Basically, then, we seem to have two different modeling principles: *power and aggression modeling* for males and *nurturance and dependence modeling* for females.

But Kohlberg says that *all* children imitate adults who are powerful and prestigious. So what we really have is a male modeling principle of power and aggression that is applied to both sexes. When females do not fit into this model, Kohlberg adds the rather dubious female modeling principle of nurturance and dependence.

Research and Common Sense

In order to substantiate Kohlberg's theory, we need to examine how children perceive both themselves and others. Do they only gradually learn that their anatomy, and hence their gender, is unchangeable? Do they then associate certain characteristics and behaviors with that gender, viewing them as naturally linked to the male or the female anatomy? And having done this, do they come to value and imitate their same-sex parents because they share the same gender and therefore share the same gender-linked interests, activities, and characteristics? At this time there are no definitive answers to these questions. But the research—combined with common sense—does permit some tentative conclusions.

LEARNING THAT I'M FEMALE

Kohlberg's major contribution lies in outlining just how knowledge of gender may develop. The earlier research on hermaphrodites (Hampson and Hampson 1961; Money and Ehrhardt 1972) and on identifying the gender of various figures (Katcher 1955) told us that young children do not understand gender categories, but not how older children develop this understanding. Kohlberg's formulation suggests that the "how" is the same as for other physical constancies such as height and weight.

The "critical period" phenomenon in hermaphrodites supports Kohlberg's contention that gender identity involves a basic cognitive structuring and hence is irreversible. Clearly, once women and men have learned to think of themselves as female or male, they continue to think of themselves that way regardless of any subsequent social, emotional, or even bodily experiences.

Katcher's (1955) study also supports Kohlberg's claim that children initially use superficial bodily appearances to determine gender. The three-year-olds made almost no errors in gender labeling when they could see the clothing or hair of the cutout figures, while 88 percent of them made errors when only the genitals were visible. Over half the four- to five-year-olds and almost one-third of the six-year-olds also made errors in gender labeling using genitals. This suggests that young children do rely on superficial differences in hair and clothing to label the gender of others and hence may think of gender as being determined by these superficial, changeable appearances. Kohlberg seems to be right in suggesting that young children have yet to learn that anatomy (and specifically the genitals) are the basis for gender categorization and that both anatomy and gender are unchangeable.

On the other hand, there is little research to substantiate Kohlberg's claim that children learn that anatomy and gender are unchangeable through the same processes by which, and at the same age when, they learn about other invariant characteristics of physical objects. Kohlberg does describe an unpublished study in which he compared the development of gender constancy with the development of other object constancies (height, weight, and quantity of physical objects) in children four to eight years old (Kohlberg 1967, reported in Kohlberg 1966a, p. 98). He reports that the gender constancy task was highly correlated with other constancy tasks ($r = .52$ to $.73$), and remained highly correlated even when mental age was taken into account ($r = .36$ to $.64$).

Unfortunately, however, no published studies repeat this comparison, and the only unpublished study I know of failed to support Kohlberg's formulation. Using seventeen children from three to six years old, the researchers found no relationship between gender constancy and various object constancies within the body—height, weight, and quantity of fingers (Rohrbaugh and Glick 1971). The gender constancy questions were similar to those reported by Kohlberg (1966b):

Are you a boy or a girl?

If you grew your hair very long (cut it very short) would you be a boy or a girl?

If you put on your brother's pants (sister's dress) would you be a boy or a girl?

Could you be a boy (girl) if you wanted to?

When you grow up, are you going to be a woman or a man?

(Rohrbaugh and Glick 1971, p. 17)

Of course, this one study does not seriously challenge Kohlberg's formulation. First of all, it is a pilot study using a small number of children. And secondly, the measurement techniques relied entirely on questions, whereas Kohlberg (1967) used a verbal exploration method based on pictured human and animal transformations. It may be easier for children to indicate their knowledge of gender constancy when they are responding to questions regarding pictorial materials.

A more important issue, however, concerns the differences between types of object constancy. When DeVries (1969) studied a cat/dog transformation using face masks, she found that species identity was acquired at an earlier age than the conservation of quantitative invariants. She interpreted this as supporting Piaget's (1968) distinction between qualitative and quantitative constancies. Qualitative invariance refers to the "identity" of external objects and requires the dissociation of permanent and variable object qualities, an ability acquired in the "preoperational period" (two to seven years of age). Quantitative invariance, on the other hand, refers to the "conservation" of various invariant characteristics of objects and requires the more sophisticated mental operations of reversibility, compensation of relations, and additive compensation; these are not acquired until the concrete operational period (seven to eleven years of age). In other words, children learn that a stick is always a stick before they learn that the number, the length, or the weight of a group of sticks remains the same regardless of changes in position, arrangement, and so on. Similarly, children probably learn that "once a cat, always a cat" before they learn that the number, weight, or other characteristics of a group of cats is also invariant. And they may also learn that "once a female, always a female" before they learn that height, weight, and number of fingers also remains constant. The invariance of species, gender, and other "identities" may thus precede the invariance of other physical properties of these animals, humans, or objects.

We can also ask whether gender constancy really involves physical characteristics as opposed to social relationships. As Rohrbaugh and Glick (1971) suggest, self-identification according to gender may involve the awareness that our basic role or relationship to others remains the same regardless of incidental changes in appearance, activity, or physical position. In other words, is gender constancy a matter of "object constancy" or is it a matter of "role constancy" or "relational constancy"?

Of course, it may be a matter of both. Knowing that one is female and will always be female may involve knowing several things: that one's anatomy is and always will be female, that this invariant female gender is the basis for a number of personal characteristics and social relationships (sister, daughter, niece), and that these social relationships are also relatively invariant.

Instead of one type of object constancy, then, there may actually be three: generic identity, or the knowledge that a gender, species, or object label is invariant; relational identity, or the knowledge that social relationships or roles are invariant; and quantitative invariance, or the awareness of the invariance of many physical properties of an object such as height, weight, and volume.

In conclusion, then, Kohlberg's formulation about the acquisition of gender identity can account for the data on hermaphrodites and has received some initial support from his own research. The kinds of learning involved in gender identity need to be considered further, however, and more research must be done to substantiate Kohlberg's hypothesis.

ANATOMICAL CONSTANCY VERSUS CASTRATION COMPLEX

How does Kohlberg portray children at four to five years of age, when Freud presents them as developing castration anxiety or penis envy after seeing opposite-sex genitals? At that age children know that there are two gender categories, but they use hair and clothing, not anatomy, to assign people to them. If they do know about genital sex differences, they do not necessarily view them as the key to gender. Most important, however the four- to five-year-old thinks gender is changeable. So if a boy this age said, "I'm going to be a Mommy when I grow up," or a girl said, "I want to have a penis," Kohlberg would interpret these remarks as examples of immature thought that allows a child to view gender as changeable; he would not interpret them as evidence of deep-seated feelings of anatomical superiority or inferiority, or as expressing fantasies based on sexual urges.

Kohlberg does point out that young children find the genitals of the other sex strange. He reminds us, for instance, that although Conn and Kanner (Conn 1940; Conn and Kanner 1947) did not find evidence of shock or trauma in response to genital sex differences, they did find that many of the children six to nine years old "(1) believed that both boys and girls 'had the same' but that the girl's was smaller, or (2) believed that the girl's had been longer or would be longer at some time, or (3) expressed the notion that the genital characteristics of the opposite sex were 'funny' or 'wrong' or that 'everyone should have the same,' or (4) believed that the girl's had been 'cut off' " (Kohlberg 1966a, p. 106).

Why do children have this reaction to opposite-sex genitals? Freud would say it is because they perceive girls as castrated and hence experience either fear or shame. Kohlberg would say that it is because they do not understand that their genitals are not going to change, and feel threatened by that possibility just as they would by the possibility of any other change in their anatomy. Thus, both Freud and Kohlberg suggest that the initial exposure to opposite-sex genitals may cause anxiety, but for entirely different reasons. As Kohlberg puts it:

> On purely cognitive grounds, the child would be expected to be un-certain about anatomical constancy. This uncertainty would be expected to cause him some concern about the integrity and constancy of his own body. It seems likely that some combination of fascination and threat is experienced when there is an awareness of the existence of a body which is like the self's but which is also basically different from it. Instead of interpreting these feelings of fascination and threat (which are also present in the attitudes of men, women and chimpanzees toward the maimed and deformed) as stemming from specific castration concerns, it seems more plausible to view them as an expression of the child's general uncertainty about anatomical constancy. (1966a, p. 107)

The idea that genital differences provoke anxiety owing to anatomical inconstancy is persuasive. But why do feelings of fascination and threat persist regarding genital differences but subside with increased familiarity regarding other physical differences such as beards? The obvious explanation is that some physical differences have more symbolic significance than others have; that is, the genitals represent other socially significant differences and hence retain their importance. This explanation is basically the same as that for "secondary penis envy": although children's initial reactions to the *physical* aspects of genital sex differences are transitory, their reactions to the *social* significance of these anatomical differences are lasting.

MALE ANATOMY AS THE BASIC HUMAN FORM: FREUD REVISITED?

Kohlberg's central argument about anatomical constancy and castration anxiety is logical. But then he goes on to say that the anxiety caused by anatomical uncertainty is intensified, because both sexes usually perceive the female body as deviating from the basic human body image. In his words:

> It also seems likely on purely cognitive grounds (de Saussure 1933) that both sexes would take the male anatomy as more basic in defining some sexually undifferentiated human-body schema, i.e., that the female body would be conceived as the negative of the masculine, rather than as a positive entity. (1966a, p. 107)

These "purely cognitive grounds" are obscure, to say the least. Given the child's natural tendency to value anything associated with himself or herself, one would expect each sex to view the other's body type as deviant and undesirable. We can still see vestiges of this childish ego-centrism in adult thought, when male psychologists attempt to define the female in purely male terms. Thus, Kohlberg's "purely cognitive grounds" for viewing the male as the basic human form might more accurately be called "purely sexist grounds."

SEXUAL STEREOTYPES AND BODY IMAGES: A NONGENITAL ANATOMICAL DETERMINISM

The major theoretical weakness in Kohlberg's model is the link between gender identity and sex typing. Having developed gender identity, the child perceives the universal connotations of nongenital body images and wants to conform to them. Kohlberg maintains that these "universal connotations" come from the body images themselves; everyone knows that the male body implies power, aggression, and competence, while the female body implies nurturance and dependence. If everyone does know this, it is probably because the culture tells them so. Thus, it seems obvious that crosscultural patterns of sex roles determine body images—not the reverse, as Kohlberg asserts. The studies of child-rearing patterns in different cultures support the cultural rather than the body image argument (Barry et al. 1957; Whiting and Edwards 1973). As we saw in Chapter 1, boys are given tasks that encourage self-assertion, independence, and aggression, while girls are given tasks that encourage altruism, nurturance, and dependence. When there is such obvious evidence of socioeconomic patterns that foster the development of sex-role stereotyping, is it not logical that body images themselves would come to symbolize these sex-role stereotypes?

Kohlberg's view of the female body image—connoting nurturance, child care, and a relative lack of activity, competence, power, and aggression—reminds me of Erikson's view of woman's "inner space." Both assert that the female body naturally implies nurturant activities and personality characteristics coupled with subservience to males. Anatomy is still destiny, and the female destiny is to be nurturant and dependent.

BECOMING LIKE MOM: COMPLEMENTARY MODELING AND FEMALE NICENESS

The second weak link in Kohlberg's theory is the transition from gender identity to parental identification. Is this a result of the child's own thought processes, as Kohlberg claims? Do boys want to be like their fathers and girls like their mothers simply because the same-sex parents share their gender-linked characteristics, interests, and behavior?

To support this basic argument, Kohlberg refers to a series of experiments in which he found that cognitive maturity was related to the development of sex-role attitudes (Kohlberg and Zigler 1967). Using intelligence quota (IQ) as a measure of cognitive maturity, he asked about thirty bright and thirty average children to perform a series of tasks involving doll play and imitation of the designs of adults in a drawing task. He then assessed their sex-typed preferences using Brown's (1956) It Scale, in which children choose activities for a stick figure called "It." Kohlberg found that the bright children preceded the average children in their development of sex-linked imitation and dependency. Whereas the average group was female-oriented at age four, the brights were already more male-oriented; and while the bright group became opposite-sex oriented at age six to seven, the average group did not turn to the opposite sex until eight to ten. All the brights, both boys and girls, were also more oriented to male adults than were the average group, and developed sex-typed interests more quickly.

Aside from the fact that a careful reading of the results suggests that Kohlberg and Zigler may have overstated the significance of the differences between the bright and the average groups, what do these studies prove? Does the more rapid development of brighter children indicate that their sex-typing and parental identification are based upon autonomous thought processes rather than upon sexual attachments or simple imitation? I think not, for the brighter children may notice the opposite-sex genitals sooner, develop castration anxiety or penis envy, and hence develop sexual identification earlier. This explanation suggests that the cognitive processes merely enable the sexual attachments to have an effect slightly earlier in life, and is hence compatible with Freudian theory. On the other hand, brighter children may be quicker to figure out what a boy or girl is expected to be like. This second explanation suggests that greater cognitive maturity simply speeds up the learning processes. Thus, it is not enough to find that cognitive maturity is associated with earlier sex-role development. Definitive support for Kohlberg's theory requires some demonstration that the child's autonomous thought processes per se are responsible for sex typing and parental identification.

Of course, Kohlberg's theory does not rely entirely on thought processes. He does suggest that children also tend to imitate powerful adults whom they perceive as like themselves. When he runs into difficulties with the contradiction between like-self and power in girls, he goes on to propose the additional female mechanisms of "niceness" modeling and complementary modeling. Here again, however, the research fails to support Kohlberg's theory.

No studies have examined "niceness" modeling directly. And small wonder. Social learning research has already established the fact that children—of both sexes—imitate powerful adults who are rewarded for their aggressive behavior. The children may express disapproval of the aggressive adult (Bandura, Ross, and Ross 1963c), much as nursery school girls resort to "prosocial aggression" by citing rules and expressing social disapproval of playmates (Sears, Rau, and Alpert 1965). But apparently girls say, "He's a bad boy" or, "You can't do that" only in order to achieve their own desires; for when such immoral aggression is displayed by adult males, both boys and girls prefer and imitate the naughty but successful adult (Bandura, Ross, and Ross 1963c). I will discuss this research in more detail in Chapter 6 but for now will simply note that no research even suggests that nurturance and dependence, which Kohlberg calls "feminine moral-niceness" (1966, p. 122), have a special, compelling appeal for little girls.

Kohlberg's idea of complementary modeling does not fare much better. Here the idea is that boys imitate the powerful adult male because they perceive him as both similar to themselves and also powerful. Girls, on the other hand, see the powerful adult male as opposite to themselves (because of his gender), and hence do the opposite of what he does. As with "niceness" modeling, no studies examine complementary modeling directly, and for the same reason. Here, too, the idea has already been refuted by social learning research. The studies that show that children imitate naughty but successful adults also show that successful aggressive behavior is imitated directly. In spite of the fact that the successful, aggressive adult models in the most pertinent study were male, both boys and girls showed moral censure combined with behavior that was the same rather than the opposite of the modeled behavior (Bandura, Ross, and Ross 1963c). Again I will leave a detailed discussion of this research for the chapter on social learning theory and simply note that girls do not show any uniquely female tendency to do the opposite of what a powerful adult male does.

Perhaps it is not fair to test Kohlberg's modeling principles in an experimental situation where there is no strong emotional bond between the child and the adult model. Maybe "niceness" modeling and complementary modeling involve more subtle interactions that occur only within a parent-child relationship. If that is the case, we should look at studies that compare children with their own parents. Kohlberg himself (1966a) cites two such parent-child studies, which he claims point to the operation of complementary modeling in girls. When we examine these studies carefully, however, we find that they do not really support Kohlberg's argument.

In the first study Hetherington (1965) asked 326 sets of parents to agree on a solution to a child-rearing problem. She scored the parental discussions for father-dominance and mother-dominance and selected 216 couples who clearly showed one or the other. She then measured parental imitation, parental similarity, and sex-typing in the sons and daughters of these 108 father-dominant and 108 mother-dominant couples. The study included thirty-six boys and thirty-six girls at each of three age levels: four to five years, six to eight years, and nine to eleven years. Half of the boys and girls in each age group came from mother-dominant and half from father-dominant homes.

In the parental imitation task Hetherington observed each child's choices of the "prettiest" picture among a set of twenty pairs in which one precoached parent had designated one from each set as the prettiest. The picture task was done in the home, once for each parent in sessions one month apart. Parent-child similarity was measured by comparing scores on rating scales completed by friends of the parents and by teachers of the children; and the children's sex-typed preferences were assessed by Brown's (1956) It Scale.

Hetherington found that both sons and daughters imitated the picture choices of the dominant parent more, regardless of which parent was dominant. She also found that the children were described as being more similar to the dominant than to the subordinant parent. Then she examined the similarity between same-sex and opposite-sex pairs of parents and children. While the girls' similarity to their mothers was not affected by the gender of the dominant parent, a dominant mother seemed to decrease the similarity between sons and fathers. And finally, Hetherington found that only the boys' sex-typed preferences were affected by parental dominance. Thus girls showed the same degree of sex-typing in their choices for "It" regardless of whether they came from a father-dominant or a mother-dominant home. Boys from mother-dominant homes, on the other hand, chose significantly fewer masculine toys and activities for "It" than did boys from father-dominant homes.

The results of Hetherington's study do not show evidence of complementary modeling in either sex. Both boys and girls seemed to copy the dominant parent, regardless of that parent's gender. And while it is true, as Kohlberg points out (1966a), that the gender of the dominant parent seemed to be more important for boys than for girls, this effect does not demonstrate the mechanism of complementary modeling. When their mother was more dominant, boys seemed to imitate her directly. Although boys may perceive a dominant mother as simultaneously powerful and opposite in gender (as Kohlberg suggests for girls and normally dominant fathers), this perception probably leads them to behave in the *same* way as the mother rather than *opposite* to her. In other words, when the perception of someone as powerful clashes with the perception of that person as opposite in gender, power may be the important dimension.

I have to say that power "may be" the important dimension in perception of parents, because the Hetherington study did not assess this perception directly. It merely compared the behavior and the characteristics of parents with those of their children. The children were not asked how they viewed their own parents. And, as I have already noted, it is the children's perceptions and thought processes that are crucial to Kohlberg's theory.

The issue of parental power is somewhat clarified in the second study cited by Kohlberg (1966a), which did assess children's perceptions of parents (Mussen and Rutherford 1963). This study used fifty-seven female and forty-eight male first-graders and was an extension and replication of an earlier study of five-year-old boys (Mussen and Distler 1959). Mussen and Rutherford used the It Scale to divide the boys and girls into two groups each: high- and low-feminine girls, high- and low-masculine boys. Then the researchers used doll play to determine the children's perceptions of their mothers and fathers as nurturant, punitive, and powerful, the last defined as both nurturant and punitive combined. The researchers interviewed the mothers to assess various child-rearing practices and had both parents fill out the femininity and the self-acceptance scales from the California Personality Inventory. In addition, Mussen and Rutherford also asked the parents whether they encouraged their children to play sex-appropriate games.

The researchers found no relationship between the sex-typing of the children and the latter's perceptions of their opposite-sex parents, but they did find significant differences in the children's perceptions of same-sex parents. High-feminine girls saw their mothers as more nurturant but not as more punitive than did low-feminine girls. And high-masculine boys saw their fathers as more nurturant and also as somewhat more punitive than did low-masculine boys; in the researchers' terms, high-masculine boys thus saw their fathers as more powerful than low-masculine boys saw them.

The effects for parental sex-typing and treatment of the child varied for boys and girls. There was no relationship between the sex-typing of boys and their parents' sex-typing or encouragement of the boys' sex-typed play and behavior. In girls, on the other hand, greater maternal self-acceptance, greater paternal masculinity, and greater paternal encouragement of sex-typed games were associated with higher femininity in the child.

These results do not point to complementary modeling in girls, as Kohlberg claims, for the girl's perception of her father was not related to her own sex-typing. On the other hand, it is true (as Kohlberg points out [1966a]) that the father's own masculinity and encouragement of the daughter's femininity were related to the daughter's sex-typing. This merely suggests that if a father encourages his daughter to act more feminine, she will show more sex-typed activities and preferences. Thus, the effectiveness of the father's encouragement points to direct learning rather than to complementary modeling.

As for boys, although perception of their parents *was* important to them, this perception again suggests direct imitation rather than complementary modeling—since boys who saw their fathers as more powerful acted more masculine themselves. The fact that parental encouragement was not related to the boy's sex-typing may also point to the power of direct imitation in girls; for if both boys and girls tend to prefer and imitate powerful adults (who are usually male), then parental pressure toward femininity may be necessary to counteract the girl's natural tendency to imitate her powerful and aggressive father.

The Mussen and Rutherford study could also be cited as evidence of "niceness" modeling in girls. High-feminine girls did tend to see their mothers as more nurturant, which at least covers one-half of the nurturance-dependence characteristics defined as "niceness" by Kohlberg. But this citation would also be misleading, for in boys, too, high sex-typing scores were associated with the perception of greater nurturance in the same-sex parent—a finding also reported in Mussen's earlier study (Mussen and Distler 1959).

Thus, closer examination of the parent-child studies leads to the same conclusions as the experimental studies. Both types of research fail to support Kohlberg's ideas about "niceness" modeling and complementary modeling. In fact, the studies we have discussed merely strengthen the impression that children directly imitate powerful and successful adults. In the next chapter on social learning theory we will see that this impression is no passing fancy but corresponds to the conclusions drawn from a considerable body of research literature.

Chapter 6

Social Learning Theory
and Female Personality

PSYCHOLOGISTS do not always view anatomy as destiny—and the female destiny as nurturance and dependence. Another major theoretical tradition in psychology focuses on learning as the crucial dimension of all human experience. This tradition grew out of behaviorism and involves a lot more than Skinner's pigeons playing ping-pong. As its name implies, social learning theory is concerned with the entire socialization process—how we learn to think and feel as well as to act.

Social learning theorists believe that "femininity" is learned in the same way as are all other behavior and personality characteristics, and do not assume that there is something inherent in the female body image—either genital or nongenital—that automatically makes women nurturant and dependent. Women learn to act and feel that way because others expect them to. These expectations are embedded in a culture. But the focus is on how the individual comes to fit the cultural expectations, not on the societal institutions and customs that shape and express those expectations.

Let us look at the basic social learning principles first. Then we can discuss the way these are applied to the area of sex roles and femininity.

The Principles of
Social Learning Theory

Social learning theory views all human behavior as learned. The child observes those around him or her and then tries out their behavior himself or herself. If the child is rewarded, he or she continues the behavior; if the child is punished, he or she does not continue it. Gradually the child develops a "habit hierarchy" of behavior through differential reinforcement (Bandura and Walters 1963, p. 21). Whatever behavior has been rewarded most frequently in a given situation in the past appears at the top of this habit hierarchy and is hence most likely to occur in that situation in the future. Other behavior has undoubtedly been rewarded in the same situation, however, even if somewhat less frequently. These responses would appear somewhat lower in the hierarchy and would be less likely to occur in an analogous situation in the future, for everyone does what he or she expects to yield the most rewards. Only if the dominant habit fails to elicit sufficient rewards will a less dominant habit or behavior be activated.

Take dependence behavior. Infants are usually encouraged to seek "contact comfort." As children grow older, however, this form of physical dependence is likely to be rewarded less frequently. Instead, parents begin to reward a child for dependence that is expressed verbally. And as the pattern of parental rewards changes, so does a child's habit hierarchy. While clinging to the parents was the dominant habit or response to stress in infancy, in later childhood the verbal attention seeking becomes more rewarded and hence becomes more dominant. This change in the habit hierarchy is reflected in a child's behavior. Thus, if an infant is frightened, he or she is most likely to cling to the parent; if an older child is frightened, on the other hand, he or she is most likely to seek attention by whining or asking questions.

Habit hierarchies change not only over time; they also vary by situation. Thus, a young child may be highly rewarded for clinging to its parents, and this dependence response would be dominant and most performed at home. In school, however, verbal attention seeking is more apt to be rewarded and hence would be dominant and most performed.

What happens when the dominant response or behavior is not sufficiently rewarded? Imagine a girl at school, for instance, who becomes frightened and raises her hand, asks a question, or seeks attention in a similar way. But the teacher pays little attention, so that the dominant response goes unrewarded. In this situation the girl will resort to a response that is lower in her hierarchy for that situation. Thus, she may cling to the teacher if asking a question fails to elicit comforting.

Habit hierarchies are not simply a matter for children. Adults, too, behave according to the basic principle of reinforcement. They do what they have been rewarded for in the past and hence what they expect to be rewarded for today or tomorrow. And they, too, exhibit their most dominant (or previously most rewarded) behavior in a given situation. If that response cannot be made or is not rewarded, they then turn to a less dominant behavior. Resorting to a less dominant behavior may cause adults in a stressful situation to behave like our hypothetical child. Failing to obtain comfort by verbal expressions of concern, adults may cling to family members who have reinforced such responses in earlier years. Thus, the personal "reinforcement history" of each of us determines how we act.*

This personal reinforcement history is summarized by the habit hierarchy adults have built up for each situation. Social learning theory focuses on the development of habit hierarchies and on the ways these hierarchies then influence behavior. We all observe the behavior of the people around us during childhood and later in life. We watch, we learn, and then we exhibit certain appropriate behavior ourselves; for of course we do not exhibit *all* the behavior we observe. What determines who we imitate, or in what situations, or in what areas of behavior? These questions have been exhaustively researched and the results incorporated in the basic principles of social learning theory (Bandura 1969; Bandura and Walters 1963). Let us consider these principles briefly.

GENERALIZATION AND DISCRIMINATION

Once one has learned a given response, one tends to generalize it to other situations that are similar to the original learning one. Take my example of dependence behavior. First the child learns to cling to his or her parents when frightened and is positively reinforced in this behavior by receiving warmth and reassurance. The child then applies this behavior to other people and situations that resemble the parents and home. In school, for instance, the same child is likely to cling to the teacher when frightened, because he or she perceives the teacher as a nurturant adult who is similar to the parents. In this case the response of clinging has generalized from the home to the school situation.

Most teachers in the lower grades do not mind if students cling to them occasionally, and view such a response as appropriate and acceptable, especially if a child is upset or frightened. But in many other situations a clinging child would be severely reprimanded or rejected.

* Bandura and Walters use this example of dependence behavior to explain why age-inappropriate responses sometimes occur. These responses do not indicate "regression" to a more primitive level of personality, as Freudian theory would suggest. They merely indicate the use of a less dominant habit or behavior when the dominant one is not rewarded, for dominant habits are not "superficial derivatives that obtain their energy from psychic forces operating in the lower levels of personality" (1963, p. 22).

At a supermarket checkout counter, for instance, the cashier may not appreciate being clutched by a strange child. When a child generalizes the clinging to a school situation, he or she is responding to cues that resemble those at home: a caretaking adult whose attention and interest are focused on the child. When the child generalizes the clinging to a supermarket, however, he or she may be responding to cues that do not really resemble those at home: a busy, distracted adult whose attention and interest are focused on the cash register, not on the child. Clinging in the supermarket is thus an example of "overgeneralization," where a response is applied to an inappropriate situation.

Responses do not always refer to overt behavior. They may also involve an emotion, an attitude, or a situational interpretation. Thus Bandura and Walters illustrate the concept of inappropriate generalization with the following letter from the advice column of a leading metropolitan newspaper.

> Dear Abby:
> My girl friend fixed me up with a blind date and I should have known the minute he showed up in a bow tie that he couldn't be trusted. I fell for him like a rock. He got me to love him on purpose and then lied to me and cheated on me. Every time I go with a man who wears a bow tie, the same thing happens. I think girls should be warned about men who wear them.
> Against Bow Ties
>
> Dear Against:
> Don't condemn all men who wear bow ties because of your experience. I know a man behind a bow tie who can be trusted.
> (Bandura and Walters 1963, pp. 8–9)

This woman's attitude about the evils of men who wear bow ties shows that she attributes a whole pattern of behavior to the bow tie. In overgeneralizing about bow-tie wearing, she has failed to discriminate between characteristics that are closely related to bow ties and those that are not. The bow tie is thus an irrelevant cue that elicits her negative attitude, much as the adult status of the supermarket cashier is an irrelevant cue that elicits a child's clinging behavior.

Thus, effective learning requires both generalization *and* discrimination. Learning a response is only the first step. One also has to learn which situations are similar enough to warrant that response, and which are so dissimilar that the response is inappropriate.

Discrimination refers to more than situations. The same response can be expressed to different people, in various ways, and with varying degrees of intensity. Subtle modifications of a response are often required, as in the case of physical aggression.

> Mild physical aggression expressed toward peers is frequently rewarded as a "sign of masculinity" in boys, but more intense responses of this kind

are usually punished. Physical aggression toward parents or siblings, even when mild, is considered undesirable and consequently goes unrewarded or, more often, is punished. On the other hand, physical aggression is permitted, encouraged, and rewarded in some social contexts, provided it is limited to specific forms. For example, in a boxing match a boy may punch with all the force he can muster, but biting or kicking even in this context will lead to prompt disapproval. (Bandura and Walters 1963, p. 9)

LEARNING VERSUS PERFORMANCE

The principle of discrimination obviously implies that we do not perform everything we learn, for the same behavior is not going to be appropriate or rewarded in every situation. Having learned a particular behavior, then, we must also learn to inhibit it in some situations while expressing it in others.

The distinction between learning and performance involves more than the inhibition of inappropriate behavior, for learning and performance operate according to radically different principles. People learn responses merely by watching others; they do not have to be rewarded during the learning period. In order to perform a response, on the other hand, they must actually be rewarded for it. Thus learning depends on *observation alone*, while performance depends on *reinforcement*.

To illustrate the difference between learning and performance, let us return to our example of dependence behavior. On the first day of school Joanne may notice that the first-grade teacher comes over to Suzy and picks up Suzy's pencil after the latter has dropped it. Joanne merely observes this from her own desk without doing anything or making the teacher notice her. The next morning Joanne is feeling lonely and upset. She drops her own pencil and finds to her delight that the teacher quickly comes over and picks it up for her. On the following days Joanne repeatedly drops her pencil. The teacher smiles at Joanne as she picks up the pencil on the first two days; on the third she tells Joanne she must learn to keep track of her own things. After that the teacher does not retrieve Joanne's pencil anymore. Joanne tries the attention-seeking behavior a few more times and then gives up. Here, then, there was no reinforcement during the learning period, when Joanne observed Suzy dropping the pencil. Then Joanne was rewarded for dropping her own pencil and so continued doing it. But when the reinforcement stopped, so did the attention-seeking behavior. Although reinforcement is not required for learning, it is essential for performance.

Social learning theory uses the distinction between learning and performance as the basic explanation for sex differences in behavior. Boys and girls learn many of the same modeled behavior patterns through observation. Their performance of learned behavior differs, however, because the prescribed male and female roles create different reinforcement contingencies. Thus, both boys and girls may learn how to apply face powder and smoke cigars by watching their parents. But when they grow up, they perform only the behavior acceptable for their sex: face powder for females, cigars for males (Mischel 1966).

A study by Bandura (1965) illustrates the difference between learning and performance. A group of children watched a movie in which an adult exhibited four novel aggressive actions accompanied by distinctive verbalizations. After the movie the boys imitated the model more than the girls did. Then the children were offered rewards for imitating the model. Now the girls imitated the model as much as the boys did. Clearly all the children learned the aggressive actions; but girls were reluctant to perform any of those actions until it was clear to them that in this unusual situation they would be rewarded rather than punished.

This study also illustrates the fact that observational learning can occur even when the imitative response is not acted out right away. The principle of *delayed imitation* means that the child can learn new behavior by observing a model and then perform it later, when the model is no longer present.

Of course, in the Bandura (1965) study, a relatively short time elapsed between learning and imitation. In real life the time period is often much longer. A little girl who watches her mother putting on face powder, for instance, probably will not be permitted to wear makeup herself until her teens. How does she manage to retain this learned behavior until she can perform it herself? The answer lies in rehearsal. The girl may try out the behavior by playing with her mother's makeup, or she may simply imagine herself doing it. This covert or vicarious role rehearsal helps her to anticipate how a powerful model would respond to her behavior and hence prepares her for various courses of action (Maccoby 1959). Vivid imagery, imagined action sequences, or other "symbolic operations" may also help her to remember a modeled behavior during a period when actual performance is not possible (Bandura 1969, p. 223).

Imagining oneself performing a behavior is not the same as actually performing it, of course. Since practice is required in order to develop skill, behavior that is only covertly practiced may not be carried out very adroitly the first few times it is actually performed. Mischel (1966) points out that males and females often practice behavior with varying frequency because of the differing reinforcement contingencies for the two sexes. As a result, the two sexes "may differ in the skill with which they execute such behaviors, particularly when the behaviors involve complex motor skills" (1966, p. 59).

DO WE IMITATE EVERYONE WE SEE?

Although the child learns simply by observing, he or she pays more attention to some models than to others. In general, a child is more likely to imitate models who are perceived as *powerful* and *successful*.

Bandura illustrated the importance of power by having children observe two groups composed of a man, a woman, and a child (Bandura, Ross, and Ross 1963b). In the first condition one adult gave toys and food to the other adult, while the child was essentially ignored. In the second condition one adult gave toys and food to the child, while the other adult was assigned a subordinate and powerless role. The powerful role alternated by sex. Once the toys and food were distributed, the two adult models exhibited different novel patterns of behavior. After the observation period, the experimenters watched to see which novel behavior the children would imitate when the adult models were no longer present. In both conditions the model who controlled the resources (passed out the toys and food) was imitated most, regardless of the model's gender and regardless of the recipient of these rewards. Clearly, children imitate models who control rather than consume resources. This experiment also demonstrates that children imitate the behavior of more than one model, and that cross-sex imitation does occur and is facilitated when the opposite-sex model has greater power than the same-sex model.*

Children also imitate models who are successful or rewarded—regardless of the means the latter use to attain success. Bandura's "Rocky and Johnny" study demonstrates this (Bandura, Ross, and Ross 1963c). Eighty nursery-school children saw a film in which an adult male, Rocky, used considerable physical aggression to swipe the possessions of another adult male, Johnny. In one condition Rocky was rewarded; in another he was severely punished; while in a third condition the film showed a highly expressive but nonaggressive model, and in a fourth condition the children did not see the models. After the film the children were tested for delayed imitation and interviewed to see which model they preferred. The experimenters found that although the girls displayed less imitative aggression than did the boys, all the children imitated the rewarded model more than the punished model. Furthermore, all the children preferred the successful (rewarded) model, even though they expressed moral censure for his aggressive actions.

While successful (rewarded) models are imitated more, unsuccessful (punished) models are imitated less. This inhibition of imitation appears to involve conditioned fear responses that children experience while watching a model being punished (Berger 1962).

A child cannot always, however, observe directly the consequences of a model's behavior. In a typical experimental situation a child watches a model perform some action and then watches the model being rewarded or punished. But in real life people are not given cookies or other re-

* The groups in this study were actually designed as prototypes of the nuclear family. The results suggest that both boys and girls imitate the father not because he is male but because he controls the family resources. They are less likely to imitate the mother, who is usually a less powerful recipient of family resources.

wards immediately after they do something. How, then, does the child know that he or she is watching a rewarded model? Apparently by noticing some tangible evidence of the model's previous successes or rewards. This evidence may take the form of fancy clothing or other symbols of economic success. Or it may be shown by an occupational title or other sign of competence, skill, and prestige. Looking at these status symbols, the child concludes that if she behaves like the models she, too, will be rewarded. This inference leads to greater imitation of high-status, high-prestige models (Bandura 1969; Bandura and Walters 1963).

Of course, the influence of status and prestige is not news to most people. The advertising industry is certainly well aware of it. Think of all those ads where a celebrity uses Brand X. The idea is essentially the same as in the laboratory studies of imitation. Noticing (and coveting) the success of a particular model, the consumer will imitate his or her behavior by buying the advertised product.

The research on status variables has concentrated on imitation of socially desirable or at least neutral behavior. There is some evidence, however, that socially disapproved behavior can also be increased by watching a high-status person doing it. In one study, for instance, two models carried out walk-light violations. The high-status pedestrian was dressed in a pressed suit, shiny shoes, a white shirt, and a tie. The low-status pedestrian was dressed in a denim shirt, pants that were dirty and patched, and scuffed shoes. Other pedestrians were more likely to jay-walk after watching the high-status violator than after watching the low-status one (Lefkowitz, Blake, and Mouton 1955).

Of course, deviant or socially disapproved behavior does not have to be performed by high-status models in order to be imitated. Bandura and Walters (1963) note that a variety of prohibitions are more likely to be ignored if other people are seen violating them freely. One interview study, for instance, suggests that adolescent boys are more likely to engage in sexual intercourse in double or multiple dating situations than in situations where they are alone with a girl (Bandura and Walters 1959). But prohibitions do seem to be ignored more readily if the observed violator has prestige.

Bandura (1969) points out that people not only imitate the behavior of a high-status model but may also adopt the model's values and attitudes. Thus, when a successful model expresses a strong preference for a certain object, the object becomes more valued by an observer. Here again, the advertising industry is ahead of us, for it expects us not only to buy a celebrity's favorite brand but also to adopt his or her evaluation of that brand. Thus, the thoughts, feelings, and behavior of powerful, successful people are all influential.

Both model power and model success are examples of *vicarious reinforcement*: the child (or adult) does not need to experience reinforcement personally; he or she can simply observe or infer the model's rewards. The observer then concludes that if the model was rewarded for a particular behavior, he or she will be, too. For this reason power and success are crucial to imitation.

There are other less important factors that facilitate imitation. A warm, nurturant relationship between child and model is one such. In one experiment Bandura and Huston (1961) exposed two groups of nursery school children to different types of interaction with the same woman. With one group the woman acted highly nurturant and rewarding, while with the other she acted distant and nonrewarding. After the interactions the model played a game with each child and exhibited relatively novel verbal, motor, and aggressive behavior that was irrelevant to the game itself. Each child's imitation of this novel behavior was then measured while the child played the game. Except for aggressive behavior that was readily imitated regardless of the nurturant quality of the model, imitation of novel responses was greater among the children with the previous warm, nurturant interaction.

Warmth and nurturance also appear to be important in increasing imitation of parents, in that children who perceive their same-sex parent as warm and nurturing show more sex-typed preferences and interests themselves (Mussen 1961; Mussen and Distler 1959; Mussen and Rutherford 1963). Bandura (1969) has suggested that parental warmth may influence children's imitation in indirect ways. Affectionate parents are likely to spend more time interacting with their children and hence provide them with more opportunities to observe parental behavior. And there is also a reciprocal quality to parent-child relationships: parental affection stimulates a child to imitation; this pleases the parent, who then becomes more affectionate, which further stimulates a child's emulation; and so on.

Similarity between child and model is yet another facilitating factor, due apparently to the fact that both children and adults pay more attention to models they perceive as being like themselves (Maccoby and Wilson 1957; Maccoby, Wilson, and Burton 1958). This increased attentiveness provides a child more opportunity to observe and learn new behavior from a model.

Before leaving the subject of model characteristics, I should note that the "symbolic modeling" provided by television and other audiovisual displays can be extremely influential (Bandura 1969, p. 249). In the classic study demonstrating this influence, Bandura and his colleagues studied imitative aggression in forty-eight boys and forty-eight girls approximately three to six years old (Bandura, Ross, and Ross 1963a). First the children watched adult models hitting an inflated doll. The models were both male and female and were presented in three ways: in person, on film, and in cartoons. After exposure to the models the children were mildly frustrated and then permitted to play without the models present. The researchers found that the children who saw the film-mediated models, whether pictorial or cartooned, imitated their aggressive behavior as much as did those children who saw the aggressive models in person. From this the conclusion was that "film-mediated models are as effective as real-life models in transmitting deviant patterns of behavior" (Bandura and Walters 1963, pp. 61–62).

This study has created quite a furor, for people are becoming increasingly concerned about the influence of the mass media. Children spend hours watching television, which is saturated with displays of violence. Will they imitate the violent aggression themselves? Perhaps, especially if they are young. Pingree (1978) has found that third-graders believe in the reality of television commercials more than eighth-graders do. For grammar-school children, then, it seems fair to say that television characters have just as much potential impact as the neighbor down the street.

DO WE ALWAYS IMITATE OTHERS?

Common sense tells us that children do not imitate others all the time. The degree of imitation must depend on the situation and on the people involved. Social learning theorists have examined this question in terms of "observer characteristics": that is, what kinds of children are more susceptible to imitation, and in which circumstances?

The most important finding is that children who have developed strong dependence habits are more influenced by social reinforcement (Bandura and Walters 1963). The usual approach is to assess dependence by measuring how readily children seek help with a simple task. Low-dependent and high-dependent children are then exposed to the same model, and imitation is assessed. High-dependents usually show greater imitation of both adults and peers.

There is also some evidence that moderate emotional arousal enhances imitation. For example, Walters, Marshall, and Shooter (1960) placed high-school boys in a stressful situation and then asked them to report how emotionally aroused they felt. The more aroused they reported feeling, the more likely they were to agree with the experimenter's incorrect statements regarding the position of a light in a darkened room.

Physiological arousal may also increase the incidence and degree of imitation. In Schacter and Singer's (1962) study of simulated emotional arousal, researchers injected college students with either a saline solution or adrenalin and told only some of them to expect the adrenalin effects of palpitations, trembling, and flushing. After injection the students waited with a confederate who acted either outraged or euphoric. The adrenalin-injected students who expected no physical effects exceeded the other groups both in reporting emotional arousal and in imitating the stooge's behavior. Thus when we feel a physical sensation for which we have no explanation, we are likely not only to label this sensation in terms of our social surroundings but also to imitate the behavior of those around us. The effects of physiological arousal may be especially marked in young children, who may not yet be able to label or understand their internal sensations.

COGNITIVE MEDIATION: WHAT GOES ON IN OUR HEADS?

Critics often maintain that learning theory presents people as empty-headed creatures who merely respond mechanically to external reinforcement without thinking or planning. Social learning theorists adamantly reject this charge.

> It is often mistakenly assumed that social-learning theories deny the existence of mediating cognitive processes. Men and women, as well as boys and girls, do think. They experience wishes, fears, and hopes; they even dream. The present social-learning view does not deny such intrapsychic activities. (Mischel 1966, p. 62)

These theorists describe thinking in terms of "higher-order conditioning" (Mischel 1966, p. 61), a concept originally developed through experiments on relatively simple responses (Mowrer 1960). These studies have repeatedly shown that if a noise or other neutral stimulus is repeatedly paired with an intrinsically rewarding or punishing stimulus (such as food or pain-producing electric shock), the initially neutral stimulus takes on the reinforcing properties of the rewarding or punishing stimulus. The initially neutral stimulus has now become "conditioned" and can in turn be used to condition other responses. If the negatively conditioned noise were later presented with a neutral object, for instance, the object would elicit avoidance responses.

When social learning theorists talk about higher-order conditioning, they focus on the way in which words and symbols function as "conditioned stimuli." The basic idea is that we start out by being rewarded for a number of discrete kinds of behavior. After a while we come to think of these behavior patterns in terms of one verbal label. This label then takes on the reward value associated with the activities it represents. And once we have such a value-laden label, we are likely to apply it to new behavior, predicting the consequences of that behavior on the basis of the rewards associated with the label.

To illustrate the principle of higher-order conditioning, let us consider what happens when a young girl engages in various forms of aggression. She is usually punished for hitting her sisters and brothers, so hitting takes on a negative value. She may also be punished for kicking and biting her playmates, so that behavior, too, takes on a negative value. The girl eventually comes to think of hitting, kicking, and biting as examples of "fighting." The verbal label "fighting" then takes on the negative value associated with being punished for hitting, kicking, and biting. When she thinks about scratching a playmate, then, the girl applies the label "fighting" to this new behavior and expects punishment.

Higher-order conditioning can continue in a hierarchical fashion, for "fighting" may become associated with other things. Let us imagine that each time the mother punishes the girl for hitting, kicking, or biting, she says something like, "Nice girls don't hit people" or even, "Nice girls don't fight." Now the girl is likely to develop new verbal labels: "nice" and "not nice." These labels, too, take on the reward value of the activities they represent. "Nice" behavior brings rewards, while "not nice" behavior brings punishments. "Nice" and "not nice" may be broader labels than "fighting" and may apply to a number of other, subordinate verbal labels, such as "sharing," "helping," "whining," and "crying."

Through the process of higher-order conditioning we gradually build up a complex system of thoughts, feelings, and anticipations. When we encounter new people, activities, or experiences, they become associated with these labels and hence take on the pleasant or the unpleasant connotations of the labels themselves. We also come to think of ourselves in terms of these labels, evaluating our own behavior and characteristics according to the connotations of the labels.

Mischel points out that higher-order conditioning can account for the development of sex differences, for the connotations of verbal labels are often dramatically different for males and females.

> Extrapolating to sex differences, it is apparent that numerous activities, goals, interests, and the like acquire differential value for the sexes by being differentially associated with positive or negative outcomes and labels. Labels like "sissy," "pansy," "tough," or "sweet" acquire differential value for the sexes, and their application can easily affect the value of other previously neutral labels. (Mischel 1966, p. 61)

Once we have attached labels to certain types of behavior, we use those labels to determine our own activities. Knowing the connotations of "sissy" or "tough," we can predict what will happen if we do things that might be perceived either way, and we act accordingly. Some of the major sex differences in behavior are based on just such self-controls. The concept of the "nice girl," for instance, causes women to limit themselves to "respectable" activities and places. This self-limitation is based on a fear of what will happen if one acts in "not nice" ways, since "in addition to forfeiture of personal physical security, the "not nice" woman becomes the target of ridicule, ostracism, and psychological punishment" (Fox 1977, p. 817).

The sex differences in connotations of verbal labels do not *cause* sex differences in behavior, however: behavior is caused by reinforcement contingencies. Labels merely serve as mediating links between the cause (previous response consequences for that behavior) and the effect (future performance or nonperformance of that behavior).

In spite of a vague similarity in terms, then, Mischel's view of "cognitive mediation" is dramatically different from Kohlberg's concept of "cognitive structures." While Kohlberg maintains that internal cognitions cause behavior, Mischel maintains that external reinforcements cause it. In explaining this difference, Mischel argues that viewing causation as external is not synonymous with viewing a person as "empty" or "passive" (1966, p. 62). Our heads are full of ideas or verbal labels. It is just that the ultimate cause of behavior lies elsewhere—in the reinforcement patterns that originally caused certain behavior patterns, activities, and objects to acquire the positive and negative connotations that then became associated with the verbal labels.

REWARDING OURSELVES

We use verbal labels not only to anticipate the consequences of our behavior but also, on occasion, to administer reinforcements to ourselves. Mischel and Liebert (1966) demonstrated this by asking children to play a game that supposedly required skill but on which scores were actually experimentally controlled. A woman first taught the game to each child using tokens that could be exchanged for rewards. The model used one strict and one lenient criterion in rewarding herself and in telling each child how to reward himself or herself when it was the child's turn to play. Three conditions combined these reward criteria differently: (1) both model and child rewarded strictly, (2) both model and child rewarded leniently, and (3) model rewarded leniently but child urged to reward himself or herself strictly. Then the experimenters observed the way each child rewarded himself or herself when playing alone. When the modeled and encouraged criteria matched, the children rewarded themselves accordingly; but when the model urged strictness and demonstrated leniency, the children adopted the lenient criterion for themselves. When the children were asked to teach the game to a younger child in a later session, they consistently imposed the same standards they had adopted for themselves. Thus, children imitate what adults *do*, not what they *say*—and continue to apply these observed self-rewards later on in life.

Mischel has pointed out that such discrepancies between what adults do and say may cause problems in sex-role development; for example, "a mother who tries to train her daughter to be 'feminine' while she herself behaves in a 'masculine' fashion might very well rear a child whose scores show conflict on masculinity-femininity scales" (1966, p. 65).

Learning to Be "Feminine"

Now I shall take a closer look at the development of sexual identification as elaborated by Walter Mischel of Stanford University (1966, 1970), and discuss it from the point of view of females, since girls become feminine in the same way that boys become masculine. Here it will not be necessary to review male development and then discuss how female development deviates from it.

LEARNING AND DISCRIMINATION: I WILL DO WHAT I AM REWARDED FOR

Sex-typed behavior patterns are simply defined as "behaviors that typically elicit different rewards for one sex than for the other" (Mischel 1966, p. 56). A girl's first task is to *discriminate* between these reward patterns, to figure out which things she will be rewarded for and which things she will be punished for. Next she must learn to *generalize* from specific learning experiences to new situations and similar behavior. And finally, she must begin to *perform* in accordance with sex-typed behavior. We could imagine a typical sequence:

Discrimination: I will be rewarded for playing with my Barbie doll at home.
I will be punished for hitting Susie at home.

Generalization: I will be rewarded for playing with my Barbie doll at school.
I will be punished for hitting Susie at school.

I will be rewarded for playing with any doll.
I will be punished for hitting all Susies (all girls, all children, anyone).

I will be rewarded for playing house (or any activity related to child care).
I will be punished for pushing (shoving, or any direct physical aggression).

Not only must the girl learn to discriminate among different types of behavior; she must also discriminate among specific situations, for particular behavior may be rewarded in one situation and punished in another. Mischel underscores this situation-specificity by pointing out "the probable differences in outcome to an American adolescent boy for sewing a dress during school recess and sewing a tent patch during a boy scout expedition" (1966, p. 67).

GENDER LABELS: I AM REWARDED FOR GIRL THINGS

Mischel accepts Kohlberg's contention that children develop gender identity during the first four to seven years of life, and that this self-categorization is irreversible; but he rejects the idea that this cognitive judgment then determines future behavior.

> Kohlberg rightly states that boys and girls label themselves as male and female, and that these judgments of sex identity, once firmly established, tend to be irreversible. However, the abundant individual differences found within each sex, and the fact that the behaviors of the sexes overlap to a great degree, suggest that there are many ways to be a boy or girl—and even more ways to be a man or woman. Sex differences in behavior are not, for the most part, universal entities. . . .
>
> In the cognitive-developmental view proposed by Kohlberg (p. 89, this volume), "once the boy has stably categorized himself as male, he then values positively those objects and acts consistent with his gender identity." *According to the present view, the child's behaviors and values are determined not by his gender role, but by his social-learning history.* (Mischel 1966, pp. 62–63; italics added)

As Mischel sees it, the gender label serves as a "cognitive mediator" that helps the child to predict probable outcomes for behavior: I am female, so such-and-such is likely to happen if I behave in this way. The cause of behavior is still reinforcement contingencies, however—not the cognitive label per se.

Knowing that she is permanently female as opposed to male does make a girl's learning more efficient. A girl no longer has to proceed by trial and error; she can use "inferred response consequences" instead; that is, she can figure out what will happen without actually performing a behavior. Using a male example again, Mischel says, "a man does not have to be arrested for wearing dresses in public to learn about the consequences for such behavior" (1966, p. 61).

PARENTAL IDENTIFICATION: IMITATING MOM AND DAD

Children imitate their parents for the same reasons they imitate other models. Parents serve as particularly important models, moreover, because young children are dependent on these powerful adults for food, toys, and emotional comfort. As we saw earlier, dependence, emotional arousal, and a warm, nurturant relationship enhance imitation.

The girl does not imitate only her mother. She learns behavior by observing both parents and then follows their behavior patterns according to her own reinforcement contingencies. Her actual behavior can thus be a mixture of specific behavior copied from both parents. Her actions will resemble her mother's more than her father's, though, since both mother and daughter are subject to female reward patterns and act accordingly. This similarity of mother-daughter performance is further enhanced by the girl's gender identity. Since she knows she is rewarded for female things, and since mother is a female, she will conclude that she is more likely to be rewarded for behavior observed in her mother than for behavior observed in her father. This conclusion strengthens the girl's tendency to try to perform maternal behavior.

According to social learning theory, then, parental identification is merely a special instance of imitation. It is based on general learning principles rather than on sexual urges and precedes rather than follows the child's development of sex-typed interests and activities.

Critique: Is This Too Simplified?

The basic principles of social learning theory have been well documented. Many critics, however, still maintain that the social learning analysis is oversimplified and cannot account for the complexities of human existence. There are two basic themes in this criticism. The first charges that learning theorists treat people like automatons, while the second questions the relationship between laboratory experiments and everyday life.

We have already seen how social learning theorists reply to the first charge in terms of higher-order conditioning. They point out that they never suggested that people are like empty "black boxes": obviously people do think, they do feel, they even fantasize and dream. But these internal events are not the essential cause of behavior; external reinforcement is. People's bodies and minds may be full of urges to action, but the form and direction of that action is determined by the environment. And this determination is made according to the same principles of learning and reinforcement that guide the behavior of animals who lack the human capacity for symbolic thought and self-conscious awareness. Thus, the uniquely human cognitive abilities do contribute to experience by providing a complex system of verbal labels that summarize reinforcement histories. But this cognitive complexity serves only as a mediator between reinforcement and behavior; it does not change the causal sequence.

The second criticism applies not just to social learning theory, but to all experimental psychology. Can a laboratory experiment ever capture the essence of real life—regardless of whether the experiment is designed to assess the presence and influence of penis envy, the development of knowledge about anatomical constancy, or the processes of observational learning and reinforced performance? Unfortunately the major strength of laboratory methods also constitutes their major weakness, for in order to isolate and examine certain processes, we often need to simplify the situation in which they occur. This simplification then raises the question of artificiality. Have we carefully eliminated something that actually causes or at least profoundly influences the phenomenon we are trying to study?

Social learning theorists are especially sensitive to this issue because they are interested in the environment in which we live. Their emphasis on external rather than on internal determinants of behavior necessitates a continuing concern with the basic reinforcing qualities of of that environment. Their experiments are designed to isolate a crucial dimension or reinforcer in order to study its effects. They are well aware that they may not have identified all the important dimensions of social interactions.

Bandura (1969), for instance, points out that many social complexities have not been examined in the social learning research. Most of the studies have focused on interactions between one child and one adult. In real life, however, we often interact with more than one person at a time. The processes of learning, reinforcement, and imitation are undoubtedly more complicated in these multiple interactions than they are in dyadic ones.

In spite of their emphasis on the environment, social learning researchers have also followed the lead of Freudians in focusing on parent-child interactions. Parents are not the only people who influence a child, however, particularly as the child gets older. In a rapidly changing society like ours, the interests, the attitudes, and the role behavior that parents learned while they were growing up often seem irrelevant to their children. As Bandura puts it, "One suspects that fox-trotting parents will not necessarily prove to be the most idolized or effective models for Watusi-swinging adolescents" (1969, p. 248). This generation gap is likely to be particularly evident in gender-linked areas today, since the role of women has undergone some dramatic shifts since World War II.

Other factors combine with general historical change to make parents less influential. Many Americans have worked hard to improve their economic circumstances, for instance. By engendering high educational and occupational aspirations, working-class parents often encourage their children to initiate or continue this upward social and economic mobility. As these upwardly mobile children grow older, however, they find that their parents cannot provide satisfactory models for class-typed patterns of speech, dress, and social skills. These ambitious children often turn to admired teachers and middle-class peers to learn the complex network of attitudes, belief systems, and behavioral repertoires necessary to achieve the desired status.

Bandura points out that symbolic modeling is also an influential but neglected source of social learning today. Television is the most obvious example here; for as I have already noted, children seem to imitate behavior portrayed on film as readily as they do that seen in real life. Another example of symbolic modeling is what Bandura calls "normative injunctions" (1969, p. 250). These complex social norms are conveyed verbally and both tell us how to behave, think, and even feel in various situations and outline what will happen to us if we do not conform.

The importance of these social complexities will become increasingly apparent as we consider the social roles and life experiences of women in the United States today. We will be looking at women's lives from a slightly different perspective from that of the social learning theorists, who focus on the imitation and the reinforcement of discrete behavior patterns. There is little attention to the whole person, much less to the network of attitudes, behaviors, and feelings embedded in social roles. Although studying small pieces of behavior has enabled these researchers to document the processes of learning and reinforcement, this atomized approach cannot convey what it is like to be a woman today.

Not that social learning theory is irrelevant. On the contrary, it has provided a persuasive explanation of the way people become "feminine" or "masculine"—an explanation based on the distinction between external behavior and internal thoughts and feelings. We learn many activities, but we perform only those we are rewarded for. This learning/performance distinction can account for the immense difference between sexually undifferentiated human potential and the behavior we observe around us every day. We all know many women who get angry but never yell, men who feel sad but never cry; we may do this ourselves. Clearly we are capable of a great variety of feelings, thoughts, and actions that we do not express in our behavior because we do not expect to be rewarded for them.

PART III

WOMAN'S PLACE
IN SOCIETY

THE THEORIES about female personality are more than empty words. They summarize the view many scientists have of the female—a male-oriented view that in turn colors the scientists' perceptions of female life experience. If the male body and personality denote much of what it means to be human, the female's feelings, attitudes, and experiences must be deviant or deficient.

Of course, not all personality theories view the male as the norm. Social learning theory assumes that males and females are basically the same. They *behave* differently, however, because other people expect them to do so; males and females live in different social worlds, which determine their different behavior and personalities.

In recent years researchers have become increasingly interested in the social factors that influence personality. Many have argued that the male-oriented theories simply translate cultural bias into psychological terms. It is time to look directly at the cultural factors that shape both female life experiences and the culture-bound theories about women.

One of the major areas of interest has been cultural variation. Do the lives and personalities of American women follow the general cross-cultural patterns? How have the social and economic changes of the past fifty years affected women? The answers to these questions lead to a new perspective on traditional women's issues such as marriage and child rearing. After considering them, I shall look at new areas of female experience that were previously ignored because they did not fit into the image of traditional femininity—women's experiences as unmarried adults, as workers, and as members of racial minorities.

Chapter 7

The Dilemma of
American Women

I HAVE ALREADY touched on the crosscultural patterns of sex differences in personality and behavior. Males are more likely to perform
the basic subsistence tasks, to control the property involved in economic
activities, and to live together in a male descent group—in other words,
they have the power. Male personality patterns reflect this dominant
position; males are usually more aggressive and sexually active and less
nurturant and emotionally expressive than females. Child-rearing customs foster these sex differences, engendering aggression and self-
reliance in males as opposed to self-sacrifice and dependence in females.

Where do American women fit into these patterns? Are they also
relatively powerless and trained to be obedient and nurturant? To some
extent they are. Although the United States is a highly industrialized
and rapidly changing society, the vestiges of these patterns remain. They
can be seen in the stereotypes or the perceptions that most people have
about men and women, in conflicting expectations about female life
styles, and in the relationships between the sexes.

Sex-Role Stereotypes Are Alive and Well

If you ask a variety of Americans to describe a typical female and a typical male, they come up with remarkably different descriptions of the two sexes. Women are affectionate, gentle, loyal, sympathetic, and warm. Men, on the other hand, are aggressive, ambitious, analytical, competitive, dominant, and independent. Although the specific adjectives mentioned by each person vary, they usually include many of those listed in Table 7.1 and revolve around four key characteristics: warmth or emotional expressiveness in females and competitiveness, aggressiveness, and dominance in males.

TABLE 7.1

Typical Views of Men and Women

Masculine Characteristics	Feminine Characteristics
Acts as a leader	Affectionate
Aggressive	Cheerful
Ambitious	Childlike
Analytical	Compassionate
Assertive	Does not use harsh language
Athletic	Eager to soothe hurt feelings
Competitive	Flatterable
Defends own beliefs	Gentle
Dominant	Gullible
Forceful	Loves children
Has leadership abilities	Loyal
Independent	Sensitive to the needs of others
Individualistic	Shy
Makes decisions easily	Soft-spoken
Self-reliant	Sympathetic
Self-sufficient	Tender
Strong personality	Understanding
Willing to take a stand	Warm
Willing to take risks	Yielding

Source: The Bem Sex Role Inventory as reported in S. L. Bem, "The measurement of psychological androgyny," *Journal of Consulting and Clinical Psychology* (1974) 42:156.

Everyone seems to share these sex-role stereotypes, or oversimplified conceptions of what men and women are like. Although their studies have been done primarily with college students, the Bems have pointed out that

today's students have challenged the established ways of looking at almost every other issue, and they have been quick to reject those practices of our society which conflict explicitly with their major values. But . . . they will find it far more difficult to shed the more subtle aspects of a sex-role ideology which—as we shall now attempt to demonstrate—conflicts just as surely with their existential values as any of the other societal practices to which they have so effectively raised objection. There is no better way to appreciate the power of a society's nonconscious ideology than to examine it within the framework of values held by that society's avant-garde. (Bem and Bem 1976, p. 181)

Furthermore, when groups that do differ in age, sex, religion, marital status, and education are studied, they generally tend to agree on this stereotype of women (Broverman et al. 1972).

ARE ALL WOMEN THE SAME?

Perhaps women are not always seen in terms of a *single* stereotype. Although the majority of the research has suggested a single stereotype, this research is usually done by presenting people with a preselected list of adjectives and asking them to rate men and women. We do not know how central those characteristics are to the subjects' own perceptions of the two sexes, or whether the subjects would have selected different adjectives if given the opportunity. Some researchers recently addressed this issue by asking students, "What words come to your mind when I say *woman*?" (Clifton, McGrath, and Wick 1976). They found adjectives applicable to five categories of woman: housewife, bunny (sex object), clubwoman, career woman, and woman athlete. When they asked another group of undergraduates to check which of the resulting 153 adjectives described these five different categories, they found three major clusters. The first two exemplified roles with high dependence on men, either as a sexually pure and maternal figure (housewife) or as a tempting sex object (bunny). The third cluster combined all the roles implying relative independence from men: clubwoman, career woman, and woman athlete. Table 7.2 shows that the descriptions of these three types of woman were quite distinctive, with only "housewife" corresponding to the traditional literature on sex roles.

These researchers also compared male and female responses to the task. While both sexes seemed to view housewife and bunny as incompatible, only men viewed housewife and independent woman (clubwoman/career woman/athlete) as mutually exclusive. The fact that women attributed many of the same characteristics to career women and to housewives suggests that they think women can be both. Men, on the other hand, seem to view career women as a breed apart, as women who have renounced their femininity by choosing "activities which carry them beyond the traditional roles which serve men" (Clifton et al. 1976, p. 145.)

TABLE 7.2

Three Types of Woman?

Housewife	Bunny (Sex object)	Independent Woman (Career woman, clubwoman, athlete)	
faithful	glamorous	active	
gentle	good-looking	aggressive	
kind	pleasure-loving	hardworking	
sensitive	romantic	alert	
sympathetic	excitable	confident	
dependent	passionate	ambitious	
cooperative	frivolous	competitive	
emotional	sensual	persistent	
tender		independent	
conservative			
casual		**Additional characteristics associated with specific types of independence**	
calm			
generous			
agreeable		*Clubwoman:*	argumentative
secure			boastful
loyal		*Career woman:*	intelligent
			logical
			tactful
			progressive
			sophisticated
			rational
			direct
		Woman athlete:	athletic
			sportsmanlike
			brave
			dominant

Source: Based on results reported in A. K. Clifton, D. McGrath, and B. Wick, "Stereo-types of woman: A single category?" *Sex roles*, 1976, 2(2): 135–48.

THE MEDIA IMAGE OF WOMEN

Sex-role stereotypes are not a weird phenomenon found only in psychology research; we see them around us all the time. The triple vision of women as housewives, sex objects, and (occasionally) mas-culinized career women is embedded in our culture. A few long evenings in front of the radio or television are enough to tell us this—as numerous studies of female media images have demonstrated.

The sex-role stereotypes are not limited to adult shows; children's programs convey them also. In a recent survey of ten of the most popu-lar children's shows in the 1971–1972 season, Sarah Sternglanz and Lisa Serbin (1974) found that female characters are relatively rare. Half of the most popular shows had no female characters at all, while the others had two male characters for every female. The female characters did not make plans and carry them out, were punished if they moved about too rapidly or were aggressive, and consistently deferred to males. The male characters, on the other hand, were physically active, aggressive, socially dominant, and able to plan. Finally, when the female characters did take some action, they were generally ignored, while a male performing the same action was rewarded. The prospects for girls watching television are dismal: either they have no female characters with whom to identify, or they have characters that are inactive, dependent, and treated as socially ineffectual.

But, one may ask, who cares about television? The truth is that we all should. Many children today spend more time watching television than they do in any other activity except sleeping. In 1963 Bandura found that filmed models were just as effective in eliciting imitation as were live models (Bandura et al. 1963a). Recently Suzanne Pingree (1978) further substantiated this finding by studying the effect of standard television commercials on 227 children in grades three and eight. She chose two five-minute sets of commercials from those broadcast during daytime and prime time in March 1975. One set showed women in traditional roles as housewives and mothers: talking about how crucial vitamins are for keeping a woman in shape for her husband; discussing the importance of using certain foods and household cleaners, since "After all, is there anything that says more about a woman than her home?"; and describing giving birth as the "ultimate experience for a woman" (Pingree 1978, pp. 265–66). The second set showed women in nontraditional roles as physician, professional car driver, dietician, golf professional, accountant, and interior designer and performing activities like bailing hay and driving a tractor. The children were randomly assigned to view the traditional or the nontraditional commercials and then given a measure of traditional attitudes toward women which asked them to rate their agreement with four statements: "Overall, women are as smart as men are," "Married women should stay home and be housewives and mothers," "Housework is really women's work," and "A woman can do the same jobs that a man can do." Those who saw the nontraditional models showed less traditional attitudes toward women after viewing.

Pingree also examined the children's perceptions of the real-life nature of the commercials by varying the instructions given at the beginning of the task. As we would expect, the reality-set group perceived the commercials as more real than did the acting-set group. In addition, younger children believed in the reality of the commercials more than did older children.

The startling thing about Pingree's study is the short time the children viewed the commercials. If five minutes of viewing time can significantly affect measures of sex-role attitudes, the profound impact television must have on children who watch it for many hours each week is almost beyond imagination.

CHILDREN'S TEXTBOOKS

We cannot dismiss the sex-role stereotypes on television as confined to commercial exploitation, for they are just as evident in the materials used in our schools. Children's textbooks clearly convey the message that girls and women are timid, overly emotional, dependent, and somewhat incompetent. In a survey of 134 elementary school readers, for instance, a task force of the National Organization for Women found that boys are portrayed as adventurous, active, and brave, while girls are portrayed as immobile, fearful onlookers. A few samples of the dialogue will illustrate the sex difference.

"I can't, I can't." Amy was crying. "It won't push! Oh, Stuey, get me out. It's so *dark* in here."

He felt a tear coming to his eye, but he brushed it away with his hand. Boys eight years old don't cry, he said to himself.

. . . Wilbur [Wright] laughed, "Whoever heard of anyone's mother building a sled?"

"Look at her, mother, just look at her. She is just like a girl. She gives up."

. . . Helplessness swept over her like a sickening wave.

"Eeek! a dog!" squealed a lady with a bag of apples. "Go away, doggie, go away."

Mrs. Allen shuddered. To think that her boy had killed such a creature made her a bit proud, but also just a little bit faint.

"No," said Pam. "The water is too deep. Grandma wouldn't like it. Some big boys are swimming out there. Let's ask them to get it!"

"Do not be afraid, Mother," said Jack, "I will do what I can."

"Oh Raymond, boys are much braver than girls."
                    (Women on Words and Images 1975, pp. 51–54)

Since this study was done, a number of groups have formed to monitor the sex-role images presented in textbooks, and many publishers have vowed to revise their publications. Lists of nonsexist materials for children are now available from groups like the American Library Association. Educators and others have become more aware of the problem and begun to rectify it, so that another generation does not have to grow up with this sexist view of Dick and Jane.

ARE SEX-ROLE STEREOTYPES CHANGING?

According to the more traditional literature, one would not think that sex-role stereotypes are changing. Yet in the past fifty years there have been significant societal changes that should affect these stereotypes, and recent research indicates some significant shifts in thinking. Two researchers recently addressed this issue by asking ninety-one college and senior high-school students in the Midwest to rate sixty-six adjectives previously found to differentiate between images of men and women (Der-Karabetian and Smith 1977). They asked the students to label each adjective as masculine, feminine, or nondiscriminatory as to sex and also asked them to rate each adjective as positive, negative, or neutral in connotation. They found that "males are still considered as aggressive, dominant, rough, enterprising and females as timid, sensitive, sociable, religious, and uncertain" (p. 195). Men and women agreed on this evaluation. Females described significantly more adjectives as nondiscriminatory than did males (46 percent female, 34 percent male), an indication that females stereotype sex roles less than males do. And finally, they found that the female students viewed feminine adjectives as more positive than masculine adjectives, whereas males rated feminine and masculine adjectives as equally positive. The authors conclude:

> It is possible that although the stereotypes as such have not changed, attitudes concerning the attributes described in these stereotypes have changed in women, such that characteristics formerly valued negatively have acquired positive value. This may indicate that women have become more accepting of feminine characteristics not previously considered socially desirable. (P. 197)

The authors do not comment on one of the most striking things about their study: between one-third and one-half of these sex-role adjectives were rated as nondiscriminatory. In other words, these students felt that many of the characteristics listed were not relevant to one's gender. The sex-role stereotypes are indeed changing if such a large portion of their content has been neutralized.

Another way to look at changing sex-role stereotypes is through their applicability rather than their content. Although people may still have the same abstract conception of what men and women are like, they may no longer feel compelled to conform to this stereotype. To get at this type of personal change or flexibility, you need to ask people what they themselves are like (or want to be like), not what they think men and women are like (or ought to be like). When this is done using the list of sex-role adjectives included in Table 7.1, we find that one-third to one-half of college students rate themselves as showing traditionally feminine and masculine characteristics equally, while about one-third rate themselves as having significantly more same-sex characteristics and about one-sixth as having more cross-sex characteristics (Bem 1976, 1977).

Of course, these students were still rating themselves on adjectives provided by the researchers. What would happen if we asked students to provide their own adjectives? Would they even think of the sex-role ones first and foremost? When I asked 233 college students to list "those qualities you would like to have" and "any things you do not like about yourself, or wish you could change," only one-third mentioned characteristics that matched the key areas of sex-role norms at their school: warmth or emotional expressiveness, competitiveness, aggressiveness, and dominance (Rohrbaugh 1976). The other two-thirds of these students presumably shared the abstract sex-role stereotypes with their peers but did not necessarily view them as crucial to their own lives.

Individuals may be changing, then, even if sex-role stereotypes remain essentially the same. There has been a flurry of research into this possibility in the past five years. The basic finding is that many people do not match the abstract stereotypes, and what is more, they are better off if they do not. Both women and men seem to cope better and feel happier with themselves if they have both traditionally feminine and masculine characteristics. I shall discuss this research in the chapters on mental health, after dealing with the way sex-role stereotypes and expectations are reflected in the everyday experiences of women in the United States.

Role Conflict and Ambivalence

Two basic roles are available to American women today: wife/mother and career woman. These two social functions are often viewed as clashing—in terms both of the activities involved and also of the personal characteristics needed to carry out those activities. Yet most women participate in both realms at various times in their lives, and many women combine the two activities simultaneously. Much research has focused on the differing demands of homemaking, mothering, and pursuing a career. In the 1950s and 1960s this research concentrated on emotional dimensions of these two roles, while more recent studies have examined the practical problems faced by working wives and mothers.

THE TRADITIONAL VIEW: STRESS AND AMBIVALENCE

This approach is reflected in the early work of Judith Bardwick and Elizabeth Douvan (1971). These psychologists emphasize the incompatibility between "feminine" personality and the characteristics needed to succeed in the workplace. They point out that women are brought up to be warm, nurturant, gentle, nonaggressive, and noncompetitive; yet successful working people need to be analytical, dominant, aggressive, and competitive—"masculine." Thus, although women are now allowed and are even encouraged to work, they are often not prepared for working.

The increasing participation of women in the workplace has also clouded the image of femininity, according to these authors, so that women end up feeling unsure of what they should be. Uncertainty compounds the problem by making women avoid the very "masculine" behaviors and characteristics they need in order to succeed in endeavors outside the home.

Finally, Bardwick and Douvan point out that the increasing emphasis on female careers has led many women to value the "masculine" characteristics associated with worldly success and to look down on the traditional female role of wife and mother. This puts women in an impossible bind: they value the male work role and the masculine characteristics that go with it, but they do not have these characteristics themselves. Bardwick and Douvan describe the female dilemma this way:

> For the girl overt freedoms, combined with cultural ambiguity, result in an unclear image of femininity. As a result of vagueness about how to become feminine or even what is feminine, the girl responds to the single clear directive—she withdraws from what is clearly masculine. In high school and increasingly in college, girls cease clearly masculine pursuits and perceive the establishment of interpersonal goals as the most salient route to identity. This results in a maximization of interpersonal skills, an interpersonal view of the world, a withdrawal from the development of independence, activity, ability, and competition, and the absence of a professional work commitment. . . .
>
> Thus, the essence of the problem of role conflict lies in the fact that up until now very few women have succeeded in traditionally masculine roles, not only because of disparagement and prejudice, but largely because women have not been fundamentally equipped and determined to succeed. Some women's tragedy is their desire to succeed in competitive achievement and their contempt for the traditional role for which they are better equipped. (1971, pp. 152, 153)

Is this rather pessimistic point of view substantiated by research on women's actual attitudes and life experiences? Yes and no. The first question is whether women do have only feminine characteristics that make them ill-equipped for the workplace. Certainly women do receive "feminine" scores on personality measures that use a single dimension for each item. These bipolar scales ask people to rate how competitive they are, for instance, and a high score indicates masculinity while a low score indicates femininity. On such measures women rate themselves as less competitive, aggressive, and dominant than men rate themselves, but this is a relative difference. It does not mean that women are not at all competitive, aggressive, or dominant. One does not have to be the most aggressive person around to succeed at work; a modicum of aggression or self-assertion is probably enough.

In the past five years the paper-and-pencil measures of individual characteristics have found only one-third of college women rating themselves as highest on feminine characteristics, as I already noted (Bem 1977). These measures treat femininity and masculinity as separate dimensions; an individual can measure high on both. Thus, one may be both very aggressive and very gentle, very competitive and very warm. The change in self-ratings may be due partially to this shift in research methodology, but also perhaps to shifts in social attitudes. Thus, sex-role stereotypes may be less compelling today, allowing more women to think of themselves as at least somewhat aggressive, competitive, and dominant at the same time as they think of themselves as warm, gentle, and nurturant.

Even self-report measures that do not treat femininity and masculinity as opposites are still slanted by what people think they *should* say or do. Women may thus perceive and describe themselves as low in aggression because they think they should be, regardless of how aggressively they act in daily life. In other words, we may be measuring women's sex-role stereotypes as much as their actual characteristics and behavior. These rating scales *are*, however, related to everyday behavior. As we will see in the chapter on mental health, women who rate themselves as much higher on feminine characteristics seem to avoid masculine behavior in everyday situations (Bem 1976). In fact, they seem hesitant to engage in *any* behavior until they are sure exactly what is expected of them. This tendency to "play it safe" supports Bardwick and Douvan's contention that many women avoid masculine behavior when they are unsure about what constitutes feminine behavior.

Here again, there are unanswered questions. What causes this avoidance—internal emotional distress about femininity or fear of external social reactions to acting unfeminine? This controversial question is still unsettled, as we will see in the chapter on achievement motivation and fear of success in women.

Then there are the women who value masculine characteristics and look down on traditional female activities, as was possibly the case with women trying to pursue careers in the 1950s and 1960s. Such an attitude is hardly surprising, given our culture's general valuing of anything male—even to the point of exalting male anatomy as the basic human form. Does valuing masculine characteristics automatically imply devaluing feminine ones? Only if you see the two as incompatible opposites—as apparently not everyone today does. As we have seen, at least some college men value feminine and masculine qualities equally, while at the same school women value feminine qualities more than masculine ones (Clifton et al. 1976). Times are indeed changing, and with them the view of sex-role characteristics. As more women are seen to manage a career, with or without a family, the idea that femininity and work-related masculinity are incompatible may begin to change also.

Bardwick and Douvan did not simply dream up the idea that femininity and masculinity are opposites. This idea is based on Freudian theory, as one can tell by reading their article carefully. Their basic argument is that masculinity has to be earned, whereas femininity is simply assumed in childhood. According to them, boys experience more parental punishment because they are more likely to masturbate, to be aggressive, and to act impulsively than are girls. These male tendencies are based on the fact that the girl's "sexuality is neither so genital nor so imperative" as the boy's (1971, p. 149). Parental punishment forces the boy to stop relying on his parents and other adults for praise and a feeling that he is worthwhile, so that he must turn inward, developing an independent sense of self-worth and valuing himself in terms of worldly achievements. The girl, on the other hand, is punished less because she masturbates and acts aggressive less often. Consequently, she continues to depend on parents and others for her sense of self, which "results in a significant delay in the girl's search for identity, development of autonomy, and development of internal criteria for self-esteem" (1971, p. 149).

The crux of the matter is female versus male sexuality. To support their view that males are more urgently and genitally sexed, Bardwick and Douvan cite Helene Deutsch. Deutsch, as I noted in the previous chapter, is a traditional psychoanalyst who maintains that female reproductive anatomy inevitably makes women passive, masochistic, and weak. Using the questionable distinction between vaginal and clitoral orgasms, Deutsch comes to the conclusion that "femininity is largely associated with passivity and masochism" (1944, p. 220). Bardwick and Douvan's argument starts with this Freudian idea that sexuality and aggression are male prerogatives and goes on to say that these two male behavior patterns cause punishment, which leads to the development of independence and achievement. Boys earn their masculinity by achieving, whereas girls are simply assumed to be feminine.

But not for long. When the girl begins to menstruate, she moves into a new phase. Now "femininity also becomes an attribute that has to be earned—this task is made crucially difficult because of the girl's ambivalent feelings toward her body" (Bardwick and Douvan 1971, p. 150). And why is the girl ambivalent about her body? Because of the "blood and pain" of menstruation, the "expectation of body distortion in pregnancy," the "threat of the trauma of birth," and the (alleged) emotional cycles accompanying menstruation that "alter the perception of

her body as secure or stable" (1971, p. 150). From the tone of their discussion Bardwick and Douvan seem to view the female reproductive capacity as a liability rather than as a gift or an advantage—a view
apparently related to the Freudian suggestion that females are more
worried about the normalcy of their own reproductive capacity than are
males, because the vagina is internal and unobservable, contributing to
"the peculiar inner uncertainty so often met with in women" (Horney
1926, p. 335).

Bardwick and Douvan also emphasize the social pressures girls face
in adolescence:

> From the very beginning of adolescence girls, as potential heterosexual
> partners, begin to be punished for conspicuous competing achievement
> and to be rewarded for heterosexual success. Socialization in adolescence
> emphasizes the use of the cosmetic exterior of the self to lure men, to
> secure affection, to succeed in the competition of dating. At the same time
> the girl is warned not to succeed too much: conspicuous success in com-
> petitive dating threatens her friendships with girls. She learns in puberty
> that she is likely to be punished for significant competition in either of her
> important spheres. (1971, p. 150)

Thus, having begun with a rather Freudian conception of male and female natures based on differences in sexual anatomy, Bardwick and
Douvan go on to examine how social pressures exaggerate these initial
sex differences. Other researchers have continued this exploration of
social factors, but without the emphasis on biology and the underlying
assumptions about sexual anatomy.

THE CURRENT VIEW: FLEXIBILITY AND FRUSTRATION

In the past five or ten years social scientists have continued to examine the social fabric of women's lives and have come to view it as ever
more crucial. They no longer assume that women start out with an
innate biological tendency to be warm, nurturant, and submissive. In
fact, these so-called feminine characteristics seem to be created by the
world in which we live. Thus, sex-role stereotypes are no longer considered to be a true reflection of biologically based reality, but rather as
oversimplified conceptions developed from social attitudes and personal
experiences. Since sex-role stereotypes are based on social learning rather
than on innate biological sex differences, they tend to change along with
the social environment that shapes them.

As sex-role stereotypes have become a subject of research in and of
themselves, we have begun to discover that they are not as simple as we
thought. The stereotype of the housewife is apparently only one view of
women, for instance, as I noted. Nor are masculinity and femininity
necessarily opposites; women appear to have many masculine qualities.

Having noticed this, the researchers have shifted their focus in examining the personal dilemmas of working women. Many women do not seem to be struggling to *attain* masculine qualities they lack, as Bardwick and Douvan imply. Instead, women are struggling for personal and social *acceptance* of those masculine qualities they already have. In this struggle sex-role stereotypes often function as part of a broader system of social control: they are part of a "nonconscious ideology" that constrains women by fostering anxiety about the consequences of being unfeminine (Bem and Bem 1976, p. 181).

Not only has attention to social factors increased, but the nature of those social factors has shifted somewhat. Rather than focus on the interaction between feminine personality and masculine career demands, recent research has broadened to consider the practical problems encountered by women today. For in spite of the general encouragement for (or tolerance of) women working outside the home, there are few institutional supports for this role change. Even if she has the ideal personality for a given job, a working mother still has difficulty arranging for child care, food preparation, laundry, and other homemaking tasks. Nor are childless women spared; they still encounter sex-role related pressures on the job. And these sex-role pressures are not limited to job situations. They influence many different areas of women's lives—how they cope with different living situations, how they deal with personal relationships, even how they view their own bodies, and what kind of treatment they receive for emotional distress. In fact, there is probably no aspect of women's lives that is not profoundly affected by society's (and by women's own) view of what women "should" be like.

The increasing concern with social factors has been accompanied by a shift in theoretical perspective. Most of the people doing research on the psychology of women today subscribe to the social learning theory of personality development. Outside psychoanalytic circles there is little discussion or support for the Freudian perspective, with its insistence on sexual anatomy as the key to differing personality patterns in women and men. Although the relationship between our minds and our bodies continues to be examined in some detail, biology is used less often as a justification for differences between the sexes. This does not mean that sexual urges, emotions, and thoughts are ignored—quite the contrary—but they are examined within the social fabric of our daily existence.

There is also a new tone to recent research. Changes in the female role tend to be viewed as an opportunity for flexibility and growth—not as a cause of confusion, emotional distress, and immobility. This more optimistic tone is related to the shift in theoretical perspective. Since Freudians view sexual anatomy as the basis for sex roles, changes in those roles are inevitably viewed as at least somewhat incompatible with female biology. If one dares to contradict biology, stress and confusion are inevitable. But when sex roles are viewed as socially derived, there is no reason for this incompatibility and resulting pessimism. In fact, this pessimism itself is sometimes viewed as a reflection of sexual bias and stereotyping; it subtly supports the status quo. Not that recent research ignores the stress involved in social change; but the emphasis is on the positive aspects of this change and the debilitating effects of the more restrictive female role.

Chapter 8

Marriage and

Motherhood

ALMOST ALL American women marry. In spite of the controversy
about changes in the female role since World War II, some 94 percent
of women in the United States marry at an average age of twenty years.
Although as many as one in three marriages may end in divorce, three-
quarters of divorcees remarry; their unmarried status is only temporary.
And most women combine marriage with its traditional complement,
motherhood. Although the size of most families is smaller today
(averaging 1.9 children in 1974), 83 percent of women are mothers.

So what has changed? Primarily the *way* in which women carry out
the traditional role. Instead of devoting all their time to homemaking
and mothering, many women now work at paid jobs outside the home.
Many writers point to the increasing number of women in the paid
workforce in the past fifty years. The increase is due to the rising cost of
living, higher rates of education for both sexes, the longer expected life
span, and smaller family size. These factors supposedly combine with
modern technology (washing machines, dishwashers, and the like) to
leave most mothers with more free time while raising children and many
more years of active life after their children leave home.

The working wife and mother is really new, however, only in
wealthier families. Poor women have always held paying jobs outside the

home. They have worked at jobs with low pay, low status, and low visibility. Most have worked in areas that are viewed as extensions of the traditional female role—waitressing, housecleaning, and (for those with more formal education) schoolteaching and nursing. While they worked, they continued to take care of their children and husbands. For them the homemaker role was still central; new activities were simply added to it. Many worked a few hours each day or off and on during the year. Because this employment was part time and seen as peripheral to their central role as wives and mothers, it was sometimes overlooked in the census reports, which are the major source of information on employment rates.

Psychologists have always focused on the problems of white, middle-class people like themselves. During the past thirty years an increasing number of middle-class women have begun to work outside the home and to view employment as an important area of their lives. The Women's Movement has focused attention on the problems facing employed women—lack of day care and other institutions that would make it easier to combine work and family responsibilities; discrimination in hiring, salaries, and promotion; and sexual harassment on the job. Psychologists like Bardwick and Douvan first responded by examining the personality characteristics they saw as necessary for homemaking and careers. Then researchers began to examine the social role conflicts of professional women with families. And now they have begun to consider the daily problems—both emotional and purely organizational—facing women who have families and who work at nonglamorous jobs. The new research has required a reexamination of the advantages and disadvantages of the traditional female role of wife/mother and homemaker that earlier writers had blithely assumed to be natural and idyllic. I shall examine this traditional role first and then consider how it has been modified by new work and living patterns.

The Joys and Frustrations
of Traditional Marriage

When I hear talk about the "modern nuclear family," I always picture something vaguely resembling the "Ozzie and Harriet" television show—two devoted parents living harmoniously with their children, usually one boy and one girl. They live in a friendly neighborhood where mothers drop in for coffee and families have weekend cookouts. There is a network of aunt, uncles, grandparents, and cousins who gather on holidays and visit regularly in between. After a hearty breakfast Dad goes to work while Mom sends the kids off to school. Mom then cleans and shops, has some time to visit with friends, and is ready with after-school milk and cookies. Supper is a time for everyone to catch up on the day's news, while the evening is taken up with the children's projects and a later time for the parents to be alone.

Does everyone live like this? Of course not. Some families have only one parent; others have older relatives or intimate family friends in their homes. There are many brother and sisters, or none. Mothers often work, and fathers are sometimes unemployed. The preceding scenario is essentially a middle-class fantasy (in which, if we are honest, the characters are usually white). There are many other images of the family, but they all have a common theme: a close-knit group of adults and children bound together by emotional, economic, and family ties. The intense nature of their involvement seems most important, as reflected in the saying, "Blood is thicker than water."

Such a family unit develops intense feelings and attachments that have the aura of permanence: the external world may be changing drastically, but family loyalty, pride, and love continue. This idea of the family also provides a sense of commitment in a changing world, a safe haven where children can be cherished and encouraged to develop as individuals. Each family member is viewed as unique, existing within a small microcosm of society (Cox 1968).

And what is life like for the woman who is wife, mother, and homemaker? She has the joy of watching her children grow, of making a warm home for her family, of feeling loved and supported by her companion/husband. She is challenged by the daily crises and the never-ending attempt to create an orderly, attractive environment with limited money, and finds satisfaction in soothing hurt feelings and frayed tempers. This nurturant task is absorbing and takes vast amounts of energy, enthusiasm, and imagination.

There is a negative side to this picture. The intensity that fosters love also fosters hatred. Family interactions are often hostile; the household chores exhausting. When the television image fades, the wife/mother often finds herself working long hours at thankless tasks. She is isolated; the family has moved often as her husband changed jobs, and she no longer has her mother, sister, or old friends to share news, advice, and feelings. She is unappreciated; no one seems to know what "good" housekeeping or mothering is, or to realize how hard she works. She feels caught up in an endless round of "stroking"—Jesse Bernard's (1972) word for attending to the emotional needs of others. As she becomes more lonely and bored, she may want to take some courses or a part-time job, but she feels hemmed in because there is no one to take on some of the household responsibilities while she is gone. She may feel like screaming, "Take care of *me* for a change! I have needs, too."

Judy Syfers (1971) expressed some of these feelings in her article "Why I Want a Wife":

> I belong to that classification of people known as wives. I am A Wife. And, not altogether incidentally, I am a mother.
>
> Not too long ago a male friend of mine appeared on the scene from the Midwest fresh from a recent divorce. He had one child, who is, of course, with his ex-wife. He is obviously looking for another wife. As I thought about him while I was ironing one evening, it suddenly occurred to me that I, too, would like to have a wife. Why do I want a wife?
>
> I would like to go back to school so that I can become economically independent, support myself, and, if need be, support those dependent upon me. I want a wife who will work and send me to school. And while I am going to school I want a wife to take care of my children. I want a wife to keep track of the children's doctor and dentist appointments. And to keep track of mine, too. I want a wife to make sure my children eat properly and are kept clean. I want a wife who will wash the children's clothes and keep them mended. I want a wife who is a good nurturant attendant to my children, arranges for their schooling, makes sure that they have an adequate social life with their peers, takes them to the park, the zoo, etc. I want a wife who takes care of the children when they are sick, a wife who arranges to be around when the children need special care, because, of course, I cannot miss classes at school. My wife must arrange to lose time at work and not lose the job. It may mean a small cut in my wife's income from time to time, but I guess I can tolerate that. Needless to say, my wife will arrange and pay for the care of the children while my wife is working.
>
> I want a wife who will take care of *my* physical needs. I want a wife who will keep my house clean. A wife who will pick up after my children, a wife who will pick up after me. I want a wife who will keep my clothes clean, ironed, mended, replaced when need be, and who will see to it that my personal things are kept in their proper place so that I can find what I need the minute I need it. I want a wife who cooks the meals, a wife who is a *good* cook. I want a wife who will plan the menus, do the necessary grocery shopping, prepare the meals, serve them pleasantly, and then do the cleaning up while I do my studying. I want a wife who will care for me when I am sick and sympathize with my pain and loss of time from school. . . .
>
> I want a wife who will take care of the details of my social life. When my wife and I are invited out by friends, I want a wife who will take care of the babysitting arrangements. When I meet people at school that I like and want to entertain, I want a wife who will have the house clean, will prepare a special meal, serve it to me and my friends, and not interrupt when I talk about the things that interest me and my friends. I want a wife who will have arranged that the children are fed and ready for bed before my guests arrive so that the children do not bother us. . . . And I want a wife who knows that sometimes I need a night out by myself.
>
> I want a wife who is sensitive to my sexual needs, a wife who makes love passionately and eagerly when I feel like it, a wife who makes sure that I am satisfied. And, of course, I want a wife who will not demand

sexual attention when I am not in the mood for it. I want a wife who assumes the complete responsibility for birth control, because I do not want more children. I want a wife who will remain sexually faithful to me so that I do not have to clutter up my intellectual life with jealousies. And I want a wife who understands that *my* sexual needs may entail more than strict adherence to monogamy. I must, after all, be able to relate to people as fully as possible. . . .

When I am through with school and have acquired a job, I want my wife to quit working and remain at home so that my wife can more fully and completely take care of a wife's duties.

My God, who *wouldn't* want a wife? (Syfers 1971, pp. 13–14)

Many unhappy housewives found they were not alone when Betty Friedan wrote about "the problem that has no name" in *The Feminine Mystique* (1963). Over the past fifteen years social scientists have begun to ask what it is about marriage that makes so many women unhappy. Rather than assume that marriage is ideal for all, that only a few "maladjusted" women do not find it idyllic, these scientists have begun to examine some of the disadvantages of the traditional female role.

Many sociologists agree with Jesse Bernard that marriage is most difficult for women whose sole activity and identity is being a wife and mother. They suggest that these women develop the "housewife syndrome," a vague malaise associated with loneliness and boredom. But not all full-time housewives have this problem; there are many happy ones. What makes some housewives flourish while others suffer?

Myra Ferree (1976) addressed this question by interviewing 135 working-class women in the Boston area. One-half of them worked outside the home in nonglamorous jobs—as waitresses, clerks in supermarkets and department stores, typists, beauticians, and the like. The wives with jobs generally felt happier and more satisfied than full-time housewives did. While both groups of women claimed to be poor homemakers (75 percent of full-time housewives, 67 percent of working housewives), none of the working wives said she felt incompetent at her paying job, and over half said they were "extremely good" at it. Ferree concluded that a regular paycheck and contact with customers probably bolsters self-esteem and provides a sense of accomplishment in paid employment, whereas there is little recognition and no clear criterion for performing homemaking well.

But some of the full-time housewives did report feeling happy and competent. Ferree found that these women saw family and friends regularly and had husbands and relatives who encouraged them and respected their homemaking responsibilities. These women were not socially isolated as some women had been before working outside the home. Previously isolated working wives talked of "going crazy staying home, not seeing anyone but four walls all day," and said that being a full-time homemaker "is like being in jail."

Ferree's study suggests that unhappiness is caused not by homemaking per se but by its context. If she has a warm, supporting social network in which her work is respected, the full-time homemaker is likely to feel valued, competent, and content. If she lacks such a network (and perhaps if she herself has doubts about the value of homemaking), she is likely to feel lonely, bored, and incompetent. Paid employment then offers another source of self-esteem and important social contacts, which can counteract loneliness and boredom. The nature of the paid employment is not necessarily crucial; Ferree's working housewives held very ordinary jobs. Social contacts and definite criteria for success seem to make the difference, not the glamor or status of the job.

The Working Wife and Mother

Women work out of financial necessity, to relieve the loneliness and boredom of the "housewife syndrome," or because they enjoy their jobs. Whatever their personal reasons, one-half of American women now work outside the home, including 44 percent of those who are married and 46 percent of those with children (Herman 1979; U.S. Bureau of the Census 1976). How does a wife's employment affect her daily living situation, her children, her relationship with her husband, her feelings about herself? As researchers have turned their attention to these questions, a complicated pattern of answers has begun to emerge. There are two central themes: the difficulty of fitting all one's activities into a twenty-four-hour day, and the crucial importance of the husband's attitude. Although most studies have concentrated on middle-class women with careers that require extensive years of training, intense emotional involvement, and long work hours, the findings also seem to apply to women who work shorter hours at lower-paying, less glamorous, and less demanding jobs.

WHOSE HOUSEWORK IS IT?

Sociologists disagree on exactly how much time women spend doing housework and taking care of children. Estimates range from fifty-three hours per week for full-time housewives to twenty-six or thirty-six hours per week for employed women with children (Robinson et al. 1977; Vanek 1974). Sociologists agree on one thing: housework is for women only. Regardless of how busy his wife may be with a paid job, the husband rarely takes on any of the household chores. In fact, Robinson and his colleagues (1977) found that husbands with working wives had *more* free time for leisure activities than did husbands with nonworking wives.

Most surprising, however, was the fact that over three-quarters of the married women in their nationwide samples said no when asked, "Do you wish your husband would give you more help with the household chores?" And there were remarkably few differences between working wives and nonworking wives. While almost one-third of the employed wives indicated a desire for more help, so did almost one-quarter of the nonworking wives.

Yet married women who worked outside the home also seemed to feel rushed, with so much to do that they had little time to themselves. They completed their housework in half the time taken by women not in the labor force—a feat that brings to mind a frazzled woman running from stove to table with a child in one hand and an iron in the other while the husband sits reading the paper. Why not ask him to help out? Perhaps the woman feels that since housework and child care are central to the female role, to share them would be unfeminine. She may be afraid that she has compromised her femininity in some way by being employed, and wants to reassert it by doing "womanly" chores. Or maybe she wants to maintain control over how and when activities are done in the home. Whatever women's motivations, there is some indication that they give husbands hidden messages to stay within certain role boundaries—to stay off their feminine turf (Poloma and Garland 1971).

Of course, many women *do* want their husbands to share responsibility for housework, but this desire is seldom realized easily. Even when a couple has agreed to divide the housework, the man may resist in innumerable ways. He may ignore the dirt and chaos, waiting for the woman to give up and do it herself. He may argue that she doesn't mind doing it as much as he minds. Or he may simply act so inept that she becomes exasperated and does the job for him. Pat Mainardi illustrates some of these male strategies in her humorous account of "The Politics of Housework":

> It seemed perfectly reasonable. We both had careers, both had to work a couple of days a week to earn enough to live on, so why shouldn't we share the housework? So I suggested it to my mate and he agreed—most men are too hip to turn you down flat. You're right, he said. It's only fair.
>
> Then an interesting thing happened. I can only explain it by stating that we women have been brainwashed more than even we can imagine. Probably too many years of seeing television women in ecstasy over their shiny waxed floors or breaking down over their dirty shirt collars. Men have no such conditioning. They recognize the essential fact of housework right from the very beginning. Which is that it stinks.
>
> Here's my list of dirty chores: buying groceries, carting them home and putting them away; cooking meals and washing dishes and pots; doing the laundry, digging out the place when things get out of control; washing floors. The list could go on but the sheer necessities are bad

enough. All of us have to do these things, or get someone else to do them for us. The longer my husband contemplated these chores, the more repulsed he became, and so proceeded the change from the normally sweet considerate Dr. Jekyll into the crafty Mr. Hyde who would stop at nothing to avoid the horrors of—housework. As he felt himself backed into a corner laden with dirty dishes, brooms, mops and reeking garbage, his front teeth grew longer and pointier, his fingernails haggled and his eyes grew wild. Housework trivial? Not on your life! Just try to share the burden.

So ensued a dialogue that's been going on for several years. Here are some of the high points. . . .

\# "I don't mind sharing the work, but you'll have to show me how to do it." MEANING: I ask a lot of questions and you'll have to show me everything every time I do it because I don't remember so good. Also don't try to sit down and read while I'M doing my jobs because I'm going to annoy hell out of you until it's easier to do them yourself. . . .

\# "We have different standards, and why should I have to work to your standards? That's unfair." MEANING: If I begin to get bugged by the dirt and crap I will say, "This place sure is a sty" or "How can anyone live like this?" and wait for your reaction. I know that all women have a sore called "Guilt over a messy house" or "Household work is ultimately my responsibility." I know that men have caused that sore—if anyone visits and the place *is* a sty, they're not going to leave and say, "He sure is a lousy housekeeper." You'll take the rap in any case. I can outwait you. ALSO MEANING: I can provoke innumerable scenes over the housework issue. Eventually doing all the housework yourself will be less painful to you than trying to get me to do half. Or I'll suggest we get a maid. She will do my share of the work. You will do yours. It's women's work.

\# "I hate it more than you. You don't mind it so much." MEANING: Housework is garbage work. It's the worst crap I've ever done. It's degrading and humiliating for someone of *my* intelligence to do it. But for someone of *your* intelligence. . . .

\# "Housework is too trivial to even talk about." MEANING: It's even more trivial to do. Housework is beneath my status. My purpose in life is to deal with matters of significance. Yours is to deal with matters of insignificance. You should do the housework.

\# "This problem of housework is not a man-woman problem. In any relationship between two people one is going to have a stronger personality and dominate." MEANING: That stronger personality had better be *me*. . . . (Mainardi 1970, pp. 28–29)

Why do men object so strongly to doing their share of the housework? Simply because it is dull? Because it is unmanly? Or because they really feel clumsy and incompetent performing tasks for which they have not been trained? It is probably a combination of these reasons. Certainly men are under some pressure to reassert their masculinity, since having a working wife can still invite caustic attacks from other men. The assumption seems to be that such a husband is hardly a man (especially if his wife is successful in her career), as reflected in comments like "How do you take not being in charge?" usually accompanied by a smirk (Nadelson and Eisenberg 1977, p. 1073).

THE OVERWORKED PARENT

In spite of current discussions about the importance of fathers to bringing up children, most parents still see women as primarily responsible for child rearing, as Kellerman and Katz (1978) recently demonstrated. They asked thirty-one middle-class parents to indicate the percentage of responsibility mothers and fathers should ideally have for various activities in the home. The eighty-nine items covered five areas: educational guidance, physical caretaking, emotional support, discipline-administrative, and active-recreational. Mothers were seen as primarily responsible for forty-seven of the items, and fathers for eight, while the responsibility for thirty-four was seen as shared. Both women and men agreed that fathers should be primarily responsible for only three things: developing a child's skill in sports, in self-defense, and in mechanical tasks.

Of course, female responsibility for child rearing is nothing new. But the popular conception of the child's nature has changed over the past fifty years from a "bundle of impulses" simply needing control to a "reservoir of rich potential" needing encouragement, tutoring, and intellectual challenges (Johnson and Johnson 1977, p. 392). The middle-class mother who reads Dr. Spock often feels that it is up to her to provide a stimulating, emotionally supporting, yet disciplined environment, so that her child will grow up to be happy, well adjusted, and famous. In order to do this, many women feel that they ought to devote all their time and energies to child rearing. And the mother is blamed if anything goes wrong—if the child is unsuccessful at school, fails on the job, or has emotional problems (Johnson and Johnson 1977; Kellerman and Katz 1978).

Working mothers are subject to the same feelings of guilt and blame as are all other mothers. In fact, they may be especially vulnerable to such feelings because of the prevalent attitude that maternal employment means maternal neglect. In spite of extensive research showing that maternal employment is not necessarily harmful to children and may even have positive effects in many instances (Hoffman 1974a), many people continue to worry about it. So, in addition to a hectic schedule, the working mother has to contend with nagging doubts about her children. When she feels overwhelmed by her many different obligations, her concern is likely to focus on child rearing problems and to be expressed as "being drained," "emotionally leeched," "overwhelmed," and "guilty" (Johnson and Johnson 1977, p. 393).

Of course not all working mothers feel guilty about their children.

Many feel that "it's the quality of the time spent with children that counts—not the quantity"—in other words, that they invest more and hence have more meaningful interactions during the time they do spend with their children (Johnson and Johnson 1977). Other mothers point out that because they can pour some of their energies into work, they do not fall into the trap of being smothering mothers (Poloma 1972). And some feel that they are providing a more active, assertive, and well-rounded model for their daughters. Altman and Grossman (1977) tested the last assertion by studying fifty-one college women who were seniors in a large urban university. Half of the women had mothers who had at least a high school diploma and had never been employed since the students' birth (noncareer group), while half had mothers who had at least a college degreee and had worked at a career while the daughter was in school—in jobs ranging from the secretarial/clerical to the professional (career group). Altman and Grossman found that the career-mother group were more oriented to having a career: they planned to work when their children were at home, and saw a full-time career as important regardless of economic need. The noncareer-mother group also thought a career was important, but to a much lesser extent: only three of twenty-six planned to devote as much or more time to a career than to a family, they were not as ambitious as the working-mother group, and they were confused about how to combine a family with a career. The authors conclude that "possibly working mothers, and not homemaking women, give their daughters the ability to imagine a comfortable accomodation between the demands of family and career" (Altman and Grossman 1977, p. 373).

MANAGING CAREER AND FAMILY

Working wives and mothers have the same twenty-four day everyone else has. How do they manage to juggle all their responsibilities to meet the sometimes conflicting demands of employment, housework, and family life? They probably use some of the following coping strategies, which focus on reconciling job and child-rearing pressures. Pressures from the marital relationship do not seem to be as much of a problem.

1. "My family comes first." The wife assigns a clear priority to the family in case of conflicting demands. If family crises and job crises occur simultaneously, the family takes precedence. When a child is sick, for instance, the mother misses work (not the father).

2. "I can settle for less success." The wife limits career ambitions and commitment to fit into the family situation: the age and number of children, the husband's job schedule, his ability (or willingness) to help with family responsibilities. This compromise may take the form of "role cycling"—temporarily lowering career involvement so that more time can be devoted to the family, and raising career involvement again when

the family situation becomes less demanding. While the children are young, for instance, the wife may work part time or take a less desirable job closer to home.

3. "Keep job and family separate." The wife may avoid bringing work home or talking about work in front of the children, in order to concentrate on her nururant and emotional role and to avoid overt competition with her husband's career.

4. "I make every moment count." The wife plans family outings and educational experiences that enrich the children's environment. Structured activities such as camping trips, bedtime stories, movies, and dinners out provide an opportunity for intense family interaction. Mothers of school-age children may also go to great lengths to participate in their children's school activities, feeling that their children should have the same family support as other children with nonworking mothers.

5. "Working mothers are better." The wife focuses on the advantages of maternal employment, such as being a nonsmothering mother and providing an assertive female role model for her children. These self-reassurances and justifications are not unique to working women, of course; everyone emphasizes the advantages of his or her own life style.

6. "Let's stick together." Couples in which the wife has a career sometimes choose friends from other two-career families and have minimal contact with relatives (especially grandparents) who may not approve of their life style. Johnson and Johnson (1977) point out that while this avoids the pressure of competing values, it also isolates the family and robs them of the emotional support traditionally provided by the kinship system.

These coping strategies are used by women who have chosen, and have the opportunity, to engage in careers that demand more time and emotional investment than a nine-to-five job. The strategies were identified in interview studies with eighty-one couples in which the wife worked in law, medicine, or college teaching (Johnson and Johnson 1977; Poloma 1972) or else in nursing, school teaching, or business administration (Johnson and Johnson 1977). Although these high-commitment and high-status careers may provide more financial and emotional rewards than other forms of employment provide, they also create more intense conflict between work and family roles than that experienced by the average female worker (Rapoport and Rapoport 1972).

Unfortunately we do not know whether most working women use the same coping strategies as these career women do, because most researchers have ignored the daily frustrations and coping mechanisms of the vast majority of working women. Certainly the idea of "role strain" may seem absurd to many women whose primary interest is their families; work is simply an added activity that they fit in as their family responsibilities permit. Yet every working woman has the problem of limited time, and many of these strategies are aimed at that difficulty. Thus, the woman with a nonglamorous nine-to-five job probably has to "settle for less" also, but the "less" is likely to be in work conditions and pay rather than in career advancement and training. The woman may also "make every moment count" by planning family activities that enhance emotional closeness and support. And she is likely to reduce or avoid conflict by saying that "my family comes first"—perhaps even more than does a career woman, who places more emphasis on employment and hence may use this strategy only in crises rather than in day-to-day living. On the other hand, most working-class women probably seek out rather than avoid contact with relatives; these are the people who often provide child care and other assistance essential to the working mother. Professional women can more easily afford to pay for help with housework and child care, while the low wages of most working women preclude this option.

BETWEEN WIVES AND HUSBANDS

How does a woman's employment affect her relationship with her husband? Although it does not seem to increase the husband's involvement in housework or child care, it often changes the couple's interaction. Many researchers have looked at this in terms of power—the ability to make important decisions that influence or control the behavior of others. In marriage such decisions include where the family will live, what job the spouse will take, where the family will spend vacations, what kind of car or major appliances will be bought, and how the children will be raised—will they be sent to public or private school; participate in sports and local scout troops; be sent to secretarial school, trade school, or college or be encouraged to marry early and be full-time housewives? Since these decisions usually involve money, family finances are crucial. As the primary provider in most families, the husband usually exercises more power than the wife. When the wife begins to work at a paid job, his financial control is weakened, and with it his control over many family decisions. The wife often feels that she should have more to say in such decisions, now that her paycheck is being spent to carry them out.

Money is not the only basis for power, of course. In our culture tradition maintains that males have the right to make most important decisions. They are expected to be the "head of the family." This expectation is not eliminated by the wife's employment; for in spite of the fact that half of American women work at paid jobs, there are very few marriages in which the wife is as dominant as the husband, much less more dominant (Bernard 1972). But the wife's paycheck can create a shift in marital power, especially if her income is crucial to the family's support. Thus, working-class wives appear to gain more power through employment than do middle-class wives (Bahr 1974).

On the other hand, the wife's employment may also decrease her control over some areas of family life. If the husband does begin to participate in housework and child care, and if people outside the family are needed to provide child care while the wife is at work, the wife may lose some of her decision-making power in these areas.

Is it really the wife's employment that causes power shifts in the family? Or are other factors just as important? We cannot really tell, because most of the research compares families in which the wife works with families in which she does not work. The balance of power in the working-wife families may have been more egalitarian *before* the wife began to work; the attitudes and the interaction patterns may have made it possible for her to work in the first place.

This possibility is suggested by the finding that the more important power is to a professional man, the less likely his wife is to be involved in a demanding career. Winter, Stewart, and McClelland (1977) had fifty-one college freshmen write stories to bland and ambiguous pictures (TAT cards) in 1960, and scored these stories for themes related to power and affiliation. Ten years after the men's graduation (that is, in 1974), these researchers assessed the career involvement of the men's wives. The stronger the husband's need for power, the less involved his wife was in a career; the stronger his motivation to be sociable and cooperative, on the other hand, the more career-involved was his wife. Furthermore, the less power-oriented husbands of career wives tended to have pleasant, intrinsically interesting jobs and to value them for their enjoyability rather than for the money and authority they provided.

Obviously a man's investment in power influences his wife's employment, whether through his choice of a wife, through his wife's choice of a husband, or through his discouragement of his wife's career after marriage. If a man's motive to be powerful during his first year of college influences his wife's employment ten years later, we can assume that it also influences the balance of power in the family. The wife's employment may thus *reflect* the marital relationship as much as it *changes* that relationship.

The question of who has the power may be especially important in middle-class, dual-career families where the status and authority of a career may be just as important as the money. A husband often feels threatened by his wife's success, especially if her career is progressing faster than his. This threat may be decreased by the wife's later start: she usually delays her training or full-time employment until her husband is well established in his career and the children are in school. Thus, the husband is able to feel that he is encouraging a "junior professional" who needs his expert "guidance" (Nadelson and Eisenberg 1977, p. 1072).

But husbands are not the only ones who have difficulty with female power. Women themselves are sometimes uncomfortable with it. High-achieving women often want to marry someone who is smarter than themselves; it is all right for them to be aggressive and successful as long as their mate is just a little more so (Horner 1970c). In spite of the egalitarian philosophy shared by many students in graduate schools today, a few women in graduate programs may still harbor an unrecognized need to feel secure by choosing a man whom they subconsciously regard as "in some way superior—older, smarter, or more popular," according to psychiatrist Ellen Berman (quoted in Meyers 1976, pp. 37–38). The marriage may run smoothly initially, but after the wife has attained professional success, her problems at home may begin. Dr. Berman attributes this to female socialization, which presents femininity and careers as incompatible.

> "Men," the psychiatrist notes, "are groomed from childhood for positions of power in middle-class American society." Pursuit of high-commitment, independent work is practically synonymous with masculinity. For a woman, on the other hand, "femininity and a career have been antithetical during most of her growing up years," she says, and characteristically the "integration of her feminine self-image with her professional self" comes only after a woman becomes launched upon a career. "She now begins to see herself as more capable, masterful, and desirable." (Ellen Berman, quoted in Meyers 1976, p. 38)

Once a woman feels competent and successful in her profession, she may begin to see her husband as only an equal instead of the superior being she imagined him to be. The professional men around her then start to look strong and challenging by comparison, and her investment in the marriage weakens. The husband, moreover, may perceive his wife's success as a threat to his masculinity and as destructive to their life together. These problems are not necessarily common, but they do appear in the couples seen at the Marriage Council of the University of Pennsylvania where Dr. Berman works.

Power is only one aspect of the marital relationship. Many other feelings and needs determine the way wives and husbands relate to each other. When it comes to the issue of the wife's working outside the home, however, it seems to be the husband's feelings and needs that are crucial, for researchers keep finding that the husband's attitude and willingness to participate in housework and child care are strongly associated with whether his wife has a paying job. This finding is so consistent that Jesse Bernard has referred to it as the "law of husband cooperation" (1974, p. 162).

THE PROS AND CONS OF JOB AND MOTHERHOOD

Many social scientists agree with Tavris and Offir's view of women as caught in a "double-bind" or "catch-22" situation: If they choose to be full-time housewives, they are likely to come down with the "house-wife syndrome"; but if they choose to work outside the home, they are susceptible to the "working-wife syndrome" (Tavris and Offir 1977, pp. 225–26). How do women themselves see their situation? Do they perceive themselves as being beset by the loneliness and boredom of full-time homemaking, on the one hand, and by the hassles of not having enough time to do anything well on the other? Do they feel forced to choose between two unattractive alternatives?

Linda Beckman (1978) addressed this issue by asking a large number of women to talk about the advantages and the disadvantages of paid employment and parenting. The women ranged from twenty-eight to thirty-nine years old, worked full time, and lived with their husbands and children in Los Angeles County. Sixty-three were professionals (scientists, physicians, lawyers, university faculty members, nurses, and librarians), while sixty were nonprofessionals in a broad range of occu-pations (secretaries, clerks, food-service workers, saleswomen, beau-ticians, factory workers, and telephone operators). In both professional and nonprofessional groups there were equal numbers of women who had no children, of women who had a small family (one child), and of women who had a large family (three or more children).

The women in Beckman's study seemed to perceive work and child rearing much as social scientists would expect them to. Interpersonal relationships were crucial for them, the single most gratifying aspect of both parenting and paid employment, although a job also offered other important benefits in terms of money, self-esteem, and inde-pendence. The central theme of the costs of both parenting and em-ployment was time: there was never enough, so that parenting and employment interfere with each other.

The pros and cons of parenting and employment looked different to women depending on the size of their family: women with larger fam-ilies placed more value on the companionship aspects of parenting and saw less of a conflict beween parenting and employment. Professionals and nonprofessionals also differed in their perception of both the areas and the amount of conflict. Professional women saw employment as interfering with parenthood, while nonprofessionals were more concerned about its interference with their housework. Professionals were more interested in the content of their work—its mental stimulation, challenge, and boost to their self-esteem—while nonprofessionals valued it for the money and social interaction it provided. And professionals tended to see work and child rearing as more conflicting than did nonprofessionals.

The differences between professionals and nonprofessionals are not too surprising. After all, if the content of work is boring (a more likely possibility with nonprofessional jobs), people will appreciate other things, such as the companionship and money a job provides. Since nonprofessional women earn less money, they may have to do their own housework, while the better-paid professionals can hire someone to ease the burden. And perhaps nonprofessionals are less likely to see themselves as "career women," and therefore experience less emotional conflict between their masculine work and their feminine parenting roles.

Beckman's findings regarding family size are more puzzling. Why did women with smaller families (no children or an only child) see work and homemaking as conflicting more than did women with large families (three or more children)? One would think that women with more children would have less time and hence perceive more conflict between the two roles.

Perhaps the answer lies in Beckman's sample. *All* the women worked full time. Perhaps the women with large families who perceive a lot of conflict do not work, so their views did not show up here. Or perhaps it it a matter of socioeconomic status and professional training. Professional women saw more conflict, and other studies have shown that professionals and wealthier women usually tend to have fewer children. Or women may choose to have fewer children because they see parenting as an emotionally demanding project of fostering creativity—these women would then see parenting as more time consuming even though they had smaller families.

If Beckman had interviewed women with medium-sized, two-child families, we would have more to go on, especially since this is the average size of American families today. Beckman herself suggests that choosing to work and choosing to have a small family seem to go together. Although this idea seems sensible, we really do not know how it works out in most women's lives.

The hectic schedules of working mothers may make some women wonder how a paying job would affect their health. Does paid employment improve health by providing more stimulation and variety, or does it cause more illness by inducing fatigue and strain? Welch and Booth (1977) examined this question by administering interviews and medical exams to about five hundred mothers in Toronto whose husbands held primarily blue-collar jobs. These researchers found that women employed full time were healthier than full-time housewives, regardless of whether the housewives had worked in the past. Surprisingly, they also found that marital instability was greatest for full-time housewives. And the health advantages of employment were greater for women with no preschool children and for those with poor marital relationships.

Welch and Booth conclude that working outside the home is good for one's health—whether one works full time or part time. On the other hand, they also note some indications that "wives in a period of transition—either by virtue of beginning full-time work or by having been employed in the recent past—are under more stress than other women" (1977, p. 391). Once a woman has made a choice and settled into a schedule, then, employment is not likely to harm her health—and may even improve it.

Paid employment does not necessarily, however, have the same beneficial effect on health and happiness at all ages. Alice Rossi (1965) has found that most bright, highly educated women in their twenties are very happy to marry and settle down as full-time housewives and mothers. They are usually excited about marriage and child rearing and feel happy and full of self-esteem. At this age women who choose careers, on the other hand, are still going through the rigors of professional training. They are full of self-doubt and anxiety, just like their male counterparts. Is this the right career for me, they wonder, and will I really be able to make it? Would I be happier if I left all this pressure and competition behind and just had babies?

Rossi predicts that the tables will turn ten or fifteen years later, though, when the full-time housewife's children are in school and her life is less full and rewarding. She will begin to envy the career woman, who is just hitting her stride, whose career is well established and has become a major source of satisfaction and self-esteem.

Judith Birnbaum (1975) confirmed Rossi's prediction of a shift in the middle adult years, by studying twenty-nine full-time homemakers who had graduated with honors from the University of Michigan fifteen to twenty-five years earlier and had not been employed since. She compared the homemakers with fifty-two career women who all had MDs or PhDs and were faculty members at Michigan—twenty-seven of them single and twenty-five married with children. All the women filled out a booklet containing autobiographical questions and wrote stories about projective cues designed to tap potential conflicts about marriage, maternity, work, and achievement.

Birnbaum found that, of all three groups, the homemakers had the lowest self-esteem and sense of personal competence. These bright, well-educated women felt generally inadequate—even at taking care of children and getting along with people. They also felt the least attractive, expressed the most concern about their self-identity, and felt the most lonely. When asked what was missing from their lives, the two groups of professional women usually talked about the familiar problem of time, while the housewives reported missing a sense of challenge and creative involvement.

Even more striking, however, was the different way homemakers and married professionals viewed marriage and child rearing. In response to the question "How does marriage change a woman's life?" 52 percent of the homemakers described marriage as restricting, demanding, and burdensome, while only 19 percent of the married career women described it so. The homemakers did not object to the limits imposed by marriage, however, but welcomed them as appropriate for a "real woman" who has learned the "art of giving herself to make someone else happy" (Birbaum 1975, p. 405). They valued the emotional and financial security provided by their traditional, successful husbands and felt that self-sacrifice and self-subordination were their proper contribution to the marriage. As one homemaker put it, "Marriage is not for the self-centered woman. It is a life of loving and giving in return for being wanted and needed and loved by her husband and later her children" (quoted in Birnbaum 1975, p. 405). Married professionals, on the other hand, saw marriage as based on having intellectual camaraderie and mutual understanding rather than on being protected and taken care of. They emphasized their husbands' achievements rather than abilities as providers and often went on to express a glowing admiration for these brilliant, sensitive men who encouraged their wives' careers.*

The theme of self-sacrifice was continued in the homemakers' responses to the question, "How does having children change a woman's life?" Most of these women had three or more children, received little help from their husbands, and spoke virtuously of the necessity for putting the children first. The married professionals, on the other hand, almost never mentioned self-sacrifice in discussing the impact of child rearing on their lives. Nor did the professionals mention the idea that children made them feel important and valuable—only homemakers did this.

Having a heavy investment in being good mothers, the homemakers feared most that their children would not turn out well. The working mothers, in contrast, were most worried about lack of time and about chaos in the home; having their work as a source of achievement and self-esteem, they did not tend to measure their own worth in terms of their children's accomplishments. Ironically, then, those women who devoted all their time to child rearing were most likely to be anxious about their own adequacy as mothers.

As for the unmarried career women, fifteen to twenty-five years after college they fared much the same as the career women who had married and had children. Their self-esteem and general emotional health were as good as those of married professionals, and they agreed with their

---

* Birnbaum suggests that the career woman's idea that her "husband is brilliant and superior and competitively out of her league" leaves her "free to do her very best only because she is convinced that her husband can do still better." The woman thus solves the dilemma of appreciating her husband's sensititivity and emotional support while worrying about "whether he is truly strong and masculine, or whether she is truly responsive and feminine" (1975, pp. 412–13). This suggestion is similar to Ellen Berman's idea that the lingering self-doubts created by conventional sex-role stereotypes cause some high-achieving career women to seek out (or create through fantasy) men who are superior to them in some way (Meyers 1976). Those career women who need to see their husbands as slightly superior are still expressing their own needs and achievement strivings, however, as compared with homemakers who justify the restrictions of marriage as part of the traditional norm of female self-sacrifice.

married counterparts in not seeing self-sacrifice as central to either marriage or child rearing. The major differences occurred in their view of careers. Although none of the married professionals felt that a career interferes with relationships with men or with having a family, 24 percent of the single professionals (and 54 percent of the married homemakers) felt that it does. And while most married women (75 percent) valued their jobs for the exciting content of the work, most unmarried women (57 percent) valued their jobs for the interpersonal relationships involved.

Birnbaum suggests that these differences stem from the fact that the unmarried professionals came from less affluent families with traditional attitudes. These women tended to feel that they had to make it on their own, and that to do this they had to choose between a family and a career. Having chosen a career, they looked to their jobs for many of the interpersonal gratifications that married professionals derived from their families.

In general, then, Birnbaum found that the typical single professional "finds herself busy, happy, and quite satisfied with life. Her self-esteem is high, she feels competent, productive and worthwhile . . . she feels lucky, pleased about the good place she has found for herself after all" (1975, pp. 417–18).*

Where does this leave the individual woman making her own life choices? Does she have to decide between job and family, or is a comfortable combination of the two possible? If she does choose full-time homemaking, will she fall victim to the "housewife syndrome"? If she chooses to pursue a career rather than marry, on the other hand, will she experience the wretched loneliness of the proverbial "old maid"?

The recent research on how women view their own lives suggests that none of these dire consequences are inevitable. Women seem to derive interpersonal satisfaction from either a family or a job and to feel challenged and creative both by watching their children grow and by exercising their talents in the workplace. Lack of time seems to be a problem for all women, whether they have families or not. And periods of transition between homemaking and employment are likely to be stressful. But it is possible to find satisfaction in a wide variety of life styles. Flexibility may be the key—both in raising one's children and in shaping one's personal life.

---

* Birnbaum's findings clearly show that a woman does not have to marry in order to be happy—especially if she has the high-status option of a professional career. I should note, however, that attitudes toward the woman's role have changed considerably in the past fifteen to twenty-five years. When the women in Birnbaum's study graduated from college in the 1950s, being a full-time housewife was "the thing to do." Thus while in their twenties the housewives probably received more social approval than did the career women; but by the time they reached their thirties and forties, the tables may have turned. These social factors probably influenced these women's feelings of self-satisfaction and competence and might account for the housewives' defensive emphasis on maternal self-sacrifice and martyrdom.

Chapter 9

Single Women—

Lives of Tragedy

or Bliss?

THE LITERATURE on women has focused on marriage and the difficulties of combining family responsibilities with paid employment. Yet Lucia Bequaert (1976) estimates that at any given point in time fully one-third of women over eighteen years old are single. Who are these single women, if about 94 percent of American women marry? Many of them are separated or divorced women between marriages—about 37 percent of first marriages end in divorce, while 59 percent of second marriages do also. Other single women are widowed. Husbands die when their wives are fifty-six years old, on the average, leaving the wives with some eighteen years of life on their own. And an increasing number of younger women are postponing marriage or choosing not to marry at all. At this time almost half the women eighteen to thirty years old have not married.

Being single does not necessarily mean having no men in one's life, for there are often fathers, brothers, sons, and lovers around. Nor is it likely to mean living alone, for many single women live with their children, other relatives, or friends. The one thing it does mean is living without a husband; beyond that there is considerable diversity in life styles (Bequaert 1976).

The traditional literature has concentrated on the negative aspects of being single. Starting with the assumption that the nuclear family is the norm for healthy adjustment, most studies have looked at the problems found in "broken homes," at the negative effects of father-absence, and at the emotional trauma of separation, divorce, and widowhood. Few studies have considered the possible advantages of being single or the growing number of adults who choose not to be married.

Bequaert (1976) set out to counteract this negative bias by attending conferences, workshops, and social gatherings for single women and by interviewing thirty women who had never married or who were separated, divorced, or widowed. She deliberately sought out women who were "copers," who were "building innovative and working lives for themselves out of the pressures and constraints of their own situations" (1976, p. xiv). Although she was careful to include women from working-class and minority backgrounds, who tend to be overlooked in the traditional literature, Bequaert's sample is small and makes no pretense of being representative of the general population. The personal accounts of these women shed considerable light on how women themselves experience being single, however, and hence contribute to our understanding of the various types of "singlehood."

Women Who Do Not Marry

Bequaert's never-married women were not the "old maids" of American folklore but saw marriage as only one of several options and decided against it. As one forty-six-year-old expressed it:

> I don't just define myself as never married. I define myself in terms of problems I'm coping with, goals I have, my relationships with other people. When I was young, I decided I did not want to get married. I made a conscious decision, which, I guess, is one of the big things that is different from a lot of other women my age who are not married. (Quoted in Bequaert 1976, p. 10)

These unmarried women did not experience conflicts between their work and family responsibilities and hence had no use for the coping mechanisms I discussed earlier. Their work was a major source of satisfaction and did not have to be sandwiched in between other responsibilities. Their lives were not without problems, however, many of which stemmed from public censure arising from the fear that the single life style makes women uppity and threatens family life. And although they seemed reluctant to admit it, these unmarried women were occasionally lonely. Yet loneliness was often valued for its growth-enhancing qualities, in that it forced them to get out and do something. And some women stressed the difference between being alone and feeling lonely, as did this black woman who lived by herself in a crowded inner city: "I like privacy. I like solitude because it gives me time to think and to write my poetry. I'm not afraid to be by myself. It's not that I don't like people—I just like to have a place to go where I can close the door" (quoted in Bequaert 1976, p. 14).

Other single women live with friends or relatives, and some have children. One woman told the interviewer how it feels to be an unwed mother:

> I'd like to explain how it feels to be single and have a child; the reason being, personally I think there's a uniqueness with that in the fact that I have my freedom. I'm very used to making decisions for myself, for a long time. I like that, especially being a black woman, I guess. We're constantly looking for a man who's stronger than we are, who can be stronger than we can, and that's very seldom and very rare. We'll wait until that comes or we'll just go through relationships that don't mean anything, or we'll marry somebody and get separated from that person, or we'll be living with somebody and really not making things work. And rather than go through that, I have my daughter. (Quoted in Bequaert 1976, p. 16)

Bequaert (1976) feels that the new morality is beginning to remove the stigma from being unmarried and having a child, and she maintains that the majority of unwed mothers are not the teenagers the media talk about, but rather women in their middle to late twenties who support themselves and their children through their own employment. Other writers, however, report that over 80 percent of the unmarried women having babies today are under twenty-five, and that a large proportion live on welfare (Rivlin 1979).

Some writers claim that there is a recent trend among women to choose not to marry but to have a child and raise it on her own. This trend has been receiving increased attention in the popular media (Marter 1979) and seems to be a middle-class phenomenon. Of course babies have always been conceived out of wedlock; the difference is that in the past a mother usually married her baby's father soon after its birth if she could; she did not deliberately choose to conceive, bear, and raise a child without a husband (Ihara and Warner 1979; Rivlin 1979; Wallace 1979).

Bequaert notes that the shift in public attitudes toward sexuality has been associated with an upsurge of advocacy programs and self-help groups for single mothers, a development that she attributes to the fact that these women no longer feel that they have to keep a low profile to avoid community disapproval and pressure. The increase in visibility raises an important point: since no extensive research has examined the trend to single motherhood, we cannot know whether the number of women choosing to become single parents has risen significantly, or whether unmarried mothers are simply becoming more open about their life style.

In some ways being a single mother is much the same as being a single woman without children. Loneliness is a problem, and money is usually short. But women report that the children provide companionship and a sense of family. On the other hand, having the sole responsibility for a child may make the mother more anxious about her daily decisions—what to do about childhood illnesses, accidents, and disciplinary problems. And many women are concerned about providing daily male companionship for the children; they may decide to stay close to male relatives, to have the children visit with a male friend, or to share communal living arrangements with men (Rivlin 1979).

The decision to have a child alone is not necessarily a decision never to get married. As a woman physician said, "I would have preferred to have the child with a partner, but it's ridiculous to wait for an external circumstance to allow you to do what's in your own power to do—to raise children by yourself" (quoted in Rivlin 1979, p. 92). This theme is echoed by others, including a middle-aged social service worker who had adopted a daughter several years before she was interviewed by Bequaert; she viewed the adoption as one of her wisest and most enriching decisions.

> I certainly hadn't given up ideas of getting married somewhere along the line, but I began to realize that what I most wanted was a family, somebody who belonged to me, someone I could take care of and love. Since marriage didn't seem to be in the cards, I decided to pursue adoption. I think it was the perfect course for me. . . . I've always had the feeling that if I had gotten married, one of the really big reasons would be to have a family. As I've said to a lot of people, I didn't want to miss the whole show, so I made a very definite decision that I would try to adopt. I think it's perhaps one of the few decisions I've made very, very consciously. (Quoted in Bequaert 1976, pp. 71–72)

This adoptive mother's tone is similar to that of all the single women interviewed by Bequaert and Rivlin. They all felt that they had made the best choices for their lives and were doing what *they* wanted. This positive attitude may not be typical of all single women, nor is it totally due to their unmarried status; for both Bequaert and Rivlin deliberately sought out women who tended to plan carefully and were enthusiastic about their life styles.

Women and Divorce

Never-married women may be doing what they really want, but what about women who are separated or divorced? Although many may have decided to leave their husbands, this choice is often viewed as an acknowledgment of failure, for most people view divorce as "permitted but quite detestable" (Epstein 1974, p. 24).

> Divorce, it is almost universally agreed, is a civilized institution . . . and as such nearly everyone now tolerates, even approves of, divorce. Except, that is, for themselves. Divorce generally seems an admirable, an altogether logical solution—for others. For oneself it is, invariably and inevitably, difficult almost beyond imagining. For if one has the least shred of introspection, the decision to divorce is to own up to one's own dismal failure. (Epstein 1974, pp. 24–25)

In spite of these feelings, however, the divorce rate has risen dramatically in the past ten years—increasing by 25 percent between 1963 and 1969 alone (Epstein 1974). There seem to be many reasons for the increase. An industrialized economy demands a large pool of workers whose primary loyalty is to their occupational advancement rather than to their familial ties. When pressures become overwhelming, job often comes before family. And the view of the family has changed. Whereas marriage used to be seen as a social responsibility, a way of fulfilling one's obligations to the community and society, now it is seen as a matter of personal happiness. This shift goes along with a general "ethic of self-realization," a feeling that one is entitled, even obliged, to maximize personal potential at all costs (Weiss 1975, p. 9).

At the same time as attitudes have changed, the barriers to divorce have weakened. Organized religion is less adamantly opposed to divorce than it once was. And the higher female employment rates since World War II mean that more women are able to support themselves; hence, divorce is a feasible alternative. All these factors have combined to create a divorce rate so high that "it is a safe prediction that about half of the American marriages now being made will at some point sustain a separation" (Weiss 1975, p. 11). And the rate continues to rise.

Knowing the social and economic reasons for divorce does not help with the personal experience of separation. The process of divorcing can be harrowing and involves at least six overlapping experiences: (1) grieving over the emotional aspects of growing apart from one's spouse, (2) dealing with the legalities of a court system that in many states still maintains that one party is at fault, (3) dividing the property and arguing over support payments, (4) arranging for child custody, visitation rights, and a new single-parent home, (5) changing patterns of friendships that have been shared as a couple, and (6) regaining individual autonomy as a person living and making decisions alone (Bohannan 1970b). Let us examine the divorce experience more closely from the woman's point of view.

By the time a couple actually separates, the warmth and fondness between them is usually a thing of the past. And yet they continue to cling to each other because of what Weiss (1975) calls "attachment"—a sense of being emotionally bound or connected. In spite of anger and hostility, they often feel comfortable only with each other and dread the loneliness of being apart.

He, who was the cause of my despair, was the only available human being, the only person I felt close to. (Woman, mid-forties)

I am at once torn between the desire to be free of all the drudgery and bitterness of this marriage and an incredible fear of separation and loneliness. (Woman, early twenties, contemplating separation)
(Quoted in Weiss 1975, p. 36)

Children are also a concern, since 60 percent of divorcing couples have young ones at home. Although Bequaert (1976) reports that many women are still caught up in the desire to stay together "for the sake of the children," Epstein (1974) and Weiss (1975) maintain that couples today are more likely to feel that a bad marriage may be worse for the children than divorce itself—a feeling that is supported by recent research (Herzog and Sudia 1968). In fact, some couples say that they decided to separate precisely because the tension-filled marriage had begun to upset the children (Weiss 1975).

Bequaert found that women also stay married because they are afraid they will not be able to manage financially after divorce. Unfortunately this fear is quite realistic; for while the income of divorced mothers typically drops to one-half or even one-third its predivorce level, their expenses remain much the same because they almost always have custody of the children (Bohannan 1970a).

In their nationwide survey of alimony and support payments, Gettleman and Markowitz (1974) found that nearly 90 percent of divorcing women waive alimony payments, and that only 2 percent of them have it awarded on a permanent basis. Even court-ordered child support is not much help. Only 38 percent of fathers continue paying the full amount after one year, and by the end of the tenth year fewer than one-fourth of them are making any support payments at all. Furthermore, the amount of child support awards is extremely low. This is poignantly illustrated by the case of one woman who found that while the Social Security Administration would give her $456 a month for her two children if her husband were dead, a judge ordered her ex-husband to pay only $70 a month in child support (Bequaert 1976).

Faced with these money problems, many divorced mothers take jobs outside the home. But now they are confronted with the high cost of child care—when, that is, they can get it at all. Licensed day-care centers have space for only one-fifth of the children under six years of age whose mothers work. And the average cost of "desirable" day care runs close to $2500 per child-year. Since only one in a hundred working mothers can afford this price tag, the vast majority of young children are cared for in private homes, watched by older siblings, or even left alone.

After summarizing these financial difficulties, Bequaert concludes that the saying, "All women are only a husband away from welfare" is based on bitter reality—which can turn into a nightmare. Monthly welfare checks are meager, averaging $49.50 per month per person for families with children. And on top of the financial strain there is the stigma of being a "welfare mother" who is seen as lazy, irresponsible, promiscuous, and living the good life. As one angry woman put it, once you have to resort to welfare, being a mother "isn't wonderful any more. Now, who's made the change here? The system. It's saying, this [more affluent] mother is wonderful, but if you're on welfare, you're trash" (Hertz 1977, p. 605).

Negative feelings do not come just from the environment, for the loss of attachment makes separating people feel depressed and abandoned. Weiss points out that "separation distress" is analogous to a child's response to threats of abandonment by parents, an analogy that few people consciously recognize. As one woman about thirty put it:

> When my husband left I had this panicky feeling which was out of proportion to what was really happening. I was afraid I was being abandoned. I couldn't shake the feeling.
>
> I remembered later that the first time I had that feeling was when I had pneumonia and my mother left me in the hospital, in a private room, in the winter. And this picture came back of this huge hospital. (Quoted in Weiss 1975, p. 49)

These feelings, of course, are more intense and painful for the spouse who is perceived as having been left behind, and for those whose marriage ends abruptly without an extended period of open dissension and discussion of impending separation. These unwillingly separated individuals are even more likely to pine for the absent spouse and to blame themselves for being unacceptable, as did this woman of about thirty: "There's somebody that knows you the best of anyone, and because of that knowledge he has made a decision about you, and you just have this idea that if everybody else knew you as well as he did, they too would feel the same way" (quoted in Weiss 1975, p. 52).

Weiss points out that blaming the self may actually serve a self-protective function. After all, if one already blames oneself, then criticism from others loses some of its sting. It can also be a way for the depressed spouse to appease the other by saying, "Look how terrible I feel. How can you be angry at me?" Or it can even be a form of retaliation: "See how thoroughly you have convinced me that it was my fault. Aren't you ashamed?" (Weiss 1975, p. 52). Of course these attitudes are not necessarily conscious, nor does the spouse have to be present for them to be expressed.

Not that all separating people are depressed all the time. Some react with euphoria, a feeling of extraordinary well-being and constant activity. This attitude seems to be a way of handling the loss by denying its importance, by saying in effect, "Who needs you anyway?" Weiss notes that the period of euphoria always ends with "separation distress" which includes pining for the former spouse (1975, p. 54). A woman in her early forties who was separated after a marriage of twenty years describes this experience:

> I found that I felt quite euphoric for about three months. I sort of did everything that I wanted to do. I hadn't gone out much, so I went to the theatre. I didn't do these things before I was married. I sat in a bar, drinking, just talking to anybody. I met just lots of different people.
>
> After three months and having met just one or two people who were really interesting, I found it was an empty life. I realized that my family meant a great deal to me and that there was no family any more. There was just the kids and myself. And the things I had done with my husband, I could no longer do them. (Quoted in Weiss 1975, p. 54)

Weiss reports that some people who have this reaction later report feeling upset and depressed during their euphoric period, in spite of the fact that they did not feel that way at the time. Regardless of its defensive quality, however, euphoria serves to keep the individual active and often helps her cope more effectively during the early period of separation.

The loss of attachment is compounded by other losses—of social status, money, and friends. Most important of all, however, is a loss of identity. This loss is particularly acute for women. While many men derive a sense of self-worth from their marriages, women are likely to perceive marriage and family as the most significant accomplishments in their lives. For women, marriage is more than a relationship; it is also a career. Even wives who work outside the home may see their jobs as peripheral, as merely "helping out." And although many women are still involved in homemaking and child rearing after separation or divorce, they seldom continue to receive adult recognition for their performance. Some women, like this one of about thirty-five, submerge themselves in the marriage so completely that they feel they have no separate identity:

> My husband was in graduate school and we had three babies and I was really up to my neck in diapers. And I was doing part-time work, very menial types of things, secretarial and typing, that sort of thing. And what he was doing was so much more interesting than what I was doing. Who wanted to hear about loads of dirty diapers and my fascinating clerical jobs? So when we broke up I felt that for all those years he had been sort of developing. And my identity was so mixed up with that, that I would find it very hard to describe myself apart from him. (Quoted in Weiss 1975, pp. 71–72)

This loss of identity is compounded by the imposition of a new identity—that of the dishonored or discredited woman. Weiss found that the woman is often blamed for the divorce and its damaging effects on the children. She is treated with new suspicion and disrespect by service and tradespeople—even those who have known her for years—and is considered fair game for uninvited sexual advances. Some landlords will not rent to her for fear she will lower the standards in the building. She often feels like an outcast, an object of contempt, as did this woman in her late thirties: "There is no dignity, no honor, in divorce. The divorced woman is pictured as a sleazy character. Men think a divorced woman is horny, or else that she's hard and cold. No landlord wants a divorced woman floating around. He has this picture of men going in and out at all hours" (Weiss 1975, p. 77).

During the distress of separation most people turn to their friends for support. But most couples socialize as a unit during marriage, and after separation many divorcées have difficulty keeping in touch and find that their friends withdraw just when they are most needed. A divorcée's married friends may fear that their husbands will become sexually involved with her, or they may be made uncomfortable by seeing that their own marriages reflect many of the divorced couple's marital troubles (Bequaert 1976).

Most couple-friends do not abandon the divorced woman right away. Weiss has found that the reactions of married friends go through three stages. In the first they "rally around" by offering sympathy, asking how they can help, and inviting the separated person to visit. Some may even make their home a temporary refuge for the divorcée.

As time goes on, however, many friends begin to feel overburdened and some even seem frightened, "as though the separation were a communicable disease" (Weiss 1975, p. 158). They may fantasize about the divorcée's experience, seeing her as they would imagine themselves as singles—bereft, wounded, and piteous, or joyously independent and perhaps sexually promiscuous. The husbands of close friends sometimes propose a discreet affair or may even paw and grab saying, "You poor thing, what are you doing for sex? You really must be hurting." The divorcée's reaction is likely to be like this woman's, who said, " 'You goddamn bastard. I'm friends with your wife. Don't you ever, ever, put your hands on me again.' And I shoved him so hard he fell off the steps. And I went in and shut the door and I threw up, I felt so degraded" (quoted in Weiss 1975, p. 160).

In the third stage couple-friends begin to withdraw. The visits and phone calls become infrequent, and gradually the friendship is allowed to fade. Weiss points out that the divorcée often blames a married couple for ending the friendship, and feels she has been condemned or rejected because of her separation or divorce. She may feel that married couples cannot tolerate her unhappiness, viewing it as manipulative self-pity. Or she may feel that other wives perceived her as sexually threatening now she is single.

These feelings of rejection are similar to those described by the divorcées Bequaert interviewed. However, Weiss goes on to point out that a divorceé may also be uncomfortable in old friendships. She no longer shares as many interests and activities with married couples; although she often has children, she is no longer part of the interests and activities that revolved around the relationship with her husband. And seeing the happiness of married friends can arouse envy and intensify a woman's own loneliness. Rather than experience these unpleasant emotions, she may prefer to stay away. But because she is upset and suffering from a loss of identity and social status, there is a natural tendency for her to ignore her own withdrawal and attribute the ending of the friendship to rejection by the couple-friends.

Many women experience divorce as a "dying process" because much of their life is wrenched away: relationships with couple-friends are ruptured, loving contact with the husband's family is sometimes ended, and the reassuring routine of daily life is disrupted. Something has indeed died—an entire social role as wife along with the personal relationships surrounding that role. But Susan Gettleman and Janet Markowitz (1974) object to the death analogy, because it obscures the fact that the ex-spouse continues to be alive and important to the lives of the children. Encouraging a woman to grieve may also result in a masking of her real relief at ending a bad living situation and foster the illusion that mourning will end only when she finds another man to take care of her.

The value of a new intimate relationship is not entirely an illusion, however. Weiss has found that a new attachment can reduce separation distress and eliminate the loneliness that follows. It also relieves some of the anguish associated with feelings of blame, guilt, and rejection. The wife who initiated the separation is often tormented with guilt at the emotional damage she has caused to someone she pledged to cherish for a lifetime. This feeling may cause her to condemn herself and to anticipate the same condemnation from others. She may question her own ability to sustain intimacy. All these feelings can be alleviated by interacting with someone who reflects a more positive view of the divorcée and offers a chance to renew intimacy and self-confidence.

The benefits of a new relationship are similar for the woman who does not choose to separate. She is likely to feel rejected by her ex-spouse and to expect the same rejection from others. She sometimes feels generally aggrieved and misused—by everyone, not just by her ex-husband. And she may accept her ex-spouse's negative appraisal of her and question her own capacity to trust or love anyone.

Some divorced women tend to delay or avoid dating men, however, because they see dating as incompatible with motherhood. They seem to feel that while it was all right and even desirable to be sexual with the children's father, sexual relationships with other men are somehow off limits, especially when their children are young. On the other hand, others come to see sex outside marriage as acceptable and do not feel the need to remarry to achieve sexual fulfillment. One divorced woman over forty with five teenage children explained this change in her attitude toward extramarital sex:

> A couple of years ago I started going to a singles' group at the Unitarian Church. There I met a real nice fellow who I've been dating steadily for two years. . . . So I can't complain now—I spend a lot of time on weekends at his place. My kids are old enough so they're just tickled pink that this came along and they can manage by themselves when I go over there. It's a very quiet haven. . . . He's really a nice guy. He cares a great deal about me and about people in general.
>
> Marriage is not in the cards at least for now. . . . I look on marriage in a very different way now. The basic question is "Why get married?" I don't feel that pressuring me. We started sleeping together almost as soon as we started dating and found it was a very beautiful, warm kind of relationship. So there's not that kind of pressure—you know, you've got to get married so you can do that.
>
> In a sense, my mores took a real flip at that point in time. . . . I could look at it and say there was no reason why we shouldn't. It's a very meaningful part of our relationship. To have gotten married so we could do that would have been a foolish thing. (Quoted in Bequaert 1976, p. 101)

In spite of the emotional trauma of becoming divorced and the financial problems of being a single mother, millions of women go through this process. And once they are established in their new life styles, some even view their divorce as a growth-enhancing experience. Bequaert reports on an interview with one such woman who was happy with her new life. She was a young professional who had divorced three years before and was now living in a middle-class suburb with her two children in a home still owned jointly with her former husband. She described being single this way:

I love it. I'm very busy but I've always enjoyed being busy and I feel that I can extend myself in each area adequately. Sometimes I feel that I don't have enough time for one thing or another, but in general I feel that I have enough time for myself, enough time for friends, enough time to take care of my work, enough time to be with my children. It works. (Quoted in Bequaert 1976, p. 2)

This woman was unusually fortunate in that she had no severe financial problems, although after the divorce she did rent the third floor of her home to another woman to help pay the bills. And she had many friends, both male and female, she found her doctor and her lawyer sympathetic, and she had always had many interests and activities of her own outside the marriage. She found congenial men to date and felt that although she did not know her neighbors well and they did not approve of divorced women, she could count on them in an emergency. Most unusual of all, however, is that she was (or became) active in the Women's Movement and felt that her women friends and her children gave her crucial emotional support. Thus, this woman had considerable strengths and independence during her marriage and existed in a generally supportive liberal or feminist environment.

The experience of this divorced woman is not necessarily typical of that of most divorced women in the United States today, but it does provide an example of how divorce can be a creative experience once the initial trauma is over, and of how divorced women can perceive being single as a positive alternative.

Widowhood

Unlike many never-married and divorced women, widows have not chosen their single status. And before they can cope with the social and economic problems of being single, they have to endure the pain of bereavement itself. This grief process is usually described as having three stages, as Parkes (1970) reported in studying twenty-two widows aged twenty-six to sixty-five. The first phase is that of "numbness," when the woman feels emotionally blunted or in shock and tries to deny her husband's death. In this phase, lasting from a few hours to a few days, there is a dramatic loss of appetite and periodic outbursts of crying and anger.

The second phase involves "yearning" and "protest." The urge to recover the lost person is expressed through pining and being preoccupied with memories of him, paying attention to things associated with him, tending to see or hear him as if he were physically present, and crying for him. This phase reaches its height in the second to fourth weeks after the loss and also includes physical restlessness, irritability, and bitterness. A widow is periodically angry (blaming this on a variety of external causes), feels that the world is now insecure and potentially dangerous, and may drive her friends and relatives away with her tendency to quick blame and irrational anger.

The third phase is called "disorganization" and features apathy and aimlessness. At this point a widow cannot see any purpose in living and has difficulty visualizing and planning for the future. Most of the widows Parkes studied were still in this third phase when the study ended after thirteen months of bereavement.

Our society's abhorrence of death aggravates the widow's difficulties. The ambiguity about what is "proper" mourning behavior confuses both the widow and those around her (Barrett 1977). And people often treat her as if she has an infectious disease. One forty-six-year-old widow commented on this isolating experience:

> I used to feel that people's faces used to change when they saw me. They didn't know how to handle me. They'd have this terribly solicitous tone. Some women even told me they went out and raised their insurance after hearing what happened to us. I got to the point where I avoided people. I felt as if every window had a face behind it, peering at me. I felt so exposed, as though there was some kind of visible stigmata. (Quoted in Bequaert 1976, p. 43)

In the midst of her grief the widow has to cope with the confusion of settling her husband's estate. Barrett (1977) points out that widows experience a dramatic drop in family income, averaging about 44 percent. Not only is their husband's income gone, but they also have to face an average of $3,900 in bills for his illness and funeral expenses. Although the majority of widows of working age are employed, they earn only three-quarters of what other women do and have an unemployment rate three times that of other *women*. The husband's pension plan may help—if it is one of the 50 percent that includes widow or survivor benefits (Bequaert 1976).

Grief, social stigma, and financial crisis combine to make loneliness the hallmark of widowhood. Widows are often nostalgic for their previous life style, chafe at their reduced social status as an unescorted female, find their established relationships strained, and have difficulty making new friends. In addition, they miss their husbands keenly: they miss interacting with them as unique individuals, having the feeling of being loved, having someone to care for, having another adult around the house, and having the opportunity to share work and a deep relationship (Lopata 1969). A number of personal accounts, such as Lynn Caine's *Widow* (1975), express the profound sense of isolation these women experience.

Since widows miss so many aspects of the marital relationship, perhaps remarriage is a good solution. Yet Barrett (1977) reports that only one-fourth of widows remarry within five years, as opposed to one-half of widowers and three-fourths of divorced people. Barrett notes that the majority of widows say they do not *want* to remarry—perhaps because their grieving arouses feelings of guilt and loyalty to their dead husbands, and also because they fear losing what meager survivor's benefits they may have. "I don't want to" may really mean, however, "I don't think I'll have the chance to," since a man usually chooses a younger wife and yet dies seven or eight years earlier than a woman of his own age. For the typical widow in her late forties and fifties, then, there simply may be no suitable mate available.

Of course, not all women react the same way to being widowed. Many writers suggest that the experience is more stressful for younger women who are less prepared for their husbands to die. The importance of anticipation was recently confirmed by Carey (1977), who found that having at least two weeks' warning was associated with less depression one year after a husband's death. Bequaert (1976), on the other hand, suggests that an older widow has more problems because she is less likely to have had a marriage which was based on companionship and in which she developed independent interests. Furthermore, Bequaert points out that, when her husband dies, an older widow is just disengaging from many social roles such as parenthood and hence is less able actively to plan for the future after his death. While a younger woman may suffer from the unexpected nature of her husband's death, she is more likely to have other interests and activities to fill the void in her life. This idea is supported by the general finding that employed women and those with more education are less depressed and isolated in widowhood.

What would help women cope with the experience of widowhood? Barrett (1977) asked widows themselves what advice they have for women whose husbands are still living, and received answers that fit in with Bequaert's emphasis on greater independence for married women. These widows suggested that a wife should participate in the management of family finances, learn occupational skills, develop her own interests and hobbies, and make sure that the couple writes wills and buys life insurance.

As for women who are already in the midst of bereavement, the most helpful element seems to be contact with other widows. A number of discussion groups have been started in recent years through church organizations, women's centers, medical schools, and colleges. All these groups stress the same thing: talk to each other, find out you are not alone or "crazy," and share ideas on how to manage, and you will be able to cope.

Lesbians: The Invisible Minority

Many single women feel isolated, stigmatized, misunderstood, and almost invisible—but no one is subject to these experiences as much as those who relate sexually to other women. Yet there are millions of gay women in the United States today.

When Kinsey and his associates studied the sexual behavior of nearly 8,000 American women in the 1940s, they found that 28 percent reported having some homosexual experience (Kinsey et al. 1953). This came as a shock to many people. Today, however, the existence of lesbianism is more recognized. Researchers estimate that 2 to 5 percent of female adults are lesbians (Money 1976), while some gay activists put the figure closer to 10 percent (Abbott and Love 1971; J. O'Leary 1978) or ten million lesbians nationwide (Martin and Lyon 1970).* More exact figures are impossible to obtain, since most lesbians are forced to hide their sexual preference because of legal sanctions and social rejection. Even the middle estimate of 5 percent leads to a startling conclusion: at any point in time there are probably as many lesbians as widows in the population and twice as many lesbians as single divorcées.†

Who are these millions of lesbians, and what are they like? The answer is that "just as there is no typical heterosexual woman, neither is there any typical Lesbian" (Martin and Lyon 1970, p. 79). As gay activists point out, lesbians come from all walks of life, hold all kinds of jobs, belong to all kinds of families and social groups, and have all kinds of personalities and characteristics. They are just like the woman next door—and may be that woman herself.

> Because the Lesbian is every woman. She is the college student preparing for a career that will make her economically independent and give her some measure of personal accomplishment. She is the dedicated nurse

* The definition of lesbianism varies. Does it mean women who sleep only with other women, or women who sleep with women as well as men? Does it involve an ability to relate to women or an inability to relate to men—a positive choice of women, or simply the only alternative for women who do not want to relate to men? Is someone who has sexual fantasies about other women a lesbian, or does she have to act on her desires to qualify? Is it a matter of self-definition, the willingness to think of yourself as "lesbian," "homosexual," or "gay"? The issue of definition is controversial, especially in the Women's Movement where many lesbians feel that some women begin sleeping with other women as an experiment or because it is "cool" and "politically correct" rather than because of strong emotional and sexual feelings. For the purpose of this discussion I will use the simplest definition: "A Lesbian is a woman who prefers another woman as a sexual partner," regardless of any other emotional and sexual involvements she may have (Martin and Lyon 1970, p. 79).

† Of course these groups of women overlap. Some lesbians are widowed, while one-quarter to one-third are currently or were previously married (Bell and Weinberg 1978). This comparison of the number of lesbians with the number of women who are widowed or divorced is based on the fact that 5 percent of women live as widows (Barrett 1977), while there are twice as many widows as single divorcées (Bequaert 1976).

or the committed social worker. She works on the assembly line of an electronics plant, drives a taxicab, or goes to night school. The Lesbian is an attorney, an architect, or an engineer. . . . She is a welfare recipient, an auto mechanic, a veterinarian, an alcoholic, a telephone operator, a civil service or civil rights worker. She may be a lieutenant in the armed forces or a beauty operator. And, being a woman in western society, she is certainly a clerk-typist, secretary or bookkeeper. (Martin and Lyon 1972, p. 7)

Lesbians as a group can be very confusing. There are lesbians whose politics are to the right of Genghis Khan. There are lesbians who make Maoists look moderate. There are lesbians who can only be described as dowdy dykes. There are lesbians who can't be described, they simply knock you out with their beauty. There are lesbians who love cats and would never be seen without one. There are lesbians who like dogs. There are lesbians who like men . . . and there are lesbians who barely know that men as a group exist. There are Baptist lesbians, born again; there are Catholic lesbians . . . Jewish lesbians . . . and all the other religious possibilities. There are even lesbians who don't believe in any religion at all. There are poor lesbians and rich lesbians. There are dumb lesbians (yes, I hate to admit it but there are) and there are smart lesbians. We come in all colors, too. Lesbians are everywhere, even in the morgue. We die like everyone else. (Brown 1978, p. 13)

In spite of this diversity, however, many people think they can describe "the Lesbian." This stereotype embodies "all the worst masculine attributes of toughness, aggressiveness, lack of emotion, lack of sentiment, overemphasis on sex, lack of stability—the need and desire to dress as a man or, at least, as much like a man as possible" (Martin and Lyon 1970, p. 79).

On the other hand, Martin and Lyon (1970) point out that a lesbian may try to fit this stereotype for a brief period in her life, especially when she is young. After all, she too grew up in our culture, which presents this image of lesbians. So when she realizes that she is gay, she may think that the only way to attract a woman is to appear masculine. Fitting the lesbian stereotype may also be a way to let other lesbians know she is gay, while at the same time defying the social mores that define her very being as abhorrent. And in previous years there was the simple reason of comfort, since "any woman who says that girdles and high heels are comfortable is simply lying" (Martin and Lyon 1970, p. 80).

The vast majority of lesbians pass beyond this stage, however, and become "indistinguishable from other women in dress, in manner, in goals and desires, in actions and in interests" (Martin and Lyon 1970, p. 80). The very fact that she is not distinguishable from other women creates problems for the lesbian, however: how will she meet other gay women, and if she does, how will they recognize each other? The "gay bar" does function as a meeting place, but few cater exclusively to women because they do not constitute a steady or a lucrative clientele.

Lesbians grew up in the same cultural milieu as heterosexual women. Many hesitate to go to bars alone, and few feel comfortable taking the initiative in starting a conversation or asking for a date. Lesbian social organizations like the Daughters of Bilitis have provided a social outlet for some lesbians in the past twenty years; but Martin and Lyon point out that these groups have offered little help to gay teenagers, since membership has had to be refused to those under twenty-one for fear of charges of "contributing to the delinquency of a minor." Although a number of women's bars, restaurants, and organizations have sprung up in large cities over the past few years, most lesbians continue to live quiet lives. They tend to find a partner, settle down, and do most of their socializing at home with a small circle of friends—usually both homosexual and heterosexual (Bell and Weinberg 1978; Martin and Lyon 1972).

Not that all lesbians share the same life style. They live their lives in a tremendous variety of ways. Some live alone, some live with a friend or a lover, others are married, and almost one-third have children (Bell and Weinberg 1978). In fact, their lives are much the same as those of other women their age with the same educational, occupational, and marital backgrounds (Oberstone and Sukoneck 1976). Almost two-thirds of gay women are involved in longterm love relationships (Bell and Weinberg 1978). Members of these gay couples meet their partners in social rather than in sexual settings (Tuller 1978) and look for the same traits in a mate as straight women do (Laner 1977).

Are the lives of lesbians the same as those of heterosexual women, then? Yes and no, for although they may be legally single, many are emotionally and socially married. In spite of the fact that these partnerships often last for years (Bell and Weinberg 1978), they receive no legal recognition and have to be carefully hidden from most of the people around them. Martin and Lyon point out that "the fact that Lesbian relationships are generally long-lasting without benefit of religious ceremony or legal sanction is indicative of a strong bond of love and respect which sees the couple through all the obstacles society places in their way" (1970, pp. 84–85).

When a lesbian loses her mate through separation or death, she may have no one to talk to about it because no one knows of her loss. Unable to work through her grief with family and friends, she may turn to a therapist to share her secret. This problem is especially acute for women who have been part of a long-term couple but have not developed any homosexual friendships for fear of being labeled "gay." Barbara Sang (1977) points out that these women often have a great deal of difficulty establishing a new relationship, because they do not know where to meet other lesbians.

The fear of being labeled "gay" is not simply paranoia, for lesbians experience severe discrimination and may suffer legal sanctions for their sexual preference. At the present time it is not possible for any state to make it illegal to *be* homosexual; but in March 1976 the U.S. Supreme Court affirmed the right of states to prohibit certain sexual *acts* between people of the same gender (J. O'Leary 1978).

These "sodomy laws" refer to a number of acts that are considered unnatural—usually oral or anal intercourse, but sometimes virtually anything other than intercourse carried out in the "missionary position" (man on top, woman on bottom). In discussing the sodomy laws, Jean O'Leary points out that "the Kinsey reports revealed that 'the abominable and detestable crime against nature,' far from being a rare 'perversion' engaged in by a tiny fraction of the population, was in fact enjoyed so widely that fair enforcement of the laws against it would put most of the country (heterosexuals, included) behind bars" (1978, p. 197).

But "fair enforcement" has not been the rule. By and large, only homosexuals are arrested under these statutes. Arrest and prosecution have been so selective that some gay activists charge that the real purpose of these laws is to prohibit homosexuality (Dobinski 1975). On the other hand, times are changing. Since the American Law Institute proposed its U.S. Model Penal Code in 1962, slightly more than one-third of the states have, as part of a general reform in criminal laws, decriminalized sexual acts carried out between consenting adults in private (J. O'Leary 1978).

Law reform has not dramatically changed the situation of lesbians, however, for few lesbians have ever been prosecuted for committing specific sexual acts. The laws are more likely to be enforced indirectly through charges of vagrancy or loitering near a gay bar, or to be used to threaten and intimidate (Dobinski 1975). The laws provide justification for the myriad forms of discrimination used against gays. Open lesbians are often refused employment, and others are fired when their sexual preference becomes known. Homosexuals are denied the right to immigrate to the United States on the grounds that they do not have the requisite moral character. If they are minors, they may be sent to prison or a mental institution simply for loving someone of the same gender.

Openly gay women and men are also refused entry into the armed forces, and those whose homosexuality is discovered are invariably discharged. This discharge usually follows an investigation that includes interrogation, harassment, isolation, and systematic punishment of anyone who is even suspected of being gay. And the discharge itself is frequently a less than honorable one that can interfere with employment and promotion throughout life (Gregory-Lewis 1978; J.O'Leary 1978).

Other forms of discrimination are less blatant. A lesbian couple often finds that its applications for apartment rentals and home mortgages are refused, for instance, even though each woman has a job and a good credit rating. Such couples are not able to take advantage of the income tax breaks given to straight, married couples. And they are frequently prevented from listing either partner as a life insurance beneficiary.

A lesbian mother experiences additional dfficulties. She must decide whether to tell her children of her sexual preference. If she does tell, she has to help them understand that although this preference is a positive aspect of her life, they must not mention it casually at school and in the homes of friends (Perreault 1975). Regardless of how she handles the issue, a lesbian mother has to live with the fear that her children will be taken away from her simply because she is gay. This fear can cause a woman to waive her right to portions of the marital property lest her ex-husband contest her fitness as a mother. If she can manage to settle things out of court, the lesbians mother is more likely to retain custody of her children (Stevens 1978).

In the face of these difficulties, many lesbians decide to pass as straight. Although it may prevent the loss of jobs, homes, and children, staying "in the closet" carries its own emotional stresses. A lesbian who feels especially threatened may expend much energy monitoring her thoughts and feelings so she will not betray her secret. The strain involved can interfere with her capacity to be open and spontaneous, as a lesbian therapist illustrates by describing one of her clients:

> S. has a high executive position in which her success depends on appearing heterosexual. When relating to the women in her office, S. closely watches her facial gestures and degree of physical contact least [sic] she be suspected of being a lesbian. Through the years S. has trained herself to appear turned on to men and to talk about heterosexual dates. On those occasions that S. brings her lover to an office affair, one would hardly recognize that these two women knew each other; they relate in such a detached manner. (S.'s lover would feel personally rejected at such events even though she understood the need for pretense.) S.'s need to be cautious about displays of feeling and affection extends to most public places. She must be discreet for fear that someone from work may be close by. (Sang 1977, pp. 271–72)

The discriminiation and social stigma that lesbians experience not only inhibits openness and spontaneity; it can also be internalized and make self-acceptance extremely difficult. In fact, some gay activists feel that self-acceptance is the most difficult problem the lesbian faces in life (Martin and Lyon 1970). As Sidney Abbott and Barabara Love put it, "Guilt is at the core of the Lesbian's life experience. It is her heritage from the past; it controls her present and robs her of her future" (1972, p. 19). They illustrate this point with their personal experience:

> In my marvelous new feelings for her I felt I had discovered myself. I went walking, celebrating sun, sky, and trees, and myself as somehow center of it all. Then I stopped as if I had come to the edge of a chasm there in the woods. A word came clawing up from the depths of my mind. I didn't want the knowledge that was coming, but my wish didn't stop it. The horror of the word burst upon me almost before the word itself—

sick, perverted, unnatural, *Lesbian.* The trees that had seemed so close drew away. The sky looked remote. I was a shadow, a wraith hurrying across the landscape as I ran home. (Abbott and Love 1972, p. 19)

These negative self-perceptions are only reinforced by the daily struggle against discrimination. And as we have already seen, hiding their sexual preference puts a great deal of pressure on both partners in a lesbian relationship—a pressure that many gay women see as a major cause of the break-up of such relationships (Tuller 1978). But a woman who stops hiding her lesbianism often encounters worse pressures. Nationwide surveys conducted in 1970, 1973, and 1974 showed that almost three-quarters of the population disapproved of homosexual relationships (Irwin and Thompson 1977; Levitt and Klassen 1974; Nyberg and Alston 1976–1977). Many people still believe the negative myths and stereotypes that were expressed by women in a course on lesbianism at San Francisco State University in 1973:

> In a very tedious and painful process, the women who identified themselves as heterosexual shared their "fantasies" concerning lesbianism. Lesbians were women who: were masculinized by some hormonal or anatomical deficiency; were ugly and therefore could not "get a man"; had been raped or brutalized by men and then rejected all men; were raised as boys by parents who really preferred boys. They believed that lesbians role-played, some (the majority) were "butch" and dressed up in men's clothing, and had very short hair cuts, that these women were attracted to feminine women who fit the stereotype of *woman* in this society. And last, the *masculine* woman was not a "real" woman, but the feminine woman who falls in love with the butch was a "real" woman. (Escamilla-Mondanaro 1977, p. 257)

Not everyone shares these attitudes and stereotypes. Recent studies with college undergraduates have shown that a more positive attitude toward homosexuality is associated with being profeminist, having a more relaxed attitude about changes in sex-role stereotypes, and having a more permissive attitude about sexual activity outside marriage (MacDonald and Games 1974; Minnigerode 1976). Contact with known homosexuals also lessens negative ideas about them (Millham, Miguel, and Kellogg 1976). On the other hand, people with more rigid, authoritarian personalities and a low tolerance for ambiguity tend to have a more negative perception of lesbians and gay men (MacDonald and Games 1974).

The way a person feels about homosexuality is not, however, necessarily the same as what he or she thinks about the rights of individual gays. Some people can think that homosexuality is wrong and perceive homosexuals negatively yet still think that they should have the same legal rights as other citizens: "I think it's wrong (sick, perverted), but that doesn't mean we should discriminate against them." In spite of the fact that a majority of Americans still disapprove of homosexuality, 56 percent of those surveyed in a 1977 Gallup poll felt that gays should have equal rights in terms of job opportunities. And a Harris poll conducted in the same year found that 55 percent felt that homosexuals suffered more discrimination than any other group in American society today (J. O'Leary 1978).

The difference between opinions about morality and those about legal rights was demonstrated in a nationwide survey of 1,500 people conducted in 1973 (Irwin and Thompson 1977). This study found that although 70 percent considered homosexual acts to be morally wrong, a majority were willing to grant at least two of the following three rights to homosexuals: to teach in college, to speak in a local community, and to borrow a local library book which was written by a homosexual and was favorable to homosexuality. Supporters of civil rights for gays tended to be the same people who supported an individual's right to express nonconformist political ideas. These civil libertarians were likely to be well educated, young, Jewish or nonreligious, and from urban areas in the Northeast or Pacific states.

For many years the negative attitudes about homosexuality were reflected and supported by psychological studies that portrayed lesbians and gay men as sick. Few people noticed that these studies were done with psychotherapy patients who would be expected to be emotionally distressed. As attitudes about sex became more liberal and less tied to the Judeo-Christian idea that sex is only for reproduction, attitudes about homosexual behavior gradually changed. And gay activists began to attend professional meetings and challenge the psychiatric "experts." Heated exchanges occurred between clinicians who thought homosexuality was pathological and those who maintained it was not. Some of these were rather humorous. Imagine the following:

> DR. A: Well, I *know* homosexuals are sick. All my homosexual patients are.
> DR. B: All my homosexual patients are sick, too. But the funny thing is, so are all my heterosexual patients.

In December 1973 the Board of Trustees of the American Psychiatric Association responded by voting that "homosexuality per se" should no longer be considered a "psychiatric disorder." "Homosexuality" was to be removed from the official list of psychiatric diagnoses used not only by psychiatrists but also by psychologists and other mental-health professionals. In its place was to be a category called "sexual orientation disturbance," reserved for those homosexuals "who are either disturbed by, in conflict with, or wish to change their sexual orientation." The American Psychological Association also issued an official statement supporting the healthy nature of homosexuality.

The change in psychiatric classification has far-reaching implications for lesbians. Psychiatric diagnoses are often used as the basis for court decisions and as justification for myriad types of discrimination. In the past numerous homosexuals have been incarcerated in mental hospitals and prisons simply because of their sexual orientation or behavior. Over the last five years research has also begun to examine the personalities and life styles of *nonclinical* lesbian populations. This research has consistently found that lesbians are just as healthy and well adjusted as heterosexual women from the same backgrounds (Riess 1974; Riess, Safer, and Yotive 1974).

Psychologists and psychiatrists however, continue to argue about the new category of "sexual orientation disturbance." Many feel that the category's very existence implies that gays will (or should) want to change their sexual orientation. Some have urged all therapists to refuse to treat anyone who wants to become straight. They argue that a request for such treatment is the result of social pressures that have induced self-hatred in gays. To agree to help them "straighten out" their lives is to reinforce this destructive self-hatred and masochism (Begelman 1977; Davison 1977, 1978; Silverstein 1977). Others, however, reply that everyone has a right to treatment, even if the treatment request is the result of negative social pressures and a poor self-image (Sturgis and Adams 1978).

Not that all lesbians feel this self-hatred. Most live quietly, happily, but invisibly—and do not come to the attention of mental health professionals. Many feel good about their sexual preference and have told friends, relatives, and employers they are gay. "Coming out" publicly is a never-ending process, however. Most lesbians tell only those close to them at first and only gradually become more open with employers and casual acquaintances. And even those who are completely "out" find themselves having to decide over and over again whom to tell and when. For lesbians, just like all women, are assumed to be "straight." There are no distinguishing features that announce their sexual preference, and even if there were, most people might prefer not to notice.

When I finally came out publicly again, shortly after my graduation from Barnard, I found it easiest to tell new people but most difficult to tell those who had presumed I was straight. Maybe it was guilt because my earlier pretense had probably caused their incorrect inference. But . . . heterosexuals have an amazing capacity for blindness, or perhaps they refuse to notice it in the way any polite person might refuse to see another's dandruff. If I had to give an award to the blindest heterosexual I've known, it would be a tough decision. The prize might go to a friend of mine for twelve years now, who stayed with my lover and me for a week, during which time we were openly affectionate, and upon leaving told me how wonderfully I got on with a roommate. . . .

The prize might also go jointly to my parents, who were surprised to discover in 1976 that I'm a lesbian (It)—their discovery occurred when they saw me on Tom Snyder's *Tomorrow Show*. How they didn't know was what surprised me. After all, I had lived with the same lover until 1975 for over five years, we had bought a car jointly, we had moved twice together, and then there was the fact that I had coedited two gay liberation anthologies. But they never had to confront it, and I never told them in explicit enough terms (although when I told them that I loved the woman I was living with—what could be more explicit than *that*—they thought it was fine to have "such good friends"), and they were doing such a wonderful job of ignoring the obvious that I let it pass. And now that they can no longer deny my lesbianism, they still don't accept It, as my lesbianism is still referred to in family circles.

The process didn't end with my parents' discovery, and it will never end, for I live in a heterosexist world where the presumption is that I'm straight, so that every time I meet a new person (and that's quite often), I have to recommence that coming-out process. . . .

Thus, we spend our lives coming out, and the reality is that none of us is completely "out" or "in." (Jay 1978, p. 29)

Other lesbians have become active in gay or lesbian groups and have begun to write articles and books about lesbian life styles (Abbott and Love 1972; Jay and Young 1975; Martin and Lyon 1972; Vida 1978). Many have shared their experiences in beginning to acknowledge and act on their sexual feelings for other women. The courage of these outspoken lesbians should not be underestimated, nor should the influence of their example. Young lesbians need to know how older gay women have lived their lives, and the general public needs to know that lesbians are not the "purple menace" or "tough dykes" of popular stereotypes.

Some gay activists urge *all* lesbians to come out of the closet and take political action. As Jill Johnston puts it, "If you're not part of the solution you're part of the problem. A personal solution or exceptional adjustment to a political problem is a collusion with the enemy" (1973, p. 181). Others, however, take a moderate position. They acknowledge that the slogan "Come Out!" is based on sound reasoning, for only when lesbians become visible, will people realize that heterosexuality is not the only possible or even the only desirable sexual orientation. On the other hand, these moderates remind militant gays that the costs of coming out can be high, and that every lesbian has to make her own personal decision.

Coming out at the wrong time to employers, to friends, to one's family, could be economically or psychologically suicidal. And the still bitter truth is that many lesbians who have come out *have* lost children, families, jobs, friends, educations. To lie and deny that possibility is to change the truth for ideological purposes, and we lesbians should recognize that old male trip. . . . Furthermore, no ideology can assuage the terror a lesbian might feel about losing whatever is at stake at that particular moment. To dismiss that terror as insignificant or to tell an impoverished lesbian that being free will be better than her paycheck is laying a trip on her and is outright oppressive. . . .

Instead, we must all get in touch with that terror within each of us, for as I have pointed out, we are all coming out, perpetually, together. (Jay 1978, p. 30)

Personal testimonials are not the only form of action. Many lesbians work within organizations that use a variety of tactics to further lesbian solidarity and to obtain social acceptance and civil rights for gays (Vida 1978). Gay professionals have begun to organize caucuses within their organizations, while others have used their professional expertise to advise lesbians and gay men about various aspects of discrimination, physical health, social and political organizations, and numerous other topics relevant to lesbian life styles (Jay and Young 1975; Vida 1978). And gay mental-health professionals have started writing books to help parents and friends of gays understand them better (Clark 1977).

These efforts have received increasing support from people outside the lesbian and gay movements. Parents of gays have begun to speak up and establish support groups (J. O'Leary 1978; Spitzer, Morgan, and Morgan 1978); the Woman's Movement has begun actively to advocate gay rights (Steinem 1978b), and many politicians, government officials, and nongay professionals have joined in supporting full human rights for homosexuals. Psychologists, for instance, are testifying before legislative bodies and courts, making statements like the following by John Money:

It is morally wrong to legislate in public the criteria by which the sexual lives of the citizens of Maryland should be conducted intimately and by mutual consent in private.

. . . There is an analogy here with native language [and] also with handedness. Some people are left-handed, some ambidextrous, and some right-handed. . . . It used to be fashionable for schoolteachers to punish left-handed children in an effort to make them right-handed. Today it is still fashionable to punish homosexual (and bisexual) people, as in job discrimination. The punishment is ineffectual, for it is not possible to force a change from homosexuality to bisexuality, any more than it is possible to force a heterosexual person into becoming a homosexual.

Homosexual and bisexual people are not a danger to society any more than are heterosexuals. The vast majority lead useful, productive lives, practicing their personal sexual preference as privately as heterosexuals do theirs. The protection of their privacy should be legal. The nobility of the law requires it. (1976, pp. 159–61)

Chapter 10

Women in
the Workplace

AMERICAN WOMEN live their lives in a variety of different ways. Some are married, some are not; some have children, some do not; some are straight, others are gay. Yes they all have one thing in common: at some point in their lives, most of them work outside the home. What kind of experience do they have on the job? What kind of work do they do, and how do they choose it? How do they handle the competition and other pressures in the workplace? Does being female influence their experience in a consistent way? Or have things changed so that gender is no longer crucial in employment?

Psychologists have looked at these questions in terms of women's motivation to succeed, their pattern of career choices, and their experiences as females in male-oriented surroundings. This research has focused on women in the professions—once again, psychologists study their own kind. Yet many of the basic issues apply to all women, as demonstrating the pervasive influence that sex roles have on yet another area of our lives.

Do Women Fear Success?

The bulk of the research on careers has focused on the achievement motive or the desire to do well in accordance with a standard of excellence. Some psychologists maintain that men have a stronger motive to achieve than do women. Others argue that women are actually afraid of success and actively avoid it. The controversy about this alleged fear of success in women has come to stand for many of the controversial issues surrounding women and careers. Do women have the personal characteristics required for the successful pursuit of a career? Is there an inherent contradiction between being feminine and having a career? Have achievement and success been defined in male terms, so that women are left in a no-win position?

WOMEN'S "MOTIVE TO AVOID SUCCESS"

Psychologists John Atkinson and David McClelland have developed a whole theory about achievement motivation (Atkinson and Feather 1966; McClelland et al. 1953). Motivation is usually measured by asking people to write a few paragraphs about a sentence or a picture that subtly suggests a work or an achievement situation. The stories are then scored for achievement themes or expressions of a desire to do well, for definite actions that lead to success, and for positive feelings about succeeding. Thus, in response to a picture of two men working on a machine, an achievement-oriented person might write: "He wants to be an inventor," "He's designing a new part," and "He feels great when it wins a prize for originality."

Innumerable studies of the achievement motive have shown that achievement imagery increases when the stories are written in a situation stressing leadership and competition. And the achievement imagery predicts a number of different behavior patterns. People with a high "need for achievement" (nAch) are more likely to get good grades in school, to do better in competitive than in noncompetitive situations, to engage in money-making activities, and to prefer tasks involving moderate difficulty and risk where one can expect to succeed and can assume that one's own efforts (not chance) were responsible for that success. The extent to which the theory can predict such behavior is impressive. There is just one problem: the theory only works for men. The results for women do not fit the theory, do not match the results for men, and are not even consistent with each other. This discrepancy did not bother the male psychologists who developed the theory; for in the book of almost nine-hundred pages outlining their research methodology, they discuss the theory as if it applied to everyone. Only a single footnote concerned with women tells a careful reader that the female data do not make sense (Atkinson 1953).

While a graduate student at the University of Michigan, Matina Horner became intrigued with this problem. Why, she wondered, do women receive higher nAch scores than men do under neutral conditions but fail to show the predicted increase of achievement imagery in response to leadership and competition? And what interferes with the expression of the achievement motive in women's behavior? Horner reasoned that since successful achievement is viewed as the result of agressively competitive behavior, it is also perceived as incompatible with femininity. Women may therefore be afraid that others will respond to their success by rejecting them as pushy and unfeminine. This fear may lead to a "motive to avoid success," or a permanant predisposition to feel anxious about the anticipated social rejection and loss of femininity that follows success. Since the anxiety is based on the incompatibility between femininity and competitive achievement, it should be more characteristic of women than of men. And since only those who want and expect to succeed are concerned about the consequences of that success, the motive to avoid success should be aroused more easily in achievement-oriented, high-ability women (Horner 1968, 1970a, 1970b, 1970c).

Horner tested her hypothesis in 1965 by having 178 undergraduates at the University of Michigan write stories to four standard achievement cues about characters of their own sex, such as "David (Carol) is looking into his (her) microscope." She added a fifth cue emphasizing the competitive aspect of achievement: "At the top of first term finals, Anne (John) finds herself (himself) at the end of her (his) medical school class." She scored the medical school stories for the presence or absence of "fear of success imagery" (FOS), defined as the expression of negative consequences or emotions about the success, of specific actions leading away from success, or of emotional conflict about the success. The FOS imagery was then interpreted as a reflection of an aroused "motive to avoid success."

Three main types of story were scored for FOS. The most common ones expressed fears of social rejection: Anne lost her friends or her eligibility as a date or a marriage partner, or became isolated, lonely, and unhappy. The second group expressed internal emotions independent of the response of others: regardless of whether anyone else knew about Anne's success, she doubted her femininity, felt guilty or in despair about her success, and wondered about her own normalcy. A third group actually denied the information given in the original sentence. For example:

Anne is a *code* name for a non-existent person created by a group of med students. They take turns taking exams and writing papers for Anne. . . .

Anne is really happy she's on top, though Tom is higher than she—though that's as it should be. . . . Anne doesn't mind Tom winning. (Quoted in Horner 1970a, p. 62)

Some FOS stories were quite bizarre, like the one that included these comments: "She starts proclaiming her surprise and joy. Her fellow classmates are so disgusted with her behavior that they jump on her in a body and beat her. She is maimed for life" (quoted in Horner 1968, p. 106). Horner commented that "the intensity, hostility and symbolic quality of the language used by the subjects in writing their stories is very clear" (1968, p. 107).

The sex differences in the medical school stories were startling: almost two-thirds (65 percent) of the women expressed FOS imagery, while less than one-tenth (8 percent) of the men did so. When Horner compared the FOS scores with the nAch scores, she found that the two went together: women with higher achievement motivation also tended to be scored for FOS. And the expression of FOS imagery was related to the student's achievement behavior. After they wrote their stories in the first session, Horner had them complete verbal and arithmetic tasks in a second session conducted under noncompetitive (solo) or competitive conditions. Achievement-oriented women displaying fear of success imagery did best in the noncompetitive condition. Achievement-oriented women without FOS, on the other hand, behaved just like the men with high nAch scores: they did best in the competitive situation.

These results supported Horner's hypothesis and led her to conclude that "Unfortunately, in American society, even today, femininity and competitive achievement continue to be viewed as two desirable but mutually exclusive ends" (1970b, p. 2). We may not need a social scientist to point this out. Horner reports that her own children were a source of inspiration for her research, as for example, "on the day when Tia, not yet 3, learned that a female friend of the family was a physician and after a lengthy silence inquired 'Is —— still a girl?' 'Well then is she still Eric's mommy?' and before going on to other things concluded, 'She must be all mixed up.' " (1968, p. iii).

WOMEN'S "WILL TO FAIL"

Horner's work was greeted with great enthusiasm by the media. Many commentators implied, "Now we know why women aren't in leadership positions in industry, in finance, in goverment, or any of the professions. It has nothing to do with discrimination or antifemale bias. It's because women just aren't cut out to succeed. In fact, they don't even *want* to. They want to fail. Look, one of them has said it herself. Women's failure to achieve equal status and success is their own fault."

In their enthusiasm for an idea that blames the victim and lets male institutions off the hook, few people have noticed that Horner's concept has been distorted. She suggested that women simultaneously want to succeed and are afraid to for fear they will be punished. This is quite different from not wanting to succeed in the first place, and from having an active desire to fail. As Horner herself said in a later article:

> I have suggested that women have a latent personality disposition or a "motive to avoid success"; i.e., that they become anxious because of success. This is not at all the same as saying that they have a "will to fail," i.e. a "motive to approach failure." This would imply that women actively seek out failure because they anticipate or expect positive consequences from failing. The [motive to avoid success], on the other hand, implies that women inhibit their positive achievement directed tendencies because of the arousal of anxiety about the negative consequences they expect will follow success. (1970b, p. 1)

The ludicrous nature of the "will to fail" idea is obvious when we recall that it was precisely those women with the strongest desire to achieve, as measured by nAch scores, who were most likely to show fear of success imagery in their stories.

THE FEAR-OF-SUCCESS CONTROVERSY

Not only journalists, but also professors, students, and researchers, have been fascinated by the idea of fear of success. In the past ten years over 150 studies have appeared attempting to repeat or extend Horner's findings. Many people have hailed fear of success as the ultimate answer to the complex problems of female achievement. Others have rushed to refute a concept that they see as reinforcing the media image of women driven by some inner compulsion to fail. Let us take a look at some of the major issues in this *cause célèbre*.

One of the most common challenges is that fear of success is not a uniquely female phenomenon: males also show this imagery in their stories. The males rates of FOS imagery have increased over the years and are sometimes found to be as high as or higher than the female rates (Tresemer 1976a). The FOS imagery in male and female stories tends to be different, however. While women fear social rejection for being unfeminine, men express negative feelings about achievement per se— two very different emotional issues (Hoffman 1974b, 1977).

Another problem is that most of the studies continue to use the cue about Anne's and John's excelling in medical school—a traditionally masculine occupation. When the sex-typed nature of the occupation is varied in the cues, we find (1) that men, too, express fear of sanctions for sex-role nonconformity if they write about males in traditionally feminine occupations (Cherry and Deaux 1978; Janda et al. 1978); (2) that both men *and* women express more FOS when writing about characters' succeeding in cross-sex-typed (Breedlove and Cicirelli 1974; Janda et al. 1978); and (3) that, in writing about female success in masculine occupations, men sometimes express *more* FOS imagery than women do (Monahan, Kuhn, and Shaver 1974).

If setting and gender of the successful character make so much difference, perhaps FOS actually taps realistic social expectations rather than deep-seated motives. The students may simply be describing the social sanctions that they expect to accompany sex-role deviance.

Another possibility is that the negative feelings expressed in FOS imagery reflect a natural envy of outstanding people, which may have nothing to do with competitive actions or academic and occupational aspirations. Thus, Shaver suggests that if Horner had used the cue, "Anne is by all accounts the most beautiful coed at the University of Michigan," she might have obtained the following results:

> Sixty-five percent of the subjects mentioned negative consequences of Anne's exceptional beauty; some saw her as "probably stupid and immature," others suspected that her friends were secretly hostile and jealous. Several mentioned that Anne found it difficult to establish normal relationships with males because "the guys are frightened by her incredible good looks; at any time she may drop them in favor of someone better." A few said that Anne wasn't really all that beautiful; she just happened to have a father in the clothing business who gave her anything she wanted. (Shaver 1976, p. 307)

Would this have indicated a fear of beauty? Of course not. It would merely have indicated the subjects' expectation that some people would be envious and hostile of anyone who excelled in the area of physical appearance.

Other writers have objected that fear of success does not necessarily affect behavior—an objection that is usually substantiated by the fact that FOS is more typical of honors students and those at outstanding, competitive colleges (Tresemer 1976b). If they fear success, why are they so successful? This objection is spurious, however, for Horner suggested that the motive to avoid success is more easily *aroused* in high-ability women with a strong motive to achieve; she did not say that it was more *debilitating* in those women (Fleming 1977). Many anxious people are successful despite their anxiety. Their simultaneous anxiety and striving for achievement may, however, be costly. They may pay a high price in terms of various psychosomatic ailments such as headaches, ulcers, colitis, and insomnia (Shaver 1976). Or they may suffer greater feelings of ambivalence about themselves, their relations with others, and their professional goals (Anderson 1978).

On the other hand, repressing or inhibiting a strong desire to achieve may cause feelings of frustration, hostility, and aggression. In one study, for instance, Horner (1970c) found that women who expressed a great deal of fear of success imagery in writing about achievement also tended to express much hostility and manipulative imagery in writing about personal relationships.

In spite of the personal anguish that may be caused by "fear of success," psychologists cannot agree on what it is. Unfortunately much of the research in this area seems to be done by people who are intensely interested in the issue of sex roles and femininity but who have only a vague understanding of the technical theory and methodology from which Horner derived her formulation of the "motive to avoid success." In order to assess individual differences in an internal motive, for instance, one has to use neutral cues. Cues that describe specific situations with conflicting demands (as for femininity and achievement) are more likely to evoke social expectations than to be expressions of more stable, internalized feelings and motives. The scoring for the stories needs to allow for a continuum of responses, not just for presence versus absence of motive. And in order to predict achievement behavior, one has to control for basic ability and motive to achieve. Horner is well aware of these issues and has developed a new scoring system that reflects them (Horner et al. 1973). Her original study was intended to be exploratory; it pointed to an important issue that may interfere with achievement behavior in women and hence may explain why the achievement research makes sense only for men. To examine this problem further, researchers have to do more than run around giving various groups the original medical school cue.

Not that nothing has been learned from this research. Regardless of whether FOS imagery reflects internal motivation or external social expectations, the underlying issues are crucial for many women today. No matter what life choices a woman makes, she tends to worry about her femininity. For one woman this may be a mild concern that emerges only fleetingly when a new wrinkle appears or when others disparage her womanhood. For another woman, however, it may be a constant source of anxiety that can make her hide her abilities and minimize her accomplishments in the male-dominated world of work.

Planning a Career

How does a woman decide whether to have a career and then what career to pursue? Is her choice based on personal ability, desire to achieve, and the opportunities provided by her economic background? Or do other things influence her decision?

In spite of the dramatic increase in female employment since World War II, most women still work at low-paying, low-status jobs, and many are "ghettoized" in a small number of fields that are seen as feminine, such as nursing, teaching, and secretarial work (Almquist 1977). Obviously job opportunities and pay scales have a tremendous amount to do with this pattern. But other factors may also be important. Psychologists have looked at this problem in terms of how women make decisions about their education and employment. Do particular personality factors and social pressures lead women to seek only certain kinds of work or careers?

MAXIMIZING FEMININITY

The research on fear of success clearly suggests that being feminine is a major concern for most women. The unspoken questions are thus, How feminine am I? Is it possible to be feminine and still have a career? Are some types of career more suitable for a woman?

Not that being feminine is something that just happens automatically. Some writers have suggested that the social skills and activities central to the stereotype of female nurturance and femininity are an important area of achievement for women. While men direct their achievement motive into worldly, task-oriented accomplishments, women direct theirs into social interactions (Stein and Bailey 1973). Thus, concentrating on marriage and children can constitute a career in and of itself. Women who choose this option are not necessarily nonachievers; they are simply directing their energies in a traditional direction.

Women who do have a strong desire for worldly achievement, on the other hand, often feel that success threatens their femininity. They handle the conflict in a variety of ways. Some choose not to work outside the home (and are economically able to do so), satisfying their need for achievement vicariously through their husbands' careers. Some choose fields whose content is seen as feminine, avoiding such traditionally masculine fields as science and engineering (Rossi 1965). Some keep a low profile by playing down their accomplishments and staying in the lower echelons of their field, fearing that more successful participation might be seen as unfeminine. And many choose a career, such as teaching, that has a flexible schedule that can be meshed with child-rearing tasks.

Other women do not commit themselves to serious involvement in a career until their children are grown, when their family responsibilities will be fewer and they will have proved their femininity. And then there is the style of the "superwoman" who "may 'compensate' for her achievement striving by being superfeminine in appearance and personality": physically attractive, nonassertive, submissive, and emotionally expressive. Such a woman avoids some of the negative sanctions associated with the stereotype of a "career woman," who is perceived as "loud, aggressive, and domineering" (Stein and Bailey 1973, p. 353). This tactic of exaggerating traditional female characteristics has also been referred to as assuming a "mask of inferiority" (Rosenberg and Sutton-Smith 1972, p. 65).

FOLLOWING MOTHER'S EXAMPLE

What makes a woman career-oriented in the first place? Many researchers report that family background is crucial. They have found that women whose own mothers worked are likely to have higher educational and career aspirations during high school and college (Marini 1978; Sutherland 1978; Tangri 1972). The idea is that the mother provides a role model, showing the daughter that women can manage successfully to combine family responsibilities with a career or paid employment. This positive example, combined with the supportive attitudes of the father and the other family members, encourages a daughter to consider a broader range of options in her own life. In other words, childhood experience fosters a less rigid or traditional view of sex-role norms which does not limit a daughter to homemaking aspirations.

But parents are not always consistent in encouraging a daughter's career. When she gets to college, a daughter often finds that her parents will not spend as much money on her as they will on their son (Sutherland 1978). Parents may feel that "a career may be okay for some women but not for our daughter." In fact, as a woman nears the end of her education, she may find that her parents reverse themselves and begin to stress the importance of marriage. Thus, many women today still share the experience reported by this college senior in 1942–43:

> I get a letter from my mother at least three times a week. One week her letters will say, "Remember that this is your last year at college. Subordinate everything to your studies. You must have a good record to secure a job." The next week her letters are full of wedding news. This friend of mine got married; that one is engaged; my young cousin's wedding is only a week off. When, my mother wonders, will I make up my mind? Surely, I wouldn't want to be the only unmarried one in my group. It is high time, she feels, that I give some thought to it. (Quoted in Komarovsky 1946, p. 185)

Other women are given a mixed message all along:

> All through high school my family urged me to work hard because they wished me to enter a first-rate college. At the same time they were always raving about a girl schoolmate who lived next door to us. How pretty and sweet she was, how popular, and what taste in clothes! Couldn't I also pay more attention to my appearance and to social life? They were

overlooking the fact that this carefree friend of mine had little time left for school work and had failed several subjects. It seemed that my family had expected me to become Eve Curie and Hedy Lamar wrapped up in one. (Quoted in Komarovsky 1946, p. 185)

When parents suddenly urge their daughter to marry, however, they do not necessarily get the response they expect. As one daughter put it: "There is a lot of pressure from my mother to get married and not have a career. *This is one reason I am going to have a career* and wait to get married. . . . There is also some pressure from my father to get married, too" (quoted in Horner 1972 [1970c], p. 65). Some women even say that they want to have careers precisely because their mothers did not. Listen to these college juniors:

> My mother is now working as a secretary, but she didn't work until now. I don't want to end up like that.
> Another reason (I am going to have a career and wait to get married) is a reaction to my mother's empty life. (Quoted in Horner 1972 [1970c], p. 65)

By the time women are in college, then, parental attitudes and life styles may have become less important (Parsons et al. 1978). The attitudes of other students are important, however—especially those of men. Women whose boyfriends encourage them are less likely to experience fear of success in college (Horner 1970c) and tend to apply to graduate school in less traditional areas (Trigg and Perlman 1976). Some women may even attribute their own ambitions to the important men in their lives:

> He wants me to be intelligent. It is a source of pride to *him* that I do so well.

> I would have to explain myself if I got a C. I want him to think I'm as bright as he is.

> *He* thinks it would be a good idea for me to go to law school.

> *He* feels very strongly that I should go to graduate school to get a Master's degree. He does not want to feel that he has denied me a complete education. (Quoted in Horner 1972 [1970c], p. 66)

A woman's orientation toward the man in her life is not necessarily due to weakness or immaturity. As we saw in the section on working wives and mothers, a husband's attitude is so important to his wife's employment that Jesse Bernard has coined the phrase the "law of husband cooperation" (1974, p. 162). College women are anticipating the realities of married life by applying the "law of boyfriend cooperation."

But what happens to a woman once she has finished her education? Are her aspirations translated into actual employment, or do they fade away along with the other dreams of youth? And is the outcome still influenced by parents and peers as much as it was while she was in school? Unfortunately we cannot really answer these questions, because the research, like most of that in psychology, has been done with (white, middle-class) college students.

The one study that did examine caeer involvement in older women suggests that parents become less important (Bielby 1978). By the seventh year after college graduation it does not matter whether mother worked, although a relatively modest financial background does seem to encourage a daughter to seek out a career. The crucial factor, however, is the daughter's own sex-role attitudes. Once a daughter is out on her own, then, she seems to make her career decisions independently of parental influences.

Women on the Job

Once a woman has decided to have a career, what is work like for her? First of all, it is not as lucrative as it should be. After a decade of equal opportunity laws, most women still bring home paychecks only 60 percent as large as those of their husbands, brothers, and lovers. After summarizing research on the "missing" 40 percent, Elizabeth Almquist (1977) concludes that this gap is due not to the characteristics of employed women—neither to their education, occupation, work experience, or marital status nor to the number of children at home—but apparently to employer discrimination against women.

If a woman is single, an employer expects her to marry. If she is married, an employer expects her to have children and drop out. Yet even if a woman does not drop out (women are doing so less and less these days), she is not paid or promoted as much as her male counterpart. When a man and a woman with identical skills and competencies apply for work, they are given different sorts of jobs, even within the same company. He enters an executive training program; she enters the secretarial pool. And the initial differences increase as, once on the job, men are urged upward and women are not. He becomes regional sales manager; she becomes his private secretary. Although there are now a number of legal remedies which women are using for these blatantly discriminatory practices, there are other, more subtle ways of keeping a woman in her place on the job. Even when a woman holds the same job title as a man, she inhabits a different social world. The fact of being female influences her daily interactions in a variety of ways that can not only be upsetting and discouraging but can also interfere with her job performance and advancement.

THE TOKEN WOMAN

Many women who enter predominantly male fields find that they are treated as outsiders whose very presence is suspect. They are constantly reminded that they do not belong to the exclusive male club of serious professionals and certainly cannot share in its camaraderie. Hazing from men often takes the form of "the putdown"—small but significant insults that range from making sexist jokes to accusing female colleagues of being "women's lib freaks" (Bernard 1976, p. 25).

The pressure often starts in graduate school and continues after the woman has completed her training. Young female attorneys, for example, report that when they enter the court house the bailiff may comment, "What are you doing here? Oh, you're a lawyer! Are you a women's lib?" And some arrogant male attorneys may say things like "that . . . Public Defender is madly in love with you" (Levezey and Anderson 1974, p. 38).

If sexist remarks were the only problem, a woman might be able to shrug them off; but they are combined with a pervasive social isolation that Bernard calls "the stag effect" (1976, p. 23). Here again the difficulty begins in graduate school, when women are much less likely to have the benefit of a close working relationship with professors (Feldman 1974; Schwartz and Lever 1973). Even a professor who does agree to be the mentor or sponsor for a female student is likely to treat her differently than he would a male student, expecting her to supply clerical help and other services (Schwartz and Lever 1973). But the woman cannot really refuse, since the work done under the guidance of such an advisor or mentor usually forms the basis for her doctoral dissertation and the publications she needs to get a job.

Once she is on the job, the isolation continues. Many business and professional decisions are made over coffee, lunch, or cocktails. Important contacts are established and maintained on the golf course, on the squash court, and in other traditionally male settings. Being excluded from these informal social occasions does not just make the female professional feel lonely; it can seriously interfere with her ability to do her job. A female attorney who is excluded from the camaraderie of the officers of the court, for instance, may have more difficulty obtaining continuances, deals, and favors for her clients (Levezey and Anderson 1974). Promotions, job openings, and professional referrals are also discussed informally; by the time the female professional finds out about them they have often been filled by that promising young man who plays squash so well. In an academic setting a woman is often excluded from the exchange of ideas and the joint projects that are essential to re-search—and hence to career advancement (Kaufman 1978). One female assistant professor comments on this problem:

> Although my research interests are clearly in line with one of the older males in my department, he has never asked me to share my ideas with him or even to read some of his research proposals. I wouldn't feel so badly but I have a male colleague who is my age and whose dissertation was much further removed from this senior professor's area of interest. My young friend has just been asked to help formulate a new research proposal with our older colleague. . . . My main contact with my older colleague is that his oldest daughter attends the same university I grad-uated from and that remains our main topic of conversation. (Quoted in Kaufman 1978, p. 16)

Why do men exclude their female colleagues from the "old boys' network" of shop talk and informal social interaction? Some men are used to relating to women only in a sexual manner and may be uncom-fortable with them in any other situation. Kaufman suggests that this is a particular problem for single women and leads them to make com-ments like "I couldn't wait until my hair turned grey. . . . I felt people could no longer accuse me of 'hunting' for a husband, least of all some-one else's" (quoted in Kaufman 1978, p. 16).

Other researchers argue that men naturally tend to band together in all-male groups because of a genetic "male bond" (Tiger 1970) or because they see other males as more powerful and stimulating because they control more resources then women do (Lipman-Blumen 1976). Whatever the reason, men seem to feel that the presence of women interferes with the natural flow of things (Schmuck 1975). A male school administrator expressed this in terms of the need for an emotional release possible only in a relaxed, all-male group:

> When things get tough and uptight and we don't seem to be making any headway we lapse into other areas of common interest—football and basketball and the like. A woman would stop that very important process from occurring because apart from the job we wouldn't have any common areas of interest. I couldn't relax if a woman were an integral part of the management team. (Quoted in Schmuck 1975, p. 351)

Not all men feel this way. When the same researcher asked other male school administrators about this "locker room" attitude, two of them said,

> I've heard it. I've seen it, but I feel sorry for districts where admin-istrators must operate on such levels of emotional catharsis.

I've heard that. There is truth in it. I just have confidence in human beings that it would change [if a woman were hired]. It's a matter of proving her skills and she would be accepted.

(Pp. 352–53)

When faced with these subtle forms of discrimination, some women become discouraged and question their own competence. Although they resent being treated differently from men in the same position, they may still tolerate or even encourage the more benevolent forms of discrimination. Thus a woman may occasionally let her male colleagues protect her from controversy and pressure, which is initially reassuring but ultimately prevents her from obtaining valuable experience (Schmuck 1975).

Other women are lucky enough to find individual men who perceive their abilities and encourage them in their work. Thus, a number of female school administrators report that they had not even considered management positions at first, because they knew no women who held such jobs; then each woman, after being encouraged by a man, took one on and was able to overcome her initial feelings of inadequacy (Schmuck 1975).

A woman who receives no encouragement from male colleagues may try to make it on her own. But this is extremely difficult, as one female professor explained to Kaufman:

Although we don't like to admit it, it's not what you know but who you know in academe. My peers who have "made it" have done so on the coattails of some prominent man. This is true for both men and women. I'm not one of those older women who's going to tell you that it's easier now than it was some twenty years ago. In some ways I think it's harder for young women today than it was then. Discrimination has simply become more subtle. Women have the illusion that they can survive professionally on their own. I watch the young women enter our department out to prove they can make it. They don't form contacts with the older women, they are not accepted by the older men, and they compete directly among themselves and with the younger men. I watch them come and go. (Quoted in Kaufman 1978, p. 20)

Although they are often isolated from their male colleagues, women do have a source of support—each other. A feeling of solidarity often develops among them even if they do not see each other often. As one woman principal describes it:

It used to be when I walked into a room full of men and only one other woman I would tend to ignore her. Now when I walk into a similar situation the woman and I at least have eye-contact. I don't necessarily sit by her and I may not even talk to her, but we have a feeling of sisterhood and we support each other. There's too damn few of us (women); we found out we need to support each other. If there were more of us we would be free to act just as folks, but because there are so few of us, there is a common bond of being women. (Quoted in Schmuck 1975, pp. 350–51)

This sisterhood may take more concrete forms. In academia, for instance, women are beginning to form "old girls' networks." The women in a department or a school often look to each other for emotional support and professional collaboration. Many of them feel that the men simply cannot be counted on. One unmarried woman who is a full professor stated this view firmly:

I have been in academia a long time and no matter how many changes occur it is still evident to me that the only colleagues one can really feel comfortable with are other women. We may start out believing differently but experience teaches us something else. You can count on your male colleagues to tell you about their personal problems and even share some ideas about departmental politics but when it really counts, when it's time to write the research proposal, when it's time to allocate the merit increases, you can count yourself out if you are a woman. . . . I've seen it happen so many times. University living is male living on male terms . . . when we try to break barriers we seem to fail. The two younger men with whom I've done research are no longer in this department, they were both denied tenure, need I say more? (Quoted in Kaufman 1978, p. 20)

As part of the attempt to build a support network, women academics seem to combine work and social lives more than men do: their close friends are more likely to be professional colleagues. But compared with the colleague-friends of men, those of women are less likely to share their specific research interests, to be older and more established, and to be helpful to the women's career advancement (Kaufman 1978). There is a loose cluster of lower-ranking women in a variety of professional specialties. Although they are able to provide crucial emotional support for each other, these women cannot provide the avenues to career advancement that are available to their male counterparts through the guidance, cooperation, and friendship of powerful older males.

ACKNOWLEDGING FEMALE ACHIEVEMENTS

Of course most women do not enter predominantly male fields and hence do not suffer putdowns and social isolation. But many women find that their accomplishments, even in traditionally female occupations, are not acknowledged as readily as are those of men, for sex-role stereotypes tend to cloud the perception of women and their work.

Researchers have approached this problem by presenting the same piece of work to different college undergraduates and telling some that the work is by a woman and some that it is by a man; the subjects then rate the work's value and the creator's competence. In this classic study Goldberg (1968) found that college women rated male authors as better than female authors even though the male and female articles were identical. He concluded that prejudice against women is so pervasive that women themselves have internalized it.

This prejudice does not mean that people think that "no woman's achievement or work is as good as a man's." When Goldberg's study was repeated on other campuses, the results were confusing. Sometimes male students showed this bias while females did not (Etaugh and Rose 1975), while at other times neither sex was influenced by a professional author's gender, yet women rated more positively student essays that they thought were written by other women (Levenson et al. 1975). And when uneducated, middle-aged women were asked to evaluate professional articles on marriage, child discipline, and special education, they viewed the work of females more positively than that of males (Pheterson 1969). This may have been due to the greater maturity of the raters or to the nature of the topics, since Mischel (1974) later found that males writing in predominately masculine fields and females writing in predominantly feminine ones received higher ratings from college students.

In trying to account for these contradictory results, researchers have focused on different aspects of achievement. Some have looked at the characteristics that observers attribute to successful men and women. When a man and a woman are both presented as successful at a masculine task, for instance, students may think that the man must be skilled whereas the woman merely worked hard or was lucky (Deaux and Emswiller 1974; Feldman-Summers and Kiesler 1974). But with a less sex-typed job such as college teaching the professor's gender may be less important. Now the important thing may be subject matter: humanities professors may be seen as more friendly, attractive, and interested in teaching, while science professors may be seen as more logical, self-assured, and conscientious and as better scholars (Hesselbart 1977).

The sex-role stereotypes an individual associates with a particular task or occupation do not always affect his or her perception of the successful person performing it. One study asked college students to watch one woman succeed and one fail in assembling a carburetor. Here the successful woman was perceived as not only having more mechanical aptitude and interest in math and science than the unsuccessful woman, but also as being more worldly, warm, emotional, and creative. Thus, the woman succeeding at this masculine task was seen not as masculinized but, on the contrary, as having more of the positive characteristics associated with both the female and the male stereotypes (Stephan and Woolridge 1977).

Some researchers have argued that the contradictory results are largely due to the way the studies have been done. Not only are different colleges used each time, but also the students are given little information about the actual behavior of the supposedly successful men and women. The student raters may resort to sex-role stereotypes simply because they do not have much else to go on. Ellyn Kaschak (1978) tried to remedy this difficulty by describing the teaching methods of a man and a woman in traditionally masculine fields (business administration and chemistry), traditionally feminine fields (home economics and elementary education), and relatively nonsex-linked areas (psychology and history). She found that the academic field was not important, but the gender of the professor was. Male students rated male professors as more effective, powerful, concerned, likable, and excellent and indicated that they would be more likely to take a course from a male than from a female professor. Female students, on the other hand, did not rate male and female professors differently except in the area of power. In spite of their perception of the female faculty as less powerful, however, the female students still preferred to take courses with women. Since the relative powerlessness of female faculty members may be a reality, this study suggests that while males are still biased, some females are not and may even be starting to band together in response to male attitudes.

Even in Kaschak's study, however, the students were responding to written descriptions of people rather than to live individuals. Faced with a real person, they may pay more attention to actual behavior rather than to abstract stereotypes. In one study, for instance, undergraduates were interviewed by male and female counselors with or without diplomas prominently displayed in their offices: while the credentials increased the ratings of expertness, the sex of the counselor made no difference in them (Heppner and Pew 1977). Thus, even though male bias continues, it may be tempered by face-to-face contact with successful women. To feel that women in general are somehow less competent than men is one thing; to refuse to acknowledge the competence of a female one is actually dealing with is quite different.

All this research is recent and confusing. One major theme has appeared, however: nothing succeeds like success, especially for women. Once the quality of an individual's work is established, sexual bias seems to disappear. Thus, some researchers found that when paintings were presented as entries in a contest, the ones supposedly done by males were rated as better. When they were presented as winners, on the other hand, paintings done by males and females were valued equally (Pheterson et al. 1971). The same effect has been found in evaluations of professors. Undergraduates are more impressed by articles supposedly written by male as opposed to female graduate students, but they show no gender bias if they think the same articles were written by associate professors (Peck 1978).

In fact, if a woman can get past the initial gender bias to become established in her field, she may actually be perceived *more* positively than a man in the same position (Abramson et al. 1977). The researchers found this in studying the perception of lawyers and called it "the talking platypus phenomenon": "that is, when an individual achieves a level of success not anticipated, his/her achievement tends to be magnified rather than diminished. After all, it matters little what the platypus says, the wonder is that it can say anything at all" (Abramson et al. 1977, p. 123).

But is it unrealistic to perceive a successful professional woman as more competent than her male counterparts? After all, the barriers to female success are often so formidable that in order to succeed a woman has to be much more determined and talented than the men around her. Other professionals know this. Thus, in one study of school administrators almost everyone interviewed, man or woman, readily agreed that a woman must be "smarter, more competent and more capable" than a man to obtain an administrative position (Schmuck 1975, p. 345). This perception may even lead some men to expect their female colleagues to be "superwomen." One male principal, for instance, said he would leave his present position only if he were promoted—with one exception. He would accept a job transfer and even a cut in pay in order to go to a school district that had a female superintendent. He explained, "She'd be a wave-breaker. It would be an exciting district to work in because she would have been used to making waves. She would really be a super-stud!" (Schmuck 1975, p. 345).

Although it may be flattering to be viewed as a superwoman, it can also make a woman feel pressured to prove her worth. Thus, when asked whether women had to be more qualified in order to get an administrative job, one woman retorted, "Of course, women are smarter and more competent. We'll have full equality in this field when we have as many mediocre women as we have mediocre men" (quoted in Schmuck 1975, p. 345).

GETTING AHEAD

How does the perception of female achievement affect a woman who is applying for a job or a promotion? If it is a job that involves a tangible product such as written material or paintings, a woman's work may not be valued as much as a man's. But how does being female influence hiring and promotion in many jobs that involve interaction with others?

This question has been asked about business managers who deal primarily with people. The approach is similar to that for professors: undergraduates are presented with fictional descriptions of work or people and asked to rate them or indicate which ones they would hire. When the criteria for evaluation are specific, both men and women evaluate applicants for managerial jobs in a gender-neutral manner (Frank and Drucker 1977; Soto and Cole 1975).

Nonetheless, unfortunately anti-female bias still affects decisions about hiring and promotion. Earlier studies have indicated that in the real world women are discriminated against by those making decisions about hiring, promotion, and salaries (Fidell 1970; Rosen and Jerdee 1974). The studies using fictional descriptions were actually done to see whether providing managerial-related information can cut down on this anti-female bias. Apparently it can; when the performance of specific tasks is considered, men and women are evaluated in the same manner.

But hiring and promotion are based on much more than task performance. The social interaction between the interviewer and the applicant is crucial, as is the whole network of relationships involved in the applicant's previous job and hence reflected in her references. Larwood and Blackmore (1978), for instance, suggest that a woman may be screened out long before she reaches the point of being evaluated for a promotion. They argue that executives and others in leadership positions employ different styles with subordinates or group members depending on how much they feel they have in common with each. A subordinate who belongs to the same "in-group" as the executive gradually learns how to be a leader himself from being given more challenging tasks and being included in decisions. A subordinate who belongs to an "out-group," on the other hand, is simply told what to do and hence learns no leadership skills. When an entry-level executive position becomes available, the in-group member is recommended for promotion while the out-group member is not. Since business organizations are controlled by men, executives tend to groom other men who also belong to the male in-group. Thus women do not have to be consciously discriminated against; their out-group status is enough to prevent their advancement.

A great deal of research on large corporations supports this "in-group grooming" theory. A sponsor is important to the success of a man in a large organization—and absolutely essential for a woman. But a leader tends to groom those subordinates who are socially similar to himself; to put it another way, he promotes the careers of those with whom he can identify. As one corporate executive said, "Boy wonders rise under certain power structures. They're recognized by a powerful person because they are very much like him. He sees himself, a younger version, in that person. . . . Who can look at a woman and see himself?" (quoted in Kanter 1977, p. 52). Kanter notes that although men do sometimes sponsor women, the motivations are different. Thus, one male executive decided to sponsor a woman to prove he could handle a tricky management problem. In another case the corporate officers were looking for a high-powered woman they could use to demonstrate the organization's willingness to promote women.

THE FEMALE BOSS

It is extremely rare for a woman to become a business manager and rarer still for her to rise beyond a first-level supervisory job such as manager of secretaries. In 1971 a national survey of 163 large companies showed that only 2 percent of first-level management jobs were held by women, while practically none of the middle- and top-management jobs were (Kanter 1975).

Now times are changing. And as increasing numbers of women obtain these jobs and do them well, the idea that women are "temperamentally unfit" for leadership is being challenged. As one male school administrator put it:

> We have a lot of myths about women; they are flighty, there is one time a month they can't be depended upon to make rational decisions, they cannot be detached, and are too emotional. Typical minority prejudices. The people in power tend to hold such myths about the minority and then work to increase the myths. We've done a brilliant job of that in our predominantly male organization. (Quoted in Schmuck 1975, p. 350)

Social scientists studying women in management are coming to the conclusion that the problem is not female biology or personality; it is the social structure of organizations. This structure affects female executives the same way it does other career women—except more so. Thus while many professional women are subjected to "the putdown" and "the stag effect," women in management often have the more extreme experience of functioning as the lone woman in an all-male work group. The "solo" woman often suffers from what Kanter calls "mistaken identity." The men with whom she works perceive her in terms of their own sex-role expectations, seeing her in four basic ways: as a "mother," as a "sex object" or "seductress," as a "pet" (group mascot), or as an "iron maiden" who is militant and unapproachable (Kanter 1975, p. 57).

Other studies have suggested that these solo women are likely to be ostracized and treated as invisible (Wolman and Frank 1975). A lone woman may aggravate her own isolation by the way in which she tries to cope with the problem. In order to avoid being treated as a sex object, for instance, she may try to minimize her sexual attributes so she can blend into the predominant male culture.

> You dressed carefully and quietly to avoid attracting attention; you had to remember to swear once in a while, to know a few dirty jokes, and never to cry if you got attacked. You fended off all attempts of men to treat you like a woman; you opened doors before they could hold them, sat down before a chair could be held, and threw on a coat before it could be held for you. (Hennig 1970, vi–21 as quoted in Kanter 1975, p. 59)

Other lone women managers may undercut the perception of their own competence by letting someone else take credit for their accomplishments. Some may even take pride in their ability to influence a group of men without the men's recognizing the source of the idea. Kanter compares this strategy with that of other minority groups who try to minimize the visibility of their success lest the majority notice it and take action against them. She suggests that lone women may thus have a concern similar to that of Jews who feel that statistics about the high percentage of Jews at elite colleges such as Yale should not be broadcast. She goes on to say that the idea of "fear of success" in women needs to be reexamined, since it may actually be "fear of visibility" (Kanter 1975, p. 60).

Sex-role stereotypes can also interfere with a woman's management functions. Women are expected to be nurturant and dependent, not task-oriented and authoritative. When they do assume a leadership position, others (especially men) are likely to ignore and circumvent their authority, going to the woman's male subordinates for information and appealing to her male superiors for decisions. Such actions reflect a problem of "legitimation," not lack of leadership skills. Both laboratory studies and field observations suggest that a clear and emphatic directive from above is important: this woman *is* your boss and we back her up (Fennell et al. 1978; Kanter 1975, 1977). While male managers also need this "reflected power" from a "godfather" or sponsor to underscore their authority, it is not as crucial for them because they do not have to counteract widespread misconceptions about and prejudices against their leadership role.

AGAINST ALL ODDS: THE SUCCESSFUL PROFESSIONAL WOMAN

In spite of the many barriers to female achievement, ever more women are engaged in successful careers. Each one of these women serves as an example of broader options for others deciding whether to work outside the home, and in what capacity. Numerous writers have commented on the importance of "role models" for young women making life decisions. But no theoretical discussion makes the point as well as personal recollections, such as this one by psychologist Elizabeth Douvan.

> The model who most impressed me—the one who provided the most startling and fresh view of what was possible in life—was an unmarried woman, a social scientist of international reputation in a specialty within her field so male-dominated that it was my impression at the time that she was the unique woman—an impression the years since have affected only slightly. . . .
> . . . I saw her and knew her because she was a much sought-after dinner guest in the [college] dormitories.

> She was sought after because of her great charm. Essentially a shy woman, she had firm convictions and an inner integrity and competence that allowed her both unambivalent self-assertion and a gentle, beautiful personhood. She was my first experience with an unmarried woman who clearly contradicted two stereotypes which I had brought to college as part of my baggage from home: a) that a woman who didn't marry was by definition unhappy and unfulfilled, and b) that unmarried women could not conceivably have chosen their status. A man might choose to be a bachelor, but outside of religious orders a woman who didn't marry had obviously never been asked. . . .
>
> My model stood as the simplest and clearest concrete evidence that these assumptions were wrong. . . . I was delighted and enlarged by the discovery. (Douvan 1976, p. 9)

Other young women find married career women to be the most compelling and illuminating models, as was true for a friend of Douvan's who felt that she would not have been able seriously to entertain the possibility of a career, without such a real-life demonstration that it is possible to commit oneself to work without abandoning marriage and motherhood (Douvan 1976).

Not that the example of a successful older woman is all it takes. Women must also have the *opportunity* to succeed. Many women may not feel ambitious because they actually have no chance for advancement. When an opportunity becomes available, however, a woman's attitude is likely to change. Kanter illustrates this by describing her interview with a woman who had spent sixteen years as a secretary in a large corporation:

> Five years ago, she would have said that she never wanted to be anything but a secretary. She also would have told you that since she had recently had children she was thinking of quitting. She said secretarial work was not a good enough reason to leave the children.
>
> Then came an affirmative action program, and Linda was offered a promotion. She wavered. It would mean leaving her good female friends for a lonely life among male managers. Her friends thought she was abandoning them. She worried whether she could handle the job. But her boss talked her into it and promised to help, reassuring her that he would be her sponsor.
>
> So Linda was promoted, and now she handles a challenging management job most successfully. Seeing friends is the least of her many reasons to come to work every day, and her ambitions have soared. She wants to go right to the top.
>
> "I have fifteen years left to work," she says. "And I want to move up six grades to corporate vice president—at least." (Kanter 1976, p. 91)

Of course, many women do not want to have a career, and many others do not have the economic advantages and education that would enable them to enter a profession. Successful professional women may still be important to them, however, as examples of female potential. When Alice Rossi (1965) asked a number of college-educated women what kinds of success they wanted for themselves, they usually mentioned things like being the "mother of several highly accomplished children" or the "wife whose husband becomes very prominent" (p. 126). When she asked them what kinds of successful women they most *admired*, however, their answers were quite different. Now they mentioned women who had received scientific, scholarly, literary, or artistic awards. Thus successful professional women may serve as symbols for all women.

Chapter 11

Third World Women

M ILLIONS of American women share not only the problems of their sex but also those of being black, native American, Puerto Rican, Mexican-American, or Asian-American. Their racial background adds another dimension to their life experience, for these Third World women suffer from the "triple exploitation" of belonging to a racial minority, of being female, and (in most cases) of being poor (Hare and Hare 1970).

Life for minority women is dramatically different from life for white women. Black women, for instance, are more often single than white women and more likely to work, to support their own households, and to live in severe poverty. But there is more to racial differences than employment rates or statistics, for belonging to a racial minority has a profound effect on every aspect of life.

Most discussions of Third World women focus on American blacks, who comprise 89 percent of the group. Since little has been written by other minority women, let us consider what black women have to say.*

---

* Not only is there little material available about women in other minority groups, but also census data and other government information usually lump other minorities together with blacks (Herman 1979). In spite of the fact, then, that things may be very different for other groups, I have only been able to mention them in passing.

Traditional Femininity—

Pedestal or Trap?

Many white women feel that the traditional homemaker role is frustrating. Over the past ten or fifteen years an increasing number of them have begun to work outside the home, not only for economic reasons but also in a search for self-fulfillment. Many black women, on the other hand, would prefer to be full-time homemakers, for most of them work at menial and low-paying jobs not out of choice but out of necessity. Black men are so discriminated against in the job market that they cannot possibly support their families with their paychecks alone. Black women see staying home with the children as a privilege, not a restriction, as a tangible and desirable benefit of dominant white status (Mayo 1973). Mae King expresses this viewpoint in commenting on a 1972 television special on discrimination against women:

> Not one black woman was featured. A white female reporter ended this special by concluding that it was true that America has placed its women on a pedestal. But, there are now indications, she admonished, that a large number of these women are no longer satisfied with this position. The protection and security that it once offered, she asserted, no longer obtain for a significant number of them. However, since America has never placed the African-American woman on a pedestal, nor provided her with protection or security, such a statement characteristically ignores the black woman's situation. (King 1973, p. 20)

Other black writers have commented that "it is hard for a black woman to imagine liberating herself from the household when she already has been forced out to work" (Hare and Hare 1970, p. 68). After striving in vain to meet society's concept of the woman's role as full-time homemaker, she is often puzzled and angry when this ideal is challenged.

> The things white women are demanding liberation from are what we've never even experienced yet. How many black women stay home bored with kids while husband is off earning a lot of money? I'm sure many black women would love to stay home and be "housewives." (Quoted in Hare and Hare 1970, p. 68)

Television, movies, and magazines heighten the black woman's feelings of deprivation by presenting traditional femininity as both alluring and the only "normal" way to live. One black woman recalls how the women in her family "all seemed to be relentless achievers, often providers," including her mother who "wanted to compel me to think for myself because she knew, whatever else she didn't know, that I would

never be able to survive if I didn't." In spite of being raised to be independent and work-oriented, however she often longed for the life of
tranquil domesticity portrayed in the media. And just as she longed for
this white middle-class way of life, so did the black men around her.

> I can't remember when I first learned that my family expected me to
> work, but it had been drilled into me that the best and only sure support
> was self-support.
>
> The fact that my family expected me to have a career should have
> made the things I wanted different from what little white girls wanted
> according to the popular sociological view. But I don't believe any so-
> ciologist took into account a man like my stepfather. My stepfather gave
> me "housewife lessons." It was he who taught me how to clean house and
> how I should act around men. "Don't be like your mother," he told me.
> "She's a nice lady but she's a bad wife. She was just lucky with me. I
> want you to get a *good* husband."
>
> Although he never managed to fully domesticate me, it was him that
> I finally listened to because he was saying essentially the same things I
> read in the magazines, saw in the movies, gaped at on television. Growing
> up in Harlem, I listened to these messages no less intently than the little
> white girls who grew up on Park Avenue, in Scarsdale, or on Long Island.
> In a way I needed to hear them even more than they did. Their alternative
> was not eternal Aunt Jemimahood, Porgy-'n'-Besshood. Mine was. (Wallace
> 1979, p. 46)

The cruel irony of this is that most whites do not actually live the way
people do in the media. Millions of white women have also been
"forced out to work." Indeed, it is precisely those little girls from the
affluent neighborhoods of Park Avenue, Scarsdale, and Long Island—
and only those girls, black or white—who will actually grow up to
marry men who can afford to have their wives stay home with the
children.

Most people also do not look like the actors and actresses on television. White women are often upset that they cannot attain the
standards of beauty expressed in all those sexy ads. They are too fat or
too thin, too tall or too short; their teeth are too crooked, their hair too
stringy. If it is upsetting for white women, however, it is infuriating for
blacks and other Third World women. Their racial characteristics have
no part in the all-American image. "A major complaint of white women
has been against . . . women as women exploited for commercialism.
But, consider the insult added to injury to black women by some of the
hair coloring advertisements, such as one in which a blond huskily
inquires, 'Don't you wish you were one, too?'" (Mayo 1973, pp.
175–76). Like poor white women, Third World women cannot afford
all the creams, lotions, and frills that are part of the image of the perfect
woman. Thus, not only the social role but also the physical characteristics of the "truly feminine woman" are outside their experience.

Black Superwoman and

the Myth of Matriarchy

There are many images of the black woman today: "Sapphire," "Mammy," "exotic tiger," a great little dancer with "natural rhythm." The predominant image, however, is that of a superwoman who can endure through it all.

> From the intricate web of mythology that surrounds the black woman a fundamental image emerges. It is of a woman of inordinate strength, who does not have the same fears, weaknesses, and insecurities as other women, but believes herself to be and is, in fact, stronger emotionally than most men. In other words, she is a superwoman. (Wallace 1979, p. 45)

This image is shared by many people—including blacks—who are now economically comfortable and want to think that although life is hard for the black woman, she can cope. For if the black woman is so strong, they need not worry about her plight, much less do anything to change it. Since it is less painful to focus on the black woman's strength than on her misery, it is often hard to let this myth go.

> I remember once I was watching a news show with a black male friend of mine who had a Ph.D. in psychology. We were looking at some footage of a black woman who seemed barely able to speak English, though at least six generations of her family before her had certainly claimed it as their first language. She was in bed wrapped in blankets, her numerous small, poorly clothed children huddled around her. Her apartment looked rat-infested, cramped, and dirty. She had not, she said, had heat and hot water for days. My friend, a solid member of the middle class now but surely no stranger to poverty in his childhood, felt obliged to comment—in order to assuage his guilt, I can think of no other reason—"That's a *strong* sister," as he bowed his head in reverence. (Wallace 1979, p. 45)

This image of the black superwoman derives partially from reality. Black women suffered terribly under slavery and since then have lived lives of severe economic and physical deprivation. Anyone would have to be strong to endure so much and still emerge with the indomitable spirit shown by many black women. This image is reinforced by the myth of "black matriarchy," which was articulated by social scientists in the 1960s and has since become highly popularized. Usually attributed to Daniel Moynihan, this theory maintains that black women "rule the roost" because black families are so unstable that they cannot count on the black male to be the breadwinner. Moynihan argued that the instability of the black family began with slavery, when blacks were not permitted to form permanent unions, and has since been aggravated by the black male's inability to find steady employment (Rainwater and Yancey 1967).

Other social scientists have elaborated on this basic idea by maintaining that the black woman, however inadvertently, perpetuates the pattern of male absence by becoming "disgusted with the financially dependent husband," which "further alienates the male from family life" (Pettigrew 1964, p. 15), and by participating in a cycle of poor mothering due to the maternal neglect and self-hatred she passes down from generation to generation (Kardiner and Ovesey 1958). They have traced black child-rearing methods back to the days of slavery, arguing that black mothers were forced to emasculate their sons in order to ensure the latter's survival in a hostile white society that would not tolerate aggression and independence in blacks, especially male blacks. "In effect, [the black mother under slavery] had to take the role of slave master, treat the child with capricious cruelty, hurt him physically and emotionally, and demand that he respond in an obsequious helpless manner—a manner she knew would enhance his chances of survival (Grier and Cobbs 1968, p. 171).* The general picture is of a black man castrated by whites—with the knowing complicity of black women.

This image of the emasculated black male is not confined to social science. Black women share it and often feel that their own suffering is insignificant in comparison with that of black men.

> The American black woman is haunted by the mythology that surrounds the American black man. It is a mythology based upon the real persecution of black men: castrated black men hanging by their necks from trees; black men shining shoes; black men behind bars, whipped raw by prison guards and police; . . . . Every time she starts to wonder about her own misery, to think about reconstructing her life, the ghosts pounce. "*You* crippled the black man. *You* worked against him. *You* betrayed him. *You* laughed at him. *You* scorned him. *You* and the white man."
>
> Not only does the black woman continue to see the black man historically as a cripple; she refuses to take seriously the various ways he's been able to assert his manhood and capabilities in recent years. . . . She sees only the masses of unemployed black men, junkies, winos, prison inmates. She does not really see the masses of impoverished, unemployed black women, their numerous children pulling at their skirts; or, if she does, she sees these women and children only as a further humiliation and burden to that poor, downtrodden black man.
>
> She sees only the myth. In fact what most people see when they look at the black man is the myth. (Wallace 1979, p. 87)

* Although Grier and Cobbs are black male psychiatrists, the viewpoint of their book is essentially the same as that of the white, male social scientists writing about black matriarchy.

This image of the castrated black man is compelling. To determine its validity, we need to look at how black women and men actually lived under slavery and how they live today.

THE HORRORS OF SLAVERY

As blacks have begun to study their own history, some have concluded that things were not quite the way white social scientists have depicted them. First of all, many slaves did live in stable families headed by a male-female partnership. While these unions were not usually sanctioned by white laws, the fact that so many of them existed "suggests that blacks, both males and females, took traditional marriage and all it entailed, including male authority, quite seriously" (Wallace 1979, p. 87).

And then there is the fact that humiliation was not reserved for the black male alone. As Michele Wallace puts it, "Yes, black men were called boys. Black women were also called girls. But the slaves thought of themselves as 'mens and womens'" (1979, p. 87). Wallace goes on to point out that while both sexes had ways to set themselves apart from ordinary slaves, the opportunities for males were actually more impressive and varied. A woman could excel at physical labor, become the sexual partner of her white master, serve as a mammy for his children, or be a house servant with a special skill such as laundering or weaving. A man, on the other hand, could excel at manual labor; become a "driver" or black overseer in the fields; work as artisan, craftsman, or mechanic; function as body servant to the white master; win influence through fighting in the American revolution; or even lead a slave revolt.

Wallace also counters the charge that only black women consorted with the enemy. Both the female mammy and the male driver were hated figures who were accused of oppressing their fellow slaves and being overloyal to their white masters. Both these figures actually provided some benefits, on the other hand, since they could intercede on behalf of their fellow slaves. The male driver, in addition, helped counter the image of the black man as a "boy" by providing a living example of a black man in a position of authority.

Slavery was horrible for all blacks, both male and female. To blame their plight on each other is senseless and condescending. As Wallace concludes:

> Viewing American slavery with any kind of objectivity is extremely difficult, mostly because the record was unevenly and inconsistently kept. Nevertheless, to suggest that the black man was emasculated by slavery is to suggest that the black man and the black woman were creatures without will, as well as that a black woman could not be equally humiliated. Slave men and women formed a coherent and, as much as pos-

sible, a beneficial code of behavior and values, based upon the amalgama-
tion of their African past and the forced realities of their American
experience—in other words, an African-American culture. (Wallace
1979, p. 88)

THE BLACK FAMILY TODAY

What about the current black life styles? Does the black superwoman
dominate the family unit, earning all the money and robbing the weaker,
unemployed male of his masculinity? Some black writers agree that this
is partially true, and suggest that the realities of life force black women
into this position, whether they like it or not.

> Toward the black man many black women must be deceptive. On
> the one hand these women must hide their conviction that black men
> have failed as liberators of the race, while on the other hand they are
> well aware of the necessity of being the backbone of the family without
> seeming to be so. They have mixed feelings about black men and speak
> of "hurting" experiences with them. They believe that they have been
> torn apart by whites and can't understand why black men do not, in
> their view, appreciate the way in which they, black women, have "helped
> the black race to survive."
>
> They generally must take pains to avoid the appearance of posing
> a threat to black men as leaders or whatever and thus feel compelled to
> express positive attitudes toward them. At the same time, however, they
> have internalized white society's low regard for black men, but they are
> troubled by their appraisals of black men and their performance. . . .
>
> Thus the burden of the family seems to fall upon the black woman, in
> her view, at the same time as she is told that the man should be superior
> and that she must "play second fiddle." (Hare and Hare 1970, p. 66)

Other black writers, however, maintain that the concept of the
matriarch is "the most pernicious of the popular stereotypes about the
black woman" (Epstein 1973, p. 156). Studies show that most black
families are actually egalitarian, with both spouses sharing in the decisions and the household work. Nor is the black woman the primary
wage earner: in 85 percent of these families husbands outearn wives
(King 1973). Tables 11.1 and 11.2 show that black women earn *less* and
are unemployed *more* than black men. In fact, black women are actually
the poorest paid of all workers, male or female, black or white. Black
female teenagers feel this the most; they suffer from unemployment far
more than any other group.

Black women have had to be strong, but this has not necessarily
caused the black family to be disorganized, or the black male to be "irresponsible" as a provider and authority. As Cynthia Fuchs Epstein points

TABLE 11.1

*Median Weekly Earnings of American Workers
Sixteen Years of Age and Older*

	May 1970	May 1978
White men	$157	$279
Black men	113	218
White women	95	167
Black women	81	158

Source: A. M. Herman, "Money: Still . . . small change for Black women," *Ms.* (February 1979) VII(8):98. Original table untitled and based on statistics provided by the U.S. Department of Labor, Bureau of Labor Statistics.

TABLE 11.2

*United States Unemployment Rates—
September 1978*

	Percentage
Black teenage women	41.2
Black teenage men	35.5
White teenage women	15.9
White teenage men	12.8
Black adult women	11.3
Black adult men	7.2
White adult women	5.6
White adult men	3.1

Source: A. M. Herman, "Money: Still . . . small change for Black women," *Ms.* (February 1979) VII(8): 96. Based on statistics provided by the U.S. Department of Labor, Bureau of Labor Statistics.

out, "strength is not the same as dominance" (1973, p. 156). She offers the following description of a black mother, given by a woman physician:

My mother was not the stronger of my parents but she was the more aggressive, always planning and suggesting ideas to improve the family's situation. A dressmaker by trade, she would slip out to do domestic work by the day when times got hard, often not telling my father about it. He was a bricklayer and carpenter but had trouble finding work because he was unable to get union membership. (P. 157)

BLAMING THE (FEMALE) VICTIM

If there is little truth to the myth of the black matriarch, why has it persisted? Mae King suggests that it is a way to blame the black woman for the oppression suffered by all blacks. "It's not our fault that blacks have been dehumanized," white Americans can say; "black women caused the problem by emasculating black men." In King's words:

> The fact that the matriarchy myth was popularized and widely accepted in this country by all segments of society, is a reflection of the depth of the cruelty that America from its inception has inflicted upon the black woman. For this myth, if carried to its logical conclusions, tends to make the black woman responsible for the creation of the social, educational, economic, and political institutions in this country which, historically, explicitly and implicitly, have been structured to deny equality in all of these areas to *all* black people. Another inference of the matriarchy notion is the exemption of white America from responsibility for the oppression of blacks and the conditions that inevitably resulted from this action. Instead, the black woman who is at the very bottom of the economic scale, earning an average wage in 1966 of $3,487 a year as compared to $4,580 for white women, is blamed for the consequences of white America's systematic efforts to dehumanize blacks. The absurdity of this myth is astounding, superceded only by its cruelty. After all, matriarchy in its historical usage denotes a position of power which, of course, neither black women nor black men have secured in America. (1973, p. 16)

King also suggests that the matriarch image permits white America to exploit black women more readily. If black women are so tough, hardworking, and dominant at home, we need not worry about protecting their fragile femininity on the job. "Such an image permits the most outrageous exploitation of black females as a cheap labor source. By 'defeminizing' them, America could subject them to the most harsh and unsafe working conditions without violating the white ethics that sustain the system" (1973, p. 16).

Not only does white America espouse the concept of black matriarchy. With the rise of the Black Movement in the late 1960s, black men took up the issue. Centuries of oppression led to an explosion of outrage—and some of this anger was directed at black women. Michele Wallace describes the powerful emotional impact this had on her as a black teenager:

> Then in 1968, the year I turned 16, blackness came to Harlem. . . . And Harlemites, who had always been divided into two distinct categories—the black bourgeoisie, and the poor—now began to split into more factions. . . . But all parties managed to agree on at least one issue: the black woman's act needed intensive cleaning up. She was one of the main reasons the black man had never been properly able to take hold of his situation in this country.
>
> I was fascinated by all of this. Not by the political implications of a black movement in a white America. I quickly realized that was a male responsibility. But by how it would affect my narrow universe. To me and

many other black women the Black Movement seemed to guarantee that our secret dreams of being male-dominated and supported women were that much more attainable. If black men had power, as in black power, then we would become the women of the powerful.

But first we had a hell of a history to live down. We had been rolling around in bed with the slave master while the black man was having his penis cut off; we had never been able to close our legs to a white man nor deny our breast to a white child; we had been too eagerly loyal to our white male employer, taking the job he offered when he would give none to our man, cleaning his house with love and attention while our man was being lynched by white men in white hoods. We had not allowed the black man to be a man in his own house. We had driven him to alcohol, to drugs, to crime, to every bad thing he had ever done to harm himself or his family because our eyes had not reflected his manhood.

I felt shocked by this history. . . . What must I do, I wondered, to atone for my errors and make myself more palatable? I must be, black men told me, more feminine, more attractive, and above all more sub-missive, in other words a "natural woman." (1979, p. 46)

Black feminists like Wallace think that although the American black's history of anguish and oppression is certainly shocking, it still cannot account for the intensity of the black male's anger, especially since much of this anger is directed at other blacks. Wallace concludes that black men identify with white America. They want all the rights and privileges white men have, including that of male dominance. She dis-cusses this in terms of the myth of black male castration under slavery:

Yet the myth of the black man's castration in slavery has been nurtured over a century. The presumed dominance of the black female during slavery would not be quite enough to explain the full extent of black male anger, especially since it was more untrue than not, and at some point the black man must have known that. Rather his actual gripe must be that the black woman, his woman, was not *his* slave, that his right to expect her complete service and devotion was usurped. She *was*, after all, the white man's slave. (1979, p. 88)

THE ENCROACHMENT OF PATRIARCHY

The myth of matriarchy demonstrates how powerful the dominant white culture is in America. In the three hundred years that blacks have been here, black women have had at least equal status with black men. Black women have always worked and been strong, independent figures within the black family. They have not been "traditionally feminine" women who stayed home with the children. But as blacks began to fight for their rights and to participate more fully in this society, they took on its values—and these values included male dominance and the traditional role of women.

Native American women have also experienced the encroachment of white patriarchy. When Europeans arrived in this country, they found that in many Indian tribes the women had considerable status and power (Jensen 1977). Among the Senecas, for instance, everyone lived in matrilocal households containing fifty to sixty people. After marriage the husband moved into the household where his wife's female relatives lived with their spouses and children. The women owned the land, which they inherited through their mothers and cultivated by hand in female groups. The women also controlled the distribution of surplus food, participated in their own political councils, and had the power to elect and depose civil rulers. The men specialized in hunting and being warriors.

After the influx of Europeans the Senecas' agricultural production fell, as lands were burned in war and the natives fell prey to strange European diseases. Missionaries came determined to teach the men to use agricultural tools and the women to spin and weave, and encouraged the Senecas to fence off their land and cultivate it in smaller family groups. The female Seneca's power was gradually weakened, as her economic function was eliminated and nuclear family units replaced communal living (Jensen 1977).

Jensen (1977) argues that the very strength of female dominance among the Senecas is demonstrated by the tremendous difficulties that missionaries, government, and reformers encountered as they attempted to "civilize" the natives by imposing on them white cultural values and customs. Perhaps the final blow was missionary boarding schools, which have served as the "cornerstone of native education, the foundation for indoctrination" (Witt 1976, p. 252). Children enter these schools at five or six years of age and are taught woodworking, car repair, house painting, or farm work—if they are male. Girls are taught only domestic and secretarial skills. Witt concludes that "the Government's master plan for women has been to generate an endless stream of domestics and, to a lesser extent, secretaries" (1976, p. 252). An old Cheyenne proverb summarizes the way the white man went about destroying the native American culture: "A nation is not conquered until the hearts of its women are on the ground. Then, it is done, no matter how brave its warriors nor how strong its weapons" (Witt 1976, p. 251).

Not that all minority groups originally had systems of female dominance. In China and Japan, for instance, the philosophy of Confucius had already eroded the position of women, who were previously scholars, warriors, and leaders. Although Asian-American women who came to the United States found the streets were not paved with gold as they had been led to expect, they did find that American customs permitted greater flexibility and opportunity than did those in their native lands (Fujitomi and Wong 1973). Adopting the values and customs of the dominant American culture has thus improved the status of women in these groups.

The status of Mexican-American women has also improved somewhat, compared with what it was (and is) in Mexico. One can trace a similar process of patriarchal encroachment earlier in Mexican history, however: when the Spanish conquered Mexico in the sixteenth century, they further debased Mexican women, who were already living in a culture where females were viewed as property (Nieto-Gomez 1976). In the United States today, Chicanas are often torn between the traditional patriarchal values of their Mexican-American culture and the more liberal white norms.

BLACK WOMEN AND SELF-ESTEEM

Social scientists have argued that mother-headed households have disastrous effects on black women: these strong women must realize that they are not "normal," that they do not measure up to the standards of femininity set by the dominant white culture; with this realization they must grow to hate themselves and develop low self-esteem. This argument assumes that black women adopt the values of the dominant white culture. Lena Wright Myers comments on the arrogance of this white male bias:

> Much of the traditional literature of social science . . . has concluded that the black woman could not possibly value herself. But this very conclusion is a function of systematic biases in social research. Some social scientists are guilty of attributing the same negative identity to black women as society at large does, and, therefore, of supporting societal stereotypes. These scholars assume that the standards of white, male society are everyone's standards; they ignore the possibility of *selectivity* among roles and reference groups for black women in the development and maintenance of self-esteem.
>
> I argue that it is time for a new view of the black woman, one that allows for the possibility of self-esteem and pride. Blacks do not necessarily measure themselves against whites, nor black women against white women. The mother-headed household has assets as well as liabilities and, in fact, may be a source of strength and pride. (1975, pp. 240–41)

Myers suggests that black women heads of households may see themselves as successful individuals precisely because they are able to provide steady incomes through their own employment. The role of head of household may thus be a source of pride and strength, not a cause for self-hatred. And in developing pride, they are likely to look to other black women to evaluate their own achievements.

To test her hypothesis, Myers interviewed 250 black women in a midwestern city and found that virtually none of them compared herself with white women as successful mother, wife, and provider. Forty percent used "black women they know" as a reference group, while 55 percent said "black women in general." Their feelings about why they were successful mothers depended on their own employment status: those who worked felt successful for being a "good provider," while those who did not work attributed their maternal success to the familial role.

Myers concludes that it is time for social science to stop evaluating the black family structure on the basis of white middle-class standards. *Black* social scientists should begin to investigate the experience of black women, for only blacks who share that experience have the knowledge and expertise to interpret it.

Black Women and Achievement

Since black women have always had to work to support their families, many people feel that the issues of achievement and success are less full of conflict for them. According to this view, black women are *expected* to work, so employment should not be considered as interfering with the wife-mother role in the black community; and with the new affirmative action programs, blacks actually have an advantage in obtaining jobs. "Let's be realistic," such people say. "Employment and careers are actually easier for black women than for white women today."

But is this the true situation? If things are easier, many black women do not know it, for their actual employment prospects are pretty dismal. Not only do they have more trouble finding work than have whites or black men; but when they do get a job, it pays less and is likely to involve domestic services, farm labor, or other menial tasks. The occupational distribution in Table 11.3 shows that, although since 1970 black women have shifted away from being maids, many more blacks than whites still work at unskilled, boring jobs. The job possibilities for other minority women may be even more depressing. Only one of ten native Americans living on a reservation can find a job in the winter, for example. And if they do leave the reservation to find work, native Americans are still trapped in the lowest-paying occupations (Witt 1976).*

Minority women encounter racial discrimination in obtaining both education and employment. But what about their personal motivations and experience on the job? Do they actually experience less emotional conflict than white women? Not necessarily, as we will see.

---

* The employment statistics in tables 11.1–11.3 are based on census data that lumps other minorities in with blacks. Nevertheless, statistics alone do not express special problems like those experienced by America's one million native Americans.

TABLE 11.3

Occupational Distribution of American Women—1970 and 1977

	Black Women		White Women	
	1970	1977	1970	1977
Professional and technical workers	10.8%	14.3%	15.0%	16.1%
Managers and administrators	1.9	2.9	4.8	6.3
Clerical workers	20.8	26.0	36.4	35.9
Sales workers	2.5	2.6	7.7	7.3
Craft and kindred workers	0.8	1.3	1.2	1.7
Operatives	17.6	15.9	14.1	11.3
Nonfarm laborers	0.7	1.2	0.4	1.1
Private household workers	17.5	8.9	3.4	2.2
Service workers (except private household)	25.6	26.0	15.3	16.7
Farmers and farm managers	0.1	*	0.3	0.3
Farm laborers and supervisors	1.5	0.9	1.5	1.1
Total	100.0%	100.0%	100.0%	100.0%

* Less than 0.05 percent.
Source: A. M. Herman, "Money: Still . . . small change for Black women," *Ms.* (February 1979) VII(8):98. Based on statistics provided by U.S. Department of Labor, Bureau of Labor Statistics; format altered by author.

FREE TO SUCCEED?

In the late 1960s, researchers found that black women showed less fear of success than did white women (Weston and Mednick 1970). In fact, the male-female pattern was actually reversed in blacks, with men showing more FOS imagery than women showed. Thus, Horner (1970c) reported the following rates of FOS imagery among college students:

| White men | 10 percent | Black men | 67 percent |
| White women | 64 percent | Black women | 29 percent |

Horner's interpretation was that "for most black men and white women, the attainment of success and/or leadership is seen as an unexpected event, making them the object of competitive assault or social rejection" (1972 [1970c], p. 63).

Most researchers have attributed the low rates of fear of success among black women to the fact that they have been encouraged to be independent and assertive and, above all, to seek the best possible educations and jobs. Not only do their working mothers provide a career-oriented model, but these strong women actively encourage their daughters to follow in their footsteps. As a black female physician put it, "From the time you could speak you were given to understand that your primary interest in life was to get the best education you could, the best job you could. There was no other way!" (quoted in Epstein 1973, p. 161).

In an interview study of thirty-one black professional women, Epstein found that parents did not push their daughters toward marriage because they saw it as "unreliable." Racial discrimination prevents black men from earning much money; so even in middle-class black families there is no "guarantee that Prince Charming will come equipped with a good profession and a suburban home, or will come at all." Consequently, "the educated black girl is prepared in both subtle and direct ways to adapt if the dream should fail"; in other words, she is pushed toward a career instead (Epstein 1973, pp. 162–63). The result is that these black career women did not feel anxious about the prospect of not getting married. Their lack of anxiety about marital prospects is related to the low rates of fear of success in black women. Why should they be anxious about how competitive achievement will affect their marriage-ability, when they are not counting on getting married anyway?

But times have changed. The black women Epstein interviewed began their careers before the rise of the Black Movement. The new emphasis on bolstering the black male's masculinity has heightened concern about femininity. Thus Horner (1970c) reported that black women started showing more fear of success in 1970. And black women are beginning to write about the new pressures to be feminine by not being competitive and career-oriented. Michele Wallace suggests that these pressures are so severe that many black women now feel that motherhood is the only acceptable activity for them.

> But the black woman, who had pooh-poohed the Women's Movement, was left with only one activity that was not considered suspect: motherhood. A baby could counteract the damaging effect a career might have upon her feminine image. A baby clarified a woman's course for at least the next five years. No need for her to bother with difficult decisions about whether or not she ought to pursue promotion or return to school for an advanced degree, both of which might attract even more hostility from black men. If she didn't find a man, she might just decide to have a baby anyway.
>
> . . . Career and success are still the social and emotional disadvantages to her that they were to white women in the fifties. There is little in the black community to reinforce a young black woman who does not have a man or a child and who wishes to pursue a career. She is still considered against nature. (1979, pp. 89, 91)

Thus, while black women have a long history of independence and employment, they are under considerable pressure to renounce this heritage. The intensity with which they discuss this issue suggests that the conflict between femininity and career-oriented achievement has become just as troublesome for them as it has for white women.

Other minority women also experience conflicts between femininity and achievement. Chicanas, Puerto Rican Americans, and Asian-Americans have a cultural heritage that is even more patriarchal than white America's. And contact with the white culture has narrowed the roles available to women in native American tribes. For instance, Navajo women, who originally had considerable status, now feel as limited as many black women; they, too, feel that their only source of prestige and gratification is in having children (Witt 1976).

THE BLACK PROFESSIONAL WOMAN: A DOUBLE TOKEN?

Although the vast majority of black women are limited to low-paying, menial jobs, an occasional black woman does manage to obtain a professional education and have a successful career. What enables this unusual woman to do so well? She must be talented, but ability alone is rarely enough.

Epstein tried to answer this question in interviews with black professional women in the New York area, and she suggests that being both black *and* female may actually be better than being either one or the other—at least in a professional job. The negative stereotypes associated with one seem to neutralize the stereotypes associated with the other. Thus, while white male professionals may feel threatened by having black men as colleagues, they do not seem to feel that way about black women. "Being a woman reduced the effect of the racial taboo" (Epstein 1973, p. 155). On the other hand, white men seldom see the black woman as potential spouse or romantic partner and thus are less likely to treat her as a sex object or belittle her career commitment. This idea is supported by the black women's reports that in black settings they encounter suspicions of their competence and motivations similar to those that white women meet in white male settings.

The perception of the black woman as neither really black nor really female makes her seem "superunique" (Epstein 1973, p. 171). She is a "stranger" who has to be treated as a person instead of a stereotype. On the other hand, being a stranger also means that she has no peers. The black professional woman often responds by developing an alternative life style that does not fit the norms of either the black community or the professional white community. She can then concentrate on her career without being distracted by community pressures. For this she pays a high price in loneliness. Many of the women studied reported, for instance, that they had "virtually no social life" in college, since most of them went to predominantly white schools (Epstein 1973, p. 162).

By her very uniqueness the black professional woman attracts attention—a visibility that often makes her feel self-conscious and determined to be better than anyone else, to be a credit to her race and her sex.

> Being a black woman. . . . It's made me fight harder. . . . I think probably one of the strengths of being black or being a black woman is that if you have the native material you really do learn to fight and try to accom-

plish and all the rest. If I had been white, with the same abilities, I'm not sure the drive would have been the same. (Quoted in Epstein 1973, p. 169)

Some of the younger women were well aware of the recent emphasis on having women and blacks in schools, hospitals, and corporations. The controversy surrounding affirmative action programs can sometimes lead to accusations that black women are simply "double tokens." Most of the women in Epstein's study referred to this idea with irony, feeling confident that they deserved whatever benefits were available from the new social awareness. As one said, "I'm a show woman and a show nigger, all for one salary" (Epstein 1973, p. 169).

The visibility and tokenism involved in being a black professional woman is essentially the same as that for white female professionals— but stronger. For such women, both black and white, visibility can be a source of both pressure and pride. And it often has some advantages, since such an outstanding person is likely to be remembered.

Women have some advantages as trial lawyers; for one thing they are well remembered, or remembered, well or not, depends on how they perform. The judge is not as likely to forget them if he has ever seen them before, because we women are in the minority. And, of course, for a Negro women, she is very likely to be remembered. It is always a help, not to be forgotten. (Quoted in Epstein 1973, p. 169)

Divided Loyalties:
Which Oppression to Fight?

Millions of black women today live in abject poverty. They work long hours at low-paying jobs only to come home to rat-infested ghetto apartments. Their race—and their sex—prevent them from getting the educations and the jobs that would improve their living conditions. And their children suffer with them.

Many black women are beginning to feel that something should be done, that they should organize—but should they do so as blacks or as women? Most feel that their experience is determined more by race than by sex. A few, however, are beginning to argue that sex is just as important. This issue is extremely controversial and is usually couched in terms of the Black Movement versus the Women's Movement.

THE BLACK MOVEMENT: A MALE DOMAIN?

The Black Movement of the 1960s was led by men. Most black women felt that although the issues were relevant to their own lives, leadership belonged to the black male. The black woman's place was "a step behind " (Lewis 1977, p. 348). Many black women shared Michele Wallace's reaction as a teenager in Harlem—the black woman had had all the advantages. "She got all the jobs, all the everything. The black man had never had a chance" (Wallace 1979, p. 48). Now it was the black man's turn. He should lead the struggle for freedom, equality, rights, wealth, and power. The black woman's place was to support him; for in the struggle he would need every ounce of his masculinity, which had suffered enough from slavery, unemployment, and inability to support his family.

These sentiments are still shared by blacks of all economic backgrounds. Thus a professional woman who was a panelist at a symposium in 1973 said, "The responsibility of the black woman is to support the black man; *whatever* he does" (quoted in Walker et al. 1979, p. 51). Other black women stress female involvement and even initiative in the Black Movement while simultaneously implying that male dominance is crucial to its success.

> The price of equality between the black sexes has been one blacks could ill afford. The psychological thrust of the saw, he who puts the bread on the table and guards the door has the right and dignity of ultimate decision, has not been misunderstood by the black female. Lower-class black women are tired of being forced to make decisions. They are tired of the exclusive right of self-determination and long for the right of shared destiny and mutual participation in family matters. . . .
>
> As past generations of black women have subtly taught sons to renounce their manhood to save their lives, present day generations are overtly teaching their sons to assert their manhood to save the race. Significantly, it was the new black feminine mystique that gave impetus to the civil rights movement by the refusal of a black woman to get out of her seat on a bus, thereby launching the now historic Montgomery, Alabama bus boycott. It was only when black women got off their feet that black men began to stand on theirs. . . .
>
> So long as black women have black sons they will remain skeptical of an alliance with women to achieve a dubious equality which guarantees less than full manhood for him for whom she has labored and given birth. For the black woman, maternalism, sexuality, and the new feminism come full circle back to the black male. (Mayo 1973, pp. 183, 185)

Black men are likely to put it in terms of women's nurturant functions. Thus Linda La Rue tells us: "It gives a great many black males pride to speak, as Dr. Robert Staples does, of '. . . the role of the black woman in the black liberation struggle is an important one and cannot be forgotten. From her womb have come the revolutionary warriors of our time' " (1970, p. 42).

THE WOMEN'S MOVEMENT: FOR WHITES ONLY?

Some black women have begun to object to the condescending attitude of black men. Thus La Rue says, "The black movement needs its women in a position of struggle, not prone" (1970, p. 41). But while these black women feel that there should be sexual equality in the Black Movement, they refuse to participate in the Women's Movement owing to their perception that it is dominated by whites (Hare and Hare 1970). In the eyes of blacks, a white woman shares the privileges of the white male's dominant status, so that for them to focus on sexual discrimination would be to belittle the crucial nature of racial discrimination. Linda La Rue forcefully expresses this point of view:

> The American white woman has had a better opportunity to live a free and fulfilling life, both mentally and physically, than any other group in the United States, with the exception of her white husband. Thus, any attempt to analogize black oppression with the plight of the American white woman has the validity of comparing the neck of a hanging man with the hands of an amateur mountain climber with rope burns. . . .
> The surge of "common oppression" rhetoric and propaganda may lure the unsuspecting into an intellectual alliance with the goals of women's liberation, but it is not a wise alliance. It is not that women ought not to be liberated from the shackles of their present unfulfillment, but the depth, the extent, the intensity, the importance—indeed, the suffering and depravity of the *real* oppression blacks have experienced—can only be minimized in an alliance with women who heretofore suffered little more than boredom, genteel repression, and dishpan hands. . . .
>
> It is time that definitions be made clear. Blacks are *oppressed*, and that means unreasonably burdened, unjustly, severely, rigorously, cruelly and harshly fettered by white authority. White women, on the other hand, are only *suppressed*, and that means checked, restrained, excluded from conscious and overt activity. And there is a difference. (1970, pp. 36, 38)

Many black women also maintain that white women would put their own interests first in a pinch. Thus, La Rue continues:

> If white women have heretofore remained silent while white men maintained the better position and monopolized the opportunities by excluding blacks, can we really expect that white women, when put in direct competition for employment, will be any more open-minded than their male counterparts when it comes to the hiring of black males and females in the same positions for which they are competing? . . .
> The black labor force, never fully employed and always representing a substantial percentage of the unemployed in the American economy, will now be driven into greater unemployment as white women converge at every level on an already dwindling job market. (1970, pp. 37, 38)

Some black women take this argument a step farther by charging that some people in the Women's Movement deliberately appeal to racist attitudes to get what they want. Mae King puts it this way:

> The non-recognition attitude also penetrates academia and the "women's liberation" movement. In fact, there is a tendency to appeal to the white male powerholders' belief in the ideology of race in order to gain support for "women's rights." White male castees are admonished by the females of their group, that evidence of the depth of the "oppression" that they inflict upon "women" is illustrated by the former's act of sometimes preferring blacks over women. This position is reflected in a statement by Alice Rossi who writes that:
>> The tenuous hold academic women without doctorates have enjoyed by way of part-time college teaching or as high school teachers without the master's degree, may therefore be reduced in the future as school systems can hire doctorates holders and what they believe to be more stable employees, men. . . .
>> [Anxiety about this possibility] is heightened among women in graduate and professional schools as the latter search their souls and markets for qualified blacks. This has lent an air of pressing and conflicting concerns in many circles of women . . . they despair of giving genuine encouragement to their women students, many of whom feel a double disadvantage; they are not black and not male. (King 1973, pp. 20–21)

The concerns expressed by La Rue and Rossi seem to be opposite sides of the same coin: that white women will corner all the jobs, or that blacks will. When faced with such an either-or choice, the majority of black women favor black men. They feel that racism is more oppressive than sexism and should be addressed first. And they are afraid that if black women should obtain better jobs before black men do, male-female tensions among blacks will be deepened (Hare and Hare 1970).

BLACK FEMINISM: WOMEN TOGETHER?

A few black women, however, are beginning to feel that sexism is a crucial issue for all women, black or white. Christine Bond expresses this feminist viewpoint.

> The only distinction between women's issues and black women's issues is the racism, and the negative image that black people have about themselves, which is compounded by the negative image that we have about ourselves as women.
> I often say that just because I was born packing a vagina doesn't mean that I want to be identified by that small space. I want people to deal with the whole of me and what I am about.
> I'd like to start a battered women's shelter in this community. My

other dream is to start a black feminist health center. . . . Feminism is about women sharing. (Walker et al. 1979, pp. 51–52)

This viewpoint is still unpopular in the black community. Sandra Flowers, who was a coordinator of the Atlanta chapter of the National Black Feminist Organization in 1974–1975, talks about how isolated black feminists can feel:

> I accept the premise that black women inherently are feminists. Our struggle makes this so, regardless of how we feel about the label. Yet, those of us who live as feminists and collaborate with the Women's Movement do so at the expense of a particular place in the black community. Let's face it—a whole lot of black women are satisfied with the male dominance of our culture. This makes feminism a risky business for black women because the options it inevitably generates tend to alienate black men as well as those black women who read feminism as antimale, hence antiblack (even black feminism, which is considered by some a white idea in blackface). (Walker et al. 1979, p. 51)

Diane Lewis (1977) points out that although black women object to the label "feminist," there are some indications that they are becoming more responsive to the issues raised by the Women's Movement. In fact, their opinions may be more feminist than those of white women, for a 1972 Harris poll showed that black women were more sympathetic than white women both to general efforts to upgrade womens' status in society (62 percent to 45 percent for white women) and to the specific strategies and work of the Women's Movement (67 percent to 35 percent for white women).

Lewis suggests that the gains of the Black Movement have created a general trend toward support for women's rights. As blacks have begun to participate in public activities previously reserved for whites, black women have encountered the sexual discrimination that pervades that arena. They have found that "the bulk of the higher-status, authoritative positions meted to blacks went to black men" (Lewis 1977, pp. 340–41). This made black women, especially middle-class ones, feel that the Women's Movement was relevant to their lives after all. One black woman put it this way: "It is clear that when translated into actual opportunities for employment and promotional and educational benefits, the civil rights movement really meant rights for black men" (Carroll 1973, p. 177). Another black woman was more blunt: "The black man grapples to achieve social justice and parity with the white male— essentially to attain the white male power, privilege and status—while black women are shoved to the back of the bus" (Eudora Pettigrew, quoted in Lewis 1977, p. 341).

National trends in education and employment have clearly favored the black male over the black female. Before 1960 black women had more education than black men had, because education did not increase the earnings of the black man as much as it did those of the black woman; and educated or not, the black man could not find a job (Epstein 1973). Now, however, the educational attainments of the two sexes are about equal (Herman 1979). In fact, Lewis argues that black males have now outstripped black females both in percentage of the black males who obtain college degrees and in prestige of institutions they attend.* And in spite of racial discrimination, black men have always earned more than black women. Table 11.4 shows that in the past fifteen years the male-female differential has increased—for both blacks *and* whites. As Alexis Herman (1979) points out, the number of black women living in poverty is *increasing*, not decreasing.

TABLE 11.4

Median Year-Round Earnings for Full-Time Workers in the United States

	1963	1970	1974
White males	$6,245	$9,447	$12,434
Black males	4,019	6,435	8,705
White females	3,687	5,536	7,021
Black females	2,280	4,536	6,371

Source: D. K. Lewis, "A response to inequality: Black women, racism, and sexism," *Signs: Journal of Women in Culture and Society* (1977) 3(2): 351. Figures provided by U.S. Bureau of the Census.

As they have experienced increasing discrimination owing to sex as well as race, a few black women have come to agree with the black feminist who said, "White women are our natural allies; we can't take on the system alone" (quoted in Lewis 1977, p. 360). White women also feel the need for female unity. A number of women's organizations, which are still predominantly white, have held conferences and established ongoing committees to focus on the issue of racism.†

The idea that racism and sexism are intertwined not only reflects the personal experience of black women but is also supported by research that suggests that attitudes toward women, blacks, and sexuality are closely related to each other. Woudenberg (1977) did a study with 350 male college students and found that many men felt guilty about sex,

* The absolute number of blacks who manage to obtain a college degree is still small. Lewis (1977) reports that in 1974, 8.8 percent of black men and 7.6 percent of black women had achieved that level of education.

† Social scientists are also responding to the crucial issues of sexism and racism. In 1978 the American Psychological Association (APA) established a permanent Minority Affairs Office, while the APA's Division 35 on the Psychology of Women established a standing committee on black women's concerns (see *APA Monitor*, Nov. 1978; *Division 35 Newsletter*, Jan. 1979).

tended to experience it without intimacy and warmth, and felt that this dangerous activity had to be carefully controlled and should not be indulged in outside of marriage. Men who felt this way also tended to have negative attitudes toward both blacks and women. Woudenberg's interpretation is that guilt-ridden men like these tend to attribute their own unacceptable feelings to both women and blacks and hence come to envy, fear, and hate them.

In spite of their support for the Women's Movement, however, black feminists have formed their own organizations (Fulcher et al. 1979), feeling that such groups reflect their experience more directly and are better able to address the problems of women from a variety of economic backgrounds. As Lewis points out, "The shared experience of racism has also tended to blur class lines among blacks [which contributes to] a greater tendency for both poor and middle-class black women to agree regarding women's rights" (1977, p. 360). This sense of unity across class lines is reflected in the sentiment that "for poor women, women's liberation is a matter of survival" (quoted in Lewis 1977, p. 359).

Not that black feminist organizations are free of many of the same pressures and divisions that beset the larger, predominantly white Women's Movement. Many blacks still feel that the fight for women's rights will divide blacks and undermine the black male's feelings of masculinity. Others charge that anyone who agitates for women's rights must be a lesbian, a charge reminiscent of the early lesbian-baiting in the (white) Women's Movement.

> With increasing regularity, the red herring of homophobia and lesbian-baiting is being used in the black community to obscure the true double face of racism/sexism. But black women sharing close ties with each other, politically and/or emotionally, are not the enemies of black men. Only to those black men who are unclear as to the paths of their own self-definition can the self-actualization and bonding together of black women be seen as a threatening development. After all, in the black community today, it is certainly not the black lesbian who is battering and raping our underage girl children, out of displaced and sickening frustration and anger.
>
> Women-identified women—those who sought our own destinies and attempted to execute them in the absence of male support—have been around in all black communities for a long time. But their presence goes largely unrecorded, except by word of mouth; for in those periods women-identified black women were doing what all black people were doing—confronting daily issues of survival . . . the unmarried aunt, childless or otherwise, whose home and resources were often a welcome haven for different members of the family, was a familiar figure in many of our childhoods.
>
> Yet within this country, for so long, we as black women have been encouraged to view each other with suspicion and distrust; as eternal competitors for the scarce male; or as the visible face of our own self-

rejection. Nevertheless, black women have always bonded together in support of each other, however uneasily and in the face of whatever other allegiances militated against that bonding. . . . We need only look at the close—although highly complex and involved—relationship between African co-wives. (Audre Lorde, in Walker et al. 1979, p. 52)

Lorde is undoubtedly correct to link "homophobia," or fear of homosexuality, with what Wallace (1979) calls "black macho." As I have said, positive attitudes toward homosexuality are associated with being profeminist and feeling more relaxed about changing sex-role stereotypes and about sexual activity outside marriage. The feelings each of us has about women, sex, and race seem to be all mixed up together. The connection between male macho and homophobia is not a problem just for black women, moreover. Lesbians who belong to other minority groups with male-dominant norms also experience considerable community rejection, as Hildalgo and Christensen (1976–1977) found among Puerto Rican Americans.

The controversy in the black community will probably continue for some time. Regardless of how a black woman feels about the issues of black matriarchy and black macho, however, she would undoubtedly agree that something should be done about the plight of millions of black women who suffer because they are black, female, and poor. It is time for social scientists to examine the black experience from the viewpoint of blacks themselves. It is time to stop imposing white, middle-class values on millions of Americans who do not necessarily share them. And it is time, some would add, for black women to act on their own behalf. As Michele Wallace puts it: "History has been written without us. The imperative is clear: either we will make history or remain the victims of it" (1979, p. 91).

PART IV

WOMEN AND
THEIR BODIES

SOCIAL EXPERIENCES are not the only important dimension of a woman's life. Her body, too, is crucial. Yet until recently little was known about a woman's experience of and feelings about her bodily functions. It was not ladylike to discuss such things, much less to treat them as an important aspect of daily life. Social scientists developed theories about female sexuality and reproduction that reflected their view of women's social role and personality. But they did not ask women how they themselves felt, nor did they pay attention to things like rape, wife beating, and the emotional aspects of birth control and abortion.

But as the view of the female role has changed over the past three decades, so have attitudes about bodily functions. The myths and taboos surrounding these functions have weakened, and women are beginning to talk more openly about what they *want* and how they *feel*. As social scientists have turned their attention to these areas they have found that what women have to say is sometimes surprising, even shocking—and has disturbing implications for the relationship between the sexes in our culture.

Chapter 12

Sexuality

FEMALE SEXUALITY has been shrouded in mystery and taboo. Our cultural heritage reflects the Victorian era, which viewed sex as dirty, dangerous, and disgusting—something to be left to men. Premarital sex was bad. Sexual fantasies were bad. And masturbation was unthinkable. Even sex between wife and husband was suspect if done too often or too enthusiastically. Sex was strictly for reproduction.

Women were divided into two groups—the pure and the sexual. No respectable woman would admit to sexual desires or feelings, even for her husband. She was to submit to sexual intercourse with him as a marital duty, remaining stoically passive and recumbent. She did have her passions—for raising children, maintaining the home, and pleasing her husband; and sex was simply a rather unpleasant way of obtaining these appropriately feminine desires.

The social and economic developments that have since altered the female role have also caused a shift in attitudes toward sexuality. No more hiding behind bedroom doors and talking in hushed whispers. Sex has gone public. It is everywhere—on television, in magazines, in movies, in novels, even on the evening news. Everyone is concerned about how sexy he or she is, and everyone wants to discuss it *ad nauseum.* Far from being reticent about sex, our culture now seems to be obsessed with it.

Yet in the midst of this "sexual revolution" many of the old myths and stereotypes linger on. Only in the past five or ten years has female sexuality begun to emerge from the mists of prejudice and taboo.

Scientists Study Sex

Eighty years ago Freud began to shock the world with his theories about sexuality. Not only were both men *and* women sexual, he claimed, but sexual desires and activities existed even in the innocence of childhood. And sex was not just an occasional whim that ensured reproduction; it was a central driving force in human nature. After the initial furor over Freud's writings, many other clinicians began to write about the sexual fantasies and practices of their patients. Although these case histories were interesting, they described a small number of distressed individuals and were not read by the general public. Most people continued to wonder, What does everyone else do?

The first study to answer this question was started in 1938 by Alfred C. Kinsey, who interviewed over ten thousand people nationwide from different religious backgrounds, ages, marital situations, and walks of life. What he found was startling. Although men were more sexually active than women, both sexes honored the Victorian norms more in word than in deed. Premarital intercourse was common, extramarital sex was not unusual, and homosexual activities were far from unheard of (Kinsey et al. 1948, 1953).

Debate raged through the 1960s. Had sexual attitudes really changed, or were people just more willing to talk about what they did? Was Kinsey's sample really representative? Many critics noted that the study participants were volunteers and hence might be "sexier" than average. Others pointed out that urban areas, affluent homes, and relatively nonreligious family backgrounds were overrepresented and also might provide "sexier" subjects than would the rest of the population. And some wondered whether the participants exaggerated their sexual exploits during the interviews.

These questions gradually died down as other studies found a continuing increase in sexual activities during the 1960s. Premarital intercourse was one indication. Kinsey found that 86 percent of the women born before 1900 had been virgins before marriage but that over one-third of the women born in the 1920s had not. And while 18 or 19 percent of the unmarried women in Kinsey's sample were no longer virgins, the percentage had risen to almost 50 percent by 1970 (Kantner and Zelnik 1972). The trend continued into the 1970s, so that by 1972 three-quarters of unmarried women and 97 percent of unmarried men had had intercourse by age twenty-five (Hunt 1974).

Apparently more and more women are coming to agree with *The Sensuous Woman*, the popular book on how to be sexy, which states: "When you grew up you put the things of childhood away. One of those things was virginity" ("J" 1969, p. 53).

The fact that the virgin bride is disappearing does not mean that women are becoming promiscuous. Although young women are less likely to insist on a formal engagement or marriage before having intercourse, they continue to have premarital sex with only one or two partners, just as they did in Kinsey's time. Men, on the other hand, are more likely to have premarital sex with more partners (Hunt 1974; Kinsey et al. 1948, 1953). Similarly, Robert Sorensen (1973) reports that only 6 percent of girls are "sexual adventurers" compared with one-quarter of boys.

What happens after marriage? Has the taboo on extramarital sex been abandoned as well? Not really. In Kinsey's day only 8 percent of married women under twenty-five had had extramarital sex, while today the figure is closer to 24 percent (Hunt 1974). In spite of this jump, fidelity is still the norm. Women now feel freer to do whatever men do, however, so that the rates of extramarital sex for women have risen to be three-fourths of those for men.

The flood of studies, books, and magazines articles on sexual behavior answered the question, What do other people do? The answer seems to be, Just about everything. Then the question became, How do they do it? For when Kinsey first began his research, little was known about how a woman responded to sexual activity. Certainly she was not an asexual being who merely endured intercourse for the sake of her husband and future children. She must enjoy sex or she would not be doing so many different things so often. But how does the female body become aroused? And what happens when it does? Are female orgasms a myth or a miracle? One-third of the women in Kinsey's study reported experiencing orgasm. What was this like for them physically and emotionally?

The first definitive answers to these questions were provided by Masters and Johnson's classic studies of the physiology of the female sexual response (1966, 1970). Later researchers have concentrated on women's own perceptions and feelings about various aspects of sexuality. These studies are beginning to provide a clearer picture of just how women experience sex—what they do, why they do it, and how they feel before, during, and after.

In one of the first such studies Seymour Fisher (1973) examined the sexual activities and personality attributes of 285 married, white women in their early or middle twenties. They were well educated (two to three years of college), middle class, had been married two to three years, and had one child or none. In 1971, Barbara Seaman (1972) gave questionnaires to a separate group of 103 independent, well-educated feminists from middle-class backgrounds. And Shere Hite (1976) conducted a nationwide questionnaire survey of 3,019 women during the years 1972–1974. Hite's respondents ranged in age from fourteen to seventy-eight, but most were well-educated professional and technical workers in their twenties and thirties, with a variety of marital statuses and religious backgrounds.* Even though Fisher concentrated on laboratory tests and multiple-choice answers, while Seaman and Hite tried to get women to talk about their sexual experiences in their own words, the results of all three studies are remarkably similar. While the experiences of these women may not be typical of every segment of our society, they provide fascinating insights into the sexual world of women today.

The Female Sexual Response

Sexual arousal can start with smelling, seeing, or thinking about something sexy. In women, however, it usually starts with physical touch on any sensitive part of the body. The most sexually responsive areas, or erogenous zones, are the genitals, breasts, mouth, and inner thighs. Once arousal begins, it can progress through four stages identified by Masters and Johnson (1966). The first is *excitement*, when nipples become erect, breasts swell, and blood begins to engorge the vessels and organs in the pelvic area. This vasocongestion causes the clitoris to swell or "erect,"

---

* The statistics in Hite's report cover only 1,844 (61 percent) of her 3,019 respondents, while the quotes are from the entire sample. Using her lists of sample characteristics, I arrived at the following percentages of the 61 percent: About one-third were married and three-quarters were in their twenties and thirties (8 percent fourteen to nineteen, 47 percent twenty to twenty-nine, 26 percent thirty to thirty-nine, 11 percent forty to forty-nine, 8 percent fifty to seventy-eight). Twenty-eight percent were housewives; while of those who worked, 38 percent held professional and technical jobs, 22 percent did secretarial or clerical work, and 22 percent were students (primarily in college and graduate school). Many were contacted through Women's Movement groups, while others responded to advertisements in church newsletters and popular magazines such as *Ms., Bride's, Mademoiselle,* and *Oui,* and also the *Village Voice.* Over all, then, Hite's respondents tended to be younger, more affluent, more educated, and more politically liberal than the general population.

A second difficulty with Hite's report is the lack of statistical analysis. When discussing the results of her study, Hite simply quotes her respondents. She does not indicate which or even how many women responded in a given way, so we cannot know how typical those responses are. Thus, Hite's report should not be viewed as a scientific study of female sexuality. On the other hand, it does provide a rich source of information about the varieties of female attitudes, feelings, and sexual behavior. For this reason I have included quotations from Hite's respondents to illustrate various points in the text.

I should also note that Hite did not inquire about the race or ethnic group of her respondents, while Seaman does not comment on race, and the data by Kinsey and Fisher do not include responses from blacks or other minorities. Thus, we should keep in mind that although the physical aspects of female sexuality undoubtedly apply to all women, many of the social and emotional experiences reported by the women in these studies may not be typical of all women in the United States today.

and wetness develops as fluid seeps through the vaginal walls. Muscle tension starts to build, and a "sex flush" or blotchy red rash may spread over the body.

As arousal continues, women enter the *plateau phase*. Now the tissues surrounding the outer third of the vagina swell, creating the "orgasmic platform." The deeper portion of the vagina balloons out to form a cavity. The clitoris retracts, becoming more difficult to see. Heartbeat and breathing become rapid and sensory awareness of the outside world is dimmed. The "sex skin reaction" turns the genitals pink, bright red, or a deep wine color.

Sexual arousal involves much more than physical sensations, however. Hite found that most women describe it with a mixture of physical and emotional terms like "tingly," "warm," "happy," and "alive" and talk about yearning to touch and be touched. In the women's own words:

I'm high—I breathe fast—also lightheaded, in a dream world, sounds are distant, time suspended.

Like wanting someone else so close you just can't touch enough.

Blood throbbing.

Like being outside of my body, outside of my mind, not really caring what is important to my usual self.

(Quoted in Hite 1976, pp. 139, 140, 141, 142)

The vasocongestion of the plateau phase sets the stage for the *orgasmic phase*. The neuromuscular discharge of orgasm requires appropriate stimulation and a massive buildup of pelvic vasocongestion. A sequence of rhythmic contractions occur at 0.8-second intervals in the uterus and the lower third of the vagina, or orgasmic platform. Rapid heartbeat and breathing continue, the entire body becomes tense, and muscle contractions or spasms may occur. The rhythmic contractions vary in number and intensity and discharge the accumulated vasocongestion and muscle tension. The subjective experience of orgasm lasts about six to eight seconds (Fisher 1973) and has been described in the following ways:

My clitoris vibrates at some unbelievable speed, and the muscles in my vagina and further back contract intensely, my head seems deburdened, my toes curl, my abdomen feels strong—and my whole body pulsates along with my clitoris and vagina.

> Waves of muscles in my vagina are pulsating, tingling, alive. Vaginal contractions radiate out over my body in waves.
>
> (Quoted in Hite 1976, p. 158)

In the *resolution phase*, after orgasm the vasocongestion decreases, but slowly. The woman returns not to an unaroused state but to the levels of arousal found in the plateau phase. The heartbeat and pulse gradually slow down, and one woman in three develops a film of perspiration over her body. Most women have a strong emotional reaction to orgasm, as Hite found when she asked them how they felt afterward. Many described feeling tender and loving, while others emphasized feeling strong, wideawake, and energetic:

> My orgasm subsides into a warm glow of well-being. This afterglow is short if I am not emotionally close to my partner, otherwise, it is long and rich and almost the best part.

> A feeling of crazy friendliness, sometimes unfounded.

> I experience a warm burning tingling—a supreme sense of health, vitality and even power immediately after.
>
> (Quoted in Hite 1976, pp. 166–67)

The Orgasmic Experience

Sexual arousal does not always culminate in orgasm; and in fact, many women have great difficulty reaching orgasm. For instance, Fisher (1973) found that almost two-thirds of the women in his studies did not attain orgasm with any consistency, while 5 percent to 6 percent had *never* experienced an orgasm. In her nationwide survey Hite (1976) found an even higher rate of nonorgasmic women—11.6 percent.

What happens if a woman becomes aroused but does not experience orgasm? If her arousal has been extensive, the pelvic congestion can cause discomfort for several hours. And she may experience her lack of orgasm as a failure that reflects on her womanhood and damages her sexual relationship. Hite found that women who never reached orgasm sometimes felt depressed and cheated.

> I feel I'm less desirable since I don't or seldom have orgasms. I often wonder if having orgasms is partly an individual physiological response.

I don't really believe that differences in this area are all psychological. I wish our culture put less emphasis on orgasm and "tiger" lovers. It would be easier for people like me to accept ourselves.

I read about orgasm and hear about it constantly. How would you like to be colorblind and keep reading about rainbows and butterflies?

I would like to have them. I do enjoy sex and feel satisfied, but maybe I'd answer differently if I knew what I was missing.

(Quoted in Hite 1976, pp. 205–6)

Other women were not sure whether they had orgasms or not, but tended to conclude that in that case they probably had not.

For a long time I didn't know if I was having them because of verbal myths surrounding them and no means of comparison with other women.

To tell you the truth, I'm not really sure. I have read so many descriptions and heard so many concepts of what an orgasm is and should feel like. I used to be terribly worried because I didn't think I could have one. I was expecting something really exciting and dynamic to happen— you know, bright lights, psychedelic flashes—but they never did. . . . Now I say—whatever happens, happens. It's usually quite nice but I don't know if it's an orgasm.

(Quoted in Hite 1976, p. 209)

Women who do not know whether they have experienced orgasm may not be sufficiently stimulated to reach the plateau phase of arousal. Masters and Johnson reported that when women were stimulated but did not reach orgasm, the pelvic engorgement persisted and caused them to experience pelvic fullness, pressure, cramping, moments of true pain, and persistent low backache and made them feel irritable, upset, and unable to sleep. These purely physical symptoms of sexual frustration would be difficult to overlook.

While many nonorgasmic women do not feel sexually frustrated, they often feel inadequate and envious; they feel they *should* be experiencing the sexual ecstasy so extensively discussed in popular literature. The new interest in female sexuality may thus be creating dissatisfaction and unhappiness where none existed before. This problem has prompted some people to say that orgasm is grossly overrated and the continual discussion of it destructive. On the other hand, Barbara Seaman argues that without such discussion many women would be unable to experience their sexuality fully, for only through sharing sexual experiences can women separate their true sexual feelings and preferences from the cultural myths about sex.

I agree with Seaman and will therefore turn to women's own experiences and discuss how they compare with the various theories and models of female sexuality.

The Clitoral-Vaginal Controversy

After Freud expounded his theory that only vaginal orgasms were mature and healthy, many women felt guilty and inadequate for finding clitoral stimulation more gratifying. Once Masters and Johnson's research had been publicized, many women responded by saying, "Clitoral orgasms are all there is. Vaginal orgasms are a myth perpetuated by men who prefer penile penetration. If women don't conform to this myth, men accuse them of being frigid." Anne Koedt expresses this point of view:

> There is only one area for sexual climax, although there are many areas for sexual arousal: that area is the clitoris. All orgasms are extensions of sensation from this area. Since the clitoris is not necessarily stimulated sufficiently in the conventional sexual positions, we are left "frigid."
> . . . The orgasm experience may also differ in degree of intensity— some more localized, and some more diffuse and sensitive. But they are all clitoral orgasms. (1970, p. 37)

How does this account compare with the actual experience of women? Do all orgasms seem to originate in the clitoris, as Koedt maintains? Or are some orgasms experienced as clitoral, while others feel centered on the vagina? The answer seems to depend on whom you ask. In spite of knowing about the clitoral-vaginal debate, some women have never experienced any difference and see the whole controversy as meaningless:

> I don't know the difference. They're all alike to me.

> I don't know what kind of orgasm I have. I just have them. I usually have an orgasm more than once. It depends on how long one makes love. In order to get an orgasm, I usually need both vaginal and clitoral stimulation.

> I'm not sure of the difference. The greater the degree of arousal, the higher the pleasure. All orgasms feel good.
> (Quoted in Seaman 1972, pp. 143–44)

Other women feel there is a difference. Some prefer what they call vaginal orgasms, and a few of these women sound rather snobby about it.

> Clitoral orgasm is mere titillation; only vaginal orgasms are real.

> I doubt that I've ever had a clitoral orgasm. I wouldn't want one.

> Clitoral is less desirable because it merely creates the desire for a vaginal orgasm.
>
> (Quoted in Seaman 1972, p. 145)

Most women, however, seem to feel that the two experiences are different, without condemning one or the other. Fisher found that women described clitoral stimulation as "warm," "ticklish," "electrical," and "sharp," whereas they usually referred to vaginal stimulation as "throbbing," "deep," "soothing," and "comfortable" (1973, pp. 197–98). One woman, for instance, explained how the two types of stimulation were gratifying in different ways:

> Clitoral stimulation has a high intensity—feelings concentrated in one spot. It's a lightness, a spark, almost ticklish sensation. I feel sort of an electricity. I feel the pleasure is all physical. In a vaginal stimulation the pleasure is mental or spiritual, a feeling of depth or meaning. A wider area of pleasurable sensation. It produces a longing or hunger. It is a comforting pleasure. Vaginal stimulation is like a warm bath of pleasure while clitoral is a spark of pleasure. My whole body responds to vaginal stimulation; and it moves and it feels. In clitoral stimulation my body is rigid with expectation of continuing pleasure. Vaginal stimulation is like a hum but clitoral is a high pitched note. From clitoral stimulation my body demands to be satisfied, from vaginal my body is content even if it's not. (Quoted in Fisher 1973, p. 197)

Although women valued both types of stimulation, most of them felt that clitoral was more important, and 64 percent said they would pick clitoral if they had to choose one or the other (Fisher 1973).

Hite explored the vaginal-clitoral difference by asking women to compare orgasm with and without intercourse. She got basically the same answer Fisher did—"a clitorally stimulated orgasm without intercourse feels more locally intense, while an orgasm with intercourse feels more diffused throughout the area and/or body" (1976, p. 191). Some women attributed the greater intensity of a nonintercourse orgasm to the possibilities of their being less self-conscious while alone and undistracted by another person, and of having greater ease in adjusting body position.

Other women, however, experienced orgasms during intercourse as more intense because their whole body was involved, while others stressed the emotional involvement, slow buildup, and greater acceptability of orgasm in intercourse. Some women described an "intense emotional peak" during intercourse, which Hite calls an "emotional orgasm." This might be "felt physically in the chest, or as a lump in the throat, or as a general opening-up sensation, a feeling of wanting deeper and deeper penetration, wanting to merge and become one person." Occasionally it was experienced as "the desire to conceive, to be impregnated, to keep the person there, inside you, mix the two as one in real flesh and blood" (1976, pp. 200–202).

By asking about orgasm with and without intercourse, Hite is actually confusing several dimensions of the sexual experience: the clitoral versus the vaginal site of stimulation, being alone versus being with someone else, and having vaginal penetration by a penis versus having it by some other body part or object. A woman often stimulates her vagina while masturbating, for instance; and penile penetration is not the only type of stimulation during lovemaking. When Hite's respondents described the entire sexual response cycle in physical rather than emotional terms, their answers tended to show a gradual buildup of excitement with sensations focusing on the clitoris and then spreading to the vagina and throughout the body.

> First, various parts of my body tingle and feel strange, then at different times there is the feeling of an orgasm but only for a split second, then all of this becomes more and more frequent until orgasm comes like waves. At that time all else is non-existent. Orgasm is centered in my clitoris releasing waves to my vagina, and ends after an intense but brief amount of time, very slowly again emitting the split-second sensations for a few minutes getting more and more infrequent and less intense.

> Before it begins, I feel a vibrant pulsing in my clitoris and pent-up tension in my vagina, then the tension explodes and I feel my vagina contracting, my heart pounding, my body moaning, and my voice going "Oh, oh ohohoh." There is a feeling of intense pleasure when it starts, then disappointment that it cannot be sustained. Then my husband becomes a person again, and I am very aware of him and the feeling of closeness.

> (Quoted in Hite 1976, pp. 160, 163)

These descriptions suggest that on a purely physical basis there is no difference between a clitoral and a vaginal orgasm—they are inextricably linked. In fact, female anatomy is such that it is physically impossible to have one without the other, for the clitoris is merely the external, visible part of an underlying *clitoral system*. These internal organs expand as much or more than the male penis during arousal, and this engorgement is discharged as a unit (Seaman 1972; Sherfey 1972).

Helen Kaplan attributes the continuing controversy about clitoral and vaginal orgasm to the fact that the female orgasm, like all reflexes, has both a sensory and a motor component. The clitoris is the sensory component whose stimulation causes arousal, whereas the vagina is the motor component whose orgasmic contractions discharge the engorgement and tension accumulated during arousal. To try to separate the two is both foolish and impossible.

> Apparently, it is this dichotomy—on the one hand, the location of orgasmic spasms in and around the *vagina* and concomitant perception of orgasmic sensation in the general vaginal and deep pelvic region; on the other hand, the location of the primary area of stimulation in the *clitoris*—which has served to perpetuate the myth that the female is capable of two distinct types of orgasms, and has also given rise to the incredibly stupid controversy surrounding female orgasm. The orgasm is, after all, a reflex and as such has a sensory and a motor component. There is little argument over the fact that the motor expression of this reflex is "vaginal." In other words everyone agrees that the clitoris is not involved in female orgastic discharge. Rhythmic contractions of the circumvaginal muscles actually constitute the female orgasm. . . .
>
> The entire argument really only revolves around the location of the sensory arm of the reflex. Is orgasm normally triggered by stimulating the vagina with the penis? Or is it produced by tactile friction applied to the clitoris? The clinical evidence reviewed above clearly points to the clitoris. . . .
>
> An analogous situation exists in the male, but it causes no controversy. Ejaculation is triggered by stimulation of the tip and shaft of the penis [but] it is the clonic spasms of muscles in the base of the penis and perineum which provide the actual orgasmic discharge. (Kaplan 1974, pp. 29–30)

When a woman talks about her preference for a clitoral or for a vaginal orgasm, then, she is actually referring to how and where she likes to be stimulated. The differences in subjective experience seem to be due both to the physical and to the emotional aspects of sexual arousal, which blend to create a tremendous variety of sensations and feelings.

How a woman experiences sexual arousal is not merely a matter of her current situation, for sexual tastes seem to be tied to one's past history and personality patterns. Seaman, for instance, found that a woman who preferred a vaginal orgasm was likely to have experienced her first orgasm during intercourse, and suggests that such a woman may have learned to be more "trusting" and thus could allow herself to experience "feeling" in her vagina and to come to orgasm through vaginal stimulation alone (1972, p. 71).

Fisher, on the other hand, found that a woman who preferred vaginal stimulation was likely to "dampen" excitement and to minimize the potentially arousing aspects of what she perceived, to report that her body felt "distant" and "not mine," and to be more anxious; and he concludes that vaginal-clitoral preferences may be tied to the interpersonal aspects of the stimulation. A woman who is anxious and uncomfortable with her body may prefer the physical intimacy and emotional fusion of intercourse, when penile penetration can signify mutual caring and the woman may be less likely to focus on her own sexuality as a separate entity. Such a woman may be less trusting and need penile penetration as a sign of love in order to proceed to climax herself.

Fisher hastens to add, however, that "although the vaginally oriented have been described as more anxious than the clitorally oriented, this in no way is meant to imply that they are less 'healthy' or that they are seriously maladjusted" (1973, p. 411). He goes on to note that "the overlap between clitoral and vaginal orientations is [extensive since] a majority of persons engaging in sexual relationships use both direct clitoral and vaginal stimulation successively and simultaneously, resulting in a complex blend of the two" and concludes that "the entire question of clitoral versus vaginal preference is obviously extremely complex" (pp. 414, 417).

"Complex" describes not only orgasms but all aspects of female sexuality. Women vary tremendously in what they do, the way they do it, and whom (if anyone) they like to do it with. The more we find out about female sexuality, the more foolish it seems to ask, What is the best (or healthiest) orgasm? Barbara Seaman puts it well: "The liberated orgasm is any orgasm *you* like, under any circumstances *you* find comfortable" (1972, p. 73).

Masturbation

Given the importance of clitoral stimulation, it should come as no surprise that most women reach orgasm faster through masturbation than through intercourse (Kinsey et al. 1953). Women, however, are brought up to view masturbation as dirty and forbidden (Fisher 1973; Hite 1976). In Fisher's sample of young married women, masturbation was rare and gave little satisfaction. The women in Hite's nationwide sample, on the other hand, masturbated more often, perhaps because two-thirds were single and hence had intercourse less frequently. But in Hite's study even those who enjoyed masturbation physically often reported feeling "lonely, guilty, unwanted, selfish, silly, and generally bad" while masturbating (p. 62).

Hite identified five basic masturbatory techniques: by the hand, by pressing against a soft object, by pressing the thighs together rhythmically, by water massage, and by vaginal entry. When she asked women why they masturbated, most indicated that masturbation was a temporary substitute for sex with a partner. Others felt it helped them know their own bodies and reactions better and was therefore beneficial in relationships with others. Some women viewed it as a means of attaining independence and self-reliance, while a few saw it as pure pleasure and important in its own right.

In spite of the variety of techniques reported by Hite, most women seem to rely primarily on direct clitoral stimulation when they masturbate. This situation has led many people (especially psychiatrists) to fear that masturbation will interfere with a woman's ability to attain orgasm during intercourse (Seaman 1972); in Freud's terms, she may become "fixated" on this "masculine" form of sexuality. Modern research on female sexuality is beginning to dispel this fear, however. Many recent sex books include detailed instructions on how to masturbate and stress the importance of knowing one's own body (for example, Kline-Graber and Graber 1975). In fact, the newest treatment programs for preorgasmic women use self-stimulation as a standard technique for enhancing sexual awareness. Some therapists are starting short-term therapy groups, where preorgasmic women can discuss their feelings about masturbation and their progress with a series of homework assignments. These assignments ask them to examine their own bodies carefully, to experiment with various masturbation techniques, and gradually to include their partners in their sexual exploration (Merriam and Parry 1978).

Intercourse

Many women do not reach orgasm regularly during intercourse. Only 20 percent (Fisher 1973) to 30 percent (Hite 1976) do so without direct clitoral stimulation; with this stimulation, the percentage rises to 60 percent (Fisher 1973), leaving 40 percent of women who do not reach orgasm regularly during intercourse.*

Given these low rates of orgasm, why does a woman engage in intercourse? Judith Bardwick (1971, 1973) explored this question by

* Hite found that the percentages of her sample who experienced orgasm regularly varied according to the type of stimulation: 30 percent in intercourse without direct clitoral stimulation, 42 percent in cunnilingus (oral-genital sex), and 44 percent in clitoral stimulation by hand.

asking 107 women, "Why do you make love?" Very few of them experienced orgasm, and consequently most felt that sex was not important in its own right. They saw physical sex as important to the man, however, and had intercourse as a way of enhancing closeness and holding onto him.

> I don't know. I think it's really necessary as a symbol of the involvement.

> It's pleasurable I guess. It's expected.

> It seems natural and because at this point it would harm the relationship not to.
>
> (Bardwick 1971, p. 55)

With the new emphasis on female sexuality, however, intercourse may not be enough. A woman often feels that she has to have an orgasm to be a "real woman" and to please the man. So if she does not actually experience an orgasm, she may fake one anyway. Hite found that 34 percent of the women in her nationwide sample faked orgasm regularly— to save the male ego, to protect their own pride, and because they were too shy to express their own sexual needs. Another 19 percent said that they used to fake orgasm but no longer did so because of the increased openness about sexuality. And 47 percent said that they rarely or never faked orgasm. Some were indignant at the very idea. As one woman put it, "No more! I think it's a testimony to male insensitivity that faking an orgasm fools them" (Hite 1976, p. 263).

Barbara Seaman also encountered numerous complaints about male insensitivity. She summarized them this way:

> The women in my survey have struggled, often valiantly, to establish their own sexual identities, to discover what it is they really like and want.
> And then they learned that most of the men don't want to hear. For as various as these women were in their tastes and proclivities, their complaints about men were depressingly repetitive. Men make love as if they are following a program. . . . They are humorless. . . . They are too fast. . . . They are cruel to women who require finger stimulation, making them feel that this is a loathsome aberration. . . . They are interested in the "target" organs only, and they fail to appreciate the total body sensuality of women. . . . And, above all, they ignore the woman's statements about what she likes. (1972, p. 101)

These concerns were reflected in the women's answers to what types of man "turned them on." The physical characteristics varied tremendously, and two-thirds of the women did not mention physical attributes at all. Instead they emphasized personality, technique, and the quality of the relationship. Seaman concludes that "the man who yearns for success with 'real' women, women who are comfortable with themselves and their own sexuality, must simply learn to be *himself*"—and to listen when women tell him about their sexual desires and preferences (p. 142).

Insatiable Woman

Masters and Johnson found not only that all female orgasms are identical physiologically, but also that women are capable of having "multiple orgasms." When a woman uses a vibrator, the number of orgasms may reach twenty or fifty in an hour, because no physical exertion is required and she does not tire easily. When a woman is stimulated by hand, however, the number of orgasms is lower. As Masters and Johnson put it:

> If a female who is capable of having regular orgasms is properly stimulated within a short period after her first climax, she will in most instances be capable of having a second, third, fourth, and even a fifth and sixth orgasm before she is fully satiated. As contrasted with the male's usual inability to have more than one orgasm in a short period, many females, especially when clitorally stimulated, can regularly have five or six full orgasms within a matter of a few minutes. (1967, p. 792).

This finding has received much publicity and caused some women to feel defensive about experiencing orgasms one at a time. Other women wonder how multiple orgasms are possible. Helen Kaplan (1974) and Mary Jane Sherfey (1972) have explained that multiple orgasms are possible because after orgasm a woman's body returns not to a resting state but to the plateau phase. Sherfey thinks that this characteristic of female physiology makes women sexually "insatiable."

> The popular idea that woman should have one intense orgasm which should bring "full satisfaction," act as a strong sedative, and alleviate sexual tension for several days to come is simply fallacious. . . . Each orgasm is followed promptly by refilling of the venous erectile chambers, distension creates engorgement and edema, which create more tissue tension, etc. The supply of blood and edema fluid to the pelvis is inexhaustible.
>
> Consequently, the more orgasms a woman has, the stronger they become; the more orgasms she has, the more she *can* have. To all extents

and purposes, *the human female is sexually insatiable in the presence of the highest degrees of sexual stimulation.* (1972, p. 112)

This does not mean that all women "should" experience multiple orgasms, for as Sherfey goes on to say "there is a great difference between satisfaction and satiation. A woman may be emotionally satisfied to the full in the absence of *any* orgasmic expression" (1972, p. 135). The personal experiences of many women appear to bear this statement out. For Hite found that some women in her study never had orgasms but enjoyed sex anyway. Others were aware of their own potential for multiple orgasms but were usually satisfied with one. And many resented the competitive flavor of much of the discussion about multiple orgasms or, as one woman called it, "The Orgasm Olympics" (Hite 1976, p. 171).

Sex After Forty

Our youth-oriented culture tends to view the older woman as asexual. Isadore Rubin points out that the "conspiracy of silence" that has maintained this stereotype of "sexless old age" is now being broken (1966, p. 252). Although Masters and Johnson found that the intensity, duration, and speed of the sexual response does decline with age, their general conclusion was that "there is no time limit drawn by the advancing years to female sexuality" (Masters and Johnson 1966, p. 247). Their conclusions have been supported by a growing body of research done by other investigators. Older women do continue to be sexually active—and to enjoy it.

In spite of this research, however, many young women cannot imagine feeling or acting sexy once they reach middle age. Many dread menopause because "for many of them menstruation has been a badge of femininity and a symbol of youth" (Rubin 1966, p. 252). To menstruate means to be a "real woman," and only a "real woman" has sex. Shere Hite (1976) points out that this attitude is related to the reproductive view of sexuality—if you are not making babies, you should not have sex.

The end of menstruation does involve hormonal change. The loss of estrogen causes the vaginal walls to become thinner, diminishing their ability to protect the internal structures next to the vagina by absorbing the mechanical irritation of penile thrusting in intercourse. When the woman is about five years past menopause, the rate and amount of vaginal lubrication caused by sexual arousal often decreases. And the contractions in the uterus, which accompany orgasm at all ages, may become painful. These changes make intercourse painful for some women. As Rubin points out, however, these problems can be remedied by localized application of simple lubricants or estrogen creams and suppositories. Hormone therapy is also available (although it is becoming controversial).

On the other hand, some of the physical changes involved in the aging process may actually *increase* a woman's sexual desire and pleasure. Mary Jane Sherfey (1972) suggests that a woman's sexual capacity generally increases with age, as a more complex system of veins develops in the genital area. This vein system enhances the pelvic engorgement that underlies female sexual response. Helen Kaplan (1974) points out that the postmenopausal woman's androgens are no longer opposed by estrogen, and hence her sex drive may increase.

Physiological changes do not seem to be as important as emotional and social factors. Rubin (1965) summarizes a number of studies showing that women become less inhibited and more interested in sex with increasing age and maintain sexual desire and activity through their fifties, their sixties, and beyond. The menopausal woman is no longer inhibited by fears of getting pregnant, is often free of family responsibilities that captured her attention and energy in previous years, and is more self-confident and relaxed about her own sexuality.

These issues are illustrated by older women's responses to Hite's questions about how age had affected their sex lives. Although to some sex was no longer particularly important, most of the women over forty felt that their sexual pleasure had increased with age.

> I am enjoying sex more in my forties than I did in my thirties; I enjoyed it more in my thirties than in my twenties. There's a liberating combination of experience, self-knowledge, and confidence, and an absence of pregnancy fears.

> I am sixty-seven and find that age does not change sex much. Circumstances determine it. I have had much more sexual pleasure, both with my husband and other mates in recent years. I love not having menstruation.

> I am sixty-six and sexual desire has not diminished. The enjoyment is as great as ever. I think it might diminish if you couldn't have sex. But enjoying it has nothing to do with age.

> (Quoted in Hite 1976, pp. 509–10)

Many of these older women had difficulty finding sexual partners, however. Some had lost their husbands through separation, divorce, or death. Some, still married, found that their desire had increased while their husband's had waned. And others talked of the general ignorance and prejudice about older women's sexuality—older women were not perceived as potential sexual partners.

Rubin points out that cultural myths often interfere with the sexual fulfillment of older women and men. One of the most persistent myths is that "one can use oneself up sexually and that it is necessary to save oneself for the later years. This myth is connected with the belief that the emission of semen through any kind of sexual activity weakens and debilitates" (1966, p. 258). Although there is absolutely no basis for this belief, many people still cling to it.

Far from recommending abstinence, sex researchers point out that it is important to engage in sex regularly in order to maintain one's sexual functioning. Rubin quotes a variety of medical experts who suggest that the more consistently one engages in sex when young, the more lively one's sexual response will be in old age. Of course, most people do not need to be told to have sex regularly. They do so because they enjoy it and know from their own experience that one does not become sexless at some arbitrary age. Many older women probably share this woman's happy discovery that their own increased pleasure enhances their partner's enjoyment: "I enjoy sex more since I no longer fear pregnancy. (I'm post-menopausal.) Also it's more enjoyable since my children are no longer home—children *can* inhibit sexual activity. Because I enjoy it more, so does my husband. He finds it a pleasant surprise—in fact I put the excitement in his life!" (quoted in Hite 1976, p. 509).

Bisexual, Straight, or Gay?

Hite asked the women in her nationwide study, "Do you prefer sex with men, women, yourself, or not at all?" A surprising 8 percent said they preferred women, while 4 percent identified themselves as "bisexual," and another 5 percent indicated that they had experienced sex with both women and men without stating a preference.*

* These percentages correspond to the gay activists' estimates that one of every ten women is lesbian, since these estimates often include women who relate to both sexes as well as women who relate only to other women (Abbott and Love 1971; Martin and Lyon 1970; J. O'Leary 1978). The percentage of women in Hite's sample indicating a lesbian preference is considerably higher, however, than the 1 to 3 percent of exclusively homosexual women in Kinsey's (1953) sample. The liberalization of sexual attitudes over the past twenty years may have made more women willing to try sexual experiences with other women and to admit to a homosexual preference. It may also be relevant that Hite's subjects were mostly under forty, and that many were sympathetic to the Women's Movement, since feminists are generally more relaxed about changes in traditional female life styles, including those involving sexuality.

What are lesbian sexual experiences like? Hite found that the descriptions were basically the same as for heterosexual experiences, except for more tender feelings and more orgasms. She summarizes the replies this way:

> What is "different" about sexual relations between women is precisely that there is no one institutionalized way of having them, so they can be as inventive and individual as the people involved. Perhaps the two most striking specific differences from most heterosexual relations, as defined in the clitoral stimulation chapter, were that there were generally more feelings and tenderness, affection and sensitivity, and more orgasms. This higher frequency of orgasm in lesbian sexuality has of course been re-marked on by other researchers going at least as far back as Kinsey. Also lesbian sexual relations tend to be longer and to involve more over-all body sensuality, since one orgasm does not automatically signal the end of sexual feeling, as in most of the heterosexual relations described earlier. (1976, p. 413)

When they explained their reasons for preferring lesbian relation-ships, a few women also said that sex with another woman could be better "because of the more equal relationship possible" (Hite 1976, p. 414). This idea echoes the words of one of Seaman's lesbian respon-dents, who said, "It is my sincere belief that the modern intelligent well-adjusted lesbian is the only person enjoying truly democratic sex" (1972, p. 75). Janis Kelly gives a fuller explanation of this viewpoint:

> All heterosexual relationships are corrupted by the imbalance of power between men and women. In order to maintain superiority, males must feed on the emotional care and economic servitude of women. To survive in a male-supremacist social order, women must cripple themselves in order to build the male ego. Due to the stifling effect of this culture and to the damaging roles it enforces, women cannot develop fully in a heterosexual context. . . .
> Love is essentially a simple phenomenon. It involves the opening-up of one person to another, the lowering of certain defenses. . . . There must be no question of conquest. There must be no imbalance of power, eco-nomic or social. This situation is clearly impossible between men and women. . . . Certain [female] defenses must be maintained simply for self-preservation.
> Love relationships between women are more likely to be free of the destructive forces which make these defenses necessary. . . . (Kelly 1972, p. 473)

Not all preferences for one gender or the other are so emphatic. What women do and who they do it with often change considerably over time. Hite actually came to the same conclusion that Kinsey had reached some twenty years earlier: there is such a broad variety of sexual experience that to label people as "gay," "straight," or even "bisexual" makes little sense. In her words:

> It is important to note that preferences can change during a lifetime, or can change several times. . . .
>
> In fact, "lesbian," "homosexual," and "heterosexual" should be used as adjectives, not nouns: *people* are not properly described as homosexuals, lesbians, or heterosexuals; rather, *activities* are properly described as homosexual, lesbian, or heterosexual. (Hite 1976, p. 396)

This opinion is shared by many psychologists today. Hite's words are similar to those used by Sandra Bem in giving the keynote address at a research conference sponsored by the National Institute of Mental Health and the American Psychological Association in May 1975:

> Let us begin to use the terms "homosexual" and "heterosexual" to describe acts rather than persons and to entertain the possibility that compulsive exclusivity in one's sexual responsiveness, whether homosexual or heterosexual, may be the product of a repressive society which forces us to label ourselves as one or the other. (Bem 1976, p. 49)

This more flexible, nonjudgmental attitude toward the expression of sexuality also seems to be shared by many women in the general population. Hite was especially struck by how frequently women volunteered the fact that they were curious about lesbian relationships and might be interested in relating to another woman sexually. They said things like:

> There are times when I feel such a warmth from my best friend that I experience it sexually and almost desire her. But I have never let her know I have this feeling, because it might make her afraid of me.

> I would like to have a sexual relationship with a woman. There is one woman I am sexually attracted to but I would never approach her in a sexual way because that would be imposing on her heterosexuality. We are very good friends and her nonsexual friendship is more important than her sexual friendship.

> I haven't had sex with another woman, except verbally—I think women often make love by talking a certain way, at least I do.

> I have several friends who are lesbians, and superficially I have no strong feelings about that one way or the other. However, when they talk about their relationships, I find myself becoming rather defensive; it seems I do have very deep and complicated feelings about it, both positive and negative.

> (Quoted in Hite 1976, pp. 398–401)

What makes some women prefer lesbian relationships? After reviewing the tremendous variety of sexual practices and proclivities of her
respondents, Hite came to the conclusion that although the argument
about the origins of homosexuality is still raging in some quarters, the
"answer" hardly matters anymore. For only when one defines "natural"
sexuality as reproductive, is it necessary to account for "unnatural" non-
reproductive sexual activities. As Hite puts it:

> It must be clear by now that female sexuality is physically "pan-
> sexual," or just "sexual"—certainly not something that is directed at any
> one type of physical organ to be found in nature. There is no organ
> especially concocted to fit the clitoral area and the kind of stimulation we
> generally need for orgasm. . . .
>
> Homosexuality, or the desire to be physically intimate with someone
> of one's own sex at some time, or always, during one's life, can be con-
> sidered a natural and "normal" variety of life experience. It is "abnormal"
> only when you posit as "normal" and "healthy" only an interest in repro-
> ductive sex. Discussions of why one becomes *heterosexual* would come to
> the same nonconclusions. To consider all nonreproductive sexual contact
> "an error of nature" is a very narrow view. (1976, pp. 389, 392)

Hite goes on to state that, in her opinion, feelings of revulsion about
lesbianism may even reflect negative feelings about oneself. If a woman
finds the thought of another woman's body repulsive, what does she
think of her own? Hite maintains that "a positive attitude toward our
bodies and toward touching ourselves and toward any physical contact
that might naturally develop with another woman is essential to self-love
and accepting our own bodies as good and beautiful" (1976, p. 416).

The Sexual Revolution

Things have changed dramatically since the Victorian era, and even
since Kinsey did his studies in the 1940s. Sex is no longer viewed as
something dirty, dangerous, and disgusting—nor is it only for men. The
double standard is gradually disappearing as women begin to explore
their own sexuality. Premarital sex is frequent. Masturbation is increasingly viewed as a positive experience. And sex is no longer reserved for
reproduction.

Not that everything has changed overnight. Many of the old attitudes
linger on and show up in—of all places—the popular sex manuals, many
of which talk about female sexuality in a mechanical way. As Barbara
Seaman comments, "Does the woman exist—anywhere—who yearns to

be 'manipulated'?" (1972, p. 80). Other books treat heightened female sexuality not as a personal goal but as a way to attract, satisfy, and keep men. "J," the "sensuous woman," introduces her book of sexual techniques by enumerating her own credentials as a man-catcher:

> Some of the most interesting men in America have fallen in love with me. . . . Yet you'd never believe it if we came face to face on the street, for I'm not particularly pretty. . . . But while those mothers, wives and girl friends are burning up over that spectacular-looking blonde undulating provocatively in the peekaboo leopard print, I'm the one that's having the wonderful time—and getting and *keeping* men.
>
> For, through intelligence and hard work, I have become a Sensuous Woman.
>
> And that's what almost every man wants. ("J" 1969, pp. 9–10)

"J" goes on to chastise women for paying too much attention to their own sexual needs.

> *By not listening to our instincts, we women made a number of mistakes.* . . . *We were so busy in bed getting "satisfied" that we forgot our responsibilities as women.* We were greedy, selfish and dumb. . . .
>
> Pin up on your bed, your mirror, your wall, a sign, lady, until you *know* it in every part of your being: *We were designed to delight, excite and satisfy the male of the species.*
>
> *Real* women know this. (1969, p. 97)

Other sex manuals are full of misinformation. Seaman reminds us of David Reuben's "mammary lie detector." In *Everything You Always Wanted to Know About Sex But Were Afraid to Ask*, Reuben suggests that women cannot be trusted not to lie about their orgasms.

> However if [a man] really wants to know, there are two accurate indicators.
>
> Immediately after orgasm, a certain number of women experience what is called the sexual flush. . . . Not every woman experiences this, but they all exhibit the other sign.
>
> Erection of the nipples always follows orgasm in the female. In spite of heaving hips, lunging pelvis, passionate groans—no nipple erection, no orgasm. It is an accurate mammary lie detector—for those who want to know the truth. (Reuben 1969, pp. 49–50)

As Seaman puts it, Reuben's mammary lie detector is a "big bust." Masters and Johnson have found that both the sex flush and nipple erection develop before orgasm and end abruptly afterward (except for a lingering nipple erection in some women over fifty).

Reuben's statement is a bit ludicrous; yet it reflects a common attitude: that men know best and should not hesitate to educate their female partners, even about *female* sexuality. Many recent writers have voiced an angry opposition to this "phallocentrism" (Rotkin 1972), arguing that men are reluctant to give up the myths about female sexuality because they allow men to meet their own sexual needs without taking any responsibility for female sexual pleasure (Shulman 1971). It is also true, however, that the two sexes share both this male-oriented assumption and the sexual limitations that it imposes. As Masters and Johnson put it:

> The most unfortunate misconception our culture has assigned to sexual functioning is the assumption, by both men and women, that men by divine guidance and infallible instinct are able to discern exactly what a woman wants sexually and when she wants it. Probably this fallacy has interfered with natural sexual interaction as much as any other single factor. (1970, p. 87)

Women need to continue exploring, sharing, and expanding their sexual sensitivities. Not only will women grow, but men, too, will benefit from greater sexual flexibility and openness.

Chapter 13

Birth Control

TRADITIONAL IDEAS about the woman's role and female sexuality have changed dramatically since World War II. And attitudes about birth control have changed along with them. Whereas conservatives, liberals, and socialists were united in calling for more population growth before the war, afterward the "population explosion" became a universal concern. Even organized medicine joined in the battle to lift the restrictions on birth control which it had helped to impose a century before (Reed 1978).

By the 1960s birth control had become—as it remains—a popular and controversial topic. People are not only more sexually active, they are talking about sexual activity. And one of their major concerns is its end product—conception. Few people—and especially few women—want every act of sexual intercourse to lead to a baby. There has thus been much controversy about the three major ways to avoid producing unwanted children: contraception, abortion, and sterilization.

Contraception

There are now available a variety of contraceptive methods whose effectiveness varies, however, as do their risks. And they all have risks, as Table 13.1 shows. Some are convenient and comfortable but work only

TABLE 13.1
Contraceptive Methods

Technique	User	Rate of effectiveness	Possible physical side effects	Psychological Advantages	Psychological Disadvantages
Birth control pill	Woman	92–100%	Nausea, weight gain, breast enlargement, blood clotting, liver tumors, cancer	Easy and aesthetic to use; not related to sex act; regularizes menstrual cycle; relieves premenstrual tension and menstrual cramps; lightens flow	Must be remembered every day; can result in loss of sex drive; continual cost
Intrauterine device (IUD)	Woman	97–100%	Heavy menstrual bleeding, irregular bleeding, cramps, uterine puncture, infection	Nothing to remember except to check string; no expense after initial insertion	May be felt during intercourse
Diaphragm and contraceptive cream or foam	Woman	80–95%	Minor irritation from cream or foam, interference with rectal and bladder function when worn for long periods	No medical side effects; minor initial and continual cost; can be inserted up to six hours before intercourse and must be left in place for six hours afterward; blocks menstrual flow	Repeated and messy insertion and removal; must be available when needed; discharge of jelly or cream afterward
Spermicidal foam, cream, or jelly	Woman	80%	Minor irritation	No medical side effects; easy to use; no prescription required	Interruption of sexual activity; messy; must be available when needed; continual expense
Condoms	Man	85%	None	No medical side effects; easy to use; no prescription required; cheap; protects against venereal disease	Reduced sensation for male; interruption of sexual activity; continual expense

Technique	User	Rate of effec- tiveness	Possible physical side effects	Psychological Advantages	Psychological Disadvantages
Withdrawal	Man	70–85%	None	No medical side effects; no cost or preparation before sex act	Requires great will power for male; may be frustrating for both sexes
Rhythm	Woman	65–85%	None	No medical side effects; no cost; acceptable to Roman Catholic Church	Requires meticulous planning and long periods of abstinence; ineffective if woman has irregular cycles
Douche	Woman	65–70%	Irritation to vagina	Inexpensive; no medical side effects; no prescription required	Interferes with sex act resolution; must be done immediately after ejaculation

three-quarters of the time. Others almost always work but cause extensive side effects that are bothersome or even dangerous. At this point there is no perfect method that is safe, convenient, and totally reliable. As Barbara Seaman says: "They tell you that every method is marvelous, and you have merely to choose. They could better put it—'Every method has drawbacks: which troubles you the least? Which can *you* live with if you want to control your fertility'?" (1972, p. 240).*

Many of these contraceptive methods have been around for a long time (Katchadourian and Lunde 1972). The diaphragm, for instance, was invented in 1882 and is similar to other early devices designed to cover the cervix and prevent passage of sperm into the cervical canal. IUDs (intrauterine devices or "coils") date back to ancient Greece and are mentioned in the writings of Hippocrates. And condoms (also known as "rubbers," "prophylactics," "French letters," and "skins") were first produced in England in the early eighteenth century. What is new in the twentieth century is the female contraceptive pill, which was invented in the 1950s and approved for contraceptive use in 1960.

THE PILL: A FALSE PANACEA?

Initially hailed as the "sexual liberator" because it is extremely convenient and almost 100 percent effective, "the pill" has recently become the subject of violent controversy. After the pill has seen eighteen years of widespread use, side effects keep turning up that are far more serious than the nausea, weight gain, and breast enlargement that were first reported.† Recent studies suggest that long-term use of the pill may cause blood clotting, liver tumors, and even cancer. And it may cause emotional as well as physical changes. Seaman (1972), for instance, reports that anywhere from 25 percent to 60 percent of women notice a loss in sex drive while on the pill, while one of three experiences mild to severe depressive changes in personality.

The frightening side effects of the pill have not only made many women hesitant to use it; they have also made some of them angry. Why, they ask, has no pill been developed for men? Seaman charges that the medical establishment is concerned less about the well-being of women than about that of men. As she puts it:

* For a summary of the advantages and disadvantages of the various contraceptive methods, see Barbara Seaman's "A Skeptical Guide to VD and Contraception" in *Free and Female* (New York: Fawcett, 1972) and *Our Bodies, Ourselves* by the Boston Women's Health Book Collective (New York: Simon & Schuster, 1973).

† Researchers and medical specialists tend to view these risks as more moderate than do feminists. Bremner and de Kretser (1975), for instance, maintain that the risks are extremely small. According to these researchers the most serious risk is excessive blood clotting. Whereas the risk of dying from abnormal blood clotting is 1 in 500,000 per year in healthy women of reproductive age not taking the pill, the same risk is approximately 1 in 60,000 for pill users. The risk of developing a clot serious enough to require hospitalization while on the pill, on the other hand, is 1 in 2,000.

There is no organ or tissue which is not affected by the pill to some degree, and the longer a woman stays on the pill, the more her organs and all her metabolic functions are apt to be subtly altered. The 20,000,000 women who take the pill—and the doctors who prescribe it—are engaged in a massive and unprecedented human experiment. We delude ourselves if we believe that a similar experiment on *males* would have been allowed. One of the cornerstones of medical ethics is "First, do no harm." Until the pill—and except for the pill—it would be unthinkable to prescribe, for continuous long-term use by healthy persons, a powerful drug of which the side effects, and even the mechanisms of action, are imperfectly known.

If you doubt that there has been sex discrimination in the development of the pill, try to answer this question: Why *isn't* there a pill for men? Studies of the male reproductive system are well advanced, and a man's organs, being handily placed outside the body, are easier to work with than a woman's. (1972, pp. 242–43)

While acknowledging that the lag in research on a pill for men is partially due to the male attitude that contraception should be a woman's responsibility, male social scientists sometimes suggest that the main reason for the lag is that the side effects for men are too objectionable. For instance, since research suggests that such pills would decrease the male sex drive, male social scientists would not expect men to use them (Katchadourian and Lunde 1972). Apparently the same side effects in women are somehow not as crucial.

On the other hand, biologists have pointed out that it is technically easier to disrupt the reproductive cycle in females than in males. In females one only has to prevent the production of one egg each month, while in males one must prevent the production of billions of sperm— even an 80 percent or 90 percent reduction in sperm production is not sufficient to cause infertility. I should also note that the most promising male pill would not act on the external genitals, as Seaman seems to imply, but rather on the pituitary gland at the base of the brain. But most important of all, feminists themselves seem to be somewhat responsible for the earlier development of a female pill. Margaret Sanger and her friend Mrs. Stanley McCormick initiated much of the early research because they felt women should be able to control their own fertility (Bremner and de Kretser 1975).*

The side effects of the pill are a serious concern for women, then, but are not necessarily the result of male indifference or malevolence. Although each woman does have to take these side effects into consideration when making her personal decision about contraception, it is not

---

* Bremner and de Kretser's summary of the research on male contraceptives also indicates that decrease in sex drive is not the only side effect. Some male pills cause abnormal red blood cell counts and other metabolic changes, some affect the bone marrow and the gastrointestinal tract, and others have been abandoned because they cause severe flushing and irregular heartbeats when alcohol is consumed along with the contraceptive drug.

particularly constructive to rant and rave about male versus female culpability.

Other women are concerned not only about the side effects of the pill, but also about the sexual pressure it can exert on them. If a woman is on the pill, she cannot refuse to have intercourse on the grounds that she might become pregnant. Thus many of Hite's respondents tended to talk of the pill as a mixed blessing:

> The pill doesn't lead to greater freedom but perhaps to greater availability to men: "Well, baby, as long as you use birth control pills, this ain't going to matter."
>
> The birth control pill allows a woman to control her fertility but also forces her to take all the responsibility for birth control and to risk her life and health and future fertility. (Quoted in Hite 1976, pp. 485–486)

Some feminists have pointed out that the answer is greater honesty and personal strength. Thus, the authors of *Our Bodies, Ourselves* say:

> The near-perfect effectiveness of the pill and the IUD can bring increased pressure on a woman to have intercourse with any man who wants it, or to do it with her husband or long-term lover any time he wants to whether she wants to or not. We used to be able to say, "No, I can't, I might get pregnant." Now we have to be more honest and say, "No, I don't want to." This takes strength, and we don't have it all the time. If both men and women can get used to saying "I don't want to this time" without being apologetic or scared, and if both men and women can get used to hearing this said without being threatened or feeling rejected, then sexual relations will probably be a lot better and more satisfying for both sexes. (Boston Women's Health Book Collective 1973, pp. 109–10).

SEXUAL ATTITUDES AND CONTRACEPTIVE USE

In spite of the variety of effective contraceptives available, thousands of unwanted pregnancies occur each year. Donn Byrne estimates that 11 million teenagers have sexual intercourse from time to time and only 20 percent of them use contraceptives regularly. "The result is almost 700,000 unwanted adolescent pregnancies a year, followed soon after by 300,000 abortions, 200,000 out-of-wedlock births, 100,000 hasty and often short-lived marriages, and nearly 100,000 miscarriages" (Byrne 1977, p. 67).

Many people have responded to the problem of unwanted pregnancies by stressing the need for more sex education. But knowledge may not be enough, for the failure to use contraceptives is not simply due to ignorance or carelessness. Negative attitudes toward sex seem to interfere with contraceptive use—and not just in teenagers.

To illustrate the problem, consider the situation at Indiana University. This enlightened institution provides an active contraceptive program through its University Health Service. Lectures about birth control are given in the dormitories, an educational movie is provided for those who are interested, and birth control pills, diaphragms, and IUDs are easily available. In spite of this effort, however, Byrne (1977) found that most of the sexually active women undergraduates do not use birth control regularly. He asked 149 women to answer an anonymous questionnaire about their sex lives. Half of the 91 who reported having intercourse had thought they were pregnant at some time. In spite of this frightening experience, however, less than one-third used contraceptives regularly while over one-half said they *never* used them. And yet these women knew about the techniques of contraception and were aware of the Health Service's birth control program.

Byrne attributes this inconsistency between information and behavior to "erotophobia," or feelings of guilt, shame, and disapproval of sex. In other studies he has found that erotophobes rate sexually explicit movies as more pornographic, shocking, and explicit than other students do. Students with these negative and anxious feelings about sex tend to be more sexually conservative, to have inadequate sexual knowledge, to have intercourse infrequently and with few partners, and to live sex lives influenced by guilt, religious belief, and fear of social rejection. They disapprove of masturbation and premarital sex, feel sex is unimportant and should always be tied to love, think erotica is potentially harmful, dislike oral-genital sex, and frown on birth control clinics and abortion. And they are less likely to use contraceptives.

Byrne suggests that erotophobia interferes with contraception in a variety of ways. Negative feelings about sex are rarely strong enough to inhibit sexual behavior completely, but they do keep people from admitting that intercourse is likely to occur. Sex then becomes an unintentional "spontaneous event." Refusing to acknowledge that intercourse is going to happen makes it even more embarrassing to obtain contraceptive devices from a drugstore or a doctor, since this would be openly admitting to sexual activity. Discussing contraception with a potential sexual partner is difficult. And using the contraceptive is also a problem since "pills require at least one daily thought about sex," while checking one's IUD, inserting a diaphragm, and slipping on a condom require some direct contact with the genitals (1977, p. 68).

Other researchers have looked at this problem in terms of "sex guilt," which is reflected in a general tendency to resist sexual temptation, to inhibit sexual behavior, and to have difficulty thinking clearly in sex-related situations (Mosher and Cross 1971). A number of studies have found that people who receive high scores on Mosher's sex guilt scales tend to have more conservative attitudes about premarital sex and to have less intimate sexual experiences. They may also know less about contraceptives, since Schwartz (1973) found that high sex-guilt people had more difficulty retaining birth control information presented in a lecture. Women with high sex guilt report less effective use of contraceptives (Mosher 1973). And when sexually active female undergraduates using various forms of contraception have been studied, those with accidental pregnancies have been found to have higher sex-guilt scores within each contraceptive group (Gerrard 1977).* Thus, negative attitudes about sex may interfere with responsible contraceptive practices all along the way: in learning about birth control, in anticipating sexual activity, and in using a contraceptive once a sexual situation arises.

Judith Bardwick (1971, 1973) came across these same issues in her study of the use of oral contraceptives. She originally intended to examine the different physical symptoms experienced by women on the pill to see whether there was a relationship between personality and physical distress. She quickly found, however, that she was really studying sexual morality. Most of the 150 women in her study were unmarried, engaged, or just-married students. They seldom experienced orgasm and engaged in intercourse for other reasons, as I have already noted. Many took the pill but felt ambivalent about it: they had made a sexual decision that forced them to perceive their sexual activity as preplanned instead of spontaneous and due to overwhelming momentary passion. Rather than feeling sexually liberated, they were likely to feel vulnerable, degraded, and fearful of being abandoned as an immoral person.

> I feel like a hard woman because taking the pill is an admission of what I'm doing. I detest these changes! Every time I have to swallow one of these pills I dislike the relationship we have a little more.

> The pill makes you aware of your sexual actions at all times.

> There's not the risk involved. This is an unselfish thing I'm doing but part of the mystique is gone. Taking responsibility brings anxiety—or sex is great but the purpose of sex is not there—and yet I'm glad.
>
> (Quoted in Bardwick 1971, p. 56)

In spite of the fact that these women made love with a husband, fiancé, or one special boyfriend toward whom they felt deeply committed, almost all of them expressed fears about sex, contraception, loss of love, and abandonment. Bardwick also found many "prostitution fantasies," or fears that they were being degraded by allowing themselves to be sexually used or by consciously seducing men in order to secure affection. Startled by these results, Bardwick gave projective measures to another 150 women and found the same prostitution anxieties and fear of abandonment. Bardwick describes the themes this way:

---

* Gerrard points out the Mosher sex guilt scales may tap transient feelings of guilt; in this case the elevated scores of women seeking abortions for unwanted pregnancies may reflect the fact that they are unmarried and have just discovered that they are pregnant. If the scales tap more generalized attitudes, however, then sexually active women with high sex guilt may be predisposed to unwanted pregnancy. We need to separate guilt feelings associated with sexual activity per se from those associated with unwanted pregnancy or the abortion procedure, as we will see in the next section.

The anxiety of these women is not simply that they will be abandoned, left alone, but that they have desecrated themselves in a nonfinancial, psychological form of prostitution. This fear we find in the psychological responses of almost all of our subjects, whether or not they are married. They generally fear that they will lose and be abandoned by their lover; a one-sided, especially a premarital, sexual relationship increases this psychological vulnerability. Without arousal and with fear of abandonment, the female is afraid of simply being used.

On a conscious level our subjects are afraid the male will leave them if they refuse intercourse; on an unconscious level they are afraid he will leave them because they have had intercourse with him. (1971, pp. 56–57)

Bardwick goes on to point out that her results are not necessarily applicable to all women. Her subjects did not attain orgasm in intercourse and still had the low self-esteem typical of some young people.

It is likely that women with high self-esteem participate in sex as free agents without fears and that they are less vulnerable to feelings of being used because they have not let themselves be used. But the age-group we studied was still dependent upon others' acceptance, with a core of fear of being rejected, and still defined themselves in terms of someone else, especially the man in their lives. (1971, p. 57)

The studies done in the past five years, however, cast doubt on Bardwick's optimism. Fisher, Seaman, and Hite all found that only one-third of adult women have an orgasm regularly in intercourse. And many different studies indicate that women continue to define themselves in terms of men—as a "proper" woman is expected to do. Thus, while women may not experience the "prostitution fantasies" Bardwick describes, many feel vulnerable and sexually used. These feelings may compound the negative effects of erotophobia or sex guilt and hence interfere with effective contraception.

Abortion

When an unwanted or accidental pregnancy does occur, a woman may choose to have an abortion rather than carry the pregnancy to term.* This is a difficult decision; for the woman has to deal with her own feelings about sexuality, reproduction, and childbirth as well as

* Some people define abortion as any termination of pregnancy before the fetus is capable of surviving on its own. This would include spontaneous abortions (miscarriages) as well as induced abortions. Here, however, I will consider only intentionally induced abortions.

with the feelings of those around her. Some people maintain that she has a "right to choose" what is best for her health and happiness. Others charge that the fetus has a "right to life," that it is selfish to consider her own feelings, and that an abortion is immoral.

The two sides in the current debate about abortion are so dogmatic that they appear to be rooted in long tradition. Actually, however, this controversy is relatively recent. James Mohr (1978) points out that abortion before "quickening" (when a woman can feel the fetus moving) was openly condoned as a means of ending pregnancy in the early nineteenth century. At that time everyone assumed that the fetus was not really alive until quickening, so abortion during the first trimester was not viewed as a particularly drastic act, much less as murder. In 1800 there were no laws prohibiting abortion, and by 1840 only slightly veiled ads for abortion techniques appeared in daily newspapers, weeklies, and even religious magazines. Sales of these products boomed, and abortion became one of the first specialties of American medicine.

It was only in the latter part of the nineteenth century that a movement to restrict abortion began. It was led by Anglo-Saxon Protestants who were worried about their own declining birth rates, and by the American medical establishment, which was eager to professionalize medical training and the delivery of health services. Feminists supported the campaign because they were worried about women's health; and they were joined by antiobscenity crusaders. The churches, however, were not active in this early movement. Even the Catholic Church was silent until 1869, when Pope Pius XI issued a decree prohibiting abortion at any stage of fetal development.

Between 1860 and 1880 new statutes were written that eliminated the traditional quickening doctrines, revoked common-law immunities for pregnant women, and made the American Medical Association (established in 1847) the judge of appropriate medical training and practice. The campaign was extremely successful—by 1900 abortion was illegal in all parts of the United States.

Half a century later, the medical establishment reversed itself and joined with the same elements of society—the Protestant elite and feminists—to push for liberalization of abortion laws. This second campaign led to the Supreme Court's 1973 decision to legalize abortion on request during the first six months of pregnancy. This decision is still extremely unpopular in many quarters, however, and is being challenged in public debate and court cases.

The woman seeking to end an unwanted pregnancy is caught in the midst of a pitched battle. Her attitudes and behavior are bound to be affected by the attitudes of those around her, and these are mixed. Shusterman (1976) points out that, in spite of the recent changes in abortion laws, in the past decade the American public has generally approved of abortion only under certain circumstances: threat to the woman's life or health, incest, rape, and possible fetal deformity. The question of abortion on request continues to be much more controversial.

In spite of this controversy, thousands of American women have abortions each year. Social scientists have looked at abortion in terms of which women have them, how they come to be pregnant, and how the abortion affects their lives.

WHO HAS ABORTIONS, AND WHY?

Shusterman (1976) reports that, when abortions were legally available in several states, almost 600,000 women had one in 1972. Many of these women were young, single and pregnant for the first time; and they had decided to terminate their pregnancies because they were concerned about the social stigma of being an "unwed mother," they felt they were not ready to handle the responsibility of caring for a child, and they did not want to be forced into marriage. If they were already engaged or living with their sexual partner, they were likely to feel that they did not want to begin marriage with a pregnancy. Others were older women who were already married and had families and felt that they were too old to raise another child or were afraid that a new baby would either create or aggravate marital and family problems. And some were separated or divorced women who could not afford to raise a child.

Thus, women who decide to terminate an unwanted pregnancy vary in many ways. They have in common their assessment that they are not in a position to raise a child at a particular moment. Their decision is to terminate one pregnancy—but not all pregnancies, for most of these women either have children already or plan to have them in the future.

REASONS FOR UNWANTED PREGNANCIES

With so many contraceptive techniques available, how does a woman become pregnant when she does not want to? One approach to this question is to ask women seeking abortions what contributed to their own pregnancies. Shusterman (1976) reports a study in which Miller (1973) did this and found that one important factor was "retrospective rhythm," or the tendency to rationalize the safety of intercourse after it is over. Many women who said they had thought they were in a safe period of their menstrual cycle actually knew practically nothing about ovulation and fertility cycles. Other women apparently ignored the possibility of getting pregnant, while some had been afraid of contraceptive devices or had used them improperly. Of the women in Miller's study, 54 percent reported using no form of contraception at the time of conception, 14 percent reported using rhythm, and 32 percent used a variety of contraceptive techniques.

Miller's results bring to mind the problems of erotophobia and sex guilt. Perhaps these women felt so guilty and full of conflict about their sexual activities that they could not bring themselves to think seriously about contraception. Even serious, responsible planning may fall through, however, for one-third of Miller's respondents reported using a contraceptive that had failed. When he interviewed a subset of 328 women to verify this claim, Miller found that their accounts sounded reasonable.* Reports such as Miller's led Shusterman to conclude that "the reported rate of contraceptive failure is surprisingly high and, although the rate needs to be validated further, it suggests that to a large extent abortion is being used as a back-up to other means of controlling pregnancy" (1976, p. 103).

IS ABORTION EMOTIONALLY TRAUMATIC?

Although some women are concerned about the physical effects of an abortion, there is no evidence that one will damage their sexuality or ability to bear children in the future. Although abortion can cause infection, hemorrhage, perforation of the uterus, and sterility, these complications are rare when the abortion is done in a sterilized setting by competent medical personnel. In fact, legal abortions done during the first six months are *less* risky than childbirth (Seaman 1972).

If the risk of physical complications is slight, why do some women continue to worry? Notman (1974) suggests that these fears may originate in guilt feelings: that is, excessive anxiety about the abortion procedure itself may reflect an individual woman's negative feelings about sex and be experienced by her as punishment.

It is now generally accepted that abortion is a medically safe procedure. But many clinicians continue to worry about its emotional impact and argue that since sexuality and reproduction are central to most women's self-identity, the strong feelings associated with them are bound to make an abortion a traumatic experience. Many of the early studies did suggest that abortion created psychological problems, but there were many methodological problems with these studies. Some simply reported one clinician's opinion about the reaction of his or her patients. Other studies asked women to recall their feelings about their abortion and perhaps led them to "overemphasize their feelings of guilt or remorse so as not to appear callous and cold-hearted" (Shusterman 1976, p. 39). Any interviews were done by males, and hence women may

---

* The rate of contraceptive failure reported by Miller is considerably higher than the usual figures, as indicated in Table 13.1. The discrepancy is particularly dramatic for pills, IUDs, and diaphragms, which usually have failure rates ranging from 3 percent to 20 percent. This suggests that Miller's respondents were using the less effective methods and/or that the failures were due to incorrect or sporadic use of contraceptive methods.

have been less frank than they might have been otherwise in discussing such a sensitive subject. And, finally, none of the studies compared abortion patients with an appropriate control group: women from the same backgrounds who carried unwanted pregnancies to term.

Many of the authors of these early studies seemed so determined to find negative results that one reviewer commented, "Deeply held personal convictions frequently seem to outweigh the importance of data, especially when conclusions are drawn" (Simon and Senturia 1966, p. 387). Perhaps most important in evaluating these studies, however, is the fact that they were done before the abortion laws were liberalized. Thus, the subjects of these studies either had to be distressed enough to qualify for "therapeutic" abortions, or else had obtained illegal abortions. In either case their emotional reaction to abortion was undoubtedly colored by the legal and social sanctions current at the time.

Several more rigorous studies have been done since legal abortion became available in 1970, however, and the results are more encouraging. In one, 250 young white women were interviewed immediately after their abortions and then one month later. One-half of them were single, while the rest were evenly divided among married, separated, and divorced. When asked how they felt about their abortions, 65 percent felt moderately happy or very happy, 21 percent felt neutral, 10 percent felt moderately unhappy, and only 4 percent felt very unhappy. The majority (76 percent) experienced no guilt, while others reported feeling some (16 percent) or considerable (8 percent) guilt. More than three-quarters were satisfied with their decision to terminate the pregnancy, and 78 percent reported that they wanted children in the future. In general, the authors concluded that "the predominant moods have been relief and happiness" (Osofsky et al. 1971, p. 231).

In another study medical students used questionnaires to conduct interviews with eighty women immediately after abortion and again one to two years later (Smith 1973). At the time of follow-up, 90 percent reported no negative feelings, and 94 percent said they were satisfied with their decision to abort. Almost half (40 percent) said that abortion had had no effect on their lives, while another 40 percent said it had actually been a positive, maturing experience. Most of these young single students said that their preabortion feelings of desperation were replaced by relief and satisfaction after the abortion, and only two of the fifteen women who had an earlier history of psychiatric problems sought psychiatric help after abortion.

Other studies have also suggested that abortion can actually be a positive, maturing experience. Notman (1974), for instance, points out that a woman's decision to have an abortion is often the first major life decision she has made on her own. No matter how supportive relatives and friends may be, the ultimate responsibility rests with the woman herself. Making such a serious decision autonomously increases her capacity to make other decisions and thereby enhances her maturity, independence, and sense of control over her life. And other women watching her may also benefit from her example. Notman points out that not only does the very availability of abortion make it clear that a woman has other options besides child bearing, but also knowing someone who has had an abortion can make the possibility of unwanted pregnancy less frightening.

> To see that a respected colleague or friend makes a decision to have an abortion and that this is a manageable experience, although this may not be public information, is important in the student's awareness of alternatives that might be available to her at a time she might be in a similar dilemma.
> The possibility of a safe, dignified abortion openly chosen confirms a woman's self-image as someone who is valued not only for her child-bearing role. Whether a particular woman ever has an abortion is not as crucial as her awareness of the possibility of having one. The existence of a choice supports the validity of other priorities. (Notman 1974, p. 220)

Not that the decision to have an abortion is ever easy. The following personal account of an abortion in 1972 illustrates how harrowing the decision-making process can be for even the most mature, thoughtful woman.

> After having two children (ages six and seven and a half) reach a point of some adjustment in school I began to feel I needed and wanted more from life. I decided to return to school, to a plan that had been inter-rupted by my marriage and children. . . . After one marvelous year (with at least one to go) I found myself pregnant. I couldn't believe it. It seemed somewhat like a very bad dream that I would wake up from at any time. The idea of a third pregnancy was suffocating. I just couldn't go through another five or six years of intensive child rearing.
> I couldn't—didn't want to—talk to anyone about my pregnancy, and I felt really alone. The burden of every anxiety and fear of childbirth, un-wanted babies, guilt about abortion, death, life—everything I could pos-sibly lay on myself, I did. I tried to accept the fact that I was pregnant so that I could make plans for my life that included a baby, but all the while I kept hoping for a miscarriage. The idea of abortion—the word—came in and out of my head, and was quickly dismissed. I felt strongly that abortion was not a choice for me. I, as a person I thought I had begun to know, did not have the freedom to make that choice. I had believed abor-tion was every woman's right, but those were hollow, liberal thoughts for me. It's so easy to be a liberal when you're comfortable. For me abortion was a whole life-death question that I could not bear to settle.
> I simply couldn't make a choice. I neither wanted to bear another child nor did I feel I could allow myself the alternative of an abortion, which I believed so strongly was a destructive, violent act. It's important to say that my husband was adamantly opposed to a third child, which

didn't help me at all in making a decision. We argued bitterly—I defending anything he was against. We really turned our backs completely on each other, and the support we had so often given to each other was gone. The situation was hopelessly deadening. It's so hard to describe those feelings. I really just wished I could die.

I went to bed at night hoping to wake up to a miscarriage, and I guess it was at this point—when I was down very low—that I realized that I was actually considering an abortion. I saw that my problem was not so much that I was having difficulty adjusting to the idea of a third child but that somewhere in the back of my mind I understood I could make a choice—and that realization was really mind-blowing.

I tried to be really honest with myself; and it seemed to me that to hope for a miscarriage was about the same as wanting a guilt-free abortion. That's really the way I looked at it. If nature would only expel this fetus, everything would be all right.

I began to talk to other women about myself—my feelings, my life, everything. They were really supportive. . . . I tried to sort out my feelings—what was real, what were the influences of my Catholic upbringing, society, my husband, myself. I couldn't stop thinking about a fetus as a child—as my six- or seven-year-old playing in the yard. I kept getting very entangled in the sanctity of life: this fetus was growing within me whether I was awake or asleep, all the time. When does one have the right to destroy life, potential or real? When is life real? I wanted to just stop and search a bit for an identity that I thought I had found but that had become confused by the realization that I could consider aborting a fetus. Fetus—to me a child.

. . . I began to think about the responsibility of making a decision. It became clear to me that my confusion was a result of my unconscious desire to avoid making a real decision. . . . I had to take on the responsibility of saying "I want to have this child and I will accept that" or "I do not want another child and I must accept the responsibility of aborting this fetus." I had to say that I was real, that my life was real and mine and important. . . . There was a certain strength in knowing that I could make a choice that was mine alone and be entirely responsible to myself. It became very clear to me that this was not the way to have a child, that in thinking about the sanctity of life I had to think about the outcome of my pregnancy, which would be a human being/child that was not wanted. On the strength that I had begun to feel as a woman I made the decision to have an abortion. There was no decision of right or wrong or morality—it simply seemed to be the most responsible choice to make. It is still upsetting to me—the logic of it all—but somewhere within me it is still very clear, and I'm still very sure of that decision.

In writing about this now it all seems so simple, but a two-month process that involved a whole spectrum of emotions is incredibly difficult to go back over. The feelings all are still within me but very hard to express verbally. . . .

My feelings the day of the abortion were in some ways very much numbed and at the same time quite clear. I was very sure of my decision that day, much more than at any other time, but my emotions were somewhat shut down. Perhaps it was in self-defense; I had questioned my decision so many times that I just had to stop. . . . What in reality had happened was that I had become a person I can control—someone who is able to say, "This is the way my life must go." I was fully awake during my abortion, and although it was difficult to go through, it was especially important, because I felt in control of the situation. I had made my decision and was able to carry it through without losing touch with what was happening to my body. (Also, being awake and aware alleviates some of those fantasies about what has happened to you, what a fetus may look like, and so on.) I also had a woman friend with me throughout the abortion, which was a really beautiful thing. . . . because of her and because of two very loving friends who accompanied me to New York, I remember that day as one of strength.

In retrospect, my feelings are very contrary and complex—some high, some low. I do not feel guilt—almost rather guilty over my astonishing (to me) lack of guilt. I have felt at many times very strong and sure in my identity as a woman—a very real person. . . . (The Boston Women's Health Book Collective 1973, pp. 152–53)

A woman who feels guilty about sex, has an especially strong desire to have children at some time, and comes from a Catholic home where abortion is considered immoral is more likely to have difficulty deciding to abort and to experience guilt afterward (Osofsky and Osofsky 1972). And a teenager who is single, is especially fond of children, feels ambivalent about her abortion, worries about its effect on her future fertility, and is not involved in a continuing relationship with her sexual partner may experience a negative reaction to abortion (Smith 1973). Although these negative after-effects seem to be short-lived and rarely intense, they suggest that abortion should not be taken lightly. The fact that many recent writers agree with Shusterman's conclusion that abortion on request is a "relatively benign procedure," does not mean that abortion is absolutely harmless. Most women have strong feelings about abortion, which are bound to influence an individual's reaction to having one herself. The availability of abortion should certainly not be used as an excuse to forget about contraceptive measures. As Seaman says, "Abortion, as an occasional backup, has much to recommend it, but at best it is not a pleasant experience, nor is it entirely safe, even when legal. You surely wouldn't want to have one every month" (1972, p. 240).

THE CONTINUING MORAL AND LEGAL DEBATE

The public controversy about abortion centers on its moral implications. The crucial question is, When does the fetus become alive? Does abortion take a life or only terminate an unwanted pregnancy? Catholic doctrine maintains that the fetus may possess a soul from the moment of conception, or that it is at least calling for a soul. In this sense, then, the fetus is indisputably alive, and to abort a pregnancy is to "take a life." Representative Henry Hyde of Illinois states this forcefully: "Abortion does not merely 'terminate a pregnancy' . . . it is the calculated killing of an innocent inconvenient human being. . . . That is a human life; that is not a potential human life; it is a human life with potential" (quoted in Neier 1979, p. 17).

The opposing view is that a fetus is not alive until it is "viable" or can survive outside the mother. Aryeh Neier explains that the difference between these two views is a matter of theology rather than of medical science:

> To accept [the idea that preventing abortions would save human lives], however, we must join Rep. Hyde in his belief that a human life with potential exists from the moment of conception and not merely a potential human life. Many Americans share Hyde's views. Most do not. For those who do not share Hyde's view that the legislation [prohibiting Medicaid funds for abortion] saves actual human lives, and who regard that view as exclusively rooted in theology and supportable only by an act of faith, [the legislation] lacks a valid secular purpose. (Neier 1979, p. 17)

In their violent opposition to abortion, "Right to Life" groups often equate abortion with murder. Suzannah Lessard points out that this equation evokes such a strong emotional reaction from "Right to Choose" groups that it becomes almost impossible for representatives of either side to communicate: "the emotional pitch of the battle is deafeningly high. That, no doubt, is because if it's difficult to discourse with someone you consider a murderer, it's equally, if not more difficult, to be open-minded toward a person who is calling you one" (1972, p. 30).

Sometimes the argument for legalized abortion is couched in terms of the morality of bringing an unwanted child into the world. How can a woman, in good conscience, take responsibility for the disadvantages and misery that such a child would suffer? Lessard expresses the discomfort that many people experience with this argument:

> While a huge proportion of the unhappy lives, and a whole network of social ills can most likely be traced to a common condition, the unwanted child, when you start arguing that the person a fetus is going to become should not exist because he or she will be unhappy and/or will be a trouble to society—because they will be damaged goods—I bale [*sic*] out. Most of us would rather be alive than not, even if being alive also means deformed, battered, half-crazy, or poor. . . .
>
> An understanding of pregnancy, wanted and unwanted, and what it means for a woman to decide whether to go through with it or not, is the proper ground on which to base a case for abortion—not the social value

of unwanted children, over-population, or any other overview which is based on conjecture of whether or not the growth of the fetus into a human being ought or ought not to be canceled. Aside from opening the door to an abhorrent utilitarianism, such arguments lead as surely as the Right to Lifer position into an intolerable intrusion into the privacy of woman's choice in matters of maternity. (1972, pp. 36–37)

Lessard goes on to call for a distinction between the legal and the personal aspects of the abortion issue. The availability of legal abortion does not mean that a woman has to have an abortion. It merely establishes her legal right to decide for herself.

Sterilization

Regardless of the contraceptive method used, accidental pregnancies do happen. Many women agree with Barbara Seaman: they do the best they can to prevent pregnancy and use abortion as a back-up when contraception fails. Some cannot contemplate having an abortion and simply hope for the best, planning to carry any unwanted pregnancy to term. Others, however, decide to use the only absolutely sure method of birth control: sterilization. This means tubal sterilization or hysterectomy for themselves or, for those with a permanent partner, vasectomy for the man.

TUBAL STERILIZATION

The surgical procedure of tubal sterilization is popularly referred to as "tying the tubes." The fallopian tubes are cut, and the ends either tied off (tubal ligation) or sealed by cauterization (laparoscopic sterilization). This operation does not affect the woman's sexual response, since it does not involve the ovaries, the uterus, or the vagina. The hormone secretions and the menstrual cycle continue as before. Each month an egg ripens and bursts out of an ovary to travel down the fallopian tube. The egg's progress is arrested before it reaches the uterus, however, and it disintegrates and is reabsorbed into the body.

Tubal sterilizations have become increasingly popular in the past five or ten years. In 1972, Katchadourian and Lunde reported that 4 percent of American women had had a tubal sterilization. Yet opinions vary about the advisibility of this method. Barbara Seaman (1972) is quite skeptical, for instance, and points out that if the fallopian tubes are imperfectly closed, the egg and the sperm may manage to join there and cause a tubal pregnancy. Such tubal pregnancies have occurred as long as twelve years after sterilization and are usually fatal. Seaman also notes that tubal ligation is major surgery requiring several days in the hospital. And, finally, she warns that sterilization is irreversible and may leave a woman feeling "depressed and mutilated" (p. 240).

Other writers are more optimistic. The authors of *Our Bodies, Ourselves*, for instance, attribute much of the general concern about irreversibility to the narrow-minded idea that a woman's major accomplishment is producing children. On the other hand, these authors warn that a woman will have to deal with her own deep-seated feelings that "someone who is infertile is inferior" (1973, p. 135); and they point out that while sterilization does mean that a woman can no longer give birth, she can always adopt if she changes her mind about wanting a child.

Both *Our Bodies, Ourselves* and Williams (1977) point out that the new procedure of laparascopic sterilization requires only two small cuts in the abdomen, and hence does not leave scars, and requires only a few hours in the hospital. Williams also refers to "reversible sterilization" in which the fallopian tubes are temporarily blocked by clips. This procedure is still being developed, however, so that most women who contemplate sterilization should expect it to be permanent.

HYSTERECTOMY

Hysterectomy involves surgical removal of the uterus and can be done through an incision in the abdominal wall or through the vagina. In either case it is major surgery and requires several days' hospitalization, followed by two or three weeks of recuperation.

Hysterectomy is usually performed because of some disease of the uterus such as uterine tumors or cancer of the cervix, although it is sometimes done solely for sterilization at the time of a caesarian section. Since the ovaries and fallopian tubes are usually left in place, menstruation stops while the sex hormones remain the same. If the ovaries are removed, hormone therapy can substitute for the missing estrogens.

VASECTOMY

The male sterilization procedure of vasectomy is relatively simple and can be done in a doctor's office in about fifteen minutes. After a local anesthetic is injected into each side of the scrotum, a small incision is made, and the two tubes that carry sperm from the testes to the penis (vas deferens) are cut and tied off. The male sex organs continue to function as usual: the sex glands secrete hormones into the bloodstream, and the man continues to ejaculate. The only difference is that the fluid is now free of sperm, which are blocked from reaching the penis. Like the female sterilization procedures, vasectomy is usually irreversible (Bremner and de Kretser 1975).

PSYCHOLOGICAL EFFECTS OF STERILIZATION

There is no physical reason why sterilization should interfere with sexual activity or lower the sex drive (unless the ovaries are removed during a hysterectomy). But the emotional reactions are highly individualized and variable. Some people feel a new sense of freedom, while others feel a vague loss of sexual identity. Research on women has focused on hysterectomy. If the operation is done because of cancer, a woman's emotional reaction will reflect not only the sterilization but also the life-threatening reason for it. Tubal sterilization is undoubtedly less upsetting than hysterectomy, since it is voluntarily chosen for birth control purposes.*

How would sterilization affect my life? Right now there is not enough research to answer this question—if indeed such a personal issue can ever be settled by knowing how others have reacted. A woman contemplating sterilization should ask herself the same questions she would in considering any birth control method. How do I feel about my sexuality? About childbirth? Do I want a child now, and am I in a position to raise one? In addition to these questions, the irreversibility of sterilization poses some others. How important is child bearing to me? Would I want another child if the circumstances of my life changed? If one of my children died? If I were with a new sexual partner? How would I feel about adopting a child if I couldn't give birth to one? All these issues are intimately related to a woman's feelings about her body. A clear knowledge of where she stands on these issues is not only crucial to a woman in making personal decisions about birth control, but it is also important to her general sense of self.

---

* Unfortunately it is not always true that sterilization is voluntary. A woman occasionally wakes up from abdominal surgery to find that her uterus has been removed or that her fallopian tubes have been tied without her consent. Women who are poor or black have been the most frequent victims of this "forced sterilization," which has been vigorously challenged in recent years.

Chapter 14

Pregnancy

and Childbirth

A BABY is not simply an occasional byproduct of intercourse, an accidental event to be guarded against by judicious use of birth control. It is also a wondrous event that is greeted with great anticipation and excitement. Throughout human history a woman's ability to give birth has been viewed with awe. It has been a source of female pride and satisfaction—and of male reverence tinged with envy. The drama of pregnancy and childbirth is as old as time and as new as the delicate fingers of the latest newborn infant. What is the experience of pregnancy and childbirth like for women today? To answer this question we need to look at social attitudes toward pregnancy and childbirth, the emotional feelings involved in becoming pregnant and bearing a child, and the experience of labor and delivery.

The Image of
the Pregnant Woman

Pregnancy and childbirth are profoundly emotional topics, which evoke many vivid images in a woman's mind: a baby crying, laughing, clinging in a fierce declaration of love; her own mother in a tender moment, or in a rage; young children helpless, infuriating, appealing; the quickening of humor, of understanding, or defiance as they grow older; her father gentle, frightening, solicitous, or aloof; her husband fumbling with diapers, tossing the baby in the air, hiding behind the newspaper, watching television amidst chaos. Other memories crowd in— of feeling nauseous, elated, cranky, or anxious when pregnant; of going into labor and being in the delivery room.

These images are not based only on personal experience but also reflect social images and stereotypes. Nor are they all focused on pregnancy: labor, delivery, infant care, and later child rearing activities are mixed together. But these images are all likely to be elicited by the sight of a pregnant woman.

MYSTERIOUS DANGER OR BLISSFUL HARMONY?

In ancient times the female reproductive capacities were viewed with a mixture of awe and repulsion, as symbolized by the "menstrual taboo." Pregnancy was perceived as a mysterious state fraught with danger. To-day pregnancy is viewed quite differently—as a blissful state infused with creativity and emotional satisfaction. The pregnant woman is ful-filling her true biological role, realizing her womanly potential. Grete Bibring explains that although these two images of pregnancy are dra-matically different, they are both based on cultural stereotypes rather than on women's own experiences.

> There are in our modern world fewer clearly animistic and magic concepts concerning the state of the pregnant woman as a mysterious, even ominous condition which has to be dealt with by ceremonial pro-cedures, yet we find that this fearful superstition has only been replaced by a different type of dogma. Our leading bias today is of the opposite nature—that pregnancy is a state of bliss and beautiful harmony, free from and untouched by inner struggles and conflicts if the woman de-serves to be called healthy and normal. This modern concept has in com-mon with the ancient and primitive ideas the fact that both are not based on scientific studies and findings concerning this important period in the life of the woman, but on culturally determined patterns of thoughts. (Bibring 1975 [1965], p. 255)

THE SOCIAL STIGMA OF PREGNANCY

The pregnant woman's personal experience may be dramatically different from this modern concept. If pregnancy is so desirable, natural, and even blissful, why are there so many euphemisms for the word "pregnant"? Why was discussion of pregnancy banned from television until recently? And why were pregnant women often legally obliged to leave work as soon as they began to "show"?

Shelley Taylor and Ellen Langer (1977) suggest that this treatment reflects an unacknowledged social rejection of pregnancy. Pregnant women are subject to the same social stigma as are crippled people: keep them out of sight so that we can be sympathetic without having to deal with them.

It may seem startling to find that pregnancy is treated like a physical disability; yet according to Taylor and Langer, there is a relatively simple reason for this treatment. They argue that since a person who is crippled or pregnant is an unusual sight, the first reaction to one is often avoidance and staring. After the initial start and feelings of discomfort, however, people gradually grow accustomed to these physical anomalies and act toward them in a more relaxed manner.

Taylor and Langer did a series of three studies that support this view of the social stigma of pregnancy. First they asked people of both sexes to participate in a study of getting acquainted. On arriving at the experiment, each person was given a fact sheet describing his or her female partner as either crippled, pregnant, or normal (no information). The subjects were divided into two groups who interacted with either a crippled or a pregnant confederate. Half of the subjects in each group, upon entering a waiting room, could see the partner through a one-way mirror and thus had a chance to get used to her appearance; the other half were seated so that they could not see the partner. When they entered the experimental room to meet the partner, the subjects reacted to the crippled and pregnant confederate in the same way: they stared and sat far away from her. If they had had a chance to look at her earlier, however, these responses were less marked (Langer et al. 1976).

In a second study the two female experimenters took turns posing as pregnant. The "pregnant" woman (equipped with a large pillow under her clothing) stood in one corner of an elevator, while the other experimenter stood in the opposite corner holding a box in front of her stomach. They found that not only did people entering the elevator stare at the "pregnant" woman, but they also stood closer to the nonpregnant confederate. Some people were almost comical in their efforts to avoid the pregnant woman.

> Several male subjects, who entered the elevator oblivious to the "pregnant" experimenter's condition, visibly backed off or moved quickly to the far side of the elevator when they saw that she was pregnant. A large curious dog was wrenched away from the pregnant confederate by his master so abruptly and so far that he spent the remainder of the ride sitting on the feet of the nonpregnant experimenter, a fact completely unnoticed by his owner, who was still apologizing to the pregnant experimenter. (Taylor and Langer 1977, p. 30)

Obviously people keep their distance from a pregnant woman. But why? Taylor and Langer thought that the reason must have to do with the traditional role of a woman. To investigate this, they did a third study in which twenty-four male-female pairs of college students were

asked to participate in a "group dynamics study." When each pair arrived they found that only one other person had shown up—a married
"pregnant" or a "nonpregnant" confederate. The confederate acted either
passive or assertive during the ensuing group discussion, after which the
participants filled out questionnaires about the study and indicated how
much they liked the confederate, how pleasant they thought she was,
and whether they would want her to participate in any later groups they
might be in. Taylor and Langer found that all the students preferred to
interact with an assertive woman, but that the female students liked the
pregnant confederate better if she was passive. As one of the female
students spontaneously wrote, "I liked her and all, but she seemed sort
of different and motherlyish. I couldn't really warm up to her. I guess
it's because she's pregnant" (Taylor and Langer 1977, p. 33). And all of
the students tended to stare at the pregnant confederate, although they
did not avoid her as much as the people in the other studies had. Taylor
and Langer think the decreased avoidance was due to the opportunity to
become accustomed to the pregnant woman's unusual appearance
through prolonged interaction.

Why did the female students express more liking for the passive
pregnant confederate but simultaneously reject her as a future com-
panion? It was not because of traditional attitudes toward women—
these bore no relationship to evaluations of the female confederates.
Taylor and Langer suggest that it is because of the social norms surrounding pregnancy. Pregnant women are *expected* to be passive. In
fact, they may be perceived as epitomizing the traditional female role—
passive, dependent, and confined to the home. These perceptions may
make pregnancy an isolating and lonely experience for many women.

> The pregnant woman is expected to withdraw from many activities where
> she would ordinarily interact with other people. As a result, the pregnant
> woman becomes a statistically rare or novel sight. Hence, when she does
> appear in public, she may well be responded to with avoidance and
> staring from men and with signs of disapproval from women. The re-
> sponses directed toward her may in turn make the pregnant woman un-
> comfortable about her physical state and cause her to withdraw from
> future activities even more. Thus, the cycle perpetuates itself. (Taylor and
> Langer 1977, pp. 34–35)

The Experience of
Being Pregnant

Contrary to the cultural image of the pregnant woman as blissfully
content, most psychiatric literature depicts her as conflict-ridden. Psychoanalytically oriented clinicians view pregnancy as arousing or intensi-

fying a woman's unconscious feelings about her femininity. In fact, these feelings are often proposed as the underlying reason for the pregnancy itself. Thus, Notman (1974) suggests that women often become pregnant accidentally just when their conscious feelings are most against it, and sees such a pregnancy as a form of escapism. By becoming pregnant the professional woman, for instance, can alleviate anxiety about working on a long-delayed project or about reentering a career and can avoid difficult decisions about training and advancement. The pregnancy is an alternate, more "feminine" way to express her creativity. It reassures her about her fertility and hence bolsters her wavering sense of feminine identity.

Once pregnant, a woman's struggle with her feminine identity continues. Psychoanalysts maintain that unresolved conflicts are reactivated as she "regresses" to childhood. As Therese Benedek puts it, "as the psychodynamic processes inherent in pregnancy revive the infantile ambivalence toward mother and motherhood, they reactivate the anxieties, frustrations, and pains referable to the pregnant woman's infancy, her oral phase of development" (1970, p. 144). The struggle is particularly difficult for a woman who is pregnant with her first child, for she must shift from being a self-contained individual to being fused with the fetus and then, after delivery, she must achieve a balance between smothering the baby and remaining connected to it. She must also change her relationship with her husband: she must learn to be his equal in parenting, to renounce some of her own dependency on him so that she can "share her husband's love with the child [and give up wanting] to be his child herself" (Bibring 1975 [1965], p. 258). And she must "work through" her symbiotic relationship with her own mother, which was previously expressed in "anxious infantile obedience" or in a "somewhat rebellious and defiant independence" (p. 266). Bibring sums it up this way: "It is our main thesis that pregnancy—this means every pregnancy—includes intrinsically an element of crisis as an indispensable factor of the process that leads from the condition of childlessness to the significantly different state of parenthood" (1975 [1965], p. 256).

This "element of crisis" does not necessarily mean that the pregnant woman is consciously upset. Therese Benedek suggests that, in spite of the stress involved in this "critical phase" of transition to parenthood, the hormonal changes of pregnancy ensure a placid emotional state (1970, p. 137). She maintains that the pregnant woman experiences "intensified receptive and retentive tendencies" that result in a "vegetative calmness" (p. 141). Only if the woman has extreme conflicts about motherhood is this biologically based balance disturbed.

Based on the psychoanalytic model, how should a woman expect to feel during pregnancy? Will she be in a state of "crisis" or a state of "vegetative calm"? Will she feel "conflict-ridden" or "lazy, cow-like, and in need of love and affection"? It is impossible to predict, since clinical opinions vary from one extreme to the other (Sherman 1971, pp. 173–74). And the empirical studies are not much clearer. After reviewing them, Fisher concluded that "the available empirical information does not justify glib generalizations concerning the nature of the average woman's psychological state during pregnancy, immediately following delivery, or during specific phases of pregnancy" (1973, p. 145). Nor could Fisher himself find any typical emotional reactions to pregnancy. When he compared 49 pregnant women with 236 nonpregnant women of the same age, marital status, and socioeconomic background, he could not find anything to differentiate the two groups. All of the women seemed to feel the same way. If any of the pregnant women was experiencing a crisis of femininity, it was thoroughly invisible, since Fisher used measures that tap both conscious and unconscious reactions.

But what about the physical reactions to pregnancy? Psychoanalytic theory has always maintained that obstetric complications reflect the emotional conflicts about femininity that are inevitably aroused by pregnancy. Here again, the "wisdom" of psychoanalysis does not seem to be reflected in everyday life. When McDonald (1968) reviewed the research of the past twenty years, he determined that there was "no conclusive proof of a causal relationship" between emotional factors and physical symptoms (p. 231). All he found was that "women with complications experience higher levels of anxiety during pregnancy than women with uncomplicated pregnancies" (p. 232). Of course this does not tell us which comes first: does anxiety cause physical complications, or do complications cause anxiety?

Even knowing how an individual woman fares during one stage of pregnancy will not necessarily help predict how she will feel at another stage. Fisher (1973) found there was little consistency among a woman's responses to the various aspects of pregnancy.

> A woman may report that she had no difficulty during pregnancy but did experience much disturbance during delivery as well as during the postpartum period. Or she may report much delivery disturbance and little at any other phase. Or she may have many distortions in body perception during pregnancy but not a corresponding amount of anxiety or pain at the same time. (1973, p. 360)

At this point, then, social science cannot tell us much about the experience of being pregnant. The available literature amounts to little more than expert theoretical opinions—and opinions, after all, when not backed up by research data, are not far removed from stereotypes. As in so many other areas of daily life, a woman's own experience and intuition are her best guide. As Shelley Taylor and Ellen Langer put it, "The pregnant woman is probably a mysterious creature to all but those who are or have been pregnant" (1977, p. 27).

The Experience of
Labor and Delivery

Our cultural images of childbirth form a stark contrast to those of pregnancy. If pregnancy is a state of "blissful harmony," childbirth is one of "horrifying anguish." As soon as her contractions become frequent, the woman is rushed to a hospital where she is subjected to numerous laboratory tests, "prepped" as if for an operation, and heavily medicated. The process of labor and delivery is usually viewed as an excruciating ordeal requiring tremendous fortitude. Common wisdom often suggests that only amnesia ensures the birth of future children; for if the woman recalled the delivery process vividly, she would never willingly endure it again.

Unfortunately this image of childbirth reflects women's actual feelings and body sensations during delivery. As one can see from the following personal account, delivery does seem to be experienced as a medical crisis that is rather dehumanizing and incredibly painful. This is not to say that it *has* to be experienced this way. But given the current American attitudes and medical practices, it usually is.

I was put in a room with two beds separated by a canvas partition. There was a patient in the other bed but she was very quiet. There was also a patient in the labor room across the hall. She was moaning and yelling and I was a little frightened by the sounds she made, but more than that I felt disgusted at her behavior. I told myself that I was not going to behave like that no matter how bad the pains got. During my pregnancy I dreaded the shave prep and enema that I knew I must have in the labor room. However, it was all done so quickly and efficiently that I didn't mind it at all. After a while my pains grew stronger and seemed to be lasting longer. I was given a shot that relaxed me and although each pain seemed unbearable, I knew it would soon go away and I was able to relax and almost sleep in between pains. A doctor came in every once in a while and gave me a rectal examination. This was very painful and I asked him to wait until my contraction passed, but he said he couldn't. When my doctor came in to examine me I felt very relieved to see him. I felt less afraid and was willing to do whatever he said. At this point my doctor and a nurse had me bear down with each contraction. I had to do this about four times and I cried because the pain was so great. They kept making me push and coaxing me and I prayed that it would soon be over. The nurse said she could see my baby and if I would push once more they would take me into the delivery room. The pain seemed constant now, never letting up. I lifted myself onto the operating table and rolled on my side for the anesthesiologist to inject the saddle block into my spine. I waited what seemed a long time but could feel no needle going in me. My doctor told me later the anesthesiologist couldn't get the needle in and that this sometimes happened. I was rolled over and my legs were tied to two bars at the end of the bed. I wanted to push now. The pain made me want to bear down but the nurses told me not to push. I was told to take deep breaths, but this was very difficult; then I was told to pant. I was extremely frightened at this time. A gas mask was put over my nose and mouth and I wanted to pass out. I remember thinking, "I must be dying. If I am I'll just have to die because I can't stand it any longer." The gas gave me the effect of being suspended somewhere—not really alive. I could hear deep long moans and I realized they must be coming from me, but I wasn't aware that I was moaning. I had no more pain. I could feel the baby coming out and I felt it stretching me. I had an impulse to close my legs but I couldn't. The next thing I remember is opening my eyes and hearing a baby cry. (Fisher 1973, pp. 352–53)

Fisher (1973) asked a number of women to write such personal accounts immediately after their hospital delivery experiences. All of the women were young, married, white, middle class, and highly educated. A few had received prenatal training in relaxation and breathing techniques, and most received anesthesia. Although the accounts were highly individual, they tended to express four major problems encountered in this type of delivery. The first is one shared by all hospital patients: the invasion of privacy. Once admitted, a patient is expected to abandon the usual standards of body modesty. Not only is she scantily covered with a sheet or hospital "johnny," but her body is subject to inspection. The invasion of privacy is intensified for the delivering woman because she is repeatedly asked to expose her genitals and to allow fingers and instruments to be poked into her rectum and vagina, and she is finally placed in the physically revealing and emotionally vulnerable delivery position. All this is done under bright lights in the presence of strangers. Most women respond to this embarrassing aspect of delivery by telling themselves that it is nothing personal, the doctors and nurses are just doing their job. This rationalization is reassuring but cannot completely remove the woman's chagrin.

The second problem can be expressed in one word: *pain*. Most women have never experienced such intense pain, and it goes on, and on, and on. The woman begins to feel that she cannot possibly endure it and, what is more, that it is inhuman to expect her to do so. She becomes "terribly angry about being expected to suffer so unreasonably" and "is deeply impressed by the uncontrollable nature of her suffering" (p. 358). She knows that there is no turning back, no way to stop the birth process once it has begun. She begs for more drugs to dull the pain and fights against the doctor who is reluctant to give them lest they interfere with the birth. Time becomes suspended—the more she longs for the whole thing to be over, the more time seems to stand still.

Fisher's descriptions also emphasize a woman's fear of losing control. "*I'm* not going to scream," she says. But she feels she has little control over her body. It has become treacherous, unresponsive, with a will of its own. Fluids pass in and out without any regulation—she is given an enema on admission to the hospital, her amniotic sac breaks with a gush, she may even lose bladder control. Muscle spasms "surge unpredictably through the body," and the pain, always the pain. Meanwhile she is often surrounded by other women whose cries indicate that they cannot contain themselves. She begins to hear herself moaning and screaming, despite the strongest resolve to be stoic and brave. Through it all she is tired, weak, and somewhat dazed from the drugs. All this combines to produce "the sensation that body processes are occurring (particularly uterine contractions) that are too powerful to be regulated voluntarily" (p. 359). She almost feels like a spectator to her own body's ordeal.

As time goes on, most women become ever more anxious. Will my baby be "deformed or retarded"? Will I be seriously injured or "ripped," even die? As the pain reaches a crescendo, many women become desperately frightened and are convinced they actually are dying. Afterward they recall this as the "weirdest sensation," as a nightmare (pp. 352, 357, 359).

Labor and delivery were apparently not this traumatic for every woman, for Fisher includes an excerpt from one account that had a much more positive tone. Although this woman was initially scared by the intensity of her labor pains, she later found that the relaxation techniques she had learned "seemed to help me a little." As we can see from the description that follows, she does not talk about fearing loss of control, feeling disconnected from her body, or being anxious about the possibility of serious injury or death; and during her unmedicated delivery she "felt nothing but complete happiness."

> The pains started to get very strong. I was in real pain and all of a sudden for the first time I got scared. I knew I was just starting my labor and I couldn't imagine my pains getting any worse. I began to grab on to the sheets as hard as I could. I tried different positions but whatever I did just seemed to make it worse. Finally I pulled myself together after about 30 minutes of twisting and turning. I was once a technician in a program where I learned the importance of lying as still as possible and trying to relax between and during contractions. So I made up my mind I was going to do it and I was very successful. All I thought about, all I concentrated on was totally relaxing. I wouldn't even allow myself to clench my fist a little. Toward the end of my labor the pain got so bad I felt my entire body was going to explode any second. When I felt a pain starting I would slowly count to myself. I would tell myself by the time I got to 10 the pain would be gone. It seemed to help a little.
>
> At around 6:30 p.m. they told me to start pushing. From then on everything was easy. Because I relaxed through my labor I had plenty of

strength left for pushing. I had the baby's head down in 20 minutes. They brought me into the delivery room where I had a "natural childbirth" (this is what I wanted). From the time they brought me into the delivery room until the time I delivered my baby I felt nothing but complete happiness because I knew the baby was going to be born any minute. . . . (P. 356)

Although this woman's program of "natural childbirth" did not eliminate the intense pain, it may have made it seem less unbearable. Fisher does not comment on the differences between this account and the others he collected. It does, however, support some of the claims made by proponents of natural childbirth techniques, as we shall see.

Theories of Childbirth

There are three major approaches to the "psychology of childbirth" that try to explain a woman's experiences during labor and delivery—the psychoanalytic, the neurophysiological, and the anthropological. These theories look at childbirth in terms of three different factors—unconscious determinants of emotion, physical bases for pain, and social customs—and are all sharply critical of the American medical establishment's approach to childbirth. All call for less use of medication and for greater participation and control by the woman herself.

PSYCHOANALYTIC THEORY: UNCONSCIOUS FEARS

According to Helene Deutsch (1944, 1945), who has written the most extensive explanation of the psychoanalytic approach, childbirth is part of a natural continuum that includes intercourse, fertilization, and delivery. This continuum constitutes female sexuality and determines the female personality: because of their reproductive anatomy, all women are passive and masochistic. As childbirth approaches, "even the most mature woman is regressively transformed into a child" (1945, p. 214). She experiences a "deep hereditary fear of death" which is aroused by "fear of separation" from the fetus and by the "unresolved and guilt-laden relation of the woman to her own mother" (1945, pp. 216–17). As a defense against this fear, a woman becomes extremely active toward the end of her pregnancy—an activity that is crucial to her resolution of her anxieties and conflicts surrounding childbirth. As Deutsch puts it:

The activity that manifests itself in the final phase of pregnancy is a mechanism of defense against fear. . . .

Woman's contribution in delivery is manifested not only by the product—the child—but above all by her active participation in the birth. . . . Direct observation of women in labor leaves no doubt that childbirth is experienced as a strenuous act of accomplishment and that it requires tremendous mastery over fear and suffering. (1945, pp. 225, 228)

Because of the importance of female activity during childbirth, Deutsch disapproves of anesthesia and other medical procedures that reduce a woman's active participation—and her experience of pain—during delivery.

Even in normal cases, the duration of delivery now depends upon the obstetric technic used, pain is mastered with the help of drugs, and fear is conquered by gradual lessening of the mother's active participation in the process. Her role as birth giver is growing ever more passive.

I question the desirability of this development. Woman's active part in the delivery process, her lasting pride in her accomplishment, the possibility of rapid reunion with her child, and some degree of gratification of that primary feminine quality that assigns pain a place among pleasure experiences in the psychic economy, are precious components of motherhood, and an effort should be made to preserve them. (1945, p. 247)

Deutsch had a profound influence on Herbert Thoms, who started the first natural childbirth program in the United States in 1947. Located at the Grace–New Haven Hospital in Connecticut, this program included prenatal instruction on pregnancy and birth processes, staff support and guidance during labor, and arrangements for keeping mother and baby together in the hospital. By trying to eliminate sources of anxiety during childbirth, Thoms hoped to encourage women to choose unmedicated delivery (Ostrum 1975).

"NATURAL CHILDBIRTH": ELIMINATING PAIN

Natural childbirth techniques emphasize prenatal preparation by teaching about the childbirth process and stressing various exercises for a woman to use during labor and delivery. These methods are part of a growing trend toward encouraging a woman to take an active part in childbirth, to use minimal or no anesthesia, to have her husband present, and to have immediate contact with her new baby. Williams points out that the term "natural childbirth" has "fallen into disfavor because of its implications that other methods, particularly those in which anesthesia is used, are unnatural" (1977, pp. 271–72). Thus, some people now refer to this general approach as the "prepared," or "participatory," method of giving birth.

The Read method of "childbirth without fear" was introduced to the United States in 1946. Based on a book by the English physician

Grantly Dick-Read (1944), it maintains that ignorance and superstition about childbirth lead to a vicious cycle of fear-tension-pain-fear. The woman's anticipation of severe pain leads to contraction of the uterine muscles, making it difficult for the cervix to expand and permit the fetus to leave the womb. This resistance leads to muscular tension in the uterus, which the woman interprets as pain. Feeling pain, she tenses up more, which creates more resistance, hence more tension, more perception of pain, and so on.

Read's method tries to eliminate anticipatory fear by instructing women about pregnancy, labor, and delivery. Without this fear there should be no initial tension, and hence the fear-tension-pain cycle will not start. Beginning in the fourth or fifth month of pregnancy, women are also trained in relaxation techniques. The idea is that if a woman can learn to relax and not struggle against the uterine action, her uterus will stay flexible, allowing for a relatively painless delivery. Deep chest breathing and muscular exercises help to achieve this relaxed state during labor.

The Lamaze method was developed in Russia in the early 1950s and then applied in France by the physician Ferdinand Lamaze. In 1959, Marjorie Karmel introduced it to the United States in her bestseller *Thank You Dr. Lamaze*. Like the Read method, the Lamaze technique also emphasizes the need for prenatal education and strives to reduce pain so women can be conscious during birth. Lamaze's view of pain is much different, however: rather than attributing pain to tension and fear, he sees it as due to activity in the cortex of the brain and, in accordance with the model of Pavlovian conditioning, this cortical activity as conditioned to speech. In other words, the pain a woman experiences in childbirth is triggered by verbal images. The reasoning goes this way: if a woman can think herself *into* pain, then she can think herself *out* of it. In the Lamaze method she is encouraged to avoid thinking of pain in connection with childbirth and taught new physical activities that become associated with labor. She then experiences the physical sensations of labor in terms of these new physical activities rather than in terms of pain. Rhythmic breathing, panting, and pushing are encouraged as responses to the sensations of labor. Rather than feeling a contraction and thinking "pain," a woman feels a contraction and thinks "breathe, push, pant."

Both these "prepared" methods assume that pain does not have to accompany childbirth. The Read method encourages a woman to respond to the sensations of labor by relaxing and dissociating herself from her body. The Lamaze method, on the other hand, encourages her to focus on the sensations and respond with activity. Although the theory behind the two methods is quite different, they may be combined in actual practice. The personal accounts gathered by Fisher (1973), for instance, show women being told to "relax" and then shortly after to "breathe deeply," "push," or "pant" (pp. 352–55). Some hospital personnel seem to have extended the basic message that pain is not necessary in childbirth: they treat pain almost as a figment of a woman's imagination and distract her from her *experience* of pain by admonishing her both to relax and to work harder to deliver her baby.

How do women themselves feel about these "prepared" or "participatory" methods? Williams (1977) reports a number of enthusiastic claims: women who use these methods recall feeling a sense of mastery and coping during delivery, and they report less pain; those whose husbands were with them are more likely to describe the whole thing as a "peak" emotional experience. Williams also quotes a study comparing the reactions of women who took these preparation programs with those of women who did not.

Takers

The ride all the way to the hospital was nice because somehow being in the car, breathing, and being with my husband, I was very much in control.

I was pushing all the way into the delivery room, and it was really the most wonderful thing in the world to watch the baby being born. It was just fantastic. And to push with all my might to get him out, and to see him, his little body.

Nontakers

I was lost . . . no medication until then . . . I was screaming purposely . . . hoping one of the doctors would give me medication. It was horrible. I kept thinking I was dying.

I remember being wheeled into the delivery room. The doctor just gave me a shot, and the next thing, he held up the baby and put her on my stomach. I remember yelling, "Take him away!"

(Tanzer 1973; in Williams 1977, p. 273)

All in all, these preparation programs seem to improve the experience of childbirth. A woman knows what to expect and has practiced some adaptive responses to the sensations of labor and delivery. She often has her husband with her, gratifying a desire expressed repeatedly in the personal accounts collected by Fisher. Although pain is seldom eliminated entirely, it certainly seems to be reduced to manageable levels. And if the pain should become overwhelming, neither method precludes the use of medication. I would agree with Williams, then: "It is difficult to see how the various components of the training could result in a worse experience than the woman would have had without them" (1977, p. 273). And chances are that they will result in a much better experience.

SOCIAL ANTHROPOLOGY: DOING WHAT IS EXPECTED

The social anthropology approach maintains that childbirth is culturally defined, and that a woman's personal experience during childbirth reflects her culture's expectations rather than her personal conflicts or physiology. Thus, Margaret Mead says that childbirth is "experienced according to the phrasing given it by the culture, as an experience that is dangerous and painful, interesting and engrossing, matter-of-fact and mildly hazardous, or accompanied by enormous supernatural hazards" (1949, p. 235).

Mead based her conclusions on both her own observations and a review of crosscultural patterns recorded in the Human Relations Area File (Mead and Newton 1967). She found that attitudes toward reproduction affect its physical dimensions: when pregnancy and childbirth are seen as times of fear and anxiety, labor is longer and more difficult. Women *learn* what to expect, how to behave, and even what to experience.

> Women may be expected to groan or shriek in a manner designed to make all young female spectators indisposed towards birth and definitely predisposed to shriek when their own "time" comes. Or women may learn that a woman in labour should behave with quite decorum, paying attention to the business in hand, and certainly not dissipating her strength or disgracing her family with a lot of loud-mouthed yelling. (Mead 1949, p. 235)

Mead suggests that this learning is strongly influenced by men, for attitudes are shaped by fantasies. Never having experienced childbirth themselves, males are apt to let their imaginations run wild. As Mead puts it, "there seems some reason to believe that the male imagination, undisciplined and uninformed by immediate bodily clues or immediate bodily experience, may have contributed disproportionately to the cultural superstructure of belief and practice regarding childbearing" (1949, p. 236). She goes on to point out that these male fantasies and attitudes are often linked to the male view of intercourse:

> Men who feel copulation as aggressive may have different phantasies about the dire effects on their wives of their dreadful uncontrolled aggressive desires from men who feel copulation as pleasant, who may share in a cultural phrasing which insists that the child "sleeps quietly until it is time to be born, then puts its hands above its head and comes out." (1949, p. 235)

In the United States males influence the childbirth experience through control of the medical profession. Mead characterizes American medical practitioners as including "males who have been very strongly influenced by their conceptions of what a female role is, and females who are strongly repelled by their conceptions of the limitations of the female role" (1949, pp. 352–53), and suggests that this combination has meant that "the men are left freer to follow their phantasies than they would have been had there been no women among them." As a consequence, the male medical establishment has developed childbirth practices and techniques that have little to do with the actual experiences or desires of women themselves.*

Mead views the trend toward natural childbirth as part of the process of males defining female experience. She points out that the fantasies of male physicians "may sometimes finally include a determination to indoctrinate women in 'natural childbirth' " (1949, p. 353). In other words, methods emphasizing relaxation and breathing exercises are not truly natural because they are not based on *women's* own experiences; they merely represent the latest male fantasy. From Mead's point of view the crucial issue is male control of the birth process—regardless of whether that process involves surgical procedures, anesthesia, or breathing and relaxation exercises.

The idea that natural childbirth is a product of male fantasies would sound like heresy to its proponents, who claim that giving birth without anesthesia is a way of "getting back to nature." They view a husband's presence during birth as a way to reassert the primacy and intimacy of family ties. And many of these advocates, feeling that the natural childbirth methods tend to reestablish a woman's control over childbirth, would probably argue that the fact that they were introduced by *male* physicians is beside the point. The important thing is how these methods affect individual women. And clearly a woman who uses natural childbirth has a greater sense of mastery and control during labor and delivery.

I would not dispute the first-hand accounts of individual women, nor that natural childbirth can be beneficial. But these methods were nonetheless produced by the male imagination. The trend toward father-presence and natural childbirth bears a striking resemblance to the ancient birth ritual of male couvade, in which the father, rather than the mother, underwent labor pains and a long recovery period. Mead found that couvade tended to exist in cultures like ours where childbirth is viewed as dangerous and painful: "The rigours of child-birth may be so exaggerated that the father shares them and has to lie beside his wife "resting" afterwards, or after pacing the floor of the hospital waiting-room take a trip to Bermuda" (1949, p. 235).

---

* The male physician's control over women's experiences in childbirth is dramatically illustrated by the doubling of caesarean births since the electronic fetal monitor was introduced in 1970. Despite a lack of long-term studies of the effects of using this machine, doctors have now broadened the reasons for performing caesarean sections to include slow contractions, slow labor, and various vague indicators of "fetal distress." Doctors often prefer caesarean sections to normal delivery, because they can schedule caesareans precisely, charge more money, and be in the spotlight during the operation. Deborah Larned charges that "in an overzealous appreciation of technology, many doctors are transforming a perfectly natural reproductive process into a surgical procedure" (1978, p. 30). And as one maverick obstetrician put it, "the most common cause of cesarians today is not fetal distress, or maternal distress, but obstetrician distress" (Larned 1978, p. 27).

Other anthropologists view the couvade as a symbolic attempt to assert paternal rights over the newborn child. In cultures where there are definite legal and economic grounds for paternity rights, these rituals are not necessary, for the male already has absolute control over his wife and any offspring. He may have paid a "bride price," for instance, which entitles him both to exclusive enjoyment of his wife's sexuality and to ownership of any offspring. Only when male ownership is not this clear do men resort to symbolic control through participation in the birth process (Paige and Paige 1973). It is as if they were saying, "That's *my* kid. I bore him" (Tavris and Offir 1977, p. 147).

These ancient rituals may have something to do with the modern practice of natural childbirth and father-presence during labor and delivery. As the female role has changed over the past fifty years, men have found themselves with less control over "their women" and "their children." Male participation in natural childbirth may thus be a symbolic way of reasserting social paternity (Tavris and Offir 1977).

The anthropological analysis does not challenge the experience of the individual woman but places it in a broader social context. Every woman has to make her own decisions about childbirth: whether to use the "preparatory" methods, to use drugs, and to have her husband present. The necessity for making individual decisions does not obviate the necessity for asking broader social questions, however; and in their search for answers social scientists need to pay more attention to the actual experiences of women. Pregnancy and childbirth are crucial female life experiences and should not be determined by male attitudes, opinions, and fantasies.

Chapter 15

Rape

MOST WOMEN live with the fear of being raped. And well they might, for rape is increasing at the fastest rate of any violent crime in the United States. In 1973, 51,000 rapes were reported, and the FBI estimates that ten times that many actually occurred (Tavris and Offir 1977). In 1974 the number of reported rapes was almost two and a half times what it had been in 1960 (Shorter 1977). By 1975 nationwide interview samples indicated that 151,000 rapes or attempted rapes had occurred; this means that *1 out of every 600* women was raped that year (Bard and Sangrey 1979).*

Rape does not happen only to other women in other places. All kinds of women are attacked—young and old, rich and poor, married and single. Staying away from dark alleys does not guarantee protection, for rape occurs in many different circumstances. One-third to one-half of rapes actually occur in the sanctity of someone's home (Frieze et al. 1978). Furthermore, the attacker is not always a stranger. Almost all

---

* Many rapes are not reported because of the victim's fear, guilt, and shame—and her realistic expectation of callous treatment by the police and courts. This situation has been changing in recent years, however, and some people think that the increase in rape merely reflects an increase in reporting. The National Crime Survey avoids this problem by conducting interviews with a random sample of household members nationwide. A comparison of these figures with the FBI statistics based on reported crimes indicates a slight increase in the percentage of rapes that were reported to the police over the past few years: 48.9 percent were reported in 1973, 51.8 percent in 1974, and 56.3 percent in 1975 (Bard and Sangrey 1979). This increase in reporting does not seem to account for the dramatic rise in rape statistics.

rapes (90 percent) occur between people of the same race, and one-third to one-half of the rapists are known to their victims, although the degree of acquiescence is usually slight (Bard and Sangrey 1979; *California Law Review* 1973; Frieze et al. 1978; Griffin 1971). The statistics provide a frightening confirmation of women's worst fears: rape can happen to a woman any time, any place, even with a man she trusts.

And when rape does occur, it is almost sure to be violent. Eighty-five percent of rapes are accompanied by physical violence or by threat of violence (Frieze et al. 1978), a weapon is used in almost one-quarter of them, and one-fifth involve a brutal beating (Amir 1971; Bard and Sangrey 1979; *California Law Review* 1973; Frieze et al. 1978). In fact, rape is not a sexual act; it is essentially an act of violence in which a man uses sex as a weapon.

The statistics about rape are shocking and difficult to accept. Women would like to believe the myth we were all brought up with: that rape happens only to a woman who flaunts her sexuality, or to a woman who is foolish and gullible, or even to a women who "asks for it." That rape happens to hitchhikers or on dark streets late at night. That rapists are deranged and not at all like the men *I* know and trust. That rape is rare, in other words, and certainly would not happen to *me*.

Unfortunately the experiences of millions of women testify otherwise. Rape is an everyday occurrence. It happens to women we know, all the time. And when a woman is raped, she is likely to feel so humiliated that she tells no one, or only her closest intimates. If she does report the incident to the police, she is likely to be subjected to even further humiliation. Even her family and close friends may blame her for the attack, leaving her feeling isolated, abandoned, and guilty as well as humiliated.

To find out the reason for this situation, we need to look at the history of rape in our culture. How do others view the victim and the rapist? And how do these ideas fit into our sex-role stereotypes and cultural norms?

Blaming the Rape Victim

The prevailing attitude in our culture is that if a woman is raped, she probably asked for it, that she secretly *wanted* to be raped and enjoyed the experience. Susan Griffin tells an anecdote that expresses this point of view:

> Still, the male psyche persists in believing that, protestations and struggles to the contrary, deep inside her mysterious feminine soul, the

female victim has wished for her own fate. A young woman who was raped by the husband of a friend said that days after the incident the man returned to her home, pounded on the door and screamed to her, "Jane, Jane. You loved it. You know you loved it." (1971, pp. 27–28)

This attitude derives principally from the notion that rape inflicts the pain and humiliation that all women unconsciously long for.

FEMALE RAPE FANTASIES

Freud maintained that women are inherently masochistic. If he was right, then what better way for a woman to satisfy such self-destructive needs than by being raped in either fantasy or fact? Helene Deutsch has elaborated on how female passivity and masochism lead naturally to fantasies of being raped:

> The fantasy life of girls in puberty reveals an unmistakably maso-chistic content. Girlish fantasies relating to rape often remain unconscious but evince their content in dreams, sometimes in symptoms, and often accompany masturbating actions. In dreams the rape is symbolic [and is] connected with fear, not pleasure. . . .
>
> The conscious masochistic rape fantasies, however, are indubitably erotic, since they are connected with masturbation. [Later in life] the masochistic tendency now betrays itself only in the painful longing and wish to suffer for the lover (often unknown). The predominance of the narcissistic element in the erotic fantasies is in itself a triumph over the masochistic element. Many women retain these masochistic fantasies until an advanced age. Such women are far removed from any manifest perversion; on the contrary, they are often extraordinarily sensitive and resentful of any psychic or physical pain. In these women especially, the narcissistic wish to be loved and desired predominates as far as their consciously sought experiences are concerned. (1944, pp. 255–56)

Deutsch goes on to say that such rape fantasies are so strong that it is often difficult to know when a woman is telling the truth. Women tend to confuse fantasy with reality, and they accuse men of raping them because that is what they *wish* had happened.

> We learn—often even without deeper analytic investigation—that rape fantasies are variants of the seduction fantasies so familiar to us in the lying accounts of hysterical women patients. Both rape and seduction fantasies are deliberately passed on to other persons as true, and they have the typical pseudologic character we found in the more romantic and fantastic lies of puberty. That is, they draw their appearance of truth from the fact that underlying them is a real but repressed experience. It is precisely rape fantasies that often have such irresistible verisimilitude that even the most experienced judges are misled in trials of innocent men accused of rape by hysterical women. (1944, p. 256)

If Deutsch were deliberately trying to absolve men from all responsibility for rape, she could not have done a better job. If rape is sexually exciting to women and they secretly long for it, then they must somehow be responsible if it actually happens. After all, rape is fun. Women really want to be raped (even if they do not realize it). They enjoy it. So what's all the fuss about?

THE FEMALE PROVOCATEUR

It is only a brief step from the notion that women *want* to be raped to the idea that they actually *do* something to encourage rapists. Thus, many people believe that women invite rape by being sexually seductive. This view assumes that men are so sexually driven that they cannot resist the temptation of a well-turned ankle, a tight sweater, or even a fashionable coat. Women should know better than to risk displaying their attractions to men, who may be unexpectedly overwhelmed by sexual desire. Throughout history, regulations have specified the proper attire to protect female modesty and virtue (Tavris and Offir 1977). And women still grow up hearing dire warnings against displaying their charms too openly. Susan Griffin's account of a childhood filled with fear and talk of a strange male menace reminds many women of their own pasts:

> I have never been free of the fear of rape. From a very early age, I, like most women, have thought of rape as part of my natural environment—something to be feared and prayed against like fire or lightning. I never asked why men raped; I simply thought it one of the many mysteries of human nature.
>
> I was, however, curious enough about the violent side of humanity to read every crime magazine I was able to ferret away from my grandfather. Each issue featured at least one "sex crime," with pictures of a victim, usually in a pearl necklace, and of the ditch or the orchard where her body was found. I was never certain why the victims were always women, nor what the motives of the murderer were, but I did guess that the world was not a safe place for women. I observed that my grandmother was meticulous about locks, and quick to draw the shades before anyone removed so much as a shoe. I sensed that danger lurked outside.
>
> At the age of eight, my suspicions were confirmed. My grandmother took me to the back of the house where the men wouldn't hear, and told me that strange men wanted to do harm to little girls. I learned not to walk on dark streets, not to talk to strangers or get into strange cars, to lock doors, and to be modest. She never explained why a man would want to harm a little girl, and I never asked.
>
> If I thought for a while that my grandmother's fears were imaginary, the illusion was brief. That year, on the way home from school, a schoolmate a few years older than I tried to rape me. Later, in an obscure aisle

of the local library (while I was reading *Freddy the Pig*) I turned to discover a man exposing himself. Then, the friendly man around the corner was arrested for child molesting. (Griffin 1971, pp. 26–27)

Popular myth maintains not only that women want to be raped and bring it on themselves, but that they can prevent it if they want to. Defense attorneys used to argue that, after all, no woman who resists can be raped (Freize et al. 1978). In her educational talks Sharon McCombie tells of the lawyer who, when defending a man accused of rape, would often hand a pencil to a member of the jury while waving a Coke bottle in his other hand. Then he would tell the juror to insert the pencil in the bottle. Of course the juror could not do so. "You see," the lawyer would exclaim triumphantly, "you can't do it unless I deliberately hold the bottle still for you."

There is no truth to these myths. Rape is not a spontaneous sexual act. In a study of 646 rape cases in Philadelphia, Amir (1971) found that most were planned well ahead of time. In group rape (the proverbial "gang bang") 90 percent of the incidents were planned; in pair rape, 83 percent; and in one-man rape, 58 percent. Furthermore, women do not use seductive acts to provoke rapists. Even though provocation can be legally defined as only a "gesture," the Federal Commission on Crimes of Violence notes that it occurs in only 4 percent of reported rapes (Griffin 1971). And then there is the issue of violence. A woman may indeed be "still," as in the Coke bottle analogy—but with a knife at her throat.

Even though the myths have no true substance, both men *and* women tend to blame the rape victim, although their reasons for placing the blame differ. Men are more likely to assume that the woman unconsciously wanted to be raped and was seductive: her clothes and appearance were too sexy, or she led the rapist on and then changed her mind. Women, on the other hand, tend to blame the woman for simply being in the wrong place at the wrong time (Selby, Calhoun, and Brock 1977): she should have followed the rules of female caution more carefully.

If there is no truth to these myths about rape, why do people believe them? Primarily because we all want to believe in a "just world" where people deserve what they get and get what they deserve (Lerner and Simmons 1966). If something unpleasant does happen to someone, we are likely to think that the victim was a "bad" person or else did something to bring on the calamity. This belief is reassuring: after all, if *I'm* "good" and do not do anything to provoke rape, it will not happen to *me* (or the women I am close to). Thus, the idea that a woman who is raped somehow asked for it shields women from their own anxiety and vulnerability; they do not have to admit that rape occurs at all, much less admit that it is happening more and more often to all kinds of women (Notman and Nadelson 1976).

Are All Men Rapists?

Over the past twenty years social scientists have begun to acknowledge that rape is a fact of life; that it is not merely a figment of women's imaginations, an expression of unconscious masochistic desires and sexual frustrations; and, moreover, that it is a violent crime whose incidence is rising at an alarming rate. In trying to find out why rape happens and how to prevent it, researchers first looked at the male rapist. What makes him attack women? Is it something in his personality? His sexual development? His social relationships? Is a rapist a "pervert" from a lunatic fringe in society? Or is he much like other men?

In asking these questions, the research of the 1950s and 1960s centered on rape as a sexual crime, with its roots in the rapist's sexual maladjustment. Gradually, however, researchers have begun to focus on the violent aspects of the crime and are now examining the social issues surrounding it: how it reflects other social relationships in our culture, expresses underlying assumptions about men and women, and serves as an extreme example of male dominance.

THE "SICKNESS" OF THE RAPIST

Research done in the 1950s focused on the personality development of a variety of sexual offenders. Rapists—along with men who exposed themselves, were peculiarly attached to unusual sex objects, molested children and so on—were generally found to be "fearful, inadequate, sensitive, shy, impulsive, irresponsible, expected too much sex, lacked social skills, had a self-concept confused in psychosexual areas of identification, and were unable to evaluate the consequences of their own behavior" (Albin 1977, p. 426).

Other studies compared rapists with other sexual offenders and concluded that the rapists were the most healthy; and some studies even stated that rapists were not really sexual deviants. To account for rape, then, some scientists suggested that a rapist's wife was at fault: she acted fearful, projecting onto men her own wish to be attacked; she competed with her husband and negated her own femininity; she refused to have sexual intercourse, causing her husband to rape out of sexual frustration and feelings of rejection. Other scientists pointed the finger of blame at the overcontrolling and aggressive mothers of rapists. All in all, these early researchers started out with the assumption that rapists were driven by sexual frustration and anger at women who did not properly meet their needs. Thus, women were still assumed to provoke rape—not directly as the victim but indirectly as the rapist's wife and/or his mother (Albin, 1977).

In the 1960s researchers began to study convicted rapists as a separate group and developed various typologies in an effort to specify which groups of rapists were the "sickest." These typologies usually differentiated between aggressive sociopaths who raped women in the same callous way they took advantage of everyone else, and men who raped in order to deny their own underlying feelings of inadequacy, fear, rage, and hostility toward women (McCaldon 1967).

More recent research has focused on the sexual and aggressive motivations of rapists. These studies generally divide rapists into three classes —those who rape out of aggression, those who rape out of sexual frustration, and those in whom sex and aggression are fused (Cohen et al. 1971). Increasingly, however, researchers have begun to note that sex is usually only an excuse—the desire to exert power and express anger is the real reason for rape. In one of the most recent studies Groth, Burgess, and Holmstrom (1977) examined 133 convicted rapists receiving mandatory treatment at the Massachusetts Center for Diagnosis and Treatment of Sexually Dangerous Persons. They also interviewed 92 women who were raped during the same time period (but by different men), and concluded that

> in *all* cases of forcible rape three components are present: power, anger, and sexuality. . . . We have found that either power or anger dominates and that rape, rather than being primarily an expression of sexual desire, is, in fact, the use of sexuality to express issues of power and anger. Rape, then, is a pseudo-sexual act, a pattern of sexual behavior that is concerned much more with status, aggression, control, and dominance than with sensual pleasure or sexual satisfaction. It is sexual behavior in the service of nonsexual needs and, in this sense, is clearly a sexual deviation. (1977, p. 1240)

These researchers identified two basic types of rape: that whose aim is power or conquest, and that whose aim is violent retaliation for perceived wrongs and rejection by women. Groth, Burgess, and Holmstrom describe power rape this way:

> *Power rape.* In this type of assault, the offender seeks power and control over his victim through intimidation by means of a weapon, physical force, or threat of bodily harm. . . . The aim of the assault usually is to effect sexual intercourse as evidence of conquest; to accomplish this, often the victim is kidnapped, tied up, or otherwise rendered helpless.
>
> This type of offender often shows little skill in negotiating interpersonal relationships and feels inadequate in both sexual and nonsexual areas of his life. Because he has few other avenues of personal expression, sexuality becomes the core of his self-image and self-esteem. Rape is the means by which he reassures himself of his sexual adequacy and identity, of his strength and potency.

. . . The assault is premeditated and preceded by an obsessional fantasy in which his victim may initially resist him but, once overpowered, will submit gratefully to his sexual embrace. She then will be so impressed by his sexual abilities that she will respond with wild abandon. . . . He does not feel reassured by either his own performance or his victim's response and therefore must go out and find another victim—this time the "right one." (1977, p. 1240)

The authors differentiate between two types of power-motivated rapist, depending on whether one rapes to assert his male prerogatives or to reassure himself that he is masculine and strong. As Groth et al. put it:

> The *power-assertive rapist* regards rape as an expression of his virility and mastery and dominance. He feels entitled to "take it" or sees sexual domination as a way of keeping "his" women in line. . . .
> The *power-reassurance rapist* commits the offense in an effort to resolve disturbing doubts about his sexual adequacy and masculinity. He wants to place a woman in a helpless, controlled position in which she cannot refuse or reject him, thereby shoring up his failing sense of worth and adequacy. (1977, pp. 1240, 1241)

Both types of power rapist have underlying feelings of inadequacy and worthlessness. They feel they are nothing and can only pretend to be something if they can humiliate someone else. Thus, the cause of rape is the rapist's secret wish to be powerful, not the victim's secret wish to be dominated. The vignette below describes this type of rapist and the way he treats his victims.

A typical power-reassurance rapist

Mr. C. is a 24-year-old married man who pleaded guilty to six charges of rape. In every case he approached the victim with a gun in a shopping mall. His fantasy was that the woman would say, "You don't need a gun. You're just what I've been waiting for," and then "rape" him. He kidnapped the women, tied them up, forced them to submit to intercourse, and then questioned them as to whether he was as good as other sex partners they had had. Mr. C had no criminal history other than the sex offenses. His background was unremarkable, but he had never felt that he did particularly well in any area of his life (academic, social, vocational, marital) with the exception of his military service. He dated actively as a teenager and indulged in pregenital sexual play, stopping short of intercourse. He found intercourse unsatisfying, partly because of premature ejaculation and partly because it never lived up to his expectations, although he could not define what was missing. He saw marriage as a solution, but since he could not be sensitive or attentive to anyone else's needs but his own, his marriage floundered. Mr. C. discovered he was sterile and began having disturbing homosexual thoughts before his offense. He described the offense as a compulsion—something he felt he must do. Although he realized the consequences of what he was doing, he could not control himself. The six assaults occurred within a 2-month period.

. . . and a typical victim

Ms. D., a 21-year-old single woman, had just stepped off a bus on her way home from work and was walking in a well-lighted area of the city. A man approached her from behind, put a knife to her back, pushed her into some bushes, and pulled her sweater over her head so that she would not see him. He raped her vaginally and kept asking her questions such as: "How does it feel? Am I as good as your boy friend?" She said, "He seemed as if he needed to be reassured and so I tried to reassure him. I was lying on my back in the gravel . . . he was odd saying those things . . . then I had to bargain with him to get my clothes back. He also wanted my address and to know if he could come and do it again. I felt if I could convince him I was being honest, he would let me go. He had my pocketbook and would know who I was so I told him where I lived but not the right apartment." The medical record indicated abrasions on lower and upper back, with no other signs of bleeding or trauma. (Groth et al. 1977, p. 1241)

The aim of anger rape is revenge, not simply domination. The anger rapist wants to get back at women and deliberately sets out to injure his victim as much as possible. The same researchers describe anger rape this way:

Anger rape. In this type of sexual assault, the offender expresses anger, rage, contempt, and hatred for his victim by beating her, sexually assaulting her, and forcing her to perform or submit to additional degrading acts. He uses more force than would be necessary simply to subdue his victim. The assault is one of physical violence to all parts of the body: the rapist often approaches his victim by striking and beating her, tears her clothing, and uses profane and abusive language.

The aim of this type of rapist is to vent his rage on his victim and to retaliate for perceived wrongs or rejections he has suffered at the hands of women. Sex becomes a weapon, and rape is the means by which he can use this weapon to hurt and degrade his victim. . . .

The rape experience for this offender is one of conscious anger or sadistic excitement. His intent is to hurt his victim, and his assault is brutal and violent. The motive is revenge and punishment; in extreme cases, homicide may result. (Groth et al. 1977, p. 1241)

There seem to be no clear precipitants to anger rapes. Such rapists use a "blitz" style of sudden attack, or else entrap their victims with a confidence ploy and then suddenly assault them in a fury of anger. They often become "blind with rage" and recall the rape only vaguely. Older or elderly women are prime targets, although victims may be of any age. The rapist gets his satisfaction and relief "from the discharge of anger rather than from sexual gratification," reveling in degrading and humiliating his victim (pp. 1241–42).

These researchers also differentiate between two types of anger rapist: some are interested primarily in revenge, while others revel in inflicting pain per se:

> The *anger-retaliation rapist* commits rape as an expression of his hostility and rage towards women. His motive is revenge and his aim is degradation and humiliation. . . .
> *The anger-excitation rapist* finds pleasure, thrills, and excitation in the suffering of his victim. He is sadistic and his aim is to punish, hurt, and torture his victim. His aggression is eroticized. (Groth et al. 1977, p. 1242)

Both types of anger rapist feel incredibly angry and humiliated. They feel that they must revenge themselves on women for having slighted, wronged, and rejected them. Here again rape is caused by the rapist's desire to humiliate and inflict pain, not by the victim's secret wish to be humiliated and hurt. The vignettes below describe this type of rapist and the way he tortures his victims.

A typical anger-retaliation rapist

Mr. E. is a 25-year-old married man and father of four. His mother abandoned the family shortly after his birth, and throughout his life his father reminded him that his mother was a "whore and never trust any woman; they are no good." During his adolescence he became acquainted with his mother and once when she was drunk she exposed herself to him and asked him to fondle her. He fled, terrified. In vain efforts to win his father's recognition and approval, he put a premium on physical toughness. In high school he played sports "like a savage." He then entered the Marine Corps and had an outstanding service record. After his discharge he married (against his father's wishes) and attended college. One day he got into a dispute with his female history teacher over the merits of the Viet Nam war and felt she was ridiculing and humiliating him in front of the class. He stormed out of the room, very angry, thinking "women are dirty, rotten bastards" and went to a bar for a few drinks. On his way to his car he spotted a 40-year-old woman (whom he described as looking older) in the parking lot. He grabbed her by the throat and hit her in the mouth; then he ripped off her clothes and raped her. Before this offense, Mr. E.'s only criminal record consisted of arrests for gambling, loitering, and drunkenness.

. . . and a typical victim

Shortly after midnight, Ms. F, a 33-year-old mother of two, was in bed reading and waiting for her husband to return from work. A man known to the family for 10 years knocked at the door and the 14-year-old son let him in. He said he was leaving town the next day and wanted to say goodbye. Ms. F talked to him from the bedroom and wished him well on his trip. Suddenly the man ordered the boy to his room, grabbed Ms. F, and forced her to go outside to another building. He beat her far more than was necessary to subdue her, choked her, and sexually assaulted her.

On follow up, Ms. F reported considerable physical pain from the beatings. She had pain and swelling of the face, neck, arms, and leg, and she reported loss of appetite, insomnia, nightmares, crying spells, restlessness, and a fear of being followed as she walked home from work. She was unable to carry out usual parenting and household tasks for the first week following the assault. There was tension within the marital relationship, delay in resuming sexual relations, and flashbacks to the assault. (Groth, Burgess, and Holmstrom 1977, p. 1242)

These researchers found that 65 percent of the rapes described by their sample were power rapes, while 35 percent were anger rapes. They note that studying convicted rapists and victims treated in a hospital emergency room probably weighted these percentages, however, in comparison with such percentages for the general population. Since the victims of anger rapes sustain more severe physical injuries, they are more likely to seek medical treatment and their attackers are more likely to be convicted if caught. This fact suggests that the vast majority of rapes are of the power type—done by insecure, inadequate males whose deliberate aim is to overpower and dominate women. The rapists are not seeking sexual pleasure per se, nor do their victims experience the rape in sexual terms. As Groth, Burgess, and Holmstrom conclude:

Clinical work with offenders and victims indicates that the initial impact of rape is not sexual for either group. Although the act is sexual, what is traumatizing to the victim is the life-threatening nature of the assault, her helplessness and loss of control in the situation, and her experience of herself as the object of her assailant's rage. (1977, p. 1243)

THE "SICKNESS" OF SOCIETY

Are the power and anger rapists in Groth's study really any different from other men? The study itself cannot tell us, since the subject men were not compared with a control group of nonrapists. But some feminists would argue that these rapists are dramatically different in only one respect—they were caught and sent to jail. These feminists maintain that not only is rape a crime of power rather than of sexuality, as those researchers found, but also that the crime of rape differs only in degree from the way men habitually treat women. Susan Brownmiller, for instance, argues that rape has always been used by men to control women: "From prehistoric times to the present, I believe, rape has played a critical function. It is nothing more or less than a conscious process of intimidation by which *all* men keep *all* women in a state of fear" (1975, p. 15). This statement is not only dramatic but rather frightening as well. Yet many social scientists are beginning to acknowledge that there is a lot of truth to it. Historian Edward Shorter, for instance, criticizes Brownmiller's historical analysis but then goes on to conclude that: "Brownmiller is brilliantly, prophetically, right in proclaiming the political nature of rape today. Violating and degrading women has become as much a political act as the stiff-arm salute or the torchlight parade" (1977, p. 481). When Shorter says that rape is a "political act," he is referring to it as a means of dominating women. In the terms of the clinical study I just discussed, this is "power rape" on a broad societal level. Not only do individual men rape specific women to assert their dominance and masculinity, but also rape and the fear of rape serve to reinforce male dominance in general.

The idea that rape is really political intimidation and power translated into an individual, sexual act is startling and upsetting. Yet an analysis of the social functions of rape suggests that it is true. Throughout history women have been treated as the property of individual men, "to be bought and sold, punished and raped, traded or married off in political allegiances" (Tavris and Offir 1977, p. 8). When a man rapes a woman, he is asserting his control over his property—or the property of some other man. Our modern laws against rape reflect this view of woman as property, for they were developed not to protect a woman's right to *her own* body, but to protect a man's right to be the sole possessor of *his woman's* body. An article in the 1952–53 *Yale Law Journal* explains that rape laws and other codifications of sexual taboos "buttress a system of monogamy based upon the law of 'free bargaining' of the potential spouses. Within this process, the woman's power to withhold or grant sexual access is an important bargaining weapon" (1952, p. 70). But the rape laws are ultimately designed to protect the woman's sexuality not as her "bargaining weapon," but as the man's "exclusive possession."

> The consent standard in our society does more than protect a significant item of social currency for women; it fosters, and is in turn bolstered by, a masculine pride in the exclusive possession of a sexual object. The consent of a woman to sexual intercourse awards the man a privilege of bodily access, a personal "prize" whose value is enhanced by sole ownership. . . . An additional reason for the man's condemnation of rape may be found in the threat to his status from a decrease in the "value" of his sexual "possession" which would result from forcible violation. . . .
>
> The man responds to this undercutting of his status as "possessor" of the girl with hostility toward the rapist; no other restitution device is available. The law of rape provides an orderly outlet for his vengeance. (*Yale Law Journal* 1952, pp. 72–73)

Both Griffin and Brownmiller go on to say that even the rules of chivalry were designed to protect male possession of female sexuality. A woman was expected to be a virgin before marriage and to remain chaste and monogamous afterward. If she behaved herself, her husband or suitor protected her against forcible violation by other men. The protection was for his own benefit, however, since it maintained the value of his exclusive sexual possession. Griffin concludes that "in the system of chivalry, men protect women against men. This is not unlike the protection relationship which the Mafia established with small businesses in the early part of this century. Indeed, chivalry is an age-old protection racket which depends for its existence on rape" (1971, p. 30).

These attitudes toward female chastity are reflected in our modern judicial system. The *California Law Review* (1973) explains that the rapist's legal defense is often based on the allegation that his victim is sexually active and hence not worthy of protection by the rape laws:

> Although evidence of past sexual acts cannot be used to impeach the male, however, it is a general rule that evidence of the "unchastity" of the female is admissible for the purpose of showing the probability of her consent to the act of intercourse. . . . Thus, legally, a man's previous sexual attacks, even if criminal, are of no relevance to his credibility, but once a woman has had sexual relations with one man, a legal presumption exists that she has consented to sexual relations with all men. . . .

> Furthermore, rape laws regard the nonmarital sexual activity of men as irrelevant to the rapist's veracity, yet the non-marital sexual activity of the woman condemns her. The sexually active woman is not only regarded as a liar, she is considered fair game. Such a double standard, which considers male sexuality normal and female sexuality abnormal, serves to enhance the dichotomy between the "good" woman, who is the sole sexual possession of one male, and the "bad" woman who, lacking status as a sole possession, functions as the outlet for "normal" male promiscuity and therefore cannot be raped. (Pp. 935–36, 938)

A common theme underlies the old rules of chivalry and the modern laws against rape: a woman who has been raped is "damaged goods." This attitude is still prevalent. Thus, when Feild (1978) studied the attitudes of over one thousand adult citizens, he found that men tended to feel that a woman was less desirable after a rape.

The idea that women are sexual property suggests that they are often treated as pawns in an elaborate male chess game. One man may take revenge on another by raping the latter's woman and hence damaging his sexual property. Or a man can simply turn his rage onto any woman he comes across: "in the act of rape, the rage that one man may harbor toward another higher in the male hierarchy can be deflected toward a female scapegoat. For every man there is always someone lower on the social scale on whom he can take out his aggressions. And that is any woman alive" (Griffin 1971, p. 34).

The use of rape as male-to-male revenge rests on a man's perception of "his" woman as an extension of himself. This perception is used not only to justify or precipitate rape; it may also be the basis for a liberal man's indignation and sympathetic outrage at the sexual violation of a woman—something he may find difficult to admit. After an academic colloquium on rape, for instance, discussion turned to what should be done with convicted rapists. I felt gratified when a prominent male psychiatrist blurted out, "They should be castrated!" I thought, that's a bit extreme, but it certainly shows a deep sympathy for the suffering of rape victims. Only later did it dawn on me that the man was not necessarily responding only to the degradation of women; he probably felt threatened by the prospect of *his* woman's being attacked, and hence by the threat to his own masculinity.

Some feminists go on to argue that rape not only reflects male dominance but is also the logical outcome of the unequal power relationship between the sexes. Thus, Brownmiller maintains that rapists are just ordinary men. "The typical American perpetrator of forcible rape is little more than an aggressive, hostile youth who chooses to do violence to women" (1975, p. 176). Susan Griffin agrees, stressing that in our culture male eroticism is defined in terms of aggression, power, and violence. This view of male sexuality has led to the phenomenon of the "armchair rapist" who enjoys the media's presentation of detailed accounts of violent rape. Griffin relates Frank Conroy's account of his own vicarious titillation in describing the Manson murders to his wife.

> "Every single person there was killed." She didn't move.
> "It sounds like there was torture," I said. As the words left my mouth I knew there was no need to say them to frighten her into believing that she needed me for protection.

Griffin points out that the pleasure Conroy felt as his wife's protector was inextricably mixed with his pleasure in the violence itself.

> I was excited by the killings, as one is excited by catastrophe on a grand scale, as one is alert to pre-echoes of unknown changes, hints of unrevealed secrets, rumblings of chaos. . . . (Frank Conroy, quoted in Griffin 1971, pp. 28–29)

Griffin goes on to note that rape is unknown in cultures where male sexuality is not defined in aggressive, violent terms. Rape was incomprehensible to the gentle Arapesh studied by Margaret Mead (1935), for instance. But in our culture "the basic elements of rape are involved in all heterosexual relationships" (Griffin 1971, p. 30).

> And in the spectrum of male behavior, rape, the perfect combination of sex and violence, is the penultimate act. Erotic pleasure cannot be separated from culture, and in our culture male eroticism is wedded to power. Not only should a man be taller and stronger than a female in the perfect love-match, but he must also demonstrate his superior strength in gestures of dominance which are perceived as amorous. Though the

law attempts to make a clear division between rape and sexual intercourse, in fact the courts find it difficult to distinguish between a case where the decision to copulate was mutual and one where a man forced himself upon his partner. (Griffin 1971, p. 29)

Other feminists have suggested that the socialization of *both* sexes contributes to rape. Men brought up to be "supermasculine" are likely to rape, while women brought up to be "superfeminine" are particularly vulnerable to attacks. Diana Russell puts it this way:

> Rape may be understood as an extreme acting out of qualities that are regarded as supermasculine in this and many other societies: aggression, force, power, strength, toughness, dominance, competitiveness. To win, to be superior, to be successful, to conquer, all demonstrate masculinity to those who subscribe to common cultural notions of masculinity, i.e. the *masculine mystique*. And it would be surprising if these notions of masculinity did not find expression in men's sexual behavior. . . .
>
> [Female socialization also contributes to rape, since] passivity, and submissiveness are regarded as typical female behavior, particularly in relation to men. . . .
>
> [Russell concludes that] with these basic incompatibilities in socialized needs and expected behavior, it is not surprising that there is often hatred between the sexes. And it is no wonder that there is rape. It is a logical consequence of the lack of symmetry in the way males and females are socialized in this country. Indeed, the remarkable thing is not that rape occurs, but that we have managed for so long to see it as a rare and deviant act when it is, in fact, so embedded in our cultural norms, as a result of the clash between the masculine and feminine mystiques. (Russell 1975, pp. 260, 271, 274)

In order to investigate the possibility that rape is caused by socialization, psychologists have examined the relationships among gender, sex-role attitudes, and beliefs about rape. Thus, two recent studies suggest that the cultural myths about rape are predominately male-oriented. Stewart and Sokol (1977) gave questionnaires about rape to 186 college students and found that males were more likely to see rape as a sexual act that a woman could control. Males were also more likely to think that women enjoy being physically overpowered by men, and that all women secretly want to be raped and enjoy it when it happens. Women, on the other hand, tended to see rape as a violent rather than as a sexual act.

Feild (1978) obtained similar results in a study of 1,056 adult citizens. He also found that men were more likely to perceive rape as sexual and to feel that it is a woman's responsibility to prevent it. These men thought that a woman's appearance and behavior provokes rape, that rapists are mentally normal, that a woman should not resist during a rape, and that a woman is less attractive after she has been raped.

Attitudes toward rape are tied to attitudes toward women. People of either sex who hold more liberal attitudes toward the female role are more likely to hold the female view of rape: it is a violent rather than a sexual act and is beyond a woman's control and outside of her desires (Feild 1978). Stewart and Sokol (1977) obtained similar results: the less students were preoccupied with power and the less they were invested in narrow, traditional sex roles, the more they saw rape as a violent act that was not an extension of normal sexual relations and could not be controlled by the female victim.

If the cultural myths about rape are associated with "male macho," does this mean that all men are rapists? Clinicians say this is not so. After describing the pseudosexual nature of rape, Groth, Burgess, and Holmstrom go on to stress the pathology of the rapist—regardless of whether he rapes to attain power or to express anger. Thus, while they acknowledge that rape is not a truly sexual act, they also argue that the use of sexuality to express dominance or anger is "sick."

> Rape, then, rather than being an expression of sexual desire, in fact is the use of sexuality to express issues of power and anger.
> . . . the etiology of the victim's trauma is the offender's pathology. Rape is more than an illegal act and more than an extreme of cultural role behavior. From a clinical point of view, it is important that rape be defined as a sexual deviation and that the pathology of the offender be recognized. (Groth et al. 1977, pp. 1242–43)

Other clinicians agree. Albin reports Cohen's vehement response to the feminist view of rape as a political act of power against women.

> Every act of rape is expressive of psychopathology; of a disturbance, moderate or severe, in the developmental history of the offender and his current adaptive efforts. . . . Cultural and subcultural factors, socio-political factors, and the characteristics and behavior of the victim play their role in the drama. The major determinants, however, reside as biological and psychological factors within the rapist. . . .
> There are some recent positions which reduce to a minimum or de-emphasize entirely the sexual component. . . . I have never studied a rapist where there was not present together with many other problems, a rather severe sexual disorder and an equally severe problem in the management of aggression. (M. L. Cohen, unpublished remarks quoted in Albin 1977, pp. 430–31)

Certainly we all would like to believe that rapists are deranged "perverts." Vinsel (1977) points out the advantages of this myth for men: since there are only a few of these uncontrollable maniacs, rape is a minor problem for which there is no social remedy. And if a man does force intercourse on a woman against her will, "he is comfortably free of worry that he might be a rapist (since rapists are crazy and he knows he is not)" (p. 185). Of course, this myth also has advantages for women, who do not want to believe that rape is common, or to think of the men in their lives as potential or actual rapists.

The Rape Victim:

Psychic Trauma

How does a woman respond to being raped? She cannot view the assault as a sexual experience, nor can she "relax and enjoy it," for both rapist and victim perceive it as an act of violence. A woman not only has to endure the rape itself, but she must cope with the painful aftermath, both physical and emotional. She feels that her life was threatened and that she escaped alive only by submitting to sexual assault. Yet others do not respond to her experience as life-threatening; they respond to it as a sexual encounter that she somehow asked for or deserved. The contradiction between the reality and the myth of rape sets the stage for intense emotional reactions that can cause major disruptions in a woman's life.

RESPONSE TO RAPE AS A STRESS REACTION

Rape is like any other crisis that threatens one's life: community disasters, war, surgical procedures, and various types of physical attack lead to predictable "stress reactions" like those found in rape victims (Notman and Nadelson 1976). In the "anticipatory or threat phase" of reaction, a potential rape victim becomes subject to such anxiety that she is able to perceive danger and try to avoid it. She notices the man lurking in the doorway and crosses the street, or she hears the threatening tone in a male acquaintance's voice and finds an excuse to leave him. At the same time, however, she defends herself against the anxiety by maintaining an illusion of invulnerability. This couldn't really happen to me, she thinks; this street is well lit, I'm at home in my own apartment, I'm minding my own business. She takes what steps she can to protect herself, while still pretending that nothing awful is about to happen.

The "impact phase" starts with the physical assault. A woman reacts in a variety of ways: she may remain cool and collected, begin to scream or cry, feel stunned and bewildered, or become so scared she cannot move. She often experiences physical reactions such as sweating, trembling, and changes in her senses of sight, hearing, and touch.

In the "recoil" phase immediately after the crisis, a woman gradually returns to herself. She still feels shocked and has not fully taken in what has happened to her. Slowly she comes to recall details, to move around, and to talk about the rape. She begins to question her own behavior: "I should have run. I should have talked him out of it. I should have . . ." Regardless of how well she handled the situation, she is often wracked by self-doubt. Group support during this phase of a crisis is crucial, for it makes the victim feel less isolated and helpless. Unfortunately the rape victim is usually alone during the attack. And even when she does see people later on, they often fail to understand her feelings.

The "posttraumatic reconstitution phase" can last for some time. Now the woman must resume her life. But the rape has shattered the illusion of invulnerability that enables most women to function easily. The woman tends to blame herself for not perceiving the danger soon enough, or for not thinking of something, anything, that could have prevented the rape. She is likely to feel helpless and unable to manage on her own, to feel defiled and worthless.

Burgess and Holmstrom (1974) describe the "rape trauma syndrome" in terms of an acute disorganizational phase and a long-term reorganization phase. They focus on the violent, life-threatening aspects of the rape and outline two general response styles that occur after the rape. Women with the "expressed style" are likely to be emotional and visibly upset. Those with a more "controlled style" are withdrawn and numb, often leading people to assume that they are not upset. Most of the victims express shock and disbelief and have anguished feelings of guilt and self-blame in the initial (acute) phase.

Like victims of any major crisis, rape victims are not likely to feel angry immediately after the attack. Clinicians suggest that this is because the crisis evokes memories of childhood punishment, so that they are too afraid of retaliation to allow themselves to feel angry. "If I'm angry," they reason, "I might be punished even more." And besides, women are not supposed to express anger (Notman and Nadelson 1976). But at some level these victims are extremely angry and are likely to displace that anger onto friends, relatives, and rape counselors (Silverman 1977).

The other striking thing about the rape victim's reaction is the intense guilt and shame she feels. Although victims of other crises also blame themselves, the rape victim's guilt is compounded by the myth that rape is sexual. She has been forced to participate in a sexual act that she sees as degrading and beyond her control—while others see her as causing it, enjoying it, and failing to control the sexual impulses supposedly underlying it.

Most pervasive of all, however, is the rape victim's feeling of helplessness. She has been subjected to a horrifying experience that was totally beyond her control. Afterward she may feel unable to manage by herself, even if she has previously lived a life of considerable autonomy and independence. Her feeling of vulnerability may cause her to turn to her parents, her husband, or other powerful people to take care of her. Although their support is important, overprotectiveness may inadvertently magnify her feelings of helplessness. The rape victim needs sympathetic understanding combined with a reaffirmation that she can manage on her own, that she has some control over her body and her life.

Bard and Sangrey (1979) point out that many of these reactions are typical of the victims of any crime—whether it is car theft, purse snatching, robbery, mugging, murder, or sexual assault. These researchers view the underlying injury as a "violation of self," an attack on the individual's sense of trust and autonomy (p. 10). A rape victim's sense of violation is heightened because the attack not only is upon her body rather than upon her physical possessions but also extends to the inner space that symbolizes the most private self.

> The criminal act of violation compromises the victim's sense of trust. It is a clear demonstration that the environment is not predictable and that it can be harmful. . . . The other essential component of a person's equilibrium is the sense of autonomy. . . .
>
> In crimes against personal property, the threat to autonomy may be somewhat muted. The victim whose purse is snatched loses control over her life for only a split second. The violation is a signal that her mastery of the world can be limited, her freedom circumscribed by the need to take precautions. It is a subtle threat.
>
> Crimes that involve personal confrontation threaten autonomy much more directly. In any face-to-face encounter with a criminal the victim is painfully aware that his or her survival is on the line. Whether the threat is stated or implied, the loss of autonomy is absolute—the victim surrenders control on pain of death. . . .
>
> Sexual assault involves further intensification—the privacy of the victim's inner body is violated. "In the crime of rape, the victim is not only deprived of autonomy and control, experiencing manipulation and often injury to the 'envelope' of the self, but also intrusion of inner space, the most sacred and most private repository of the self. It does not matter which bodily orifice is breached. Symbolically they are much the same and have, so far as the victim is concerned, the asexual significance that forceful access has been provided to the innermost source of the ego" [Bard and Ellison 1974, p. 70].
> (Bard and Sangrey 1979, pp. 14–15, 19–20)

In fact, the sense of violation experienced by rape victims is so excruciating that this crime has become a metaphor for the violation experienced by victims of other crimes. Thus, one man who had been beaten and robbed in his apartment said,

> If a woman talked to me about being raped, she'd never believe it if I said it to her, but I know what it's like. My home was taken over; my body was taken over; I was violated; I mean I was literally raped. It's an incredible feeling of impotence, when your body is in somebody's else's control, and you're the slave. It's an incredible outrage. (Bard and Sangrey 1979, p. 20)

RELATING TO MEN

Most victims report feeling distrustful toward men after being raped. Notman and Nadelson (1976) suggest that this reaction is due to women's unconscious fantasies. Women often expect men to be protectors and providers but see them simultaneously as potential aggressors and exploiters. Rape may profoundly damage the protector fantasy while providing a terrifying fulfillment of the aggressor fantasy.

Unconscious rape fantasies may confuse things further. While a woman may fantasize about submission to a stronger man, this fantasy does not involve violence and danger. The reality of rape is dramatically different from the fantasy; on a conscious level the woman knows that she submitted to the sexual assault because any other behavior would have endangered her life. The rape not only confronts a woman with another person's uncontrolled aggression and sadism, but it also arouses the woman's fears of being unable to control her own unconscious wishes. She may become afraid of acting out her own aggressive, destructive, and masochistic fantasies.

Even without unconscious fantasies, the vicious attack is enough to create distrust. As Bard and Sangrey point out, all crime victims experience this response. The personal assault and the invasion of inner space intensifies the reaction in rape, however. And the pseudosexual nature of the crime makes gender relevant: it is not the entire world that seems untrustworthy; it is primarily the male part of that world. All men are now on trial. Will they be protectors or aggressors, friends or enemies? The warmth and support of the men in her life thus become crucial to a woman recovering from the rape trauma.

Unfortunately these men are the people most likely to have difficulty helping her, for men tend to identify with the rapist as well as the victim. A man may feel that his masculinity is treatened by the attack on "his" woman and have trouble with his own impulses to seek revenge. His own feelings of helplessness may be aroused by his failure to prevent the attack. Men often become overprotective—as a way of handling their own guilt feelings and also as a way of dealing with their anger at both the rapist and their wife, daughter, or girlfriend for somehow allowing the rape to happen. And they sometimes have difficulty with their own rape fantasies and perceptions of a woman as "used merchandise."

All men share these mixed feelings about rape. When a man finds that a woman close to him has been attacked, his emotional reaction is usually intense. To share her pain in an intimate way arouses his own feelings of vulnerability and threat, and he is likely to withdraw in response to this anxiety (Notman and Nadelson 1976; Silverman 1977). He may not even be aware that he is doing this, however, for his own turmoil makes him minimize the experience in order to forget it as quickly as possible. While his withdrawal helps him to cope, it can have a devastating effect upon the rape victim, for this is the time when she needs him most. His withdrawal reinforces her feelings of shame, guilt, and isolation. And it may also compound her distrust of men— they not only fail as protectors and even turn out to be aggressors, but they also fail to come through in an emotional crisis.

LIFE STAGE ISSUES

Most women feel guilty, ashamed, and helpless after a sexual assault. Their ability to cope with these feelings depends not only on their personal strengths but also on their life situations (Notman and Nadelson 1976). A young woman who has just left her parental home may retrace her steps, feeling that she cannot make it on her own after all. Her experiences with men are limited, and thus she is extremely vulnerable to feelings of disappointment and distrust. And she is likely to experience as a "second rape" the gynecological exam required by clinics and police.

A woman who has recently separated or divorced is also particularly vulnerable to feelings of helplessness and dependence. She is already struggling with new demands for autonomy and may feel isolated and overwhelmed. If the end of the marital relationship was bitter, she is more susceptible to a profound distrust of men. And if she has children, she must decide when, where, and how much to tell them about the rape.

A middle-aged woman is also especially at risk. She is often in the process of reevaluating her life and may be worried about the changes that accompany menopause. She, too, is likely to have children, who may well be old enough to be intensely affected by their mother's rape.

Thus, life transitions magnify the emotional impact of rape. Regardless of her age or life situation, however, every woman is likely to be traumatized. The rape casts doubt on her sexuality, her independence, and her relationships with men. And her distress is often compounded when she seeks help, for the personnel in medical and legal settings tend to emphasize the sexual aspects of the rape and to question the victim's credibility and responsibility. Others who are more sympathetic may try to overcompensate for her negative experience by offering help too aggressively. A rape victim often experiences such behavior on the part of men as a "symbolic recreation of the rape" (Silverman 1977, p. 95).

Prosecuting the Rapist

Taking legal action against the rapist can alleviate a woman's anger and allows her to reassert her control. It also helps to underscore the fact that she is the victim, not the perpetrator, of the crime. But the process of reporting a rape and prosecuting the rapist can be so frustrating and humiliating that it only compounds the emotional trauma.

WHAT IS RAPE?

The experience of rape has little to do with its legal definition.* Until recently a woman had to have bruises and other physical evidence of violence and resistance in order to prove that she had not encouraged and enjoyed the rape. If a mugger holds a knife to someone's throat, no one questions the victim's motives for giving up his money. But if a rapist holds the same knife to a woman's throat, the police and the courts continue to ask: "Why didn't you resist? Didn't you secretly want to be raped? Didn't you actually enjoy it?"

Some states also require a witness to substantiate a rape charge. Since the only witnesses to a rape usually are the victim and the rapist, this rule makes many rape laws unenforceable. No witness, no rape. Period.

And then there are the millions of rapes involving coercion that stops short of physical force. And the rapes committed by men who have the legal right to have sex with a particular woman whether she wants to or not. Legally rape does not exist in marriage, where the husband is viewed as legally entitled to exercise his "conjugal rights" at any time and in any place *he* chooses. Thus, in most states rape is defined as "unlawful sexual intercourse or attempted sexual intercourse by a male with a female other than his wife by force or without legal or factual consent" (Bard and Sangrey 1979, p. 194).

But times are changing. Many states have now adopted new laws like the one in Massachusetts, which defines rape as the performance of sexual intercourse or unnatural acts without consent and with the use of or threat of force. This means that vaginal penetration is no longer a stipulation, nor is evidence of physical injury. Both men and women can be raped, and the rapist can technically be of either sex. In some

* The definition of rape accounts for some of the controversy over whether rapists are "perverts" or simply normal men who carry male aggression a little too far. Feminists like Brownmiller and Russell define rape as sexual assault against a woman's will. They feel that "assault" includes nonphysical coercion. The clinical literature, on the other hand, is based on studies of convicted rapists. The definition of rape used to convict these men is much more narrow, and only the most violent and "sick" offenders are likely to be convicted and imprisoned.

jurisdictions rape within marriage is beginning to be recognized, although no husband has yet been convicted.*

DEALING WITH THE POLICE

Many women hesitate to report a rape because they expect the police to be almost as brutal as the rapist. Many police officers treat a rape victim with suspicion and contempt, subjecting her to a second, psychological rape by challenging her report of the incident. "What were you doing there?" they ask, "and what did you expect when you're dressed like that? Did you enjoy it?" And so on.

Women are right to be skeptical about police attitudes. Feild (1978) found that police officers have the same views of rape as have rapists themselves—that is, that rape is a sexual act, that rapists are normal, and that women are less attractive after being raped. Feild notes that the suspicion that many police officers display in interviewing rape victims may be exaggerated by their training. For many police recruits are told to handle rape cases this way:

> The victim should be interviewed as soon as possible after the occurrence. . . . The victim should be questioned thoroughly concerning the occurrence, the circumstances surrounding it and her movements before and after the commission of the offense.
>
> Where a vigorous woman alleges ravishment, it is to be expected that signs of violence such as wounds, bruises and scratches will be present and their absence should induce a moderate degree of skepticism, unless the girl avers that she fainted from fear, became panic stricken, or was otherwise rendered incapable of physical resistance. The acts and demeanor of the female immediately after the alleged commission should be subjected to very critical investigation in these cases. (O'Hara 1973, pp. 305, 306)

Here again, however, times are changing. Women's Movement groups have been working with the police to increase the latter's sensitivity to rape victims. Many police departments maintain a cooperative relationship with rape crisis centers. And the attitudes of individual policemen can change. Thus, Feild (1978) found that patrolmen who received some training in rape casework came to believe that women should not resist a violent attack—an opinion they shared with rape counselors.

---

* In December 1978, an Oregon case attracted nationwide attention. Although John Rideout was acquitted of raping his estranged wife Greta, the case nevertheless set a precedent, because the judge recognized the validity of the new statute under which a man can be charged with raping his wife. The first such case in Massachusetts was heard a short time later, in March 1979 (*The Boston Globe*, 29 March 1979, p. 13).

GOING TO COURT

In those rare instances when a rape case reaches the courtroom, the woman is likely to feel as if *she* were on trial: *her* life style and sexual behavior become a major issue. She is put on the defensive and has to prove that she is not really to blame for being assaulted. It is an uphill battle, and the conviction rate is very low.*

Psychologists have begun to investigate the reasons for the low conviction rates by using jury simulations. This technique involves showing written case histories to a large group of people and asking them to answer a number of questions. How do they see the rape victim? The defendant? Would they vote guilty or not guilty? If guilty, how many years in prison would they recommend? The results of this research match women's own experiences in court. For instance, physical appearance is indeed relevant. An attractive plaintiff does not affect the jury's perception of a victim's credibility and responsibility or change the verdict, but both sexes perceive an attractive woman as relatively promiscuous (Dermer and Thiel 1975; Thornton 1977). On the other hand, they also see her as relatively respectable, and men assign a harsher sentence to her attacker. (Thornton 1977). Perhaps men feel that when an attractive woman is raped, a valuable sexual asset has been damaged.

A woman's marital status is also relevant (Jones and Aronson 1973). Although a divorcée is perceived as less respectable than a virgin or a married woman, she is also likely to be perceived as less responsible for her rape. Jones and Aronson's interpretation follows the "just world" hypothesis: since a respectable woman's character cannot be blamed for the rape, her behavior must be suspect. On the other hand, men who rape married women receive harsher sentences than those who rape virgins or divorcées. Jones and Aronson suggest that raping a married woman is viewed as more serious because it affects the husband as well as the wife. In other words, it infringes on another man's sexual property.

The sexual composition of a jury is also important. Feild (1978) suggests that since men perceive rape differently from the way women do, male jurors may identify with the rapist rather than with the victim. Although sex differences do not seem to affect the perception of the victim's credibility or responsibility, they do affect the verdict. Women tend to vote for conviction more than men do, but also choose more lenient punishment (Thornton 1977).

* During the 1950s and 1960s, only about 10 percent of those originally charged with rape went to prison (*California Law Review* 1973). In the cases of forcible rape that women reported to the police in 1975, only 49 percent led to an arrest. Of those suspects arrested, 33 percent were found guilty as charged, 10 percent were found guilty of a lesser charge, 37 percent were acquitted or dismissed, and 21 percent were referred to the juvenile court (Bard and Sangrey 1979).

The shift in attitudes about rape has altered the court experience for women. Nevertheless, the victim still has to "defend her virtue." Tavris and Offir (1977) suggest that dramatic changes in this situation will occur only when women share equal status with men—and when rape cases are presented, heard, and judged by women as well as by men. Mandel points out that in the Soviet Union, where women are fully employed and hold higher-status jobs than in the United States, a rape victim is not treated as if *she* were on trial.

A husband can get two weeks in jail for "gross behavior" toward his wife, simply on her say-so. Similarly, a man can get three to seven years for rape on the woman's say-so, with no witness needed. This does not mean that Russian courts ignore such realities as the woman who seeks to entrap a man into marriage, which still happens, or that they fail to weigh the credibility of the testimony of both parties, or that attorneys and judges are miraculously free of the prejudices that hang on among other human beings. But . . . the fact that one third of prosecutors, judges, and lawyers and one half of citizen juror-judges are women immediately makes a difference.* (Mandel 1975, p. 272)

* By December 1972 one-third of the judges in the Soviet Union were female; this forms a marked contrast to the United States, where only "two judges in a hundred are female" (Mandel 1975, p. 132).

Chapter 16

Domestic Violence:

The Battered Woman

MANY PEOPLE THINK that if a woman wants to avoid being attacked, she should stay at home. But a woman is not always safe from violence at home: one out of every four or five wives is beaten by her husband. The FBI estimates that one and a half million women are physically abused each year—three times the number who are raped (Tavris and Offir 1977). These figures are based only on abuse so brutal that it causes serious injury. Studies that define wife abuse as anything from an occasional hard slap to repeated, severe beatings suggest that there are 26 million to 30 million abused wives in the United States today (Langley and Levy 1977). Many researchers in this field agree with Judge Stewart Oneglia's estimate that "50 percent of all marriages involve some degree of physical abuse of the woman" (Langley and Levy 1977, p. 20). These statistics are grim and lead some people to conclude that "wife-beating is almost as much of a national pastime as baseball" (Women in Transition 1975, p. 413).

The immediate response to these statistics is often, "Ridiculous!" "Impossible!" "I don't know anyone who's treated like that." Many women *are* treated like that, however; they simply do not talk about it. Wife abuse is a taboo subject, just like rape and sexuality. Women go to great lengths to hide their bruises—and the feelings of shame, guilt, and humiliation that go with them. As with so many other areas of women's daily lives, however, there has been an increase of publicity and research over the past ten years. Wife abuse is "coming out of the closet." And as it does, people are appalled at the pain and suffering millions of women experience at the hands of the men they love.

Women Should Be Beaten

When people do talk about wife beating, they tend to treat it lightly. Many even view it as a good thing. "A man needs to hit his wife every now and then," they say. "It's his responsibility to keep her in line." It is all in the family, after all, and the man is the head of the family. As sociologist Murray Straus says, "There are informal norms that make a marriage license also a hitting license" (Langley and Levy 1977, p. 24).

In a nationwide poll done in 1968, Louis Harris found that one-fifth of Americans approve of slapping one's spouse on appropriate occasions—and the approval rate increases along with education and income (Langley and Levy 1977). People also feel that such slaps are a private, family matter. It the violence does occur in public, it tends to be ignored. Three psychologists at Michigan State University demonstrated this attitude by staging a series of three fights on a sidewalk. They found that men rushed to the aid of another man being assaulted by a man or a woman. Men also rushed to the aid of a woman being assaulted by another woman. But if a woman was assaulted by a man, it was strictly "hands off"—not one man tried to assist her (cited in Pogrebin 1974). Langley and Levy (1977) compare the results of this study to the infamous incident that occurred several years ago in New York City, when Kitty Genovese was stalked, repeatedly stabbed, and finally killed while thirty-eight people looked on from their windows. Not one person came to her aid, and afterward some said they had not done anything because they assumed the man was her husband.

Del Martin points out that the hands-off attitude reflects the idea of wife as property. She tells an anecdote that dramatically illustrates the strength of this popular belief.

A feminist friend learned this lesson in an incident in Oakland, California. She witnessed a street fight in which a husband was hitting his pregnant wife in the stomach (a recurring theme in stories of wife-abuse). She saw the fight as she was driving by, stopped her car, and jumped out to help the woman. When she tried to intervene, the male bystanders who stood idly by watching the spectacle shouted at her, "You can't do that! She's his wife!" and "You shouldn't interfere; it's none of your business." Although the wife had begged the gathered crowd to call the police, no one did so until my friend was struck by the furious husband. (Martin 1976, p. 19)

Wife beating is not only condoned, it is even considered humorous. Political writer Richard Reeves thinks he is being witty when he tells *Time* magazine, "Politicians, like wives, should be beaten regularly." But as Langley and Levy point out, "there's nothing funny about wife beating in the real world." They note that wife beating is not likely to get a laugh from:

> Elizabeth M., who was hacked with a ceremonial sword wielded by her husband, a West Point graduate, or from:
> Rosemary G., who walks with a limp because her right leg was crushed when her husband pushed a refrigerator over on her as she lay unconscious on the kitchen floor, or from:
> Niki R., who was blinded in the right eye by the rage in her husband's fists, or from:
> Virginia K., whose baby was stillborn after her husband knocked her down and repeatedly kicked her in the stomach, or from:
> Sue Anne B., whose right cheek has a deep depression in it because her husband extinguished his cigarette there. (Langley and Levy 1977, p. 24)

Who Beats His Wife,

and Why?

What are wife beaters like? They are rich and poor, young and old, fat and thin. They live in cities, in suburbs, in rural areas. They work at all occupations and come from all racial and ethnic groups. In fact, they are pretty much like all other men (Gelles 1972; Langley and Levy 1977; Martin 1976; Pizzey 1974). As Langley and Levy put it:

> The answer to the question "What kind of man beats his wife?" is: *Every* kind and they can be located in so-called "normal families." . . .
> The simple fact is that in America today almost every man is a potential wife beater. (1977, pp. 65, 70)

Much as we would like to, we cannot brush wife beating aside as the work of a demented few: It is far too widespread for that. Yet researchers have identified some themes in the personalities of the worst offenders. (These descriptions are based on studies of the rare wife beater who is arrested and convicted, and on descriptions offered by wives who have been so severely beaten that they seek help in desperation.) In general, these men feel that they are less than what they ought to be, that they cannot live up to society's ideal of masculinity (Langley and Levy 1977). Some show a "compulsive masculinity" that divides the world into virile males who ferociously defend their honor and property, and the females who "belong" to these males and are seen as either madonnas or sluts (Toby 1975).

Some researchers suggest that the wife beater is immature, transferring his dependence from his mother onto his wife (Schultz 1960). He then feels both hostile and dependent on his wife; when she fails to meet his dependence needs, he beats her. Others point to the consuming, infantile jealousy experienced by many of these men (Langley and Levy 1977; Martin 1976), and to their heavy use of alcohol and drugs. In general, wife beaters are depicted as insecure men who are threatened by any change in their lives—especially change that involves greater family responsiblity for them or increasing independence and autonomy in their wives. Thus, a man is likely to beat his wife when she becomes pregnant, goes back to school, obtains a job, or even changes her physical appearance by dying her hair or losing weight (Langley and Levy 1977).

Thus the beatings are often provoked by something the wife does, but her behavior rarely seems to justify the violence of the attack. She may have been late in fixing dinner, failed to keep the children quiet enough, or said the wrong thing at the wrong time. Often the attacks appear totally arbitrary. Judge Stewart Oneglia reports: "My worst case was the wife of a physician in Montgomery County, Maryland, the richest county in the nation, whose husband jumped on her spine causing paralysis because she left the door open and let the cool, air-conditioned air escape" (quoted in Langley and Levy 1977, p. 58).

Why does a man respond to the frustrations of daily life by beating his wife? Again we come to the question of "male macho." After all, *real* men do not cry. Nor do many of them know how to argue and discuss. They tend to respond immediately by hitting something—and the wife is usually the target. Not only is this violent response condoned; it is learned. For according to Judge Oneglia, husbands who beat their wives often come from violent homes themselves:

> I think violence is learned and that it's based on a man maintaining a superior position in the family. The wife is usually economically dependent. He knows he can hit her and get away with it. In general, these are men who are respectable in every other way. But they tend to come from homes where their mothers were beaten, where the father was absolute ruler and the mother submissive. (Quoted in Langley and Levy 1977, p. 105)

Why Does a Woman Take It?

Social custom, childhood upbringing, and threatened masculinity may explain why so many men beat their wives. But then the question is, Why do these wives stand for it? Of course the man is usually larger and more powerful. Even though the wife cannot do much to fend off a violent attack, however, she can leave afterward. Yet most women stay to endure repeated beatings, often over many years or an entire lifetime. Some people maintain that women stay because they really want to be beaten—the old masochist argument again. We often hear that an abused wife who stays is as "sick" as the husband who beats her. In her popular advice column Ann Landers states this emphatically:

> Dear Ann: My husband bruises me during quarrels. Yes, I mean physically. Divorce or separation? No, most of the time he is good to me. Joint counseling? Several years didn't stop the hitting. Karate? It's an invitation to escalation. Besides, he's stronger than I am. Police? NG in a small city where people talk.
>
> Meanwhile, is there some quiet legal device to restrain or penalize him short of being so badly beaten up that I have to go to the hospital?
>
>   Black and Blue
>
> Dear Black and Blue: If you've had several years of counseling and your husband is still beating you and you're still living with him, he is kinky beyond hope and you, my dear, have a deep-seated need for punishment. Obviously you two feed on each other's neurosis.
>
> According to the experts, a man who gets his jollies beating up women can always find someone who will tolerate it and they are both sick. (Quoted in Langley and Levy 1977, pp. 136–37)

I wonder which "experts" Landers consulted. Freud perhaps? For the research on battered women clearly indicates that they do not have a "deep-seated need for punishment." On the contrary, many "are literally trained by their parents to become battered wives" (Langley and Levy 1977, p. 126). They grow up in families where the father beats not only the wife but the children as well. If a daughter asks her mother why she puts up with the father's violence the mother is likely to answer: "Claudia, that's just the way men are. You just have to take it" (Dreifus 1973, p. 72). The message is clear: men are naturally aggressive. The beatings are natural, indeed inevitable, and there is no way out.

Not that all women think that men should beat their wives. A woman often feels that the beatings show that her marriage is a failure—but if it is a failure, then she is a failure as a woman. This reasoning makes many women feel deeply ashamed and guilty about being abused. As one woman put it:

> When I came to, I wanted to die, the guilt and depression were so bad. Your whole sense of worth is tied up with being a successful wife and having a happy marriage.
>
> If your husband beats you, then your marriage is a failure, and you're a failure. It's so horribly the opposite of how it's supposed to be. (Quoted in Langley and Levy 1977, p. 130)

The importance of being a female nurturer also leads to the "oh but he needs me" syndrome (Martin 1976, p. 83). Having promised to stick by her husband in sickness and health, the abused wife concludes that the more violent he is, the more he needs her. She tries to reason with him, he beats her to a pulp, she tries again, he beats her again. With each beating she perceives him as sicker—and as needing her all the more. "This rationalization forms its own tight little circle of logic: The more he beats me the sicker he is; the sicker he is the more he needs me. In some cases, alas, the circle is closed with 'the more he needs me the more I love him'—a peculiar but very common permutation of marital affection" (Martin 1976, p. 83).

On top of the guilt there is fear. Fear that if she defends herself or seeks help, the violence will only get worse. Fear that her husband will begin to beat the children as well. Fear that she will not be able to make it on her own—who is she, this debased, worthless woman whose "failure" is marked by the bruises and scars all over her body? This fear immobilizes the woman, creating more passivity and depression (Martin 1976). She becomes "afraid to go and afraid to stay" (Langley and Levy 1977, p. 135).

If a battered wife does leave, the fear follows her. Her husband is often consumed by an infantile jealousy that makes him pursue his wife and then beat her for leaving (Langley and Levy 1977). He cannot tolerate the blow to his macho pride, for when his wife leaves "he loses 'his' woman, the scapegoat that is living proof of his superiority" (Martin 1976, p. 79). Paradoxically, this very fear of pursuit often makes a woman return to her abusing husband. It is somehow better to know what to expect, to know that he is there and will continue to beat her at his usual times, rather than be haunted by the specter of an enraged hunter who may strike at any moment. Erin Pizzey explains how this fear of pursuit "blots out all reason":

> Lucy did go to social workers for help and they put her into temporary welfare accommodations, but when the social workers went home there was no one to protect her. Her husband often got into the huge unlit block of flats, broke into her room and threatened her. She explained that it was better to be at home where she knew where he was than sitting night after night not knowing if the footstep passing her door was him, if the car idling on the street was him waiting to catch her.
>
> Very few people understand this kind of fear. It is the fear of knowing that someone is searching for you and will beat you when he

finds you. In the mind of someone who has been badly beaten, this fear blots out all reason. The man seems to be omnipotent. I know the fear of streets that could possibly contain my enemy. Even now a particular cough or gesture can freeze me. (Pizzey 1974, p. 39)

If she can overcome the guilt and the fear, the woman still faces an even greater problem: she has nowhere to go. The typical battered wife has no money, no job, and no way to take the first step toward getting them. She may reach out for help again and again, only to find that people blame her for being attacked and urge her to patch things up with her husband. Some women make a private resolve to get an education so they can leave and support themselves and their children—as did the battered wife whose letter follows. Millions of others see no way out, however, even with hard work and careful planning; they feel they have no choice but to endure—and endure, and endure.

> I am in my thirties and so is my husband. I have a high school diploma and am presently attending a local college, trying to obtain the additional education I need. My husband is a college graduate and a professional in his field. We are both attractive and, for the most part, respected and well-liked. We have four children and live in a middle-class home with all the comforts we could possible want.
>
> I have everything, except life without fear.
>
> For most of my married life I have been periodically beaten by my husband. What do I mean by "beaten"? I mean that parts of my body have been hit violently and repeatedly, and that painful bruises, swelling, bleeding wounds, unconsciousness, and combinations of these things have resulted. . . .
>
> I have had glasses thrown at me. I have been kicked in the abdomen when I was visibly pregnant. I have been kicked off the bed and hit while lying on the floor—again, while I was pregnant. I have been whipped, kicked and thrown, picked up again and thrown down again. I have been punched and kicked in the head, chest, face, and abdomen more times than I can count.
>
> I have been slapped for saying something about politics, for having a different view about religion, for swearing, for crying, for wanting to have intercourse.
>
> I have been threatened when I wouldn't do something he told me to do. I have been threatened when he's had a bad day and when he's had a good day. . . .
>
> Hysteria inevitably sets in after a beating. This hysteria—the shaking and crying and mumbling—is not accepted by anyone, so there has never been anyone to call. . . .
>
> Now, the first response to this story, which I myself think of, will be "Why didn't you seek help?"
>
> I did. Early in our marriage I went to a clergyman who, after a few visits, told me that my husband meant no real harm, that he was just confused and felt insecure. I was encouraged to be more tolerant and understanding. Most important, I was told to forgive him the beatings just as Christ had forgiven me from the cross. I did that, too.

Things continued. Next time I turned to a doctor. I was given little pills to relax me and told to take things a little easier. I was just too nervous.

I turned to a friend, and when her husband found out, he accused me of either making things up or exaggerating the situation. She was told to stay away from me. She didn't, but she could no longer really help me. Just by believing me she was made to feel disloyal.

I turned to a professional family guidance agency. . . . I found I had to defend myself against the suspicion that I wanted to be hit, that I invited the beatings. . . .

I called the police one time. They not only did not respond to the call, they called several hours later to ask if things had "settled down." I could have been dead by then!

I have nowhere to go if it happens again. No one wants to take in a woman with four children. Even if there were someone kind enough to care, no one wants to become involved in what is commonly referred to as a "domestic situation." . . .

I know that I do not want to be hit. I know, too, that I will be beaten again unless I can find a way out for myself and my children. I am terrified for them also. . . .

My situation is so untenable I would guess that anyone who has not experienced one like it would find it incomprehensible. I find it difficult to believe myself.

It must be pointed out that while a husband can beat, slap, or threaten his wife, there are "good days." These days tend to wear away the effects of the beating. They tend to cause the wife to put aside the traumas and look to the good—first, because there is nothing else to do; second, because there is nowhere and no one to turn to; and third, because the defeat is the beating and the hope is that it will not happen again. A loving woman like myself always hopes that it will not happen again. When it does, she simply hopes again, until it becomes obvious after a third beating that there is no hope. . . .

For many the third beating may be too late. Several of the times I have been abused I have been amazed that I have remained alive. . . . What saved me?

I don't know. I only know that it has happened and that each night I dread the final blow that will kill me and leave my children motherless. I hope I can hang on until I complete my education, get a good job, and become self-sufficient enough to care for my children on my own. (Quoted in Martin 1976, pp. 1–5)

Legal Protection?

In spite of the popular attitudes condoning wife abuse, it is now illegal. But implementing the appropriate laws is difficult. When a battered wife does decide to take steps to protect herself, she is likely to encounter a morass of official indifference, apathy, and red tape. As Erin Pizzey says:

> It would probably take a Charles Dickens to do full justice to the labyrinth of indifference, red tape, callousness, and simple incompetence that exists between people in need and so many of the agencies that are meant to help them. . . .
>
> . . . when a woman tries to gather herself and her children away from the muggings of a brutal husband [she is likely to find] only a babble of conflicting advice and not one jot of practical help. (1974, p. 91)

Pizzey is talking about the situation in England, but things are much the same in the United States.

LAWS FOR WIFE BEATERS

The legal system in the United States was developed from the eighteenth-century British common law, which gave a husband the right to "chastise" or "correct" his wife because he was answerable for her behavior. Marriage made the husband and wife into one person— and that person was the husband (Prosser 1971). Langley and Levy explain how the legal fusion of husband and wife made the wife into a nonperson who had no rights and could not charge her husband with beating her:

> One of the most bizarre Catch 22 conditions imposed on women by men was the legal concept that when two people married, they became one in the eyes of the law. This prevented a woman from suing her husband—regardless of what he did to her property or her person— because under the law a man and wife were one, and it is impossible to sue yourself.
>
> "By marriage the husband and wife are one person in law, that is, the very being or legal existence of the woman is suspended during marriage or at least is incorporated and consolidated into that of the husband," wrote Blackstone in 1768.
>
> And by extending this concept, it was easy to conclude that a husband couldn't be charged with beating his wife because he and his wife were one. How can you arrest someone for beating himself? And a nonperson whose "very being" was "legally suspended" certainly could have no business before the courts. How can someone who isn't there be beaten? (1977, pp. 50–1)

In the nineteenth century things began to improve for women in the United States. After the Civil War the Married Women's Property Acts were passed, giving women the right to seek employment, to keep their earnings, to set up a separate residence if they wished, and to own property separately from their husbands. The trend toward legal rights for women continued into the 1880s, when it was established that a husband no longer had the right to beat his wife.

Now a new barrier to wife-beating charges was introduced. Although the twentieth-century courts maintained that a husband had no right to beat his wife, they also maintained that she could not sue him for doing so. According to these jurists, such a suit would interfere with the "peace and harmony of the home" (Prosser 1971, p. 863). This argument created "the paradox that the courts would allow violence in order to keep the peace" (Langley and Levy 1977, p. 55). Apparently the courts could not bring themselves to acknowledge that in these violent homes there was no peace to preserve.

By the 1960s, however, some courts were beginning to recognize that this argument made little sense. Thus in 1962 a California court observed, "The contention that immunity is necessary to maintain conjugal harmony is unsound because after a husband has beaten his wife, there is little peace and harmony left to be disturbed" (*Self v. Self*, quoted in Langley and Levy 1977, p. 55).

Current laws clearly state that it is illegal for a husband to beat his wife. Some of them even state that it is a felony to injure one's wife or children (Martin 1976). But the old attitudes about the sanctity of the family linger on, as the battered wife soon discovers in dealing with police departments and the judicial system.*

THE POLICE: KEEPING THEIR DISTANCE

A battered wife usually rationalizes the first beating: "He was just overtired, upset, desperate. It won't happen again." But it does—and again, and again. Each time the beating gets worse. The woman wants to call for help but is ashamed and afraid of exacerbating the situation. Finally she works up her courage and calls the police. But instead of the compassion and protection she expects, she often gets indifference and cynicism, even hostility, for the police are extremely reluctant to get involved in "family problems." Erin Pizzey points out that the woman would be much better off if she had been viciously attacked on the street. Then everyone would be sympathetic, and the attacker would receive a

---

* Under the common-law doctrine that husband and wife are one, women did receive some protection against wife beating under the criminal statutes "since the criminal law, at least, regarded the husband and wife as separate individuals" (Prosser 1971, p. 859). But criminal charges are extremely difficult to substantiate and prosecute in a domestic situation. The recent rulings on spousal immunity from civil "tort actions" have only slightly improved the situation. By 1971 only sixteen states had recognized a woman's right to sue her husband for "intentional physical attacks"; the vast majority of American courts still maintain that to allow wife-beating suits would damage the "peace and harmony of the home"—even if the marriage has already been terminated by separation, divorce, or annulment (Prosser 1971, p. 863).

severe prison sentence. But the same act committed behind closed doors is minimized or ignored (Pizzey 1974).

What makes the police respond this way? Many share the attitude of the general public toward wife abuse: it is not all that bad and may actually be necessary from time to time to "keep her in line" (Martin 1976). The police do not take wife-beating investigations seriously, as indicated by the euphemisms they use for them: "domestic disturbance," "family squabble," "family trouble," "lovers' quarrel," and "family spat" (Langley and Levy 1977, p. 176).

Then there is the idea that a "man's home is his castle." If a man wants to beat his wife, it is his business and his right. The violent husband feels this strongly: he may even turn his attack on a policeman who tries to intervene to protect the wife. This makes it very risky for the policeman, and he knows it. FBI statistics show that more officers are killed in family disputes than in any other type of call (Langley and Levy 1977).

If he does intervene and is assaulted by the husband, the policeman has little recourse. The "castle" idea is codified in the right-to-privacy laws. Courts consistently rule in favor of the husband's rights in his own home, as they did in this case:

> An attorney related the following incident as an example of the legal community's interest in the area of family disputes. A policeman accompanied a woman back to her home to pick up her belongings. The husband told the policeman to leave and later assaulted him.
> The policeman brought assault charges against the man. When the case was brought to court, the judge dropped the charges because the man had told the policeman to leave and he stayed. (Eisenberg and Micklow 1974, quoted in Langley and Levy 1977, p. 171)

Of course this interpretation of the law focuses on the *man's* rights in *his* home. What about the *woman's* rights in *hers*? Langley and Levy point out that the right to privacy does conflict with the right to freedom from attack. "No one, however, has asked the battered wife which of her Constitutional rights—privacy or equal protection under the law—she wants enforced and which she wants suspended" (1977, p. 171).

Even if he wants to intervene, a policeman may not know how. Commander James Bannon of the Detroit Police Department feels that "the real reason that police avoid domestic-violence situations to the greatest possible extent is because we do not know how to cope with them" (Langley and Levy 1977, p. 179). Many police departments have instituted training programs to alleviate this difficulty. These programs are not aimed at assisting the wife in filing charges or obtaining legal assistance, however. On the contrary, they teach techniques designed to calm things down, to talk the wife out of pressing legal charges, to get the spouses to "kiss and make up," and to minimize the time spent on "family disturbance" calls.

All this means that when a woman calls the police during a beating, they do not show up for anywhere from twenty minutes to several hours. As the battered wife in the letter (page 356) points out, by then it is too late: the woman has already been severely beaten, if not killed. And when the police do arrive, they are likely to conduct the investigation in a manner that immediately puts her on the defensive. While establishing a bond of male camaraderie with the husband, they usually ask the wife questions like these.

> Who will support you if he's locked up?
> Do you realize he could lose his job?
> Do you want to spend days in court?
> Why don't you kiss and make up?
> Why did you make him slug you?
> Why do you want to make trouble? Think of what he'll do to you next time. (Langley and Levy 1977, p. 183)

As Commander Bannon has pointed out, the disinterested attitude of the police officers only serves to reinforce the wife beater's behavior (Martin 1976). He thinks to himself: "After all, if the police treat the beating so lightly, it can't really be that bad. Obviously they agree with me—a little wife beating every now and then is all right."

THE COURTS

A few battered wives persevere in their determination to press legal charges—only to find that lawyers, prosecutors, and judges share the same attitudes as the police, who feel that wife beating is part of life and press her to reconcile with her abusing husband. They cross-examine her to ensure that she will really follow through and testify against her husband. All along the way, they tell her what *they* think she should do.

> An attitude pervades the judicial system that the woman doesn't know what's best for her, that she is incompetent and must be treated in a condescending, "Papa knows best" manner. She is talked down to like a child. It's assumed best if she listens to older and wiser men who will set her straight and advise her in her own best interest. (Langley and Levy 1977, p. 183)

Some of these men are not merely condescending. Many are openly hostile, like the family court judge who refused a woman's warrant with the comment, "Any woman dumb enough to marry such a jerk deserves what she gets" (Langley and Levy 1977, p. 185). And these attitudes are not necessarily limited to males. The few female attorneys, prosecutors, and judges sometimes share them as well. Justice Yorka C. Linakis of the Queens (New York) Family Court, for instance, objects to the practice of issuing a court order to get the violent husband out of the house during the pretrial period, and bases this objection on the welfare of the children: "All the havoc that can be created by the absence of the father from the home can be tremendous, and Family Court Judges are most reluctant to order spouses from the house" (quoted in Martin 1976, p. 116). Martin responds by asking, "Is the presence of a violent father psychologically more healthy than no father at all?" She then notes that the judge's opinion is "based on shaky emotional grounds at best," as demonstrated by the judge's remarks to a 1975 conference on the abused wife: "There is nothing more pathetic than to see a husband going to his home—usually in the company of a policeman—to collect his meager belongings." Again Martin asks, "Is a woman who trembles in anticipation of her husband's next attack any less pathetic?" (1976, p. 116).

Even if she does succeed in obtaining a court order against her abusing husband, however, a woman is not necessarily safe. She may still have to "tremble in anticipation of her husband's next attack," since "enforcement is practically nonexistent" (Martin 1976, p. 104). Langley and Levy came to the same conclusion as Martin and noted that although legal notices are designed to scare the husband, they are usually "meaningless pieces of paper" (1977, p. 189). The wife beater simply ignores them. He is going to beat *his* woman, no matter what any judge says.

Battered Men

Men are not the only violent ones. Women also strike their husbands. Langley and Levy (1977) report an unpublished study by sociologist Suzanne Steinmetz that suggests that women may actually match men in the minor kinds of physical force. Using a random sample instead of reported cases of domestic violence, Steinmetz found that 39 percent of the husbands and 37 percent of the wives admitted throwing things at their spouses, while 20 percent of each group said they hit with their hands. Husbands outstripped wives (31 percent to 21 percent) in pushing, shoving, and grabbing. But there were no sex differences in striking the other spouse with a hard object: 10 percent of each sex admitted doing this.

Interviews done by Steinmetz and others also indicate that a woman sometimes strikes the first blow in a family fight. Langley and Levy attribute this to a vague notion of chivalry:

It appears that some women, still harboring some dim memory of idealized chivalry, feel that they can strike a male since "no gentleman would ever hit a lady." Correspondingly, many men interpret this code of conduct to mean "no gentleman should ever hit a lady *first*." Once a woman smacks such a man, he often concludes, "I can't let her get away with that." (1977, p. 200)

And he does not let her get away with it, for these fights often escalate into vicious brawls. Now the woman is at a dramatic disadvantage and can do little to protect herself from the brutality of her husband's attack. Steinmetz suggests that the husband's greater size and strength account for the battered-wife syndrome: it is not that men are more aggressive, it is simply that they are physically stronger and hence can inflict more damage. As evidence of this she cites the police figures on spousal homicide:

Data on homicide between spouses suggests that an almost equal number of wives kill their husbands as husbands kill wives. Thus, it appears that men and women might have equal potential toward violent marital interactions, initiate similar acts of violence, and in the extreme, when differences of physical strength are equalized by weapons, commit similar amounts of spousal homicide. (Steinmetz, quoted in Langley and Levy 1977, p. 207)

Other researchers, however, argue that women are not as aggressive as men but are simply desperate. Not being a match for their husbands in physical combat, they grab whatever weapon is handy. This is often a gun, and their defense becomes a fatal one. Sue Eisenberg and Patricia Micklow (1974) put it this way:

The lack of any meaningful protective measures available to the assaulted wife, as well as a minimizing of the seriousness of her situation, often produces drastic results—homicide. Faced with a violent husband and no alternatives, she may equalize the situation herself by using a deadly weapon such as a gun or knife. The wife killing her husband is not a rare crime. (Quoted in Langley and Levy 1977, p. 208)

Does this mean that women *only* strike their husbands in self-defense? No, for there *are* cases of husband abuse. These are rarely reported, however, for what man wants to admit that his wife is beating him up? She may be doing it for a variety of reasons. Some husbands claim that their wives want to be beaten as part of a dominant-submissive relationship. When her husband does not beat her, the wife takes to beating him instead. Or she may be deliberately trying to provoke him in order to gain an advantage in a divorce action. Langley and Levy (1977) report that some lawyers have even been known to advise their female clients to do this in order to establish the "cruel and unusual punishment" needed as grounds for divorce, or as a way to set the husband up for a financial settlement that will be more advantageous to the wife.

Regardless of a woman's reasons for attacking her spouse, however, the husband with a physically abusive wife is faced with a dilemma. Should he just sit and take it or strike back? If he hits her, will her manipulations be successful in getting whatever advantage she is angling for? Will his children view him as a brutish wife beater? Will he himself feel guilty and demeaned? If he "lets her get away with it," on the other hand, will he feel debased and worthless? Will his children see him as a passive milquetoast who allows his wife to push him around? Both alternatives are unpleasant and upsetting.

Escape from Battering

What can a woman do to avoid being beaten? Many researchers suggest that she should make it clear from the beginning that she will not tolerate physical abuse, for once it starts, it only escalates. Others suggest that she avoid trading verbal insults and blows with her husband, since arguments can lead to violent battles in which the wife inevitably suffers the worst injuries. And if her husband does beat her, she should wait to talk with him until he has calmed down, since he is likely to be "blind with rage" during the attack and oblivious to her attempts to communicate.

Once a pattern of marital violence has been established, it is up to the female victim to initiate any change. Most wife beaters view their behavior as justified and normal and resist any attempts at change or reform. Various strategies have been recommended for the battered wife. She can try to have a relative or a friend in the home when she expects an attack, since the husband's violence is usually inhibited when another person is present. This inhibition wears off quickly, but it can provide a brief, nonviolent interlude in which the wife can try to establish some communication. She can attend meetings of Alcoholics Anonymous or Alanon to learn better ways to cope with the drinking and drug abuse that often accompany her husband's violence. She can join a women's group to share her "secret" and obtain invaluable emotional support from others in the same predicament. If her husband is willing, she can try marital counseling. She should avoid isolating herself and use what little police and legal protection is available. And as a last resort there is always separation and divorce.

The underlying problem with all these remedies is that the abused wife is often trapped in her violent home. Even if she should decide that she has had enough, that she has to get out to save herself and her children, she has *nowhere to go*. This problem is gradually being alleviated, however. A number of shelters for abused wives and their children now exist where "battered women find solace and support. These houses are havens where she can recuperate from her wounds, recover her sense of self, and re-evaluate her situation" (Martin 1976, p. 197).

One or two of these refuges were started in the late 1960s. With the resurgence of the Women's Movement in the 1970s, women began to use the new women's centers and other gathering places as emergency facilities. These temporary shelters were only stopgap measures, however, since they were not designed specifically for battered women and their children. When Erin Pizzey started Chiswick Women's Aid in 1971, many women were intensely interested; Pizzey's account of this refuge received much attention, especially in feminist circles (Pizzey 1974). Del Martin (1976) points out that there are now similar shelters all over Europe and in Australia, Canada, and the United States.

Such shelters are a recent phenomenon and are still poorly funded and located primarily in large cities. More of them are desperately needed so that *all* battered women will have some place and someone to turn to. In order to use the shelters, of course, women also have to know about them and view them as a positive alternative. Abused wives need to know that they are not alone, that their beatings are not due to a secret desire to suffer, and that wife beating is not a man's prerogative and a woman's fate.

To make a serious change in the lives of battered women, then, broad social action is required. The first step is for society to acknowledge that there *is* such a thing as the battered-wife syndrome, and that it is appallingly common. Social scientists need to turn their attention to this problem and change their unrealistic assumptions about the prevalence of male violence and aggression. Too many of them share the wishful thinking of Eleanor Maccoby and Carol Jacklin who, in their book, *The Psychology of Sex Differences*, provided a thoughtful review of almost every other area but skirted the issue of battered wives. After quoting a report of wife beating from a 1973 issue of the *Manchester Guardian*, they commented:

> Although incidents of this kind exist as an ugly aspect of marital relations in an unknown number of cases—an aspect that tends to be unseen or deliberately ignored and denied, by outsiders—there can be little doubt that direct force is rare in most modern marriages. Male behavior such as that described above would be considered pathological in any human (or animal!) society and, if widespread, would endanger a species. (1974, p. 264)

Of course we would all like to believe that "direct force is rare." But as with rape, the experiences of millions of women tell us otherwise.

What research has already been done suggests that eliminating wife beating will not be easy. A whole cycle of violence is often perpetuated within a family. Most wife beaters and battered wives grew up in violent homes themselves. We do not have to infer the cycle of violence in retrospect, however, for Erin Pizzey has observed it directly in the children of the battered women who seek refuge at the Chiswick Home:

> We find that the girls of the families who come to the house tend to be passive and withdrawn, in contrast to the boys who are aggressive and destructive. However, it does not mean that the girls are any less damaged. . . .
> You've only to watch the boys in the house to see that they are the next generation's potential batterers. Many of them are extremely violent by the age of three. By eleven they are potential criminals. Where ordinary children would have a tussle or just shout in annoyance, they fight to kill. . . .
> Violence goes on from generation to generation. (1974, pp. 67, 74)

It is not merely the observation of violence that engenders violence in the child. Physical methods of discipline also communicate the message that violence is acceptable. Langley and Levy feel that these child-rearing techniques reflect a broader attitude toward violence as a perfectly acceptable way to solve any problem: "The root of the problem is our acceptance of violence as a legitimate means of solving problems. It's been said that every time we spank a child, we teach the lesson that violence is acceptable. It is almost universally accepted in America that, under certain circumstances, it's proper to spank a child" (1977, pp. 236–37).

While some researchers suggest that men beat their wives to assert their dominance and control over the family, they do not necessarily think that eliminating male dominance would also eliminate wife beating. Even egalitarian relationships contain some conflict, so that as long as violence is used as a method of conflict resolution, men will continue to abuse their wives. Straus, Gelles, and Steinmetz expressed this point of view in a paper presented before the American Association for the Advancement of Science in 1976:

> A great deal of the physical violence between husband and wife is related to conflict over power in the family and specifically to attempts by men to maintain their superior power position. One might therefore expect that as families become more egalitarian, violence between husband and wife will decrease. However, this will be the case only to the extent that men voluntarily give up their privileges. To the extent that sexual equality comes about by women demanding equal rights, the movement toward equality could well see a temporary increase in violence rather than a decrease. Aside from struggles over changing rules of the marriage game, there is nothing inherent in an equal relationship which precludes

conflict and violence over substantive issues. In fact, in the past, to the extent that women accepted a subordinate position, much overt conflict may have been avoided by not contesting the husband's view of an issue. (Straus et al. 1976, quoted in Langley and Levy 1977, pp. 237–38)

A few people maintain that a woman should accept her lot, since asserting her own independence would threaten the male's "compulsive masculinity," and that threatened males respond with violent aggression—it is part of their nature. But *are* aggression and violence inevitable, even in men? Feminists do not think so. They attribute male violence to the cultural stereotype of male macho and consider it no more inevitable than female passivity and dependence. Both male aggression and female passivity result from socialization, as Del Martin points out:

> I contend that an "adequate male role model" may actually incorporate a good dose of "compulsive masculinity." In fact, it may be safe to say that the standard male role model endorsed by our society is *synonymous* with compulsive-masculinity, and that only boys who *escape* that model will emerge as fair-minded human beings able to view women as equals and wives as partners. Those who are successfully socialized in schools, families, churches, and other institutions according to prevailing standards of masculinity may very well grow up to be dominating bullies. . . .
>
> It is inevitable that some of the boys trained by society to be "masculine" aggressors will grow up to be women-beaters. By the same processes those girls who are taught to be passive, submissive, docile, and dependent, are being set up as "feminine" victims. (1976, pp. 63, 67)

Martin goes on to say that the fact that violence is evident early in life does not mean it is inherent in human nature. In fact, the idea that violence is inevitable may simply reflect the male bias of social scientists themselves. As Martin puts it:

> The violent behavior of men toward women may be an understandable result of the socialization process, but I contend—against growing opposition—that violence is in no way inevitable. Because of the ever-increasing violence in our society, male theorists and doomsayers are trying to convince us that aggression is inherent in human nature, rather than the result of conditioning and reinforcement by a male-dominat society. (1976, p. 67)

I agree. Wife abuse is not an isolated phenomenon. It occurs in a cultural context that condones and even encourages the use of physical violence to keep women in their place. The idea that a woman *should* be beaten reflects the idea of woman as property. A man's home is still viewed as his castle, and if he chooses to beat *his* woman there, it is considered his business. Wife beating is nothing new, the wife beater says, so what's all the fuss about? No one takes it seriously, he points out; they even joke about it.

But people are beginning to take it seriously. And, as more and more battered women talk about their "secret," the concern can only deepen. Wife beating is so common that it can no longer be laughed off or dismissed as the work of a deranged few. It is a serious social problem that demands immediate attention.

Chapter 17

Women and Sports

SPORTS have long been a national enthusiasm in the United States. Over the past ten years, however, there has been a dramatic change in the sports scene. Now people do not just watch, they participate. And the new enthusiasts are not just men; they are women, too. Millions of women are now involved in competitive athletics, and female athletes even appear on television.

This new female participation is controversial. Some people hail it as an important victory for women's rights. At last, they say, women have the opportunity to develop their physical potential, to experience the strength and beauty of their own bodies, to feel the exhilaration of competition and victory. Sports are a crucial learning experience, a way to develop self-confidence and a feeling of mastery over the environment. And sports are fun. Many women envy the young female athlete whose physical exploits express the daring, the mastery, and the assertiveness they wish they had. They imagine the female athlete as carefree and self-assured, the youthful beneficiary of changing attitudes toward women.

There is a less idyllic view of the female sports experience, however, which pictures the female athlete as fraught with conflict and anxiety. Competitive athletics are still a male preserve, after all, and the popular image of the athlete is that of a youthful male (Spears 1978). As Marie Hart (1971) points out, any woman who participates in sports places herself outside the social mainstream. By entering such an eminently male activity she risks her own femininity. Dorothy Harris compares the situation of the female athlete with that of other female pioneers who have dared to violate the unspoken rules regarding proper female conduct:

> When a female chooses to participate in vigorous competitive activity she may be risking a great deal. She is laying on the line everything she may represent as a female in much the same way as the girl who first smoked in public risked her image, or the female who first appeared in public wearing pants. The female who has the courage of her convictions and the security of her feminine concept is still taking a risk when she wins a tennis match from her male opponent or outperforms any male whether it be in sports, business, or a profession dominated by the male. Competitive sports are still primarily the prerogative of the male in this society. (1973, p. 193)

The basic idea is that serious athletic competition is stressful for a woman because it creates a role conflict. How can a woman be both feminine and a "jock"? Will extensive participation in sports masculinize a woman, both physically and mentally? And even if she is not masculinized, will others perceive the female athlete as such and thus cause her to feel defensive and unhappy?

To answer these questions, we need to look at the personal experiences of women in sports today. How are female athletes viewed by others—and by themselves? Do competitive sports create emotional conflict and distress? Or do they create a positive experience which enhances feelings of confidence and self-worth?

The Amazon Myth

Some writers have suggested that a woman who competes seriously in sports is often preoccupied with the idea that her athletic activities will masculinize her body: she worries about becoming "muscular," "large," "thick," or "mannish" (Mathes 1978, p. 69). Some female athletes may even go to great lengths to counteract the "Amazon" stereotype. Knowing that others may perceive them as masculine, they try to counteract this perception in various ways—by wearing hair ribbons, pastel-colored outfits, or having a "feminine" hair style (Harris 1974; Hart 1972).

Apparently there is no objective basis for these fears of masculinization. Female athletes do not seem to have markedly different physiques from those of nonathletes. Sociologists Eldon Snyder and Joseph Kivlin demonstrated this by comparing 275 undergraduate nonathletes with 328 women who participated in the 1972 Women's Intercollegiate Championships in a variety of sports or else in the 1972 Olympic tryouts in gymnastics (Snyder and Kivlin 1975). Although the athletes were slightly larger, the differences were hardly dramatic—one inch in height (5 feet 6 inches versus 5 feet 5 inches) and three pounds in weight (129 pounds versus 126 pounds).

Nor is there any truth to what Marie Hart calls "the muscle myth" (1972, p. 296). When women engage in organized swimming or even in weight-lifting programs, the major changes in body composition involve decreases in subcutaneous fat (Mayhew and Cross 1974; Wade, 1976). And exercise physiologists point out that athletic competition does not cause excessive muscle development (Hart 1972).

Perhaps the fear of masculinization reflects a subjective experience of one's body: that is, even though athletes do not look any different, maybe they are more critical of their bodies than nonathletes because of subtle physical differences. Here again, however, research does not support anecdotal observations. For sociologists Snyder and Kivlin also asked these college women to indicate whether they felt positive, neutral, or negative about their energy levels, appetites, health, and eighteen different body parts or aspects of physical appearance; these athletes rated their bodies much more positively than did the nonathletes, especially in terms of energy level and health. When Snyder repeated this measure with 556 high school students, he again found that athletes had much more positive body images than had nonathletes (Snyder and Spreitzer 1976). And perhaps most dramatic of all, the high school athletes actually rated themselves as equally or even more feminine than the nonathletic high school students.

It is possible that these findings mean that an athlete's body-image concerns are mainly a matter of worrying about how *others* will perceive her, although there has been no carefully designed research that shows that even this worry is pervasive. Nor is it clear that feelings about the body are the same in all contexts. Sharon Mathes, who teaches physical education at Iowa State University, suggests that the positive feelings of female athletes may apply only to sports. Asked about their bodies in a social setting, these women might respond differently (Mathes 1978).

It does not seem likely that an athlete's positive body image is sports-specific, for Snyder's data were collected from mailed questionnaires, not administered in locker rooms or social settings. And female athletes have commented that they are made to feel especially unfeminine in the male-dominated sports world: whenever they do something well, they are likely to be praised not for their ability per se, but for their ability to perform "like a man" (Hart 1974). Thus, a female athlete may be subjected to even more negative pressures about her body image in athletic contexts than in social settings. At the present time, however, there is no indication that these negative pressures are reflected in a negative female body image.

The Ladylike Sports

A number of writers have suggested that an athlete's concern about her femininity may vary according to the sport, for the general public views some sports as more acceptable than others because they are more compatible with the popular image of femininity.

Eleanor Metheny (1965) first presented this idea systematically by analyzing the underlying characteristics of sports that were either forbidden to women in the Olympics or else disapproved by the general population. The predominant theme was that women should not use physical force, especially to overpower or subdue an opponent; they should avoid shows of strength; and they should have no direct bodily contact during competition. Thus, acceptable sports for women are those that rely on skill rather than on strength or force, that employ a spatial barrier between opponents, that use light implements to manipulate light objects, and that display the body in graceful, flowing movements which are attractive to men.

According to Metheny's analysis, a woman who wants to maintain a feminine image should stick to tennis, racquet ball, gymnastics, and diving, and avoid sports involving face-to-face competition, body contact, handling a heavy object, and propelling one's body through space over long distances. In other words, she must stay away from basketball, softball, volleyball, long distance running, and certainly lacrosse and soccer. This advice corresponds to popular stereotypes about women's sports. Eldon Snyder and his colleagues asked a cross section of over 500 adults from the general population whether participation in a number of sports would enhance a woman's femininity. The percentages answering yes were 67 percent for swimming, 57 percent for tennis, and 54 percent for gymnastics. Less than one-fifth indicated that softball, basketball, and track would have this positive effect. When the same people were asked whether these sports would actually detract from feminine qualities, the percentages were reversed: 30 percent for track, 21 percent for basketball, 20 percent for softball, and less than one-tenth for gymnastics, tennis, and swimming (Snyder, Kivlin, and Spreitzer 1975)

Female athletes are well aware of these popular attitudes. The same sociologists asked their sample of 328 college athletes "Do you feel there is a stigma attached to women who participate in the sport you specialize in?" The responses varied by sport and in a pattern corresponding to the popular stereotypes: 54 percent of the basketball players and 47 percent of the track and field participants said yes, while only 38 percent of the swimmers and divers and 27 percent of the gymnasts did so. All of these rates were lower than those found in the control group of 275 college women, however, of which 65 percent indicated that there was a general stigma attached to women's participation in sports (Snyder and Kivlin 1975).

Studies such as these substantiate the general picture of the female athlete as beleaguered by negative social sanctions, as a social reject who suffers from severe anxiety and conflict about her femininity and social acceptability. This picture may be exaggerated, however, for this general social prejudice is not necessarily translated into personal reactions to individual athletes.

This hopeful possibility is suggested by a recent study done by a physical education professor, a psychologist, and a doctoral student in higher education (Kingsley, Brown, and Seibert 1977), who asked 240 female undergraduates at Arizona State University to rate the social acceptability of a softball player or a dancer described in a brief vignette. Half of the women were athletes and comprised virtually all of the varsity and junior varsity players on the female college teams. The other half of the women were nonathletes who had never been on such a team and were selected at random from the university's enrollment lists. Each group of 120 was randomly divided into four groups who read a vignette describing a low-aspiration softball player, a high-aspiration softball player, a low-aspiration dancer, or a high-aspiration dancer. Both the vignettes and the rating scale were pretested. The results should surprise many who believe in the beleaguered-athlete image: there was no evidence of social stigma in the responses. The level of competitive ambition made no difference, the athlete-nonathlete character of the rater made no difference, and the nature of the activity depicted in the vignette made no difference. Apparently these college women found nothing wrong with being a softball player, even though it is a relatively "tough" sport. Nor did they perceive serious competition as unacceptable. For them, it seemed acceptable to be a female athlete.

This study is one of the most sophisticated in the sports psychology literature; few others use a relatively large sample, a random design, and carefully pretested measures. Although the study needs to be replicated, it certainly suggests that responses to individual athletes may not be as negative and anxiety-provoking as the popular stereotypes suggest. Times are changing. While the old stereotypes may linger on, they do not determine all social interactions.

An Athletic Personality?

A number of writers have suggested that the conflict between femininity and athletics is expressed in emotional as well as in physical terms. Sports have always been viewed as a way to "build men" by developing independence, assertiveness, a strong motive to achieve, and a sense of control over oneself and the environment. Seldom have sports been viewed as a way to build women as well. After all, *real* women are not supposed to be independent, assertive, competitive, or oriented to mastering their physical environment.

If the athletic personality is seen as a male personality, then the woman athlete must fear that her participation in sports implies that her personality is also rather male or unfeminine. Felshin (1974) has suggested that this female discomfort leads to an "apologetic" in which the woman athlete tries to emphasize her femininity so that she can afford to participate actively in sports. She may dress in particularly feminine ways, specialize in the more socially acceptable sports, act as if she does not take sports seriously, or even espouse more traditional attitudes toward a woman's role. All these strategies communicate the same message: See, I may be an athlete, but I'm still very feminine.

To test Felshin's suggestion, Patricia Del Rey gave the Attitudes toward Women Scale to 102 female varsity team members at three branches of the City University of New York (Del Rey 1977). She expected to find that women participating in traditionally masculine sports would espouse more traditional attitudes toward women than would those participating in traditionally feminine sports; for these masculine sports would create conflict in the female players and thus call for greater compensation or "apology." Her results provided partial support for the hypothesis: at two of the schools, women playing tennis (a ladylike sport) expressed more liberal attitudes than did women swimming or playing the less ladylike sports of basketball and softball.

Snyder and Kivlin's study of 603 college women also points to the existence of an "apologetic" in female athletes. These researchers asked eight questions about the female role and found that the athletes were more conservative than the nonathletes in their attitudes about the importance of family life, women working outside the home, women holding positions of authority over men, and women competing for the same jobs as men (Snyder and Kivlin 1977).

The difficulty with both of these studies is that we do not know how the various groups of women differed before some of them entered competitive sports. Some women may feel free to participate precisely because they think they are sufficiently feminine in their other interests and attitudes. They may choose a particular sport because of the sex-role attitudes they already have, or change those attitudes after sports involvement in order to reassert their femininity. Further research is obviously needed to substantiate the existence and the mechanisms of a female "apologetic."

Other writers have approached the issue of sex roles and sports by arguing that the "athletic personality" should be viewed not as a "male personality" but rather as an "androgynous personality" combining the positive attributes of both masculinity and femininity. For instance, Mary Duquin of the University of Pittsburgh challenges the Western cultural view of sport as an agent for developing male instrumentality. She calls for the "neutralization of instrumentality as a male preserve," so that it would be considered appropriate for females as well. At the same time she calls for more attention to the "expressive" (that is, emotional and feminine) aspects of athletics. As she puts it:

> Western culture perceives sports as primarily instrumental. The question to ask is whether only instrumental qualities are inherent in sports or whether Western societies have merely inhibited or ignored what might be termed the more expressive aspects of the sport experience. According to an androgynous perspective, sport can involve the following expressive experiences:
> 1. Moving with child-like joy and cheerfulness
> 2. Experiencing passive, defensive, yielding movements
> 3. Moving and responding to others by understanding what they are communicating non-verbally
> 4. Moving delicately, tenderly, gently
> 5. Becoming aware and sensitive of others, their presence, their movements, their emotions
> 6. Creating beauty with movement, sensing the aesthetic nature of human movement
> 7. Sensing the introspective quality of becoming absorbed in one's bodily movements and feeling at one with one's body.
> (Duquin 1978, pp. 100–101)

Carole Oglesby also argues for an androgynous view of sport, but from a slightly different perspective. She maintains that athletics already do encourage the development of both instrumental and expressive behaviors—a reality that viewing sports as a male domain has simply obscured. Using a less poetic approach to expressiveness than Duquin's, Oglesby says:

> We call off the masculinity-femininity game in sport by recognizing and publicizing that sport is *not* masculinity training, nor femininity training but androgyny training. All the qualities of fully functioning human beings are potentially communicable/reinforceable in sport. . . .
> For example, we have long proposed that sport participation can assist the development of independence and dominance (two qualities of the so-called masculine principle). I believe it is equally possible to demonstrate that sport can and does assist the development of such qualities as dependence and subordination. In softball or baseball, when the squeeze play is on, the runner at third base breaks running with the pitch trusting/depending that the batter will do what she/he must to make the play successful. In the many sacrifice situations (and scores of other instances) a player learns the benefits of subordination of personal glory to team victory. (1978, pp. 82, 84)

Although no empirical studies establish that sports encourage androgynous as opposed to purely masculine behavior, there is some indication that women with androgynous personalities are more likely to participate in competitive sports. In one study two Canadian psychologists gave the Bem Sex Role Inventory (BSRI) to twenty-three female and twenty-five male competitors in the Canadian National Racquetball Championships (Myers and Lips 1978). Since competitive sports are viewed as a masculine activity, Myers and Lips thought that a woman would have to have a flexible view of herself in order to enter one, whereas this would not be necessary for a man. Therefore, they expected that the men would describe themselves as higher on masculine than feminine characteristics (masculine sex-typed), while the women would describe themselves as having masculine and feminine characteristics to an equal extent (androgynous sex-typed).

In this competitive setting this expectation was indeed borne out: 60 percent of the males were masculine or near-masculine, while 24 percent were androgynous; whereas 39 percent of the women were feminine or near-feminine, while 44 percent of the women were androgynous. This female distribution is significantly more androgynous than that found in Bem's (1975) normative samples. Furthermore, fewer husbands of the androgynous women played in the tournament, which the researchers interpret as indicating that these women felt freer to enter this male domain without spousal support.

In a second study Myers and Lips gave the BSRI to twenty-seven female and twenty-four male competitors in local badminton, squash, and handball tournaments. In this less competitive setting they divided the participants into competitive and noncompetitive groups on the basis of their reasons for entering the tournament: to win or simply to have fun. All of the males fell into the competitive group. Among women, those in the competitive group tended to be androgynous, while those in the noncompetitive group tended to be feminine. The researchers conclude that "these results suggest that defining the situation in a noncompetitive way makes it less masculine and therefore allows participation by traditionally sex-typed women" (1978, pp. 575–76).

Since the competitive nature of the local tournaments was defined by the participants' own reasons for entering them in the second study by Myers and Lips, the results suggest that women who describe themselves as traditionally feminine may participate in sports for noncompetitive reasons and/or tend to perceive sports less competitively. In addition, as the researchers suggest, a woman may select a particular sport and setting according to how competitive it is.* Whether participa-

---

* Socioeconomic factors also influence which sport a person chooses to participate in. Individual and dual sport athletes tend to come from more affluent backgrounds than do team sport athletes (Greendorfer 1978).

tion itself then encourages androgyny in both sexes remains to be seen (although it apparently had not done so in the male samples studied by these researchers).

The idea of a female apologetic does not imply that sports actually foster masculine personality characteristics in women. Women try to re-assert their femininity simply because they fear that they will be mascu-linized, or that others will think they have been. The idea that participa-tion in a sport enhances androgyny, on the other hand, does imply that competitive athletics actually affect the personalities of the participants. The desirability of the masculinization is simply asserted; the mascu-linization itself is not challenged.

Other researchers have also assumed that sports actually change the personalities of female athletes, although some view this change as dubious, regrettable, or even deplorable. The studies in this area have been full of methodological flaws and have yielded contradictory results, as Christopher Stevenson concluded in 1975. There just does not seem to be an easily identified "athletic personality."

The Athletic Superelite

There are contradictions and tensions in female athletics. At the same time as more women have started to enjoy sports, organized athletics have become increasingly oriented toward the small group of women who are extremely talented and compete seriously—in other words, toward women who are superathletes.

The controversy surrounding this trend is most marked in college athletics. The 1975 Federal Guidelines for Title IX of the Educational Amendments of 1972 now require colleges to provide women with equal athletic opportunities. While this requirement has increased the funding of female sports programs, it has also changed their character. The introduction of women's athletic scholarships over the past five years has been a tremendous boon, for "an athletic scholarship is a job that pays a student's way through college, and women athletes certainly deserve the same chance as men to work their way through school" (Diamant 1979, p. 21).

On the other hand, these scholarships have intensified competition. As part of the effort to equalize athletic opportunities for both sexes and comply with the Title IX Guidelines, the women's sports programs have been merged with the men's. And the philosophy of these men's pro-grams is clear: winning is everything. Averill Haines, assistant athletic director and basketball coach at Boston University, explains that athletic scholarships are essential to this effort—and that the woman who receives one had better realize it.

> A scholarship is a contract. It's a business contract. If a student isn't willing to live up to that, then you have a breach of contract.
>
> One of our philosophies at BU is to compete in Division I, which means we're not going to be content with the state title or just a New England title. We want Eastern ranking, eventually national ranking. We've got to get the committed athlete to realize this before she comes in. It's five and a half months of her life here at BU for four years, and that's what she's got to understand. (Quoted in Diamant 1979, p. 21)

Of course, playing to win has its benefits. It legitimizes competition, for one thing, as Diamant points out.

> But for women who played hard and played to win during all those years when winning wasn't supposed to be important, there's enormous relief in being able to say, "Everybody wants to win." . . .
>
> The denial of competition in the name of fun cut women's sports off at the knees for decades. It "excused" women's physical education with slogans of moral superiority that were really based on theories of relative female weakness and an apology to pristine femininity. No one in athletics regrets the demise of those ideas or apologetics. (Diamant 1979, p. 21)

Playing to win instead of for fun also has its drawbacks. Women's sports programs used to emphasize physical fitness for everyone; now they emphasize competitive excellence for superathletes only. And while the emphasis on competitive excellence can be exhilarating, it can also lead to the view of sports as simply a job. Louise O'Neal, assistant athletic director and basketball coach at Yale, feels that the problem is worse than this. For in adopting the male focus on competitive excellence, women also seem to have adopted other, less desirable male attitudes.

> I don't care for the way it feels to compete today. I don't enjoy having to beat people up to play and I don't like fighting and scrapping as if we were out on Wall Street. It's not what we're supposed to be about . . . Everybody is unhappy because of the climate. I hear the women complaining and they can't quite put their finger on what it is. . . .
>
> In the late '60s and early '70s, I really felt that the athletes were my equals. They wanted to be treated that way and they acted that way. Today they want to be treated in this militaristic, autocratic kind of fashion. I keep thinking maybe I'm getting older and they can't see me as their equal. But I don't think it's that. I think it has to do with where women are today in sports. They've copped out for role models that are exactly like the men. (Quoted in Diamant 1979, p. 24)

Play for Happiness

and Equality

Although competitive athletics do not seem to foster specific personality characteristics, they do appear to enhance a general sense of confidence and well-being. In comparing athletes and nonathletes at the college level, Snyder and Kivlin found that the athletes reported that they "generally feel in good spirits," are "very satisfied with life," and "find much happiness in life" more of the time than nonathletes (1975, p. 195).

Marilyn Vincent also asked college women to describe themselves (Vincent 1976) and used the Tennessee Self-Concept Scale which includes one hundred statements to be rated by varying degrees of truth or falsehood as applied to oneself. She found that 248 athletes at a variety of southern colleges received the same scores as 212 nonathletes at the same institutions. When she analyzed the responses according to athletic participation in high school, however, differences did appear. Regardless of their activities during college, those women who participated in high school sports scored higher. This finding suggests that sports may foster self-confidence and identity, especially when they are part of the adolescent growth experience.

Two physical education instructors at Whittier College did a similar study using both the Tennessee Self-Concept Scale and Shostrom's Personal Orientation Inventory which assesses self-actualization (Ibrahim and Morrison 1976). They found no differences in self-concept among two hundred students: one hundred male and one hundred female athletes and nonathletes at the high school and college levels. Differences in self-actualization did appear, however, in the female college athletes. Compared with nonathletic college women, the athletes were less dependent on the opinions of others, held more growth-enhancing values, were more flexible in applying those values, were more sensitive to their own needs and feelings, were more likely to see people as essentially good, and were able to see the contradictions in life as meaningfully related. Thus, the female athletes were more self-actualized—surer of themselves, of their world, and of their ability to relate meaningfully to that world.

Sports, then, seem to enhance a general sense of well-being and self-identity; but they are not alone in this effect. When Snyder and Spreitzer (1978) studied over six hundred high school athletes and musicians, they found that these two groups of highly accomplished and ambitious girls were equally likely to describe themselves as happy, satisfied, and generally in good spirits. Furthermore, parental encouragement seemed to be instrumental in the girls' participation and enjoyment of both types of activity. Thus, serious involvement in any challenging activity may be the secret of self-confidence and a feeling of well-being. The specific content and apparently feminine nature of that activity may not be important. As these authors put it, "We suggest that the whole notion of a role strain surrounding the female athlete needs to be re-evaluated" (p. 349).

Many feminists, on the other hand, argue that there is something uniquely valuable about competitive athletics—and part of this unique-ness is their supposedly masculine nature. These feminists feel that all women should have the opportunity to participate in sports because such competition brings a sense of mastery and accomplishment that has a profound impact on the rest of their lives. Some women athletes have written personal accounts, like this one by Wilma Scott Heide, a former president of N.O.W. and also a registered nurse, a semanticist, and a college professor. She feels that sports played an important part in developing her self-confidence, leadership abilities, and strength to fight for what she believes in. In her own words:

> In spite of the sexism and discrimination encountered throughout life, I have functioned as an athlete in several sports and had some gratifying experiences. Remember the "in spite of" . . .
> Nonetheless, my experiences as a sportswoman provided enormous self-confidence and feelings of self empowerment. In countless instances in my decades as a human rights activist, this background has provided the self-confident courage to participate in and lead in necessary dem-onstrations, confrontations, sit-ins, microphone liberations, conference takeovers, often unpopular decisions and actions reflecting individual and organizational integrity. . . .
> There is no doubt that the experiences as a sportswoman (when even more than now sports was considered primarily a male preserve with girls and women as marginal participants and/or cheerleaders) provided the courage of my convictions in spite of criticism, misunderstanding and overt actions to keep me and my sisters "in our place." (1978, pp. 196–97)

Heide is basically suggesting that defying rigid sex-role norms as a youthful athlete enabled her to continue defying them as an adult. By learning how to assert herself physically, she also learned how to assert herself verbally and emotionally.

Leanne Schreiber has suggested that this process applies to all women. When Schreiber was editor of the now defunct magazine *womenSports*, she dedicated an entire issue to the "Great American Tomboy": "I wanted to validate this hunch that women who had been tomboys, a tomboy being defined as a child who had defied sex roles at the level of play, is more likely as an adult woman to defy sex role limitations on occupation" (Quoted in Diamant 1979, p. 25).

To check out her hunch, Schreiber got in touch with many accomplished women in a variety of fields. She found that 80 percent of them had indeed been tomboys as children "and they very clearly connected in their minds the experience of the adventuring and challenging as a tomboy with the things they had dealt with as adults" (Diamant 1979, p. 25). As further proof of her claim, Schreiber points out that when the researchers who wrote *The Managerial Woman* contacted the one hundred most highly placed women in American business, they found that all of them had been tomboys and participated in whatever organized sports were available.

Many feminists would agree with Heide and Schreiber: sports are a training ground for female assertiveness and defiance of sex-role restrictions. And others would agree with Heide when she goes on to say that females and males should participate in sports together—in both contact and noncontact sports. First of all, she points to the demonstrated fact that "separate is inherently unequal, to the disadvantage of women and girls" (1978, p. 198). More important, however, sexual integration of contact sports would demythologize heterosexual encounters. People would learn that when female meets male, the purpose and end result is not always sexual arousal and intercourse. And finally, Heide argues that mixed-sex sports would decrease men's use of physical brutality to dominate women. As she puts it:

> Protect us from any more male "protectors." As girls and boys, women and men learn and exercise feminist perspectives in sports and elsewhere, I predict that rape, the political act via physical brutality, the true original sin, will disappear. Sex inequality, sexual apartheid, sports as domination and submission will increasingly be seen as barbaric and primitive. Men and boys will finally learn how to become good sports which should strengthen some currently fragile egos. (1978, p. 201)

Heide is not suggesting that all girls and women should be forced to participate in sports, whether in single-sex or mixed-sex settings, but that the availability of sports is important. When we stop seeing the world in terms of male athletes and female cheerleaders, we may also stop experiencing it in terms of male tyrants and female subordinates, male wife beaters and female victims, male achievers and female admirers.

In discussing women's sports with Anita Diamant, Leanne Schreiber pointed out that sexual equality in sports is not just a matter of money; in fact it is not even sports as such that matter, but rather the issue of female "physicality."

> The ex-tomboy elaborates: "Women have been systematically encouraged to divorce their identities from their bodies and in so doing they have been divorced from the most basic sense of power and the most basic source of power. When you divorce a whole class of people from that very

primary sense of their own power, you've created a sort of ruptured identity, a psychological instability, a very primary disconnection with the world.

"Because I genuinely believe that the physical discrepancy between men and women is the root and source of all later forms of discrimination; economic, political, educational, sexual, it's going back to that root and re-establishing a sense of control that is ultimately going to be the most potent means of women reclaiming a sense of their own value.

"And sports," says Leanne Schreiber, "is the route for physicality in this country." (Diamant 1979, p. 25)

The feminist arguments about physicality and defying sex-role norms essentially reverse the usual arguments about whether sports masculinize women. These feminists are implying that they do—and that that is a good thing. For defiance builds strength. And who is to say what will happen as ever more women begin to feel the strength of their bodies—and hence the courage of their convictions?

PART V

WOMEN AND

MENTAL HEALTH

M ENTAL HEALTH is very "in" these days. Everyone, it seems, has his or her own "shrink" or pretends to have one. Woody Allen has built his entire career around the charm of his neuroticisms. Thousands of how-to books have been written on attaining personal happiness and growth by eliminating one's emotional hang-ups. Many others address the problems of those in crisis—after losing a loved one or suffering one or another of life's tragedies, both large and small.

Much of this interest is justified. With current more isolated life styles, mental health professionals often replace the confidants of yesterday—the warm older relative, the familiar and well-loved neighbor, the local priest or minister. Many of the remedies and solutions offered in popular how-to books are valuable and sensible. However, the search for personal growth sometimes turns into a vindictive search for self-justification, an indirect way to prove that "I'm OK, you're a slob." This dark side of the mental health boom is not merely personal and private, moreover. On a societal level, mental illness functions as a basic method of social control. Whereas social rejects used to be called "bad," "immoral," or "incorrigible," now they are often called "mentally ill" or "crazy." While the concept of mental illness has removed much of the stigma attached to social deviance, it carries a stigma of its own. Someone who is too upset to work is no longer automatically dismissed as a malingerer. On the other hand, someone who wants to do something unusual may also be labeled and treated as "mentally ill" and therefore not be taken seriously.

When unconventional behavior can be labeled as a symptom of mental illness and hence dismissed, those who are trying to find a life style that differs somewhat from the traditional socially prescribed ones are particularly at risk. Since sex roles contain some of the most rigidly enforced and yet changing conventions of society, sex-role behaviors are particularly subject to this labeling process.

Am I saying that "mental illness" is merely a label for defying social conventions? Not entirely, for there is ample clinical evidence of mental illness as a personal rather than social phenomenon. But social labeling and stigma are not irrelevant to mental illness, as we shall see.

Chapter 18

Are Women Sicker

than Men?

I BEGIN with this provocative question because more women than men are treated for mental illness. The exact ratio varies from about one to one to as much as three to one, depending on the type of treatment facility: residential, outpatient, public, or private. But women are always in the majority. Are women, then, really the weaker sex? After all, Freud suggests that women are less able to resolve the oedipal complex and hence tend to have weaker superegos as well as to be passive, self-destructive, and generally immature throughout their lives.

Although this rather simplistic view was once prevalent, today we know that many factors are involved in becoming an identified patient who seeks help for certain symptoms of emotional distress. We cannot assume that the quantity of people in treatment is the same as the quantity of people who are actually sick. Many people show behavior and feelings that psychotherapists would label as symptoms of an emotional illness—but these people are not sick in that they have not become identified patients by seeking treatment. Perhaps they cannot afford it or feel it is shameful to be a mental patient. Or maybe their feelings and behavior are considered natural in their social group, something to be expected in the circumstances, perhaps even helpful and adaptive. What is being "sick" with an "illness" anyway? Researchers are beginning to realize that the answer to this question depends on one's social surroundings.

We cannot assume that a treated patient resembles his or her untreated counterparts in all major ways save for being in treatment. The most obvious difference is economic: the more money one has, the more likely one is to seek psychiatric treatment for a particular degree of emotional distress—but the less likely one is to be forced to participate in psychiatric treatment as part of legal sanctions for antisocial behavior. But even within a particular economic group, there is great variation in the feelings and behavior with which individuals respond to the same stress, in the tendency to perceive emotional difficulties and behavior as "symptoms" that would benefit from professional help, and in an individual's willingness to seek treatment even if he or she thinks it would be helpful or appropirate. Many of these variations are affected by one's sex.

Female Emotionality

First, let me return to the assumption that treatment rates accurately reflect illness rates. Many major studies have started with this assumption and looked for reasons why women would be more likely to become emotionally ill than men. One suggestion is that when subjected to extensive stress and emotional tension, women tend to become emotionally ill while men tend to become physically ill. Gove and Tudor (1973) tested this assertion by comparing the sex ratios of patients in treatment for "transient situational personality disorders" with those in treatment for "psychophysiologic disorders." The first type of disorder is characterized by acute emotional symptoms that develop in response to an overwhelming situation and disappear when the stress is withdrawn. The second includes physical illnesses known to be especially responsive to emotional tension (headache, ulcers, arthritis, and so on). Assuming that the two sexes are exposed to roughly equivalent amounts of stress, women should show higher rates of "transient situational personality disorders" and lower rates of "psychophysiological disorders" than men. Contrary to this suggestion, Gove and Tudor found that women are treated for *both* emotional and physical symptoms at a higher rate than men.

A second suggestion is that women are more willing to express their emotional distress and symptomatology than men are (Phillips and Segal 1969). Although this suggestion is consistent with women's generally greater willingness to admit to anxiety and other "undesirable" emotions, there is no indication that being more willing to admit emotional distress makes one more willing to seek professional help. Furthermore, the Dohrenwends (1974) have pointed out that the items included in the most widely used symptom scales tend to represent more female than male modes of expressing distress. Thus although the question of greater female expressiveness remains unresolved, it is unlikely that it could account for the strikingly higher rates of female psychiatric treatment.

Labeling Illness

If the sex differences in treatment rates are not due to women's greater tendency to admit unpleasant emotions, perhaps the differences are due to the way others perceive women as opposed to the way they perceive men. This theory grows out of the societal reaction perspective on mental illness (Scheff 1966), which maintains that an individual becomes mentally ill and seeks treatment primarily because others perceive him or her as mentally ill. Phyllis Chesler (1972) has applied this analysis to women, arguing that female mental illness is a matter of underconformity or overconformity to the prescribed female sex role. As she puts it:

> Men are not usually seen as "sick" if they act out of the male role fully— unless, of course, they are relatively powerless contenders for "masculinity." Women are seen as "sick" when they act out the female role (are depressed, incompetent, frigid, and anxious) and when they reject the female role (are hostile, successful, sexually active, and especially with other women). (1972, p. 118)

Chesler then quotes from public records and her own interviews with women hospitalized for violating sex-role norms, apparently with no other indication of emotional distress or emotional illness. Here are a few typical examples of these female sex-role offenders:

> A widening wave of shocked horror is sweeping Britain following disclosures that two sane women were kept confined in a mental hospital for about 50 years each simply because they had borne illegitimate children. . . . The women's parents went to local government officials for help with their "wayward" daughters and, Sheridan said, "the local authority to whom the parents turned did not have a department to deal with unmarried mothers." . . . Miss Baker was 23 when committed to the hospital in 1921: Miss Kitson was 22 when committed in 1928. (New York *Post*, May 27, 1972)

> CARMEN: I was so sad [after my daughter's birth] and so tired. I couldn't take care of the house right any more. My husband told me a maid would be better than me, that I was crazy. . . . He took me to the hospital for what they called observation.

> KATHRYN: After my husband left me and the baby, I was too de-
> pressed to do anything. I was a twenty-year-old mother, and back home
> dependent on my parents. . . . I didn't go to college because my mother
> didn't think I was smart enough. My father was very violent to me. . . .
> It was a shitty family and I escaped it by getting married. . . . So I came
> back home and said "I'm home," and my mother said, "Like hell you are.
> You made your bed, lie in it." So I had to threaten that I'd kill myself to
> get some sympathy and my mother said, "Okay, if you're crazy you belong
> in a hospital. If you're depressed, go get some tests to find out why." . . .
> My father knew the director of this loony bin and they all told me to sign
> myself in and be grateful. (Quoted in Chesler 1972, pp. 162, 165–66)

Chesler supplements her argument by pointing out that the "cure"
for mental illness in women often involves forced compliance with the
sex-role norms whose violation was used to attach a label of mental illness in the first place; that is:

> Those women remanded to state asylums were involved in sex-typed
> forced labor. They worked as unpaid domestics, laundresses, ward aides,
> cooks, and commissary saleswomen. If they refused these jobs they were
> considered "crazy" and "uncooperative" and punished with drugs, shock
> treatments, beatings, mockery, and longer hospital stays. If they accepted
> these jobs, and performed them *well*, the hospital staff was often reluctant
> to let them go. (1972, p. 168)

Furthermore, looking "feminine" and being "cooperative" are often
used as a measure of recovery, as Chesler illustrates:

> LAURA: Fix yourself up, they told me. So every morning I got the hot
> sweats [insulin therapy] and every afternoon I spent in the beauty parlor
> with the other women. Of course, you had to pay for it. . . . You have to
> hide your feelings, pretend everything is wonderful, if you want to get
> out.
> LAVERNE: I finally figured it out. You weren't supposed to be angry.
> Oh no. They lock you up, throw away the key, and you're supposed to
> smile at them, compliment the nurses, shuffle baby—so that's what I did
> to get out. (1972, pp. 169–70)

The experiences these women relate are chilling indeed and make one
wonder if any woman is ever safe from an arbitrary charge of insanity.
But the basic argument itself does not provide a compelling explanation
of the higher rates of psychiatric treatment for women. Men, too, can
be labeled as metally ill purely on the basis of socially disapproved behavior. Many psychologists feel that sex-role norms are actually *more*
stringently enforced for males, especially during the childhood years.
In fact, Gove and Tudor (1973) have summarized both theoretical speculations and empirical data that indicate that when men and women both

perform acts indicative of mental illness, *men* are much more likely to be perceived and reacted to as mentally ill. This may be because symptoms of emotional distress are more antithetical to the masculine than to the feminine role. It is hard to act independent, assertive, competitive, and calm while acting extremely anxious, depressed, or nervous.

This is not to say that social labeling may not play a major role in determining which—and how many—women are viewed as mentally ill and enter psychiatric treatment; for sex roles appear to be crucial in both the definition and the treatment of mental illness. Nonetheless, the social labeling process is not applicable only to women, or to women more than to men, and cannot be taken by itself as an adequate explanation for the sex differences in psychiatric treatment rates.

Sex and the Social Context

If the sex differences in treatment rates cannot be attributed to sex differences in expressive styles and social reactions, perhaps the difference lies in the amount of stress the two sexes encounter in daily life; that is, the higher treatment rates for women may actually reflect higher rates of mental illness in women, and these higher rates may be due to greater stress rather than to greater female weakness.

This line of reasoning has led many social scientists to focus on the idea of "role strain," or the contradictory and confusing expectations involved in the activities required of the typical American woman. Gove and Tudor (1973) have discussed this possibility in terms of married women who are restricted to one major societal role and hence do not have the variety of activities and sources of satisfaction available to the man who is both a worker and a family member. These researchers claim that "a large number of women find their major instrumental activities— raising children and keeping house—frustrating [since] being a housewife does not require a great deal of skill" (p. 52). They argue further that because the role of housewife is relatively unstructured and invisible, a woman may tend to brood over her troubles and hence magnify them. If a married woman does work, she is in a less satisfactory position than a married man because of sexual discrimination on the job and the typical pattern of continuing female responsibility for household chores. The working mother thus has two jobs, one of them often underpaid and the other entirely unpaid, while the working father has only one fully paid job.

Gove (1972) has expanded on this argument with an empirical study of the mental health of single and married men and women. He found that while men appear to benefit psychologically from marriage, women do not appear to. While there are much higher rates of mental illness among married women than among married men, there are no appreciable sex differences in illness rates for the divorced, the widowed, or the never-married. He concludes that marriage is a more difficult experience for women than for men and attributes this greater difficulty to the confused, contradictory, and frustrating expectations of marriage for women today.

I do not intend to proclaim that marriage is dangerous to every woman's emotional health, for studies have repeatedly shown that married adults of both sexes have lower rates of mental illness than have unmarried adults. The usual interpretation is that marriage provides a stable set of intimates who are generally helpful in a crisis. The fact that women fare better as singles than do men has been attributed in part to a woman's greater tendency to form close friendships, thus providing herself with a network of support similar to that found in a marriage or a family (Seiden 1976).

The issue of who gets married is also relevant. Do emotionally unstable people tend to lose out in courtship and dating and remain unmarried, hence raising the illness rates of singles? Since the man usually takes the initiative in courtship, his faults (emotional instability) are likely to be more visible and inhibiting than a woman's; this situation may lead to a larger pool of unstable bachelors than of unstable spinsters. Srole (1962, p. 180) suggested a related possibility: that men want to dominate their wives and hence bypass women with "strong, independent personalities"; these healthier females then remain single. Both of these explanations suggest that unstable males are more likely to be screened out of the marriage market than are unstable females, leaving a pool of healthier males to be married. These healthier males would then deflate the mental illness rates for married males, regardless of the stress involved in being a husband and father as opposed to being a wife and mother.

On the other hand, if unstable people tend not to marry, those previously married individuals who are now divorced or widowed should resemble their married counterparts more than they resemble never-married people, since they won in the marriage market. However, the illness rates of these once-marrieds are just as high as those of never-marrieds. Is this due to the stress of single-parenthood and the emotional trauma of losing one's spouse—and social identity—through divorce or death?

Other writers have extended Gove and Tudor's analysis to include the problems of the shrinking nuclear family network. For instance, Anne Seiden (1976) talks about the new situation of "crowding-in-isolation," where a single set of parents and children are crowded into a few small rooms, and the housebound mother is relatively isolated from relatives and other adults. Seiden calls the resulting tensions and frustrations the "trapped young mother syndrome" and points out that frequent job-related moves, isolated living arrangements, and decreased contact with those outside the nuclear family unit place increased importance on the husband-wife bond just at a time when its stability is decreasing, as evidenced by current divorce rates (1976, p. 1111). Furthermore, the woman bears the strain of total responsibility for child care and, for the half of American women who work outside the home, the problems of combining occupational and maternal roles.

Seiden's discussion highlights stresses that have increased for American women since World War II, and that may underlie mental illness rates. Men must also be experiencing some stress from changing family patterns, however, and hence these stresses alone cannot account for the higher treatment rates of females as compared with males.

The Patient Female Role

If differential environmental stress levels cannot be clearly established for female versus male social roles, perhaps something about the nature of the female sex role per se leads a woman to become a patient, and remain one, in psychotherapy. Phyllis Chesler has written the most scathing and broadly publicized articles on this issue. She maintains that a woman is encouraged to lean on a superior man throughout her life: first father, then husband, and then therapist. Thus, psychotherapy is considered appropriate for a woman because it matches and perpetuates her "one down" position in society. As Chesler puts it:

> It may be that more women than men are involved in psychotherapy because it—along with marriage—is one of the only two socially approved institutions for middle-class women. That these two institutions bear a strong similarity to each other is highly significant. For most women the psychotherapeutic encounter is just one more instance of an unequal relationship, just one more opportunity to be rewarded for expressing distress and to be "helped" by being (expertly) dominated. Both psychotherapy and marriage isolate women from each other; both emphasize individual rather than collective solutions to woman's unhappiness; both are based on a woman's helplessness and dependence on a stronger male authority figure; both may, in fact, be viewed as reenactments of a little girl's relation to her father in a patriarchal society; both control and oppress women similarly—yet, at the same time, are the two safest havens for women in a society that offers them no others.
>
> Both psychotherapy and marriage enable women to safely express and defuse their anger by experiencing it as a form of emotional illness, by translating it into hysterical symptoms: frigidity, chronic depression,

phobias, and the like. Each woman as patient thinks these symptoms are unique and are her own fault. She is neurotic, rather than oppressed. She wants from a therapist what she wants—and often cannot get—from a husband: attention, understanding, merciful relief, a *personal solution*—in the arms of the right husband, on the couch of the right therapist. The institutions of therapy and marriage not only mirror each other, they support each other. . . .

The institutions of psychotherapy and marriage both encourage women to talk—often endlessly—rather than to act (except in their socially prearranged roles as passive women or patients). (1971, pp. 260–61)

Chesler supports her viewpoint with data from a study of a thousand middle-income people who were clinic outpatients in New York City from 1965 to 1969 (Chesler 1971). Most of the 258 patients, both male and female, who voluntarily expressed a sex-of-therapist preference requested a male therapist and stated that they trusted and respected men more than women. The preference for a male therapist was particularly marked in single women. Chesler concluded that these women were seeking an intimate male authority figure in their lives in place of a husband. She elaborates on this idea by stressing the commonplace nature of sexual intercourse between male therapists and their female patients.

"Sex" between private female patients and their male psychotherapists is probably no more common—or uncommon—an occurrence than is "sex" between a female secretary or housekeeper and her male employer. Both instances generally involve an older male figure and a young female figure. The male transmits "unconscious" signals of power, "love," wisdom, and protection, signals to which the female has been conditioned to respond automatically. Such a transaction between patient and therapist, euphemistically termed "seduction" or "part of the treatment process," is legally a form of rape and psychologically a form of incest. The *sine qua non* of "feminine" identity in patriarchal society is the violation of the incest taboo, i.e. the initial and continued "preference" for Daddy, followed by the approved falling in love with and/or marrying of powerful father figures. There is no real questioning of such feminine identity in psychotherapy. More often, an adjustment to it is preached— through verbal or sexual methods. (1972, pp. 138–39)

Chesler goes on to say that most therapists in the United States are white, middle-aged, married men who subscribe to Freud's belief that "the psychoanalyst-patient relationship must be that of 'a superior and a subordinate.' " (1971, p. 262). She also talks about more general criticisms leveled at psychotherapy by people like Irving Goffman and Thomas Szasz: that psychotherapy fosters the illusion that individual psychological solutions can be found to what are actually collective, political problems; that it discourages socially isolated people from seeking acceptance, security, and emotional gratification through more accessible channels such as friendship; and that it serves as a form of social and political control by offering temporary emotional relief and the illusion of self-knowledge and self-control to those who can pay for it, while consigning other unhappy people who cannot pay to asylums that provide custodial care rather than therapeutic illusions. Chesler acknowledges that these general criticisms of psychotherapy apply to both male and female patients but insists that psychotherapy is particularly damaging for women because it corresponds to the institution of marriage and perpetuates the Freudian view of women.

Chesler's basic argument is dramatic: more women than men enter psychotherapy because it reinforces the subordinate position of a woman to a man by providing a relationship similar to that of traditional marriage. To support this idea, she points to the predominance of male as opposed to female therapists, to the overwhelming preference of both female and male patients for male therapists, and to the frequent sexual exploitation of female patients by male therapists. Recent research data, however, do not clearly support these assertions. For instance, a 1977 study showed that in community mental health centers nationwide, psychiatrists provide about 15 percent of the therapy hours, while psychologists provide about 8 percent; the rest of the therapy hours are provided by psychiatric social workers and general clinic staff. While only about one-tenth of psychiatrists and one-third of psychologists are female, two-thirds of social workers and other staff are female. These statistics mean that in the public clinics that provide the bulk of outpatient psychotherapy in this country, approximately one-half of the services are provided by women. Thus, although psychotherapy is indeed a male-dominated field in the sense that the most influential and well-paid positions are held by men and the theory has been developed by men, a female patient is just as likely to be talking to another woman as to a man. This is not to say that the superior-inferior relationship in therapy may not be oppressive and reinforce female helplessness, dependence, and subordination; but such oppression is not necessarily carried out by males and hence is not necessarily parallel to a marriage.

The issue of a patient's preference for a male or female therapist is fascinating. When Chesler wrote her original articles in the early 1970s, the little available data suggested an almost universal preference for male therapists—a preference based on a desire to see the most expert, authoritative, and powerful person, who would therefore have the magical ability to cure one's ills. Preference for a male therapist hence goes along with preference for a therapist with other signs of power and authority: more extensive credentials (Ph.D. or M.D.), higher fees, fancier offices.* In the past five or ten years, however, this situation has

---

* This is not to say that there are not *other*, valid reasons to seek out a credentialed therapist: credentials reflect formal training and hence may be a necessary, although not a sufficient, condition for competent treatment.

begun to change as more women have become aware of the power underlying many social relationships and have started to challenge the value of such traditionally male values as power, competition, authority, and control. Today many women request a female therapist precisely to avoid the power-authority dimension they had previously sought in therapy. I shall put off a detailed examination of this issue until my discussion of feminist therapy, in order to consider it along with related issues.

Chesler's contention that sex between patient and therapist is "commonplace" is provocative and difficult to refute. Two recent studies asked 450 physicians (including 112 psychiatrists) and 666 psychologists to answer a questionnaire about their own opinions and sexual activities with patients (Holroyd and Brodsky 1977; Kardener, Fuller, and Mensh 1973, 1976). About 5 percent, or 50 of 1,000, male psychologists and psychiatrists reported that they themselves had had sexual contact, including intercourse, with one or more opposite-sex patients; while only 0.6 percent, or 6 of 1,000, female psychologists reported doing this. Between 96 and 99 percent of these respondents believed that erotic contact would *never* benefit a patient. Yet the small group of (mostly male) therapists who did have sexual contact with a patient tended to have done so with more than one patient.

These studies suggest that only a few male therapists have sexual relationships with female patients. However, one must remember that these therapists were asked to report their own participation in activities that are widely considered to be unethical and frequently carry severe legal penalties. Furthermore, 54 percent of the physicians and 30 percent of the psychologists originally contacted did not return their questionnaires, leaving almost one nonrespondent for every respondent. Since those who reported engaging in such sexual activities returned their questionnaires much more slowly than did other respondents, the rate of nonreturn strengthens the suspicion that the actual rate of sexual contact is much higher than 5 percent for male therapists.

This possibility has not escaped psychologists and psychiatrists, who have become so concerned about the issue of sexual contact that it has been specifically banned in recent revisions of their ethics codes (American Psychiatric Association 1973; American Psychological Association 1977), and professional insurance carriers are no longer willing to assume liability for suits stemming from sexual contact. The very idea of sexual contact between a male therapist and a female client has come to be viewed by most women as a form of exploitation, as the American Psychological Association's Task Force on Sex Bias and Stereotyping in Psychotherapeutic Practice reported in 1975 (Brodsky et al. 1975). And, often with the help and encouragement of other mental health professionals, women are beginning to sue their therapists for this kind of exploitation.

Thus the available research does not clearly support Chesler's assertion that women enter therapy seeking a male authority figure similar to a husband or a father. Although most patients have preferred male therapists in the past, many of the available therapists are female, and actual sexual contact in therapy can seldom be documented. On the other hand, the patient role *is* rather powerless and hence appropriately feminine, and the mental health establishment is male-dominated. A male doctor is in charge at most facilities, so that a woman may perceive therapeutic wisdom and support as male-controlled. And a woman may indeed enter therapy to find a powerful person to lean on, even though her specific therapist may turn out to be another female. Given the stereotype of the helpless female, a woman is undoubtedly more likely to want or accept such a "one down" position than is a man.

How, then, are we to account for the higher treatment rates among women? Although no one explanation seems to stand by itself, the predominant themes of female emotionality, sanctions for sex-role conformity, role strain, and perpetual powerlessness are striking. They have aroused the interest—and often the fury—of clinicians and researchers alike. More and more, people are asking themselves not *whether* sex roles are related to mental illness, but just *how* these roles influence behavior, diagnosis, and treatment.

Researchers in this area have now turned from social issues surrounding the female role to the personality characteristics associated with that role, and have found that the elements of traditional femininity—nonaggression, noncompetition, warmth, and dependence—are related to many areas of mental health. A woman's traditionally feminine characteristics not only are reflected in her behavior but also seem to determine how clinicians perceive and diagnose her, what treatment goals they will establish for her, and what type of interaction will occur in the therapy sessions. Although the male sex role is also relevant to mental health, traditional masculinity is not as detrimental to a man's health as traditional femininity is to a woman's.

Chapter 19

The "Female" Illnesses

SOME PEOPLE THINK there is something sick about the typical female personality. Others say this is a ridiculous assumption. Yet there *is* a pattern of "female" symptoms of emotional distress—that is, symptoms that are far more likely to occur in females than in males. And conversely, there are symptoms that are "male" in that they tend to occur more in males. The sex differences begin in grammar school, when boys are more likely to be referred to child guidance clinics for physical behavior of an aggressive, destructive, antisocial, and competitive nature, while girls are more likely to be referred for personal attitudes and feelings such as excessive fears and worries, shyness and timidity, lack of self-confidence, and feelings of inferiority. The sex differences continue into adulthood, when men's symptoms may reflect destructive hostility toward others and pathological self-indulgence, while women's symptoms may express destructive hostility and criticism aimed at the self, such as self-deprecation, depression, and suicidal thoughts and actions.

The striking sex differences occur not only in single symptoms but also in clusters of symptoms that make up diagnostic categories or "illnesses." Some illnesses are found primarily in women, while others are found primarily in men. The pattern of these sex differences suggests a close relationship between sex roles and mental illness.

Hysteria as Superfemininity

Hysteria refers to the existence of an obvious bodily dysfunction that does not have a physical cause. Thus, someone might be blind but have nothing detectably wrong with the eyes, or another might have a paralyzed hand that is apparently physically healthy. The traditional interpretation of hysteria has focused on the emotional meaning of the dysfunction as a symbol of psychological conflict, especially a sexual conflict. For example, the sight of something traumatic could cause hysterical blindness, or guilt about masturbating or engaging in some other forbidden activity could lead to hysterical paralysis of the offending hand.*

Hysteria is *the* female disease. The very word "hysteria" is derived from the Greek *husterikos*, which means uterus. The famous physician Hippocrates (460–357 B.C.) thought such disturbances were caused by a uterus that became unattached and moved around the body pining for children, and finally lodged in a position that obstructed whatever bodily organ was afflicted. He felt that sexual difficulties were often involved and recommended marriage as the best remedy.

The concept of a "wandering uterus" seems preposterous today. Yet the idea that only females can be hysterics remains. While a specific physical disability with no known organic cause might be labeled hysterical in a man, there is much less awareness of a broader hysterical personality in men. And this is where most current attention is focused, since the more dramatic hysterical symptoms are now rare because of the increased medical sophistication of the general population. For instance, it is unusual to see someone who has a hand paralyzed from the wrist down in a "glove paralysis," because most people are now aware that the nerve fibers run down the arm into the wrist and hand, making paralysis that cuts across this bundle of fibers extremely unlikely physiologically. Hysterical responses are thus likely to be more subtle, combining isolated physical symptoms into a pattern that is medically unusual or improbable.

Hysterical character is a personality style found in people who tend to respond to stress or conflict by developing physical symptoms that have little or no organic cause. Donald Klein describes hysterics as

---

* Freud emphasized the sexual nature of the underlying conflicts and used the term "conversion hysteria" to indicate that the psychological-sexual conflict was converted into a bodily disturbance. Modern psychiatry has retained this concept of conversion but includes many other types of psychological conflict besides sexual ones. The current meaning of the term "conversion reaction" includes this broader conception of the cause of these symptoms.

fickle, emotionally labile, irresponsible, shallow, love-intoxicated, giddy, and short-sighted. They tend to be egocentric, narcissistic, exhibitionistic, vain, and clothes-crazy. They are seductive, manupulative [*sic*], exploitative, sexually provocative, and think emotionally and illogically. They are easy prey to flattery and compliments. Their general manner is histrionic, attention-seeking, and may be flamboyant. In their sexual relations they are possessive, grasping, demanding, romantic, and foreplay-centered. When frustrated or disappointed they become reproachful, tearful, abusive, and vindictive, and often resort to alcohol. (1973, p. 152)

Klein calls this behavior pattern a "caricature of femininity" and attributes it to a chemical imbalance that creates emotional lability and oversensitivity to rejection.

Other writers have emphasized the way in which normal upbringing creates this typical personality style in female children. Howard Wolowitz, for instance, describes the hysteric as someone who is histrionic and uses real and imaginary suffering to elicit tokens of sympathetic attention such as material gifts. Such hysterical women also typically show an intense envy of others who receive more attention, so that they are likely to respond to another's tale of misfortune with, "Oh, that's nothing. You should have seen what happened to me (or my husband, or my child, etc.) . . ." Competition for attention makes it difficult to make close same-sex friends, so these women turn to men with a great show of sexual interest and attractiveness that covers up their own rather repressed sexual response. In other words, hysterics are women who relentlessly seek attention and get caught up in "an aim to be immediately (but often not deeply) pleasing which generates an other directedness, social charm and a radar-like (though often inaccurate) sensitivity to other's emotional states" (Wolowitz 1972, p. 309).

Wolowitz argues that female children typically develop hysterical traits because in controlling children, it is more common for people to manipulate the emotions of girls than those of boys. Thus parents, teachers, and peers tend to get boys to do socially acceptable things by making use of rules, authority, physical punishment, and material rewards, while they tend to get girls to do socially acceptable things by showing approval and disapproval in an emotional way. This reinforcement leads the female child to form a sense of self-identity and self-worth that is based more on the ability to get positive emotional responses from others than it is on a sense of autonomy.

Wolowitz is not decrying these child-rearing methods for girls, nor is he critical of the end results. Indeed, he maintains that they are important in preparing the female child for her proper role as an adult. As he puts it:

> In moderate intensity these latter [hysterical] qualities seem particularly well suited to the complexities inherent in the roles of mother

and wife (in our culture) whose major tasks focus on fulfilling the ever changing, conflicting daily round of complex emotional, interpersonally mediated needs of family members. . . . It is difficult to imagine, on hearing even the surface details of a typical day in the life of an involved wife and mother, how this all could be carried out successfully without a rather enormous investment in the wish to please others at the sacrifice of her own individual needs. It is not surprising then that the mother is often stereotyped as a masochistic martyr. (1972, p. 309)

The essential claim here is that other-directedness, social charm, and sensitivity to the emotional needs of others are important to the nurturing female role as wife and mother. But do wives and mothers use social skills more than everyone else? How about adult males in work situations? Do not these situations involve interpersonal interactions that have to be managed in the same manner as interactions within the family? And then there is the nature of the social skills Wolowitz describes. He seems to be talking about superficial and manipulative charm rather than genuine emotional warmth and empathy. Why are these pseudo-social skills useful at all, not to mention more useful in the intimate interpersonal setting of the family than in the less intimate but often more socially complex setting of the workplace? And finally, I wonder whether Wolowitz is not falling into that familiar male trap of leaving the management of personal relationships to women while men go about the "serious" business of doing task- and object-oriented work. Such division of human beings leads to men who cannot feel and women who cannot think.

Psychopathy:

A Male Hysteria?

Women do not have a monopoly on superficial social charm and pseudo-emotionality. There is a group of men who are known for these qualities, who are also unable to form close personal relationships, and who are likely to be good looking, intelligent, and impulsive, to manipulate and defraud others (especially women), and to have no guilt feelings. These men, if caught in their illegal activities, are diagnosed as psychopaths.* Stories about these "con artists" typically involve a series

---

* Other terms used interchangeably with "psychopath" are "sociopath" and having an "antisocial personality." Over the past few years there has been a growing awareness that females may be psychopaths and males may be hysterics, but this is a new trend that has not yet affected most clinicians. At this point, psychopathy and hysterical personality remain as almost prototypical male and female illnesses, respectively.

of slightly illegal or unethical schemes in which an adoring woman is involved. The admirer defends her man against accusations of dishonesty and general sleaziness; when her patience and credulousness have been exhausted, the man typically finds another gullible female sponsor.

Descriptions of male psychopaths emphasize their social charm and manipulation of others and infer an accompanying lack of guilt feelings. Descriptions of female hysterics also emphasize social charm and manipulation of others but add the element of sexualizing interpersonal relationships and infer an accompanying lack of a sense of autonomy or identity. The theories about the causes of the two conditions also differ. The failure of psychopaths to develop guilt feelings has been attributed either to their escaping punishment because they were so attractive as children, or to their inability to learn from punishment because of a defect in their central nervous systems (Maher 1966). Hysterical personality structure is usually attributed to unresolved sexual conflicts of an oedipal nature or to extensive use of love withdrawal as a childhood punishment, perhaps exaggerated by a chemical imbalance that sensitizes the child to this treatment.

Male psychopaths and female hysterics both obviously use social charm to manipulate others. They differ most in their *un*observable or inferred characteristics—lack of guilt versus lack of autonomy, and a history of no punishment (too much love) versus a history of love withdrawal (too little or too-conditional love). Perhaps sex roles can account for the discrepancy between these similar behavioral observations and these different inferred personality correlates. For a man to manipulate others, especially women, indicates that he has no moral feelings but not that he is overly dependent on the opinion of others or that he has a weak sense of self-identity. On the contrary, he is viewed as a selfish loner who sees himself as above the law and social norms. For a woman to manipulate others, however, apparently indicates that she has many sexual conflicts and no sense of herself apart from others.

Wolowitz suggests that such a woman is selfless almost to the point of being masochistic and, far from being a loner above social norms, is incredibly self-effacing in her attempt to fulfill her obligations as a wife and mother. The sexual tone of such a woman's manipulations is attributed to sexual conflict rather than to her use of sex as one of her few weapons or tools with which to attain social power. Thus, a man is permitted and encouraged to be direct in his social aggression; when he carries this behavior too far too often, he is thought to be a selfish loner who lacks a conscience. A woman is permitted only indirect social aggression; when she uses sexual manipulation too obviously and too often, she is thought to be a dependent, selfish clinging vine rather than the selfless creature society meant her to be.

This comparison of hysterics and psychopaths is simplified—so much so, in fact, that it will probably infuriate many clinicians who would prefer to delve into the subtle differences between the two personality types. But these subtleties do not change the basic question of why superficial charm and pseudo-emotionality are interpreted so differently in the two sexes.

Depression

MOURNING, GRIEF, AND DEPRESSION

Depression is a fact of human existence. Everyone has felt "down" at least occasionally, and some people have repeatedly and severely. Feelings of sadness, disappointment, frustration, and discouragement are ordinary and "normal" when one is faced with the loss of a job, of a loved one, of an important personal function or ability, or of another source of self-esteem. But if these feelings are unusually severe or persistent, a clinician might see the individual as sick—that is, as having a "depressive syndrome" involving a number of physical and emotional symptoms, such as:

> feelings of worthlessness, guilt, helplessness and hopelessness, anxiety, crying, suicidal tendencies, loss of interest in work and other activities, impaired capacity to perform everyday social functions, and hypochondriasis, accompanied by such physical alterations as anorexia [loss of appetite], weight change, constipation, psychomotor retardation or agitation, headache, and other bodily complaints. (Klerman 1975, p. 1008)

Of course, these feelings and kinds of behavior also occur in everyday life, as we have already seen in Parkes' (1970) study of bereaved widows. And it is not always easy to differentiate normal mourning from depressive symptoms and illness. The major factor used to distinguish between the two is the existence of a precipitating event. Has something happened in a person's life to bring on this reaction? Is the reaction unduly prolonged? But who is to say what is a reasonable reaction or an event significant enough to warrant such a grief reaction? The object of mourning may not be a loss that occurred at a specific point in time. It may not even be a loss at all but a yearning for something never attained. Phyllis Chesler, for instance, maintains:

> Women are in a continual state of mourning—for what they never had—or had too briefly, and for what they can't have in the present, be it Prince Charming or direct worldly power. It is not very easy for most women to temper, idle, or philosophize away their mourning with sexual, physical,

or intellectual exercises. When female depression swells to clinical proportions, it unfortunately doesn't function as a role-release or respite. . . .
[Women's] "depression" may serve as a way of keeping a deadly faith
with their "feminine" role. . . . It is safer for women to become "depressed" than physically violent. Physically violent women usually lose
physical battles with male intimates; are abandoned by them as "crazy"
as well as "unfeminine"; are frequently psychiatrically or (less frequently)
criminally incarcerated. Further, physically strong and/or potentially
assaultive women would gain fewer secondary rewards than "depressed"
women; their families would fear, hate, and abandon them, rather than
pity, sympathize, or "protect" them. (1972, pp. 44–46)

Chesler is suggesting not only that female depression may sometimes
be a grief reaction or yearning for things never attained, but also that
women are more likely than men to respond to such deprivation by
turning their anger against themselves—that is, by converting that anger
into depression. Women are responding to the well-established fact that
among people clinically diagnosed as depressed, there are from two to six
women for every man (Arieti 1979; Arieti and Bemporad 1978; Scarf
1979; Weissman and Klerman 1977). This disproportionate rate of depression in women raises the obvious question of what in the female
condition leads to depression. Is it biology? Is it female personality
styles? Or is it female social roles?

FEMALE BIOLOGY AND DEPRESSION

Some attempts to find a biological basis for depression in women
focus on "raging hormones." Not only are the monthly cycles blamed for
depression and other emotional discomforts, but also the cessation of
menstruation in middle age is blamed for major depressive reactions.
In discussing the research on the monthly cycles in my earlier chapter
on biology, I concluded that the lack of research on male cycles and the
numerous flaws in the research on women themselves make this explanation seem weak at best. The idea about menopause (the "climacterium")
appears to be more valid, but here major life changes coincide with the
hormonal ones. It is difficult to say whether children leaving home, a
woman's own reentry into the job market, or her view of herself as
aging and hence less sexual may be more important than the physical
effects of the level of circulating hormones in the body.

Pauline Bart (1971) tested the hormonal explanation for menopausal
depression by examining the role of women throughout the life span in
thirty-three different cultures. She found that women's status usually
rises in middle age; only in the two cultures where it falls did she find
evidence that this life period was viewed as stressful. Bart concluded
that the social-status changes coinciding with menopause are the major
factors that cause depression in middle-aged women. This data is rather

sketchy, however, for we need to know more about the psychological processes involved in the depressive response to the physical and social changes accompanying menopause. And we need to remember that the hormonal and social role explanations are not necessarily mutually exclusive. Menopause is obviously both a physical *and* a social event that is accompanied by a complex network of emotional reactions.

A more convincing biological explanation for the high rate of female depression concentrates on a genetic linkage. Genetic research has suggested that a predisposition to depressive illness may be transmitted as an X-linked dominant gene; hence, it would be inherited through the mother and would give females twice the vulnerability of males (Mendlewicz et al. 1972).* This research is still in the early stages, however, and has so far only demonstrated a clear genetic linkage for manic-depressive psychosis (Arieti and Bemporad 1978), which involves marked mood swings accompanied by loss of contact with reality (hallucinations and delusions) and is much different from the mild or "neurotic" depressions treated in most outpatient settings.

Other biological bases for depression have also been proposed. Arieti and Bemporad (1978) suggest that the most promising line of research has followed the "catecholamine hypothesis," which connects depression with decreased activity of some neurotransmitters in the brain. A tendency in women to have lower levels (or more easily disrupted functioning) of these chemicals than men might explain the higher rates of depression in women. As Arieti and Bemporad point out, however, biochemical hypotheses such as this one "have not gone beyond the hypothetical stage" (1978, p. 5).

At the present time, then, no evidence establishes a biological cause for depression, much less a cause that is sex-linked. On the other hand, there is plenty of evidence that depression is always accompanied or caused by psychological factors (Arieti and Bemporad 1978). This does not mean that biological factors do not accompany or even contribute to depression, but it does suggest that the social and emotional aspects of depression are crucial—and that these factors *are* sex-linked.

WOMEN AND LEARNED HELPLESSNESS

Some researchers emphasize the personality styles of women as opposed to their biology, and suggest that women have learned to respond to adverse circumstances with depression rather than with positive action (Weissman and Klerman 1977). This argument is based on an animal model of depression called "learned helplessness." Martin Selig-

---

The research suggests that not only depression (unipolar depressive illness), but also mood swings from depression to mania and back (bipolar affective illness), may be linked to an X gene.

man and his associates (1972) developed the model by subjecting dogs to unavoidable shocks in their hind paws. These traumatized dogs were later placed in a shuttle box with a shoulder-high partition and shocked on the paws again. Unlike other dogs placed in the shuttle box, the traumatized dogs almost never learned to jump over the partition to avoid the shock. On the contrary, they seemed to give up and passively accept the shock, huddling and whining in a corner. The basic argument is that the experience of being unable to control the original traumatizing shock led to passivity in the face of future trauma, to slow learning of responses that would permit escape from the future trauma, and to a higher degree of emotional distress in response to the future trauma, as measured by defecation, fearful behavior, decreased appetite, and weight loss.

Seligman (1974) believes that learned helplessness in animals may parallel the lack of initiative and the hopeless attitude about the effectiveness of one's actions that are typical of depression in humans. The logical link between the cause of learned helplessness and depression is thus a previous experience of uncontrollable trauma that sets the stage for passivity in the face of future traumas. The analogue has been applied to women in particular, with the argument that childhood experiences teach girls to think of themselves as powerless, helpless, and ineffective, and that therefore as women they respond to stress and trauma with passivity and the hopelessness of depression. As Aaron Beck and Ruth Greenberg explain it:

> According to Seligman, it was not trauma *per se* "that produced failure to escape, but having learned that no response at all can control trauma." Many female children are taught that their personal worth and survival depend not on effective responding to life situations but on physical beauty and appeal to men—that is, that they have no *direct* control over the circumstances of their lives. Throughout adolescence they are subjected not to physical shock, but to parental and institutional supervision that both restricts their alternatives and shelters them from the consequences of any disapproved alternatives they do choose to pursue. Perhaps women, like dogs who have learned that their own behavior is unrelated to their subsequent welfare, lose their ability to respond effectively and to learn that responding produces relief. (1974, pp. 120–21)

Beck and Greenberg then go on to outline a "cognitive therapy" for depressed women, which revolves around the effort to increase the patient's awareness of "automatic thoughts" about her own worthlessness and incompetence and the hopeless nature of her situation, and encourages her to gradually to explore actions and feelings that can change things. This therapeutic process can be viewed as an attempt to reeducate or resocialize women to think of themselves as active, competent, and effective rather than as passive, helpless, and powerless.

The difficulty with this analogy, however, is that the learned help-lessness model is not based on a general trait of helplessness in animals; that is, the experimental animals were not encouraged to be generally helpless and dependent, as the argument maintains that women were while growing up. Rather, the experimental animals were subjected to specific circumstances that inflicted physical pain with no possibility of escape. To make a powerful argument that learned helplessness underlies the higher rates of depression in women, therefore, one would have to specify what painful experiences—at least emotional, if not physical—occur only to girls, with no hope of escape. A vague, general encourage-ment to act helpless may not be sufficient.

Much as we may deplore the encouragement of clinging, dependent, passive behavior in females, we should not forget that this behavior usually influences the situation in some way; it is not quite comparable with an animal that is shocked in a situation where *no* behavior in-fluences the amount or the duration of shock. Many girls are indeed taught that they can control their lives only indirectly by appealing to or manipulating men. The manipulation of males through "feminine wiles" may be indirect or even devious, but it is often effective. To treat indirect action and control as totally ineffective or inactive is to imply that the only effective—or even recognized—behavior is that carried out in the openly aggressive male mode.

THE EMPTY-NEST SYNDROME AND ROLE LOSS

In the past ten years more attention has been focused on the ways in which the female role itself actually fosters depression. One of the major problems appears to be the "empty-nest syndrome," or the feeling a mother has of having lost her identity when her children leave home. Pauline Bart (1971) investigated this explanation for depression by com-paring the hospital charts of over 500 women aged forty to fifty-nine who were hospitalized for the first time for either depression or a physical illness. She found that, shortly before hospitalization, the de-pressed women were more likely to have had a child leave home and that they also had had overinvolved and overprotective relationships with their children. Bart concluded that the depressives were supermoms from the facts that they were more likely to be housewives who did not work outside the home, to be middleclass rather than working class (so that they had the time to devote to child-centered activities), and to be Jewish, Anglo-American, or black in that order. To test her impressions further, Bart interviewed twenty of the depressed women and found that, in spite of their children's now being grown, they ranked "helping children" as first or second in importance of seven roles available to them, while they did not choose as valuable helping their parents, being a sexual partner to their husbands, or working outside the home (even though eight actually did work). In other words, these depressed women valued only the homemaker and mother role which had just been dramatically constricted by the departure of their children.

Bart goes on to speculate about a martyr dynamic in these women. Like all "involutional depressives," or people showing depressive illness for the first time in middle age, they tended to be rigid, conventional martyrs who had trouble handling their own aggressive feelings and needed to be useful in order to feel worthwhile. Bart therefore suggests that these women were very angry at their children for leaving home and in effect flouting their efforts as supermom and superwife, and thus depriving them of both role and function by which to feel themselves worthwhile. Since a woman is not "allowed" to be hostile to her children, these women turned the anger onto themselves in the form of depression, which then served to induce guilt and greater attentiveness in their children.

Bart points out that her theory of role loss can also explain involutional depression in men, which tends to occur in the sixties when retirement deprives a man of his central role and identity as a worker-breadwinner. She goes on to make the important point that the tragedy of depressed women is that they were *expected* to be supermoms and superwives. As Phyllis Chesler would say, it is their very compliance and conventionality that has done them in.

> It is very easy to make fun of these women, to ridicule their pride in their children and concern for their well-being. But . . . these women are as much casualties of our culture as the children in Harlem whose I.Q.'s decline with each additional year they spend in school. They were doing what they were told to do, what was expected of them by their families, their friends, and the mass media; if they deviated from this role they would have been ridiculed (ask any professional woman). Our task is to make their sacrifices pay off, though in a different way from what they expected. As their stories are told, other women will learn the futility of this life style. (Bart 1971, p. 115)

MALE DOMINANCE AND FEMALE DEPRESSION

Other writers have suggested that it is not the *loss* of the female role but the *role itself* that causes so many women to be depressed. According to this view, a woman does not have to be a martyred supermom to be depressed, nor does depression strike only when her children leave home. The relationship between the sexes causes female depression, and this experience of oppression starts in childhood and persists throughout a woman's life.

This approach focuses both on the social role of women and on the personality characteristics which that role fosters. Thus Weissman and Klerman (1977) discuss the "learned helplessness" model of female depression and the "social status" hypothesis. The latter suggests that sexual discrimination and inequality lead to economic and legal helplessness and dependence on others—qualities that are accompanied by low self-esteem, low aspirations, and eventually depression.

Scarf (1979) has proposed a model of female depression which reflects both the learned helplessness and the social status hypotheses. According to her, "Being female means (frequently) never being encouraged to become a self-sufficient individual" (1979, p. 52). Instead, women are encouraged to be dependent on others and, at the same time, to be more emotionally expressive, warm, and involved in personal relationships than are men. Their early "femininity training" thus encourages women to throw themselves into a small number of intensely important relationships. "To fail in those relationships is, then, equated with 'failing in everything' " (1979, p. 52). In other words, women not only learn to be dependent and helpless; they also learn to define themselves in terms of the dominant male. When the relationship with such an all-important male is disrupted, depression ensues.

Arieti has suggested a more extensive model of depression which encompasses many of the themes touched on by others (Arieti & Bemporad 1978). According to this model, someone with a depressive personality is always trying to recover the "Paradise Lost" which he or she experienced during the first two or three years of life (Arieti 1979, p. 57). In this early period the mother gives the child a lot of love and attention—an attention that is dramatically decreased when a younger sibling is born, or else when the duty-oriented parents decide that the child is old enough to manage on his own. The child feels bereft and abandoned and, owing to this lingering feeling, responds in either of two ways later in life:

> One is by doing his best to live up to the expectations of the adults—by doing hard work, or by becoming a goody goody, by attempting to placate them. Striving to regain paradise, he thus lives not for himself but for others. He believes that love is not available now, but that if he can live up to the expectations of adults, it will be. He becomes a compliant person, a person with a strong sense of duty. When he does not succeed in obtaining what he wants, he tends to blame himself. He feels that he has not done enough. He could do more. . . .
>
> At other times, the ideology has to do not with the Dominant Other but with a Dominant Goal. The kind of person motivated by a Dominant Goal has decided in early adolescence that to regain love, he or she must achieve something great in life: to become a famous actress, to win a Nobel Prize, to become the mother of six children, or something like that.
>
> So the person may live only to be a great conductor, a Toscanini. His whole life becomes filled with the fantasy of being Toscanini. When he realizes later in life that he isn't going to be Toscanini, he becomes depressed. Whereas a normal person would be able to find alternative goals

in life, he cannot. The fantasy has occupied his whole life and the empti-ness cannot be filled. (Arieti 1979, pp. 57–58)

Arieti maintains that the sex differences in depressive illness stem from the sex differences in response to early maternal deprivation. Fe-males are encouraged to be dependent and hence become obsessed with the Dominant Other. Men, on the other hand, are encouraged to be independent and hence become oriented to the Dominant Goal. De-pression in women is thus associated with loss of attachments, while depression in men is associated with career disappointments, much as Scarf (1979) suggests.

Arieti goes on to attribute female dependence to male dominance, or the patriarchal nature of our society:

> Women really are depressed more often than men, and the reason is that we still live in a patriarchal society in which women are raised to be dependent on another person. Women more often than men have the relation of submission to the Dominant Other, who doesn't have to be a male, incidentally. There are many women who have another woman as their Dominant Other—a sister, or a friend, or their mothers. (Arieti 1979, p. 58)

Although both males and females experience the traumatic loss of parental love and attention in these warm but duty-oriented families, Arieti suggests that a number of sociocultural factors may intensify the female's experience of that loss. The first involves the greater valuation of male children:

> I can only postulate in the most hypothetical way that in families which practice gender prejudice, and in which a girl has already been born, the birth of a boy is experienced with great joy and leads to neglect of the older girl. A great deal of attention is devoted to the newborn boy and the girl experiences the trauma of the loss of love. (Arieti and Bemporad 1978, pp. 365–66)

While acknowledging that this hypothesis is "purely speculative" (1978, p. 366), Arieti notes that a number of other factors are well established, some of which I have discussed in earlier chapters. First there is the fact that girls are pressured to be more nurturant and re-sponsible than boys and thus grow up to be more "duty-bound." A girl is expected to serve the needs of others and to be submissive to a "male-dominant other." Being feminine is often "confused with being dependent," so that "the man often depicts himself as the pillar, the ruler, or the directionmaker to the point of fostering a state of helpless-ness in the women in his life" (Arieti and Bemporad 1978, pp. 366–67). And finally, there is the fact that society teaches the woman that her subordinate position and depressed feelings are both normal and proper.

In a patriarchal society the woman often represses the sorrow, the anger, and the frustration which accompany her subordinate way of living. The repression, however, in the best circumstances leads to neurotic defenses; in the worst, to facilitating serious mental disorders, especially depression. Although it is true that the very beginning of a pattern of female dependency can be traced back to the first two or three years of life, it is also true that this pattern would not persist and become ingrained in many cases if society at large did not promote it. (Arieti and Bemporad 1978, p. 366)

Arieti goes on to point out that the woman is caught in a no-win situation. Once she has become dependent as expected, she is criticized for her dependence. Yet she has no way to express or foster her own independence, since "as a rule, only in the areas of motherhood and homemaking is the woman allowed to assert herself fully. Homemaking, however, is decreasing in value in modern society, and many functions which in a pre-industrial society were entrusted to the woman are now relegated to other agencies" (Arieti and Bemporad 1978, p. 367).

Since she is often barred from having a career herself, a woman often adopts marriage and romantic love as her Dominant Goal. This choice, however, exposes her to "double jeopardy" (Arieti and Bemporad 1978, p. 368). Now she becomes depressed not only from vainly striving to please her husband but also from his vain attempts to attain his (and hence her) Dominant Goal. And if the couple separates, the wife has lost everything: her Dominant Other, his (and her) Dominant Goal defined in terms of his career, and her Dominant Goal defined in terms of the marital relationship itself.

Arieti notes that this double jeopardy has a profound effect on the woman, who mourns not only for adoration from the Dominant Other but also for the privileges and opportunities that that (usually male) Dominant Other enjoys.

At this point it is worthwhile to reconsider the theory which from time to time has appeared in classic psychoanalytic literature, that a castration complex can explain the greater occurrence of depression in women. I think it is easier to affirm that depressed women are more likely to mourn not for the castration of their penis, which would be pure fantasy on their part, but because they really have been castrated—although in a metaphorical sense. The symbolic penis of which they have been deprived is the male role in the world, including all opportunities connected with that role, from becoming president of the United States to being the director of a small bank. (Arieti and Bemporad 1978, p. 368)

This view of women as mourning for the male role is remarkably similar to Phyllis Chesler's view of women as "being in a continual state of mourning—for what they never had—or had too briefly, be it Prince Charming or direct worldly power" (1972, p. 44). It is also reminiscent of Elizabeth Janeway's (1974) argument that Freud saw women as "social castrates."

On a personal level, then, the key to greater female depression is greater female dependence. And a woman's unconscious attempt to recover the paradise lost through her dependence on the Dominant Other is reinforced by cultural images of women, which reflect ideas that prevailed in the nineteenth century and continue as the unconscious basis of our thoughts and feelings today. To illustrate this point, Arieti outlines the six major ways in which women are depicted in operas.

1. Women are victimized, exploited, insulted, and brutalized by men; and they are prevented by society from redeeming themselves.
2. Women are sick or frail.
3. Women are infantile, vain, and dependent.
4. Women are loose and promiscuous.
5. Women are mechanical, insincere, and untrustworthy.
6. Women are beautiful and lovely when young, but their youth is of brief duration.

(Arieti and Bemporad 1978, p. 370)

Arieti says further that if this is what women expect life to be like, even unconsciously, no wonder they are more depressed than men.

> My conclusion . . . is that if women were in situations as depicted in the lyric operas or if they were conceived of as they were in operas, they had good reason to be sad and were certainly facilitated in a trend toward depression. To the extent that these ideas continue in our conscious or unconscious, women are still affected in this way. . . .
>
> If we consider all six categories, we can conclude that either a woman's life is made miserable by men and therefore she is right in being depressed, or she is regarded by men in such a negative way as to justify being in a state of despondency. . . .
>
> In summary, in a world which sees women in the role of victim, or as sick, gullible, and naive, or loose, as a prostitute, it is no wonder women are bound to feel despondent about their lot and more inclined than men to become melancholic. (Arieti and Bemporad 1978, pp. 369, 370, 372)

Anorexia Nervosa:

Femininity on a Rampage?

Anorexia nervosa is a disease of self-starvation. People suffering from this disorder have a normal appetite but refuse to eat because of an aversion to food or to weight gain. When the amount of their deliberate weight loss reaches about 25 percent of their normal body weight, they are considered to be "anorexics." At this point they have also begun to show a number of physical symptoms, such as cessation of menstruation (amenorrhea), repeated and often self-induced vomiting, constipation, intolerance to cold, a decrease in or cessation of sex drive, an extensive growth of downy body hair (lanugo), low blood pressure, a sluggish heart beat, periods of overactivity, and a denial of fatigue. They have an extremely distorted body image and agonize over how fat they are at a time when they have already become grotesquely emaciated. Their eating behavior may be bizarre, including food hoarding and alternating periods of fasting and gorging. When they are gorging, they eat everything in sight, often to the point of becoming hideously bloated. Then they resort to vomiting and taking handfuls of strong laxatives to lose weight as they embark on a period of fasting.

Anorexia nervosa is a life-threatening disease. If left to her own devices, an anorexic will literally starve herself to death. Furthermore, severe depression and suicide attempts are common in anorexic patients. The incidence of this rare disorder has risen dramatically in the past twenty years, and mild forms may now be relatively common, if only because of heightened awareness of the disorder and hence the greater likelihood of a physician's diagnosing it. The victims are usually adolescents or young adults, and almost invariably female. Current studies estimate that 85 percent to 95 percent of diagnosed anorexics are women (Bemis 1978).

The refusal to eat is not simply a symptom of some other psychiatric disorder, for although appetite disturbances frequently accompany a variety of physical and mental illnesses, the diagnosis of anorexia nervosa is appropriate only when no evidence of another illness is found (Feighner et al. 1972). Nor can the refusal to eat be blamed on the physical and emotional disturbances typical of anorexics, for the refusal to eat appears to *cause* these symptoms, not vice versa. Almost all of the behavior, feelings, and physical symptoms of anorexics are similar to those caused by involuntary starvation (Bemis 1978; Bruch 1978). Thus, the singular aspect of anorexia nervosa is the determination not to eat. Once this determination is made, all the other symptoms follow.

FEMALE BIOLOGY AND ANOREXIA NERVOSA

A bewildering variety of medication has been used to treat anorexia nervosa, usually with little success. The essential problem in medical management of the disease is to differentiate cause from effect. Treatment of the myriad physiological symptoms of the disease remains only a palliative as long as we do not know whether these physical abnormalities *cause* the refusal to eat or are the *result* of that refusal.

The difficulty in knowing lies in the fact that, although most of the physical symptoms found in anorexia nervosa are also found in starva-

tion, there are discrepancies. For instance, in anorexia nervosa, amenorrhea frequently appears before food restriction, while in starvation
amenorrhea appears only after severe weight loss. Bemis (1978) points
out the implausibility of the suggestion that "early" amenorrhea is
actually due to dieting before weight loss becomes perceptible, because
amenorrhea may precede visible weight loss by several years. It is also
improbable that the emotional stress of self-starvation causes the amenorrhea, since menstrual disorders in anorexics are long-lasting, while
those due to psychological factors are usually transient even when the
stress continues. Bemis goes on to point out other complicated chemical
and neurological changes that occur only in anorexia nervosa, and suggests the hypothalamus as the most likely site of organic disturbance
since it controls eating patterns.

On the other hand, if organic dysfunction causes anorexia nervosa,
we would expect some evidence of genetic transmission of the disease;
but studies of identical twins and sisters have failed to provide any.
Women who have an anorexic identical twin or sister are not necessarily
more likely to be anorexic than is the average woman.

The research into biological causes of anorexia nervosa is recent, so
that for the present we have only theoretical speculations which do not,
however, rule out a biological mechanism. As with most psychiatric
disorders, the predominant interpretations have been psychoanalytic.

REJECTION OF FEMININITY

Traditional views begin with the premise that eating is a symbolically
sexual behavior. Although self-starvation can be interpreted in a variety
of ways (Deutsch and Murphy 1955; Fenichel 1945), it is most commonly
attributed to underlying preoedipal or oedipal conflicts (Bemis 1978).
Thus, anorexics refuse to eat because they are afraid of oral impregnation. Their periodic gorging behavior is seen as a breakthrough of unconscious (and contradictory) desires to become pregnant. The absence
of menstruation is seen in two ways: first as a symbol of pregnancy, and
second as a denial of femininity. Thus the refusal to eat expresses the
anorexic's severe psychological conflicts about being feminine. Traditional psychology attributes these conflicts to unconscious hostility
toward the mother, and that hostility in turn to unresolved conflicts from
the preoedipal period. In other words, an anorexic has failed to identify
with her mother and hence is extremely ambivalent about the emotions
and behavior that characterize the truly feminine woman.

Clinical literature usually describes anorexic female patients as
sensitive, dependent, introverted, anxious, perfectionistic, selfish, and
intractably stubborn. As children they were conscientious, well-behaved,
and shy—"good girls" who gave no trouble at school or home and were
generally eager to please. Their mothers are usually depicted as dominant

and intrusive, with an emotionally intense but ambivalent relationship with the child. The fathers are vaguely described as passive, intellectual, and emotionally removed from the family. It is sometimes suggested that these girls have few social skills and react to new social situations, such as beginning college or getting married, with dieting as a way to control some aspect of their behavior. Since these situations also coincide with increased sex-role pressures, the self-starvation response can also be viewed as a reaction to arousal of the underlying conflicts about femininity (Bemis 1978; Bruch 1978).

Unfortunately no controlled studies contrast the families and childhoods of anorexic women with those of nonanorexic women, so that we cannot know whether the backgrounds of the anorexics are unusual.

A CARICATURE OF FEMININITY

A group of researchers have recently proposed a feminist analysis of anorexia nervosa that suggests that the anorexic "doesn't reject her femininity, she becomes a caricature of it" (Boskind-Lodahl and Sirlin 1977, p. 52). The researchers studied 138 college women who reported habitual eating binges followed by purging rituals of self-induced vomiting, diarrhea, or fasting. One student described this process: "After a binge I force myself to vomit. I do this for a long as I can, continually. After about three days I simply can't vomit any more . . . and then I start the binging" (quoted in Boskind-Lodahl and Sirlin 1977, p. 50). The researchers named this behavior pattern "bulimarexia," after *bulimia* for insatiable appetite and *anorexia* for lack of appetite. They maintain that since anorexia nervosa is often accompanied by periodic eating binges, its fasting and binging aspects need to be studied together.

Nearly all of their bulimarexic patients reported that a perceived or an actual male rejection triggered their first big diet, which was followed by their first binge. The binge made them feel out of control, guilty, and ugly, leading to a renewed compulsion to lose weight by fasting or purging. Once the cycle was well established, they came to fear and avoid sexual contact with men not because they feared getting pregnant, but because they were terrified of performing inadequately and being rejected again. The following story of Anne provides a poignant example of how fear of male rejection and hence of intercourse can lead to the binging-purging behavior.

The connection between the fear of rejection and the binge was dramatically illustrated in a session with Anne. She had spoken earlier of her first attempt at sexual intimacy.

"When I was 15 I was on a cruise down the Snake River. I impulsively decided I didn't want to be a virgin any more, and since I liked the boatman, I decided to let him make love to me. The only thing is, I got drunk

and passed out, and that's when he did it to me. I didn't remember anything the next day and felt miserable and disgusted with myself. And the
worst part was this guy didn't want to have anything to do with me after
that. I began to diet then because I thought maybe I was too fat and that's
what had turned the guy off. I think my binging started around that time."

To clarify what was happening here, we asked Anne to play the role
of the food she ate, to enact the food's assault on her body. She described
it this way:

"I'm your food, and I'm going into you now, stuffing you, making you
disgusting, fat. I'm your shame, and I'm making you untouchable. No one
will ever touch you. That's what you want, that no one will touch you."
(Boskind-Lodahl and Sirlin 1977, p. 52)

Like anorexics, the bulimarexic women studied came from affluent
families in which beauty and success were all important. The typical
mother was intelligent and well educated but gave up her career possibilities to raise a family. This frustrated, hostile, and domineering mother
was joined by a father whose interests lay mostly outside the home. The
typical bulimarexic woman adored her father and tried to please him by
doing well in school and by being physically perfect. She consciously
despised her mother, however; and the authors suggest that the bizarre
eating patterns might have been one of the few ways such a daughter
could rebel against a suffocating mother.

This feminist analysis does not argue with the psychoanalytic view
that eating disorders express sexual conflicts. The difference lies in the
sexual conflicts expressed. Freudians emphasize the fear of impregnation
and the underlying rejection of femininity, while the feminists emphasize the fear of rejection and the underlying eagerness to be feminine. As
Boskind-Lodahl puts it:

The sexual conflicts that are evident in these women do not reflect a rejection of femininity or a bizarre fear of oral impregnation. Rather, these
women have already learned a passive and accommodating approach to
life from their parents and their culture. This accommodation is combined
with two opposing tensions: the desperate desire for self-validation from
a man, and an inordinate *fear of men* and their power to reject. Since most
of the women have already experienced a real or perceived rejection by a
male or males, this perpetuates that already larger than life belief in the
power and importance of men. The sexual fears of these women are often
associated with intercourse, which is viewed as an act of surrender exposing their vulnerability to rejection. Rather than finding an obsession
with bizarre fantasies (oral impregnation), I found a preoccupation with
the fear of rejection in sex, of not being good enough to please a man.
(1976, pp. 353–354)

The Freudians and the feminists also differ dramatically on the *origin*
of this sexual conflict. While the former point to an unresolved oedipal

conflict and a resulting failure to identify with the mother, the latter point to a natural socialization process within a culture in which the only meaningful relationships are with men. In such a male-dominated society, to be like (to identify with) one's mother means to be male-oriented just as she is. If one derives a sense of identity and self-worth only from pleasing men, the desperate search for male approval can certainly lead to overwhelming fear and, in its wake, hatred of those all-powerful men.

THE GOLDEN CAGE

Hilde Bruch (1974, 1978) has proposed a third interpretation of anorexia nervosa that differs from both the traditional psychoanalytic one and the feminist analysis offered by Boskind-Lodahl and Sirlin. According to Bruch, a pervasive sense of helplessness and lack of autonomy leads to the central symptom of refusing to eat in spite of being obsessed with food.

Bruch (1978) presents an analysis of over one hundred anorexic patients whose family backgrounds and symptomatology were quite similar to those of the patients described by Bemis (1978) and Boskind-Lodahl (1976). These adolescents came from affluent, high-achieving homes where they were given all the material possessions they could possibly need. They experienced such a home as a "golden cage" of privilege, however, in which they felt "undeserving," "unworthy," and "ungrateful": "Their common complaint is that they received too many privileges and felt burdened by the task of living up to the obligation of such specialness" (1978, p. 39).

These girls often had a symbiotic relationship with their parents. They were not only pressured to excel in scholastic achievements and physical beauty, but they also felt responsible for making life more rewarding for their parents. The response of each was to be the proverbial "good girl."

> A common feature is that the future patient was not seen or acknowledged as an individual in her own right, but was valued mainly as someone who would make the life and experiences of the parents more satisfying and complete. Such expectations do not preclude a relationship of great warmth and affection. Usually clinging attachment and peculiarly intense sharing of ideas and feelings develop. . . .
>
> The distressing situation (in receiving parental gifts) is to guess what the parents want to give and to accept it with enthusiastic gratitude. . . . These episodes express more than attitudes toward receiving gifts. They illustrate the oversubmissiveness, abnormal considerateness, and lack of self-assertion characteristic of anorexics. Deficient in their sense of autonomy, they have difficulties in making their own judgments and opinions. (1978, pp. 34, 44–5)

When these overly dependent girls reach puberty and are sent away to a new school, to camp, or to college, they feel helpless and incapable of relating to their peers on an equal basis. They begin to diet as a way to exert control over their biological urges, to become special by accomplishing an extraordinary feat, and, most important of all, to retain their childlike body, which symbolizes their childish dependency.

Bruch notes that there is a sexual dimension to the anorexic's self-starvation. Thus, for some girls "reaching puberty may be the end of a secret dream of growing up to be a boy" (p. 69), while for others refusing to eat may express "antagonism toward menstruation" (p. 80). And many anorexics see their excessive thinness as a way of pleasing their parents, especially the father. But the basic cause is an underlying sense of helplessness and panic in the face of demands for autonomy; it is not a disturbance in sexual identity.

Bruch goes on to point out that many of the symptoms that have traditionally been attributed to unconscious conflicts are actually due to the effects of starvation itself. The literature has examined the physiological effects (Bemis 1978) but has overlooked the pervasive psychological effects—a distorted sense of time, interference with conceptual functioning, and a distortion of both external and internal stimuli. Thus, the anorexic not only has a distorted body image but also overestimates distances and the size of objects as well. And although she almost always says that she cannot eat more than a token morsel because of "feeling full" (p. 86), this feeling does not represent a fear of pregnancy. It is due to a distortion of physical sensations "which expresses the conviction that the mind can do anything and can control the body in every way it wants" (p. 86). As further evidence that fear of pregnancy is not the basic dynamic of the refusal to eat, Bruch notes that several of her patients "had pregnancy fantasies with a positive connotation" (p. 83).

Thus, Bruch agrees with other writers that the central symptom of anorexia nervosa is a refusal to eat. But she does not attribute this refusal to a fear of pregnancy (which may symbolize unconscious oedipal conflicts and rejection of femininity). Nor does she attribute it to a fear of sexual rejection (which may represent a caricature of femininity). Instead, she attributes it to a fear of becoming a teenager, of growing up and becoming autonomous.

Bruch's analysis applies to males as well as to females. Both sexes, after all, may perceive their affluent homes as "golden cages." Both sexes may have a symbiotic relationship with their parents. And both sexes experience increasing demands for autonomy in adolescence. Why, then, are 85 to 95 percent of diagnosed anorexics female? The answer is similar to that for depression: females are encouraged to be more dependent than males. In this sense, then, even Bruch's analysis revolves around sex-role issues, in that traditional femininity is often synonymous with dependency and a lack of assertiveness and autonomy.

Phobias: The Irrational Fears

There are many things to fear in everyday life—being killed by a reckless driver, being raped on a dark city street, becoming ill from eating contaminated food or from touching someone with a highly contagious disease. When a fear swells out of all proportion to the objective danger and causes severe anxiety and involuntary avoidance of an object or situation, however, it is considered a phobia. Both men and women often show such irrational fear and avoidance of some *specific* activity, object, or place, such as heights, thunder, darkness, driving, or certain social activities; but three-quarters of the patients who seek help for a *generalized* fear of open spaces are women. This relatively common female fear is called *"agoraphobia"* (from the Greek *"agora"* for marketplace) and usually affects a number of activities such as shopping, traveling, and social situations. Agoraphobia is usually accompanied by severe anxiety, panic attacks, dizziness, and depression.

Phobias are not associated with any particular bodily malfunction or personality pattern but seem to be due to specific personal experiences and psychological conflicts. Since women with agoraphobia outnumber men by three to one, perhaps there are common female experiences or emotional conflicts that make women more vulnerable to this generalized, irrational fear.

UNRESOLVED OEDIPAL CONFLICTS

Freud attributed phobias to unresolved oedipal conflicts and their accompanying castration anxiety.* These conflicts contribute an anxiety-provoking incestuous tinge to sexual arousal. A woman first tries to put the disturbing sexual arousal out of her mind. When this repression fails, she displaces the sexual conflict from the person who aroused it onto a seemingly unimportant or irrelevant object or situation. This situation then comes to symbolize the sexual conflict, so that contact with it stirs up the repressed feelings of sexual arousal and anxiety. The symbolic object or situation has become the feared and avoided phobic object.

The following case illustrates how this psychoanalytic interpretation is applied to a young woman's phobia of boats, which is attributed to

---

* Freud's final formulation of the phobic neurosis, which he continued to call "anxiety hysteria," was published in 1926 in *Inhibitions, Symptoms and Anxiety,* and it reflects his revision of his earlier idea that repression causes anxiety. These later writings of Freud's suggest that anxiety's major function is to signal the ego to strengthen its defenses against a forbidden unconscious drive that is pushing for conscious expression. Thus, in the end Freud considered anxiety to be the *cause* rather than the *result* of repressive defenses.

her underlying fear of intercourse, which, in turn, is linked to her unconscious sexual desire for her father.

> . . . . she gradually revealed her intense interest in, but fear of, sexuality, which was colored by frightening fantasies of the mutilation of the female genital that, she imagined, resulted from sexual intercourse. . . . [Her phobia] symptoms had started after a brief experimental sexual affair in adolescence that had taken place on her boyfriend's boat. . . . Ultimately, her associations led her back to loving feelings and sexual feelings about her father during her childhood, which at the time had been a source of intense guilt and anxiety. . . . [Thus] because of their association with the sexual activity which had initially aroused her anxiety, boats, through the mechanism of displacement, had come to be the symbol of the patient's sexual conflict. . . . (Nemiah 1975, p. 1237)

Modern psychoanalysts have introduced a new emphasis on preoedipal conflicts in phobic neurosis and now view phobias as expressing not only oedipal sexual conflicts but also preoedipal sex drives (related to the mother), separation anxiety (also usually related to the mother), and aggression. The analysis remains essentially the same as before, however, as we can see in the preceding case history which is taken from the *Comprehensive Textbook of Psychiatry, Second Edition* (1975), which is one of the bibles of modern psychiatry.

CONDITIONED REFLEXES

John B. Watson has applied the principles of stimulus-response conditioning to the development of phobias in suggesting that, when an inherently frightening stimulus occurs simultaneously with a second, inherently neutral stimulus, anxiety aroused by the frightening stimulus becomes associated with the neutral one. The neutral stimulus then arouses the anxiety by itself.

Watson's famous experiment with little Albert is a dramatic illustration of this process (Watson and Rayner 1920). Albert was a healthy eleven-month-old boy who was fond of animals. Watson showed Albert a white rat and, as the boy reached for the animal, struck a steel bar with a hammer behind the boy's head. The loud noise scared Albert and made him cry. After several repetitions of this experience Albert became extremely disturbed at the sight of a white rat even without the loud noise, and his fear spread to include other furry animals and objects as well. The originally neutral—and even enjoyable—white rat had become a feared and avoided object, along with many other things that apparently reminded Albert of the rat.

Deliberate conditioning of fear and avoidance responses in an experiment is extremely rare—and is now strictly controlled by the ethical standards of the American Psychological Association. But everyday life is full of traumas, large and small, that can lead to fear and avoidance of objects and events surrounding the traumatic event. For instance, the following case study shows how, after such a natural trauma, one young woman developed a phobia of large social gatherings:

> The woman was at the Coconut Grove night club in Boston on the night the entire building was destroyed by fire. This fire was one of the worst disasters of the last 30 years, resulting in almost 500 people being burned to death and hundreds of others being seriously injured. Temporarily trapped by the roaring fire, the woman suffered severe burns of her face and hands. Like everybody else who was able to do so, she dashed for the exit, but it was already blocked by other panic-stricken people. The frantic crowd shoved her over the injured and dead bodies in front of the door, until finally she was outside.
>
> In the hospital, she showed the typical symptoms of traumatic neurosis. She complained particularly about anxiety attacks, nightmares, and daytime reveries during which her thoughts involuntarily returned to the disaster. Months later, after recovering physically and being discharged from the hospital, she continued to show symptoms of traumatic neurosis, the most pronounced being phobic reactions (excessive fear and avoidance of situations or objects that are not dangerous). Specifically, she was unable to go to any large gathering place. A sociable person, she attempted repeatedly to overcome this phobia, but each time she suffered overwhelming anxiety attacks. For example, once when she was at a restaurant with her family she suddenly recollected fire breaking out and tables and chairs being tipped over, just as they had in the Coconut Grove disaster, and she had to flee the room, in a frantic state of terror. Another time she attempted to sit through a movie, but she had a similar anxiety attack as she looked at the people sitting around her; again she had to return home. (Janis 1969, pp. 48–49; based on the report by Cobb and Lindemann 1943)

SEX-ROLE CONFLICTS

Iris Fodor (1974) has suggested that female phobias reflect sex-role, rather than unresolved oepidal, conflicts. Her feminist analysis focuses on agoraphobia and maintains that phobic women usually have dependent personality patterns and avoid independent, self-assertive behavior. They have particular difficulty expressing anger, and they fear situations that require them to engage in typically masculine behaviors involving competence, mastery, and competition.

Fodor attributes this dependency to parental treatment, especially by a "smothering mother" who encourages her daughter to be dependent and clinging. This parental treatment is reinforced by the way females are depicted in school readers and in the popular media—as helpless, incompetent, and fearful children who rely on boys, while the boys master fear by contrasting themselves to girls and feeling good about their male superiority.

Fodor presents an agoraphobic woman as being handed from her parents to her husband, who in turn assumes the function of eliciting helpless, dependent behavior from her. After a few years, such a woman often develops a trapped feeling. She wants to become independent but is afraid to leave because she has nowhere to go and lacks the skills to make it on her own. The bottled-up anger and anxiety stemming from this conflict over strivings toward self-assertion, independence, and separation from a protective parent or husband is then expressed in agoraphobia. The woman begins to avoid the (phobic) situation of going out alone.

The feminist analysis of agoraphobia is similar to that of anorexia nervosa in that it does not contest the Freudian idea that the symptom expresses sexual conflict; but it views the *nature* of that conflict as social or sex-role linked: an agoraphobic woman simultaneously wishes for and fears masculine independence and assertiveness, rather than simultaneously wishing for and fearing incestuous sexual intercourse. The feminists also reinterpret the *origin* of the sexual conflict: they see it as due to sex-role socialization rather than to unresolved oedipal desires. The issue, once again, is whether the woman showing phobic symptoms is rejecting her femininity or, on the contrary, has embraced that femininity to an excessive and self-destructive extent.

The Freudian and the feminist interpretations of agoraphobia are clearly incompatible, but they can be based on the same material, as the case of Ethel H. illustrates rather dramatically. This case study was written (and interpreted) in a Freudian manner, yet it is clearly just as amenable to a feminist analysis.

Ethel H., a married woman of twenty-six, had suffered her first acute anxiety attack two years before she began therapy. She was arriving alone by plane from England after visiting her parents there. As she entered the high-ceilinged terminal, where no one met her, she suddenly felt terrified at the huge empty spaciousness. She began "shaking like a leaf"; she could not get her bags through customs without constant help; she had the impulse to tell everyone around who she was in case she went mad. A porter, sensing her anxiety, expressed his concern over her openly and this comforted her. She managed the rest of the trip by train without mishap, but reached home exhausted and unnerved, certain that something awful was happening to her. She told her husband nothing of this when he returned from work because she was afraid of expressing her resentment at not having been met.

During the ensuing two years Ethel felt nervous a great deal of the time, uneasy about driving on parkways and highways, and lonely when walking along strange streets. Then she made another trip to England, intending to stay three months with her parents. As time went on, however, she heard from her husband less and less frequently, while his letters seemed more and more impersonal, until she began to fear that she would lose him. Her fear was confirmed when he finally wrote that he wanted a divorce. Her immediate reaction was to become depressed, to weep bitterly, lose sleep and appetite, and declare that she was alone in the world.

The day after this letter arrived, Ethel was crossing a moor toward dusk when she was suddenly struck by the desolate surroundings. She felt isolated from the world and terribly frightened. She told herself that she might as well be exiled to Siberia as stranded here. Then she became afraid that she would step into a bog and disappear. Her legs were so weak that she could scarcely walk on to the house. Following this experience Ethel could not cross large open spaces anywhere without acute anxiety, unless someone whom she knew accompanied her. She avoided concerts because of the "emptiness" of concert halls. On the advice of a physician friend she returned at once to the United States. At the air terminal she repeated her experience of two years earlier even though this time her sister was there to meet her.

Because of the impending divorce Ethel moved to another city, terminating therapy, which she believed would be unnecessary once the reality situation was cleared up. During the brief period of treatment certain matters of dynamic interest came out. Ethel's feeling of desolation, which now permeated all her thinking, she ascribed not only to her husband's desertion but also to the lifelong neglect of [by] her father. She had always wanted to be close to him but he had never shown a genuine interest in the family. Now, she said, his only concern about her was a worry that her divorce might hurt his professional standing.

Ethel had had earlier phobias which reflected her frustrated unconscious wishes for a father's love. Around pubescence she often dreamed that burglars had broken into her bedroom. She would wake up with the feeling that someone was in the room; she was too frightened then to move, turn over in bed, or even to breathe, for fear of disclosing her position. She was also afraid that somebody was hiding behind the door when she entered a room. She would push the door hard against the wall to make sure before going in. When she was a little girl, Ethel was often frightened that something was in bed with her and creeping up toward her. Whenever this happened she would run to her parents' room for comfort and insist upon sleeping with them the rest of the night. Thus, although the irrational fears in early childhood and pubescence were different in kind, the phobic pattern of defense against desire and loneliness was one that she had used in one form or another most of her life. (Cameron 1963, pp. 291–92)

Sex Roles and the "Female" Illnesses

I have only discussed the major illnesses that are most obviously female in that women are diagnosed as having them far more often than are men.* Clear themes emerge from studying these few illnessses, however. Women suffering from them are likely to be extremely de-

* I have also focused on the ways in which these illnesses reflect sex differences in personality and socialization. For a thorough discussion of all the psychodynamics and treatment issues involved, the reader should consult the clinical literature itself.

pendent, passive, and helpless and to derive a sense of identity only through others—primarily men but also children. In a frantic attempt to please others, some of these women become conventional, martyred caretakers who are then vulnerable to the depression that can accompany the empty nest syndrome. Some become depressed trying to conform to the expectations of their Dominant Other. Some women starve themselves in response to demands for autonomy or in a vain attempt to attain a distorted image of physical beauty that they see as the path to happiness and fulfillment through male attentions. And still other women rely on superficial social charm and emotional appeals to manipulate the men in their lives.

As a group these women tend to shun traditionally masculine behavior involving self-assertion, competition, and mastery. They are especially loath to express their anger: they turn it on themselves in depression or self-starvation; they try to deny and block it out, and hence develop pervasive phobias; or they turn it on others through the subtle manipulations of superficial charm.

The striking thing about all of these women is their extreme—and conflicted—expression of traditionally feminine characteristics. While Freudians interpret their distressing symptoms as a *denial* of femininity stemming from unresolved oedipal conflicts, feminists interpret them as a *caricature* of femininity stemming from socialization pressures and resulting social role conflicts. The Freudians and the feminists appear, however, to agree on one central point: *femininity may be harmful to a woman's health*. The continuing disagreement focuses on whether too little or too much femininity causes the problem.

Chapter 20

Sexism in Therapy

IF PHYLLIS CHESLER is correct in comparing psychotherapy with marriage, there should be evidence of an oppressive, patriarchal bias in treatment methods. Researchers have begun to explore this issue by examining the sex-role attitudes of psychotherapists and how these are expressed in therapy.

Mental Health
as Masculinity

The major research to date has examined the definitions of mental health that are used by practicing clinicians. The classic study was done by Broverman and her colleagues (1970) with seventy-nine clinically trained psychologists, psychiatrists, and social workers twenty-three to fifty-five years old, forty-six of them male and thirty-three female. These clinicians were given a 122-item questionnaire containing thirty-eight sex-role-stereotypic items such as "aggressive," "independent," "hides emotions," "competitive," "acts as leader," "talkative," "tactful," "gentle," "religious," and "expresses tender feelings." Each item had two poles, such as "not at all aggressive" and "very aggressive." The instructions asked the respondents to indicate which pole would be closer for a "mature, healthy, socially competent" adult. One-third of the clinicians filled out the questionnaire for any adult (sex unspecified), one-third for a man, and one-third for a woman.

Broverman found that both male and female clinicians gave the same descriptions for healthy adults and healthy men but described healthy women as differing from healthy men "by being more submissive, less independent, less adventurous, more easily influenced, less aggressive, less competitive, more excitable in minor crises, having their feelings more easily hurt, being more emotional, more conceited about their appearance, less objective, and disliking math and science" (1970, pp. 4–5). The authors go on to say that "this constellation seems a most unusual way of describing any mature, healthy individual." Indeed it is, and it makes us wonder whether this view of female "health" is something women should want to work toward in therapy.

Should I See

a Female Therapist?

The Broverman study is repeatedly used to bolster the argument that women should not see male therapists because the latter impose undesirable and demeaning stereotypes on their female patients. Yet both male and female clinicians described "healthy" women in the same way in Broverman's study, indicating that these sexist stereotypes are shared by clinicians of both sexes, who have of course grown up and worked in the same sexist culture. Thus, Broverman's study does not constitute evidence that only male clinicians impose sex-role stereotypes on patients.

Another study, on the other hand, does suggest that it is primarily male therapists who have an implicitly sexist (and demeaning) view of female health. Alice Aslin (1977) gave Broverman's sex-stereotyping measure to fifty-five male and seventy-five female therapists in community mental health centers and also administered it to eighty-two female therapists who belong to the feminist Association for Women in Psychology. She asked each therapist to complete the questionnaire for a mentally healthy adult, female, wife, or mother. Only the male therapists described healthy adults as different from females, wives, or mothers—and thus expressed a double standard for mental health.

In response to the charge that they are sexist and hence can harm their female patients, many male therapists argue that, on the contrary, *female* therapists are *too* radical for their female patients: by encouraging their female patients to overcome sex-role stereotyping, female therapists may be enforcing sexism in reverse. Some of these male clinicians go even further by saying that it is the sex-role conflicts and underlying doubts about their own femininity that drive these female clinicians to try to convert their female patients to their own career-oriented life styles.

George Stricker (1977), for instance, suggests that female therapists have severe conflicts about their own sex roles, which cause them to misperceive the attitudes of men in general and especially of their male colleagues. He cites the crosscultural research of Anne Steinmann (1974), who found that women see themselves as balanced between self-fulfillment values and family values and want to be in that position. However, women perceive men as wanting them to be much more strongly oriented toward the family and as more passive and submissive than women see themselves, while men themselves actually want women to be balanced between the two orientations much as they actually are. Steinmann found that this discrepancy was heightened in a group of fifty-four feminist psychologists who were not interested in the family, saw themselves as not living up to their ideal of an achieving woman, and perceived men as wanting women to be even more passive than the general female population did (Steinmann and Rappaport 1970). Steinmann felt that the female perceptions of male desires were based on faulty communication and unwarranted mistrust between the sexes and concluded that "taken together, the results of *this* study, compared with those of the national composite, suggest the depth of conflict and confusion in educated feminist women" (Steinmann 1974, p. 66).

Stricker extends Steinmann's viewpoint to the issue of whether female patients should seek out female therapists:

> Thus, for professional women the [sex-role] conflict is strong in reality and even more severe in their perceptions, in that these women feel they do not conform to the ideal of men. This is not to say that male therapists impose these discordant views; in fact, the conflict for the great majority of female patients, if I may extend these data, would lie in their [female] therapists' wishing them to be more self-oriented than they desire for themselves. (1977, p. 19)

Stricker goes on to suggest that "the solution, of course, is that the effective therapist should not impose his [her?] stereotypic views on any of his patients. . . . Rather, each woman should be aided to find her own position of greatest satisfaction and comfort." This is reasonable enough, but his characterization of female therapists as being conflict-ridden smacks of the old Freudian idea of "masculine protest." These uppity women must have an underlying wish to be men, or at least a deep conflict about how to be women, and they are in danger of passing this unnatural enthusiasm for autonomy and achievement on to their female patients. Stricker overlooks the reality issues of male bias and pressures on the job and elsewhere. Female therapists could reasonably be expected to have encountered a lot of these pressures in their own careers and personal lives as well as in the experiences of their patients, and hence to be more rather than less accurate in their perception of male attitudes.

From Stereotypes to Practice:

Sexism on the Couch

Knowing that most male, and some female, therapists harbor sexist and rather derogatory definitions of female mental health does not automatically tell us how this sex-role bias influences their treatment of women. Most writers have simply cited Broverman's results and asserted that they prove the point, without considering exactly how this bias is transmitted to the patient. Others have tried to defend male therapists by arguing that abstract sex-role stereotypes may not be transmitted to the patient at all. These male apologists contend that a professionally trained therapist interacts with each patient as an individual, suspending his views of women in general (Stricker 1977). This argument not only seems unlikely on its face value but is also contradicted by research indicating that a therapist's judgments of improvement in therapy are a function of the extent to which the patient has modified his or her values to be more like those of the therapist (Rosenthal 1955). Other writers have suggested that value shifts are not merely coincidental to therapy but actually constitute a central *aim* of therapy:

> The aim of psychotherapy can be conceptualized, at least in part, as an attempt to bring about value change or value reeducation in a client or patient. . . . If therapy is to be successful, it must surely be manifested as changes or rearrangements of value priorities and as changes in the degree of integration of the client's or patient's value system. (Rokeach 1973, p. 333)

Psychiatrist Seymour Halleck has written extensively about the pervasive influence of a therapist's values upon both the process and the outcome of treatment. He views the problem as one of essentially *political* influence:

> Even if a psychiatrist pretends to be nonpolitical, he is usually influencing his patient to accept the status quo; this, in itself, is a form of political indoctrination. . . . Ultimately, the only protection the patient has is his

knowledge of where the therapist stands politically, of what kinds of therapeutic outcome the therapist would welcome. (Halleck 1971, p. 56)

Halleck suggests that the "therapeutic outcomes" that most therapists would welcome for their female patients actually reinforce female oppression.

> The writings and teachings of psychiatry have helped to provide a rationale for keeping women in a subservient position. The founders of psychoanalysis saw women as basically masochistic and passive—as needing a certain degree of masculine domination in order to feel comfortable and whole. Many outstanding psychiatrists still refer to women in terms of their needs for passivity, to be companions to men, or to be mothers; little mention is made of their need to be active contributors to the larger society. A woman who enters psychotherapy will usually be exposed to a system of values that emphasizes the virtues of passivity; if she rejects these values her therapist may interpret her attitude as immature. (1971, p. 109)

AM I FEMININE ENOUGH?

Can a therapist, as George Stricker suggests, suspend his or her sex-role stereotypes for an individual client? Two researchers tried to answer this question recently by having a man and a woman tape-record an identical interview session in which each expressed concerns about work. Twenty male and twenty female counselors then listened to the tapes; half of the counselors of each sex listened to the male, and half to the female voice. After listening, each counselor rated the client using Broverman's Sex-Role Stereotype Questionnaire. Both male and female counselors rated the female clients as more "masculine" on sixteen of the thirty-seven items—that is, as more aggressive, independent, dominant, competitive, and self-confident; as making decisions more easily; as being less easily influenced, less excitable in minor crises, less gentle, less passive, and less home oriented; and as having less need for security (Hayes and Wolleat 1978).

The researchers suggest that since clinicians view traditional masculinity in males and traditional femininity in females as healthy, perhaps they tend to perceive clients, who have acknowledged some difficulties by seeking treatment, as unhealthy and therefore as deviating from their proper sex-role stereotypes. This reasoning suggests that a woman client may be automatically viewed as sick and hence as too masculine, regardless of individual characteristics and behavior.

On the other hand, the content of the taped interviews may have interacted with the sex-role stereotypes of these clinicians. Since the workplace tends to be viewed as a male domain, a woman expressing work concerns may be viewed as masculinized. (A career woman, after

all, is engaging in "masculine protest.") A man expressing work concerns, on the other hand, may be viewed as having difficulty with his
masculinity, for not only is a career often closely identified with maleness, but also any admission of weakness or personal difficulty is often
viewed as unmanly.

Neither of these interpretations is encouraging, and both suggest
that the sex-role stereotypes of male *and* female clinicians may affect
their perception of potential clients: a woman seeking treatment is unhealthy and hence too masculine, while a man seeking treatment is
unhealthy and hence not masculine enough.

TREATMENT GOALS

After an initial interview the therapist analyzes the client's major
problems, assigning a label or diagnosis for the latter's difficulty or
personality pattern, and assesses what changes are desirable and possible. Then he or she usually outlines one or more goals to work on in
therapy. Here again we have the same question: Are the therapist's own
sex-role stereotypes reflected in this process?

Donna Billingsley (1977) asked this question in a recent study with
sixty-four male and female psychotherapists. She first prepared descriptions of four fictitious clients who displayed two levels of pathology.
Two clients were described as only mildly disturbed, with a recent inability to go to work because of fear of being in a car accident, with
no previous psychiatric problems, and with a general motivation to
understand the symptoms. The second two clients were described as
severely disturbed, with difficulties in all areas of living including
marital problems, a recent job probation for "idiosyncratic behavior,"
persistent mental confusion, potential emotional explosiveness, and a
history of similar difficulties. All four clients were described as being
twenty-five to thirty-five years old and married, while one at each level
of pathology was described as male and one as female. After reading
either two male or two female client descriptions, (one at each level of
pathology), each therapist was asked to choose six initial therapy
goals from a checklist of eighteen items. Half of the eighteen goals were
based on the feminine and half on the masculine items from Broverman's
Sex-Role Stereotype Questionnaire. Other measures were used to assess
each clinician's opinion about diagnosis, degree of severity, and expectations for recovery.

Billingsley found that the sex of the fictitious client had no effect on
treatment goals: women and men showing the same behavior were
seen similarly. The level of pathology was important, however. For the
severely disturbed, explosive client, both male and female clinicians
chose significantly more treatment goals that would increase traditionally
feminine behavior. This study suggests that the degree and nature of

distress, not the sex of the client, determines what will happen in psychotherapy. Perhaps a clinician tends to perceive clients in terms of sex-role stereotypes only when the presenting problems are mild or vague. When the presenting problems are more severe or more clearly delineated, a clinician may focus on the behavioral problem or pathology rather than on the client's sex.

This does not mean that sex-role stereotypes have no impact on treatment goals, for although the *client's sex* had no effect on treatment goals, the *therapist's sex* did. There was a general difference between male and female therapists that cut across level of pathology and sex of client. Female therapists chose a greater number of masculine treatment goals, while male therapists chose a greater number of feminine treatment goals. Thus, these clinicians appeared to be encouraging cross-sex-role behavior in clients of both sexes.

Billingsley suggests that clinicians may consider themselves atypical in terms of sex-role stereotypes. After all, since therapists must be sensitive, nurturant, warm, and emotive ("feminine") as well as independent, assertive, and dominant ("masculine"), they may encourage adoption of their own cross-sex characteristics in their clients. Thus, male therapists may encourage feminine behavior in both males and females. Since most therapists are male and most clients are female, the sex bias found in other studies may simply reflect this tendency to encourage cross-sex behaviors in clients who happen to be female.

We cannot evaluate the idea that a therapist encourages all clients, both male and female, to adopt his or her own cross-sex-role characteristics unless we know the therapist's particular sex-role characteristics and self-perceptions. The tendency to foster cross-sex-role characteristics in clients may have little to do with a clinicians' own self-perceptions but could reflect the power relationships in therapy itself. A male therapist may act more domineering and less emotional in therapy, encouraging his clients (of both sexes) to be submissive, dependent, and emotionally expressive (more "feminine"). A female therapist, on the other hand, may act less domineering and more emotionally expressive in therapy, encouraging her clients (of both sexes) to become equals and act less submissive and dependent (more "masculine").

Of course the use of power within therapy may be related to the personality of the therapist. A male therapist may indeed perceive himself as rather feminine and be defensive about this, leading to a more determined attempt to dominate all his clients. A female therapist, on the other hand, may perceive herself as rather masculine and be defensive about this, leading to an attempt to minimize her dominance over clients. A simpler explanation would link the power aspects of therapeutic relationships to the social roles and the expectations of therapists rather than to their personality characteristics and defenses. Men are expected to be dominant and are accustomed to this role, while women are not. Therapists are no exception and might be expected to carry this behavior into the therapeutic situation.

LENGTH OF TREATMENT

Women tend to stay in treatment longer than men do. Some writers have attributed this difference to the male therapist: he fosters dependency in the female client and may even prolong treatment to indulge his own sexual curiosities (Abramowitz et al. 1976). Should women, then, seek out female therapists to shorten the time in therapy?

Janet Helms (1978) considered length of treatment in a study of actual treatment records of thirty-two university women who saw different counselors for personal-interpersonal, educational, and vocational problems. She found that the female counselors perceived more difficulties in the clients after an initial session and met with them twice as many times as did male counselors (for an average of five to six visits). By comparing her results with those of an earlier study using videotapes of fictitious women with similar problems (Hill et al. 1977), Helms concluded that the female counselors seemed to be completing what would be considered an ideal number of visits. Something seemed to interfere in the interaction between the male therapists and their clients, however. Although Helms does not speculate about the nature of this interference, it could be that the women did not feel comfortable sharing their difficulties with a male; thus, the male therapist would not rate problems as important, and therapy would be terminated prematurely.

Although Helms' study is exploratory and deals with a limited, relatively well-adjusted group of female clients, it does raise an interesting question. As women become more aware of the male bias and dominance embedded in many therapeutic relationships, will they become increasingly reluctant to reveal their personal feelings and problems to male therapists? If so, women may leave therapy early or not become emotionally involved in treatment with a male in the first place. Various authors have suggested that women are indeed beginning to prefer women counselors (Fabrikant 1974; Simons and Helms 1976), and this may well be one of the reasons.

Is Psychotherapy
Always Sexist?

Some feminists conclude that psychotherapy will always compound a woman's suffering rather than relieve it, and warn women that all psychotherapy is hazardous to their health. Other feminists, however, have begun to explore other possibilities for using the knowledge and the skills of psychotherapy in a constructive manner. These efforts involve a redefinition of mental health and a careful examination of the benefits of existing psychotherapeutic techniques.

ANDROGYNY: A NEW DEFINITION OF MENTAL HEALTH

Feminists urge the adoption of "androgyny" as the norm for mental health. Derived from the Greek *andro* for man and *gyne* for woman, androgyny denotes an integration of positive masculine and feminine behaviors or traits. Alexandra Kaplan describes it this way:

> Androgyny . . . signifies behavior that is not delimited or constrained by prevailing sex-role stereotypes about what is or is not proper for each sex. An androgynous woman would respond to any situation in a manner that best meets her personal needs and situational demands, not according to what is best for her simply because she is female. An inherently strong and forceful woman might be tough and insistent with her boss, firm but gentle with her children. A quieter, more emotionally expressive woman would still be able to hold her own when challenged, while being openly tender and loving with those for whom she feels deep affection. Both of these women's styles would be characterized by flexibility and a wide repertoire of behavioral and emotional possibilities from which they might draw. Both would also be free from the extreme caricatures of sex-typed behavior that tend to be manifested when one's options are arbitrarily restricted. (1976, p. 354)*

The idea that an individual can embody both masculine and feminine qualities is not new. Carl Jung (1953) described the *anima* (feminine component) and the *animus* (masculine component) present in us all, and the psychological literature of the last decade is full of references to the concept of androgyny. Janet Spence, for instance, has assessed the way college students describe themselves in terms of characteristics viewed as part of masculine or feminine stereotypes (Spence and Helmreich 1978; Spence, Helmreich and Stapp 1975). She found that scores for both male-valued and female-valued items were positively correlated with a separate measure of self-esteem. Not only were masculinity and femininity in *both* sexes associated with higher self-esteem, but the masculinity and the femininity scores were also positively related to each other. Spence concluded not only that an individual can be both highly masculine and highly feminine, but also that such an androgynous person is likely to view himself or herself more

---

* The model of androgyny applies to both sexes, for men also suffer from rigid sex-role norms and expectations. Since I am concerned with the interaction between the female role and mental health, however, I shall discuss only the androgynous woman.

positively than someone who scores high on only masculinity *or* femininity.

Although the idea that androgyny is *possible* is not new, the claim that androgyny is *essential* to psychological well-being is, however, and reflects the research of Sandra Bem of Stanford University, who devised the Bem Sex-Role Inventory (BSRI).* When describing himself or herself on the BSRI, an "androgynous" person endorses masculine and feminine characteristics equally, while a "feminine" person has a significantly higher score for feminine than masculine items, and a "masculine" person has a significantly higher score for masculine than feminine items. In studies of over two thousand college students, Bem has found that one-third to one-half are androgynous and one-third are sex-typed ("masculine" men and "feminine" women). Less than one-tenth receive higher scores for the characteristics of the opposite sex ("masculine" women and "feminine" men).†

Bem did a series of studies to determine how sex typing on the BSRI was related to actual behavior in a variety of situations. She found that sex-typed individuals were more reluctant to engage in activities commonly associated with the opposite sex and showed more discomfort when they did so. The activities were rather mundane, such as preparing a baby bottle, oiling squeaky hinges, ironing cloth napkins, and nailing two boards together. She then created an experimental situation that assessed resistance to conformity, and found that both masculine and androgynous students (of both sexes) were more nonconforming or "independent' than feminine students.

Finally, Bem devised a series of situations to assess nurturant behavior in the expectation that feminine women would excel. First she observed students playing with a kitten, then with a baby, and finally she asked them to listen to a same-sex student talking about the typical problems of transferring to their school. In all three situations androgynous and feminine men acted more nurturant than masculine men. But

---

* The masculine and feminine adjectives used for self-descriptions in the BSRI are listed in Table 7.1. This list does not include twenty items from the BSRI that are neutral (non-gender-linked), nor does it include the two BSRI adjectives "masculine" and "feminine." The BSRI is often given with instructions to rate the adjectives both for oneself and for a typical man and a typical woman.

† In her early work Bem defined androgyny as a balance between "masculine" and "feminine" characteristics and found that one-third to one-half of her college sample fell in this category. However, Janet Spence (Spence and Helmreich 1978; Spence, Helmreich, and Stapp 1975) has pointed out that people who are high on both masculine and feminine qualities are different from those who are low on both these qualities. Spence argues that only high-highs should be called "androgynous" while low-lows should be called "undifferentiated." Bem (1977) reanalyzed her data using a median split and found that only 24.4 percent are high-highs (29 percent of females and 20 percent of males), while 23.9 percent are actually low-lows (20 percent of females and 27 percent of males). Bem has now come to agree with Spence and would label only one-quarter of her college samples "androgynous."

feminine women did not act more nurturant than either androgynous or masculine women. Androgynous women touched the kitten the most, followed by masculine women; feminine women touched the kitten the *least*. There were no differences among the female groups when playing with the baby. Only when listening to the student did feminine women excel: here they were more attentive and responsive than either androgynous or masculine women.

Bem points out that only androgynous students were capable of acting both independent and nurturant. Nonandrogynous students showed a behavioral deficit of one sort or another: masculine men did well only on the independence task that matched their masculine self-image, while feminine women did well only on the nurturant task that matched their feminine self-image, and even then only under rather limited conditions. It is these limited conditions that particularly concern Bem, for she thinks that the feminine women failed to excel in "nurturing" the kitten and the baby because the expectations and the rewards in these situations were not explicit. In listening to the fellow student, on the other hand, the instructions spelled out what was to be done. As Bem puts it:

> What this pattern suggests to me is that the major effect of femininity in women—untempered by a sufficient level of masculinity—may not be to inhibit instrumental or masculine behaviors per se, but to inhibit any behavior at all in a situation where the "appropriate" behavior is left ambiguous or unspecified. . . .
>
> This leads me to speculate that the feminine woman may be overly concerned about the possible negative consequences of her behavior, regardless of whether that behavior is masculine-instrumental or feminine-expressive. Hence, when it is unclear whether a particular behavior will yield a positive evaluation or a positive outcome, feminine women become inhibited. Either they withdraw from the situation or, if withdrawal is not feasible, they engage in the "safest" behavior or as little behavior as possible. . . . In other words, they take no risks; they play it safe. (1976, p. 59)

"Playing it safe" by doing only what you are sure others want you to do reminds me of the women suffering from the "female illnesses." As a group, these women tend to shun masculine behavior involving self-assertion, competition, mastery, and especially the expression of anger. If striving to be feminine also means avoiding all other behavior that involves taking the initiative and deciding what one wants to do, nothing is left but immobility, dependence, and depression. Thus while femininity is restrictive and may even be harmful to health, androgyny promises a flexibility and range of self-expression that is more fulfilling and hence more healthy.

If mental health were defined in such individual and flexible terms, a woman would no longer be perceived and treated in terms of her degree of femininity, a basic source of sexism would be eliminated from all psychotherapies, and a woman could obtain help with her real social and emotional problems.

THE CREATIVE USE OF POWER

Phyllis Chesler argues that psychotherapy matches and perpetuates women's "one down" position in society by encouraging them to depend on yet another male authority figure: "For most women the psychotherapeutic encounter is just one more instance of an unequal relationship, just one more opportunity to be rewarded for expressing distress and to be 'helped' by being (expertly) dominated" (1971, p. 260).

Other feminists have extended Chesler's argument to all therapists, male or female, and insist that traditional psychotherapies always involve a destructive power relationship that keeps women dependent and helpless. Edna Rawlings and Dianne Carter (1977b) call this therapeutic style "unilateral influence." Using Argyris and Schön's (1975) model of how psychologists *actually* behave, as opposed to how they say they behave, Rawlings and Carter argue that therapists manipulate their clients by defining the problem and therapy goals for them, by suppressing all negative feelings, by providing no valid feedback or information, and by discouraging responses that would challenge the therapist's actions. In other words, the therapist controls the situation, and the client, from a position of professional authority and expertise. The emotional distress that brought the client to therapy makes her particularly susceptible to these power tactics, which play upon feelings of helplessness, dependence, worthlessness, and despair.

This condemnation of professional power and authority stems from the tenets of "radical psychiatry," which blames mental health professionals for "mystifying" or confusing clients about the real social sources of their emotional distress (Wyckoff 1977). Rawlings and Carter state unequivocally that "unilateral control in therapy is incompatible with feminist values" (1977b, p. 41), and advocate an egalitarian relationship between client and therapist where there is "reciprocal influence": decisions are arrived at together, all information and feelings are shared mutually, and the client is encouraged, and expected, to confront and test the therapist's views and opinions.*

Is a therapist's power always destructive, as these writers claim? Or is it an important asset that can be used for the client's benefit? Psychoanalyst Jean Baker Miller takes a positive view of power in therapy when

---

* Although other writers have suggested that the client and the therapist should make a "contract" specifying treatment methods and goals, it is unusual to insist on the desirability (or even the possibility) of establishing a totally egalitarian client-therapist relationship.

she distinguishes between relationships of "permanent inequality" and those of "temporary inequality." In the former, dominance is expected to go on forever and is based on inherent qualities such as race, sex, economic class, nationality, or religion. The dominant group or individual defines social reality in such a way that the subordinate person or group is kept dependent, helpless, and inferior. Relationships of temporary inequality are quite different:

> Here, the lesser party is *socially* defined as unequal. Major examples are the relationships between parents and children, teachers and students, and, possibly, therapists and clients. There are certain assumptions in these relationships which are often not made explicit, nor, in fact, are they carried through. But they are the social structuring of the relationship.
>
> The "superior" party presumably has more of some ability or valuable quality, which she/he is supposed to impart to the "lesser" person. While these abilities vary with the particular relationship, they include emotional maturity, experience in the world, physical skills, a body of knowledge, or the techniques for acquiring certain kinds of knowledge. The superior person is supposed to engage with the lesser in such a way as to bring the lesser member up to full parity; that is, the child is to be helped to become the adult. Such is the overall task of this relationship. The lesser, the child, is to be given to, by the person who presumably has more to give. Although the lesser party often also gives much to the superior, these relationships are *based in service* to the lesser party. That is their *raison d'être*.
>
> It is clear, then, that the paramount goal is to end the relationship; that is, to end the relationship of inequality. The period of disparity is meant to be temporary. (1976, p. 4)

Therapy can thus be viewed as a relationship of temporary inequality. The client seeks out the therapist precisely because the latter is seen as an authority whose expertise the former expects to be beneficial. In the course of successful therapy, the client's initial dependence should be dramatically reduced, so that therapy ends when the client no longer needs the therapist's assistance. Thus, the therapist's power can be used creatively rather than destructively, with the specific purpose of eliminating the client's initial dependence and helplessness.

PSYCHOANALYSIS WITHOUT PENIS ENVY

Is it possible to practice psychoanalysis without assuming that a patient suffers from penis envy? Would such a form of psychoanalysis be nonsexist? Most feminist writers have answered with a resounding *no*, in view of the general conservatism of psychiatrists and psychoanalysts (about 95 percent of whom are male). Recently, however, female psychoanalysts have begun to defend their specialty; they emphasize the value of psychotherapeutic techniques based upon the concept of the unconscious, while calling for a new emphasis upon social factors.*

Feminist revisions of psychoanalysis begin by redefining penis envy as a social rather than a physiological phenomenon: the penis serves as a symbol of the social status and the power of men and hence is desired by women. Rather than interpret hostile and envious comments about men as evidence of a desire to have a penis, which in turn indicates an unresolved oedipal complex, these writers interpret them as a rebellion against the real oppression of women and then go on to emphasize the social factors in female oppression, in order to help women perceive and combat male aggression and dominance in their everyday lives. Feminists point to the crippling effects of female degradation, such as low self-esteem and a weak sense of self, and apply them to uniquely female issues like reproduction, sexual inhibitions, and mother-daughter relationships.

Esther Menaker (1974), for instance, emphasizes the negative, derogatory self-images that are passed down from mother to daughter, and urges female therapists to enhance separation from this negative "introject" and provide a new positive "introject" (that is, object for identification, or role model). Natalie Shainess (1977) presents positive self-assertion as the key to mastering interpersonal situations, and hence life issues, and argues that without self-assertion, a strong sense of self, and equal power in intimate relationships, there can be no "uninhibition" or healthy sexual expression for women.

This new emphasis on cultural factors is fine in and of itself, but it does not solve the problem of male bias. All psychological conflicts are still seen within the context of Freud's theory of psychosexual stages, which make no sense without the concept of penis envy to explain a woman's progress through the psychosexual stages. To redefine penis envy as a social rather than a physiological phenomenon eliminates the force Freudian theory attributes to biology without substituting another cause for female development.

It is extremely difficult for a psychoanalyst to ignore the issues of

* "Psychoanalysis" should be distinguished from the "psychodynamic," "insight-oriented" talking therapies. In psychoanalysis the patient is expected to come in every day and, lying on a couch, to relate dreams, to make free associations to everyday words, and to explore the sexual and emotional relationships of early family life. The psychoanalyst typically says little, leaving the patient free to project on him or her the parental figures who provoked these early emotional reactions ("transference"). In a psychodynamic talking therapy the patient comes in once or occasionally twice a week and sits up to talk about both current and childhood experiences. The therapist is more active here, but both the underlying theory and the techniques are the same. The aim is to uncover unconscious (and primarily oedipal) conflicts that psychoanalysts think cause current emotional distress and distorted relationships. Most attacks on psychoanalysis actually discuss psychodynamic therapy, which is the former's modern, and less expensive, derivative. I shall use the word "psychoanalysis" here to refer broadly to both types of Freudian-based therapy.

penis envy and oedipal conflicts and to focus instead on other unconscious conflicts underlying specific behavior and symptoms. As in the cases of hysteria and phobia, a Freudian cannot assign any diagnosis without simultaneously attributing a host of oedipal conflicts to a patient.

Yet discrete symptoms and behavior can be examined for unconscious determinants without relying on assertions about penis envy and oedipal conflicts. Such an approach would focus on the symbolic quality of a behavior pattern as an indication of unconscious conflicts. The exact nature of the symbols and the corresponding content of the unconscious would be an individual matter, heavily influenced by cultural factors. For example, Alice W. once came to see me and complained of chronic headache for which repeated tests had revealed no physical cause. As she talked about her pain, she spoke of being "confined," "punished," and "helpless." The headache had started about two months before, shortly after her daughter's first birthday. Alice had originally planned to return to work when the girl was six months old, but found that, with her husband's unexpected promotion he was unable to take over the household tasks he had agreed on. Alice was angry, but she felt guilty because they both had hoped so much for this promotion, and his salary was twice what hers had been. Unable to express her anger, she developed the headache. Once her mixed feelings about her situation surfaced, and she was able to discuss the problem with her husband, the headache eased and became intermittent. Here the symptom (headache) has some symbolic aspects that express an unconscious conflict about independence-dependence; the symptom does not necessarily express an unconscious sexual conflict stemming from the oedipal complex.

The exploration of the unconscious determinants of a symptom is a traditional psychoanalytic technique. One of the most widely used psychiatric textbooks provides detailed transcripts of interviews with patients to train therapists in "the faculty of listening attentively to follow 'the red thread of the unconscious' in a patient's verbal productions and behavior." The authors call this method "associative anamnesis" and explain that it is "an interviewing method based on the concept of free associations as used in analysis" and "consists in recording not only what the patient said, but also how he gave the information" (Deutsch and Murphy 1955, pp. 11, 19). Although the interpretations offered in the text rely heavily on Freud's concept of psychosexual stages (and hence on penis envy), the associative technique itself can be used to explore any unconscious material.

We still, however, cannot have a nonsexist psychoanalysis. Specific psychoanalytic techniques based on Freud's concept of the unconscious are amenable to a nonsexist therapy, but psychoanalysis per se is wedded to the broader theoretical framework of the psychosexual stages (and penis envy). Without the psychosexual stages there can be no psychoanalytic interpretations of symptoms and illnesses.

Some clinicians do use Freudian techniques without subscribing to the psychoanalytic interpretation of all symptoms and illnesses and thus may be providing a nonsexist therapy, especially if they are aware of the broader social issues as well as of the subtle influence of sexism and power within the therapeutic relationship itself. These therapists are struggling to develop new theories and techniques that will reflect both the accumulated wisdom of psychoanalysis and more recent information about the psychology of women. At the present time this combination of rigorous traditional training and sensitivity about women's issues in therapy may well offer the best treatment for many women in distress.

THE FEMALE GESTALT

In most people's minds psychotherapy is almost synonymous with psychoanalysis. There are, however, several other therapies that are not based upon Freudian theory—although some of them borrow and adapt aspects of Freud's theory and techniques. For instance, Frederick Perls has extended the principles of gestalt psychology into a special form of psychotherapy (Perls 1969). Gestalt therapy emphasizes the importance of perceiving oneself and one's environment as a unified whole. Life is naturally composed of many polarizations, such as the dichotomies of mind versus body, self versus nonself, conscious versus unconscious, activity versus passivity, and love versus aggression. These splits produce conflict and sometimes immobilization. The purpose of gestalt therapy is to enhance one's awareness of immediate personal experience, which is expected to lead to a natural and healthy integration of opposites within the personality. The focus is on the here and now, on becoming aware of one's own perceptions and conflicting needs. A recent summary of gestalt therapy techniques gives the general flavor of this process:

> The patient is trained to observe himself by bringing his ongoing experience into awareness and keeping it there. . . . Efforts are not directed toward finding out why he experiences what he does but how he does it. The focus is on his behavior at as many levels as possible—all that he is expressing verbally and nonverbally, all indications of avoidance, and, particularly, all discrepancies in different forms of expression as they occur. He may, for example, speak of someone with love but in a hostile tone of voice. . . . Discrepancies of this kind indicate to the therapist that the patient is avoiding part of his actual experience and is thus not responding as a whole person. (Thetford and Schucman 1975, p. 709)

Its proponents think that gestalt therapy is inherently less sexist than psychoanalysis. They argue that its emphasis on the present rather than the past, on how rather than why, and on ways to enhance one's growth are particularly appropriate for women, to say nothing of the fact that it has no complex theory of female personality that begins with the wonders of male anatomy as opposed to the deficits of female anatomy. And the primary goal of self-awareness is crucial for women because:

> In our society men know much more about what they want. They are raised to develop their creative and earning power through education and work. They ask themselves constantly what they want to do with their lives. Women, in contrast, are raised to look for a man! Seldom do they look at themselves as whole, creative persons. Rather, they see themselves fitting into a man's life and career. Our experience in working with many women is that they are out of touch with who they are and what they want from themselves and from others. Our initial task is to help them find this out. (Brien and Sheldon 1977, p. 123)

Once a woman knows what she wants, she still may be reluctant to go after it. Miriam Polster (1974) has outlined a number of ways in which women often keep themselves "stuck," experiencing their present situation as dissatisfying or painful but feeling that there is nothing they can do to change it. They may project outside themselves their unwillingness to change, they may play dumb or be vague to keep themselves unaware of what they do not like about their present situation, they may direct their disapproval of something back onto themselves as inadequate or unworthy, or they may make their goals so grandiose that they cannot get beyond fantasizing and take action. Although men also use this self-defeating behavior, it is reminiscent of the helpless stance ingrained in women through years of striving to be feminine. Gestalt therapy's focus on self-awareness, self-definition, and the elimination of self-destructive tactics may thus make it an appropriate, nonsexist therapy modality for many women.

BEHAVIOR THERAPY FOR WOMEN

In the past twenty-five years the principles of learning theory have been systematically applied to clinical problems and have thus given rise to a cluster of techniques loosely defined as "behavior therapy." This approach involves an examination of symptoms or behaviors that distress the patient, including an analysis of the various situations that elicit the troublesome behavior. A program of positive and negative reinforcements is then designed to change the patient's response to those situations.

Since the social learning theory on which it is based views sex differences as learned behavior, behavior therapy has no theoretical investment in innate sex differences. The analysis and treatment of each symptom are supposed to be determined by each patient's individual needs, not by a social or a psychological definition of what is right or healthy. For this reason behavior therapists maintain that this treatment modality is culturally neutral and hence nonsexist. As Arnold Lazarus puts it:

> Long before it was fashionable to do so, behavior therapists questioned why so many women believe that "femininity" necessarily implies a range of indirect, docile, subservient, emotionally labile, and deliberately inept behaviors. It is unfortunate that we live in a culture that promotes various types of hypocrisy, that discourages personal openness, that favors numerous social inhibitions, and that upholds a tradition of personal dishonesty in the name of tact, or considerateness. Within these corruptive confines, women have the doubly demanding task of skillfully playing these nefarious societal games while pretending to be stupid at the same time.
>
> Therapists (unlike theorists) inevitably place positive or negative value upon various categories of behavior—e.g., adaptive, deviant, asocial, etc. The value judgments of behavior therapy are such that "assertive behavior" is generally preferred over unassertive or submissive behavior—for men and women. There are no double standards. (1974, p. 218)

Having made the point that behavioral theory and techniques are nonsexist, Lazarus goes on to acknowledge that there is more to a therapy session than the mechanical application of reinforcements. An emotional relationship is inevitably established between patient and therapist. And, I might add, this relationship is subject to the same sexist interactions and expectations as all other patient-therapist relationships. In fact, the power aspects of the therapeutic relationship may be even more problematic in behavior therapy than in other therapy modalities, for the therapist administers "reinforcements" to the patient in what Rawlings and Carter (1977b) might call a highly "unilateral" way. The female patient is cast in a relatively passive role as the person who is acted upon. Thus while there is nothing inherently sexist about either the theory or the techniques of behavior therapy, the techniques may inadvertently foster passivity and dependence in the female (and the male) patient.

Behavior therapy is the answer to sexism on the couch only in the sense that the treatment goals are not determined by a sexist theory of femininity. Furthermore, I should note that, aside from the issue of sexism, controversy rages about the long-term effectiveness of this treatment modality. More psychoanalytically oriented therapists charge that when one symptom is eliminated, another will simply take its place, since the underlying emotional conflict causing the symptom has not been dealt with. This charge of "symptom substitution" is still hotly debated. It now appears, however, that relatively discrete symptoms affecting only a limited area of one's life can indeed be removed without another's taking their place. When the behavioral problem is more widespread or severe, however, a more emotionally oriented therapy is probably called for.

ASSERTIVENESS TRAINING

"What do women want?" The answer to this question is getting clearer. Women want both freedom and ability to define themselves in a positive, independent way. They want to be able to express anger as well as warmth, strength as well as gentleness. Yet how are they to achieve these goals after spending years learning to be gracefully compliant? Many writers feel that a woman must learn to assert herself, to insist on her own needs and desires. These writers are careful to distinguish assertiveness both from aggression, which harms others, and from nonassertion, which harms ourselves. As Patricia Ann Jakubowski puts it:

> *Assertion* involves standing up for one's basic interpersonal rights in such a way that the rights of another person are not violated in the process. It is a direct, honest, and appropriate expression of one's thoughts, feelings, and beliefs. In contrast, *aggression* involves standing up for one's rights in such a way that the rights of the other person are violated. It is an attempt to dominate, humiliate, or put the other person down. *Nonassertion* is failing to stand up for one's rights and, consequently, permitting one's rights to be violated by others. It is failing to express one's honest thoughts, feelings, or beliefs, or expressing these in such an anxious, diffident way that permits the other person to disregard them. (1977a, p. 147).

In the past five or ten years assertiveness training (AT) has become a popular fad. Dozens of how-to-assert-yourself books have been published with catchy titles like *Stand Up, Speak Out, Talk Back!*; *I Can If I Want To*; and *Don't Say Yes When You Want to Say No*. Assertion training workshops have sprung up on college campuses and community centers as well as in clinical settings. The variety of techniques used in these training groups seems endless, yet most are actually derived from the learning principles of behavior therapy.

Assertiveness training groups often progress from analysis of personal situations and behavior, through discussion designed to develop a positive attitude toward assertiveness and reduce anxiety about honest self-expression, to role playing of sample situations in order to practice new behavior (Jakubowski 1977b). Behavior therapists use this sequence of self-analysis, discussion, and behavioral practice to treat many different problems. Assertiveness training thus resembles a limited behavior therapy, in which standard techniques are applied to one specific problem in a group setting. When a behavior therapist works with a woman who needs to assert herself, the treatment seems indistinguishable from assertion training, as in the following report:

The wife of a wealthy lawyer was rendered miserable by the fact that her husband refused to allow her to pursue part-time work. She desired to escape from "domestic drudgery" for a few hours each day, but her husband stubbornly insisted that her place was in the home and glibly argued down her objections and protestations. He refused an invitation to discuss matters with the therapist on the grounds that he was too busy. A program of behavior rehearsal remedied the situation after three sessions. The therapist role-played the husband and easily argued down the wife's pleadings and protests. The dialogue was tape-recorded, and the playback was described by the client as "typical of our arguments at home." The therapist played the tape again, stopped it at judicious points, and suggested appropriate rejoinders that the client might have inserted. The scene was rehearsed several times. Occasionally the therapist modeled appropriate responses by playing the client's role. After the third session, the therapist was unable to win the argument by means of rhetoric or verbal abuse. The client was then pronounced capable of confronting her husband. At the next session she reported having won his consent and duly obtained part-time employment. The husband, in turn, reduced dissonance by outspokenly supporting the virtues of "working wives." (Lazarus 1968, p. 53)

In spite of its growing popularity, assertiveness training has its critics. Clinicians worry that its goals are the same for everyone rather than being individualized as goals are in behavior therapy. Although many women need to become more assertive, some need to develop other new behavior as well. Other clinicians feel that underlying emotional conflicts need to be dealt with before significant change can take place (a criticism leveled at behavior therapy as well as assertiveness training).

Another major difficulty stems from the fact that once a woman learns to act more assertive, her social environment does not necessarily change. Her self-assertion may be perceived as aggression and hence as inappropriately masculine behavior, leading to a whole new set of social and emotional problems for her.

From a political point of view AT seems to promise individual solutions to group problems. Leigh Marlowe (1978) has elaborated on this criticism, charging that AT expresses a number of dangerously incorrect political attitudes. First, it "blames the victim" by implying that women are imposed upon because they do not have the right behavioral techniques, not because they are part of an oppressed group. Second, AT tends to create the illusion of "tokens," women who have beaten an oppressive, sexist system through their clever self-assertive techniques. And third, AT offers an "interpersonal fix": it sells the illusion that by changing interpersonal relationships a woman will change her second-class status. Many feminists would agree with Marlowe's characterization of AT as a "quick shrink" that fails to offer the profound emotional growth of psychotherapy while undercutting political activism.

Chapter 21

Feminist Therapy:

The Radical Alternative

IF TRADITIONAL PSYCHOTHERAPY is pervasively sexist, perhaps we should discard it entirely and establish a new therapy for women. A number of people advocate such a "feminist therapy" as one radical alternative to the mental health establishment. Although the precise definition of this therapy varies, the central themes reflect the major criticisms of traditional psychotherapy.

Feminist versus Nonsexist Therapy

Feminist therapy incorporates the political tenets of feminism, whereas nonsexist therapy merely eliminates sex-role bias without adding any new political elements. Edna Rawlings and Dianne Carter state this difference clearly:

> Although feminist and nonsexist therapies are often used interchangeably, we make a distinction between the two. The major distinction is that feminist therapy incorporates the political values and philosophy of fem-

inism from the women's movement in its therapeutic values and strategies while nonsexist therapy does not. Feminism insists that (1) males and females should have equal opportunities for gaining personal, political-institutional, *and* economic power; and that (2) interaction between persons should be egalitarian. Feminist therapists, therefore, are intolerant of the mysticism and authoritarian power of traditional therapists. Nonsexist therapists may function in an egalitarian model also, but they do so from humanistic motivations and not, as feminist therapists, from a political position. (1977a, p. 50)

In other words, although an individual therapist may be a feminist, she practices feminist therapy only when she brings her politics into the therapy session.

Although there is quite a range of opinion and belief within the Women's Movement, discussions of feminist therapy usually focus on several key elements, which are expressed in the values and assumptions of feminist therapy as summarized by Carter and Rawlings. Their major points are:

1. The inferior status of women is due to their having less political and economic power than men. Feminists all agree that the basic problem is the power differential between males and females. However, they disagree on which social factors account for the power difference.
2. A feminist therapist does not value an upper- or middle-class client more than a working-class client.
3. The primary source of women's pathology is social, not personal: external, not internal.
4. The focus on environmental stress as a major source of pathology is not used as an avenue of escape from individual responsibility.
5. Feminist therapy is opposed to personal adjustment to social conditions; the goal is social and political change.
6. Other women are not the enemy.
7. Men are not the enemy either. [Although] some radical feminists do identify men as the enemy . . . both sexes are victims of sex-role socialization. There are many negative aspects to the male sex role. . . . However, since men benefit more from sexism than women do and since most men are loath to give up their position of privilege, women cannot count on help from men in changing the social role system. Women will have to liberate themselves.
8. Women must be economically and psychologically autonomous.
9. Relationships of friendship, love, and marriage should be equal in personal power.
10. Major differences between "appropriate" sex-role behaviors must disappear. This is necessary in order to avoid sex-role expectations and stereotyping. Sex-roles should become androgynous.

(Rawlings and Carter 1977a, pp. 54–57)

Feminist therapy has not developed any new therapeutic techniques; rather, each therapist chooses existing methods that are compatible with

feminist political values. Several surveys of women who claim to practice feminist therapy show that they use a wide variety of techniques
(DuBois 1976; Brodsky et al. 1975; Thomas 1977); but they have common aims: to get rid of power and dependence, to share uniquely female experiences with other women, and to change the political and
social environment.*

Let Us Dispense with Power

One of the central tenets of feminist therapy is that the therapeutic
relationship should not involve power. A therapist should neither be a
patriarch nor dominate or intimidate a client. Women have been trained
to be helpless and dependent; the last thing they need is to have their
dependence encouraged and prolonged in therapy. Many feminist therapy
techniques and practices reflect this theme.

EQUALIZING STRATEGIES

A number of suggestions derive from the idea that the client knows
herself best. The therapist should not "mystify" or confuse her by
using psychological jargon, should avoid psychological tests and diagnostic labels that are dehumanizing and sexually biased, and should
offer no interpretations of the client's behavior based on these technical
ideas. The client should have access to her own records and be encouraged to discuss them with the therapist. At the beginning of treatment a contract should be made specifying what the client's goals are
and how she plans to attain them; in this way the therapist is less likely
to impose her own values and goals on the client. Group, rather than
individual, treatment is often recommended, since it dilutes the client's
dependence on the therapist and encourages trusting, helpful relationships with other women. The language of therapy should reflect the
equality of the relationship: "client" rather than "patient" should be
used, and the therapist should usually be addressed by her first name.

POWER VERSUS AUTHORITY AND EXPERTISE

Many therapists I have talked with feel that since social science and
the mental health establishment are sexually biased and dominated by

---

* Although some male therapists follow the tenets of feminist therapy, many
feminists feel that women should see only female therapists and couch their discussions of feminist therapy in female terms. I have followed this convention in my
discussion by referring to all therapists as female.

men, technical training in psychotherapy should be eschewed. These therapists maintain that women need to develop entirely new ideas and treatment methods that reflect the more helpful, egalitarian nature of woman-to-woman relationships. I feel this course would be more harmful than not, however, for there is much we can learn about the human personality from such training.

It is also necessary to distinguish between authority derived from technical expertise and power derived from interpersonal dominance. A woman in emotional distress goes to a particular therapist as to an expert knowledgeable enough to help her. Since expectation of recovery is one of the most important factors in progress in psychotherapy, it seems both naive and foolish to discard the therapist's authority and expertise.

It is better not to attempt to eliminate the therapist's power entirely. If a therapist does not exaggerate the power difference, then she can use her initial power to bring the client up rather than to put her down, as Jean Baker Miller (1976) suggests in her discussion of relationships of "temporary inequality."

If the therapist is indeed inherently powerful, it can even be dangerous to pretend that the client-therapist relationship is totally equal. Female therapists who are uncomfortable with a position of authority are not necessarily any the less caught up in the joys of power than a man is, and may be less alert to its effects upon the therapy. Better to acknowledge and discuss power openly with the client, and thereby give her a chance to examine how she relates to authority figures and how she can begin to become less dependent and subordinate.

Self-Disclosure: Therapists

Talk about Themselves

Many radical feminists maintain that therapists should be willing to answer any questions about their politics or personal lives. In part, they are rebelling against the haughty "Um hmmm" of the traditional, opaque therapist who, they feel, is guarding her position of authority and control. This approach also reflects a strong feeling that a woman in distress needs role models to help her visualize how to deal with her own personal problems. There are some difficulties with this approach, however. The therapist, given her acknowledged power, may inadvertently influence the client and produce a carbon copy of herself. Freudians would add that an opaque therapist offers a client the opportunity for "transference."

Some radical feminists go further and argue that the therapist should volunteer information about herself rather than wait to be asked. This argument usually refers to the therapist's political views and reflects the assumption that bias is less potent when it is stated openly. Rawlings and Carter (1977a), for instance, state that the therapist should explain her own values right away, only holding off a session or two if the client is in a crisis. Whether the information volunteered is personal or political, the same problem arises: Is the therapist abusing her authority by inadvertently suggesting herself as a role model to the client?

There is also the danger that the therapist (being only human) will occasionally forget that a session is the client's. I have heard many complaints from women who went to a radical therapist and sometimes found themselves listening to her more than to themselves. After a while they stopped going, feeling that the therapist should be paying them rather than vice versa.

Rawlings and Carter go on to say that the therapist herself must be politically active and urge the client to be also. Not only do I wonder whether this might be coercive, but I also wonder why therapy cannot be seen as a political contribution in itself. Women in severe distress are seldom able to be productive. By helping others clarify their goals and deal with their emotional problems, the therapist can be seen as making a valid (although invisible) contribution to the intentions and the ideals of the Women's Movement. It seems unrealistic to expect everyone, whether therapist or client, to have the time or the inclination to be an organizer or an activist.

Who Can Be a

Feminist Therapist?

With their emphasis on role models, sharing common female experiences, and avoiding interpersonal dominance, it comes as no surprise that most feminist therapists insist that women should be treated by other women. This principle is sometimes extended further: women for women, gays for gays, black for blacks. . . . The assumption is that client-therapist similarity will enable the therapist to empathize with the client more readily, and will enhance an egalitarian relationship. This assumption is supported by clinical research: greater similarity in demographic variables (age, socioeconomic status, and ethnic group) does improve therapeutic outcome. Similarity implies not only common experience but a shared value system as well.

Some feminists are more extreme and maintain that a woman should *never* see a male therapist because he cannot serve as a role model and he automatically elicits subordinate behavior (Chesler 1972). Other writers have pointed out that while shared experience is beneficial in short-term therapy, in more emotionally absorbing long-term therapy the sex of the therapist is not as important (Goz 1973). Even those holding a more moderate position would probably agree, however, with Rawlings and Carter's unequivocal statement that men should never lead all-female therapy groups because this reinforces dependence and competition for male attention.

A Sliding Scale of Fees:

Serving Those in Need

It is an established fact that while poverty increases the probability of emotional distress and illness, it also diminishes the availability of treatment (Srole et al. 1962). Only the relatively well-to-do can afford private therapy in the United States today. Radical feminists have responded to this problem by suggesting that therapists charge a client according to his or her ability to pay. To make therapy available to all women, fees should be as low as possible.

Traditional therapists, on the other hand, staunchly maintain that it is therapeutic for a client to pay high fees. In our money-oriented society one values only what one pays (dearly) for. Furthermore, paying a high fee demonstrates that one takes therapy seriously and feels one's personal growth is important. High fees thus make one work harder and progress faster in therapy. Many feminists discount these arguments as mere justifications for greed.

Money is a touchy subject in our society because it symbolizes so many things—including power, independence, and self-worth as well as dirtiness and greed. Therapists of all types sometimes feel guilty because they make their living from other people's suffering and are paid for emotionally nurturant behavior that should, ideally, be free. Feminists sometimes labor under the additional fear of "ripping off" their sisters.

The symbolic quality of money has implications for the authority, prestige, and self-worth of the female therapist. A woman who charges low fees may be perceived as less expert and powerful, which can limit her usefulness as a role model for female clients. Charging unusually low fees may also have an adverse effect on the therapist herself: she may come to feel that she is not really worth the usual, higher fees. At the same time the therapist may feel uncomfortable with her own authoritative role and hesitate to charge higher fees. These emotional issues are not unique to female therapists. All mental-health professionals experience conflicts about charging money for their services; but these conflicts may be particularly severe for female therapists, especially ones who think of themselves as feminists and believe in the egalitarian philosophy of the Women's Movement.

At a 1978 conference on feminist psychology, women from several therapy collectives tried to grapple with this problem. While they still felt strongly that therapy should be available to all women, they were growing tired of living hand-to-mouth themselves. The clients, they felt, did sometimes tend to denigrate the value of such cheap therapy, while the therapists felt that their work was innovative and valuable and should be compensated in a way similar to that of other professionals. The problem was complicated by the fact that many of the therapists in these alternative settings did not have the traditional training or credentials that would make insurance payments possible and would also enhance the therapists' prestige and acceptability in parts of the community (including the feminist community). As a temporary solution, these therapists decided to extend the high end of their sliding scale and to insist that women who could afford it should pay more.

Further Controversy

There is really no one feminist therapy. I have presented here a composite of many different points of view. Any individual feminist therapist would agree with some points and object to others. As therapists struggle to find ways to integrate their professional work with their feminist convictions, controversies and questions abound. Let us take a look at some of the major criticisms that may not be popular but are certainly important.

PSYCHOTHERAPY AS SCIENTIFIC OR POLITICAL

The idea that psychology and the other social sciences have unstated political biases and assumptions is not unique to feminist therapy. Nor is the idea that society causes mental illness; so that if people are freed from coercive social pressures, their natural psychological health will emerge. These ideas are also expressed in the antiestablishment stance of radical psychiatry and in the self-actualizing notions of humanistic psychology and the human potential movement.

These other movements also view much of professional training as social indoctrination rather than as the acquisition of technical knowledge, and condemn diagnostic labeling as inaccurate and stigmatizing. Thus, we can ask them also whether effective treatment is possible without some type of diagnosis, focused either on specific individual behavior per se or on theoretical interpretations of those kinds of behavior that use social role analysis or psychoanalytic concepts. And in considering all these movements, we may wonder whether it is effective or even safe to ignore the unconscious determinants of emotions and behavior and to focus solely on the client's stated understanding of her own difficulties.

Feminist therapy does raise some unique therapeutic issues that reflect this view of science and psychology, however. One particularly troublesome idea is that political ideology is more important than any other aspect of therapy. When asked where women should seek help, many feminist therapists say that if forced to choose they would send someone to a poorly trained feminist therapist rather than to a well-trained but politically conservative therapist. Rawlings and Carter, for instance, state:

> . . . An ineffective therapist with nonsexist or feminist values will do minimum harm to female clients. In contrast, a skillful sexist therapist can do a great deal of damage to women. . . . Feminists believe that skill, expertise, and a commitment to a feminist philosophy are more important credentials than formal degrees and titles. (This attitude is consistent with the egalitarian philosophy of feminism.) Therefore, having a professional degree is not a sufficient qualification nor is believing that women and men should be equal. Commitment to the principles of feminism is suspect if a therapist does not apply feminist principles to her/his personal as well as her/his professional life. Any therapist, female or male, is not qualified to treat women if s/he does not read the literature by women concerned with feminist issues and the subtle oppressions women experience. In addition, a therapist is not qualified to treat women unless s/he has participated in a consciousness-raising group. (1977a, pp. 58, 70–71)

Psychotherapy is an intense experience that can cause dramatic personal change in both a positive *and* a negative direction. Technical training sensitizes the therapist to subtle changes in the client and in the therapeutic relationship. For instance, willing power away is seldom sufficient; one needs skill and experience to make it happen. Furthermore, women who seek therapy are sometimes in severe crisis and need immediate—and expert—help. If they are seriously suicidal or mentally confused, medication and occasionally hospitalization are indicated. Formal degrees and titles are not merely status symbols; they do indicate specialized training in both crisis intervention and long-term therapy. Every therapist knows horror stories about patients who have seen well-meaning but incompetent therapists. These therapeutic casualties warn many of us against a cavalier dismissal of technical expertise.

I should also note in passing that although many psychological tests that analyze personality structure and functioning are indeed sexist, those that are designed to detect physical problems are not. Some tests, for instance, use the drawing of geometric shapes to detect possible brain damage. It would be irresponsible, to say the least, to fail to administer these tests when they are indicated merely because other psychological tests are sexist. Moreover, even tests with sexually biased scoring procedures can be interpreted in a nonsexist manner by trained clinicians. Rather than dismiss all diagnostic testing as part of an oppressive, sexist labeling system, we need to differentiate the tests that are simply sexist and stigmatizing from the tests that are nonsexist and essential to accurate determination of appropriate treatment methods.

In talking with feminist therapists, I also formed the impression that many of them view therapy as a special kind of friendship. Although many people seek out a therapist where once they would have talked with a friend or a relative, talking with a therapist is not just like talking with either. Therapy is a unique relationship which is both caring and businesslike. The client and the therapist have a common goal: to work on the *client's* problems. They are not to work on the therapist's problems nor to become involved in a social, an emotional, or a sexual relationship outside the therapy hour. Therapy is a one-way relationship, not a two-way one. If the nonreciprocal and working nature of the relationship is ignored or minimized, the client may not be free to concentrate on herself; she may feel that she has to take care of the therapist just when she herself is most needy. The therapist, on the other hand, may become too emotionally involved to be objective and to carry out the confrontations and other work of therapy.

INDIVIDUAL VERSUS POLITICAL GOALS

"Feminist therapy is opposed to personal adjustment to social conditions; the goal is social and political change." This statement by Rawlings and Carter (1977a, p. 56) sounds fine in the abstract, but how does it relate to the problems of an individual client? If a woman's emotional distress is caused by social conditions, only changing those social conditions will ultimately eliminate the distress. But each woman has to live her life day to day. The individual woman entering therapy needs to find some individual solution or compromise now; she cannot wait for the revolution to end her depression or her self-destructive behavior patterns.

Furthermore, the client may want to work toward a solution that a feminist would not perceive as liberated or androgynous. Some radical therapists would refuse to work on such nonfeminist goals. Hogie

Wyckoff, for instance, says, "An example of a contract I would not agree to is: 'I want to learn to be satisfied with being a housewife' " (Wyckoff 1977, p. 392).

Feminist therapy, then, is not appropriate for all women. Although many feminists do not acknowledge that this is so, others would agree with Rawlings and Carter's more moderate position:

> In regarding feminist and nonsexist therapies as different, we do not imply that one is better than the other. Rather, we believe that one may be more appropriate than the other, depending upon the client. Nonsexist therapy should be used with traditional female clients for whom the tenets of feminism are threatening; feminist therapy should be used for female clients who are dissatisfied with the constriction of the culturally defined role for women and are seeking alternatives. . . .
>
> The higher the woman's level of consciousness, the more appropriate feminist therapy is for her. As a woman's consciousness develops, treatment may evolve from nonsexist to feminist therapy. Good therapy always starts where the client is and keeps pace with her progress. (1977a, pp. 50–51)

I would certainly agree that therapy should begin where the client is. But I would add that it should also move toward where she wants to go. Although psychotherapy certainly has political biases and undercurrents, just like other social institutions, its primary purpose is to help the individual client with her personal problems.

Chapter 22

Therapeutic Aspects

of Consciousness-

Raising Groups

M ANY FEMINISTS are now suggesting that, to solve her personal problems, a woman should join one of the all-female consciousness-raising (CR) groups, which have been a vital part of the Women's Movement for the past ten years. A group usually has four to twelve members who meet in each other's homes once a week for anywhere from two to four hours, and is either organized by an existing women's group, such as the National Organization for Women (NOW) or a local women's center, or established by word of mouth among a group of women who already know each other. In order to stress the unity of all women, many CR groups strive for a diverse membership that varies in age, race, class, education, work experience, marital status, and sexual orientation (gay or straight). Although some focus on specific areas, such as the problems of widows or divorced women with children, most discuss the general topic of women's experiences and women's roles in the current cultural context.

In keeping with the norm of egalitarianism, most CR groups are leaderless. Sometimes a woman who has been in a CR group before meets with a new group a few times to help it get started. After that the members are on their own. This emphasis on self-direction makes for great diversity among CR groups; but common to both structure and discussion topics, however, is the unifying philosophy of feminism and the suggested guidelines published by the Women's Movement. Barbara Kirsh describes the essence of the CR experience:

> Political and social realizations arise in interaction with the telling of personal experiences and feelings. Each woman must view herself as an "authority" since she knows her own experience best; the ideology of the group is developed as an outcome of personal experience—thus, the popular slogan that "the personal is political." This process is akin to R. D. Laing's (1967) "politics of experience."
>
> Some norms that commonly evolve in rap groups include allowing a member to speak without interruption and without criticism; not dwelling on personal problems without generalizing the source or manifestation of the problem to the rest of the group and other women; not dominating the discussion or competing for speaking time; feeling that the group is important enough to arrive on time and only miss meetings for valid reasons; being tolerant of other group members' feelings, different life-styles and backgrounds; being supportive of the other women and yet not offering specific advice.
>
> The discussion topics are sometimes decided upon a week in advance, or they can appear spontaneously at a meeting if a woman presents an issue of personal importance that arose during the week. Some guidelines for rap groups that circulate in women's movement publications offer topic suggestions. Examples of discussion starters are the following: what do you like most and least about being a woman; do you interact differently with men than with women; do you compete with women; how did you learn about sex and what were your first sexual experiences; what would you like to be and what would you like to change about yourself; when did you first perceive discrimination and when do you experience it now; what is the division of labor in your family? (Kirsh 1974, pp. 342–43)

All CR groups insist on confidentiality: nothing said in a group is to be shared outside, either during or after its life span. In the first few months the members share personal experiences and begin to establish mutual trust and a feeling of intense emotional closeness. As the members become comfortable with each other, the focus gradually shifts from individual experiences to shared group experiences. The members find that women can indeed work together and like each other, that deep friendships with other women are possible and rewarding, and that their self-doubts and frustrations are shared by others. This sharing makes them realize that they are "normal," that their problems are due to social pressures stemming from sexism rather than to personal short-comings or "craziness."

Common group experiences lead naturally to discussions of the general position of women in society. In the process of these discussions many women become increasingly angry at the innumerable manifestations of sexual bias and discrimination. They become more and more sensitive to the way women are portrayed on television and in textbooks, to the male-biased nature of our language and art forms, and to the way they themselves are treated at work, at home, and on the street. Cary Cherniss calls this "finding one's anger" and suggests that a woman usually goes through a period of catharsis, after which she turns her energies to changing herself and society (1972, p. 121). Although people outside the Women's Movement often claim that CR arouses anger, women who have been through CR report that it merely frees them to recognize anger they once ignored or repressed. One woman put it this way:

> A common complaint about women's groups is that they make women angry. My own experience is that the group didn't "make" me angry. It just helped me discover that I was. I had told myself I felt depressed. Now I have some sense of being angry and can begin to ask myself what I'm angry about and work on the problem. (Quoted in Whiteley 1973, p. 42)

Annette Brodsky (1977) suggests that this anger is aroused when the women try to transfer their newly learned behavior and attitudes outside the group, only to find that nothing out there has changed. Employers, friends, families, and lovers continue to act in the old chauvinistic ways. Anger is sometimes followed by depression and withdrawal from the CR group. If the group can weather this period of frustration, however, it usually passes into the last stage of its development when it makes concerted plans to change society.

A group thus begins with discussion of personal experiences of being female, progresses to discussion of common group experiences, goes on to analyze broad societal issues and institutions, and finally passes into a stage of political activism. These stages overlap, and not all groups conclude by planning political action. My impression is that most groups that are successful in establishing the initial feelings of trust and closeness last anywhere from three to eighteen months; ones that last longer usually make the transition from personal discussion to group activism.*

---

* A number of personal accounts of the CR experience are now available, such as *Woman's Fate: Raps from a Feminist Consciousness-raising Group* by Claudia Dreifus (New York: Bantam Books, 1973). I should note that the National Organization for Women has developed a more structured method of running CR groups, which involves a recognized and trained leader, specific discussion topics, and a ten-week time period. These groups are described in NOW's pamphlet, *Guidelines to Feminist Consciousness Raising*, prepared by Harriet Perl and Gay Abarbanell (Perl and Abarbanell 1976).

The Self-Help Movement
in Mental Health

Over the past decade people with similar emotional and behavioral problems have begun to organize their own support groups, which are usually modeled after Alcoholics Anonymous (Schizophrenics Anonymous, Weight Watchers Anonymous, and Gamblers Anonymous) and focus on specific problems for which traditional psychotherapy has proved ineffective, such as drug addiction, alcoholism, gambling, over-eating, and smoking. The loosely defined self-help movement charges that the mental-health establishment is oppressive, stigmatizing, and ineffective, and it advocates reliance on the support, encouragement, and example offered by more experienced group members who share one's personal experience of distress.

Irvin Yalom's analysis suggests that shared experience is crucial to these groups (Lieberman, Yalom, and Miles 1973; Yalom 1975). The members find that they are not alone, they share information about how to manage from day to day, and they learn to view endurance and recovery as possible. They imitate the strategies of their successful colleagues and practice new kinds of social behavior within the group. In the process of group give-and-take they become less self-absorbed and find that they have something to offer, that their problem does not make them worthless. And they develop a shared rationale for the source of common difficulties and for the best procedures for over-coming them. The result is to enhance a group member's self-respect, confidence, and determination, which in turn assist in his or her recovery.

CR groups have much in common with these self-help groups, including a general condemnation of the mental-health establishment as oppressive, a common group philosophy regarding the source of members' problems, an opposition to hierarchical relationships, and a primary focus on shared personal experience. The mechanisms of individual change are therefore similar in CR and other self-help groups. This does not, however, make CR (or other self-help groups) identical to group psychotherapy.

CR versus Group Psychotherapy

CR differs from group psychotherapy both in purpose and structure. As Barbara Kirsh puts it:

> The basic difference in the structures is that the patient-therapist relationship is unequal and hierarchical, contrasted with the peer equality among women in consciousness-raising groups. The basic difference in

the ideologies is that traditional psychotherapy stresses adjusting the inner workings of individuals to fit society; consciousness-raising groups emphasize the need to change society by showing individuals that their "personal" problems are rooted in sociocultural phenomena. . . .

[In psychotherapy] the woman expresses her dissatisfactions or unhappiness to the male authority and asks for his help. Her frustrations are kept under control by the interpretation that they are symptoms of a personal "mental illness"; no comparison with other women's problems is made and organization to change objective social conditions is not considered. The therapist traditionally reinforces talking rather than motivation for social action as a cure. (1974, pp. 336–37)

Kirsh goes on to say that the purpose of CR is to resolve role conflict and to enhance a woman's motivation to change both herself and society. The purpose is not to clarify and eliminate other emotional difficulties a woman may have.

These basic differences in structure and ideology from group psychotherapy have implications for the personal interactions and the mechanisms of individual change in the CR group. While Yalom points out that the processes found in self-help groups operate in the initial stages of group psychotherapy, therapy groups also enhance individual change through "interpersonal learning" and "group cohesiveness" (1975, pp. 19ff, 45ff). Interpersonal learning in group therapy relies on the view of the group as a social microcosm representing an individual's typical interactions in the world at large. A group member goes through a sequence where he or she does or says something, receives feedback from the others about the appropriateness of that behavior and its impact on their feelings and opinions, and alters his or her behavior and self-perception. Much discussion centers around the group interactions, with accompanying emotional arousal and expression. The individual gradually becomes aware of what he or she does, takes responsibility for it, and tries to change. Individual change thus evolves through cycles of interpersonal learning in an emotionally charged but supportive environment which is representative of everyday life.

Yalom (1975) describes group therapy as a "corrective emotional experience" which relies on a combination of intellectual insight into personal motivations and emotional arousal through here-and-now interactions (pp. 25ff). Transference is also involved in the working through of interpersonal distortions, especially those related to perception of the therapist and of other authority figures (p. 41). The individual relives earlier emotional experiences, such as the competition among group members that echoes sibling rivalry for parental love and attention. In the group, early experiences are clarified and their accompanying emotions neutralized, so that the member can learn to deal with analogous situations in a more realistic, mature manner.

"Group cohesiveness" is the rather vague term that Yalom uses to refer to the sense of belonging which keeps people in the therapy group. He points out that while group cohesiveness does not cause individual change, it is a necessary condition for other "curative factors" such as interpersonal learning. Cohesive groups are able to express both intermember hostility and hostility toward the group leader. This expression is important because it demonstrates that anger does not destroy other members or the group itself; on the contrary, it increases group cohesiveness and frees the members to feel and express positive, warm emotions for each other. If anger and hostility are not expressed openly, they become suppressed, resulting in a "creeping irritation" within each member or toward the group and often emerging in attacks on convenient scapegoats such as another group member or outside people or institutions (p. 65).

How does CR compare with Yalom's description of group therapy? First of all, CR does not begin with the assumption that the group represents society as a whole. On the contrary, relationships and interactions in the group are viewed as atypical: only here do women discover the positive value and support of women-to-women relationships. Furthermore, the focus on social institutions and sexism as the source of female personality and behavior implies a corresponding emphasis on changing society rather than the individual. Although women in CR groups strive to become less sexist and less restricted by the demands of femininity, their primary purpose is not to reexamine their personal relationships and feelings. Finally, the norm of nonconfrontation in CR combines with the societal focus to inhibit discussion and emotional arousal about the personal interactions within the group. Although CR emphasizes warm, helpful women-to-women relationships, it does not give equal latitude to examining the more uncomfortable or destructive aspects of group interactions.

To put it in Yalom's terms, CR is not a "corrective emotional experience." There is little or no emphasis on correcting interpersonal distortions ("transference") by reliving analogous situations in a positive manner, or on the individual's feelings or behavior within the group. Although each woman does receive feedback in CR, this feedback is focused on the relationship between personal experience and sexism rather than on the relationships among personal experience, behavior, and interactions within the group. CR participants develop strong feelings of belonging or "cohesiveness" but seldom either examine them for their own sake or express their "negative," hostile aspects. What-ever hostility and anger is felt within the CR group is likely to be expressed outward, toward institutions reinforcing sexism in society. While traditional therapists would view as displacement or "scapegoating" this turning outward of anger, feminists view it as one of the most distinctive and valuable aspects of CR, an important antidote to the tendency of traditional psychotherapy to encourage women to continue turning their anger inward against themselves.

Personal Change
Through CR

Although CR is clearly not the same as group therapy, it can be therapeutic—when "therapeutic" is defined as facilitating positive personal change and growth rather than as "curing" symptoms of emotional distress. Although there are innumerable personal testimonials about the positive benefits of CR, systematic studies are still rare because most Women's Movement groups will cooperate only with researchers who are sympathetic to their goals and activities. Feminists are suspicious of both men and social scientists in general, fearing that their research will be biased and used to discredit the Movement as much media coverage has tried to do. The grass-roots nature of CR adds to these problems: there is no central place to contact a CR group.

Of the interview studies that have been published, the one done by Cary Cherniss (1972) is a good example. Cherniss, a male psychologist, interviewed twelve women actively involved in women's liberation and eight nonpolitical women who were matched for age (twenty-one to twenty-eight years old), occupation, and marital status. He found that the women's liberation group showed more autonomy, assertiveness, push to achieve, and self-acceptance. These women were also less focused on being wives and mothers than were the nonpolitical women, had other roles available to augment their self-definition and, in their accounts of participation in the Women's Movement, stressed the process of " 'finding' one's anger" and redefining their mothers' roles (p. 121). As each Movement woman became more sensitive to sexual discrimination, she grew less harsh in evaluating the maternal relationship and recognized the common female oppression that made her mother (and herself) act as she did.

Cherniss also found that while the Movement women found personal meaning and growth through a feminist analysis of society, the nonpolitical women structured reality in more personal and nonpolitical terms. This difference led him to suggest that the most important dimension of the Women's Movement experience was the "pursuit of meaning" (1972, p. 123). The particular women he studied seemed to enter the Movement after a crisis of personal identity in which they felt that the conventional models of femininity were not appropriate or satisfying for them. Other psychologists have posited such a "restoration of meaning" as a central aspect of psychotherapy, as Cherniss points out (p. 124).

Although the Cherniss study suggests ways in which CR may be therapeutic for many women, it is not definitive. First of all, it is not clear whether the twelve women's liberation participants were members of CR groups or of groups that focused on political activism rather than on personal discussion. Even if they were members of CR groups, the positive effects they felt cannot be attributed to CR specifically rather than to feminist ideas in general. To determine the source of these effects, one would need to interview three groups: feminists in CR, feminists not in CR, and nonfeminists.

In the past five years, some researchers have given both personality and attitude measures to many women who either volunteered for a "Psychological Growth for Women" class (Sprinthall and Erikson 1974) or were participating in women's studies and other courses as part of their regular college curriculum (Scott, Richards and Wade 1977). Although these researchers' studies found increases in profeminist attitudes and general psychological adjustment over time, the differences may be due to natural maturation and attitude differences inherent in group membership before the study. To sort out these effects, one needs random assignment of women to CR and non-CR groups.

Four recent studies have used random assignment to groups designed to simulate CR. High school, college, or community volunteers were either put on a waiting list or enrolled in a discussion group focusing on sex roles. In two of the four studies, comparison of CR and wait-listed control groups showed that CR increased self-reported profeminist attitudes (Abernathy et al. 1977; Follingstad et al. 1977) and behavior (Follingstad et al. 1977), while self-esteem was not affected. The CR participants did show greater increases in general measures of self-actualization and self-concept in all four studies (Abernathy et al. 1977; Berman et al. 1977; Follingstad et al. 1977; Kincaid 1977).

Even these studies using random assignment have their shortcomings, for the CR groups were more like women's studies courses than like self-help groups. They were led by an academician with considerable authority, and they focused on topics she assigned. This arrangement automatically sets up a hierarchical relationship, which is not typical of most CR groups and may have led the study participants to fill out the paper-and-pencil measures the way they thought they should. The changes may have been more a matter of learning the proper response than of real personal development.

Barrett (1978) tried to get around these problems in a study of recently widowed women randomly assigned to four groups: (1) a "self-help group" whose leader encouraged the members to initiate the topics and seek solutions from each other, (2) a "confidant group" in which the women were paired and asked to complete tasks to foster intimacy, (3) a "consciousness-raising group" where the leader introduced sex-role topics and asked each member to respond in turn without confrontations or interruptions, and (4) a "control group" that was placed on a waiting list.* Eighteen self-report measures of personality, attitudes,

* Barrett's CR group was run according to the "Los Angeles" method of CR, as outlined in NOW's pamphlet *Guidelines to Feminist Consciousness Raising* (Perl and Abarbanell 1976).

and behavior were given before and after group participation. Barrett found that *all* the women showed a substantial increase in self-esteem, a shift to more negative attitudes toward remarriage, and an increased intensity of grief. Among the four groups, however, CR was the most effective in enhancing these changes.

These studies support the anecdotal reports of CR as a powerful experience. CR is especially helpful for women who are questioning their attitudes, their values, and their life decisions—and who wish to examine these within the broader social framework of woman's role in society. For such women, CR can provide emotional support, the opportunity to share experiences with other women, and a vital sense of community.

On the other hand, CR lacks many characteristics of group therapy that are important to a woman experiencing severe or even moderate emotional distress. There is little opportunity to focus on one's private emotional experiences that are not directly related to sexual discrimination and social roles. There is little emphasis on reliving painful experiences so as to enable the individual to change those deeply ingrained attitudes and behavior patterns that may be maladaptive. And although positive feelings are often expressed in a CR group, members are discouraged from sharing the hostile or negative feelings they may arouse in each other. Hence, there is an opportunity to express anger toward absent people and institutions but no opportunity to learn that anger expressed or heard face to face is not always overwhelming. Most important of all, however, there is no emergency back-up for severely distressed or suicidal members. Such women should seek help from a mental-health professional.

In summary, then, I would say that CR is not group therapy, nor is it appropriate for everyone; but it is a positive alternative to traditional psychotherapy for the millions of women who are seeking personal growth.

CONCLUSION

THE IMPLICATIONS
OF BEING FEMALE

IN TALKING ABOUT the human experience, people tend to rely on broad generalities. They discuss philosophies of life; the common anguish and joys of birth, illness, love and death; problems of poverty, ignorance, and unemployment; and the cultural norms and institutions that shape our lives. But, looking at the daily lives of individual women and men, we find something different. It is not simply that the broad themes are translated into individual experience in a multitude of ways. It is also the fact that the experience of each human being is always colored by gender.

Gender determines our lives from the moment of birth. Not that male and female infants differ in any way other than their genitalia, but each is treated differently from the first day of life. A female is perceived as more fragile and is pressured to be nurturant, dependent, and passive. A male, on the other hand, is perceived as physically hardy and is pressured to be aggressive and self-reliant. As the child grows, she or he learns to act, to think, and even to feel only in certain ways. Learning extends to physical gender itself; as is clear from the studies of her-

462

maphrodites, biology is no match for learning even in this area. If an infant is brought up as female, that infant becomes a woman regardless of biology; the same infant, brought up as a male, becomes a man and goes on to have a man's interests, activities, and privileges. Gender determines whether you or I should be dependent or independent, passive or aggressive, noncompetitive or competitive. In other words, whether you or I must be feminine or masculine.

Women and men are basically different. The question is, What causes their differences? A decade of research has shown that both the biological and the personality differences are more myth than reality. Thus, to answer this question, researchers have turned to the myths themselves. Instead of asking, How are females different from males? they have begun to ask, Why do we think they are different?

Researchers have found that the gender dichotomy is all pervasive. Psychologists have always begun with the general social attitudes about women and men and then set up studies destined to perpetuate these attitudes. If a behavior pattern was considered to be male, it was studied in men only; if it was considered to be female, it was studied in women only.

When the two sexes were compared, men always seemed to be better, for whatever they did, felt, or thought was defined as the norm for everyone, regardless of gender. If a male scored higher in math and spatial tasks, then these tasks must be more important; the female verbal advantage was simply different, not better. To be aggressive, independent, and fascinated by worldly achievement was to be masculine—and hence more desirable and even more psychologically healthy. Sexuality was a male domain. A woman was frigid if she could not obtain gratification through the purely vaginal contact preferred by men. If a woman insisted on clitoral stimulation, she was weird, clearly immature, and obsessed with pretending to be a man.

This male bias has created a "Catch 22" for women. A woman cannot win when she is defined and evaluated in totally male terms. In this sense, then, psychology has been a male, rather than a human, science. The theories have been developed by males, the values have been male, and the studies have perpetuated myths about sex differences and male superiority. Women are the losers.

Why has the female always been defined in male terms? The answer can be expressed in one word: *power*. Since males are viewed as more powerful, females are automatically viewed as passive, dependent, and even somewhat helpless. In the traditional theories of personality development, for instance, maleness is equated with power. Freud expresses this in anatomical terms: a woman wants what she basically lacks—a penis. As the neo-Freudians have pointed out, penis envy is really social envy or power envy—and powerlessness is the core of Freudian femininity.

Kohlberg's theory also equates maleness with power; but in it the

entire male anatomy, not the penis alone, connotes power and dominance. Kohlberg does not claim that women wish their bodies were
male, but he argues that females want to be nurturant and dependent as
a natural consequence of their body image. This theory is merely the
obverse of Freudan penis/power envy. The basic premise of both theories
is the same: a man is naturally more powerful and dominant than a
woman, as is obvious from a comparison of their anatomies.

These psychologists did not create the idea of male power. They
were reflecting the male bias in the real world. In almost every culture
men are more likely to perform the basic subsistence tasks, to control the
property involved in economic activities, and to live together in a male
descent group. The man is viewed as the head of his household who
owns the objects and the people within it. And although we would like
to think that the idea of woman as property is antiquated, the statistics
on rape and battered women show that it is clearly still with us.

Male power is not always expressed through physical brutality, but
it is active nevertheless: in a wife's need to elicit her husband's approval
and assistance in order to work outside the home; in a young woman's
tendency to defer to the "superior" guidance and ability of her boyfriend; and in the working woman's need for an older, powerful male
mentor in order to advance. Men are dominant even in bed; their sexual
needs usually determine what happens, indeed even what is accepted as
sexual.

Today, however, women are no longer entirely powerless, nor do
they totally accept the male view of themselves. Many women are turning to each other for support and guidance, and some even express a
rather defiant attitude toward male dominance. One often sees slogans
like the popular one asserting that "a woman without a man is like a fish
without a bicycle." Although this statement reflects a courageous
(and angry) determination to be independent, the realities of life for
most women are starkly different. All too often, a woman without a
man is a socially isolated, invisible individual with no money, no clear
social role, and few emotional supports. In equating maleness with
power, psychologists have translated a social and economic reality into
psychological terms.

The social and economic realities of male dominance not only shape
the day-to-day lives of most women; they also have a profound impact
on how a woman feels about herself. Femininity is not just an abstract
notion found in personality theories. It represents a view of women that
is shared by the majority of the population, both male and female. And
this view presents *real* women as inherently nurturant, emotional, passive, gentle creatures who are happiest when they have a man to lean
on and who may even enjoy a little suffering.

Gender roles are central to the identity of most Americans. And
women are no exception. Most women want to be as feminine as pos-

sible. Whatever a woman decides to do with her life, she often tries to maximize her femininity. She worries about whether worldly success will lead to envy and social rejection; whether her gender will isolate her on the job and elsewhere; whether becoming too assertive, competitive, or athletic will cause her to be perceived as—or even to become—masculinized. This fear of masculinization can become a constant preoccupation. A woman may go to great lengths to reassure others, and herself, that even though she may seem to be doing things traditional women do not, she is not really stepping beyond the pale. Some women try to compensate for unconventional behavior by becoming superwomen—those paragons of virtue who can be supermoms and superworkers simultaneously, who manage to get all their "womanly" chores done and still add a full day of "unwomanly" activities on the side, who emphasize their sexual charms and feminine gestures at every available opportunity. Thus are many women trapped into a compulsive femininity that complements the male's compulsive masculinity: the simpering female plays to her macho male.

Femininity in moderation, of course, is a perfectly acceptable part of a woman's life; but carried to extremes, it is a hazard to a woman. The dependence and passivity that go with the female stereotype make a woman vulnerable—to rape and beating; to depression, phobias, and hysteria, to a general self-deprecation that can cause pervasive feelings of worthlessness and hopelessness. A woman may inhibit her intellectual development lest she outstrip the men around her. She may even ignore her own body lest she challenge the male view of female sexuality. Femininity exaggerated can destroy her health and happiness—and, ultimately, the health and happiness of those close to her.

Not all these hazards are uniquely female. Economic and social pressures elicit behavior patterns and personality characteristics that go with subordinate status. A less powerful group is usually perceived and defined in terms of the dominant group, whether the lens is gender-linked, racial, or economic and cultural. The stereotypes applied to powerless groups have much in common—passivity, dependence, a happy-go-lucky emotionality, and a certain tolerance for and even enjoyment of suffering. "They don't mind," a member of the dominant group is likely to say. "After all, women [or blacks or the poor] are different from us. They just don't see things the same way we do. They don't mind housework [or menial labor or various other forms of drudgery]. After all, they're used to it. In fact, they're really pretty happy the way they are." The attitudes, feelings, and perceptions surrounding major power and status differences can thus be termed a "psychology of oppression." In discussing women, this oppression is based on gender. But the other oppressions are felt no less keenly by their victims.

Although a woman may suffer from her social role and status in society, she gets little sympathy and is held responsible for her own victimization. Of a woman raped, people—especially men—say, "She must have asked for it," or even, "She probably enjoyed it." If she is beaten repeatedly by her husband or boyfriend, other men say, "Why doesn't she leave? She must provoke him beyond all endurance. She's as sick as he is." If her husband is threatened by her career and she decides not to fight for a promotion, they say, "See, I told you she wasn't really cut out for success. She must have a secret will to fail, like so many women." If she complains about her sex life, her husband or lover says she is unfeminine and demanding. And if she is assertive and independent, her husband or lover accuses her of being castrating.

The tendency to blame the woman herself serves a useful function. It treats sexual discrimination and harassment as a personal problem. Each incident represents a minor difficulty for which there is no social remedy. "After all," a man says, "if women bring these awful experiences on themselves, what can I do about it?"

Blaming the victim is not a purely male-female phenomenon, but prevails in every dominant group as a social mechanism to keep subordinate groups in a perpetual "one down" position. The fact that it is a common phenomenon does not mean, however, that we should continue to put up with it. Women can effectively challenge the male view of the female experience—and they have been doing so more and more.

Women's challenge has coincided with many changes in their social role since World War II. More women are now working at paid jobs outside the house and in less traditionally feminine areas. There is greater flexibility in what a woman is expected to do, to think, and to feel on the job, at home, in social settings, and even in bed. Marriage is no longer perceived as the only option for a woman, and some women are beginning to explore other living arrangements.

Social scientists have responded to these changes and to the issues raised by the Women's Movement over the past ten years. Social learning theory has become popular among psychologists, who have begun to examine what it is like to grow up female in America today—how women learn to be feminine and what that means to people in different localities, different social and economic groups, and different subcultures. Psychologists have begun to examine the myths surrounding the concepts of femininity and masculinity and their effect on our everyday lives. In other words, many psychologists are no longer content to view the female through the lenses of cultural myth and sex-role stereotype but are questioning the male bias implicit in both and are revising their theories about women.

As part of the recent emphasis on the psychology of women, psychologists and other social scientists have begun to ask women about their own experiences, and have often been surprised by the results. A woman does not always perceive femininity and achievement as incompatible; a working wife and mother is much more concerned about job discrimination and scheduling problems than about personality factors. She is not striving to become more masculine; she simply wants recognition and acceptance of the abilities and characteristics she already has. Women are far from frigid; indeed, many researchers now think that the physiology of the female sexual response makes women insatiable. And domestic relationships involve much more than a struggle over who does the dishes; physical abuse of women is appallingly common. The world is obviously not like "The Ozzie and Harriet Show," and psychologists are beginning to realize it.

As research has progressed over the past decade, there has been a shift from examining internal personality factors to examining external barriers to female achievement, to role change, and to personal satisfaction. Psychologists no longer blithely assume that a woman's anatomy is her destiny, that her reproductive organs make her inherently passive, dependent, and even masochistic; that her "feminine" nature determines her life style; or that she wants and deserves whatever she gets. Psychologists are attending more to the social surroundings in which women live and to how those shape women's lives and personalities.

Nor do psychologists assume that women are all alike (or if they do, they will not be able to much longer). If we have learned anything about women today, it is that they are extremely diverse. They have many different life styles, personalities, and interests. What some love, others hate. What some value, others deplore. The thing all have in common, is the limitations imposed on them by gender. Women today are under a lot of stress, as they strive for change. It is not the change that is debilitating; it is the rigidity of compulsive femininity, which is no more adaptive than compulsive masculinity.

Not every woman shares the view that flexibility and change are positive and growth-enhancing. Many women feel threatened by the shifts in the female role and have responded by exaggerating the traditional feminine values. This "female backlash" has spawned a number of books like Marabel Morgan's *Total Woman* (1975), which implores women to flatter the male ego by at least pretending to "accept him," "admire him," "adapt to him," and "appreciate him." This backlash is partially due to the militant and angry tone in which some women discuss their plight; in order to compensate for years of oppression, they castigate the male and treat him as "the enemy." These women admire only the most aggressive, independent, and dominant woman and consider that all others are buying into the male system. If she is a housewife, a woman must be suffering from the "housewife syndrome," even if she thinks she is happy. If she works, she is far better off; and if she can manage without a man at all, she is doing splendidly.

Although the angry desire to manage without a man may sometimes be justified, it does not reflect most women's feelings or the everyday realities of their lives. Women are changing, but gradually.

Men are changing too, but also gradually. As flexibility becomes more acceptable and more commonplace than rigidity, everyone should be able to find his or her own way to deal with the gender-role issues. Some women will choose to combine traditional motherhood with the less traditional activity of paid employment. Others will decide to remain single and devote their energies to a career. Some will undoubtedly decide that they are happiest and most productive in the traditional role of full-time housewife and mother. The important thing is for a woman to have the freedom and the opportunity to decide for herself, without fear of social rejection and stigma. To change from a rigid adherence to femininity to a rigid avoidance of femininity is not the point. The point is to permit greater flexibility and hence greater personal fulfillment.

There are no ideal personal solutions. Full equality between the sexes must await basic social and economic changes. But each and every woman can begin to reexamine her assumptions about what it means to be female, and how she wants to live her own life. She can begin to search for solutions that reflect her own experiences and the experiences of the women around her.

Millions of women have already begun to reevaluate their assumptions, attitudes, and value systems. They have turned to other women to share, to give support, to define themselves in female rather than in male terms. They gather in each others' homes, at schools and churches, in Women's Movement offices. They meet in groups for widows, divorcées, and mothers as well as in abortion clinics, rape crisis centers, and groups of battered women. In talking with each other, these women are doing more than reevaluating their own feelings and life styles; they are creating a female solidarity and activism that reflects a positive view of the female experience. Women are not simply dependent, passive, and weak; they are also independent, assertive, and strong.

Female solidarity has a tremendous social impact; it gets things done. Pressure from the Women's Movement forced male social science to reexamine its assumptions and its cavalier treatment of women's lives and personalities. Pressure from women and from sympathetic men has initiated changes in the laws governing women's rights—rape, wife-beating, divorce, and broader changes such as those of the Equal Rights Amendment. In female solidarity lies not only a woman's personal strength, but also her social force.

References

In the text when a direct quotation from reprinted material is used, both the original date of publication and the reprinted date are given, and the page numbers of the citation refer to the latter source.

Abbott, S., and Love, B. 1971. Is women's liberation a lesbian plot? In *Woman in sexist society* (pp. 436–51), edited by V. Gornick and B. K. Moran. New York: Basic Books.

Abbott, S., and Love, B. 1972. *Sappho was a right-on woman: A liberated view of lesbianism.* New York: Stein & Day.

Abernathy, R. W.; Abramowitz, S. I.; Roback, H. B.; Weitz, L. J.; Abramowitz, C. V.; and Tittler, B. 1977. The impact of an intensive consciousness-raising curriculum on adolescent women. *Psychology of Women Quarterly* 2(2): 138–48.

Abramowitz, S. I.; Abramowitz, C. V.; Roback, H. B.; Corney, R.; and McKee, E. 1976. Sex-role related countertransference in psychotherapy. *Archives of General Psychiatry* 33: 71–73.

Abramson, P. R.; Goldberg, P. A.; Greenberg, J. H.; and Abramson, L. M. 1977. The talking platypus phenomenon: Competency ratings as a function of sex and professional status. *Psychology of Women Quarterly* 2(2): 114–24.

Albin, R. S. 1977. Psychological studies of rape. *Signs: Journal of Women in Culture and Society* 3(2): 423–35.

Almquist, E. M. 1977. Women in the labor force. *Signs: Journal of Women in Culture and Society* 2(4): 843–55.

Altman, S. L., and Grossman, F. K. 1977. Women's career plans and maternal employment. *Psychology of Women Quarterly* 1(4): 365–76.

American Psychiatric Association. 1973. The principles of medical ethics with annotations especially applicable to psychiatry. *American Journal of Psychiatry* 130: 1057–64.

American Psychological Association. 1977. Ethical standards of psychologists. *APA Monitor* (March) 8(3): 22–23.

Amir, M. 1971. *Patterns of forcible rape.* Chicago: University of Chicago Press.

Anderson, R. 1978. Motive to avoid success: A profile. *Sex Roles: A Journal of Research* 4(2): 239–48.

Argyris, C., and Schön, D. A. 1975. *Theory in practice: Increasing professional effectiveness.* San Francisco: Jossey-Bass.

Arieti, S. 1979. Roots of depression: The power of the dominant other (interview). *Psychology Today* (April) 12(11): 54, 57–58, 92–93.

Arieti, S., and Bemporad, J. 1978. *Severe and mild depression: The psychotherapeutic approach.* New York: Basic Books.

Aslin, A. L. 1977. Feminist and community mental health center psychotherapists' expectations of mental health for women. *Sex Roles: A Journal of Research* 3(6): 537–44.

Atkinson, J. W. (ed.) 1958. *Motives in fantasy, action, and society: A method of assessment and study.* New York: Van Nostrand.

Atkinson, J. W., and Feather, N. T. (eds.) 1966. *A theory of achievement motivation.* New York: Wiley.

Bahr, S. J. 1974. Effects on power and division of labor in the family. In *Working mothers* (pp. 167–85), written by L. W. Hoffman and F. I. Nye (with S. J. Bahr, A. C. Emlen, J. B. Perry, Jr., and M. G. Sobol). San Francisco: Jossey-Bass.

Bandura, A. 1965. Influence of model's reinforcement contingencies on the acquisition of imitative responses. *Journal of Personality and Social Psychology* 1: 589–95.

Bandura, A. 1969. Social-learning theory of identificatory processes. In *Handbook of socialization theory and research* (pp. 213–62), edited by D. A. Goslin. Chicago: Rand McNally.

Bandura, A., and Huston, A. C. 1961. Identification as a process of incidental learning. *Journal of Abnormal and Social Psychology* 63: 311–18.

Bandura, A.; Ross, D.; and Ross, S. A. 1963a. Imitation of film-mediated aggressive models. *Journal of Abnormal and Social Psychology* 66: 3–11.

Bandura, A.; Ross, D.; and Ross, S. A. 1963b. A comparative test of the status envy, social power, and secondary reinforcement theories of identificatory learning. *Journal of Abnormal and Social Psychology* 67: 527–34.

Bandura, A.; Ross, D.; and Ross, S. A. 1963c. Vicarious reinforcement and imitative learning. *Journal of Abnormal and Social Psychology* 67: 601–7.

Bandura, A., and Walters, R. H. 1959. *Adolescent aggression.* New York: Ronald.

Bandura, A., and Walters, R. H. 1963. *Social learning and personality development.* New York: Holt.

Bard, M., and Ellison, K. 1974. Crisis intervention and investigation of forcible rape. *Police Chief* 41: 68–73.

Bard, M., and Sangrey, D. 1979. *The crime victim's book.* New York: Basic Books.

Bardwick, J. M. 1971. *Psychology of women: A study of bio-cultural conflicts.* New York: Harper & Row.

Bardwick, J. M. 1973. Psychological factors in the acceptance and use of oral contraceptives. In *Psychological perspectives on population* (pp. 274–305), edited by J. T. Fawcett. New York: Basic Books.

Bardwick, J. M., and Douvan, E. 1971. Ambivalence: The socialization of women. In *Woman in sexist society* (pp. 147–59), edited by V. Gornick and B. K. Moran. New York: Basic Books. Reprinted in *Readings on the psychology of women* (pp. 52–58), edited by J. M. Bardwick. New York: Harper & Row, 1972.

Barrett, C. J. 1977. Women in widowhood. *Signs: Journal of Women in Culture and Society* 2(4): 856–68.

Barrett, C. J. 1978. Effectiveness of widows' groups in facilitating change. *Journal of Consulting and Clinical Psychology* 46(1): 20–31.

Barry, H.; Bacon, M. K.; and Child, I. L. 1957. A cross-cultural survey of some sex differences in socialization. *Journal of Abnormal and Social Psychology* 55(3): 327–32. Reprinted in *Readings on the psychology of women* (pp. 205–9), edited by J. M. Bardwick. New York: Harper & Row, 1972.

Bart, P. B. 1971. Depression in middle-aged women. In *Woman in sexist society* (pp. 99–117), edited by V. Gornick and B. K. Moran. New York: Basic Books. Reprinted in *Readings on the psychology of women* (pp. 134–42), edited by J. M. Bardwick. New York: Harper & Row, 1972.

Beck, A. T., and Greenberg, R. L. 1974. Cognitive therapy with depressed women. In *Women in therapy: New psychotherapies for a changing society* (pp. 113–31), edited by V. Franks and V. Burtle. New York: Brunner/Mazel.

Beckman, L. J. 1978. The relative rewards and costs of parenthood and employment for employed women. *Psychology of Women Quarterly* 2(3): 215–34.

Begelman, D. A. 1977. Homosexuality and the ethics of behavioral intervention: Paper 3. *Journal of Homosexuality* (Spring) 2(3): 213–19.

Bell, A. P., and Weinberg, M. S. 1978. *Homosexualities: A study of diversity among men and women.* New York: Simon & Schuster.

Bem, S. L. 1974. The measurement of psychological androgyny. *Journal of Consulting and Clinical Psychology* 42: 155–62.

Bem, S. L. 1975. Sex-role adaptability: One consequence of psychological androgyny. *Journal of Personality and Social Psychology* 31: 634–43.

Bem, S. L. 1976. Probing the promise of androgyny. In *Beyond sex-role stereotypes: Readings toward a psychology of androgyny* (pp. 48–62), edited by A. G. Kaplan and J. P. Bean. Boston: Little, Brown.

Bem, S. L. 1977. On the utility of alternative procedures for assessing psychological androgyny. *Journal of Consulting and Clinical Psychology* 45(2): 196–205.

Bem, S. L., and Bem, D. J. 1976. Training the woman to know her place: The power of a nonconscious ideology. In *Female psychology: The emerging self* (pp. 180–90), edited by S. Cox. Chicago: Science Research Associates.

Bemis, K. M. 1978. Current approaches to the etiology and treatment of anorexia nervosa. *Psychological Bulletin* 85(3): 593–617.

Benedek, T. 1970. The psychobiology of pregnancy. In *Parenthood: Its psychology and psychopathology* (pp. 137–51), edited by E. J. Anthony & T. Benedek. Boston:

Little, Brown. Reprinted in *Readings on the psychology of women* (pp. 246–51), edited by J. M. Bardwick. New York: Harper & Row, 1972.

Bequaert, L. H. 1976. *Single women, alone and together.* Boston: Beacon Press.

Berger, S. M. 1962. Conditioning through vicarious instigation. *Psychological Review* 69: 450–66.

Berman, M. R.; Gelso, C. J.; Greenfeig, B. R.; and Hirsch, R. 1977. The efficacy of supportive learning environments for returning women: An empirical evaluation. *Journal of Counseling Psychology* 24(4): 324–31.

Bernard, J. 1972. *The future of marriage.* New York: Bantam.

Bernard, J. 1974. *The future of motherhood.* New York: Penguin.

Bernard, J. 1976. Where are we now? Some thoughts on the current scene. *Psychology of Women Quarterly* 1(1): 21–37.

Berne, E. 1966. *Principles of group treatment.* New York: Oxford University Press.

Bibring, G. L. 1965. Some specific psychological tasks in pregnancy and motherhood. In *Premier Congrès International de Médecine Psychosomatique et Maternité, Paris, 8–12 Juillet 1962*, edited by L. Chertok. Paris: Gauthier-Villars. Reprinted in *Women: Body and culture* (pp. 254–61), edited by S. Hammer. New York: Harper & Row (Perennial Library), 1975.

Bielby, D. 1978. Maternal employment and socioeconomic status as factors in daughters' career salience: Some substantive refinements. *Sex Roles: A Journal of Research* 4(2): 249–66.

Billingsley, D. 1977. Sex bias in psychotherapy: An examination of the effects of client sex, client pathology, and therapist sex on treatment planning. *Journal of Consulting and Clinical Psychology* 45(2): 250–56.

Birnbaum, J. A. 1975. Life patterns and self-esteem in gifted family-oriented and career-committed women. In *Women and achievement: Social and motivational analyses* (pp. 396–419), edited by M. T. S. Mednick; S. S. Tangri; and L. W. Hoffman. New York: Wiley (Halstead Press).

Blum, G. S. 1949. A study of the psychoanalytic theory of psychosexual development. *Genetic Psychology Monographs* 39: 3–99.

Bock, D. R., and Kolakowski, D. 1973. Further evidence of sex-linked major-gene influence on human spatial visualizing ability. *American Journal of Human Genetics* 25: 1–14.

Bohannan, P. (ed.) 1970a. *Divorce and after: An analysis of the emotional and social problems of divorce.* New York: Doubleday (Anchor Books, 1971).

Bohannan, P. 1970b. The six stations of divorce. In *Divorce and after: An analysis of the emotional and social problems of divorce* (pp. 29–55), edited by P. Bohannan. New York: Doubleday. Revised reprint in *Readings on the psychology of women* (pp. 156–63), edited by J. M. Bardwick. New York: Harper & Row, 1972.

Boskind-Lodahl, M. 1976. Cinderella's step-sisters: A feminist perspective on anorexia nervosa and bulimia. *Signs: Journal of Women in Culture and Society* 2(2): 342–56.

Boskind-Lodahl, M., and Sirlin, J. 1977. The gorging-purging syndrome. *Psychology Today* (March), pp. 50–52, 82–85.

Bosselman, B. C. 1960. Castration anxiety and phallus envy: A reformulation. *Psychiatric Quarterly* 34: 252–59. Reprinted in *Readings on the psychology of women* (pp. 251–54), edited by J. M. Bardwick. New York: Harper & Row, 1972.

The Boston Women's Health Book Collective. 1973. *Our bodies, ourselves.* New York: Simon & Schuster.

Breedlove, C. J., and Cicirelli, V. G. 1974. Women's fear of success in relation to personal characteristics and type of occupation. *Journal of Psychology* 86: 181–90.

Bremner, W. J., and de Kretser, D. M. 1975. Contraceptives for males. *Signs: Journal of Women in Culture and Society* 1(2): 387–96. Reprinted in *Psychology of women: Selected readings* (pp. 266–74), edited by J. H. Williams. New York: Norton, 1979.

Brien, L., and Sheldon, C. 1977. Gestalt therapy and women. In *Psychotherapy for women: Treatment toward equality* (pp. 120–27), edited by E. I. Rawlings and D. K. Carter. Springfield, Ill.: Charles C. Thomas.

Brodsky, A. M. 1977. Therapeutic aspects of consciousness-raising groups. In

Psychotherapy for women: Treatment toward equality (pp. 300–309), edited by E. I. Rawlings and D. K. Carter. Springfield, Ill.: Charles C. Thomas.

Brodsky, A. M.; Holroyd, J.; Payton, C.; Rubinstein, E.; Rosenkrantz, P.; Sherman, J.; and Zell, F. 1975. Report of the task force on sex bias and sex-role stereotyping in psychotherapeutic practice. *American Psychologist 30*(12), 1169–75.

Bronson, F. H., and Desjardins, C. 1968. Aggression in adult mice: Modification by neonatal injections of gonadal hormones. *Science 161*: 705–6.

Broverman, D. M.; Klaiber, E. L.; Kobayashi, Y.; and Vogel, W. 1968. Roles of activation and inhibition in sex differences in cognitive abilities. *Psychological Review 75*: 23–50.

Broverman, I. K.; Broverman, D. M.; Clarkson, F. E.; Rosenkrantz, P. S.; and Vogel, S. R. 1970. Sex-role stereotypes and clinical judgments of mental health. *Journal of Consulting and Clinical Psychology 34*(1): 1–7. Reprinted in *Readings on the psychology of women* (pp. 320–24), edited by J. M. Bardwick. New York: Harper & Row, 1972.

Broverman, I. K.; Vogel, S. R.; Broverman, D. M.; Clarkson, F. E.; and Rosenkrantz, P. S. 1972. Sex-role stereotypes: A current appraisal. *Journal of Social Issues 28*(2): 59–78.

Brown, D. G. 1956. Sex-role preference in young children. *Psychological Monographs 70*(no. 14).

Brown, P. 1976. *Mood fluctuation and the menstrual cycle.* Unpublished undergraduate honors thesis, Department of Psychology and Social Relations, Harvard University, April 1976.

Brown, R. M. 1978. Foreword to *Our right to love: A lesbian resource book* (pp. 13–14), edited by G. Vida (in cooperation with women of the National Gay Task Force). Englewood Cliffs, N.J.: Prentice-Hall.

Brownmiller, S. 1975. *Against our will: Men, women and rape.* New York: Simon & Schuster.

Bruch, H. 1974. Eating disturbances in adolescnce. In *American handbook of psychiatry* (2nd ed.), editor-in-chief S. Arieti. Vol. 2: *Child and adolescent psychiatry, sociocultural and community psychiatry* (pp. 275–86), edited by G. Caplan. New York: Basic Books.

Bruch, H. 1978. *The golden cage: The enigma of anorexia nervosa.* Cambridge, Mass.: Harvard University Press.

Buffery, A. W. H., and Gray, J. A. 1972. Sex differences in the development of spatial and linguistic skills. In *Gender differences: Their ontogeny and significance,* edited by C. Ounsted and D. C. Taylor. Baltimore: Williams & Wilkins.

Burgess, A. W., and Holmstrom, L. L. 1974. Rape trauma syndrome. *American Journal of Psychiatry 131*: 981–86.

Byrne, D. 1977. A pregnant pause in the sexual revolution. *Psychology Today* (July) *11*(2): pp. 67–68.

Caine, L. 1975. *Widow.* New York: Bantam.

California Law Review. 1973. Comment on rape and rape laws: Sexism in society and law. *61*(3): 919–41.

Cameron, N. 1963. *Personality development and psychopathology: A dynamic approach.* Boston: Houghton Mifflin.

Carey, R. G. 1977. The widowed: A year later. *Journal of Counseling Psychology 24*(2): 125–31.

Carroll, C. M. 1973. Three's a crowd: The dilemma of the black woman in higher education. In *Academic women on the move* (pp. 173–85), edited by A. S. Rossi and A. Calderwood. New York: Russell Sage Foundation.

Cavell, M. 1974. Since 1924: Toward a new psychology of women. In *Women and analysis: Dialogues on psychoanalytic views of femininity* (pp. 162–68), edited by J. Strouse. New York: Grossman.

Cherniss, C. 1972. Personality and ideology: A personological study of women's liberation. *Psychiatry 35*(2): 109–25. Reprinted in *Beyond sex-role stereotypes: Readings toward a psychology of androgyny* (pp. 364–80), edited by A. G. Kaplan and J. P. Bean. Boston: Little, Brown, 1976.

Cherry, F., and Deaux, K. 1978. Fear of success versus fear of gender-inappropriate behavior. *Sex Roles: A Journal of Research 4*(1): 97–101.

Chesler, P. 1971. Patient and patriarch: Women in the psychotherapeutic relationship. In *Woman in sexist society* (pp. 251–75), edited by V. Gornick and B. K. Moran. New York: Basic Books.

Chesler, P. 1972. *Women and madness.* New York: Doubleday.

Clark, D. 1977. *Loving someone gay.* Millbrae, Cal.: Celestial Arts.

Clifton, A. K.; McGrath, D.; and Wick, B. 1976. Stereotypes of woman: A single category? *Sex Roles: A Journal of Research* 2(2): 135–48.

Cobb, S., and Lindemann, E. 1943. Symposium on management of Coconut Grove burns at Massachusetts General Hospital: Neuropsychiatric observations. *Annals of Surgery* 117: 814–24.

Cohen, M. L.; Garofalo, R.; Boucher, R.; and Seghorn, T. 1971. The psychology of rapists. *Seminars in Psychology* 3: 307–27.

Conn, J. H. 1940. Children's reactions to the discovery of genital difference. *American Journal of Orthopsychiatry* 10: 747–54.

Conn, J. H., and Kanner, L. 1947. Children's awareness of sex differences. *Journal of Child Psychiatry* 1: 3–57.

Corah, N. L. 1965. Differentiation in children and their parents. *Journal of Personality* 33: 300–08.

Cox, R. D. 1968. Marriage and the family. In *Role and status of women in the Soviet Union* (pp. 130–36), by D. R. Brown. New York: Teachers College Press. Reprinted in *Readings on the psychology of women* (pp. 128–30), edited by J. M. Bardwick. New York: Harper & Row, 1972.

Crawfurd, R. 1915. Notes on the superstitions of menstruation. *Lancet* (18 December) (vol. 2 of 1915), pp. 1331–36.

Dalton, K. 1968. Ante-natal progesterone and intelligence. *British Journal of Psychiatry* 114: 1377–82.

Dalton, K. 1969. *The menstrual cycle.* New York: Pantheon Books.

D'Andrade, R. G. 1966. Sex differences and cultural institutions. In *The development of sex differences* (pp. 173–204), edited by E. E. Maccoby. Stanford, Cal.: Stanford University Press.

Davison, G. C. 1977. Homosexuality, the ethical challenge. *Journal of Homosexuality* (Spring) 2(3): 195–204.

Davison, G. C. 1978. Not can but ought: The treatment of homosexuality. *Journal of Consulting and Clinical Psychology* 46(1): 170–72.

Deaux, K., and Emswiller, T. 1974. Explanations of successful performance on sex-linked tasks: What's skill for the male is luck for the female. *Journal of Personality and Social Psychology* 29: 80–85.

de Beauvoir, S. 1953. *The second sex.* New York: Knopf (Bantam Books, 1961).

Del Rey, P. 1977. The apologetic and women in sport. In *Psychology of motor behavior and sport,* Vol. 2, edited by D. M. Landers and R. W. Christina. Champaign, Ill.: Human Kinetics Publishers. Reprinted in *Women and sport: From myth to reality* (pp. 107–11), by C. A. Oglesby. Philadelphia: Lea & Febiger, 1978.

Der-Karabetian, A., and Smith, A. J. 1977. Sex-role stereotyping in the United States: Is it changing? *Sex Roles: A Journal of Research* 3(2): 193–98.

Dermer, M., and Thiel, D. L. 1975. When beauty may fail. *Journal of Personality and Social Psychology* 31: 1168–76.

Deutsch, F., and Murphy, W. F. 1955. *The clinical interview* (Vol. 1: *Diagnosis*). New York: International Universities Press.

Deutsch, H. 1925. The psychology of women in relation to the functions of reproduction. *International Journal of Psycho-Analysis* 6(4): 405–418. Reprinted in *Women and analysis: Dialogues on psychoanalytic views of femininity* (pp. 147–61), edited by J. Strouse. New York: Grossman, 1974.

Deutsch, H. 1944. *The psychology of women.* Vol. 1. New York: Grune & Stratton.

Deutsch, H. 1945. *The psychology of women.* Vol. 2. New York: Grune & Stratton.

DeVries, R. 1969. Constancy of generic identity in the years three to six. *Monographs of the Society for Research in Child Development* 34(no. 3, serial no. 127).

Diamant, A. 1979. The women's sports revolution: Change for the better? Or only for the best? *The Real Paper* (Cambridge, Mass., 24 March) 8(12): 20–21, 24–25.

Dick-Read, G. 1944. *Childbirth without fear.* New York: Harper & Brothers.

Dobinski, K. 1975. Lesbians and the law. In *After you're out: Personal experiences of gay men and lesbian women* (pp. 152–60), edited by K. Jay and A. Young. New York: Links Books.

Dohrenwend, B. P., and Dohrenwend, B. S. 1974. Social and cultural influences on psychotherapy. *Annual Review of Psychology* 25: 417–52.

Douvan, E. 1976. The role of models in women's professional development. *Psychology of Women Quarterly* 1(1): 5–20.

Dreifus, C. 1973. *Woman's fate.* New York: Bantam.

DuBois, B. R. 1976. *Feminist perspective on psychotherapy and the psychology of women: An exploratory study in the development of clinical theory.* Unpublished doctoral dissertation, Harvard University, November 1976.

Duquin, M. E. 1978. The androgynous advantage. In *Women and sport: From myth to reality* (pp. 89–106), by C. A. Oglesby. Philadelphia: Lea & Febiger.

Ehrhardt, A. A., and Baker, S. W. 1973. *Hormonal aberrations and their implications for the understanding of normal sex differentiation.* Paper presented at the meetings of the Society for Research in Child Development, Philadelphia.

Ehrhardt, A. A., and Money, J. 1967. Progestin-induced hermaphroditism: IQ and psychosexual identity in a study of ten girls. *Journal of Sex Research* 3(1): 83–100.

Eisenberg, S. E., and Micklow, P. L. 1974. *The assaulted wife: Catch 22 revisited (A preliminary overview of wife-beating in Michigan).* Unpublished study. Ann Arbor, Mich.: University of Michigan. Reported in *Wife beating: The silent crisis*, by R. Langley and R. C. Levy. New York: Pocket Books, 1977.

Epstein, C. F. 1973. Positive effects of the multiple negative: Explaining the success of Black professional women. In *Changing women in a changing society* (pp. 150–73), edited by J. Huber. Chicago: University of Chicago Press.

Epstein, J. 1974. *Divorced in America: Marriage in an age of possibility.* New York: Dutton.

Erikson, E. H. 1968. Womanhood and the inner space. In *Identity, youth, and crisis* (pp. 261–94), by E. H. Erikson. New York: Norton. Reprinted in *Women and analysis: Dialogues on psychoanalytic views of femininity* (pp. 291–319), edited by J. Strouse. New York: Grossman, 1974.

Escamilla-Mondanaro, J. 1977. Lesbians and therapy. In *Psychotherapy for women: Treatment toward equality* (pp. 256–65), edited by E. I. Rawlings and D. K. Carter. Springfield, Ill.: Charles C. Thomas.

Etaugh, C., and Rose, S. 1975. Adolescents' sex bias in the evaluation of performance. *Developmental Psychology* 11: 663–64.

Fabrikant, B. 1974. The psychotherapist and the female patient: Perceptions, misperceptions, and change. In *Women in therapy: New psychotherapies for a changing society* (pp 83–109), edited by V. Franks and V. Burtle. New York: Brunner/Mazel.

Farber, L. H. 1979. Merchandising depression. *Psychology Today* (April) 12(11): 63–64.

Feighner, J. P.; Robins, E.; Guze, S. B.; et al. 1972. Diagnostic criteria for use in psychiatric research. *Archives of General Psychiatry* 26: 57–63.

Feild, H. S. 1978. Attitudes toward rape: A comparative analysis of police, rapists, crisis counselors, and citizens. *Journal of Personality and Social Psychology* 36(2): 156–79.

Feldman, S. 1974. *Escape from the doll's house.* New York: McGraw-Hill.

Feldman-Summers, S. A., and Kiesler, S. B. 1974. Those who are number two try harder: The effect of sex on attributions of causality. *Journal of Personality and Social Psychology* 30: 846–55.

Felshin, J. 1974. The social view. In *The American woman in sport* (pp. 179–282), edited by E. Gerber; J. Felshin; P. Berlin; and W. Wyrick. Reading, Mass.: Addison-Wesley.

Fenichel, O. 1945. *The psychoanalytic theory of neurosis.* New York: Norton.

Fennell, M. L.; Barchas, P. R.; Cohen, E. G.; McMahon, A. M.; and Hildebrand, P. 1978. An alternative perspective on sex differences in organizational settings: The process of legitimation. *Sex Roles: A Journal of Research* 4(4): 589–604.

Ferree, M. M. 1976. The confused American housewife. *Psychology Today* (September) 10: 76–80.

Fidell, L. S. 1970. Empirical verification of sex discrimination in hiring practices in psychology. *American Psychologist* 25: 1094–98.

Fisher, S. 1973. *The female orgasm: Psychology, physiology, fantasy.* New York: Basic Books.

Fisher, S., and Greenberg, R. P. 1977. *The scientific credibility of Freud's theories and therapy.* New York: Basic Books.

Flavell, J. H. 1963. *The developmental psychology of Jean Piaget.* New York: Van Nostrand Reinhold.

Fleming, J. 1977. On "Do women fear success?" Letter replying to David Tresemer. *Signs: Journal of Women in Culture and Society* 2(3): 706–17.

Fodor, I. G. 1974. The phobic syndrome in women: Implications for treatment. In *Women in therapy: New psychotherapies for a changing society* (pp. 132–68), edited by V. Franks and V. Burtle. New York: Brunner/Mazel.

Follingstad, D. R.; Robinson, E. A.; and Pugh, M. 1977. Effects of consciousness-raising groups on measures of feminism, self-esteem, and social desirability. *Journal of Counseling Psychology* 24(3): 223–30.

Fox, G. L. 1977. "Nice Girl": Social control of women through a value construct. *Signs: Journal of Women in Culture and Society* 2(4): 805–17.

Frank, F. D., and Drucker, J. 1977. The influence of evaluatee's sex on evaluations of a response on a managerial selection instrument. *Sex Roles: A Journal of Research* 3(1): 59–64.

Freud, A. 1946. *The ego and the mechanisms of defense.* New York: International Universities Press.

Freud, S. 1923. The ego and the id. In *The standard edition of the complete psychological works of Sigmund Freud*, edited by J. Strachey. Vol. 19, pp. 3–66. London: The Hogarth Press, 1961.

Freud, S. 1925. Some psychological consequences of the anatomical distinction between the sexes. In *The collected papers of Sigmund Freud*, edited and translated by J. Strachey. Vol. 5, pp. 186–97. New York: Basic Books, 1959. Also reprinted in *Women and analysis: Dialogues on psychoanalytic views of femininity* (pp. 17–26), edited by J. Strouse. New York: Grossman, 1974.

Freud, S. 1931. Female sexuality. In *The collected papers of Sigmund Freud*, edited by J. Strachey, translated by J. Riviere. Vol. 5, pp. 252–72. New York: Basic Books, 1959. Also reprinted in *Women and analysis: Dialogues on psychoanalytic views of femininity* (pp. 39–56), edited by J. Strouse. New York: Grossman, 1974.

Freud, S. 1933a. Anxiety and instinctual life. In *New introductory lectures on psychoanalysis*, edited and translated by J. Strachey. New York: Norton, 1965, pp. 81–111.

Freud, S. 1933b. The dissection of the psychical personality. In *New introductory lectures on psychoanalysis*, edited and translated by J. Strachey. New York: Norton, 1965, pp. 57–80.

Freud, S. 1933c. Femininity. In *New introductory lectures on psychoanalysis*, edited and translated by J. Strachey. New York: Norton, 1965, pp. 112–35.

Friedan, B. 1963. *The feminine mystique.* New York: Dell.

Friedman, S. M. 1952. An empirical study of the castration and oedipus complexes. *Genetic Psychology Monographs* 46(1): 61–130.

Frieze, I. H.; Parsons, J. E.; Johnson, P. B.; Ruble, D. N.; and Zellman, G. L. 1978. *Women and sex roles: A social psychological perspective.* New York: Norton.

Fujitomi, I., and Wong, D. 1973. The new Asian-American woman. In *Asian-Americans: Psychological perspectives* (pp. 252–63), edited by S. Sue and N. N. Wagner. Palo Alto, Cal.: Science and Behavior Books. Reprinted in *Female psychology: The emerging self* (pp. 236–48), edited by S. Cox. Chicago: Science Research Associates, 1976.

Fulcher, P.; McHenry, S.; and Thom, M. 1979. Black women united: sororities, alliances, and pressure groups. *Ms.* (January) *VII*(7): 90.

Gelles, R. 1972. *The violent home: A study of physical aggression between husbands and wives.* Beverly Hills, Cal.: Sage Publications.

Gerrard, M. 1977. Sex guilt in abortion patients. *Journal of Consulting and Clinical Psychology* 45(4): 708.

Gesell, A.; Halverson, H. M.; Ilg, F. L.; Thompson, H.; Castner, B. M.; Almes, L. B.;

and Amatruda, C. S. 1940. *The first five years of life: A guide to the study of the preschool child.* New York: Harper's.

Gettleman, S., and Markowitz, J. 1974. *The courage to divorce.* New York: Simon & Schuster.

Ginsburg, H., and Opper, S. 1969. *Piaget's theory of intellectual development: An introduction.* Englewood Cliffs, N.J.: Prentice-Hall.

Goldberg, P. 1968. Are women prejudiced against women? *Transaction* 4: 28–30.

Gove, W. R. 1972. The relationship between sex roles, marital status, and mental illness. *Social Forces* 51(1): 34–44. Reprinted in *Beyond sex-role stereotypes: Readings toward a psychology of androgyny* (pp. 282–92), edited by A. G. Kaplan and J. P. Bean. Boston: Little, Brown, 1976.

Gove, W. R., and Tudor, J. F. 1973. Adult sex roles and mental illness. In *Changing women in a changing society* (pp. 50–73), edited by J. Huber. Chicago: University of Chicago Press.

Goy, R. W. 1970. Experimental control of psychosexuality. In *A discussion on the determination of sex* (pp. 149–62), edited by G. W. Harris and R. G. Edwards. London: Philosophical Transactions of the Royal Society (series B, vol. 259).

Goz, R. 1973. Women patients and women therapists: Some issues that come up in psychotherapy. *International Journal of Psychoanalytic Psychotherapy* 2(3): 298–320.

Greendorfer, S. L. 1978. Social class influences on female sport involvement. *Sex Roles: A Journal of Research* 4(4): 619–25.

Gregory-Lewis, S. 1978. Lesbians in the military. In *Our right to love: A lesbian resource book* (pp. 211–15), edited by G. Vida (in cooperation with women of the National Gay Task Force). Englewood Cliffs, N.J.: Prentice-Hall.

Grier, W. H., and Cobbs, P. M. 1968. *Black rage.* New York: Basic Books.

Griffin, S. 1971. Rape: The all-American crime. *Ramparts* (September) 10(3): 26–35. Reprinted in *Female psychology: The emerging self* (pp. 290–303), edited by S. Cox. Chicago: Science Research Associates, 1976.

Groth, A. N.; Burgess, A. W.; and Holmstrom, L. L. 1977. Rape: Power, anger, and sexuality. *American Journal of Psychiatry* 134(11): 1239–43.

Hall, C. S., and Domhoff, B. 1963. A ubiquitous sex difference in dreams. *Journal of Abnormal and Social Psychology* 66: 278–80.

Hall, C. S., and Van de Castle, R. L. 1966. *The content analysis of dreams.* New York: Appleton-Century-Crofts.

Halleck, S. L. 1971. *The politics of therapy.* New York: Science House.

Hamburg, D. A., and Lunde, D. T. 1966. Sex hormones in the development of sex differences in human behavior. In *The development of sex differences* (pp. 1–24), edited by E. E. Maccoby. Stanford, Cal.: Stanford University Press.

Hampson, J. L., and Hampson, J. G. 1961. The ontogenesis of sexual behavior in man. In *Sex and internal secretions* (vol. II, pp. 1401–32), edited by W. C. Young. Baltimore: Williams & Wilkins.

Hare, N., and Hare, J. 1970. Black women 1970. *Trans-action* (November/December) 8(1/2): 65–90. Reprinted in *Readings on the psychology of women* (pp. 178–81), edited by J. M. Bardwick. New York: Harper & Row, 1972.

Harlow, H. F. 1962. The heterosexual affectional system in monkeys. *American Psychologist* 17(1): 1–9.

Harlow, H. F., and Suomi, S. S. 1970. Nature of love—simplified. *American Psychologist* 25(2): 161–68.

Harlow, H. F., and Zimmerman, R. R. 1959. Affectional responses in the infant monkey. *Science* 130(3373): 421–32.

Harris, D. V. 1973. *Involvement in sport.* Philadelphia: Lea & Febiger.

Harris, D. V. 1974. The sportswoman in our society. In *Sport and American society: Selected readings,* 2nd ed. (pp. 310–14), edited by G. H. Sage. Reading, Mass.: Addison-Wesley.

Hart, M. M. 1971. Women sit in the back of the bus. *Psychology Today* 5: 64–66.

Hart, M. M. 1972. On being female in sport. In *Sport in the socio-cultural process* (pp. 291–302), edited by M. M. Hart. Dubuque, Iowa: Wm. C. Brown Company.

Hart, M. M. 1974. Stigma or prestige: The all American choice. In *Issues in physical education and sport,* edited by G. McGlynn. Palo Alto, Cal.: National Book Press.

Hartlage, L. C. 1970. Sex-linked inheritance of spatial ability. *Perceptual and Motor Skills* 31: 610.

Hayes, K. E., and Wolleat, P. L. 1978. Effects of sex in judgments of a simulated counseling interview. *Journal of Counseling Psychology* 25(2): 164–68.

Heide, W. S. 1978. Feminism for a sporting future. In *Women and sport: From myth to reality* (pp. 195–202), by C. A. Oglesby. Philadelphia: Lea & Febiger.

Helms, J. E. 1978. Counselor reactions to female clients: Generalizing from analogue research to a counseling setting. *Journal of Counseling Psychology* 25(3): 193–99.

Hennig, M. 1970. *Career development for women executives.* Unpublished doctoral dissertation, Harvard University Graduate School of Business Administration.

Heppner, P. P., and Pew, S. 1977. Effects of diplomas, awards, and counselor sex on perceived expertness. *Journal of Counseling Psychology* 24(2): 147–49.

Herman, A. M. 1979. Money: Still . . . small change for Black women. *Ms.* (February) VII(8): 96, 98.

Hertz, S. H. 1977. The politics of the welfare mothers movement: A case study. *Signs: Journal of Women in Culture and Society* 2(3): 600–11.

Herzog, E., and Sudia, C. 1968. Fatherless homes: A review of research. *Children*, (September–October) 15: 177–82.

Hesselbart, S. 1977. Sex role and occupational stereotypes: Three studies of impression formation. *Sex Roles: A Journal of Research* 3(5): 409–22.

Hetherington, E. M. 1965. A developmental study of the effects of sex of the dominant parent on sex-role preference, identification, and imitation in children. *Journal of Personality and Social Psychology* 2(2): 188–94.

Hidalgo, H. A., and Christensen, E. H. 1976–1977. The Puerto Rican lesbian and the Puerto Rican community. *Journal of Homosexuality* (Winter) 2(2): 109–21.

Hill, C.; Tanney, M. F.; Leonard M. M.; and Riess, J. A. 1977. Counselor reactions to female clients: Types of problems, age of client, and sex of counselor. *Journal of Counseling Psychology* 24: 60–65.

Hite, S. 1976. *The Hite report: A nationwide study of female sexuality.* New York: Dell.

Hoffman, L. W. 1974a. Effects of maternal employment on the child: A review of the research. *Developmental psychology* 10(2): 204–28. Reprinted in *Beyond sex-role stereotypes: Readings toward a psychology of androgyny* (pp. 294–318), edited by A. G. Kaplan and J. P. Bean. Boston: Little, Brown, 1976.

Hoffman, L. W. 1974b. Fear of success in males and females: 1965 and 1971. *Journal of Consulting and Clinical Psychology* 42(3): 353–58.

Hoffman, L. W. 1977. Fear of success in 1965 and 1974: A follow-up study. *Journal of Consulting and Clinical Psychology* 45(2): 310–21.

Holroyd, J. C., and Brodsky, A. M. 1977. Psychologists' attitudes and practices regarding erotic and nonerotic physical contact with patients. *American Psychologist* 32(10): 843–49.

Horner, M. S. 1968. *Sex differences in achievement motivation and performance in competitive and non-competitive situations.* Unpublished doctoral dissertation, University of Michigan.

Horner, M. S. 1970a. Femininity and successful achievement: A basic inconsistency. In J. M. Bardwick; E. Douvan; M. S. Horner; and D. Gutmann, *Feminine personality and conflict* (pp. 45–74). Belmont, Cal.: Brooks/Cole.

Horner, M. S. 1970b. *Follow-up studies on the motive to avoid success in women.* Symposium presentation, American Psychological Association, Miami, Fla., September 1970.

Horner, M. S. 1970c. The motive to avoid success and changing aspirations of college women. In *Women on campus: 1970 a symposium* (pp. 12–23). Ann Arbor, Mich.: Center for the Continuing Education of Women. Reprinted in *Readings on the psychology of women* (pp. 62–67), edited by J. M. Bardwick. New York: Harper & Row, 1972.

Horner, M. S.; Tresemer, D. W.; Berens, A. E.; and Watson, R. I. 1973. *Scoring manual for an empirically derived scoring system for motive to avoid success.* Unpublished manuscript, Harvard University, August 1973.

Horney, K. 1926. The flight from womanhood: The masculinity complex in women as viewed by men and by women. *International Journal of Psycho-Analysis* 7(3/4): 324–29. Reprinted in *Feminine psychology* (pp. 54–70), by K. Horney. New York: Norton, 1967. Also reprinted in *Women and analysis: Dialogues on psychoanalytic views of femininity* (pp. 171–86), edited by J. Strouse. New York, Grossman, 1974.

Hudson, J. 1978. Physical parameters used for female exclusion from law enforcement and athletics. In *Women and sport: From myth to reality* (pp. 19–57), by C. A. Oglesby. Philadelphia: Lea & Febiger.

Hunt, M. 1974. *Sexual behavior in the 1970s.* Chicago: Playboy Press.

Ibrahim, H., and Morrison, N. 1976. Self-actualization and self-concept among athletes. *The Research Quarterly* 47(1): 68–79.

Ihara, T., and Warner, R. 1979. Making illegitimacy legitimate. *Ms.* (April) 7(10): 92–93.

Inhelder, B., and Piaget, J. 1958. *The growth of logical thinking from childhood to adolescence.* New York: Basic Books.

Irwin, P., and Thompson, N. L. 1977. Acceptance of the rights of homosexuals: A social profile. *Journal of Homosexuality* 3(2): 107–22.

Ivey, M. E., and Bardwick, J. M. 1968. Patterns of affective fluctuation in the menstrual cycle. *Psychosomatic Medicine* 30: 336–45.

"J." 1969. *The sensuous woman.* New York: Dell.

Jakubowski, P. A. 1977a. Assertive behavior and clinical problems of women. In *Psychotherapy for women: Treatment toward equality* (pp. 147–67), edited by E. I. Rawlings and D. K. Carter. Springfield, Ill.: Charles C. Thomas.

Jakubowski, P. A. 1977b. Self-assertion training procedures for women. In *Psychotherapy for women: Treatment toward equality* (pp. 168–90), edited by E. I. Rawlings and D. K. Carter. Springfield, Ill.: Charles C. Thomas.

Janda, L. H.; O'Grady, K. E.; and Capps, C. F. 1978. Fear of success in males and females in sex-linked occupations. *Sex Roles: A Journal of Research* 4(1): 43–50.

Janeway, E. 1974. On "Female Sexuality." In *Women and analysis: Dialogues on psychoanalytic views of femininity* (pp. 57–70), edited by J. Strouse. New York: Grossman.

Janis, I. L. 1969. Stress and frustration. In *Personality: Dynamics, development, and assessment* (pp. 1–198), by I. L. Janis; G. F. Mahl; J. Kazan; and R. R. Holt (edited by I. L. Janis). New York: Harcourt, Brace & World.

Jay, K. 1978. Coming out as process. In *Our right to love: A lesbian resource book* (pp. 28–30), edited by G. Vida (in cooperation with women of the National Gay Task Force). Englewood Cliffs, N.J.: Prentice-Hall.

Jay, K., and Young, A. (eds.). 1975. *After you're out: Personal experiences of gay men and lesbian women.* New York: Links Books.

Jensen, J. M. 1977. Native American women and agriculture: A Seneca case study. *Sex Roles: A Journal of Research* 3(5): 423–42.

Johnson, C. L., and Johnson, F. A. 1977. Attitudes toward parenting in dual-career families. *American Journal of Psychiatry* 134(4): 391–95.

Johnston, J. 1973. *Lesbian nation: The feminist solution.* New York: Simon & Schuster (Touchstone Books).

Jones, C., and Aronson, E. 1973. Attribution of fault to a rape victim as a function of respectability of the victim. *Journal of Personality and Social Psychology* 26(3): 415–19.

Jones, E. 1955. *The life and work of Sigmund Freud* (vol. 2). New York: Basic Books.

Joslyn, W. D. 1973. Androgen-induced social dominance in infant female rhesus monkeys. *Journal of Child Psychology and Psychiatry* 14: 137–45.

Jung, C. G. 1953. Anima and animus. In *Two essays on analytical psychology: Collected works of C. G. Jung* (vol. 7, pp. 186–209). New York: Bollingen Foundation (Pantheon Books).

Kagan, J., and Kogan, N. 1970. Individual variation in cognitive processes. In *Carmichael's manual of child psychology* (3rd ed., vol. 1, pp. 1273–1365), edited by P. H. Mussen. New York: Wiley.

Kagan, J., and Lemkin, J. 1960. The child's differential perception of parental attributes. *Journal of Abnormal and Social Psychology* 61: 440–47.

Kando, T. 1974. Males, females, and transsexuals: A comparative study of sexual conservatism. *Journal of Homosexuality* 1(1): 45–64.

Kanter, R. M. 1975. Women and the structure of organizations: Explorations in theory and behavior. In *Another voice: Feminist perspectives on social life and social science* (pp. 34–74), edited by M. Millman and R. M. Kanter. Garden City, N.Y.: Anchor Books.

Kanter, R. M. 1976. Why bosses turn bitchy. *Psychology Today* (May) 9(12): 56–57, 59, 88–89, 90.

Kanter, R. M. 1977. Power games in the corporation. *Psychology Today* (July) 11(2): 48–53, 92. Excerpted from *Men and women of the corporation*, by R. M. Kanter. New York: Basic Books, 1977.

Kanter, J. F., and Zelnik, M. 1972. Sexual experience of young unmarried women in the United States. *Family Planning Perspectives* 4: 9–18.

Kaplan, A. G. 1976. Androgyny as a model of mental health for women: From theory to therapy. In *Beyond sex-role stereotypes: Readings toward a psychology of androgyny* (pp. 353–62), edited by A. G. Kaplan & J. P. Bean. Boston: Little, Brown.

Kaplan, H. S. 1974. *The new sex therapy: Active treatment of sexual dysfunctions.* New York: Brunner/Mazel.

Kardener, S.; Fuller, M.; and Mensh, I. 1973. A survey of physicians' attitudes and practices regarding erotic and nonerotic contact with patients. *American Journal of Psychiatry 130:* 1077–81.

Kardener, S.; Fuller, M.; and Mensh, I. 1976. Characteristics of "erotic" practitioners. *American Journal of Psychiatry 133:* 1324–25.

Kardiner, A., and Ovesey, L. 1958. *The mark of oppression: A psychosocial study of the American Negro.* New York: Norton.

Karmel, M. 1959. *Thank you, Dr. Lamaze.* Philadelphia: Lippincott.

Kaschak, E. 1978. Sex bias in student evaluations of college professors. *Psychology of Women Quarterly* 2(3): 235–43.

Katchadourian, H. A., and Lunde, D. T. 1972. *Fundamentals of human sexuality.* New York: Holt, Rinehart, & Winston.

Katcher, A. 1955. The discrimination of sex differences by young children. *Journal of Genetic Psychology 87:* 131–43.

Kaufman, D. R. 1978. Associational ties in academe: Some male and female differences. *Sex Roles: A Journal of Research* 4(1): 9–21.

Kellerman, J., and Katz, E. R. 1978. Attitudes toward the division of child-rearing responsibility. *Sex Roles: A Journal of Research* 4(4): 505–12.

Kelly, J. 1972. Sister love: An exploration of the need for homosexual experience. *The Family Coordinator* 21(4): 473–75.

Kincaid, M. B. 1977. Changes in sex-role attitudes and self-actualization of adult women following a consciousness-raising group. *Sex Roles: A Journal of Research* 3(4): 329–36.

King, M. C. 1973. The politics of sexual stereotypes. *The Black Scholar* (March-April) 4(6–7): 12–23. Reprinted in *Beyond sex-role stereotypes: Readings toward a psychology of androgyny* (pp. 339–51), edited by A. G. Kaplan and J. P. Bean. Boston: Little, Brown, 1976.

Kingsley, J. L.; Brown, F. L.; and Seibert, M. E. 1977. Social acceptance of female athletes by college women. *The Research Quarterly* 48(4): 727–33.

Kinsey, A. C.; Pomeroy, W. B.; and Martin, C. E. 1948. *Sexual behavior in the human male.* Philadelphia: W. B. Saunders.

Kinsey, A. C.; Pomeroy, W. B.; Martin, C. E.; and Gebhard, P. H. 1953. *Sexual behavior in the human female.* Philadelphia: W. B. Saunders (New York: Pocket Books, 1965).

Kirsh, B. 1974. Consciousness-raising groups as therapy for women. In *Women in therapy: New psychotherapies for a changing society* (pp. 326–54), edited by V. Franks and V. Burtle. New York: Brunner/Mazel.

Klein, D. F. 1973. Drug therapy as a means of syndromal identification and nosological revision. In *Psychopathology and psychopharmacology* (pp. 143–60), by J. O. Cole; A. M. Freedman; and A. J. Friedhoff. Baltimore: Johns Hopkins University Press.

Klerman, G. L. 1975. Overview of depression. In *Comprehensive textbook of psychiatry* (2nd ed., Vol. 1, pp. 1003–12), edited by A. M. Freedman; H. I. Kaplan; and B. J. Sadock. Baltimore: Williams & Wilkins.

Klerman, G. L. 1979. The age of melancholy? *Psychology Today* (April) 12(11): 36–38, 42, 88.

Kline, P. 1972. *Fact and fantasy in Freudian theory.* London: Methuen.

Kline-Graber, G., and Graber, B. 1975. *Woman's orgasm: A guide to sexual satisfaction.* New York: Bobbs-Merrill.

Koedt, A. 1970. The myth of the vaginal orgasm. In *Notes from the second year: Women's liberation* (pp. 37–41), edited by S. Firestone and A. Koedt. New York: Radical Feminism.

Kohlberg, L. 1966a. A cognitive-developmental analysis of children's sex-role concepts and attitudes. In *The development of sex differences* (pp. 82–173), edited by E. E. Maccoby. Stanford, Cal.: Stanford University Press.

Kohlberg, L. 1966b. Stage and sequence: The developmental approach to moralization. In *Moral processes*, edited by M. Hoffman. Chicago: Aldine Press.

Kohlberg, L. 1967. *Stages in the development of physical and social concepts in the years four to eight.* Unpublished manuscript, Chicago, Ill. (Cited as "Kohlberg, 1966a" in L. Kohlberg, A cognitive-developmental analysis of children's sex-role concepts and attitudes. In *The development of sex differences*, edited by E. E. Maccoby. Stanford, Cal.: Stanford University Press, 1966 (pp. 82–173).

Kohlberg, L. 1969. Stage and sequence: The cognitive-developmental approach to socialization. In *Handbook of socialization theory and research* (pp. 347–480), edited by D. A. Goslin. Chicago: Rand McNally.

Kohlberg, L., and Zigler, E. 1967. The impact of cognitive maturity on the development of sex-role attitudes in the years 4 to 8. *Genetic Psychology Monographs* 75(1): 89–165.

Komarovsky, M. 1946. Cultural contradictions and sex roles. *American Journal of Sociology* 52(3): 184–89. Reprinted in *Readings on the psychology of women* (pp. 58–67), edited by J. M. Bardwick. New York: Harper & Row, 1972.

Laing, R. D. 1967. *The politics of experience.* New York: Ballantine.

Landy, E. E. 1967. Sex differences in some aspects of smoking behavior. *Psychological Reports* 20: 575–80.

Laner, M. R. 1977. Permanent partner priorities: Gay and straight. *Journal of Homosexuality* (Fall) 3(1): 21–40.

Langer, E. J.; Taylor, S. E.; Fiske, S. T.; and Chanowitz, B. 1976. Stigma, staring and discomfort: A novel stimulus hypothesis. *Journal of Experimental Social Psychology* 12: 451–63.

Langley, R., and Levy, R. C. 1977. *Wife beating: The silent crisis.* New York: Pocket Books.

Larned, D. 1978. Cesarean births: Why they are up 100 percent. *Ms.* (October) VII(4): 24, 27–28, 30.

La Rue, L. 1970. The Black movement and women's liberation. *The Black Scholar* 1(7): 36–42. Reprinted in *Female psychology: The emerging self* (pp. 216–25), edited by S. Cox. Chicago: Science Research Associates, 1976.

Larwood, L., and Blackmore, J. 1978. Sex discrimination in managerial selection: Testing prediction of the vertical dyad linkage model. *Sex Roles: A Journal of Research* 4(3): 359–68.

Lazarus, A. A. 1968. Behavior therapy and marriage counseling. *Journal of the American Society of Psychosomatic Dentistry and Medicine* 15(2): 49–56.

Lazarus, A. A. 1974. Women in behavior therapy. In *Women in therapy: New psychotherapies for a changing society* (pp. 217–29), edited by V. Franks and V. Burtle. New York: Brunner/Mazel.

Lefkowitz, M. M.; Blake, R. R.; and Moulton, J. S. 1955. Status factors in pedestrian violation of traffic signals. *Journal of Abnormal and Social Psychology* 51: 704–6.

Lerner, M. J., and Simmons, C. H. 1966. Observers' reaction to the "innocent victim": Compassion or rejection? *Journal of Personality and Social Psychology* 4(2): 203–10.

Lessard, S. 1972. Aborting a fetus: The legal right, the personal choice. *The Washington Monthly* (August) 4(6): 29–37. Reprinted in *Beyond sex-role stereotypes: Readings toward a psychology of androgyny* (pp. 144–52), edited by A. G. Kaplan and J. P. Bean. Boston: Little, Brown, 1976.

Levenson, H.; Burford, B.; Bonno, B.; and Davis, L. 1975. Are women still prejudiced against women? A replication and extension of Goldberg's study. *Journal of Psychology* 89(1): 67–71.

Levezey, B., and Anderson, J. 1974. Trials of a woman lawyer. *Women's Rights Law Reporter* 1(6): 38.

Levin, R. B. 1966. An empirical test of the female castration complex. *Journal of Abnormal Psychology* 71: 181–88.

Levitt, E. E., and Klassen, A. D. 1974. Public attitudes toward homosexuality: Part of the 1970 national survey by the Institute for Sex Research. *Journal of Homosexuality* 1(1): 29–43.

Levy-Agresti, J., and Sperry, R. W. 1968. Differential perceptual capacities in major and minor hemispheres. Paper presented at fall meetings, National Academy of Sciences, California Institute of Technology, Pasadena. *Proceedings of the National Academy of Sciences* 61.

Lewis, D. K. 1977. A response to inequality: Black women, racism, and sexism. *Signs: Journal of Women in Culture and Society* 3(2): 339–61.

Lieberman, M. A.; Yalom, I. D.; and Miles, M. B. 1973. *Encounter groups: First facts.* New York: Basic Books.

Lipman-Blumen, J. 1976. Toward a homosocial theory of sex roles: An explanation of the sex segregation of social institutions. *Signs: Journal of Women in Culture and Society* 1(3, part 2): 15–31.

Lopata, H. Z. 1969. Loneliness: Forms and components. *Social Problems* 17: 248–61.

Lydon, S. 1970. The politics of orgasm. In *Sisterhood is powerful: An anthology of writings from the women's liberation movement* (pp. 197–205), edited by R. Morgan. New York: Vintage Books.

McCaldon, R. J. 1967. Rape. *Canadian Journal of Corrections* 9: 37–59.

McCance, R. A.; Luff, M. C.; and Widdowson, E. E. 1937. Physical and emotional periodicity in women. *Journal of Hygiene* 37: 571–605.

McClelland, D. C.; Atkinson, J. W.; Clark, R. A.; and Lowell, E. L. 1953. *The achievement motive.* New York: Appleton-Century-Crofts.

Maccoby, E. E. 1959. Role-taking in childhood and its consequences for social learning. *Child Development* 30: 239–52.

Maccoby, E. E., and Jacklin, C. N. 1974. *The psychology of sex differences.* Stanford, Cal.: Stanford University Press.

Maccoby, E. E., and Wilson, W. C. 1957. Identification and observational learning from films. *Journal of Abnormal and Social Psychology* 55: 76–87.

Maccoby, E. E.; Wilson, W. C.; and Burton, R. V. 1958. Differential movie-viewing behavior of male and female viewers. *Journal of Personality* 26: 259–67.

MacDonald, A. P., Jr.; and Games, R. G. 1974. Some characteristics of those who hold positive and negative attitudes toward homosexuals. *Journal of Homosexuality* 1(1): 9–27.

McDonald, R. L. 1968. The role of emotional factors in obstetric complications: A review. *Psychosomatic Medicine* 30(2): 222–37. Reprinted in *Readings on the psychology of women* (pp. 269–77), edited by J. M. Bardwick. New York: Harper & Row, 1972.

Maher, B. A. 1966. *Principles of psychopathology: An experimental approach.* New York: McGraw-Hill.

Mainardi, P. 1970. The politics of housework. In *Notes from the second year: Women's liberation* (pp. 28–31), edited by S. Firestone and A. Koedt. New York: Notes from the Second Year, Radical Feminism. Reprinted in *Sisterhood is powerful: An anthology of writings from the women's liberation movement* (pp. 447–54), edited by R. Morgan. New York: Vintage Books, 1970.

Mandel, W. M. 1975. *Soviet women.* Garden City, N.Y.: Anchor Books.

Mandler, G. 1962. Emotion. In *New directions in psychology* (pp. 257–343), edited by R. Brown; E. Galanter; E. H. Hess; and G. Mandler. New York: Holt, Rinehart & Winston.

Marini, M. M. 1978. Sex differences in the determination of adolescent aspirations: A review of research. *Sex Roles: A Journal of Research* 4(5): 723–54.

Marlowe, L. 1978. *Assertive training: Caveat emptor.* Paper presented at Fifth Annual National Conference on Feminist Psychology: Theory, Research and Practice, The Association for Women in Psychology, Pittsburgh, Pennsylvania, March 1978.

Marter, J. 1979. "Unwed motherhood" for the whole family: Two TV specials. *Ms.* (April) 7(10): 70.

Martin, D. 1976. *Battered wives.* San Francisco: Glide Publications.

Martin, D., and Lyon, p. 1970. The realities of lesbianism. In *The new women* (pp. 78–88), edited by J. Cooke; C. Bunch-Weeks; and R. Morgan. New York: Bobbs-Merrill. Reprinted in *Psychology of women: Selected readings* (pp. 255–61), edited by J. H. Williams. New York: Norton, 1979.

Martin, D., and Lyon, P. 1972. *Lesbian/woman.* New York: Bantam.

Masters, W. H., and Johnson, V. E. 1966. *Human sexual response.* Boston: Little, Brown.

Masters, W. H., and Johnson, V. E. 1967. Orgasm, anatomy of the female. In *The encyclopedia of sexual behavior* (pp. 788–793), edited by A. Ellis and A. Abarbanel. New York: Hawthorn Books.

Masters, W. H., and Johnson, V. E. 1970. *Human sexual inadequacy.* Boston: Little, Brown.

Mathes, S. 1978. Body image and sex stereotyping. In *Women and sport: From myth to reality* (pp. 59–72), by C. A. Oglesby. Philadelphia: Lea & Febiger.

Mayhew, J. L., and Cross, P. M. 1974. Body composition changes in young women with high resistance weight training. *The Research Quarterly* 45(4): 433–40.

Mayo, J. 1973. The new black feminism: A minority report. In *Contemporary sexual behavior: Critical issues in the 1970s* (pp. 175–86), edited by J. Zubin and J. W. Money. Baltimore: Johns Hopkins University Press.

Mead, M. 1935. *Sex and temperament in three primitive societies.* New York: Dell.

Mead, M. 1949. *Male and female.* New York: Dell. (New York: Morrow, 1949).

Mead, M. 1974. On Freud's view of female psychology. In *Women and analysis: Dialogues on psychoanalytic views of femininity* (pp. 95–106), edited by J. Strouse. New York: Grossman.

Mead, M., and Newton, N. 1967. Cultural patterning of perinatal behavior. In *Childbearing, its social and psychological aspects* (pp. 142–244), edited by S. A. Richardson and A. F. Guttmacher. New York: Williams & Wilkins.

Menaker, E. 1974. The therapy of women in the light of psychoanalytic theory and the emergence of a new view. In *Women in therapy: New psychotherapies for a changing society* (pp. 230–46), edited by V. Franks and V. Burtle. New York: Brunner/Mazel.

Mendlewicz, J.; Fleiss, J.; and Fieve, R. 1972. Evidence for X-linkage in the transmission of manic-depressive illness. *Journal of the American Medical Association* 222: 1624–27.

Merriam, B. W., and Parry, S. M. 1978. *Group treatment of pre-orgasmic women.* Paper delivered at the Fifth Annual National Conference on Feminist Psychology: Theory, Research and Practice, The Association for Women in Psychology, Pittsburgh, March 1978.

Metheny, E. 1965. *Connotations of movement in sport and dance.* Dubuque, Iowa: Wm. C. Brown.

Meyers, M. A. 1976. Like husband, like wife. *The Pennsylvania Gazette* (October) 75(1): 37–40.

Miller, J. B. 1976. *Toward a new psychology of women.* Boston: Beacon Press.

Miller, W. 1973. *Psychological antecedents to conception in pregnancies terminated by therapeutic abortion.* Unpublished manuscript. Reported in The psychosocial factors of the abortion experience: A critical review, by L. R. Shusterman. *Psychology of Women Quarterly* (1976) 1(1): 79–106.

Millett, K. 1970. *Sexual politics.* New York: Doubleday.

Millham, J.; San Miguel, C. L.; and Kellog, R. 1976. A factor-analytic conceptualization of attitudes toward male and female homosexuals. *Journal of Homosexuality* 2(1): 3–10.

Minnigerode, F. A. 1976. Attitudes toward homosexuality: Feminist attitudes and sexual conservatism. *Sex Roles: A Journal of Research* 2(4): 347–52.

Mischel, H. 1974. Sex bias in the evaluation of professional articles. *Journal of Educational Psychology* 66: 157–66.

Mischel, W. 1966. A social-learning view of sex differences in behavior. In *The development of sex differences* (pp. 56–81), edited by E. E. Maccoby. Stanford, Cal.: Stanford University Press.

Mischel, W. 1970. Sex-typing and socialization. In *Carmichael's manual of child psychology* (3rd ed., vol. 2, pp. 3–72), edited by P. H. Mussen. New York: Wiley.

Mischel, W., and Liebert, R. M. 1966. Effects of discrepancies between observed and imposed reward criteria on their acquisition and transmission. *Journal of Personality and Social Psychology* 3: 45–53.

Mitchell, J. 1974. On Freud and the distinction between the sexes. In *Women and analysis: Dialogues on psychoanalytic views of femininity* (pp. 27–36), edited by J. Strouse. New York: Grossman.

Mohr, J. C. 1978. *Abortion in America: The origin and evolution of national policy, 1800–1900.* New York: Oxford University Press.

Monahan, L.; Kuhn, D.; and Shaver, P. 1974. Intrapsychic versus cultural explanations of the "fear of success" motive. *Journal of Personality and Social Psychology* 29(1): 60–64.

Money, J. W. 1961. Sex hormones and other variables in human eroticism. In *Sex and internal secretions* (3rd ed., vol. 2, pp. 1383–1400), edited by W. C. Young. Baltimore: Williams & Wilkins.

Money, J. W. 1976–77. Statement on antidiscrimination regarding sexual orientation. *Journal of Homosexuality* (Winter) 2(2): 159–61.

Money, J. W., and Ehrhardt, A. A. 1972. *Man and woman, boy and girl: The differentiation and dimorphism of gender identity from conception to maturity.* Baltimore: Johns Hopkins University Press.

Morgan, M. 1975. *The total woman.* New York: Pocket Books.

Morris, J. 1974. *Conundrum.* New York: New American Library (Signet Books).

Mosher, D. L. 1973. Sex differences, sex experience, sex guilt, and explicitly sexual films. *Journal of Social Issues* 29: 95–112.

Mosher, D. L., and Cross, H. J. 1971. Sex guilt and premarital sexual experiences of college students. *Journal of Consulting and Clinical Psychology* 36: 27–32.

Moss, H. A. 1967. Sex, age, and state as determinants of mother-infant interaction. *Merrill-Palmer Quarterly* 13: 19–36. Edited reproduction in *Readings on the psychology of women* (pp. 22–29), edited by J. M. Bardwick. New York: Harper & Row, 1972.

Moulton, R. 1970. A survey and reevaluation of the concept of penis envy. *Contemporary Psychoanalysis* 7(1): 84–104. Reprinted in *Psychoanalysis and women: Contributions to new theory and therapy* (pp. 207–30), edited by J. B. Miller. New York: Brunner/Mazel, 1973.

Mowrer, O. H. 1960. *Learning theory and behavior.* New York: Wiley.

Mussen, P. H. 1961. Some antecedents and consequents of masculine sex-typing in adolescent boys. *Psychology Monographs* 75(2, whole no. 506).

Mussen, P. H., and Distler, L. 1959. Masculinity, identification, and father-son relationships. *Journal of Abnormal and Social Psychology* 59: 350–56.

Mussen, P. H., and Rutherford, E. 1963. Parent-child relations and parental personality in relation to young children's sex-role preference. *Child Development* 34: 589–607.

Myers, A. M., and Lips, H. M. 1978. Participation in competitive amateur sports as a function of psychological androgyny. *Sex Roles: A Journal of Research* 4(4): 571–88.

Myers, L. W. 1975. Black women and self-esteem. In *Another voice: Feminist perspectives on social life and social science* (pp. 240–50), edited by M. Millman and R. M. Kanter. Garden City, N.Y.: Anchor Books.

Nadelson, T., and Eisenberg, L. 1977. The successful professional woman: On being married to one. *American Journal of Psychiatry* 134(10): 1071–76.

Neier, A. 1979. Abortion: Civil law vs. religious code. *The Boston Globe*, 18 January 1979, p. 17.

Nemiah, J. C. 1975. Phobic neurosis. In *Comprehensive textbook of psychiatry* (2nd ed., vol. 1, pp. 1231–41), edited by A. M. Freedman, H. I. Kaplan, and B. J. Sadock. Baltimore: Williams & Wilkins.

Newton, E., and Webster, P. 1973. Matriarchy: As women see it. *Aphra* 4(3): 6–22. Reprinted in *Female psychology: The emerging self* (pp. 72–87), edited by S. Cox. Chicago: Science Research Associates, 1976.

Nieto-Gomez, A. 1976. Heritage of La Hembra. In *Female psychology: The emerging self* (pp. 226–34), edited by S. Cox. Chicago: Science Research Associates.

Notman, M. T. 1974. Pregnancy and abortion: Implications for career development of professional women. In *Women and success: The anatomy of achievement* (pp. 216–21), edited by R. B. Kundsin. New York: Morrow. Reprinted in *Women:*

Body and culture (pp. 243–53), edited by S. Hammer. New York: Harper & Row (Perennial Library), 1975.

Notman, M. T., and Nadelson, C. C. 1976. The rape victim: Psychodynamic considerations. *American Journal of Psychiatry 133*(4): 408–13.

Nyberg, K. L., and Alston, J. P. 1976–77. Analysis of public attitudes toward homosexual behavior. *Journal of Homosexuality* (Winter) 2(2): 99–107.

Oberstone, A. K., and Sukoneck, H. 1976. Psychological adjustment and life style of single lesbians and single heterosexual women. *Psychology of Women Quarterly* 1(2): 172–88.

Oetzel, R. M. 1966. Classified summary of research in sex differences. In *The development of sex differences* (pp. 323–51), edited by E. E. Maccoby. Stanford, Cal.: Stanford University Press.

Oglesby, C. A. 1978. The masculinity/femininity game: Called on account of. . . . In *Women and sport: From myth to reality* (pp. 75–88), by C. A. Oglesby. Philadelphia: Lea & Febiger.

O'Hara, C. 1973. *Fundamentals of criminal investigation* (3rd ed.). Springfield, Ill.: Charles C Thomas.

O'Leary, B. 1978. A mother's support. In *Our right to love: A lesbian resource book* (pp. 269–72), edited by G. Vida (in cooperation with women of the National Gay Task Force). Englewood Cliffs, N.J.: Prentice-Hall.

O'Leary, J. 1978. Legal problems and remedies. In *Our right to love: A lesbian resource book* (pp. 196–207), edited by G. Vida (in cooperation with women of the National Gay Task Force). Englewood Cliffs, N.J.: Prentice-Hall.

Osofsky, J. D., and Osofsky, H. J. 1972. The psychological reaction of patients to legalized abortion. *American Journal of Orthopsychiatry 42*: 48–60.

Osofsky, J. D.; Osofsky, H. J.; Rajan, R.; and Fox, M. R. 1971. Psychologic effects of legal abortion. *Clinical Obstetrics and Gynecology 14*(1): 215–34.

Ostrum, A. 1975. Childbirth in America. In *Women: Body and culture* (pp. 277–92), edited by S. Hammer. New York: Harper & Row (Perennial Library).

Paige, K. E. 1969. *The effects of oral contraceptives on affective fluctuations associated with the menstrual cycle.* Unpublished doctoral dissertation, University of Michigan. Reported in *Psychology of women* (pp. 36–37), by J. M. Bardwick. New York: Harper & Row, 1971.

Paige, K. E. 1973. Women learn to sing the menstrual blues. *Psychology Today* (September) 7(4): 41, 43, 45–46.

Paige, K. E., and Paige, J. M. 1973. The politics of birth practices: A strategic analysis. *American Sociological Review 38*: 663–76.

Parke, R., and O'Leary, S. 1974. Mother-father-infant interaction in the newborn period: Some findings, some observations, and some unresolved issues. In *Determinants of behavioral development* (vol. 2), by K. Riegel and J. Meacham.

Parkes, C. M. 1970. The first year of bereavement: A longitudinal study of the reaction of London widows to the death of their husbands. *Psychiatry 33*(4): 444–67. Reprinted in *Readings on the psychology of women* (pp. 143–56), edited by J. M. Bardwick. New York: Harper & Row, 1972.

Parlee, M. B. 1973. The premenstrual syndrome. *Psychological Bulletin 80*(6): 454–65.

Parlee, M. B. 1973–74. *Sex differences in perceptual field dependence: A look at some data embedded in theory.* Unpublished manuscript, Radcliffe Institute.

Parsons, J. E.; Frieze, I. H.; and Ruble, D. N. 1978. Intrapsychic factors influencing career aspirations in college women. *Sex Roles: A Journal of Research* 4(3): 337–48.

Peck, T. 1978. When women evaluate women, nothing succeeds like success: The differential effects of status upon evaluation of male and female professional ability. *Sex Roles: A Journal of Research* 4(2): 205–14.

Perl, H., and Abarbanell, G. 1976. *Guidelines to feminist consciousness raising.* Prepared for the National Task Force on Consciousness Raising of the National Organization for Women. Los Angeles: published by the authors.

Perls, F. S. 1969. *Gestalt therapy verbatim.* Moab, Utah: Real People Press.

Perreault, J. 1975. Lesbian mother. In *After you're out: Personal experiences of gay men and lesbian women* (pp. 125–27), edited by K. Jay and A. Young. New York: Links Books.

Peterson, A. C. 1973. *The relationship of androgenicity in males and females to spatial ability and fluent production.* Unpublished doctoral dissertation, University of Chicago.

Pettigrew, T. F. 1964. *A profile of the Negro American.* Princeton, N.J.: Van Nostrand.

Pheterson, G. I. 1969. *Female prejudice against men.* Unpublished manuscript, Connecticut College. Reported in Prejudice against women: A new perspective, by D. H. Soto and C. Cole. *Sex Roles: A Journal of Research* (1975) 1(4): 385–93.

Pheterson, G. I.; Kiesler, S. B.; and Goldberg, P. A. 1971. Evaluation of the performance of women as a function of their sex, achievement, and personal history. *Journal of Personality and Social Psychology* 19(1): 114–18.

Phillips, D., and Segal, B. E. 1969. Sexual status and psychiatric symptoms. *American Sociological Review* 34(1): 58–72.

Phoenix, C. H.; Goy, R. W.; and Young, W. C. 1967. Sexual behavior: General aspects. In *Neuroendocrinology* (vol. 2, pp. 163–96), edited by L. Martini and W. F. Ganong. New York: Academic Press.

Piaget, J. 1929. *The child's conception of the world.* New York: Harcourt, Brace.

Piaget, J. 1952. *The origins of intelligence in children.* New York: International Universities Press.

Piaget, J. 1954. *The construction of reality in the child.* New York: Basic Books.

Piaget, J. 1968. *On the development of memory and identity.* Barre, Mass.: Clark University Publishers.

Pingree, S. 1978. The effects of nonsexist television commercials and perceptions of reality on children's attitudes about women. *Psychology of Women Quarterly* 2(3): 262–77.

Pizzey, E. 1974. *Scream quietly or the neighbours will hear.* Middlesex, England: Penguin Books.

Pogrebin, L. C. 1974 Do women make men violent? *Ms.* (November) 3(5): 49–52.

Poloma, M. M. 1972. Role conflict and the married professional woman. In *Toward a sociology of women* (pp. 187–99), edited by C. Safilios-Rothschild. Lexington, Mass.: Xerox College Publishing.

Poloma, M. M., and Garland, T. 1971. On the social construction of reality: Reported husband-wife differences. *Sociological Focus* 5: 40–54.

Polster, M. 1974. Women in therapy: A gestalt therapist's view. In *Women in therapy: New psychotherapies for a changing society* (pp. 247–62), edited by V. Franks and V. Burtle. New York: Brunner/Mazel.

Prosser, W. L. 1971. *Handbook of the law of torts* (4th ed.). St. Paul, Minn: West Publishing.

Rainwater, L., and Yancey, W. J. 1967. *The Moynihan report and the politics of controversy.* Cambridge, Mass.: Massachusetts Institute of Technology Press.

Ramey, E. 1972. Men's cycles (They have them too, you know). *Ms.* (Spring), pp. 8–14. Reprinted in *Beyond sex-role stereotypes: Readings toward a psychology of androgyny* (pp. 138–42), edited by A. G. Kaplan and J. P. Bean. Boston: Little, Brown, 1976.

Rapoport, R., and Rapoport, R. N. 1972. The dual-career family: A variant pattern and social change. In *Toward a sociology of women* (pp. 216–45), edited by C. Safilios-Rothschild. Lexington, Mass.: Xerox College Publishing.

Rawlings, E. I., and Carter, D. K. 1977a. Feminist and nonsexist psychotherapy. In *Psychotherapy for women: Treatment toward equality* (pp. 49–76), edited by E. I. Rawlings and D. K. Carter. Springfield, Ill.: Charles C. Thomas.

Rawlings, E. I., and Carter, D. K. 1977b. Unilateral and reciprocal influence in psychotherapy. In *Psychotherapy for women: Treatment toward equality* (pp. 34–45), edited by E. I. Rawlings and D. K. Carter. Springfield, Ill.: Charles C. Thomas.

Reed, J. 1978. *From private vice to public virtue: The birth control movement and American society since 1830.* New York: Basic Books.

Reuben, D. 1969. *Everything you always wanted to know about sex but were afraid to ask.* New York: Bantam (originally published by McKay).

Riess, B. F. 1974. New viewpoints on the female homosexual. In *Women in therapy:*

New psychotherapies for a changing society (pp. 191–214), edited by V. Franks and V. Burtle. New York: Brunner/Mazel.

Riess, B. F.; Safer, J.; and Yotive, W. 1974. Psychological test data on female homosexuality: A review of the literature. *Journal of Homosexuality* 1(1): 71–85.

Rivlin, L. 1979. Choosing to have a baby on your own. *Ms.* (April) 7(10): 68–70, 91–92, 94.

Robinson, J. P.; Yerby, J.; Fieweger, M.; and Somerick, N. 1977. Sex-role differences in time use. *Sex Roles: A Journal of Research* 3(5): 443–58.

Rohrbaugh, J. B. 1976. *The psychodynamics of sex-role orientation: Response to deviation from traditionality.* Unpublished doctoral dissertation, Harvard University.

Rohrbaugh, J. B., and Glick, M. 1971. *Sex-role constancy and object constancy within the body in children 3 to 6 years old.* Unpublished manuscript, Boston University, May 1971.

Rokeach, M. 1973. *The nature of human values.* New York: Free Press.

Rose, R. M.; Holaday, J. W.; and Bernstein, I. S. 1971. Plasma testosterone, dominance rank, and aggressive behavior in male rhesus monkeys. *Nature* 231: 366–68.

Rosen, B., and Jerdee, T. H. 1974. Influence of sex-role stereotypes on personnel decisions. *Journal of Applied Psychology* 59: 9–14.

Rosenberg, B. G., and Sutton-Smith, B. 1972. *Sex and identity.* New York: Holt, Rinehart & Winston.

Rosenberg, M. 1973. The biologic basis for sex role stereotypes. *Contemporary Psychoanalysis* 9(3): 374–91. Reprinted in *Beyond sex-role stereotypes: Readings toward a psychology of androgyny* (pp. 106–23), edited by A. G. Kaplan and J. P. Bean. Boston: Little, Brown, 1976.

Rosenthal, D. 1955. Changes in some moral values following psychotherapy. *Journal of Consulting Psychology* 19(6): 431–36.

Rosenthal, R. 1966. Experimenter effects in behavioral research. New York: Appleton-Century-Crofts.

Ross, M. W.; Rogers, L. J.; and McCulloch, H. 1978. Stigma, sex, and society: A new look at gender differentiation and sexual variation. *Journal of Homosexuality* 3(4): 315–30.

Rossi, A. S. 1965. Barriers to the career choice of engineering, medicine, or science among American women. In *Women and the scientific professions* (pp. 51–127), edited by J. A. Mattfeld and C. G. Van Aken. Cambridge, Mass.: Massachusetts Institute of Technology Press.

Rossi, A. S. 1974. *Psychological and social rhythms.* Paper presented at the meeting of the American Psychological Association in Detroit, Michigan, 9 May 1974.

Rotkin, K. F. 1972. The phallacy of our sexual norm. *RT: A Journal of Radical Therapy* (formerly *Rough Times, Radical Therapist*) (September), 3(1). Reprinted in *Beyond sex-role stereotypes: Readings toward a psychology of androgyny* (pp. 154–62), edited by A. G. Kaplan and J. P. Bean. Boston: Little, Brown, 1976.

Rubin, I. 1966. Sex after forty—and after seventy. In *An analysis of human sexual response* (pp. 251–66), edited by R. Brecher and E. Brecher. New York: New American Library (Signet). Reprinted in *Women: Body and culture* (pp. 211–22), edited by S. Hammer. New York, Harper & Row (Perennial Library), 1975.

Rubin, J. Z.; Provenzano, F. J.; and Luria, Z. 1974. The eye of the beholder: Parents' views on sex of newborns. *American Journal of Orthopsychiatry* 44(4): 512–19. Reprinted in *Beyond sex-role stereotypes: Readings toward a psychology of androgyny* (pp. 179–86), edited by A. G. Kaplan and J. P. Bean. Boston: Little, Brown, 1976.

Russell, D. 1975. *The politics of rape: The victim's perspective.* New York: Stein & Day.

Sang, B. E. 1977. Psychotherapy with lesbians: Some observations and tentative generalizations. In *Psychotherapy for women: Treatment toward equality* (pp. 266–75), edited by E. I. Rawlings and D. K. Carter. Springfield, Ill.: Charles C. Thomas.

Sarnoff, I., and Corwin, S. M. 1959. Castration anxiety and the fear of death. *Journal of Personality* 27: 374–85.

Scarf, M. 1979. The more sorrowful sex. *Psychology Today* (April) 12(11): 44–45, 47–48, 51–52, 89–90.

Schachter, S., and Singer, J. E. 1962. Cognitive, social, and physiological determinants of emotional state. *Psychological Review* 69: 379–99.

Scheff, T. 1966. *Being mentally ill: A sociological theory.* Chicago: Aldine Press.

Schmuck, P. A. 1975. Deterrents to women's careers in school management. *Sex Roles: A Journal of Research* 1(4): 339–53.

Schultz, L. G. 1960. The wife assaulter. *The Journal of Social Therapy* 6(2): 103–12.

Schwartz, P., and Lever, J. 1973. Women in the male world of higher education. In *Academic women on the move* (pp. 57–77), edited by A. S. Rossi and A. Calderwood. New York: Russell Sage Foundation.

Schwartz, S. 1973. Effects of sex guilt and sexual arousal on the retention of birth control information. *Journal of Consulting and Clinical Psychology* 41: 61–64.

Scott, R.; Richards, A.; and Wade, M. 1977. Women's studies as change agent. *Psychology of Women Quarterly* 1(4): 377–79.

Seaman, B. 1972. *Free and female.* Greenwich, Conn.: Fawcett Crest Book.

Sears, R. R.; Rau, L.; and Alpert, R. 1965. *Identification and child rearing.* Stanford, Cal.: Stanford University Press.

Seiden, A. 1976. Overview: Research on the psychology of women. II. Women in families, work, and psychotherapy. *American Journal of Psychiatry* 133(10): 1111–23.

Selby, J. W.; Calhoun, L. G.; and Brock, T. A. 1977. Sex differences in the social perception of rape victims. *Personality and Social Psychology Bulletin* 3(3): 412–15.

Seligman, M. E. P. 1972. Learned helplessness. *Annual Review of Medicine* 23: 407–12.

Seligman, M. E. P. 1974. Depression and learned helplessness. In *The psychology of depression: Contemporary theory and research* (pp. 83–113), edited by R. J. Friedman and M. M. Katz. Washington, D.C.: Winston-Wiley.

Shainess, N. 1977. The equitable therapy of women in psychoanalysis. In *Psychotherapy for women: Treatment toward equality* (pp. 104–19), edited by E. I. Rawlings and D. K. Carter. Springfield, Ill.: Charles C. Thomas.

Shaver, P. 1976. Questions concerning fear of success and its conceptual relatives. *Sex Roles: A Journal of Research* 2(3): 305–20.

Sherfey, M. J. 1972. *The nature and evolution of female sexuality.* New York: Random House.

Sherman, J. A. 1967. Problem of sex differences in space perception and aspects of intellectual functioning. *Psychological Review* 74(4): 290–99.

Sherman, J. A. 1971. *On the psychology of women: A survey of empirical studies.* Springfield, Ill.: Charles C. Thomas.

Shorter, E. 1977. On writing the history of rape. *Signs: Journal of Women in Culture and Society* 3(2): 471–82.

Shulman, A. 1971. Organs and orgasms. In *Woman in sexist society* (pp. 198–206), edited by V. Gornick and B. K. Moran. New York: Basic Books.

Shusterman, L. R. 1976. The psychosocial factors of the abortion experience: A critical review. *Psychology of Women Quarterly* 1(1): 79–106.

Silverman, D. 1977. First do no more harm: Female rape victims and the male counselor. *American Journal of Orthopsychiatry* 47(1): 91–96.

Silverstein, C. 1977. Homosexuality and the ethics of behavioral intervention: Paper 2. *Journal of Homosexuality* (Spring) 2(3): 205–11.

Simon, N. M., and Senturia, A. G. 1966. Psychiatric sequelae of abortion. *Archives of General Psychiatry* 15: 378–89.

Simons, J. A., and Helms, J. E. 1976. Influence of counselor's marital status, sex, and age on college and noncollege women's counselor preferences. *Journal of Counseling Psychology* 23: 380–86.

Smith, E. 1973. A follow-up study of women who request abortion. *American Journal of Orthopsychiatry* 43: 574–85.

Snyder, E. E., and Kivlin, J. E. 1975. Women athletes and aspects of psychological well-being and body image. *Research Quarterly* 46(2): 191–99.

Snyder, E. E., and Kivlin, J. E. 1977. Perceptions of the sex role among female athletes and nonathletes. *Adolescence* 12(45): 23–29.

Snyder, E. E.; Kivlin, J. E.; and Spreitzer, E. 1975. The female athlete: An analysis of objective and subjective role conflict. In *Psychology of sport and motor be-*

havior (pp. 165–80), edited by D. Landers. University Park: Pennsylvania State University Press.

Snyder, E. E., and Spreitzer, E. 1976. Correlates of sport participation among adolescent girls. *The Research Quarterly* 47(4): 804–9.

Snyder, E. E., and Spreitzer, E. 1978. Socialization comparisons of adolescent female athletes and musicians. *The Research Quarterly* 49(3): 342–50.

Sorensen, R. C. 1973. *Adolescent sexuality in contemporary America (The Sorensen report)*. New York: World Publishing.

Soto, D. H., and Cole, C. 1975. Prejudice against women: A new perspective. *Sex Roles: A Journal of Research* 1(4): 385–94.

Spears, B. 1978. Prologue: The myth. In *Women and sport: From myth to reality* (pp. 3–15) by C. A. Oglesby. Philadelphia: Lea & Febiger.

Spence, J. T., and Helmreich, R. L. 1978. *Masculinity & femininity: Their psychological dimensions, correlates, & antecedents*. Austin, Texas: University of Texas Press.

Spence, J. T.; Helmreich, R. L.; and Stapp, J. 1975. Ratings of self and peers on sex role attributes and their relation to self-esteem and conceptions of masculinity and femininity. *Journal of Personality and Social Psychology* 32: 29–39.

Spitzer, C.; Morgan, E.; and Morgan, K. 1978. Parents of gays. In *Our right to love: A lesbian resource book* (pp. 272–79), edited by G. Vida (in cooperation with women of the National Gay Task Force). Englewood Cliffs, N.J.: Prentice-Hall.

Sprinthall, N. A., and Erickson, V. L. 1974. Learning psychology by doing psychology: Guidance through the curriculum. *Personnel and Guidance Journal* 52: 396–405.

Srole, L.; Langner, T. S.; Michael, S. T.; Opler, M. K.; and Rennie, T. A. C. 1962. *Mental health in the metropolis: The midtown Manhattan study* (vol. 1). New York: McGraw-Hill.

Stafford, R. E. 1961. Sex differences in spatial visualization as evidence of sex-linked inheritance. *Perceptual & Motor Skills* 13: 428.

Stein, A. H., and Bailey, M. M. 1973. The socialization of achievement orientation in females. *Psychological Bulletin* 80:(5): 345–66. Reprinted in *Beyond sex-role stereotypes: Readings toward a psychology of androgyny* (pp. 240–62), edited by A. G. Kaplan and J. P. Bean. Boston: Little, Brown, 1976.

Steinem, G. 1978a. If men could menstruate: A political fantasy. *Ms.* (October) 7(4): 110.

Steinem, G. 1978b. The politics of supporting lesbianism. In *Our right to love: A lesbian resource book* (pp. 266–69), edited by G. Vida (in cooperation with women of the National Gay Task Force). Englewood Cliffs, N.J.: Prentice-Hall.

Steinmann, A. 1974. Cultural values, female role expectations and therapeutic goals: Research and interpretation. In *Women in therapy: New psychotherapies for a changing society* (pp. 51–82), edited by V. Franks and V. Burtle. New York: Brunner/Mazel.

Steinmann, A., and Rappaport, A. 1970. Self achieving vs. family orientation of "professional-liberated" women. (Perceptions of female sex roles among members of association of women psychologists.) Paper presented at the 78th Annual Convention of the American Psychological Association, Miami Beach, Florida, 3–7 September 1970.

Stephan, W. G., & Woolridge, D. W. 1977. Sex differences in attributions for the performance of women on a masculine task. *Sex Roles: A Journal of Research* 3(4): 321–28.

Sternglanz, S. H., and Serbin, L. A. 1974. Sex-role stereotyping in children's television programs. *Developmental Psychology* 10(5): 710–15. Reprinted in *Beyond sex-role stereotypes: Readings toward a psychology of androgyny* (pp. 233–38), edited by A. G. Kaplan and J. P. Bean. Boston: Little, Brown, 1976.

Stevens, M. 1978. Lesbian mothers in transition. In *Our right to love: A lesbian resource book* (pp. 207–11), edited by G. Vida (in cooperation with women of the National Gay Task Force). Englewood Cliffs, N.J.: Prentice-Hall.

Stevenson, C. L. 1975. Socialization of participation in sport: A critical review of the research. *The Research Quarterly* 46(3): 287–301.

Stewart, A. J., and Sokol, M. 1977. *Male and female conceptions of rape*. Paper presented at Eastern Psychological Association Convention, Boston, Massachusetts, April 1977.

Straus, M.; Gelles, R. J.; and Steinmetz, S. 1976. *Violence in the family: An assessment of knowledge and research needs.* Paper given before the American Association for the Advancement of Science, Boston.

Stricker, G. 1977. Implications of research for psychotherapeutic treatment of women. *American Psychologist* 32(1): 14–22.

Strouse, J. 1974. Introduction to *Women and analysis: Dialogues on psychoanalytic views of femininity* (pp. 3–13), edited by J. Strouse. New York: Grossman.

Sturgis, E. T., and Adams, H. E. 1978. The right to treatment: Issues in the treatment of homosexuality. *Journal of Consulting and Clinical Psychology* 46(1): 165–69.

Sutherland, S. L. 1978. The unambitious female: Women's low professional aspirations. *Signs: Journal of Women in Culture and Society* 3(4): 774–94.

Swyer, G. I. M. 1968. Clinical effects of agents affecting fertility. In *Endocrinology and human behavior* (pp. 161–72), edited by R. P. Michael. London: Oxford University Press.

Syfers, J. 1971. Why I want a wife. In *Notes from the third year: Women's liberation* (pp. 13–14), edited by A. Koedt and S. Firestone. New York: Notes From the Second Year, Inc.

Talbot, H. S. 1955. The sexual function in paraplegics. *Journal of Urology* 73: 91–100.

Tangri, S. S. 1972. Determinants of occupational role innovation among college women. *Journal of Social Issues* 28: 177–99.

Tanzer, D. 1973. Natural childbirth: Pain or peak experience. In *The female experience*, edited by C. Tavris. Del Mar, Cal.: Communications/Research/Machines.

Tavris, C., and Offir, C. 1977. *The longest war: Sex differences in perspective.* New York: Harcourt Brace Jovanovich.

Taylor, S. E., and Langer, E. J. 1977. Pregnancy: A social stigma? *Sex Roles: A Journal of Research* 3(1): 27–36.

Terman, L. M., and Tyler, L. E. 1954. Psychological sex differences. In *Manual of Child Psychology* (2nd ed., pp. 1064–1114), edited by L. Carmichael. New York: Wiley.

Thetford, W., and Schucman, H. 1975. Other psychological personality theories. In *Comprehensive textbook of psychiatry—II* (2nd ed., vol. 1, pp. 687–711), edited by A. M. Freedman; H. I. Kaplan; and B. J. Sadock. Baltimore: Williams & Wilkins..

Thomas, S. A. 1977. Theory and practice in feminist therapy. *Social Work* 22(6): 447–54.

Thompson, C. 1942. Cultural pressures in the psychology of women. *Psychiatry* 5: 331–39. Reprinted in *Psychoanalysis and women* (pp. 49–64), edited by J. B. Miller. New York: Brunner/Mazel, 1973.

Thompson, C. 1943. "Penis envy" in women. *Psychiatry* 6: 123–25. Reprinted in *Psychoanalysis and women* (pp. 43–48), edited by J. B. Miller. New York: Brunner/Mazel, 1973.

Thornton, B. 1977. Effect of rape victim's attractiveness in a jury simulation. *Personality and Social Psychology Bulletin* 3(4): 666–69.

Tiger, L. 1970. *Men in groups.* New York: Vintage Books.

Toby, J. 1975. Violence and the masculine ideal: Some qualitative data. In *Violence in the family*, edited by S. K. Steinmetz and M. A. Straus. New York: Dodd, Mead.

Torg, B. G., and Torg, J. S. 1974. Sex and the Little League. *The Physician and Sports Medicine* 2(5): 45–50.

Tresemer, D. W. 1976a. The cumulative record of research on "Fear of Success." *Sex Roles: A Journal of Research* 2(3): 217–36.

Tresemer, D. W. 1976b. Do women fear success? *Signs: Journal of Women in Culture and Society* 1: 863–74.

Trigg, L. J., and Perlman, D. 1976. Social influences on women's pursuit of a nontraditional career. *Psychology of Women Quarterly* 1(2): 138–50.

Truninger, E. 1971. Marital violence: The legal solutions. *The Hastings Law Journal* (November) 23(1): 259.

Tuller, N. R. 1978. Couples: The hidden segment of the gay world. *Journal of Homosexuality* 3(4): 331–44.

U. S. Bureau of the Census, Population Division. 1976. *A statistical portrait of women in the United States*. Special Studies Series P-23, no. 58 (April).

U. S. Department of Health, Education and Welfare, Office for Civil Rights. 1975. Final Title IX Regulations (June).

Vandenberg, S. G. 1968. Primary mental abilities or general intelligence? Evidence from twin studies. In *Genetic and environmental influences on behavior* (pp. 146–60), edited by J. M. Thoday and A. S. Parkes. New York: Plenum Press.

Vanek, J. 1974. Time spent in housework. *Scientific American* (November) 231(14): 116–20.

Vida, G. (ed., in cooperation with women of the National Gay Task Force). 1978. *Our right to love: A lesbian resource book*. Englewood Cliffs, N.J.: Prentice-Hall.

Vincent, M. F. 1976. Comparison of self-concepts of college women: Athletes and physical education majors. *The Research Quarterly* 47(2): 218–25.

Vinsel, A. 1977. Rape: A review essay. *Personality and Social Psychology Bulletin* 3(2): 183–89.

Waber, D. P. 1977. Sex differences in mental abilities, hemispheric lateralization, and rate of physical growth at adolescence. *Developmental Psychology* 13(1): 29–38.

Wade, C. E. 1976. Effects of a season's training on the body composition of female college swimmers. *The Research Quarterly* 47(2): 292–95.

Walker, A.; Flowers, S.; Bond, C.; and Lorde, A. 1979. Other voices, other moods. *Ms.* (February) 7(8): 50–52, 70.

Wallace, M. 1979. Black macho and the myth of the superwoman. *Ms.* (January) 7(7): 45–48, 87–89, 91. Adapted from M. Wallace, *Black macho and the myth of the superwoman*. New York: Dial Press, 1979.

Walsh, B. 1977. Letter to the editor of 5 February 1977. *Newsletter of the Society for Family Therapy and Research* (Waban, Mass.), April 1977, p. 4.

Walters, R. H.; Marshall, W. E.; and Shooter, J. R. 1960. Anxiety, isolation, and susceptibility to social influence. *Journal of Personality* 28: 518–29.

Watson, J. B., and Rayner, R. 1920. Conditioned emotional reactions. *Journal of Experimental Psychology* 3(1): 1–14.

Waxenberg, S. E.; Drellich, M. G.; and Sutherland, A. M. 1959. Changes in female sexuality after adrenalectomy. *Journal of Clinical Endocrinology* 19: 193–202.

Weideger, P. 1975. *Menstruation and menopause: The physiology and psychology, the myth and the reality*. New York: Knopf.

Weiss, R. S. 1975. *Marital separation*. New York: Basic Books.

Weissman, M. M., and Klerman, L. 1977. Sex differences and the epidemiology of depression. *Archives of General Psychiatry* 34: 98–111.

Weisstein, N. 1971. Psychology constructs the female. In *Woman in sexist society* (pp. 133–46), edited by V. Gornick and B. K. Moran. New York: Basic Books.

Welch, S., and Booth, A. 1977. Employment and health among married women with children. *Sex Roles: A Journal of Research* 3(4): 385–98.

West, D. J. 1967. *Homosexuality*. Chicago: Aldine.

West, D. J. 1977. *Homosexuality re-examined*. Minneapolis: University of Minnesota Press.

Weston, P. J., and Mednick, M. T. Race, social class, and the motive to avoid success in women. *Journal of Cross-Cultural Psychology* 1(3): 284–91. Reprinted in *Readings on the psychology of women* (pp. 68–71), edited by J. M. Bardwick. New York: Harper & Row, 1972.

Whiteley, R. M. 1973. Women in groups. *The Counseling Psychologist* 4(1): 27–43.

Whiting, B., and Edwards, C. P. 1973. A cross-cultural analysis of sex differences in the behavior of children aged three through 11. *Journal of Social Psychology* 91(2): 171–88. Reprinted in *Beyond sex-role stereotypes: Readings toward a psychology of androgyny* (pp. 188–205), edited by A. G. Kaplan and J. P. Bean. Boston: Little, Brown, 1976.

Williams, J. H. 1977. *Psychology of women: Behavior in a biosocial context*. New York: Norton.

Winter, D. G.; Stewart, A. J.; and McClelland, D. C. 1977. Husband's motives and wife's career level. *Journal of Personality and Social Psychology* 35(3): 159–66.

Witelson, S. F. 1976. Sex and the single hemisphere: Specialization of the right hemisphere for spatial processing. *Science* (30 July) *193*(4251): 425–27.

Witkin, H. A. 1950. Individual differences in ease of perception of embedded figures. *Journal of Personality 19*: 1–15.

Witt, S. H. 1976. Native women today: Sexism and the Indian woman. In *Female psychology: The emerging self* (pp. 249–59), edited by S. Cox. Chicago: Science Research Associates.

Wolman, C., and Frank, H. 1975. The solo woman in a professional peer group. *American Journal of Orthopsychiatry 45*: 164–71.

Wolowitz, H. M. 1972. Hysterical character and feminine identity. In *Readings on the psychology of women* (pp. 307–14), edited by J. M. Bardwick. New York: Harper & Row.

Women in Transition, Inc. 1975. *Women in transition: A feminist handbook on separation and divorce.* New York: Scribner's.

Women on Words and Images. 1975. *Dick and Jane as victims: Sex stereotyping in children's readers.* Princeton, N.J.: published by the author.

Woudenberg, R. A. 1977. The relationship of sexual attitudes, attitudes about women, and racial attitudes in white males. *Sex Roles: A Journal of Research 3*(2); 101–10.

Wyckoff, H. 1977. Radical psychiatry for women. In *Psychotherapy for women: Treatment toward equality* (pp. 370–91), edited by E. I. Rawlings and D. K. Carter. Springfield, Ill.: Charles C. Thomas.

Yale Law Journal. 1952. Comment on forcible and statutory rape: An exploration of the operation and objectives of the consent standard. *62*(1): 55–83.

Yalom, I. D. 1975. *The theory and practice of group psychotherapy* (2nd ed.). New York: Basic Books.

Zeitlin, A. B.; Cottrell, T. L.; and Lloyd, F. A. 1958. Sexology of the paraplegic male. *Fertility and Sterility 8*: 337–44.

Index